Cairo of the Mamluks

CAIRO of the MAMLUKS

A History of the Architecture and its Culture

Doris Behrens-Abouseif

I.B. TAURIS

LONDON · NEW YORK

Published in 2007 by I.B.Tauris & Co Ltd
6 Salem Road, London W2 4BU
175 Fifth Avenue, New York NY 10010
www.ibtauris.com

In the United States and Canada distributed by Palgrave Macmillan,
a division of St. Martin's Press, 175 Fifth Avenue, New York NY 10010

ISBN: 978-1-84511-549-4

A full CIP record for this book is available from the British Library
A full CIP record for this book is available from the Library of Congress
Library of Congress catalog card: available

Designed by Paula Larsson
Typeset in Minion by Dexter Haven Associates Ltd, London
Printed and bound in the Czech Republic by FINIDR, s.r.o

Contents

List of Illustrations

Unless otherwise indicated, all plans, maps and views are by Nicholas Warner. 'BO' denotes Bernard O'Kane. Photographs without attributions are by the author.

Preface

In 1961 the Egyptian scholar and polymath Husayn Fawzi published his book *Sindbad Misri*. It was immediately a great success. The Sindbad of this book is the author, who travels through Egypt's long history in search of the Egyptian identity, all the while asking himself which period is the one closest to his heart? His answer is the Mamluk period. Having grown up in the Jamaliyya quarter, in the heart of medieval Cairo, with its Mamluk monuments brought to life in the histories of Maqrizi, Suyuti and Ibn Iyas, he felt most at home in that era of Egypt's history. There he was among his own people.

Despite the cruelty, extortion, dirt, smells, epidemics and other dark aspects of medieval life, when seen from the distance of history, Mamluk Cairo is, according to Husayn Fawzi, a city that offered many pleasures to the common man. From Cairo an empire that embraced Asia Minor, Libya, Nubia and Arabia was ruled and efficiently governed. People from the most exotic and remote places came there to pursue their careers and earn a living. It was a centre of scholarship, commerce and art, where books and beautiful things were produced. With its recreation venues, a profusion of celebrations, amusements, waterfront festivities, glamorous processions and parades, music and poetry, Cairo was a brilliant and bustling metropolis that maintained its Mamluk identity even after four centuries of Ottoman rule.

Cairo of the Mamluks is a homage to Sindbad's choice.

I dedicate it to the memory of my father, who opened my eyes on Sindbad.

Acknowledgements

The research carried out for this book has been supported by grants from SOAS, University of London, and the British Academy, who both also sponsored the production of the book. I am very grateful for their support.

The publication was also subsidized with grants from the Barakat Trust, the Alessandro Bruschettini Foundation and the Max van Berchem Foundation. The Max van Berchem Foundation is a scientific foundation established in Geneva, Switzerland, in memory of Max van Berchem (1863–1921), the founder of Arabic epigraphy. Its aim is to promote the study of Islamic and Arabic archaeology, history, geography, art, epigraphy, religion and literature.

I am deeply grateful to Hussam al-Din Isma'il for the wealth of information he generously shared with me and for his help on so many occasions. Our excursions to the Mamluk monuments have been a memorable experience.

Bernard O'Kane's pertinent comments were enlightening. I thank him for giving me access to the epigraphy database compiled under his leadership and not yet published at the time of the preparation of my manuscript.

I am also indebted to my colleagues: Howyda al-Harithy for generously giving me access to her unpublished survey of the madrasa of Sultan Hasan – her drawing of the sections of the eastern wings have been integrated in the section published in this book; Christel Kessler for allowing me to consult her unpublished paper on the mosque of al-Nasir Muhammad; Chahinda Karim for her prompt response to my queries; and Stephen Vernoit for his valuable editorial contribution to the manuscript and sagacious comments.

As indicated in the list of illustrations, many of the photographs were taken by Bernard O'Kane. Nicholas Warner drew the axonometric views and all the maps and plans in this book. The plans are based on originals by the Egyptian Antiquities Organization, K.A.C. Creswell and Michael Meinecke. I am indebted to the Research Centre for Mediterranean Archaeology of the Polish Academy of Sciences for the axonometric drawing of the Qurqumas complex.

Note to the Reader

This book presents the Mamluk architecture of Cairo in its social and urban context. It is not my aim to provide a comprehensive survey of monuments in the entire Mamluk territories; this has already been done by Michael Meinecke in his monograph on Egypt and Syria, which also provides a list of buildings recorded in the literary sources.

In the first nine chapters of this book I examine the cultural background and the patronage of the pious foundations that shaped the architecture of Cairo during the Mamluk period. The use of Cairo's urban space by the sultans as a theatre for their practice of kingship established a strong link between urban and architectural planning and design, which contributed to the singularity of Mamluk architecture in Cairo; this has stimulated me to take a close look at the urban evolution of the capital and its significance in determining the character of the metropolitan architecture. A general view on the arts and crafts and symbols of status should elucidate Mamluk aesthetical and artistic approaches before dealing with the structure and material aspects of the building craft, the evolution of the architecture and its techniques, and the construction methods documented by Philipp Speiser in an appendix. In the second part of the book 60 entries are dedicated to the major monuments and other buildings of interest. Some of these buildings have not survived. Many have not been examined before.

This book is focused on religious architecture not only because of its greater social and political significance in Mamluk society, but also due to the scarcity of extant secular architecture from this period. The few remaining residences are in a fragmentary state and have been modified in later periods, and, most of all, a number of studies, including the collective publication by Garcin, Maury, Revault and Zakarya on the residential architecture of this period, made it unnecessary to discuss this topic in the present context.

I hope that this book will stimulate more studies in this field, and more concern for the conservation of the Mamluk architectural legacy. It is sad to recall that the magnificent portal of the mosque of Emir Husayn (Fig. 30) and the mosque of Qanibay al-Rammah at Nasiriyya have been demolished in recent years.

Note on technicalities

Waqf documents have been a major source for this study and crucial to the understanding of the functions and the urban context of Mamluk foundations and monuments. Unpublished documents are cited in the notes; published deeds are included in the bibliography.

In order not to overload the text with diacritic signs, transliteration had to be limited to long quotations and difficult phrases. Also for the aesthetics of the text, Arabic architectural terms are not italicized.

References to the 'Comité' indicate the Comité de conservation des monuments de l'art arabe, which was in charge of the preservation of the monuments of Cairo from 1882 to 1963, when it was replaced by the Egyptian Antiquities Organization.

Some monuments that have not been discussed in individual entries are identified with their index number adopted in the maps and publications of the Antiquities Organization. The monuments discussed in individual entries are numbered by chronological order and indicated by these numbers on the map and the accompanying key.

Regarding the conversion of Hijra dates to the CE equivalent, whenever it was not possible to determine the exact corresponding month or year, I have indicated a double CE month or year.

–1–

The Mamluk Sultanate (1250–1517)

The Mamluk system

The Mamluks entered history as military slaves recruited by the Ayyubid sultan of Egypt, al-Malik al-Salih Najm al-Din Ayyub (r.1240–49), to form an elite corps in his army. This corps, which al-Salih had already begun to recruit during his father's reign, consisted of Kipchak Turks from southern Russia. They were known as the Bahri Mamluks. The term 'Bahri' is usually interpreted as referring to the location of their barracks on the island of Rawda on the Nile; in Egyptian Arabic, the river is called *bahr*, which also means 'sea'.[1] The Bahri Mamluks were succeeded after 1390 by Circassian Mamluks, who were purchased in the Caucasus.

The Mamluk system of military recruitment was a tradition in Muslim lands that pre-dated by some centuries the creation of the Mamluk State of Egypt and Syria. Although the word 'mamluk' literally means 'owned', and indicates that the Mamluks were purchased, the status of a Mamluk was not identical to that of ordinary slaves, who were not allowed to carry weapons and were usually restricted to menial tasks. Paradoxically, the Mamluks were the true lords, with a social standing far above that of their freeborn Egyptian, Syrian and other subjects.

The Mamluks were purchased while still young boys of pagan, or perhaps also Christian, origin. They were trusted because of their particular status – without social ties or political affinities – and for their high military skills. The recruits were brought up in the barracks of the Citadel of Cairo, where they received a strict religious and military education as prerequisites to becoming good Muslim horsemen and fighters. After their training they were manumitted but their career

remained attached to the patron who had purchased them. In equal measure, the power and prestige of a patron depended upon his recruits. Sultan Qalawun (r.1279–90) was reported to have declared: 'All kings accomplish things with which to be commemorated, either fortunes or monuments; I have erected sturdy bastions for myself, my children, and all Muslims: these bastions are the Mamluks'. Besides allegiance to his master, a Mamluk was also tied by a strong *esprit de corps* to his peers in the same household.

Royal succession was conducted through the election of one of the great emirs from among the sultan's Mamluks, rather than on a hereditary basis. This almost invariably led to rivalry between Mamluk factions upon the death of a sultan, which sometimes escalated into destabilizing military confrontations. The Mamluk principle that succession should not be hereditary did not prevent many sultans from attempting to appoint their sons as their successors. Qalawun managed to establish a dynasty that continued to rule until 1382; the sultans of the fifteenth century were less successful in their endeavours.

The Mamluks took pride in their origin as slaves and in principle only those who had been purchased were eligible to attain the highest positions. The privileges associated with their status were such that a free Turk might arrange for a dealer to sell him as a Mamluk in order to gain access to this privileged society.[2] The fifteenth-century traveller Felix Fabri reported that some Mamluks let their children pretend to be Christians so that they would be eligible to the status of Mamluk, and could be recruited.[3] As alternatives to the military establishment, the sons of Mamluks turned to other activities, integrating themselves into the local population

Fig. 1. Three Mamluk dignitaries by Mansueti.

and participating in its cultural and economic activities. They bore Muslim names, unlike the true Mamluks who cultivated their identity by retaining their Turkish names. In practice, however, the system could not entirely exclude the sons of Mamluks in high positions. The Mamluks owned by civilians did not join the aristocracy.

The Mamluks spoke Turkish, which was also the *lingua franca* among the Circassians; not all were proficient in Arabic. Despite their humble origins and their exclusive attitude, they managed to earn the respect of their Arab subjects thanks to their zeal in sharing with them the values of Islam. They earned admiration and prestige as the true guardians of Islam during a most critical period of history by repelling both the Crusaders and the Mongols. The historian and philosopher Ibn Khaldun praised the Mamluk military system for having created one of

the best armies in the world, and described them as a blessing from God to the Muslims.

In the eyes of the Muslim rulers, however, the origin of the Mamluks was a subject of scorn, and it was used against them. The Mongols, who boasted of their descent from Chingiz Khan and other exalted ancestors, did not value the Mamluks' obscure origins. Neither did the Aq Qoyunlu Turcomans or the Ottomans, who deplored the fact that the Holy Cities of Islam were governed by former slaves instead of kings of royal descent. In response to such challenges, and also to the fact that the Shafi'i rite of Islamic law does not acknowledge the rule of Turks,[4] some Circassian sultans referred to fabricated genealogies that traced their ancestry to the Quraysh, the tribe of the Prophet.[5] The pious Sultan Jaqmaq considered upon his access to the throne that he should change his name to Muhammad. However, being aware of the awe that the Mamluks inspired in the world, and fearing the 'greed of other rulers' (*ṭamaʿ al-mulūk fīhi*) who might think he was not a Turk, he preferred instead to call himself Muhammad Jaqmaq.[6]

The Mamluks in history

The first phase of Mamluk history began in 1250 after the Ayyubid sultan al-Salih Najm al-Din had died, while fighting the Crusader invasion under the leadership of Louis IX at the Egyptian city of Damietta. Although al-Salih's son and designated heir Turanshah was at that time absent in the Jazira (in Mesopotamia), the Mamluk army achieved a decisive victory and captured the French king. The victory of al-Salih's army of Mamluks at the battle of Mansura in February 1250 led to the retreat of the defeated Crusaders, who were forced to pay a ransom for their captured king, and it opened a route to power for the Mamluks. Their allegiance to their former patron al-Salih did not prevent them from eliminating his son and heir al-Muʿazzam Turanshah in May 1250, and installing his widow and former slave Shajar al-Durr on Egypt's throne with the title of sultan. She was not Turanshah's mother, and her own son Khalil died as a baby. Nevertheless, she added to her name on coinage the official title of 'mother of the victorious king Khalil', and the *khutba*, or Friday prayer, referred to her as the wife of al-Salih.

Facing opposition from the Ayyubids in Syria, Shajar al-Durr had to abdicate three months later in favour of the Mamluk commander-in-chief of the army, al-Muʿizz Aybak, whom she married. The rivalry between factions, and most of all the conflict with the members of the Ayyubid dynasty who still held power in Syria, prompted the Mamluks to enthrone the Ayyubid child al-Ashraf Musa as a shadow-sultan alongside al-Muʿizz Aybak – the initiative came from Baybars al-Bunduqdari, the future sultan. Musa's enthronement was a gesture to pacify rivals and opponents for a while, and a means by which the Mamluks emphasized continuity and allegiance to their Ayyubid origins and to their patron al-Salih. Aybak eventually sent Musa into exile, but the de facto ruler during his reign continued to be Shajar al-Durr, until she had him assassinated in 1257, upon hearing that he planned to marry the daughter of Badr al-Din Lu'lu', the ruler of Mosul. She was herself killed immediately afterwards.

Meanwhile, more than one pretender laid claim to the throne and Baybars, who had sought refuge in Syria, braced himself to fight the Mamluk rulers in Cairo. However, the Mongol invasion of Syria that followed the fall of Baghdad in 1258 created a new situation, which required urgent help from Egypt. Qutuz, a Mamluk of Aybak and the regent of Aybak's son, responded by appointing himself sultan in November 1259, and allying himself with Baybars. Their alliance eventually succeeded in repelling the Mongols in September 1260 at the famous battle of 'Ayn Jalut. One month later, Baybars assassinated Qutuz and seized the Mamluk throne.

When the Mamluks took power, Egypt and Syria had been separately governed by different members of the Ayyubid dynasty. Unlike Egypt, which was ruled by one sultan, Syria was divided into several principalities. Sultan al-Zahir Baybars (r.1260–77) eventually united Syria and the Hijaz with Egypt under his authority. In a series of campaigns he seized major strongholds from the Crusaders and raided Little Armenia. From Egypt he expanded Mamluk authority to include Nubian territory. Besides his heroic performance in warfare, Baybars established himself as a great statesman able to consolidate his authority and cultivate extensive diplomatic alliances. With administrative reforms, extensive infrastructure works, and a large programme of pious foundations, he confirmed his role as the de facto founder of the Mamluk State, and the designer of the Mamluk court and its hierarchy.

Following Baybars' death, two of his sons succeeded him, and in 1279 Qalawun, the de facto ruler, became sultan. He continued the fight against the Crusaders by conquering three of the four Frankish capitals in Syria, and he died on his way to conquer Acre. This final victory was achieved in the following year by his son al-Ashraf Khalil (r.1290–93), who seized the remaining Frankish strongholds.

Qalawun succeeded in doing what Baybars had strived for; against Mamluk principles, he established a hereditary succession that lasted a century. His son al-Nasir Muhammad came to the throne as a child and, unlike the previous infant rulers, his reign from 1293 to 1341, with interruptions in 1294–99 and 1309–10, was long. He inherited a kingdom free from foreign occupation and he managed to protect it from external threats. In 1303, during his second reign, the Mamluk army repelled a Mongol invasion of Syria by the Ilkhanid ruler Ghazan, and in 1313 during his third reign a renewed attempt to conquer Syria by Ghazan's successor, Uljaytu, was thwarted. Al-Nasir's third reign was a post-war era

of stability and prosperity, to which he added glory and brilliance with a highly ambitious building programme and considerable work in developing the infrastructure.

During the second half of the fourteenth century, however, the reigns of his weak descendants over a period of four decades resulted in a period of political instability and civil war. The reign of Sultan al-Ashraf Sha'ban saw the devastating sack of Alexandria in 1365 by the Crusaders, under the leadership of the king of Cyprus, Pierre de Lusignan.

The world of the Bahri Mamluks was dominated at the outset by the Crusaders and the Mongols, but their containment opened the way for diplomatic and trade relations with these former enemies, so that the Mamluks could concentrate their resources on internal development. Al-Zahir Baybars was keen to promote commerce and encourage international merchants to trade with his kingdom. He entertained friendly relations with Constantinople, which were later consolidated by a treaty concluded by his successor Qalawun. This entente secured the import of Mamluks from the Black Sea, which was of vital and strategic importance to the state. The conversion to Islam of the Crimean Tatars facilitated friendly relations with the Golden Horde, with whom the Mamluks shared their hostility towards the Ilkhanid dynasty of Iran. However, the marriage of al-Nasir Muhammad in 1320 to a princess from the clan of Chingiz Khan sealed an entente with the Ilkhanids and boosted trade with the Mongols and China.

The diplomatic and commercial network that linked Africa, Asia and Europe facilitated the spice trade, which was the major source of Mamluk wealth besides agriculture. This network stretched into the Indian Ocean via the Red Sea, which was now fully under Mamluk control with ports in the Hijaz as entrepôts, and the connection with Yemen secured. The predominance of the Mamluks in the Indian Ocean trade was secured by the Egyptian branch of the Karimi merchants, a kind of corporation of overseas wholesale dealers, some of whom were among the wealthiest in the world. Their role declined, however, in the fifteenth century. Despite the papal sanctions the Venetians, Genoese, Catalans and French all traded with the Mamluk State, purchasing Indian spices and selling European agricultural and luxury products.

The great period of prosperity was brought to an end by Timur's brutal invasion of Syria in 1400, which had a devastating effect on Mamluk military and economic resources in the ensuing period. The disaster, which was coupled with natural catastrophes and famine, coincided with the beginning of the rule of the Circassian sultans, and consequently accentuated the perception of historical rupture between the Turkish or Bahri and the Circassian periods.

Qalawun had been the first sultan to recruit Mamluks of Circassian origin from the Caucasus. Following a revolt of this corps against al-Ashraf Sha'ban and a subsequent period of disorder, Sultan Barquq (r.1382–99, with interruption), himself of Circassian origin, seized the throne and ushered in the rule of the Circassian sultans, which lasted up to the close of the Mamluk period. In the following century, which witnessed as many as twenty-five sultans on the throne, the reigns of al-Mu'ayyad Shaykh, al-Ashraf Barsbay, al-Zahir Jaqmaq, al-Ashraf Inal, al-Zahir Khushqadam and al-Ashraf Qaytbay stand out as periods of relative stability, which earned positive assessments by contemporary chroniclers. Barsbay even managed in 1426 to extend his territory by annexing Cyprus, which remained a tributary of the Mamluk sultans until the end of their rule. Like al-Mu'ayyad Shaykh he managed temporarily to reform the monetary system, which remained nonetheless a permanent challenge to the Mamluk State. In an attempt to redress the economic situation and improve his resources, Barsbay implemented a controversial policy of monopolizing foreign and major local trade.

Most of the problems the Circassians had to confront were due to factors beyond their control. In addition to its effect on the economy, Timur's invasion altered the geopolitical landscape of the world around the Mamluks. The eastern connections that were formerly cultivated with the Mongols were interrupted. The emergence of the Turcoman principalities in south Anatolia following Timur's withdrawal, and the growing power of the Ottomans in this area, began to challenge Mamluk territorial integrity. Qaytbay managed to halt an attempt by Uzun Hasan (r.1457–78), the Aq Qoyunlu ruler of Iraq and Tabriz, to encroach upon Mamluk hegemony in southeast Anatolia. Although he achieved a victory in the first military encounters with the Ottomans in the Taurus between 1485 and 1490, these confrontations took a heavy toll on the Mamluk economy. In addition to warfare, a series of plague epidemics weakened the demographic resources, while bedouin raids in Syria and Egypt severely affected agricultural production. Moreover, the discovery of a sea route around the Cape of Good Hope by the Portuguese and their commercial expansion in the Indian Ocean substantially undermined the Mamluk monopoly on the spice trade.

While the vigour of the Mamluk State was dwindling, the expansion of the Ottomans in Anatolia and southeast Europe, crowned by their conquest of Constantinople in 1453, inevitably aroused their desire for the heart of the Muslim world, the Mamluk sultanate of Egypt, Syria and the Hijaz. In 1516 Sultan al-Ghawri fell in battle against the Ottomans at Marj Dabiq near Aleppo, and in 1517 the last Mamluk sultan, al-Ashraf Tumanbay, was executed at the gate of Bab Zuwayla in Cairo by order of Sultan Selim, who annexed the Mamluk territories to the Ottoman Empire.

The cultural environment

The Mamluks were in an ambiguous situation; they were strangers in the territory they governed and spoke a language that was foreign to their subjects. In Arabic historiography, the Mamluk regime was designated as *dawlat al-turk*, or 'the regime of the Turks', *al-turk* being the generic term for the Mamluks as a system, including the Circassians.

Although faith united the Mamluks with their subjects, some secular and cultural differences remained between them. The Turkic Mamluk culture at the court coexisted with the dominant Arabic culture of the Egyptian and Syrian populations.[7] At the court of the Bahri Mamluks, translation was necessary to facilitate communication between the rulers and their subjects. Under their Circassian successors, who also spoke Turkish at the court, translation took place on an even broader scale, extending to Persian and Turkish literature. Unlike their predecessors, who were recruited at a very young age, the Circassian Mamluks arrived as adolescents or adults and already had a sense of identity formed by their native background.

Despite the attempts of the Mongols to conquer Mamluk territory and the wars between the two powers, the Bahri Mamluks felt an affinity for the Mongols, with whom they considered themselves ethnically and culturally related, in contrast to their relationship with their subjects. The Mamluk army included Mongols, who came in large numbers as refugees to Cairo following the entente between Baybars and Baraka Khan of the Golden Horde, both of who were united by their antagonism to the Ilkhanids of Iran. Al-Zahir Baybars' wives were Mongolians, and Qalawun married a Mongol woman from among the refugees who settled in Cairo in 1263. He married a second Mongolian in 1283 from the refugees who settled in Damascus, and she gave birth in 1285 to al-Nasir Muhammad. Qalawun's son al-Ashraf Khalil married Mongol women, and one of his sisters married the Mongol ruler Baraka Khan in 1276. Among the several Mongol women al-Nasir Muhammad married, one was a princess from the Ilkhanid dynasty.[8] Such family alliances could not fail to consolidate cultural affinities with the Mongols. Although the numerous concubines of a sultan or emir were of diverse origins, Egyptian wives are not mentioned in the Bahri period. The situation changed, however, with the Circassian sultans, who occasionally married into families of Egyptian notables, as in the cases of Barquq and Jaqmaq. The Circassian sultans often married Greek and Turkish women from Anatolia.

Maqrizi reported that Baybars introduced the Mongol code, or *yasa*, of Chingiz Khan in the secular legislation governing intra-Mamluk matters.[9] In this context he commented, 'their traditions and manners became widespread and filled the hearts of the kings, emirs, and soldiers of Egypt, whose fear of Chingiz Khan and his descendants, mingled in their flesh and blood with awe and glorification,' and he added that, despite their Muslim education, the Mamluks were mixing good with evil, as a result. Histories and legends of Mongol and Turkic Central Asian origin also found their way into texts written by authors of Mamluk stock. The influence of the Mongol lifestyle is confirmed in the costume of the period.[10] Similarly, the Circassian sultans encouraged Turkish scholars from various regions to join their court and sponsored their literary works. However, this court literature remained confined to Mamluk circles; it was snubbed by the native scholars and had no noteworthy impact on the Arabic-speaking culture of Syria and Egypt. There is no evidence to suggest that the endowed teaching institutions of the Mamluks were involved in the dissemination of Turkic culture; this remained confined to the secular and courtly domain.

While some sultans and emirs hardly spoke or read Arabic, others among them were highly educated in Islamic sciences and Arabic literature. Among the second and subsequent generations of Mamluks, who did not participate in government and were more culturally integrated, some were prominent Arabic-Islamic scholars, such as Ibn Aybak al-Dawadari, Baybars al-Mansuri, Ibn Taghribirdi and Ibn Iyas. Eventually Arab stereotypes that portrayed the Mamluks as crude and barbaric could not be upheld.[11]

The significance of the Mamluks to the history of Arab culture cannot be over-emphasized. By assuming the role of guardians of Islam, their patronage of pious foundations had a tremendous impact on Egyptian and Syrian urban culture for the centuries to come. The promotion of institutions of learning on an unprecedented scale activated academic endeavour, stimulated the visual arts and enriched urban life. The pious foundations, which were equipped with substantial libraries, boosted scholarship and book production, and, while in principle dedicated to the study of the legal and religious sciences, they disseminated a broad range of knowledge. The biographies of the notables of Mamluk society show that scholars of the time were learned in a large array of disciplines in addition to the strictly religious ones. This included medicine, astronomy, arithmetic, accountancy, land surveying, history and belles-lettres. It is interesting to note that a fourteenth-century astronomer (*muwaqqit*), 'Ala' al-Din Ibn al-Shatir, employed in the Umayyad mosque of Damascus to calculate prayer times, achieved a major breakthrough in the study of astronomy, which revised the Ptolemaic views. His findings became known to Copernicus, who integrated them in his work.[12] This example shows how Mamluk religious institutions could also provide a fertile ground for non-religious studies and thinking.

Rather than being princely paraphernalia or a collector's item, the book in Mamluk culture was the product of pious endowments and a common commodity. Waqf documents indicate that all religious foundations were equipped with libraries, often managed by an appointed librarian.[13] Considering the number of religious foundations, books were available to a wide audience. Biographical literature also refers to substantial libraries owned by scholars and emirs, and physical evidence indicates commissions of books for royal libraries.[14] Yashbak min Mahdi, Qaytbay's great secretary, collected and commissioned books, and when necessary acquired them by coercion.[15] The library of the madrasa founded by Jamal al-Din Mahmud, the *ustadar* or majordomo of Barquq, which was originally the collection of the Shafi'i chief judge and polymath Ibn Jama'a (d.1416), was described by Maqrizi as unparalleled in Egypt and Syria and covering all disciplines.[16] Another majordomo, Jamal al-Din, who was described as a notorious evildoer, purchased the substantial library of the former sultan al-Mansur Hajji, which included rare and lavish manuscripts, for his private collection and for the library of his madrasa. After confiscating his estate, Sultan Faraj transferred many of these books back to the Citadel,[17] but his successor al-Mu'ayyad helped himself from this collection to equip the library of his own mosque. Little is known about the royal library of the Citadel.

Waqf documents and physical evidence indicate that all religious foundations included a maktab or charitable primary school for orphan boys, which spread literacy at an early age among the needy. The maktab gradually became a prominent architectural feature of Mamluk religious monuments.

Access to the metropolitan teaching institutions, being philanthropic and in principle open to all, offered an opportunity for the local urban and rural population to ascend in the social scale as 'men of the pen'. They provided the basis for the education of the ulema, who came from various social backgrounds including the rural, mercantile and craftsmen's milieus. They were either local subjects, arabized migrants from other Muslim countries, or sons and descendants of Mamluks. A number of them were of Christian birth and converted to Islam. Those who did not accede to the highest administrative positions practised mercantile and artisanal trades as their main means of earning their living or to improve their income. Besides constituting the religious establishment, the 'men of the pen' provided the civil servants, who administered religious, political and financial matters, along with the intelligentsia and the circles of historians, encyclopedists and poets.

Through their close association with their patrons' pious foundations, the ulema tended to bridge the cultural divide between the ruling aristocracy and their subjects. This was not an insurmountable problem in medieval Islamic society, which traditionally integrated a multitude of races and cultures. At the same time, however, social segregation between the military elite and the rest of the population was maintained; under Circassian rule, however, the boundaries between classes became increasingly permeable.

Along with the ulema, the merchants connected the aristocracy with the city and its population. Investment in trade was practised by the Mamluk establishment as well as the urban bourgeoisie. The sultans and emirs participated in commercial business by delegating merchants and administrators. Some ulema were merchants or came from mercantile families, and some merchants were also scholars. With the spread of learning, the middle class expanded, contributing to and participating in the wealth that the aristocracy held from land resources and trade.

The historians among the ulema examined and assessed their socio-political environment in a lucid and critical manner, most of them working on a freelance basis rather than being hired as court historians. Only a few historical works were directly commissioned by the rulers or dedicated to them. Although the ulema had to rely on princely patronage for their living and for their employment in government offices or religious foundations, which naturally cost them much of the non-alignment they were eager to uphold towards their Mamluk masters, their accounts testify to a remarkable boldness and independence of thinking.

Facing the military and political power of the Mamluk ruling elite, the ulema articulated a strong sense of their identity as the learned elite, as is reflected in the plethora of biographical works dedicated to persons of their cultural background. It is generally acknowledged that the major achievements of the Mamluk period were historiography and architecture, and the two disciplines were more interconnected than might at first appear. The massive patronage of funerary architecture as memorials to the patrons must have had an impact on the historians and intellectuals of the period, who were similarly concerned with the cultivation of their own literary memorials. In one of the scholarly gatherings that Sultan al-Ghawri hosted, the *Shahnama* of Firdawsi was discussed, and it was concluded that the patronage of such a book was a better memorial to the patron than a monument that would fall in ruins after three or four hundred years.[18]

The belief that a book was more durable than a monument was not new in Arabic literature; through their chronicles and biographical encyclopedias the Mamluk historians aimed to immortalize their own elite. Al-Sakhawi praised the value of biographical literature for reviving the memory of the deceased: reading about the life of a Muslim was like visiting him, and reading about the life of a saint was like receiving his blessing.[19] By making this analogy between reading a biography and visiting the tomb of a dead person or a saint, a link was established between biographies and the culture of mausoleums cherished by the Mamluk patrons. Sakhawi's words: 'No one is dead whom memory keeps alive', 'the kings and the rich spent money on buildings, fortresses and castles only for the perpetuation of their memory', and 'a tale is all a person leaves behind; strive that your tale be known as good and kind', reveal the link between the monument and the book in the Mamluk period.[20]

Thus, the proliferation of literary commemoration cannot be dissociated from the funerary architecture of the Mamluks; rather, it should be seen as the intellectuals' response to it. It is also interesting to recall that al-Sakhawi dedicated an entire volume with 1,075 entries of his biographical encyclopedia to women, most of whom were from the circle of the urban and learned bourgeoisie to which he belonged.

Due to the difference of language between the rulers and their subjects, the Mamluk sultans and emirs did not involve themselves in the patronage of Arabic poetry, although it was the foremost art of the Arabic-speaking population. The professional court poet who represented princely refinement and classical connoisseurship was out of fashion, and poetry turned to a non-princely audience and dealt with daily life. Mamluk historians inserted poems extensively in their texts to enhance and flavour their accounts. Poetry thereby became a spontaneous expression and the pastime or hobby of scholars, historians, bureaucrats, and even commoners and craftsmen.[21] Ibrahim al-Mi'mar, who was a builder, had the privilege to be listed in Safadi's biographical encyclopedia, not for anything related to his profession, but rather because he was a poet, who composed a famous *diwan* or collection of his vernacular poems. His status as a poet did not make him deny his profession, which rather inspired some of his poetical images.[22] The emergence of freelance literati and hobby poets was a social phenomenon that reflected the aspirations of many individuals towards self-expression and the dissemination of their personal opinions and critiques of social and political issues. This dissemination of freelance literature was a further consequence of the patronage of charitable educational institutions by the Mamluk aristocracy.

Mamluk Cairo was the home of a mixed population: besides the elements of the Mamluk army, which also included Turcomans, Kurds, Anatolians, Greeks and Caucasians, refugees from the entire Muslim world were drawn to the Egyptian capital. Migrants from al-Andalus left their traces in architectural decoration, and a Maghrebi community existed already prior to the Mamluks. Even captured Crusaders lived with their families in a quarter of the city during al-Nasir Muhammad's reign. Besides scholars and students, the migration of other elements from various provinces of Iran was a constant phenomenon in Mamluk territory.[23] After the first wave pushed forward by the Mongols in the early fourteenth century, which introduced artists from Iraq to Egypt and Syria, a second one followed Timur's invasion, which also led the Jalayirid sultan Ibn Uways to seek refuge in Mamluk territory. With his retinue he settled for several years in Damascus. Maqrizi mentioned 'weavers from the East' (*al-mashariqa al-huyyak*), who settled in Cairo.[24] The number of Iranians in Cairo in 1418 had increased to such an extent that orders were issued on more than one occasion to evict them.[25] During the reign of al-Mu'ayyad many Iranians occupied high positions in the bureaucracy. Refugees also came from Baghdad and Mosul after the Qara Qoyunlu ruler Isbahan took Iraq from his brother Shah Muhammad in 1434. According to reports reaching Cairo, these cities were being deserted at that time.[26] Turkish scholars and Sufis from Anatolia and Iran also settled in Cairo, the latter increasing after the emergence of the Shi'i Safavids.[27] In the late fifteenth century, travellers reported the presence of a large number of converted Europeans of diverse origin among the Mamluk aristocracy.[28]

The geographical variety in the urban population, the wide commercial network, and the refinement of the Mamluk cities had a significant impact on secular culture, which found expression in the collection and compilation of the tales of *The Thousand and One Nights*. The earliest documented edition of the tales, as we know them today, goes back to the thirteenth century,

and was produced either in Syria or Egypt. Their vernacular Arabic, interspersed with classical and popular poems, combined fantastic fairy tales from India and Iran, anecdotal urban stories from the bazaars of Cairo, Damascus and Baghdad, bourgeois romances, adventures of rogues and seafarers, true historical accounts and mythology. Their syncretistic character reflects the wealth of Egyptian and Syrian cities in Mamluk times, and the commercial network that spread between China, India and the Mediterranean. They celebrate the mercantile culture of an urban society accustomed to consuming goods from all over the world and dealing with merchants of various origins, and they express a secular culture in which morality and faith played a minor role and where women could be protagonists. Cairo of the Mamluks was the natural environment of *The Thousand and One Nights*.

– 2 –

Pious Patronage

Institutions, scholars and waqf

Far from confining their zeal to military achievements, the Mamluks sought from the outset to consolidate their legitimacy through the patronage of both orthodox religious practice and Sufism, and by cultivating a high standard of urban culture within their territory.

The institution of a neo-Abbasid caliphate in Cairo bestowed an aura of tradition and orthodoxy on the pagan-born Mamluks. Shortly after the sack of Baghdad in 1258 and the fall of the Abbasid caliphate, al-Zahir Baybars appointed an Abbasid prince to be the first of a line of shadow caliphs whose task was to fulfil ceremonial functions in the Mamluk State and legitimize Mamluk rule. The caliph invested the new sultan, and, conversely, he himself was invested by the ruling sultan. He was present on all solemn occasions. However, aside from his ceremonial function, the Mamluks did not allow the caliph to exert any authority in court or society.[1] Baybars kept the caliph he had himself invested in captivity in one of the Citadel towers. Most subsequent sultans maintained this attitude towards the caliphs, who, with their families, led rather humble lives.[2] The pious Qaytbay did not refrain in a fit of anger from evicting the caliph from his residence in the Citadel, to punish him for having let a fire break out in his kitchen; it spread to the sultan's warehouse, destroying most of his valuable tents.[3] The caliphs were not even given the privilege of a dedicated mausoleum; rather, they were collectively buried in a mausoleum probably built by al-Zahir Baybars for his sons in the cemetery of Sayyida Nafisa. Many of them dwelt nearby in a palace built by Shajar al-Durr.[4] It is a remarkable fact that none of the Abbasid caliphs of Cairo is associated with monumental patronage; their modest resources did not allow them to sponsor any religious foundations or build any representative monuments. The caliphs were granted for their living the supervision of the endowment of the shrine of Sayyida Nafisa, along with the right to collect its donations and the monopoly on its sale of oil and candles.

A complement to their reinstatement of the caliphate was the Mamluks' control of the Hijaz and their role as the 'servants of the Haramayn', i.e. of the holy cities of Mecca and Medina, which they jealously protected from interference from other Muslim rulers. The most significant symbol of their presence in the Haramayn was their prerogative to dispatch the cover for the Ka'ba from Cairo. It was woven in the black colour of the Abbasid caliphate, which was also the colour of the caliphs' and the sultans' investiture gowns. The building zeal of the Mamluks in Mecca, Medina, Jerusalem and Hebron is well documented in archives and literary sources, and supported by physical evidence. No less significant than the pious foundations the Mamluks established was their continuous maintenance of the infrastructure and hydraulic installations along the pilgrimage road and at the holy sites.

Besides their sponsorship of Sufis, who migrated to their territory, the sultans and emirs demonstrated their reverence for the traditional local saints of their realm; they participated in their cults, and constantly rebuilt, embellished and endowed their shrines in Egypt and Syria.[5] In addition, the mosques of 'Amr Ibn al-'As and al-Azhar, venerated as the first Muslim sanctuaries of Fustat and Qahira, were regularly restored and refurbished, and their curriculum enlarged to fulfil functions comparable to contemporary madrasas.

Unlike the Ottomans, who adopted Hanafism as their official *madhhab*, the Mamluks, following the initiative of al-Zahir Baybars, appointed four chief qadis to represent the four *madhhab*s of Sunni law.[6] The Shafi'i judge had the additional task of supervising the waqfs or pious endowments.[7] This apparently even-handed policy towards the four schools was in fact a means of enhancing the status of Hanafism, to which they themselves adhered, and which previously had not played a significant role in Egypt and Syria, where the Shafi'i prevailed alongside the Maliki school.

There was more than one reason behind the Mamluks' preference for Hanafism. Besides the fact that this *madhhab* was dominant in Central Asia and was generally adopted by Turkic peoples, it suited the Mamluk regime politically, because in principle the Shafi'is did not acknowledge the legitimacy of Turkish rule; they required the ruler to be of Qurayshi[8] descent and a *mujtahid*, i.e. qualified for theological and juridical interpretation, both of which did not apply to the Mamluks. Commenting on Sultan al-Muzaffar Qutuz, who ruled for less than a year before his assassination by Baybars in 1260, the Syrian historian Abu Shama said that his assassination was the inevitable fate of a sultan who did not adhere to the *madhhab* of Imam Shafi'i, the patron saint of Egypt (*sahib misr*). Abu Shama believed that the premature death of Qutuz was a consequence of the spell (*sirr*) of the imam.[9] From the opposite perspective, in a defence of Hanafism against Shafi'ism, the jurist al-Tarsusi vehemently rejected such opinions. Moreover, he emphasized the advantage of Hanafism in conceding to the ruler more authority than Shafi'ism, allowing him to exert his power with less constraint.[10] The Mamluks also found supporters among Shafi'i scholars; in the late fifteenth century Abu Hamid al-Qudsi compiled a tract devoted to fervent praise of the moral and political virtues of the Mamluks, in which he described them as the 'salt of Egypt' (*al-turk milh misr*).[11]

The multi-rite policy enhanced the Mamluks' religious authority in the Muslim world, and was appropriate for the Mamluk capital as the seat of the neo-Abbasid caliphate. Many royal madrasas taught the four schools, following the model of the madrasa founded by the last Ayyubid sultan, al-Salih Najm al-Din, who in turn followed the imperial model of the madrasa founded by Caliph al-Mustansir in Baghdad. This encouraged students and scholars from other parts of the Muslim world to study and teach in Cairo. The pluralism of *madhhab*s was not a consistent feature of the Mamluks' politico-religious attitude, since some Mamluk foundations were exclusively dedicated to Hanafism. Whereas Friday prayer in royal foundations was held by a Shafi'i preacher, and the Shafi'i teacher had the privilege to sit in the qibla hall or sanctuary, the heads of the Sufis in royal religious foundations were mostly Hanafis. The patronage of Sufism thus strengthened Hanafism, departing from the Ayyubid policy, which promoted the Shafi'i and Maliki schools. Occasionally, financial incentives were used by the Mamluk patrons to boost the recruitment of Hanafis to the detriment of Shafi'is, as was the case at Sultan Barsbay's funerary complex in the city.[12] The endowments of the sultans Hasan and al-Mu'ayyad provided hospitality for more students of the Hanafi rite than others.

In his function as supreme authority over religious and secular matters, the sultan appointed the rectors of the great religious foundations, thus maintaining his grip on religious and academic life at the same time as controlling the administration of pious endowments and the upkeep of their buildings. The sponsorship and maintenance of teachers and students consolidated their allegiance to, and hence their dependence on, the Mamluk patrons. For their diplomatic missions the sultans often appointed Sufis and scholars as envoys to other Muslim courts.

The Mamluks practised scholarly hospitality as a sign of royalty and a demonstration of piety and learning. Acting as the central religious authority in the Muslim world, they pursued a persistent policy of encouraging foreign scholars and mystics to join their religious foundations. One of the most notable examples of

Mamluk scholarly patronage was Sultan Barquq's promotion of Ibn Khaldun, the great Tunisian historian and philosopher, who was offered the office of Maliki chief judge in Egypt and a teaching position in the sultan's funerary madrasa. Ibn Khaldun moreover acted as Barquq's ambassador at Timur's court.[13]

Prior to the Mamluks, Sufism in Egypt had already been associated with mystics of foreign origin. When in 1173 Salah al-Din founded the first khanqah in Egypt, he specified that it should house foreign Sufis in preference to local men. The second earliest khanqah mentioned by Maqrizi was founded in 1284–5, during Qalawun's reign, by the emir Aydakin al-Bunduqdar. In the absence of a waqf document its stipulations are not known, but the next funerary khanqah to be built, by al-Muzaffar Baybars al-Jashnakir, gave priority to foreigners.[14] Although the waqf document of al-Nasir Muhammad's khanqah in Siryaqus is not explicit regarding such preferences, its first rector, Nizam al-Din Ishaq, was of Iranian origin, albeit of Arab Qurayshi descent, as his full name indicates.[15] Likewise, Qawam al-Din Muhammad, the rector of the Sufis at al-Nasir's New Mosque, al-Jami' al-Jadid, originated from Shiraz. Al-Nasir moreover dedicated two zawiyas, the Qubbat al-Nasr and the zawiya of Taqiyy al-Din, to Sufis from Iran.[16] The khanqahs of his great emirs Baktimur and Qawsun also had foreign rectors.

The chroniclers regularly report foreigners, sometimes adventurers, coming to Cairo to pursue a scholarly career in one of the princely foundations. Maqrizi wrote that, in 1340, 'a group of Iranians, wearing a strange outfit with very tall hats with turbans looking like *tarturs*',[17] arrived with their shaykh called Zada. The emir Qawsun welcomed them and hosted them in his khanqah, and then spoke to the sultan, al-Nasir Muhammad, about them. The sultan appointed Zada as rector of the Rukniyya khanqah founded by al-Muzaffar Baybars, which he then administered and where he held a weekly chanting and recitation session (*sama'*) sponsored by Qawsun.[18]

The scholarly immigration from Iran and Central Asia did not diminish in the fifteenth century. Janibak, the great secretary of Sultan Khushqadam, dedicated an important foundation to Sufis from Iran, and the shaykh of Yashbak's mosque in Matariyya was called Sinan al-Azarbayjani.[19] Surprisingly, however, the rector of the Sufis of Qaytbay's funerary madrasa was a Maghrebi of the Maliki *madhhab*.[20]

The native elite sometimes resented the massive presence of foreign scholars, in particular Iranians and Central Asians, in Cairo's religious institutions.[21] The great merchant al-Kharrubi stipulated in his endowment for a madrasa, founded in 1374–5, that it should be dedicated exclusively to Arabs, not admitting any *a'jam*.[22] Maqrizi accused the *a'jam* of trying to impose Hanafism in Egypt during the late Bahri period.[23] Since they were Hanafi, these *a'jam* were most likely of Turkic origin.

A significant outcome of Mamluk pious patronage was the full integration of Sufism in religious and academic life.

The ruling elite had a strong inclination for Sufism, and in particular an affinity for Turkic and Iranian Sufi shaykhs. The madrasa and the khanqah inherited from the Ayyubids were initially two distinct, if not antagonistic, institutions, whose purpose was to teach orthodox Islam and Sufism respectively. By the late fifteenth century, however, as the result of a gradual development stimulated by Mamluk patronage, the madrasa and the khanqah had merged in the multifunctional madrasa-khanqah-mosque, where the Sufis were scholars and the scholars were Sufis. This development counteracted initial orthodox hostility against the Sufis for being idle and secluded from common religious life.[24] Besides the khanqahs, most turbas or mausoleums, and many mosques, provided Sufi services or hosted a Sufi community. As a result, Sufism had permeated religious and academic life and Mamluk culture in general. Although the chronicles and biographical encyclopedias point to the significance of the orders (*tariqa*) in Sufi culture – the order affiliation being sometimes part of a person's name – waqf documents do not mention any specific *tariqa* affiliation in connection with the khanqahs. Perhaps, by avoiding a specific affiliation, at least formally, the foundations could address a wider audience.

A pioneer initiative in the direction of merging the khanqah with the madrasa was the emir Shaykhu's religious complex, which was the first to be founded after the Black Death. Its curriculum combined the four schools of Sunni law with the programme of a khanqah. Three decades later, Sultan Barquq followed Shaykhu's example at his own funerary complex. In the meantime, however, Sultan Hasan, for some reason still to be investigated, did not include any provision for Sufism in the foundation deed of his madrasa. Instead, he enhanced the status of the madrasa by combining it for the first time with a Friday mosque. The endowment he made for his wife's funerary madrasa did not include a Sufi service either.[25]

At the same time as Sufism merged with orthodoxy, it continued to have a special and somehow talismanic association with funerary culture. Funerary foundations, even when they were not teaching institutions, generally included a Sufi service, and the chronicles always mention turba and Sufis in conjunction. The sultans Barquq and Barsbay, who both built a multifunctional complex with a mausoleum within the city, preferred to be buried in their respective mausoleums in the cemetery in the vicinity of Sufis and scholars.

Waqf documents indicate that the religious foundations of the late fifteenth century generally included a Sufi service without a specified curriculum for other religious studies. The explanation for this might be that there was no more need for additional madrasa teaching due to the ample opportunities already available.

In addition to the khanqah, which was an exclusively princely foundation, the sultans and emirs also indirectly sponsored a number of zawiyas, smaller Sufi foundations of a more individual character, focused on the person of a shaykh as the spiritual leader of a community. Unlike the khanqah, the zawiya and the ribat were often associated with specific Sufi orders.

The patronage of the Mamluks, however, did not bridge the gap between the Turco-Persian mysticism that they favoured and the local Sufism of Egypt and Syria, which was more conservative, less esoteric and closer to orthodoxy.[26] Indeed, the Mamluk patronage of Sufism might even have unintentionally promoted the antagonism between the indigenous and the foreign schools of mysticism, which persisted well into the Ottoman period.

The waqf or the Islamic system of trust based on the principle of perpetuity, promised continuity in issues of religious and political significance, and provided a framework to protect and maintain great philanthropic projects as well as commercial family enterprises. It thereby enabled the founder to play a role in socio-religious life beyond his death, thus compensating the rotating Mamluk aristocracy for its non-hereditary status. The waqf was not only applied to educational foundations and philanthropic services, for in the late Mamluk period even fortifications were endowed through waqf, as a deed in the name of the emir Yashbak regarding a fort in Alexandria attests.[27] However, the waqf could not prevent the evolution of the institutions it was intended to preserve; the system allowed for modifications. The founder's successors or subsequent supervisors could make additions and enlargements to the waqf's assets and to the curriculum, adding a course, or a Sufi service or the khutba to a madrasa, thus modifying the patron's initial scheme. Maqrizi's listing of religious foundations shows that an evolution in the function of religious foundations had taken place over time. He described some early fourteenth-century foundations as a combined madrasa and khanqah, although according to the evidence of waqf documents this combination is unlikely to have occurred in the early period, and must have been rather a later evolution of the fifteenth century. Qalawun's endowment was repeatedly enlarged by his descendants, and Faraj enlarged the endowment of his father Barquq.[28]

In addition to the building of mosques, the sultans and emirs included a large array of social services in their endowments, such as the distribution of alms and food for various occasions and places. Sultan Hasan's endowment offered medical care and clothes to its own community as well as to outsiders.[29] Barsbay included in his waqf the distribution of bread in the mosque of al-Zahir Baybars, and of sacrificed animals to the hospital of Qalawun.[30]

The obsessive zeal of the Mamluks in sponsoring religious and funerary monuments, which did not always emanate from consistent and fervent piety, had to have also other, more prag-matic, motivations. Besides pious intentions and the pursuit of immortality, material benefits that could be achieved through the waqf system were another incentive for the Mamluk ruling establishment to sponsor religious foundations. The waqf framework allowed the sponsor to reserve part of the endowment's revenue as a tax-free income for himself or his family, and circumvented the non-hereditary iqta' system that left the descendants of the Mamluks without privileges or secure financial resources.[31] Most Mamluk waqfs were a combination of a charitable and a family endowment. For example, al-Zahir Baybars endowed his madrasa with a large apartment complex, reserving one third of its revenue for his son Baraka.[32] Barsbay's estate was particularly large to allow sufficient surplus to revert to his descendants. Qaytbay included in his endowment residences for members of his family. Also, the frequency of confiscation in Mamluk ruling practice created the need to protect funds in beneficial pious endowments.

Ibn Khaldun recognized the double purpose of the Mamluks' pious foundations but did not blame them for this stratagem. More sceptical jurists, such as Suyuti, looked upon it more severely, and questioned the legitimacy of the Mamluks' endowments considering the fact that they did not own the land they were endowing, which belonged to the public treasury or bayt al-mal.[33] He even went so far as to add that, as the Mamluks themselves had been purchased with the funds of the treasury, their property also belonged to it!

A major and controversial issue concerning pious foundations was the methods used by the Mamluks to acquire the estates to be endowed. The building zeal of the ruling aristocracy throughout the period increased the demand for prestigious locations in the city suitable for their religious monuments and the commercial structures that financed them. The magnitude of the estates needed for the upkeep of the large number of pious foundations designed for perpetuity ultimately exceeded the resources available to the next generations. This was particularly problematic in the case of the agricultural land that was supposed to provide the iqta' to pay the army.[34] An attempt by Barquq to reform the system and dissolve the endowments of agricultural land and return them to the bayt al-mal met with the tough resistance of the Shafi'i chief qadi Siraj al-Din al-Bulqini.[35] The situation regarding commercial estates was no easier. The sultans and emirs regularly used their power to acquire land and commercial structures in the city that already belonged to pious endowments, thereby depriving the latter of their resources.

Aware of the threat that a foundation might face over time, their founders often sought to protect its buildings in the first place. The hierarchy of stipulations listed in waqf documents confirms the significance of the building's upkeep. In many waqf deeds the first priority on the list of stipulations is the preservation of the architecture. Furthermore, the sultans, being well aware of the risks associated with the waqf, often nominated their successors or high-ranking officials as supervisors of their endowments. Non-princely patrons also preferred to nominate persons with political power rather than jurists, because the latter were more likely to succumb to corruption.[36] Al-Nuwayri explained that the reason for publishing the waqf of al-Nasir Muhammad's madrasa in his chronicle was as a means of countering the corruption of supervisors and administrators, who concealed the documents and tampered with them, modifying their stipulations and embezzling their resources.[37] In fact, the waqf documents, with all their importance to the understanding of social history, convey an ideal image of how the patron envisaged his foundation. In reality, multiple factors could lead to the exhaustion of the waqf's resources, and eventually to substantial modifications in the foundation's programme. The large estates in Syria and Egypt, with which Sultan Hasan endowed his mosque, had considerably shrunk at the time of Maqrizi in the first quarter of the fifteenth century. The fact that a few years after Sultan Hasan's death, in 1377, an emir settled two hundred of his Mamluks in the dwellings of the madrasa, which were dedicated to students, and decades later al-Mu'ayyad moved the door and the chandelier to his own mosque, demonstrates the precarious situation of such trusts.[38]

Ultimately, the waqf system was not compatible with the vicissitudes of time. Neither the pious foundations nor their buildings could last for ever, as planned. Even so, if not the foundations, many monuments have lasted long enough to challenge contemporary Egyptian society, which is hardly able to cope with their conservation.

The ulema, who found employment and gained prestige through association with princely foundations, acknowledged the benefits to the community, and took it for granted that sultans and emirs built monuments to demonstrate their power and legitimize their rule, using even illegal methods to achieve their purpose. Moreover, many judges connived with the ruling establishment by issuing the fatwas necessary to achieve such goals,[39] as for example when al-Ghawri was allowed to transfer the relics of the Prophet from a dedicated shrine to his own mausoleum, thus breaching the stipulations of the original waqf.[40] Ultimately, consensus held that the community should take advantage of the pious endowments, notwithstanding the dubious means by which some were established. In response to those who wished to avoid praying in mosques erected by illicit means, the disillusioned Maqrizi noted that if one were to apply such criteria, worshippers would find no place left to perform their prayers.[41] On the other hand, when writing about al-Azhar mosque he commented: 'On entering this mosque one finds intimacy with God, comfort, and peace of mind unlike in any other,'[42] thereby raising the value of the 'anonymous' al-Azhar above the mosques of the Mamluks. This attitude might have been a reaction to the fact that the continuous creation of new religious foundations was reducing the role of the great old sanctuaries, the mosques of 'Amr in Fustat and al-Azhar in Qahira. Maqrizi's long and detailed entries on those two sanctuaries read as a statement whose purpose is to emphasize their significance as the true religious centres and the major shrines of the Egyptian capital. It is also interesting to note that, when Ibn Iyas blamed al-Ghawri for taking the marble of a dignitary's palace to decorate royal palaces in the Citadel, he found that 'it would have been more worthwhile to use it for his madrasa'. This comment implies a kind of justification or flexibility towards wrongdoing for a pious cause.[43]

Even when overstepping legal bounds for the benefit of their foundations and monuments, the sultans and emirs were keen to maintain an image of law-abiding pious Muslims, and not challenge openly the authority of the religious establishment. Rather than clearly break the law, they just bent it when necessary with the collaboration of lenient, corrupt or perhaps fatalistic judges and bureaucrats.[44] This was not always an easy task and cooperative judges had to be found. Ultimately, confrontation between the Mamluks and the jurists could not always be avoided, nor the conflicts among the jurists themselves, which could become heated and acrimonious. However, considering their absolute power, the efforts of the Mamluk rulers to gain the authorization of the jurists was in itself a demonstration of goodwill with the result that, despite their selective criticism, the historians did not question the legitimacy of the Mamluk regime. A *modus vivendi* prevailed according to which the rulers managed to tame those who held the moral authority, whether they were judges, teachers or chroniclers. As urban development and philanthropic activities greatly enhanced the opportunities for the Muslim community to thrive, the rulers who provided such benefits were assessed as good Muslims.

Ibn Taghribirdi's statement that 'people follow their kings',[45] whether they demonstrate piety or pursue pleasure, confirms the moral expectations of the Mamluk watchdogs towards the sultans, while Ibn Khaldun's homage to Cairo as the 'assembly of nations, ant-hill of peoples, garden of the world, throne of royalty, stronghold of Islam and symbol of its glory' attests to the acquired legitimacy of the Mamluks.

—3—

Motivation and Perception of Monumental Patronage

Prestige, memory and urban development

'When a human being dies, his doings come to an end except in three cases, [if he leaves behind] an ongoing charity, or beneficial knowledge, or a virtuous offspring to pray for him', says a frequently quoted Hadith (*idhā māta banī ādam inqaṭaʿa ʿamaluhu illā min thalāth: ṣadaqa jāriya aw ʿilm yuntafaʿ bihi aw wild ṣāliḥ yadʿū lahu*). This Hadith is often included in the preambles of waqf deeds, to define the ultimate goal of a charitable foundation. For the non-hereditary military Mamluk aristocracy, the third option was the least significant; rather, they chose to immortalize themselves by concentrating their endeavours on the first and second options, combining an ongoing charity with the dissemination of beneficial knowledge. This is the core of the intensive Mamluk patronage of religious-funerary foundations. Regardless of whether they were judged to be good or bad sultans, and pious or not, almost all sultans who were given enough time to rule sponsored religious foundations and erected monuments. This patronage stimulated architectural and artistic achievements that added brilliance to the charitable deed and prestige to the founder.

The importance of princely patronage in architectural history is rooted in the very nature of Islamic political concepts. The pre-modern Muslim ruler was per se the foremost patron of construction and urban development. This is rooted in Islamic law and in the rules of *siyasa* or statesmanship. The ruler, in his function as the trustee and administrator of the public treasury, the *bayt al-mal*, has the competence and the duty to oversee the major religious foundations, build fortifications, undertake civil projects and boost urban development, sponsor scholars, and support the needy. He assumed religious, military, economic and social tasks, and the responsibility to stimulate all activities necessary for the community to thrive.[1] Because the princely patronage of pious foundations required representative monuments, architecture occupied a central position in Muslim art. It was the most visible and most effective medium of philanthropy, legitimization and commemoration.

Muslim authors viewed the city as a cultural identity and the epitome of a superior quality of life. Only a flourishing city provided adequate opportunities for learning and scholarship, i.e. for leading the right Muslim life. The Mamluk author Ibn ʿAbd Allah al-Hasan equated building with life, as opposed to decay and death (*al-kharāb mawt wa'l-ʿimāra ḥayāh*).[2] Urban development was a source of life of which the ruler was the caretaker. There were no optimal limits for urbanization; the larger the city the higher its importance and value. Not only the foundation of mosques was expected to be useful to the community, but commercial and residential buildings as well. Ibn Iyas reported that when the two most prominent emirs, Yashbak al-Dawadar, the great secretary, and Azbak, the chief of the army, invited Sultan Qaytbay to visit their new quarters, where each welcomed him with a banquet and hosted him for the night, the sultan gave his preference to Yashbak's complex at Matariyya over Azbak's quarter, Azbakiyya. Although the reason for Qaytbay's choice was not explicitly given here, Ibn Iyas himself judged that Azbakiyya neither served a pious cause nor was of any use to the Muslim community (*wa kāna dhālika fī ghayr ṭāʿa li-'llāh taʿālā wa lā bihi manfaʿa li'l-muslimīn*).[3]

The Mamluk attitude of urban *horror vacui* was in full accord with the expectations of the moral monitors of the time. The fact that the building zeal of the Mamluks did not diminish, and that the quality of their architecture was hardly affected by political and economic decline, attests to the obstinate and unshakable priority of monumental patronage in their concept of rule.

Ibn Khaldun's philosophical ideas regarding historical evolution and civilization were inspired by Mamluk Cairo, where he spent the latest and best part of his career. His statement on the accumulation of urban culture in the true madina points to Cairo. He viewed the madina as the place where history is perceived and documented, where the achievements of monarchs complement each other over generations. Artistic refinement and scientific progress required long procedures to mature, therefore the longer the urban tradition of a city the higher the quality of its culture. Great monumental works are the collective achievements of successive generations and the product of accumulated knowledge, which itself is an addition of learning. They require large-scale organization and a massive concentration of labour and resources, which only a powerful state can realize. Architecture is thus a manifestation of power.[4] Ibn Khaldun emphasized the central role of political power in the patronage of cities, in the sponsorship of religious and scholarly institutions and in stimulating economic growth.[5] He praised the Mamluks for attracting scholars and craftsmen to Cairo, a city 'beyond imagination', the splendour of which epitomized the very greatness of Islam.[6]

Ibn Khaldun spoke as a newcomer, who was dazzled by the Mamluk metropolis, and flattered by the privileges Sultan Barquq bestowed on him. Maqrizi's perspective was more skeptical; in his assessment of the religious foundations, he measured the beauty of a monument according to its patron's moral integrity rather than by the aesthetics of its architecture. Likewise, Ibn Taghribirdi judged the madrasas of the vizier Fakhr al-Din 'Abd al-Ghani, Jamal al-Din al-Ustadar and another unnamed patron, all of whom he considered as evildoers, as less 'soothing to the heart', despite their fine decoration, than the plain stone vestibule of the khanqah of Salah al-Din.[7]

While the historians, as mentioned earlier, acknowledged the benefits for the community despite the legal transgressions committed by the patrons,[8] they did not refrain from criticizing the sultans for building mosques with the mere purpose of perpetuating their names.[9] Ibn Kathir blamed Sultan Hasan for brutally extorting money from people in order to erect unnecessary buildings. Ibn Iyas blamed Sultan al-Ghawri for having spent a fortune on the lavish decoration and the gilding of monuments that were of no use to the Muslim community.[10]

Although Mamluk historians referred to princely building activity largely in terms of its religious and social role, they were not indifferent to its more mundane physical aspect. They often praised the monuments of their time, emphasizing the speed of their construction as a sign of power and majesty, and reporting the founder's presence on the construction site as a token of his dedication. The 'men of the pen', however, were not familiar with construction practices, and, accordingly, they provided very little information on the history or concepts of architecture. Unlike the Ottoman traveller and bureaucrat Evliya Celebi, who described Cairo and its monuments in the seventeenth century with acumen in respect of architectural styles, the Mamluk authors entirely lacked the knowledge of architectural technicalities. Maqrizi wrote that the minaret of Aqbugha, erected in 1340, was the first to be built of stone after the minaret of Qalawun,[11] disregarding the minaret of Ibn Tulun, the Fatimid minarets of al-Hakim, the minarets of al-Nasir Muhammad at the Citadel and the minaret of Bashtak (1336). The most flagrant ignorance, however, can be attributed to Ibn Iyas, who praised Barquq's initiative to build a stone dome for his mausoleum in the city, and to have been the first to build a stone dome in Cairo, all previous domes being made of wood covered with lead![12] Barquq's waqf deed and the physical evidence leave no doubt that the original dome was made of wood covered with lead. Even if it had been built of stone it would have been far from being the first. The ignorance of the historians in architectural matters is also evident in their descriptions, which rarely provide exact details. A 'who's who' of the building craft also remained unknown to the chroniclers. Architecture was not a discipline accessible through literature, like medicine or mathematics, but a practitioner's craft remote from the circles of the historians. The Mamluk elite, who were often directly involved in the construction business and management, were probably more knowledgeable in the art of building than most historians. One might think that Ibn Taghribirdi's sagacious remark, that the mosques of Sultan Hasan and Faraj are the most outstanding monuments in Cairo, may have been due to his education as the son of a Mamluk emir. Ibn Iyas was also of Mamluk stock, but only a great-grandson of an emir![13]

Being named after their founders, each of the Mamluk mosques had an individual identity. The sultans usually founded their funerary structures immediately after gaining the throne, and the construction was normally completed within a year. It is interesting to note that, instead of completing the unfinished mosque of his uncle, Sultan Hasan, al-Ashraf Sha'ban founded two new ones, one for his mother and another for himself. He died, however, before his mosque was finished, and no successor completed the work; instead, the mosque was eventually dismantled by Faraj for its building materials. When the emir Yashbak died before completing his domed mosque at Raydaniyya, Qaytbay took care of its completion, but not gratuitously, however; he appropriated the monument by inscribing his own name on it, without mentioning the founder. Emirs and members of the civilian elite built their religious monuments close to their residences to form part of the quarter where they dwelt; in this way they ingratiated themselves in their neighbourhood and earned prestige and authority there.

Unlike the patronage of the Ottoman sultans, whose religious foundations had to be justified by conquest and jihad, very few Mamluk mosques were associated by contemporary historians with the commemoration of specific religious or historic occasions. Al-Nasir Muhammad's victory against the Mongols in 1303 and his subsequent campaigns in Cilicia have not been linked by contemporary historians with any of his monuments. The founding of his great khanqah in Siryaqus was, rather, associated with the mundane fact that the sultan was once relieved from acute pain while riding in that area. Likewise, despite all its philanthropic significance, the founding of Qalawun's hospital was associated with that patron's personal experience. After suffering from a colic attack while fighting in Baybars' army in Syria, he recovered with medical care provided by Nur al-Din's hospital in Damascus, which prompted him to vow that he would build a hospital if he became sultan. Contemporary critics noted that unlike Nur al-Din, who built his hospital with the booty of cities captured from the Crusaders, Qalawun's funds were acquired by dubious means.[14] Lajin's restoration of the mosque of Ibn Tulun was also motivated by a personal experience: the fact that he found shelter within it when pursued for his involvement in the assassination of al-Ashraf Khalil. Realizing that the mosque was in bad disrepair, he vowed to restore it if he was ever rehabilitated, and did so upon his accession to the throne in 1297. Similarly, the founding of al-Mu'ayyad Shaykh's mosque was linked to his detention in a prison there and his pledge to build a mosque on the site if released. Such pledges represented the founder's individual experiences rather than a cause significant to the community.

The construction of the mosque of Sultan Hasan, which occupied an enormous site for several years, posing unprecedented challenges to the builders and other craftsmen from various regions, was not perceived by contemporary chroniclers as an outstanding event in the daily life of Cairo's population that was worthy of being documented. Neither did they associate this greatest monument of the time with any exalted cause, not even with the end of the Black Death, the horror of which they had reported a few years earlier. This attitude suggests that during its construction the mosque of Sultan Hasan was perceived as the sultan's monument rather than a collective cause of the people of Cairo, quite unlike the way medieval cathedrals were perceived in their cities. Only later, after the sultan's brutal death and when the mosque's architectural significance was established, did it become an attribute of Cairo and a symbol of its glory.

There are, however, a few exceptions, which link the foundation of mosques with a collective cause. Such associations were particularly significant in the age of the Crusades; for example, the mosque of al-Zahir Baybars, which displayed spoils from a Crusader fortress in its monumental dome, celebrated a significant victory of Islam. Al-Ashraf Khalil's waqf document stressed that he endowed his father's and his own pious foundation with land he had conquered from the Crusaders. Maqrizi vaguely associated the foundation of the mosque of the emir Aydumur al-Khatiri in Bulaq built in the 1340s and the earlier mosque and khanqah of Bashtak, with the eviction of Christians from their respective areas.[15] The mosque of Mughultay al-Jamali at Bayn al-Surayn was called *jami' al-tawba* or 'mosque of redemption' because it was built on the site of a quarter inhabited by *ahl al-fasad* or bad people.[16] When Maqrizi reported the demolition of Khazanat al-Bunud, a quarter inhabited by Europeans and Armenians, by the emir Almalik following al-Nasir's death, and his foundation of a mosque for a Muslim community he settled there, he praised this act as equivalent to the capture of Tripoli and Acre from the Crusaders.[17] The mosque of the emir Muhsin al-Shahabi, built in the 1340s in Bulaq al-Takruri, a village in the area of Giza, was dedicated to a saint venerated by the local population.[18] The inscriptions of Qaytbay's funerary mosque have been interpreted as a celebration of a military victory.[19] A more obvious monument to a victory is the cistern and fountain of Ya'qub Shah al-Mihmandar, with its extensive and unusual historical inscription lauding Qaytbay's victory against the Ottomans.[20]

Although the attitude of most sultans was devout and reverential towards scholars and Sufis, the princely mausoleums were generally exclusive to the founder's family and members of his clan. Sufis and scholars could be buried in the graveyard of a princely complex, such as the khanqah of al-Nasir Muhammad in Siryaqus and that of Barsbay in the cemetery, but generally they did not share a princely mausoleum. The tomb of the Sufi Hasan Sadaqa in the funerary complex of Sunqur al-Sa'di is an exception, as was Sultan Khushqadam's decision in 1463 to transfer the remains of the shaykh 'Umar al-Kurdi al-Babani to his own mausoleum so that he could benefit from the Sufi's blessing.[21] The case of the highly venerated shaykh Akmal al-Din, the first rector of the khanqah of Shaykhu, who was buried in this khanqah, might be another exception; how far this was in compliance with Shaykhu's waqf stipulations cannot, in the absence of a document, be established; the burial took place during Barquq's reign.[22]

It is interesting to note that the mausoleums built by Mamluk emirs for holy men are not always of the same architectural quality as the princely mausoleums, as shown by the domed mausoleum of the Sufi saint 'Umar Ibn al-Farid (d.1235), and that of the shaykh 'Abd Allah al-Minufi (d.1348), both erected in the fifteenth century.[23] The first was sponsored by two emirs, Timur al-Ibrahimi and Barquq al-Nasiri in the 1460s; the sponsor of 'Abd Allah al-Minufi's mausoleum is unknown. One may speculate that Sultan Qaytbay built it when he founded his funerary complex in the vicinity.[24] Compared with princely domes, the respective dimensions and decoration of these mausoleums for holy men belong to a more modest category. Mamluk princely mausoleums included a crypt (*fisqiyya*) for burial, like the Seljuk gunbads or tomb towers, which was an innovation in Egypt. Ibn al-Hajj rejected the crypt strictly as a *bid'a* or heretical departure from orthodoxy. Ordinary people and religious men and saints were simply interred.[25]

Unless they were dedicated to saints, the building of mausoleums was a matter of controversy among religious scholars. Some scholars allowed the building of funerary structures as long as they were on land owned by the founder and not taken from a waqf.[26] By founding funerary mosques the Mamluks fulfilled individual aristocratic aspirations, as the founder's pretext to insert his mausoleum in the urban fabric. At the same time they affiliated themselves in the tradition of *ziyara* or pilgrimage to the tombs of saints that the Fatimids had already cultivated in the cemetery,[27] adding a new urban dimension to the Cairene funerary culture. The mausoleums were integrated in the mosques, and furthermore, as the waqf deeds stipulate, they were declared as oratories with their own imam to lead prayer and often also provided a teaching curriculum. A staff was appointed to perform Koran recitations day and night in the mausoleum; the readers sat in the window recesses to spread the holy words to the street thus perpetuating the founder's presence and his piety in the city.

Unlike the Ottoman *külliye*s, where the funerary, residential and educational structures were set apart from the mosque in a hierarchic order, the Mamluk religious complexes, which were not enclosed, were merged in the urban fabric without a clear-cut separation between religious and profane space. Not only funerary structures but residential rooms and dwellings were also integrated in the architecture of Friday mosques.

Waqf documents show that the patrons often used their pious foundations to award their manumitted slaves and eunuchs with positions that served as a kind of pension for the rest of their lives. This was the case in the foundations of Qalawun, his son al-Nasir Muhammad and grandson al-Nasir Hasan, and of Baybars al-Jashnakir and many others.

The impact of the waqf framework on urban development is well documented. The mosques of the Mamluks were largely financed by urban estates, mainly in Cairo. Although agricultural lands with their towns and villages in the Egyptian and Syrian provinces often figure as endowed estate, the endowment of land, which was needed for the *iqta'* and the upkeep of the army, could be problematic and controversial. The great waqfs relied, therefore, largely on urban commercial structures; virtually all commercial buildings and dwellings in the major markets in Qahira's centre belonged either to the estate of the great pious foundations or were the private property of the Mamluk elite. As a result, the merchants and craftsmen of the bazaars were

the tenants and not the owners of their shops and workshops, as were the inhabitants of all types of domestic and residential structures, including mansions and palaces. Facades were tied together without physical separation between religious and profane structures, creating a homogeneous streetscape.

Although the foundation of Friday mosques contributed to urban development and the upgrading of their neighbourhood, not all great pious waqfs were conceived in terms of projected quarters with all their commercial structures and dwellings grouped around the mosque. Rather, the most current pattern in a royal foundation was that of diversified investments, which included, among other items, commercial and residential structures in the vicinity of the mosque. Al-Zahir Baybars endowed his madrasa at Bayn al-Qasrayn with a large apartment complex near Bab Zuwayla, as well as a qaysariyya and a house in other quarters.[28] Part of al-Ashraf Khalil's endowed estates to the benefit of his madrasa and his father's mausoleum consisted of rented land in the western suburbs alongside a variety of commercial structures in other parts of Cairo and land in Syria. Al-Nasir's estates for his madrasa in the city or his khanqah in Siryaqus were also mixed, including agricultural land, commercial structures and factories in Alexandria and Syria; the two hammams in the northern suburb that belonged to the estate of the madrasa must have been a useful service to this neighbourhood. The waqf of Sultan Hasan's madrasa, which consisted mainly of agricultural land and villages in Egypt and Syria, also included the revenue of half the city of Antakia (Antioch), part of which had remained in a ruined condition since al-Zahir Baybars recaptured it from the Crusaders in 1268. The waqf deed stipulated that these estates should be restored and upgraded to secure the revenue of the sultan's mosque.

Qaytbay's and al-Ghawri's waqfs also consisted of a mixture of dispersed commercial structures and agricultural land. The diversified investments, by which the ruler acquired estates anywhere in underprivileged or marginal areas, or dilapidated buildings to upgrade them, had the advantage of decentralizing building and reconstruction initiatives, allowing the founder to generate or regenerate urban structures where they were needed. Qaytbay rehabilitated a number of commercial structures in the centre of Qahira for his endowment of the Prophet's mosque in Medina.[29] As the religious foundations of the emirs and members of the civilian elite were located near their residences,[30] their commercial estates tended also to be concentrated in the same neighbourhood, though not exclusively. As a result of the princely involvement in urban development, either through the creation of new quarters or the upgrading of old ones, or simply by adding commercial structures and dwellings wherever needed, the urban fabric was continuously renewed.

Qahira's main thoroughfare was gradually transformed into a royal funerary-religious precinct. The density of religious monuments there reached such proportions that when the emir Uljay in 1372 wished to add a Friday sermon to Qalawun's madrasa, his scheme was rejected by religious scholars, who argued that al-Salih's madrasa on the opposite side of the street had a *khutba* already, and its pulpit could be seen from within Qalawun's madrasa![31] A century later, in 1494, however, the *atabak* Azbak succeeded, despite legal concerns, in introducing the Friday prayer to this madrasa. Sultan Barquq took a new direction in Mamluk monumental patronage when he demonstrated his affinity to the cemetery, where he wished to be buried in the vicinity of Sufis and saints rather than in his urban mausoleum. Faraj, Barsbay and Qaytbay, who established funerary mosques in the cemetery, did not fail at the same time to signal their presence with a pious foundation in the city.

The considerable number of multifunctional Friday mosques erected during the Mamluk period led inevitably to a gradual change in their status and function and to a popularization of the *khutba*. By the time of Qaytbay's reign, the royal complexes were reduced to a combined mausoleum with a neighbourhood Friday mosque of smaller dimensions and no elaborate teaching curriculum. While the size of the mosque diminished, the rab' or apartment building became a regular feature of the complex. In the absence of a large community of students or Sufis with permanent maintenance and stipends, these foundations were less costly to sustain. The rab', which the supervisor was entitled to manage according to his estimation, could be rented to provide revenue to the foundation. However, all late Mamluk mosques continued to provide primary education and to supply drinking water to their neighbourhoods, as indicated by the omnipresent sabil-maktab at the building's corner, both services being of substantial value to the inhabitants of the quarter.

The Mamluk patrons also perpetuated their names in the monuments of the past. The Azhar mosque, with its three Mamluk minarets built by Aqbugha, Qaytbay and al-Ghawri, and the madrasas of Taybars, Aqbugha and Jawhar al-Qanqaba adjoining it, proclaims the Mamluk heritage to the present day. Al-Zahir Baybars returned the *khutba* to al-Azhar, which had been abolished by Salah al-Din, who, following the Shafi'i rite, had authorized only one *khutba* in the city, in the mosque of al-Hakim; on this occasion he refurbished the building.[32] Bashir al-Jamdar, an emir of Sultan Hasan, added Hanafi teaching to al-Azhar's curriculum. On these occasions the premises were substantially renovated. Barquq built a new minaret and al-Mu'ayyad replaced it with one made of stone, which did not survive, and Barsbay added a cistern.[33] Qaytbay's restorations and additions were substantial; they included, besides con-solidation work, two gates and his minaret.[34] The mosque of 'Amr at Fustat was restored by the sultans al-Zahir Baybars, Qalawun and Qaytbay,[35] and by the emir Salar.[36] Sultan Lajin

renovated the mosque of Ibn Tulun in 1365–6, and endowed it with the curriculum of a madrasa for the four schools of law.[37] When the earthquake of 1303 damaged many buildings in the city, and decapitated a number of minarets, Sultan al-Nasir Muhammad immediately delegated several emirs with the task of restoring them.

Al-Nasir Muhammad built a Friday mosque at the shrine of Sayyida Nafisa and restored the mausoleum of Imam Shafi'i, which was refurbished also by Qaytbay and al-Ghawri.[38] Likewise, the shrine of Imam al-Layth was among the sanctuaries maintained by Mamluk sultans and emirs.[39] The Ribat al-Athar, founded in 1307 to house relics of the Prophet, was regularly restored and endowed by sultans, until al-Ghawri transferred the relics to his mausoleum.[40] When the great mystic and poet 'Umar Ibn al-Farid died in 1235, he was buried in the southern cemetery without a mausoleum, having refused an offer by the Ayyubid sultan al-Malik al-Kamil to erect a memorial monument for him. As the saint enjoyed great popularity and his grave was a major pilgrim site in the cemetery, in the mid-fifteenth century two emirs erected a domed mausoleum over his grave and sponsored a zawiya and an annual celebration of his birthday (*mawlid*).[41]

Jaqmaq believed that restoring what was in disrepair was preferable to the creation of new buildings (*iṣlāḥ mā yushrif 'alā 'l-hadm awlā min al-ibtikār*). Accordingly, he deliberately refrained from erecting a funerary complex, and concentrated his patronage on the maintenance and reconstruction of old, dilapidated monuments, commemorating his works with inscriptions in his name.[42] This attitude might have inspired Qaytbay, who likewise made a significant contribution to restoring the legacy of his predecessors.[43]

Ladies of the Mamluk aristocracy were also associated with the founding of funerary and religious monuments. Shajar al-Durr, al-Zahir Baybars' daughter,[44] Qalawun's wife Fatima Khatun, Aydakin al-Bunduqdar's daughter,[45] Aydakin,[46] Bukja' al-Nasiri's wife, al-Nasir Muhammad's daughter Khawand Zahra,[47] Sitt Miska,[48] Tatar al-Hijaziyya,[49] Tughay,[50] the anonymous princess of Turbat al-Sitt,[51] Sultan Hasan's mother (Sultaniyya mausoleum), his wife Tulubiyya[52] and Sha'ban's mother Baraka all figure in the Bahri period. In the Circassian period, Inal's wife,[53] Qaytbay's concubine Asalbay, who was the mother of his successor al-Nasir Muhammad, and Fatima Shaqra are mentioned as having founded religious monuments.[54] A ruined oratory of the late fifteenth century is attributed to a lady also called Fatima.[55]

Although Mamluk princesses could accumulate great fortunes, the names of the monuments alone do not define the modality of their patronage. In some cases the foundations were sponsored by the husband or the son, as was the case, according to the chroniclers, with the funerary madrasa of Qalawun's wife. A waqf of Sultan Hasan[56] indicates that he also sponsored a mausoleum for his unnamed wife, who could have been Tulubiyya. He probably did the same regarding his mother's mausoleum, the Sultaniyya. Also, the inscriptions of the madrasa of Sha'ban's mother identify the sultan as the sponsor. It is interesting that an unknown inscription in the mausoleum attached to the khanqah (1285–6) attributed to the emir 'Ala al-Din Aydakin al-Bunduqdar refers to his unnamed daughter as the founder of the turba. However, nothing about her is mentioned by Maqrizi.[57] The mosque named to Fatima Shaqra located in the street of Taht al-Rab', where Qaytbay, according to his waqf deed, built a mosque, is dated Jumada II 873/December 1468–January 1469. It could have been dedicated by Qaytbay to his only legitimate wife Fatima. However, Ibn Iyas, who said a great deal about her and her father, a scholar of Mamluk descent and the librarian of Qaytbay's mosque, did not call her Shaqra, nor did he attribute a mosque to her.[58]

The chroniclers sometimes associated the foundation of mosques with the provision of pleasure and amusement, using such terms as *muftarajat* or *muntazahat*, which mean 'promenades' and 'venues of leisure'. Maqrizi used the latter for the mosques of Taybars, Sultan al-Nasir Muhammad and the emir al-Khatiri, which were all located on the waterfront amid greenery.[59] In the late fifteenth century, the prominent bureaucrat Ibn al-Ji'an refurbished an old pleasance complex along the Khalij in the northern suburb of al-Zawiya al-Hamra with a palace, pavilions and a Friday mosque, to which a fountain and a trough were attached, amid gardens. Ibn Iyas described this complex, which attracted the masses during the flood season, as one of the *muftarajat* or sightseeing spots of Cairo. Qaytbay's master builder, Hasan Ibn al-Tuluni

sponsored a monthly event at the sultan's mosque at Rawda; on this occasion the mosque was decorated with festive lights, and tents were pitched beside it along the Nile shore to accommodate people who came by boat to attend Koran recitations and lectures. The visitors could, moreover, enjoy the attraction of a waterwheel drawn by a donkey, which Ibn al-Tuluni had set up at this venue. In this instance, al-Suyuti was cited as having objected to the building of mosques on the Nile shore, basing his argument on the precepts of the Shafi'i school, but this objection was rejected as being baseless.[60]

Qaytbay was so pleased by the village called al-Marj wa'l-Zayyat when he rode there one day that he decided to endow it with a zawiya, fountain and trough for animals, which were then built 'in best fashion'.[61] Such a pious foundation of course upgraded the neighbourhood. Al-Ghawri's founding of a small Friday mosque next to the gate of the hippodrome beneath the Citadel bestowed piety on his ceremonial venue. The combination of piety and entertainment might have been a Sufi component, aimed at integrating devotion in all aspects of life, including pleasure. This combination could be taken to extremes, as shown by the case of Shaykh Haydar, who was allowed to establish a zawiya in the premises of al-Mu'ayyad's palace, the Khamas Wujuh, but had to face accusations that he was leading a promiscuous lifestyle there, which eventually led to the demolition of this zawiya during Inal's reign in 1454.[62]

With their multifunctional monuments the Mamluks asserted themselves in many aspects of the religious and secular life of their capital, and secured at the same time their posthumous place in its architecture and history.

— 4 —

The Patronage
of the Civilian Elite

Functionaries, shaykhs and merchants

Pious patronage was not exclusive to the Mamluk class; members of the religious establishment, merchants and professionals also contributed to social and philanthropic works, albeit in a different manner. Their patronage was less associated with commemorative monuments than was the case with the Mamluk aristocracy. Wealthy individuals in the capital tended, rather, to sponsor existing foundations by restoring or renovating their buildings, or by enlarging their endowments, or they directly made donations and distributed alms. The high-ranking bureaucrats could ingratiate themselves with the sultan by contributing to and consolidating his foundations, as did, for example, al-Barizi with Sultan al-Mu'ayyad. The wealthy merchant 'Abd al-'Aziz al-Kharrubi (d.1399/1400) donated 100,000 dirhams for the restoration of the mosque of Mecca after a fire.[1] Another merchant called 'Abd al-Wahhab al-'Ayni sponsored Jaqmaq's restoration of the Fatimid mosque of al-Salih Tala'i'.[2] The wealthy notable Sadaqa al-Sharabishi, who, according to his name, came from a family of textile merchants who produced ceremonial caps, sponsored the khanqah of the emir Sunqur al-Sa'di.[3] The master builder of Sultan Qaytbay, al-Badri Hasan Ibn al-Tuluni, added, as mentioned earlier, a monthly service at the sultan's mosque on the island of Rawda.[4] An Ottoman merchant from Bursa, the *khawaja* Mustafa Ibn Mahmud Ibn Rustum al-Rumi al-Bursawi, sponsored Qaytbay's substantial refurbishing of al-Azhar mosque in 1494–5, which cost him about 15,000 dinars.[5] He was, like his father before him, the sultan's merchant (*tajir al-sultan*). He spent many years in Mecca, an important commercial

centre for the Mamluks, and in Cairo but he returned to his homeland, where he died in 1500. His name is recorded on several inscriptions at al-Azhar, which state that the restorations were carried out by him by order of the sultan.[6] This sponsorship included a new gate and the addition of a minaret in the sultan's name.

The hospital of Sultan Qalawun owed its long history not to Qalawun's endowment alone but also to the contributions of generations of donors, among them a chief of the physicians and orthopædists in the fifteenth century, who endowed it with a share of his family waqf.[7] Similarly, the mosques of 'Amr at Fustat and al-Azhar benefited from the ongoing sponsorship of individuals along with members of the ruling class. Maqrizi praised the great achievements of the chief of the merchants, Burhan al-Din Ibrahim, during the reign of Sultan Barquq for having totally refurbished the mosque of 'Amr and rescuing it from decay.[8] Because of its location at Fustat, which had gradually become marginal, the mosque of 'Amr seems to have relied more on the civilian elite for its maintenance than on the Mamluk aristocracy.

Maqrizi and Ibn Duqmaq mentioned members of the civilian elite in the Bahri period as founders of religious monuments. These patrons, who included individuals of diverse career and background, were mostly associated with the ruling establishment and entitled to participate in its privileges, which made them wealthy and enabled them to act as patrons of pious foundations. Among the high-ranking civilian patrons was a dynasty of powerful and wealthy viziers and bureaucrats, the Banu Hanna from Fustat, who sponsored great projects in their city in the early Mamluk period.[9] Most of these buildings subsequently disappeared due to the shift of the urban centre to Qahira.

The chief physician of al-Nasir Muhammad, Ibn al-Maghrabi, built a funerary mosque in the western suburb and a madrasa within the city. Sitt Miska, the sultan's nanny and the master of his private household, and 'Ali Ibn al-Tabbakh, his chief cook, also built Friday mosques. Al-Nasir's cook became rich by selling on the market the leftover meat and offal of the royal kitchen, which earned him 20,000 dirhams per day. He owned twenty-five houses on the Nile shore and a lavish residence. However, he founded his mosque not by endowing it with a waqf but financing it with direct donations. When he fell in disgrace after al-Nasir Muhammad's death, his entire estate was confiscated and the mosque was left without resources, until eventually an emir took it over and endowed it in his own name.[10]

Among the bureaucrats mentioned in the Bahri period as founders of Friday mosques are Ibn 'Abd al-Zahir, the historian and head of the chancellery during Qalawun's and Khalil's reigns, whose mosque was built in 1284.[11] Muhammad Ibn Fadl Allah al-Fakhr (d.1332), the secretary of the army (*nazir al-jaysh*) of al-Nasir Muhammad, built three Friday mosques in Cairo, at Bulaq, Rawda and Jazirat al-Fil, in addition to other philanthropic foundations in the province, including a hospital in the town of Bilbays, which earned him the praise of Maqrizi although he was a Christian convert. Another convert, who managed a great career in the state service, Ibn al-Baqari (d.1374/5), the supervisor of Sultan Hasan's treasury and the waqfs, founded a madrasa with a domed mausoleum, which in 1420 acquired the status of a Friday mosque.[12] Qadi Shams al-Din Muhammad (d.1348/9), the supervisor of the *bayt al-mal*, founded the Jami' al-Asyuti near Bulaq. This mosque was restored in 1419 by Sultan al-Mu'ayyad's private secretary, Nasir al-Din Muhammad, of the Barizi family, who turned it into a Friday mosque.[13]

From the fifteenth century the mosques of al-'Ayni,[14] 'Abd al-Ghani al-Fakhri, Qadi 'Abd al-Basit and Zayn al-Din Yahya, all of whom were high-ranking bureaucrats, are handsome monuments with the princely attributes of the time, built in locations worthy of emirs. Qadi 'Abd al-Basit's sister, Marhaba, restored the shrine of Imam al-Layth in 1428–9.[15] The complex mentioned, of Ibn al-Ji'an along the Khalij, has not survived, but Ibn Iyas described it in laudatory terms.

Whereas civilians were not often associated with the founding of khanqahs, except for Shaykh Nizam al-Din Ishaq, the *shaykh al-shuyukh* or superior of all Sufis and rector of the khanqah of al-Nasir Muhammad at Siryaqus, who founded a khanqah of his own at the foot of the Citadel in 1356,[16] they often sponsored zawiyas. It is not exactly clear, however, who were the sponsors of the zawiyas associated with the Sufi shaykhs Zayn al-Din Yusuf and Ibn Sulayman al-Rifa'i.

Although many zawiyas dedicated to mystics were sponsored by princely patrons, such as the zawiya of Shaykh Khidr,

which was founded by Sultan al-Zahir Baybars, some shaykhs preferred to do without princely support. A number of zawiyas are identified only by their shaykh, who was also the founder. The majority of zawiyas were built in the cemeteries or the suburbs rather than the urban centre.

In the early fifteenth century, the *khutba* was added to many zawiyas alongside turbas and madrasas, giving them the status of a jami' or Friday mosque.[17] The Friday mosques founded in the fifteenth century by Sufis are likely to have fulfilled the function of a zawiya as well. The mosques of al-Hanafi,[18] al-Zahid, Hajj Ibrahim al-Hummusani and al-Ghamri were founded by Sufis in 1414, 1415, 1427 and 1440 respectively. Most of these civilian constructions have disappeared. The mosque of al-Ghamri (d.1447) had a beautiful minaret, depicted by David Roberts.[19] The mosque of the Sufi shaykh Madyan is a small building comparable to others built by Mamluk dignitaries of its period.[20]

Shaykh Dashtuti completed in 1506 a fine funerary mosque to which he conducted water from the Khalij to form a pond beside it. According to Ibn Iyas, he received considerable donations, which he spent on building several mosques in various places.[21] The zawiya of the Sufi shaykh Damirdash, one of the latest of the Mamluk period, was financed by the shaykh's orchard.

The role of the merchants should be also mentioned in this context. A substantial amount of Mamluk wealth was earned in international trade, in which the Karimi merchants are believed to have made some of the largest fortunes in the world. They were wholesale spice merchants who also played the role of bankers. Court purveyors, such as the slave and Mamluk dealers, were also among the wealthiest men in the state, who shared the privileges of the ruling establishment; the strategically significant import of Mamluks was exempted from taxes. The spice trade, because of its importance, was under the sultan's supervision through an office annexed to the vizierate or the privy,[22] and he bestowed the title of *kabir al-tujjar*, or head of the merchants, on the most prominent men in the business. Nevertheless, the merchants did not endow the Egyptian capital with a monumental legacy, although some contributed to the buildings of Fustat and other cities of Egypt and Syria. Nasir al-Din Ibn al-Harrani al-Sharabishi founded a mosque in the southern cemetery near the mausoleum of Imam Shafi'i.[23] Badr al-Din Muhammad al-Kharrubi, a sugar merchant, founded a madrasa in Fustat around 1349.[24] His nephew, Muhammad Ibn Salah al-Din, also planned a madrasa in Fustat, but he died before completing its endowment.[25] Nasir al-Din Muhammad Ibn Musallam (d.1374/5), one of the most prominent Karimi merchants of Egypt, who traded in India, Africa and Yemen, also sponsored a madrasa in Fustat that was estimated to have cost 16,000 dinars. Ibn Musallam, who was born the son of a porter, was wealthy enough to lend Sultan

Sha'ban money.[26] Najm al-Din Abu Bakr Ibn Ghazi, who was in the slave trade, *dallal al-mamalik*, founded a Friday mosque near Bulaq in 1340.[27] Some Karimi merchants also appear as patrons of religious foundations in Alexandria.[28] Ibn al-Zaman, a prominent merchant, and at the same time the supervisor of Qaytbay's constructions in Medina, built a madrasa in Jerusalem, another in Medina, and in Cairo he founded in 1492 a mosque at Bulaq and a turba, probably in the cemetery.[29]

Ibn Hajar judged the merchants to be not generous as sponsors,[30] and al-Jawhari commented about Burhan al-Din al-Mahalli (d.1403), the chief of the Karimis, that his only charity was the restoration of the mosque of 'Amr at Fustat,[31] although Maqrizi, as mentioned above, praised him for his substantial contribution. The absence of monuments built by merchants within Qahira may be due to the fact that they were aware their foundations would have a precarious status. One may also assume that, fearing confiscation and extortion, the merchants preferred to hide their wealth, and to channel their philanthropy into deeds that were less visible than monuments. As individuals who belonged neither to the Mamluk aristocracy nor to the religious or scholarly establishment, they had less leverage to protect their foundations, as the case of Fath Allah al-'Ajami indicates. Initially al-Mu'ayyad's physician, later his father-in-law and private secretary, and eventually one of the most influential men in the bureaucracy, his estate and turba were confiscated by the sultan upon his death in 1413, after he had been tortured in jail.[32] The foundations of those who had no roots in the Mamluk aristocracy had little chance of surviving.

Occasionally, patrons of common origins are mentioned, such as the provincial Egyptian of undefined qualifications (*shakhs min al-nas*) called Nasir al-Din Muhammad Ibn Muhammad Ibn Budayr, from the town of al-'Abbasa in the eastern Delta, who founded a small Shafi'i madrasa in 1357 in Cairo's centre, where the eminent Shakyh al-Bulqini studied, and a madrasa in the city of Bilbays in the eastern Delta.[33]

The fifteenth century witnessed an increase of commoners' patronage. In 1400 the Kimakhti mosque was founded by a master (*mu'allim*) of the craft of *kimakht*-makers.[34] In 1414 the mosque of al-Basiti was founded by a man described merely as a scholar. Maqrizi mentioned a Friday mosque built by Shakir al-Banna', who might have been a builder unless al-Banna' was only a nickname,[35] and a madrasa built by a grain broker.[36] These buildings no longer exist, but the mosque and mausoleum built in the 1480s by the merchant Nur al-Din 'Ali Ibn Muhammad al-Qanish al-Burullusi for the Sufi shaykh Abu 'l-'Ila, as stated in an inscription above the mihrab, still reveals fine workmanship in spite of the substantial restoration works it underwent.[37] Hasan 'Abd al-Wahhab praised its signed minbar as one of the masterpieces of late Mamluk woodwork.

The proliferation of Friday mosques founded by individuals who did not belong to the ruling establishment indicates an increasing social flexibility in the Circassian period. It should be recalled that the sultan's permission was necessary for a patron to introduce a *khutba* in his mosque.[38]

It thus appears that in the Bahri period the foundation of religious monuments in the metropolitan area was rather restricted to the ruling aristocracy and their administrative establishment, but the situation changed in the fifteenth century, which witnessed a more diverse patronage under the rule of Circassian sultans.

−5−

Ceremonial Culture

The spectacle of the Sultan

The Mamluk sultan was the protagonist in a sophisticated ceremonial culture with well-defined rituals ruled by a strict protocol. His apparel (*hay'a*) was designed to be suitable for the occasion, and his performance attuned to the venue. Cairo's streets were the main theatre of such performances.

Despite the variations and innovations introduced over time, the chroniclers conveyed an aura of tradition in their descriptions of Mamluk ceremonial. Being led by a first-generation aristocracy, the Mamluk regime needed regal traditions to emphasize the royal status of the former slaves and to demonstrate continuity. When Ibn Iyas described the procession of Sultan al-Ghawri on his way to the battlefield in Syria to fight the Ottomans, he recalled the customs of previous sultans, noting the novelties and variations that were introduced over time;[1] ceremonials meant the traditions of the kings.

The sultans' display of pomp and glory in their processions through the capital was viewed as a serious responsibility, and a demonstration of concern and attention towards their subjects. Notwithstanding their bad record in other matters, the cultivation of ceremonial rituals earned the monarchs a positive echo in the chronicles. In the obituaries of the sultans, the historians weighed their good and bad features before offering a final assessment, which usually expressed mixed feelings. In his obituary of al-Ghawri, Ibn Iyas commented on his revival of the lancers' parade with the words: 'it was considered as one of the positive deeds of al-Ghawri to have shown people things that had been forgotten, and which he revived in order to be commemorated among the kings'.[2] In Ibn Taghribirdi's view,

ceremonies 'glorified the kings and celebrated events'; the cultivation of regal traditions (*shi'ar al-mamlaka*) such as the sultans' sportive excursions to Siryaqus, or their tournaments and parades at the hippodromes, made the difference between a sultanate and a provincial government.[3]

Ibn Taghribirdi, who was the son of a Mamluk emir, listed with dismay all the ceremonies that the austere Sultan Jaqmaq cancelled in 1451. These included the audiences in the Qasr, one of the two major palaces of the Citadel, dispensing justice in the Palace of the Stables, and the ceremonial fanfare at dawn and sunset in the Citadel. He described these musical performances as bestowing beauty on the Citadel when in the morning its gates were opened. The orchestra could be heard from afar, trumpeting glory and greatness, and inspiring awe and respect in those who were not familiar with the Citadel (*kāna yaṣīru bihi ubbaha wa 'aẓama zā'ida wa ru'b wa hayba li-man lā ilmām lahu bi-ṭulū' al-qal'a*). The author also deplored that Jaqmaq cancelled the royal hunts in Giza and elsewhere, the lancers' parades during the month of Rajab, which were among the beauties and wonders of the world, and that he neglected the paraphernalia of power.[4] However, in his obituary of the same sultan, Ibn Taghribirdi respectfully acknowledged his extreme piety and virtuousness. He was frugal in his appearance and orthodox to the extent of never wearing the colour red, or fur, or using gold trappings.[5]

Sultan Khushqadam's taste for ceremonial spectacles was more worthy to win Ibn Taghribirdi's approval. The latter once accompanied the sultan to watch a tournament of lancers directed by Qaytbay, the future sultan. At the end of the spectacle, Qaytbay let the lancers dismount and kiss the floor before the sultan, who was delighted by this reverential gesture, which was not a custom. The historian commented that such reverence should henceforth become a tradition, because kings loved to be glorified and the audience would also enjoy it.[6]

In his panegyric of the Mamluks, al-Qudsi wrote: 'Their costume is more beautiful and sumptuous than any other in any country'.[7] In his view, the luxury of the Mamluks' lifestyle, the beauty of their palaces, horses and attire, were signs of their excellence.

Mamluk costume included various styles called Mongol or Islamic, and it was subject to multiple fashions and innovations. Colours played a significant role in ceremonial outfits, each regiment wearing the appropriate colour for the occasion. Zahiri reported proudly that the rigour of the Mamluk dress codes made a great impression on an envoy of Timur, who had to admit that in his own country all people wore the same type of clothes.[8] The Mamluks had two emblematic colours: black, the colour of the Abbasid caliphate, which seems to have been used for dress only; and yellow, the colour inherited from the Ayyubids, which characterized Mamluk paraphernalia, notably their flags and banners. For his investiture ceremony, in which the sultan was formally confirmed by the caliph, the sultan, like the caliph, wore a religious outfit with a gold-embroidered black turban, displaying no military emblems. When al-Zahir Baybars celebrated the new Abbasid caliphate in Cairo, he appeared in black and gold, including the trappings of his horse. On secular occasions, the sultans wore various colours in winter and mainly white in summer. White was also the colour of mourning at the Mamluk court, as it had been under the Ayyubids. Unlike the Fatimids, whose ceremonial was defined by the religious and spiritual supremacy of the caliph, the Mamluks, following their Ayyubid predecessors, presented themselves as men of the sword.

Riding in state, a Bahri Mamluk sultan would be shaded by the royal gold-embroidered silk parasol crowned with a gilded silver bird, preceded by a horseman carrying the *ghashiya*, an emblem of royalty in the shape of a gold-embroidered leather saddle. The parasol, like the *ghashiya*, was yellow. The neck of the royal horse would be clad with brocaded yellow silk. Ahead of the sultan was the royal standard amid a set of banners, also of brocaded yellow silk and embroidered with the name and titles of the sultan. Also ahead of him rode the carriers of halberds while others behind him displayed different weapons. The sultan was preceded by a pair of pages on white horses, fully dressed in yellow silk including their headgear, and accompanied by solemn music.[9] To open the Khalij, in celebration of the Nile annual flood, the sultan rode in a less solemn procession, without the parasol and the neck brocade on his horse. The Circassian sultans rode in state in winter wearing a velvet gown, which could be red or violet, lined with sable. A yellow belt was a further insignia of royalty. The shape

and size of the royal turban varied according to the occasion. Sultan al-Ghawri introduced a new style of large turban with an upward-pointing double-ended knot, which might have been a reference to Dhu 'l-Qarnayn, or 'the One with Two Horns', meaning Alexander the Great.[10] The protocol dictated that the sultan's clothes had to be embroidered with his blazon, in a colour that contrasted with the ground material.[11] The blazon was embroidered with gold threads like the epigraphic bands with princely titles, which also adorned his gown.

Maqrizi and Ibn Taghribirdi took a rigorous attitude towards issues of protocol and often criticized inconsistencies or short-comings in the sultans' performances, as when Barsbay appeared in a procession wearing the outfit dedicated to his audience sessions (*bi-thiyab julusihi*).[12] Barsbay was not, however, the first to do so; Faraj had already set a bad example, and was followed by al-Mu'ayyad, who often rode out in audience outfit.[13] Ibn Taghribirdi criticized Sultan Jaqmaq for inaugurating the winter season in the Qasr of the Citadel instead of the hippodrome known as Mat'am al-Tayr, in the northern suburb of Raydaniyya. To make matters worse, that sultan wore an unsuitable outfit in the wrong colours. The historian, however, was pleased to report on a later occasion that the sultan finally adhered to the rules of protocol and rode to the Mat'am properly dressed.[14]

Ibn Iyas reported that Qaytbay was criticized for having inaugurated the summer season on a Monday instead of the customary Friday.[15] Unlike Ibn Taghribirdi earlier, who associated the celebration of the new season exclusively with the Mat'am al-Tayr, Ibn Iyas shows that the protocol had become more flexible on this issue, allowing a choice between two venues, the Citadel's mosque or the Mat'am; however, it had to be on a Friday. On that occasion the winter-coloured woollen clothes, consisting of a green gown with a red velvet robe, would be exchanged for the white linen summer attire.[16] Al-Jawhari remarked that in 1470–1 Qaytbay did not follow the canonical dates for the new season but wore the white clothes seven days earlier, as he did also for the winter clothes.[17] Qaytbay's son al-Nasir Muhammad was criticized for having performed the Friday prayer wearing a small headgear instead of the traditional *kalaftah*.[18]

When Qalawun's favourite son died, the sultan's grief was so deep that he took off his headgear and refused to wear it again. Only through the insistence of his emirs did he finally agree to cover his head and wear white, the colour of mourning.[19]

Alongside their outfit and blazon, the Mamluks also reserved for themselves the exclusive right to ride horses. The 'men of the pen' were distinguished by their own distinct costume, which al-'Umari described in detail. They usually avoided wearing the unorthodox silk and gold; black and white were the colours of their official dress, which consisted of a robe called a *farajiyya* and a specific form of turban that varied according to their office and rank.[20] They were allowed to ride mules. Transgressions in these matters were not tolerated by the ruling establishment, and not even by the ulema themselves. Some were as desirous to maintain their distinct identity as were the Mamluks with their own, and they would not change their dress even if transferred to a military position. In the fifteenth century some of the 'men of the pen' occupied positions initially reserved for the 'men of the sword', which entitled them to the rank of emir, to have an *iqta'*, and to dress as Mamluks, ride horses and display a blazon.[21]

Fashions changed, and it seems that the 'men of the pen' got bored with their black and white outfit, for Ibn Hajar reported that in 1397 the *katib al-sirr*, the sultan's private secretary, asked Sultan Barquq on behalf of the 'turbaned people', as the 'men of the pen' were called, for permission to wear coloured gowns on official occasions instead of the customary white, which he was granted.[22] In the khanqah, Sufis were invested in a special ceremony with a mantle called *khirqat al-tasawwuf*. Each Sufi order had its own banner with a specific colour and emblems. Christians and Jews also had, in principle, to follow dress codes with specific colours.

The chronicles refer to a series of other solemn occasions, besides those listed in 'Umari's, Qalqashandi's and Maqrizi's rubrics that belonged mostly to the Bahri period. Zahiri's longer, but less detailed list refers to the Mamluk ceremonial as it was in the mid-fifteenth century, modified by the Circassian sultans.[23] The ceremonial culture of the Circassians has not been documented in the same systematic and detailed manner available for the Bahri period. For the fifteenth century we have to rely, rather, on dispersed information in the chronicles.

Mamluk ceremonial consisted of outdoor and indoor performances. Among the outdoor ceremonies were the annual Opening of the Khalij in the summer, hippodrome events, hunts and other excursions.[24] The indoor ceremonies were staged in the Citadel, the sultan's residence and office, and consisted of various categories of audiences and military reviews. The protocol was focused on the palatial complex created by al-Nasir Muhammad around the Great Iwan and the Qasr. These ceremonies included the weekly Monday audience, when the sultan acted as supreme judge to deal with petitions from the population, daily business audiences and meetings, and reviews of the Mamluks. The corteges to Friday prayer and religious feasts were scheduled in the hippodrome beneath the Citadel.

The close connection between ceremonial and venue is confirmed in Ibn Taghribirdi's description of al-Nasir Muhammad's involvement with the transformation of the Citadel. He designed the architecture of his Great Iwan, and he designed the furnishings of the Qasr and the choreography (*haraka*) to be followed by the dignitaries serving there.[25] In the course of his architectural transformation of the palace complex, al-Nasir Muhammad set the rules that continued to prevail under his descendants.

The first Circassian sultan, Barquq, introduced major modifications in the ceremonial culture of the Mamluks; he shifted the indoor ceremonial centre of gravity from the Qasr-Iwan area to the Palace of the Stables, to which he transferred the audition of the Petitions or *mazalim*.[26] At the same time he revitalized this institution, which brought secular justice within closer reach of the populace; it served as a court of appeal, in which the ruler played the role of an arbiter for the common people.[27] When the transfer of this tribunal to the Stables was announced, the high dignitaries were scared because 'the rabble began to defy the grandees' (*wa ijtara'a 'l-asfāl 'alā 'l-akābir*).[28] To distinguish himself and his handling of the *mazalim* from his predecessors, Barquq also changed the schedule from the traditional Mondays and Thursdays to Sundays and Wednesdays, and then to Tuesdays and Saturdays. His zeal went so far as to add a third day, Friday afternoons.[29] Both Maqrizi and Ibn Taghribirdi praised Barquq for having personally supervised this petition court (*yataṣaddā li 'l-aḥkām bi-nafsihi*), paying as much attention to small cases as to important ones, and for protecting people's rights.

Barquq's change of schedule and venue for the *mazalim* sessions could not have been accidental; Maqrizi used the term '*a'rada 'an*' when reporting Barquq's refusal to hold this tribunal in the Bahri Great Iwan, which implies a deliberate intention of reform; by transferring the petitions venue to the Stables, he meant to enhance this institution. His choice of the Stables must be related to the beginning of his career as master of the stables (*amir akhur*), when his residence was in this area of the Citadel. His successors continued to hold their tribunal in a loggia (maq'ad) attached to the Royal Stables, which henceforth acquired a prominent place in the royal ceremonial of the fifteenth century.[30] Although the Great Iwan was restored by Barsbay and later by Qaytbay to host festive and solemn occasions, including the reception of embassies, it did not recover its function as tribunal again.[31] The palatial centre of the Bahri sultans had ceased to be at the heart of Mamluk ceremonial, being used rather sporadically.

Barquq's son Faraj built a new structure in the Hawsh, formerly the private section of the Citadel, where he held the celebration of the Prophet's birthday in the presence of religious dignitaries. Al-Mu'ayyad added a domed audience hall to it, and Qaytbay held his court in the Bahra compound there, which, as its name indicates, included a pool, where he built a lavish loggia. Sultan al-Ghawri introduced the last major innovation in the court ceremonial by restructuring the hippodrome beneath the Citadel and transferring his audiences to its premises, where the proximity of water and greenery created an ambience of pleasance.

The sultans performed their Friday prayer in the Citadel's mosque, where they appeared in state. The prayer of the two religious feasts was scheduled in the hippodrome; however, information on this subject is rather scarce. Qalqashandi mentioned the maqsura of the mosque among the insignia of royalty. In the Umayyad period, the maqsura was a kind of grille that surrounded the mihrab area of the mosque to seclude the ruler and protect him from attack while praying.[32] In the mosque of the Citadel it was made of iron, and probably resembled contemporary window grilles. Al-Nasir Muhammad emphasized the maqsura area of this mosque with a dome covered with green tiles. Barquq introduced the celebration of the Prophet's birthday in the Citadel, to which the religious dignitaries were invited. The venue was a ceremonial tent pitched especially for the occasion in the Hawsh area. Notwithstanding the importance of the governmental and diplomatic tasks that the sultans performed within the Citadel, the royal ceremonial extended across the entire city of Cairo. Fustat, however, did not figure in the itinerary.

The Sultan in the city

When Ibn Aybak al-Dawadari wrote that al-Nasir Muhammad 'crossed the well-protected Qahira, who was adorned like a bride' (*shaqqa 'l-qāhira 'l-maḥrūsa wa 'l-qāhira bi-zinātihā ka 'l-'arūsa*),[33] his image of the Mamluk capital reveals its intimate relation to the sultan. The appearance of the sultan in the city's streets was a major and yet regular event, carefully covered by the chroniclers of the time, celebrated by the poets, and eagerly awaited by the population. When describing the main avenue, the qasaba, of Qahira, Maqrizi viewed it as the venue of royal rituals ('awayid).[34] Indeed, the occasions when the city was decorated to celebrate a procession are beyond enumeration.

The first *rukub* or ceremonial ride of the sultan after ascending the throne, which was his first encounter with the population, was an event of special importance. If a sultan delayed or failed to perform the expected *rukub*, people would begin to worry and speculate whether he had any reason to fear showing himself (*khashiya al-nuzūl li-amr min al-umūr*), as was the case with Sultan Khushqadam's rather belated first public appearance.[35]

Barquq's first *rukub* started at the Citadel and took him to Matariyya in the northern suburbs and further to the Abu 'l-Manajja bridge outside the city, and back through the northwestern gate of Bab al-Sha'iriyya.[36] On his first *rukub*, Barsbay rode to Raydaniyya for the distribution of the winter clothes to the emirs. He rode back to the Citadel, passing through Bab al-Nasr and Bab Zuwayla.[37] On his way he threw gold and silver coins to the populace. It also happened that the notables would throw silver and gold to greet the sultan on the occasion of his visit to a mosque or one of his friends. On the occasion of solemn processions, silk carpets were spread before the sultan's horse; after he passed, these were collected by the master of the wardrobe. But it also happened in 1390, on the occasion of Barquq's return from Syria, that the populace rushed to seize them, and the sultan, in order to divert their attention, threw silver and gold coins on the street.[38]

Barquq was the first to introduce this ceremony at Mat'am al-Tayr at the beginning of the winter, which became a tradition under all his successors.[39] This novelty, which launched the Mat'am al-Tayr as a major venue of Mamluk regal spectacles, is likely to have required new constructions or a major refurbishment of the place. Barquq probably built the mastaba, which seems to have been an elaborate dais that is henceforth regularly mentioned in the chronicles.

On their processions the sultans would stop at one of the madrasas or khanqahs, meet and debate with scholars, and even spend a night there. Residential structures were available in Mamluk religious buildings to host princely guests. The sultans also often rode to the city for private reasons, to attend a wedding or a funeral, or simply to pay a visit to a friend or a relative. It was common practice for a sultan to spend a night in the summerhouse of one of his courtiers on the riverside or the shore of a pond.[40] The sultans regularly attended funerary prayers for dignitaries and scholars, traditionally held in the oratory or musalla of al-Mu'ini beneath the Citadel. Barquq went to visit the Sufi shaykh Akmal al-Din when he was dying in 1383, and he walked in his funerary cortege from the musalla to his tomb in the khanqah of Shaykhu. His emirs had to prevent him from carrying the shaykh's bier.[41]

When Khushqadam went to inspect his funerary mosque in the northern cemetery, he stopped on his way to visit one of his courtiers; the visit was unexpected and the host was not at home. The sultan might distribute money or food to the poor on his way. Such visits could be also onerous to the host, who had to present gifts to the sultan, for example horses.[42]

The sultan's outings were not confined to specific places but could include any part of Qahira, the hippodromes, the cemetery, the island of Rawda, the port of Bulaq, the shore of the Khalij or any of the ponds. On his way out and back he followed a traditional itinerary, which unfolded the highlights of Qahira's architecture before him.[43] The royal cortege coming down from the Citadel would take the road through the cemetery if the sultan aimed north, or through Saliba street if he took a western or southern direction. On his way back he would enter the city from the northern gate, the Bab al-Nasr, cross the main avenue passing through Bab Zuwayla to Tabbana street, and head further towards the mosque of Sultan Hasan before turning to the Citadel. Slight variations in the procession itinerary were possible, such as using the western gate, the Bab al-Qantara, instead of the northern Bab al-Nasr.

On his tours through the capital the sultan had ample opportunity to hear people's complaints, and sometimes he would be handed a petition.[44] Qaytbay, who was more peripatetic than any other sultan, avoided the city centre on one occasion because he feared he would be confronted with people's complaints about inflation. There were even reports that he went incognito in Maghrebi dress to pray in al-Azhar mosque and talk to people on the street, hearing the most negative opinions about his government.[45] Although the appearance of the sultan in the city was always described as a merry event with crowds cheering in the streets, Cairo's populace was not undiscriminating. Ibn Taghribirdi reported that in 1459 the populace, entirely against their custom of 'exaggerated cheering on the least occasions', demonstrated their discontent to Sultan Inal when he went to launch a naval parade on the Nile. The reason for their anger was that the sultan had imposed heavy extortion and tyrannical measures on the population for the construction of the ships, including the felling of trees in people's gardens without compensating them, and forcing craftsmen to work without wages.[46]

Political events were major occasions for a sultan to display pageantry to his subjects and to foreigners. The arrival in Cairo of the Jalayirid sultan Ahmad Ibn Uways, who had come from Baghdad on Barquq's invitation following Timur's invasion of his territory and the capture of Tabriz, received extensive coverage.[47] Barquq went in full regalia to meet his guest at the Mat'am al-Tayr. The desert was filled with spectators, who watched the guest arrive. The sultan descended from his dais to greet his guest, and invited him to sit down next to him on the ceremonial carpet. The two sultans eventually rode in pomp to the guest residence at the pond of Birkat al-Fil.

The sultan's return from a victorious campaign, or the display of captured prisoners of war, were major occasions for metropolitan celebrations.[48] One of the most celebrated events was the return of al-Nasir Muhammad from Syria in July 1299 after having repelled the Mongol invasion led by Ghazan. Accompanied by all his emirs in full ceremonial pomp, shaded by the royal parasol surmounted by a bird, he rode from Bab al-Nasr to the Citadel on silk carpets spread all the way under his horse's hooves. Fettered Mongol emirs were displayed with the heads of their fallen comrades hanging around their necks, while other heads were paraded on the points of lances, and their smashed drums displayed; musicians from all over Egypt accompanied the event. A major attraction that day was the display of the so-called decorative citadels (*qila' al-zayna*), which was customary in the celebration of military victories. These consisted of decorative structures made of wood and palm branches in the shape of fortresses. On that occasion, the emirs ordered seventy of them to be suspended from buildings along the procession route. To ensure their manufacture, orders had been issued forbidding people to hire carpenters until the citadels were ready.[49]

Barsbay displayed Janus, the captured king of Cyprus, in a parade through Cairo's decorated streets before a crowd of cheering men and women.[50] The Cypriot king rode in chains behind his officers and a thousand other prisoners, including women and children. The booty was carried on camels, mules and donkeys, one of which was bearing the Cypriot crown and the enemy's lowered banners. The procession started at the port of Bulaq and entered the city from the western Bab al-Qantara gate, continuing through Bab Zuwayla, Saliba street and Rumayla square, from where it reached the Citadel through the Bab al-Mudarraj gate.[51]

Similarly in August 1472, when Shah Suwar of the Dhu-'l-Qadir principality in southern Anatolia was captured by Emir Yashbak in a campaign to suppress his rebellion against Mamluk hegemony, he was paraded in Cairo. The city was decorated, and the gates of Bab al-Nasr and Bab Zuwayla painted and adorned with gilded blazons. Spectators had to pay high fees to get a place along the main street to watch Suwar head the procession with his family and retinue, fettered on mules. Dancers and musicians awaited the victorious Yashbak at the entrance of the Citadel, where, inside, a military fanfare punctuated the ceremony of handing Suwar over to the prefect. The finale of the celebration was Suwar's ride on a camel, wearing a white cap, to be hanged at Bab Zuwayla.[52]

When Qaytbay returned from pilgrimage he was greeted by Azbak, the commander-in-chief of the army, who held the parasol with the bird over him, while the emirs and the chief judges preceded him in ceremonial attire. A military orchestra and other musicians (including female singers standing along the streets) and poets hailed the sultan, whose horse stepped on silk carpets that were laid out from Tabbana street to the Citadel. There, the sultan's wife had spread silk carpets from the main gate to his residence in the Hawsh compound, and she showered gold and silver coins over him. The eunuchs waved yellow silk banners and anointed themselves with saffron. In the domed hall of the Hawsh, the deputy sultan Yashbak received the sultan with a banquet. Qaytbay distributed robes of honour and gifts to his dignitaries. He himself received during his pilgrimage gifts worth 200,000 dinars from the merchants and dignitaries of Mecca and Medina.[53]

On the days of great parades, notably on the occasion of the pilgrimage, gender segregation was forgone in the decorated city, where crowds of men and women gathered. Women would sit on vendors' benches and sometimes even spend the night in a shop in order not to miss the spectacle next morning. Such behaviour was condemned as promoting promiscuity.[54] When Inal and his wife visited Bulaq the streets were crowded with men and women, as on the days of the pilgrimage procession or the Opening of the Khalij.[55]

There always seems to have been an audience waiting to be entertained by any kind of spectacles. When, in 1375, Sultan

Sha'ban ordered that two huge columns, found in a residence located on the site of the Fatimid palace in the city, be transported to the construction site of his madrasa near the Citadel, the task proved impossible for ordinary carriers. The sultan therefore summoned technicians from the navy, who produced a mechanical device that facilitated their transport, and the populace got so excited by this event that they accompanied the transported columns with drums and flutes, improvising songs that continued to circulate in Egypt for years. The event was commemorated in popular culture with a fabric being named *jarr al-'amud* or 'dragging the column', probably implying sturdiness![56] Perhaps equally thrilling for the masses were the processions of criminals, and other individuals, when they were paraded on a donkey or a camel across the city on their way to execution, after being tortured.

The hippodromes occupied a prominent place in Mamluk ceremonial life and entertainment. The 'hippodrome' is listed as an event that required the sultan to ride in ceremonial brilliance, back and forth, to attend tournaments or other spectacles. Princesses were allowed to watch such spectacles during the reign of al-Nasir Muhammad, who built loggias for the ladies of his harem at his great hippodrome along the Nile.[57]

When the urban centre of gravity moved from Fustat to Cairo, the Khalij and the connected ponds provided Cairo with its waterscape. The yearly opening of the Khalij to celebrate the Nile flood was a great popular event with a long pre-Mamluk tradition. Although Egypt has always celebrated the flood, which is vital to her existence, the scenario of cutting the dyke to conduct water to Cairo's Khalij and its tributaries that feed the ponds surrounding the city should be attributed to the Fatimids. The Mamluks inherited this festival but the Bahri sultans usually delegated an emir for the solemn opening of the dyke. According to Maqrizi, Barquq was the first sultan after al-Zahir Baybars to participate personally,[58] but this was not the rule among his successors.

Khushqadam, however, went himself to open the dyke. On his way to the Nilometer, where the ceremony started, he rode from the Citadel through the cemetery towards Fustat, where he stopped to visit the shrine of the Prophet's relics (*al-athar al-nabawiyya*). On his way back he halted at the newly built palace of al-'Ayni (Qasr al-'Ayni), and he visited the zawiya of Janibak nearby. From the window of the palace he threw fruits, sweetmeat and silver coins to the gathered populace.[59] The sultan then navigated in the golden barge or *dhahabiyya* to the island of Rawda, where he anointed the column of the Nilometer with saffron, according to custom. From there the naval parade proceeded with a large escort of boats to the mouth of the Khalij to cut the dyke and usher in the flood.[60]

During the reign of Sultan al-Mu'ayyad, the Nile shore began to appear as a venue of royal leisure. The sultan showed a remarkable liking for the river, where he would even go for a swim at Bulaq.[61] He would spend as many as thirty days on the Nile sailing on his *dhahabiyya* between his khanqah in Giza, the residence of his secretary al-Barizi at Bulaq and the island of Rawda, where he rebuilt the mosque of the Nilometer.[62] On one occasion, while residing in his palace near his pasture ground on the Nile shore of Ambuba northwest of Cairo, he ordered his emirs to provide oil and naphtha in large quantities to light floating lamps made of eggshells, orange peel and clay. After sunset they were set afloat on the river while fireworks lit up the sky. The spectacle, as usual attended by a large crowd, went on until the oil was exhausted or the lights extinguished by the wind. On this occasion the emirs were asked to contribute with fireworks, illuminations and ornamented boats. Boats were on hire for those who did not have their own.[63] In the last years of his life, when he was ill, al-Mu'ayyad was itinerant between the Barizi palace, the hippodrome and his own new residence, called the Khamas Wujuh, or Pentagon, along the Khalij.[64]

Al-Ghawri also celebrated lavish feasts on the Nile shore.[65] On such an occasion, his palace on the island of Rawda alongside the Nilometer and the mosque with its minaret, and all the houses on the Nile shores of Rawda and Fustat, including the aqueduct he had recently restored, were illuminated. The golden barge anchored nearby was likewise covered with lanterns on all its masts. While fireworks were fired from fifty boats surrounding the Nilometer, the sultan's twenty-four great emirs were in their boats with their music bands accompanying the royal orchestra. The sultan watched the spectacle from the roof of his palace.

The *dhahabiyya* is first mentioned in the late fourteenth century as the royal barge and one of the insignia of the sultanate.[66] It was a grand vessel, entirely golden in appearance, with masts and sixty oars.[67] It is not clear why Qaytbay abolished it, but in 1513 al-Ghawri ordered the construction of a new one and revived the naval festivities associated with it.[68] The notion of a golden barge recalls the Venetian Bucintoro, the golden ship used by the Doge of Venice in naval ceremonies, notably the celebration of the marriage of the city with the sea.[69]

While most of the spectacles that involved the sultans in the city were rather secular in nature and displayed the sultans' glory, some circumstances required pious ceremonies. In times of hardship, such as drought or plagues, the sultan and the populace came together to pray. Two such occasions occurred during the reign of al-Mu'ayyad. On one of these, in May 1419, people were summoned to attend a collective prayer in the northern cemetery to end the plague. The sultan arrived accompanied by the caliph, the heads of the religious establishment and officials. Wearing the simple white wool gown of the Sufis, without any emblem of royalty or accessory, and riding an unadorned horse, he was met by a crowd carrying banners and Koran fascicles invoking God's mercy. He dismounted and, after prostrating himself, began to sacrifice animals for distribution to the poor. He then rode to visit the tomb of Sultan Barquq in the khanqah of his son Faraj nearby.[70] A similar spectacle in June the following year, during a period of drought, was dedicated to the invocation of water (*istisqa'*).[71] The sultan, again in a Sufi garment, led the crowd to the cemetery, where he knelt down to pray on the dusty ground without a carpet or mat.[72]

The only religious festivity to be celebrated in the city with great pomp was the departure of the pilgrimage caravan. Only four Mamluk sultans are reported to have performed the pilgrimage: Baybars, al-Nasir Muhammad (three times), al-Ashraf Sha'ban and Qaytbay. Sultan al-Mu'ayyad set out on pilgrimage but was prevented from completing it because of a Turcoman threat at the Syrian border.[73] The head of the pilgrimage caravan, the *amir al-hajj*, represented Mamluk authority and patronage of the pilgrimage and the Holy Cities. In 1464 Ibn al-'Ayni, the *amir al-hajj*, started in full pomp and 'solemn beauty never seen before' at al-Nasir's hippodrome north of Fustat, crossed Saliba street to Rumayla square beneath the Citadel, where Sultan al-Zahir Khushqadam could watch him from the window of his palace. He then crossed Qahira from south to north accompanied by the notables of the city, to reach his encampment in the northern outskirts. The procession returned in the evening to Rumayla square through the city, this time accompanied with the lights of torches and lanterns.[74]

Qaytbay's departure for pilgrimage in 1480 took place in a remarkably unobtrusive way. He rode out through the cemetery, unnoticed, with a small escort; however, his return was duly celebrated.[75]

Several sultans' wives performed the pilgrimage to Mecca. Their processions were an uninhibited display of luxury, which Mamluk historians seemed to have enjoyed describing. It was a rare occasion for the Cairene population to celebrate ladies of the Mamluk court, who otherwise made no public appearances. The exception to this rule was Tughay, al-Nasir Muhammad's favourite wife, who joined her husband on a hunting excursion to Giza. Even then, the princess was not supposed to be seen, and an order was given that, on her way across Cairo, all shops should be closed and people kept away from the streets.[76] The pilgrimage was therefore the only occasion for a sultan's wife to be honoured with a procession of her own.[77] Historical accounts of the pilgrimage of Mamluk ladies dwell on descriptions of the luxury and beauty of their convoys. Tughay, who travelled in 1321, was the first to display such pilgrimage glamour.[78] Baraka, Sultan Sha'ban's mother, was escorted by a crowd of high dignitaries and a ceremonial orchestra.[79] Qaytbay's wife Fatima travelled in 1475 in a palanquin, described at length by Ibn Iyas as embroidered with silk and encrusted with rubies, turquoises and pearls.[80] Her caravan included an orchestra performing religious music.

When Sultan al-Ghawri's wife went on pilgrimage with her ten-year-old son, the sultan himself went to her encampment outside Cairo to oversee the arrangements of her caravan and tents according to protocol.[81] Her equipment included a portable bath made of copper, and utensils for heating water. Although the sultan's wives were not supposed to cross the city but ride out through the cemetery, al-Ghawri created a new scenario, which allowed the camel with his wife's palanquin to join in a procession through the city; however, the palanquin was empty, and the princess waited in the Citadel for its return in order to depart from there according to the conventional manner.[82]

Sultan Inal's wife enjoyed a special status in her husband's life, which was also reflected in her social status. Zaynab was the only wife Inal ever had, and, moreover, the only woman in his life and the mother of all his children; he had no concubines either, which was exceptional.[83] Usually the sultans kept four wives, although not always the same ones, as they were regularly divorced and replaced – in addition, of course, to numberless concubines. On her recovery from a bad illness during which she moved to her own residence at Bulaq, where all the great dignitaries went to visit her, Inal's wife was honoured with an extraordinary celebration. Her cortege to the Citadel was accompanied with fanfares, fireworks, torches, lanterns and candles, which were lit as for the celebrations of the pilgrimage or the Opening of the Canal.[84]

Although Ibn Iyas' assessment of al-Ghawri's reign was not particularly favourable because of his frequent use of extortion and confiscation, he praised him for having revived the tournaments that accompanied the departure of the pilgrimage caravan, which Qaytbay had abolished. On that occasion a group of lancers dressed in red paraded in the city accompanying the *mahmal*, the symbolic pilgrimage palanquin, and games were performed in Rumayla square under the eyes of the sultan, who watched from a loggia while masses of people from villages and towns came to celebrate. After sunset there were fireworks, and Ibn Iyas found it 'a memorable evening'.[85]

Al-Ghawri also introduced elephants in the parades of the Khalij festival.[86] The first elephant arrived from Africa in 1510; it was one year old, and the populace, which had not seen an elephant in over four decades, was delighted. Another one followed a few months later.[87] The last procession of al-Ghawri, which took him to meet the Ottoman sultan and his army in Syria, fills seven pages of Ibn Iyas' chronicle, with detailed description of the convoy and the names of the dignitaries involved.[88] Three elephants decorated with banners led the procession, which also included fifty camels carrying the entire treasures of the Mamluks that were kept in the Citadel, and which Sultan Selim was fortunate to capture.[89]

The Sultan as overseer

As a rule the sultans and the emirs personally inspected the construction of their religious foundations and celebrated their inauguration, sometimes with a banquet.[90] In cases of public works of vital significance they even demonstrated active participation. Al-Mu'ayyad ordered work on the Nile bed, which had shifted too far to the west, causing the branch between the island of Rawda and Fustat to dry out.[91] All shops had to be closed for a while, and the population of the city was summoned to contribute to help dig the riverbed. The emirs came with their Mamluks and servants, neighbours and whoever belonged to their household. They set an example by digging with their own hands, and the sultan, who was camping on the shore, gave the signal to start by taking a *quffa* or basket in his hands.[92] With the same gesture al-Mu'ayyad enticed people to join in work on the canals.[93] The personal supervision and participation of the sultan on construction works, in particular civil works concerning the river, which often required popular participation and volunteers, was a tradition that went back to the Ayyubids. Al-Malik al-Kamil is reported to have summoned his emirs and Mamluks, and to have joined them digging the Nile bed with his own hands,[94] and al-Salih Najm al-Din oversaw personally the construction works at his citadel at Rawda.[95]

On his way to inspect the construction of his madrasa, Barsbay stopped at al-Azhar to have a look at its cistern and to visit scholars.[96] Jaqmaq undertook regular inspection tours in the city, and, although he was himself not a great builder, he renovated many mosques and gave orders to clear the mounds of Rumayla and restore its hippodrome. He also severely punished a chief qadi when a minaret collapsed and killed people.[97] On another occasion he gave orders to demolish the house of a shaykh that was built illegally in the ziyada or exterior courtyard of the mosque of Ibn Tulun. He went in person to the premises to oversee the demolition of the house and two latrines in this ziyada, then rode to inspect the construction of a new wall in the hippodrome. While reporting the demolition of the house, Maqrizi recalled that Sultan Hasan earlier on had taken similar measures to demolish an apartment built in the ziyada of al-Hakim's mosque.[98]

Inal likewise was directly involved in maintenance and upkeep, and earned high praise for building his commercial structures in the city's main street in such a way as to widen the street, which had been encroached upon.[99]

Qaytbay's inspection tours were a characteristic feature of his rule.[100] He would ride to inspect the main mosques of Cairo and order the necessary repairs; even the latrines would not escape his attention. On one occasion he scolded the Shafi'i chief judge with the words: 'Go and look at the Taybarsiyya

madrasa, which is under your supervision, people are drowning in the latrines!'[101] Concerned about the encroachment of the Sayfiyya madrasa on neighbouring buildings, he regularly inquired about the issue, which he discussed with his jurists and bureaucrats.[102] On one of his inspection tours he found the mouth of the Khalij in disrepair. He became angry and scolded his vizier and great *dawadar* Yashbak min Mahdi, the most high-ranking of his emirs, ordering him to supervise the work personally. Yashbak obeyed immediately and supervised the works himself ('*amala fihi bi-nafsihi*).[103] Al-Jawhari was surprised at the sultan's concern about the construction of a dam, to the extent that he designated high-ranking emirs and other Mamluks to deal with the task at a time when the country was facing more serious problems.

The Mamluks' involvement in legal matters was not only confined to looking into petitions at the Citadel, but increasingly took a more everyday and casual form that intensified their presence in the city. Sultan Jaqmaq interfered in the case of a man who killed a burglar in self-defence, judging that he should be brought before the Hanafi qadi because Hanafi law would be more lenient in this case.[104] Maqrizi criticized the fact that already in the Bahri period the secular justice of the emirs had increasingly widened its competence at the expense of the judge's jurisdiction. The great chamberlain of Sultan al-Kamil Sha'ban (r.1345–46) was appointed to dispense justice (*li-yahkuma bayn al-nas*),[105] and under Sultan al-Salih Salih (r.1351–54) the qadi was no longer allowed to handle cases of commercial litigation.[106] In reaction to this development, the Hanafi judge al-Tarsusi reiterated the ruler's duty to respect the domain of Islamic law (*shar'*), while practising the *mazalim* jurisdiction, and he required that the sultan forward to the qadi all cases that belonged to his competence.[107] However, the enlarged role of Mamluk justice was not always perceived as tyranny; in the late Mamluk period it responded to the needs of people who preferred to rely on the highest executive authority rather than on the judges.[108] During the reign of Sultan al-Ghawri the Mamluk involvement in dispensing justice increased to such an extent that it could not be done without. Benches (*dikak*) were placed in front of the residences of Mamluk emirs, as the seat of tribunals; these emirs were called *umara' al-hukm*, or 'emir-judges'. When al-Ghawri tried to abolish the jurisdiction of the benches or *dikak*, arguing that plaintiffs should present their cases to the qadis, and the criminals be sent to the police, there was an outcry among people who feared that they would be deprived of their rights. The sultan was eventually compelled to reinstitute the 'tribunals of the benches'.[109] The significance of Mamluk justice is best illustrated in Ibn Iyas' criticism of al-Ghawri, blaming him for transferring litigation cases to the qadi's justice, thus depriving people of their rights (*wa yadfa' al-ahkam ila 'l-shar' wa yudi' huquq al-nas*)![110]

The grooming of the Mamluks as horsemen and soldiers rather than noblemen defined the nature of their artistic patronage, which they designed to be acknowledged and admired from the street in the first place, where they themselves were visible on a regular basis. The lifestyle of the sultans was far from being defined by splendid isolation in the royal precinct. Unlike the Ottoman sultans, who, inspired by the Byzantine *genius loci*, cultivated imperial seclusion, and laid down in their code of state ceremonial that the sultan's majesty excluded intimacy with his subjects,[111] the Mamluk sultans administered their capital in a direct manner, involving themselves in various and even minor aspects of urban life. The sultans' constant appearance in the capital was, therefore, not just a display of ceremonial glamour and power but an inherent aspect of Mamluk government, and the streets of Cairo were not only the stage on which the sultans played the role of glorious monarchs and Muslim philanthropists, but also a platform for regular interaction between the ruling establishment and its subjects.

Fig. 3. Qaytbay sitting on his throne (dikka) (from The Pilgrimage of Arnold von Harff*).*

– 6 –

Treasures, Status and Style

Treasures

Besides architecture, a variety of arts and crafts developed under Mamluk rule in response to the requirements of religious patronage, urban expansion and the secular lifestyle of the aristocracy and urban bourgeoisie.

The Mamluk patrons honoured their religious foundations with lavish manuscripts and luxurious artefacts. The khanqah of Baktimur, for example, owned a remarkable collection of inlaid metal vessels and gilded glass.[1] It also owned the famous Koran manuscript commissioned by the Ilkhanid ruler Uljaytu, which was probably sent to al-Nasir Muhammad as a gift, and he gave it to Baktimur, his son-in-law and once his favourite emir.[2] Later it belonged to the mausoleum of al-Ghawri.[3] Koran volumes dedicated to religious foundations were the finest manuscripts ever produced under Mamluk patronage. While Mamluk calligraphy did not decline, the fine quality of the illuminations of the fourteenth century, displayed in the work of Abu Bakr or the famous Sandal and his pupils, was not maintained in Cairo but cultivated instead in Damascus; there, the Koran fascicles made for Sultan Sha'ban and his mother, which are among the finest in Islamic art, were produced.[4] In the fifteenth century, Barsbay's Koran manuscripts reveal Timurid influences, perhaps from metalwork.[5] As in other arts, the book illuminations of the reign of Qaytbay, including the frontispiece of his main waqf book, display a new style, which was maintained under al-Ghawri. The designs, without the traditional geometric star and polygon compositions, were composed instead of interlocking cartouches and roundels against a ground of naturalistic floral motifs, also favoured

on contemporary metalwork.[6] The few known signatures of calligraphers and illuminators indicate that individuals of Mamluk origin were involved in this craft. Moreover, the barracks of the Mamluks included scriptoriums, which produced fine manuscripts.[7]

The Mamluk rulers were not particularly renowned for being bibliophiles, however, and their patronage lacked the production of lavishly illustrated manuscripts. Considering the significance of this art in the contemporary Mongol, Timurid, Turcoman and Ottoman courts as a medium of regal self-representation, the Mamluk sultans' abstinence in the promotion of illustrated manuscripts must have been a deliberate decision, aimed at cultivating an orthodox image. Even the great patrons of the arts al-Nasir Muhammad and al-Ashraf Qaytbay, were not associated with commissions of illustrated manuscripts. The elaborate illustrated manuscripts attributed to the first half of the fourteenth century remained a relatively short episode in the history Mamluk art, and their patronage is not clear, which in itself is an indication of a low profile. They mostly follow the pre-Mongol Abbasid traditions of Iraq and Syria, and their subjects, among which are the *Maqamat al-Hariri and Kalila wa Dimna*, were also the ones favoured in the Abbasid tradition. Sultan Jaqmaq is reported to have collected precious books, although, considering his strict orthodoxy, these could not have been illustrated.[8] Sultan al-Ghawri's initiative to commission an illustrated Turkish translation of the *Shahnama* was an exceptional case. It is one of only two known illustrated manuscripts of the Circassian period; the other one is the *Iskandarnama* of the Turkish poet Ahmedi produced for Khushqadam, the secretary of Sultan

Timurbugha, in 1467–8.[9] Both productions show the influence of the Turcoman school of painting and an affinity with Turkish culture. By contrast, the manuals of horsemanship (*furusiyya*) of the fifteenth century were not intended to be works of art; they seem to have been illustrated for didactic purposes, without the aesthetic ambitions of their Bahri predecessors.

While endowing their religious foundations with luxury items and art objects, including enameled glass lamps, which are among the outstanding specimens of Mamluk art and Islamic art in general, as well as bronze lamps, chandeliers and carpets, the sultans, emirs and other dignitaries were also promoting a refined lifestyle. Such objects were of dual use. Indeed, the high costs of palaces, which appear to have exceeded those of contemporary mosques, were probably due to their lavish furnishings and decorative items. The palaces of the Mamluk emirs, although they were often granted as a form of remuneration and were returned at the end of their tenure, were nonetheless symbols of status. As Sultan Baybars was told by one of his emirs, the magnificence of a Mamluk's palace enhances the fame of his master the sultan in the eyes of his enemies.[10] The few remaining residences and the abundant waqf documentation indicate that the construction and decoration of urban residences in Mamluk Cairo, which were maintained throughout the Ottoman period, were executed with the same kind of materials and decorative devices used in religious architecture.[11]

Mamluk artefacts now occupy a prominent place in all major museum collections of the world, but they convey only a partial picture of the aesthetic values and material culture of the society that produced them. Information about what constituted the symbols of status in Mamluk society can be found in the chroniclers' accounts of the confiscation of rich individuals' estates, which figure on a regular basis. Confiscation was a measure of punishment and at the same time a form of extortion that helped the sultans replenish the treasury. Some individuals experienced confiscation many times in their career. On these occasions the historians provide a glimpse into the possessions of the wealthy. The estate of a wealthy individual was described as consisting of 'inanimate and animate' riches (*samit wa natiq*), the latter being slaves and animals. For obvious strategic reasons, Mamluks and slaves were the most significant indicators of power and affluence, and their importation was among the most important trades of the Mamluk period.[12] Horses, mules, gold, precious stones, jewellery and luxury textiles were other major signs of wealth, most of which were also imported.

Whether they were members of the Mamluk aristocracy or the civilian elite, the dignitaries hoarded a share of their wealth in precious metals and stones, which they hoped to preserve from confiscation and other arbitrary measures, and bequeath to their descendants. Leo Africanus, who described Cairo

during the Ottoman campaign, wrote that the trade in precious stones from Asia occupied a prominent place in Cairo's luxury markets. Precious metals and copper were imported from Asia and Europe.[13]

Tuhaf (sing. *tuhfa*) also featured among the treasure of a Mamluk high dignitary; these were outstanding objects of a particularly artistic or material value, which could also be collector's items and antiquities.[14] When Sultan Qaytbay went on pilgrimage, he received gifts from the merchants and dignitaries of the Holy Cities that included money and *tuhaf*.[15]

The chronicles and Maqrizi's descriptions of Cairo's markets[16] indicate that textiles, as elsewhere in the medieval world, were a major symbol of status and a prime investment in the estate of a wealthy person. They included raw fabrics, gowns, carpets, furnishings, tents and palanquins, many of which would have been imported from Asia and Europe, although local Syrian and Egyptian textile manufacture was significant.[17] Some princesses' costumes studded with precious stones could cost a fortune compared to which the price of constructing a mosque appears modest. In the fifteenth century, *qumash*, which literally means 'textile', is mentioned as equivalent to ceremonial costume, and often also in a context that suggests a material value with almost the same significance as cash.[18] As a bonus, the sultans bestowed robes of honour (*khil'a*) on multiple occasions to persons of all classes, to invest them or confirm them in office, or as a prize for excellence or a token of acknowledgment, or even as a sign of reconciliation or rehabilitation (*khil'at al-rida*).[19] The honourees wore such robes on solemn occasions.

Because of their universal use in military campaigns, as well as in times of peace, tents belonged to the most highly esteemed treasures of a sultan or emir. Some were very elaborate, being essentially a portable palace, and consisting of multiple structures.[20] They were valued as insignia of royalty and cherished as royal gifts. Qaytbay's tent for the celebration of the Prophet's birthday in the Citadel, made of multicoloured appliqué patterns, needed, according to Ibn Iyas, three hundred sailors to pitch it.

The list of the Salar's confiscated estate, which is typical for an emir of this period, includes gold, a large variety of precious stones, jewellery, vessels of gold and silver, gold trappings, a ceremonial silk tent, a multitude of gowns of silk brocade, and furs.[21] Since the costume reform of Barquq, fur had become a major import on the market as well as a necessary item in every lady's wardrobe.[22] Qawsun's treasure included a large collection of Anatolian carpets, together with Egyptian carpets made in Fustat in the workshop of al-Sharif, rock crystals, *sini* or Chinese porcelain, vessels of gold and silver, and horse trappings.[23] Qawsun hoarded so much gold that the gold value in relation to silver almost halved when the hoard was sold following the looting of his estate.[24] When the estate of the emir Bardabak

Fig. 4. Detail of the Baptistère de St Louis.

al-Farisi, the governor of Damascus, was sold after his death in 1471, the sale, which went on for weeks, caused a glut of luxury goods on the markets to the detriment of Cairo's dealers.[25]

The trousseau of a Mamluk lady was one of the major symbols of status for her father and the bridegroom.[26] On the occasion of princely weddings, the dowry (*jihaz* or *shiwar*) of a princess would cross the city in a long procession of porters accompanied by the notables of the city. When Anuk, the son of al-Nasir Muhammad, married Baktimur's daughter, her trousseau included furniture made of ebony and silver, palanquins, inlaid brass and Damascus brass vessels, textiles, gilded glass, jewellery and *sini*. It was paraded in the city, carried by a long procession of mules.[27]

Maqrizi mentioned among typical trousseau items, before the great crisis of the early fifteenth century, a set of seven inlaid metal vessels, bowls and trays of decreasing size, one inside the other. The trousseau items were displayed on a kind of table (*dikka*) made either of wood inlaid with ebony and ivory, or lacquer, or porcelain or silver. He also mentioned a *dikka* of rock crystal made for a princess during the reign of al-Ashraf Sha'ban with a vase of the same material.[28]

When Sultan Jaqmaq's daughter married, her dowry was displayed in her uncle's house, to be admired by the guests. Although Jaqmaq himself was renowned for his austerity, this trousseau was lavish, with textiles brocaded and embroidered

with pearls, jewellery, furs, rock crystals, silver and *sini*. Ibn Taghribirdi admitted never having seen the like of it, although several ladies in his family married sultans. The author was amazed in particular at the pearl-embroidered textiles. He also referred to undefined *tuhaf* and a type of porcelain that he called '*sini mukattab*', which is difficult to identify, but may be Chinese porcelain with Islamic inscriptions made for export.[29] Scanlon's archæological finds in Fustat have revealed an overwhelming proportion of imitations of Chinese celadon, thus confirming the chronicles' regular mentions of *sini*. Whether it was imported or a local imitation, *sini* indicates the Mamluk appreciation of the aesthetics of Chinese tableware.

Along with architecture and the furnishings of religious monuments, military paraphernalia constituted the artefacts that a medieval urban citizen had ample opportunity to admire, as displayed in Mamluk attire and trappings. The attire of emirs and their soldiers, often described in detail by the chroniclers, was a major and integral aspect of the sultan 's advent.[30] Sultan Qalawun's Mamluks wore silver belts. His son al-Nasir Muhammad, who pursued the policy of motivating the Mamluks' zeal by keeping them as prosperous and content with their material conditions as possible, replaced the silver belts with golden ones that could be encrusted with precious stones.[31] Sultan Barquq is reported to have replaced inlaid bronze in horse trappings with gilded silver, and he also introduced the fashion of the Mamluks to wear gowns lined with fur, usually sable.[32] According to Maqrizi, gold and silver stirrups were commonly used before the calamities of the early fifteenth century, except among orthodox civilians who rejected the personal use of gold. Despite the economic decline, the Mamluks were reported throughout the entire Circassian period to have been riding on saddles of silver and gold, also studded with gems.[33] Ibn Iyas mentioned saddles of rock crystal (*billawr*) and agate (*'aqiq*),[34] which were presumably encrusted with these stones. Finely crafted weapons naturally belonged to the attire of a Mamluk.

Although the chroniclers might have exaggerated the value of certain items that glittered but were not pure gold, the almost total absence of extant objects made of precious materials from this period is remarkable and requires an explanation. The non-hereditary system of the Mamluk aristocracy prevented the continuity and accumulation of estates in individual possession; estates were continuously recycled. At the death or dismissal of an emir, not only his *iqta'* was given to his successor but his palace, and in principle also his portable valuables reverted to the sultan, who after choosing some items for himself or the *bayt al-mal* put the rest on sale; the successor in office would be the main heir. The system prevented the development of individual hereditary estates and palaces that might have included art collections. However, a Mamluk *Schatzkammer* collected by the sultans over the centuries existed in the Citadel of Cairo until it fell into the hands of the Ottomans, and it is likely that some of the Chinese porcelain of the Topkapi collection came from the Mamluk booty.

Status and style

On festive occasions gilded blazons were displayed on the monuments of the city. Blazons were also embroidered on ceremonial gowns, and they adorned many artefacts. More than any other visual symbol, the blazon embodied the identity of the Mamluks, and complemented their proud titular inscriptions. Although Mamluk heraldry was never as canonical as its European homologue, and had no dynastic associations, it was a characteristic feature of Mamluk material culture and the visual arts in general. The blazon, which had already appeared in the Ayyubid period, seems to have emerged under the influence of European heraldry during the warfare with the Crusaders.[35] It included the symbol of the emir's initial function, and represented the earned, not inherited, social prestige of the Mamluks. In a society that purchased its

aristocracy, including the monarch, on the slave market, rank based on merit identified social status.

The metal vessels of the Bahri period, which have survived in large numbers, had a high status among the arts of the Mamluks, bearing representative features that bestowed on them an official ceremonial character. The basin known as the Baptistère de St. Louis, which should be attributed to the reign of al-Zahir Baybars, is a ceremonial art object that represents Mamluk pomp, and might have also had a commemorative purpose. A festive procession of Mamluks on foot and enthroned figures are depicted on its exterior, while horsemen engaged in hunting and warfare decorate the interior (Fig. 3). The individuality of the physiognomies and the costume details suggest what the mural paintings of al-Zahir Baybars' pavilion in the Citadel, which Ibn Shaddad described as representing a procession of the sultan and his emirs, might have looked like.[36] A contemporary poem described the painted warriors of this pavilion as surrounded by birds and stepping on their enemies' bodies, as is also shown on the basin. In the basin, human representation reached a monumentality and individuality never achieved before on a vessel and never tried again in Egyptian or Syrian art, and which could well compete with contemporary European pictorial art. The basin marks simultaneously the apogee and the end of the figural tradition in Mamluk metalwork.[37]

A different iconography characterizes the vessels of the reign of al-Nasir Muhammad and his descendants; it expresses the glory of the Mamluk aristocracy through the medium of epigraphy. Calligraphic inscriptions predominate, displaying a long series of honourific titles, which bear the attributes to which the Mamluks aspired: knowledge, scholarship, piety, jihad, chivalry, valiancy, equity, charity, benevolence and nobleness. The titles of a Mamluk emir, accompanied by his

Fig. 5. Tughra of Sultan al-Nasir Muhammad in Qalqashandi's Subh al-a'sha.

Fig. 6. Blazon of Sultan Qaytbay.

blazon, also referred to his royal master; they emphasized his own rank and status and at the same time glorified the sultan. The sultan's name was propagated on the buildings, furnishings and other portable possessions of his emirs. A large number of fourteenth-century art objects bear princely titles without a name; however, the inclusion of the title 'al-Nasiri' reveals the pedigree of the unnamed owner as a Mamluk of al-Nasir Muhammad.

The political symbolism of the epigraphic decoration is revealed in the similarity between the style of the inscriptions of al-Nasir Muhammad's reign and the *tughra* or royal seal of that sultan. In the *tughra* depicted in Qalqashandi's book on chancellery, the letters of al-Nasir's name and titles were elongated and tightly arranged to emphasize verticality,[38] as in contemporary inscriptions on art objects. Al-Nasir's higher esteem for the written word rather than for the image was reiterated in the royal epigraphic blazon, which he introduced into Mamluk heraldry to distinguish it from the icon blazon of the emirs (figs 4,5). Another epigraphic innovation of his was the writing of his name like the image of the sun, a universal symbol of royalty, with radiating golden letters on silver inlaid brass.[39] The radial motif was inspired by the coins of al-Zahir Baybars, and al-Nasir adopted it also in his own coinage.[40]

The princely epigraphic style, which shows little variation throughout the fourteenth century, was always executed with high-quality craftsmanship; many masterpieces of metalwork bear the names of al-Nasir Muhammad and his emirs. This style was also adopted on a type of pottery, known as sgraffiato ware, and on glass lamps and vessels of the period (Fig. 6). The sgraffiato vessels, made of incised, glazed red earthenware and probably manufactured in the upper Egyptian town of Bahnasa, seem, according to their inscriptions, to have been used in the households of the Mamluk sultans and emirs. Al-Zahir Baybars had a yearly budget of 1,500 dinars for the clay pottery of his household, not including other pottery (*qashani*) and porcelain (*sini*);[41] this clay pottery is most likely the sgraffiatto ware. The *qashani* probably refers to painted vessels made of frit, which was of a different style. Although most likely it was not made for princely use, but was perhaps 'barracks pottery',[42] the official epigraphic style of the sgraffiato ware did publicize a sense of pride in the Mamluk identity.

Glass production was not only associated with mosque lamps but also had a significant secular role. Lamps without Koranic inscriptions were probably used in residences. Drinking vessels, cups and bottles, adorned with poetical inscriptions or glorious titles, celebrated profane pleasures with scenes of drinking and music, gorgeous horsemen involved in equestrian tournaments or hunting, and fabulous landscapes with fantastic birds and animals. Bottles and beakers were exported to Europe, but they also had a local clientele, as their inscriptions suggest. There may have been several centres of glass production in Syria and Egypt; Maqrizi mentioned markets of glass dealers (*zajjajun*) in his description of Cairo.[43] These are likely to have included factories, as was the case with other crafts in the bazaar; glass kilns can well be accommodated within the markets. The disappearance of enameled glass in the fifteenth century has been attributed to Timur's devastation of Syria, traditionally a

Fig. 7. Enamelled glass lamp, fourteenth century.

Fig. 8. Inlaid brass ewer in the name of Sultan Qaytbay's wife.

Fig. 9. Late Mamluk inlaid bowl (Khalili Collection).

major glass-producing region; however, Alexandria, an ancient centre of glass production, might have also contributed to this craft under the Mamluks before it was devastated in 1365 by the raid of Pierre de Lusignan from Cyprus. This would explain why the glass lamps of Sha'ban's reign are almost plain and hardly enameled, in contrast to the lavish specimens of his predecessor Sultan Hasan.[44] Al-Nasir Muhammad had founded a factory in Alexandria, but it is not known what kind of glass it produced.[45] The craft regained vitality during Barquq's reign before it finally disappeared.

Unlike architecture, which continued with unabashed vigour through all crises, the economic and social changes of the fifteenth century brought about a rupture in the evolution of the decorative arts. Many of the arts and crafts that were the pride of Cairo's markets came to an end, according to Maqrizi. The Circassians ceased to produce enameled glass, sgraffiato pottery, and inlaid brass in the epigraphic style. The end of Bahri metalwork may not have been due only to shortages of metal, as has been assumed; sultans and emirs always managed to get what they wanted. A change of taste and ceremonial practices, which began with Barquq's reign, may have been decisive. The transfer of the sultans' audiences from al-Qasr al-Ablaq after the end of the Qalawunid dynasty to other venues in the Citadel, alongside the costume reform, suggest a deliberate renewal that might have involved various aspects of material culture, including the use of vessels. The revived fifteenth-century metalwork reflects the social changes revealed in the chronicles. Aristocratic inscriptions make room

for other designs where names and titles are absent or occupy a subordinate position, while poetical texts proliferate and arabesques dominate. Names of commoners appear as patrons, with the phrase 'made by order of' ('*mimma 'umila bi-rasm*') that used to be exclusive to the aristocracy.

A variety of novel styles appeared during the reign of Qaytbay, including some princely vessels of unprecedented decoration.[46] The so-called 'Veneto-Saracenic' vessels, anonymous, but often signed by a *mu'allim*, are among the most interesting innovations of this period.[47] Created for export to Europe, where they are mostly found, and often displaying European shapes, they represent a new vision of the arabesque and curved geometry (figs 7,8). Naturalistic flower motifs appear for the first time in Mamluk metalwork, in manuscript illumination and in architectural decoration. Although a pluralism of styles characterizes the artistic revival of this period, we also find common patterns on various media, like the marble inlaid rosette of Qijmas al-Ishaqi's mihrab, which recalls the decoration of Veneto-Saracenic metal objects, and the compositions of interlocking ribbons, which appear on metal vessels and in book illumination.

The strict geometry of Mamluk carpets cannot be related to any other Mamluk art, except perhaps to marble pavements. We do not have specimens of the carpets produced in fourteenth-century Fustat by the workshop of al-Sharif. The name of Sharif is associated with carpets made for the emir Qawsun, and more than forty years later for the mosque of Sultan Barquq (1386).[48] It is not possible to establish their relationship to the late Mamluk carpets known from European collections, which continued to be made after the Ottoman conquest. These carpets, which seem to emerge in the late fifteenth century, suggest yet another initiative in Qaytbay's reign to revive a craft that had flourished in the fourteenth century. A large carpet found in the Generalife in the Alhambra, which must have been sent to the Nasrid court just before its fall, points to Qaytbay.[49] His attempt to revive the art of enameled glass, however, was unsuccessful, as a unique and ugly piece in his name reveals.[50] Considering Qaytbay's interest in trade, the artistic revival of his reign might have been guided by export interests; however, this could not have been his exclusive motivation. Rather, the simultaneous florescence of architectural decoration reveals a general sense of artistic ebullience that he is likely to have promoted. The fact that Qaytbay's name on some metal objects is inscribed in a new distinctive style, with curls atop the vertical letters in a manner that distinguishes his from all other sultans names, reveals a certain coquettishness and a sense of style.

The involvement of the Mamluk ruling elite in shaping and regulating the urban markets, and their major role as investors and patrons had an undeniable impact on the taste and styles of the major arts and crafts. In the Bahri period it is almost impossible to distinguish, on mere aesthetic grounds, princely from non-princely objects; only the absence of titles may suggest a non-Mamluk patron. In the Circassian period both categories, the high-quality and the more ordinary-looking vessels, include a few specimens inscribed with names of dignitaries, while the majority are anonymous. It appears that the significance of Mamluk titles diminished with time. Anonymous vessels without princely titles but with a blazon may or may not have been made for emirs. One may only speculate to what extent the blazon was usurped by non-Mamluks.

Although the sultan and his emirs might have had craftsmen under contract working for them, there is no information to suggest the existence of royal ateliers directly attached to the court creating designs for royal artefacts. Neither al-Nasir Muhammad's epigraphic style, which had a centralized official character, nor Qaytbay's artistic revival can be associated with such an institution, as it existed at the Timurid and Ottoman courts.

The only workshop known to have been under direct courtly patronage was the tiraz factory in Alexandria, which had produced ceremonial textiles since Fatimid times, but it was not the exclusive provider. Another case is the *zardakhana* in the Citadel, a workshop overseen by an emir that manufactured and repaired weapons, although weapons were also produced in the markets.[51]

The sultan could at any time order the craftsmen of the bazaars of Cairo or Damascus to supply whatever he needed, and in urgent circumstances he could compel certain craftsmen to keep themselves available and not take on other commitments until they had completed his own order. The *suq al-sharabshiyyin* or Sharbush market in Cairo produced the ceremonial caps introduced by Barquq, along with a new type of robe of honour and its accessories, which the sultan bestowed on the dignitaries of state. During the economic crisis of the early fifteenth century, the dealers, who used to sell such items to the court, were eliminated, so that the sultan could buy directly from the producers.[52]

On the eve of a military campaign, many of the workshops in the city would be busy producing textiles and other goods necessary for military supply.[53] When Sultan Sha'ban ordered for his pilgrimage cortege a long list of luxury items in Damascus, the craftsmen were summoned and given the raw materials and specifications for their work. The governor of Damascus, Baydumur, sent him embroidered silks, horse trappings, gold and silver chains, and jewellery. Slightly later, the sultan commissioned the chandeliers and other metal furnishings for his madrasa in Cairo. Despite economic problems, and a famine that forced people to eat dogs in Aleppo, Baydumur sent to Cairo large quantities of metal taken from doors and windows, keys, locks and dome finials, along with metal vessels inlaid with gold and silver and carried on 160 camels.[54] The chronicles regularly report that the governors of Damascus arrived in Cairo with riches for the sultan. Although Syria played a major role in supplying the Mamluk court and the urban bourgeoisie with refined artefacts, an exact assessment of the extent of the Syrian contribution to Mamluk decorative arts is not possible.

The Mamluks did not need to establish court ateliers, because the major markets of Cairo and Damascus with their well-established artistic traditions, being under their control, fulfilled this function. The magnificent minbar of the mosque of Abu 'l-'Ila, founded by a merchant, and that of Qaytbay's mosque are most likely to have been produced in the same workshop. Even the designers, the *rassamin*, who created decorative patterns worked in shops in Cairo's markets.[55] The markets produced artefacts for the court as well as the urban bourgeoisie, following the trends set by the princely patrons; as Maqrizi and Ibn Taghribirdi on more than one occasion commented, '*al-nās 'alā dīn mulūkihim*', i.e. people emulate their rulers.

– 7 –

Construction:
Organization and Cost

Supervisors, master builders and builders

For the construction of royal buildings, the Bahri Mamluks instated the office of supervisor, the *shadd al-'ama'ir al-sultaniyya*, who was traditionally a low-ranking 'emir of ten'.[1] His task was to oversee the builders and craftsmen involved in the state's constructions. The *shadd al-'ama'ir al-sultaniyya* must have been associated with the *diwan* created by al-Nasir Muhammad to co-ordinate his building programme.[2] In addition, high-ranking emirs or bureaucrats were appointed to administer the construction of individual royal and princely buildings.

Aqsunqur al-Rumi min 'Abd al-Wahid[3] was the supervisor of the royal constructions of al-Nasir Muhammad between 1315 and 1318. Not much is reported about his career except that he was master of the stables before this appointment, which gave him the opportunity to amass a great fortune. The emir Aqbugha min 'Abd al-Wahid (d.1343) was promoted to the office of supervisor while serving at the same time as royal majordomo and master of the wardrobe. The fact that he was the brother of Princess Tughay, the sultan's favourite wife, contributed to his prestige.[4] He was, moreover, in charge of the construction works of Yalbugha's fabulous palace, and one may speculate that, being known for corruption, his involvement in this project might have contributed to its exceptionally high costs![5] Maqrizi severely criticized him for his unscrupulous and tyrannical methods. The emir Iyas (d.1350) was another *shadd al-'ama'ir*, who worked in Syria, where he held high offices including the governorship of Safad and Aleppo. He was of Christian Armenian origin.[6] Sultan

Hasan appointed one of his ten 'emir of thousand' to oversee the construction of his mosque.

Qalqashandi also mentioned a *muhandis al-'ama'ir* or construction engineer among the professionals (*arbab al-waza'if min ahl al-sina'at*). On the same level as the chiefs of the physicians, the ophthalmologists and the shipyard, he was lower down in the hierarchy, and on a more technical level than the supervisor.[7] Like these professionals, the chief *muhandis* was a technician in charge of overseeing his craft, controlling the qualifications of the craftsmen and issuing authorization for their employment. A fifteenth-century protocol of the restoration of Baybars' apartment complex at Taht al-Rab' street names four *muhandis*, or surveyors, who were in charge of assessing the state of the building and the cost of its repair.[8] A *muhandis* named Hujayj accompanied the emir Aqbugha to Hama to survey the Duhaysha palace of the Ayyubid sultan al-Mu'ayyad in order to build a similar one in Cairo.[9] The term *muhandis* referred also to builders; Maqrizi mentioned the *ra'is al-muhandisin* of al-Nasir Muhammad, *al-mu'allim* al-Suyufi, who built the madrasa of Aqbugha and the mosque of al-Maridani.[10]

Virtually nothing is known about the simple builders, their organization or their wages, except for the wages of the *mi'mar* attached to pious foundations and mentioned in waqf documents; a *mi'mar* was a simple builder, who belonged to the regular staff, to be in charge of the maintenance and restoration work of buildings, alongside a plumber and a carpenter. All three received the same salary, which was the lowest on the salary scale of the foundation. Ultimately, however, the supervisor of the waqf and the chief judge who oversaw all pious foundations were also responsible for the safety of the endowed buildings.

Sultan Jaqmaq punished the deputy Shafi'i qadi Nur al-Din al-Qalyubi when the minaret of the Ayyubid Fakhriyya madrasa, of which he was the waqf supervisor, collapsed, demolishing an adjoining apartment building and killing many people. The intercession of an emir might just have prevented the supervisor from being whipped; however, he along with the Shafi'i chief qadi had to endure the sultan's most virulent insults and curses, and eventually both of them were dismissed from their offices. Nur al-Din was, moreover, condemned to pay a high sum for the restoration of the minaret.[11]

In the fifteenth century there seems to have been a fusion between the office of the *shadd al-'ama'ir* and the sultan's master builder, who was called *mu'allim al-sultan*. The first *mu'allim* to have climbed the social ladder was Ahmad Ibn al-Tuluni, also called *muhandis, kabir al-sunna'* (chief of the builders) and *shadd al-'ama'ir*, who served Sultan Barquq.[12] He belonged to a family of carpenters, stonecutters and contractors, and was one of the wealthy notables of Cairo. Although he built Barquq's madrasa, the overseer of its construction was the emir Jarkas al-Khalili, the sultan's master of the stables, whose name is included in an inscription on the building. Barquq appointed Ahmad Ibn al-Tuluni an 'emir of ten', and married his sister and his daughter. Ahmad built a mausoleum for himself in the southern cemetery.[13] His descendants, who were educated as scholars, succeeded him in office, and they continued to play a prominent role in the building craft to the end of the Mamluk period. Although Ahmad Ibn al-Tuluni experienced this extraordinary career, Barquq's reign did not produce the most outstanding Mamluk monuments. The main function of the master builder, however, was not confined to erecting handsome monuments but also included military and civil engineering works, and he was in charge of hydraulic constructions in Cairo and the Holy Cities.

The title *mu'allim al-mu'allimin* appears in the fifteenth century in connection with high-ranking native bureaucrats who supervised royal construction works, but at the same time Mamluk names also figure in this function. In the fifteenth century merchants are mentioned among the supervisors of royal construction works, such as the sultan's merchant (*tajir al-sultan*) 'Ali al-Kaylani, who was appointed by Barsbay to be a member of the team in charge of restoring the Mecca shrine.[14] Badr al-Din (also called al-Badri) Hasan Ibn al-Tuluni, who held the position of *mu'allim al-mu'allimin* during Qaytbay's and al-Ghawri's reigns, was described in his biography and obituary mainly as a scholar knowledgeable in various religious and theoretical disciplines rather than a practitioner.[15] Also during Sultan Qaytbay's reign, a prominent merchant, Ibn al-Zaman, led the restoration of the mausoleum of Imam Shafi'i, the reconstruction of the Prophet's mosque in Medina after a fire, and the foundation of the sultan's madrasa and ribat beside it.[16] The involvement of merchants and scholars in the supervision of royal construction works suggests that supervision did not require full-time involvement with architectural matters and was mainly administrative; it also leads to the conclusion that architectural innovations should be credited, rather, to the master masons. At the same time and as in the Bahri period, several emirs were appointed to oversee various branches of the royal constructions in Egypt and the Hijaz, including civil and military buildings. The emir Inal is mentioned as the *shadd al-'ama'ir al-sultaniyya* of Sultan al-Ghawri, while Khayrbak al-Mi'mar was involved in fortification works. Syria had its own local *mu'allim al-sultan*.

Unlike the decorative arts, builders' or masons' signatures are rare in Mamluk architecture. Only the portal of Qawsun's palace[17] and al-Mu'ayyad's minarets bear builders' signatures; their names are not recorded in the literary sources unlike the supervisors, emirs or high-ranking bureaucrats, whose names are regularly mentioned and sometimes also figure in the monumental epigraphy as well. The following emirs are mentioned in the inscriptions of royal buildings: Muhammad Ibn Biylik al-Muhsini, one of the royal emirs, in Sultan Hasan's mosque; Jarkas al-Khalili, the master of the stables, in Sultan Barquq's funerary complex, Lajin al-Turantay is mentioned without title in Faraj's khanqah; Qadi 'Abd al-Basit, the secretary of the army, in Barsbay's madrasa; an unnamed secretary of the army and the sultan's household in Inal's madrasa; Azbak, the commander-in-chief of the army, on Qaytbay's causeway in Giza; and Shaykh 'Abd al-Qadir al-Dashstuti, the famous scholar and Sufi, in Asalbay's mosque in Fayyum.[18] The rarity of master builders' names, by contrast, may be explained by the collective copyright of a construction project, in which the patron himself along with his supervising emirs and bureaucrats participated, leaving little room for the creativity of an individual designer. In terms of acknowledgement, administration was given the priority over design.

The existence of a supervising office of royal constructions does not imply that the building craft was organized into corporations or autonomous self-governing guilds with workshops that travelled from one place to another, as was the case in medieval Europe. The recruitment of builders on the market was organized by the *shadd* or the *mu'allim*, whereas the corvée required the authority of a mighty emir or a sultan. Judging by the chroniclers, who found it noteworthy to report when a patron treated his workers with fairness, it seems that building craftsmen were often subjected to arbitrary measures. The *diwan al-'ama'ir*, which was the authority administering royal constructions, seems to have employed a building staff on a permanent basis. When the financial situation became critical during Sultan Hasan's first reign, the budget of the royal construction works, including the salaries of the employed craftsmen (*al-mustakhdimin fi 'l-'ama'ir*), was annulled.[19]

Sultan al-Nasir Muhammad made systematic use of the corvée. Aqbugha, his overseer of the constructions, forced all builders involved with royal buildings to work without pay one day each week on the construction of his own madrasa. Moreover, he used his position to acquire building materials and furnishings without paying for them. He also used forced labour for the construction of Yalbugha's palace.

The emirs related to al-Nasir Muhammad through marriage, such as Maridani, Aqsunqur, Baktimur al-Saqi and Aqbugha, enjoyed special privileges that facilitated their building schemes. The sultan promoted the building activity of his in-laws to realize his own monumental vision of Cairo. Qawsun, the sultan's brother-in-law and son-in-law, and one of the most glorious emirs of the Bahri period, like other emirs close to the sultan, was privileged by having his mosque overseen by the royal *shadd al-'ama'ir* and having access to prisoners of war for its construction.[20]

Al-Nasir Muhammad used Frankish and Armenian prisoners of war.[21] Some of them were settled in the Citadel and others in the city. This community must have been captured during his military campaign in the kingdom of Little Armenia or Cilicia in 1322, where he took many prisoners, which might have included Franks as well, who were there in great number. Their descendants seemed to have succeeded them in the craft, perhaps also joined by new recruits; this Frankish–Armenian community, which enjoyed a privileged status, still existed in Cairo in the early fifteenth century. As late as the second half of the fourteenth century, Europeans captured during naval raids on Alexandria were sent to Cairo to work in the building craft.[22]

When the sultans required manpower for their public works the emirs helped out with their own Mamluks. When al-Nasir Muhammad envisaged digging a canal from the Nile at Hilwan to the foot of the Citadel across the Muqattam hill, he intended to recruit soldiers for the gigantic task.[23] The royal majordomo 'Abd al-Ghani al-Fakhri contributed to the construction of al-Mu'ayyad's mosque by sending his Mamluks to build the latrines. In 1472 hundreds of people from Cairo were recruited alongside peasants to work on the reconstruction of the bridges of Giza, which had collapsed several times under the pressure of the Nile flood, costing Qaytbay considerable sums. The project required two hundred qualified builders (*mi'mar*) and engineers (*muhandis*) and two thousand workers, in addition to the Mamluks of Azbak, the commander-in-chief of the army. The recruitment of civil workers was not met with enthusiasm by the population; the patrons had to use the stratagem of announcing a public execution, and, according to Jawhari, a murderer was in fact crucified and paraded to attract a large crowd of spectators. At that point all the men present were fettered in chains and dragged to the construction site. They were told that they would be paid fairly for their work![24]

Taming the Nile has been a major concern throughout Egypt's history, including Cairo's history as well.[25] The annual flood in the summer could have unpredictable consequences. Too much or too little water could lead to a catastrophe. The chronicles provide abundant details about the civil engineering works that the Nile required from the Mamluk State, which was responsible for constructing dykes to protect the embankments, dams to moderate the flood, and quays to consolidate constructions along the Nile shores. During al-Nasir's reign, the riverbed needed to be channelled westwards to protect the eastern bank from flood. A couple of decades later, under Sultan Hasan, corrections were made in the other direction after the riverbed had shifted too far to the west and people could walk to the island of Rawda; the water supply for the urban population had also been disrupted. This kind of infrastructure maintenance required a formidable manpower of engineers and labourers, and most of all an efficient central authority. The emirs assumed the major responsibility in such situations to plan and organize the work, raise the necessary funds and recruit labour. They contributed with funds and manpower from their household of soldiers and peasants from their *iqta'* land, as well as with the transportation of animals and tools. Many thousands of labourers were involved in such undertakings.[26] 'The whole army' is reported to have been engaged in 1313 in the construction of the bridge of Giza.[27] The emirs' control of military and rural manpower enabled them to mobilize human resources to cope with emergency situations, and to participate in great building projects.

Time and money

The Mamluks built their monuments with astonishing speed, even by modern criteria. Because of their individual and commemorative character and the absence of hereditary succession, their monuments needed to be completed quickly within the time-span of a career that might for a variety of reasons end early or abruptly. Qalawun's monumental complex of mausoleum, madrasa and hospital was built within less than a year. Al-Nasir Muhammad's reconstruction of Baybars' hippodrome, replacing wood with masonry structures, took two months.[28] The two stone bridges of Qaytbay in Giza carried inscriptions that indicated a construction period of two and three months respectively.[29] This rapidity by no means implied cheap, poor-quality construction. The monuments were planned for perpetuity to immortalize their founders and maintain the ongoing charity recommended by the Hadith. They were built of stone and rubble, and the thickness of their walls exceeded structural requirements. The Mamluk heritage attests to the scrupulousness of the building craft.

The financial aspect of Mamluk pious and monumental patronage is difficult to establish. Waqf documents do not mention building costs, or the revenue produced by a waqf estate. The chronicles, on the other hand, do provide a great deal of financial information, ranging from the building costs of a mosque to the value of small items, such as the slipper of a princess. However, the analysis of these figures and their interpretation faces several obstacles that make clear conclusions difficult.

The first such difficulty is the evaluation and comparison of sums given in dirhams and dinars over a period of time. This poses the double problem of defining the purchase value of the currency, along with its appreciation or depreciation, and also the development of the conversion rate between the two currencies during the period under investigation. Whereas the Bahri dinar was almost constantly equivalent to 20 dirhams, by 1458 the ratio had reached 1 to 460.[30] In the following analysis I have therefore converted the dirham sums given for the Bahri period into one twentieth of a dinar. Fortunately for this investigation, the conversion problem does not arise for the Circassian period, because the sources indicate all amounts only in gold dinars, without reference to their silver dirham equivalent.

The range of sources that sultans and emirs could tap to achieve their monumental schemes also makes it difficult to evaluate and compare the actual building costs. Despoliation, confiscation, coercion and forced labour contributed to reduce substantially the cost of a building. The Mamluk aristocracy used its power and authority to quarry uninhibitedly the ancient monuments of Egypt and Syria, as is attested by the monuments themselves and confirmed in the chronicles. They were not the first to be associated with such practices, however. The Fatimids, for example, demolished Pharaonic temples in Lower Egypt to build Qahira's walls; Salah al-Din dismantled a number of small pyramids to erect the Citadel. Al-Nasir Muhammad used stones from the 'small pyramid' to build a bridge.[31] The Mamluks did not restrict their spoliation to pre-Islamic monuments; they also quarried mosques whose estates were exhausted or had fallen to ruin for various reasons.[32]

The integration of pre-existing structures or the reuse of their foundations contributed to the reduction of construction costs. The complex of Qalawun was built with material and marble removed from al-Salih's citadel at Rawda, which itself had been built with pre-Islamic spoils. The funerary madrasa of al-Ashraf Sha'ban, built with stone blocks from ancient monuments, was dismantled by the emir Jamal al-Din Yusuf for the building of his own madrasa and of Sultan Faraj's oratory-cum-fountain, the Duhaysha. Jamal al-Din also dismantled the madrasa of al-Ashraf Khalil and used its stone for a new minaret at al-Azhar.[33] Faraj himself took the marble of the madrasa built by Baha' al-Din Ibn Hanna in Fustat in 1256,[34] which at that time was abandoned, as was the whole area. When al-Nasir Muhammad

ordered the reconstruction of al-Zahir Baybars' hippodrome in 1331, its wooden debris was sold for 102,000 dirhams or 5,100 dinars.[35] The value of reused building materials should not be underestimated; when Barsbay demolished the commercial complex known as Khan Masrur, which was decayed, its debris was sold for 12,000 dinars.[36]

Sultans and emirs could confiscate marble and wood from other people's residences, as did al-Mu'ayyad and Barsbay. Al-Mu'ayyad also took columns from Qawsun's mosque; Barsbay took marble from the palace of al-Baysari; and Aqbugha confiscated a residence to build his mosque on its site. The list of such cases is long. The cenotaphs of Princess Tulubiyya (1364)[37] and Sultan al-Mu'ayyad Shaykh, both with Koranic inscriptions in beautiful early Kufic script, had obviously belonged to earlier tombs.

The bronze door of the mosque of Abu Bakr Ibn Muzhir was originally made for the madrasa of Mankutimur built in 1291, and the door of Barsbay's mosque in the village of Khanka outside Cairo was in the name of Shams al-Din Sunqur al-Tawil, an emir of Qalawun.[38] A more famous case is the present door of al-Mu'ayyad's mosque, which belonged to Sultan Hasan's mosque. Ibn Taghribirdi described the sultan's appropriation of the chandelier and door of Sultan Hasan's mosque as showing a lack of manners and chivalry (qillat adab wa qillat muruwwa); the sultan could well have commissioned better ones.[39]

It is not clear, however, whether the dismantling of older monuments was always an illegal despoliation or, rather, a legitimate reuse of materials from buildings that were already in disrepair and abandoned. Maqrizi's polemic against Mamluk practices, and his view of sariq min sariq, 'a thief stealing from another', might have been occasionally exaggerated, and should be treated with caution. The historian also regularly drew attention to patrons who built mosques without reverting to such methods, praising them in order to highlight his critique of the more common and dubious methods of acquisition.

For the acquisition of a desired plot of land, sultans and emirs, by their own often despotic terms, could force people to sell properties, as did Qalawun, Maridani, Qawsun and many others, or they could bend the law to acquire waqf estates, or simply confiscate what they wished to take. The most controversial measures were those involving waqf property because of their detrimental effect on the pious foundations.

By applying the stratagem of istibdal, which in exceptional situations or emergencies authorized the exchange or sale of a waqf property to rescue a foundation from ruin, the sultans and emirs could manipulate without a legal justification the transaction to their advantage, and acquire valuable estate at a low price. With the help of false testimony, the coveted waqf estate would be assessed as being in a ruined condition and hence available for purchase. This required the collaboration of corrupt jurists.[40] The emir Qawsun applied this method to acquire the palace of al-Baysari.[41] The case of Jamal al-Din al-Ustadar is well documented by Maqrizi, because the emir eventually fell in disgrace, and his transactions, which included the acquisition for his own madrasa of an entire quarter in the heart of the city, with residences and commercial structures belonging to pious waqfs, were eventually annulled by Sultan Faraj.[42] Barsbay, while acquiring waqf property to build his madrasa in the city, allegedly offered the owners a fair deal.[43] Sultan al-Ghawri combined various forms of illegal acquisition, including illicit *istibdal* and the confiscation of land and building materials, so that his mosque was nicknamed *al-masjid al-haram*, playing on the word *haram*, which means 'holy' as well as 'sinful'.[44] The usurpation of endowed property had already led to the decay and disappearance of major foundations by sultans and emirs at that time. Meanwhile, many sultans were willing to redress the harm that was done or even reform the system. As their duty as supreme overseers of the pious endowments required, they contributed to the support of foundations and repaired the monuments of their predecessors.[45]

The cost of a mosque

The Bahri Mamluks

Only occasionally do the chroniclers report how much it cost to build a mosque. Safadi indicated that the mosque of al-Zahir Baybars at Husayniyya cost one million dirhams (50,000 dinars),[46] which was a relatively high price. By comparison, the budget of that sultan's private household was 40,000 dinars a year.[47]

Maqrizi reported that the building costs of the mosque of the emir Aydumur al-Khatiri, built in 1337, which he described as a lavish monument with a marble pulpit, amounted to 400,000 silver dirhams, which was equivalent to 20,000 dinars. Al-Maridani's mosque, which is one of the most richly decorated of the period, is reported to have cost more than 300,000 dirhams or 15,000 dinars, not including the wood and marble provided by the sultan, and the columns taken from the Fatimid mosque of al-Rashida.[48] The spoils and the sultan's contribution must have been a significant subsidy; by comparison, the renovation of the complex of Qalawun, which lasted from December 1325 to April 1326, cost 60,000 dinars, which is triple Maridani's contribution to the costs of his mosque.[49]

The mosque of Sultan Hasan was the most costly ever built by the Mamluks. Although the decoration was never completed, it took three years to construct without a single day of rest, which was longer than any other religious monument needed. The allocated construction costs amounted to 20,000 dirhams per day, equivalent to 1,000 gold *mithqal*s or dinars. On the basis of a Hijra year of 354 days, the total expenses for

this period would have amounted to more than 21,240,000 dirhams or 1,062,000 dinars. Maqrizi was told that the mould used for the construction of the sanctuary, which was dumped after completion of the work, had cost 100,000 dirhams alone. The total amount for the salaries to be paid annually by the waqf to the staff of the madrasa-mosque amounted to 558,600 dirhams or 27,930 dinars. The founder stipulated that the waqf supervisor should keep a reserve fund of 200,000 dirhams or 10,000 dinars for the maintenance of the foundation.[50]

Information concerning the running costs of a pious foundation, or the costs of the estate with which a religious foundation was endowed, is rather scarce. Maqrizi estimated that one million dirhams (50,000 dinars) was the annual revenue of the estates dedicated by Qalawun for the upkeep of his complex.[51] Aqsunqur endowed his mosque with land in the region of Aleppo, which produced the annual revenue of 150,000 dirhams or 7,500 dinars. However, in the absence of a waqf document it is not possible to tell whether the mosque was entitled to the entire revenue or only part of it.[52] During the Mamluk rebellion in the late fourteenth century following Barquq's death, the revenue was blocked, and the mosque decayed until it was refurbished in 1412 by the emir Tughan.[53] The endowed estate of the zawiya of Shaykh Khidr, sponsored by al-Zahir Baybars, produced an annual income of 30,000 dirhams. The land purchased by Manjaq from the treasury for the endowment of his cistern and fountain cost 25,000 dinars.[54]

An examination of the costs of Bahri Mamluk palaces[55] during the reigns of al-Nasir Muhammad and his sons reveals a great discrepancy in comparison with the costs of mosques. As the following figures will show, the discrepancy seems to be less in the cost of construction than in the high expenses usually incurred for luxury items such as furnishings and decoration, which seem to have been more significant in residential buildings than in mosques. At the palace called Dar al-Qurdumiyya, the gate alone was worth 100,000 dirhams or 5,000 dinars.

The grand palace of Baktimur al-Saqi took ten months to build at a cost of 1,500 dirhams per day, not including the labour of prisoners and the stones provided by al-Nasir Muhammad. Maqrizi estimated that it would have otherwise cost twice as much, i.e. 3,000 dirhams per day. On the basis of months of 29 and 30 days alternately, this would make a total cost of 442,500 dirhams (22,125 dinars) excluding the costs of labour and building material, or 885,000 dirhams (44,250 dinars) including them. Maqrizi's estimate of the total building costs of this palace at 1,000,000 dirhams or 50,000 dinars[56] is equivalent to the price of the mosque of al-Zahir Baybars, a royal monument, and as much as one and a half times the cost of building the mosque of al-Khatiri or al-Maridani. Not quite consistent, however, with the general prolific spending on palaces is the example of Tankiz's palace in Cairo. Its decoration cost only 17,000 dirhams or 700 dinars, and the same palace was sold in unknown circumstances in 1418/19 for less than 1,000 dinars.

Al-Nasir Muhammad paid one million dirhams or 50,000 dinars to build a stable for the cows that operated the waterwheels of the Citadel's aqueduct, which is more than double the price of the Khatiri mosque. This was, however, not merely a stable; it belonged to a residential complex with a garden.[57]

When Qawsun forced the owners to sell the Baysari palace at an arbitrary price, he paid them 200,000 dirhams (10,000 dinars), which suggests that the actual value was much higher.

The palace of Yalbugha al-Yahawi stands out as a legendary and almost unbelievable case. It was sponsored in 1337/8 by al-Nasir Muhammad himself, who wished to see a grand monument beneath the Citadel, and he paid the costs from his private purse. Its foundations alone cost 400,000 dirhams (20,000 dinars),[58] as much as al-Khatiri's lavish mosque, and the lapis used in its decoration was worth 100,000 dirhams (5,000 dinars). The total building costs amounted to 400,060,000 dirhams or over 20 million dinars! This amount dwarfs the costs of Sultan Hasan's mosque, being approximately twenty times as expensive, which is hard to believe. It is even harder to believe if we bear in mind that Sultan Hasan's mosque was already some fifty times more expensive than al-Khatiri's mosque. Although Maqrizi was a historian of great acumen in matters of finance and currency, one should not exclude the possibility that, writing seven decades later, he might be mistaken with these figures. On the basis of the Mamluk dinar, which weighed normally c.3.4g, the gold equivalent to 20 million dinars would weigh more than 68,000 kg or c.2.2 million Troy ounces; this quantity is today worth c.1.3 billion US dollars![59] Obviously, the costs of Yalbugha's palace were extraordinary, which might be explained with the fact that they included furniture, textiles and other portable items of exceptionally high value.

The Duhaysha hall built by Sultan 'Imad al-Din Isma'il in the Citadel in 1344 cost over 500,000 dirhams[60] (25,000 dinars), not including the 40,000 dirhams or 2,000 dinars for the white and red stones imported from Syria for its striped or ablaq facing. Two thousand white stone blocks were ordered from Aleppo at twelve dirhams each, and the same number of red stones from Damascus at eight dirhams each.[61]

The gilding of Sultan Hasan's hall in the Citadel, the Baysariyya, built in 1355, cost 38,000 *mithqals*/dinars alone. The silver used for the inlay of its 49 chandeliers was worth 220,000 dirhams (11,000 dinars). The building material and the workers amounted to 100,000 dirhams (5,000 dinars).[62] The total costs thus exceeded one million dirhams (50,000 dinars).

According to Maqrizi, the daily expenses of al-Nasir Muhammad's *diwan* for the royal constructions amounted to between 8,000 and 12,000 dirhams, which would be equivalent to 141,600 and 212,400 dinars in a Hijra year of 354 days.[63]

Other figures of the same period indicate that the Bahri Mamluk aristocracy led such lavish lifestyles that the construction of a mosque appears as a rather modest expense. The eleven daughters of al-Nasir Muhammad each received a trousseau worth 800,000 dinars, one of them including a bed curtain worth 100,000 dinars,[64] which corresponds to five times the building costs of al-Khatiri's mosque! One of his daughters paid 40,000 dirhams or 2,000 dinars for a pair of encrusted *qubqab* (bath footwear).[65] The *tarha* (veil) of a lady in his harem, probably embroidered with precious stones, was worth between 5,000 and 10,000 dinars.[66]

When Aqbugha fell in disgrace after al-Nasir's death and his estate was confiscated and put on sale, one pair of his wife's trousers went for 200,000 dirhams or 10,000 dinars, which was half the cost of al-Khatiri's mosque, some of her shoes for 75,000 dirhams and a gown for 100,000 dirhams (5,000 dinars). The value of tableware, copper and furnishings that a high bureaucrat had to sell in 1311, when his property was sequestrated, was 300,000 dirhams or 15,000 dinars, which again was about half the cost of a mosque.[67]

The inaugural celebration of al-Ashraf Khalil's palace, the Ashrafiyya hall in the Citadel in 1293, cost 300,000 dinars,[68] which was twenty times the amount al-Maridani paid to build his mosque. The inauguration costs of al-Nasir's palace in the Citadel, al-Qasr al-Ablaq, amounted to 500 million dirhams (25 million dinars), including thousands of robes of honour for all high dignitaries and generous bonuses to all emirs.[69]

The Circassian Mamluks

During the reign of Sultan Barquq, in 800/1397, the cost of the minaret he built at al-Azhar mosque amounted to 15,000 dirhams or c.750 dinars.[70] This was probably made of brick, as it had to be replaced later with a masonry construction. Shortly before his death, Barquq allocated 80,000 dinars for the construction of a funerary monument in the cemetery and the purchase of an estate for its endowment. We do not know whether his son Faraj increased this amount when he undertook the construction of the double mausoleum in the northern cemetery. By comparison with the 220,000 dinars that this sultan bequeathed at the same time to his wives and concubines, the amount dedicated to the funerary monument was not considerable.[71] The turba of Barquq's great *dawadar* Qalamtay al-'Uthmani, which has not survived, cost 20,000 dinars; his estate at the time of his death amounted to four million dinars.[72]

When Sultan Faraj annulled in 1411 the endowment of Jamal al-Din al-Ustadar and returned its illegally acquired estates to their owners, he reimbursed Jamal al-Din's heirs for the building costs of the mosque before re-endowing it in his own name, which he estimated at 10,000 dinars. This estimation, which amounts to half the building costs of the contemporary Qalamtay's turba, which did not survive,[73] is rather low; it probably excluded the building materials and marble, assuming that Jamal al-Din had taken them free of charge from other monuments.

Al-Mu'ayyad's mosque is reported to have cost 70,000 dinars. In addition, he acquired building materials through the confiscation of properties, and he received financial support and manpower from his subordinates. Yet the mosque complex was never completed; neither the second dome nor the Sufi dwellings were built in the lifetime of Maqrizi (d.1446), for which 20,000 dinars had been allocated.[74] It is not clear whether this amount was included in the 70,000 dinars; this dwelling complex must have been sizeable considering that, a few years later, Barsbay paid 9,000 dinars for the construction of an apartment building in the city centre.[75] Although Maqrizi credited the sultan for not using forced labour, al-Mu'ayyad's methods were not quite licit. He acquired the bronze door and chandelier from Sultan Hasan's mosque for 500 dinars, and the Dar al-Tuffah, an important commercial building, for 1,000 dinars.[76] In 1418 al-Mu'ayyad allocated 40,000 dinars to a complex in the city of Malatya consisting of a zawiya, two mills, a khan and a qaysariyya with forty shops.[77] For the restoration of the Fatimid palace, the Khamas Wujuh, as a venue for his audiences, he paid 20,000 dinars, which is rather low.[78] Each of the birthday celebrations of his sons Musa and Muhammad cost over 15,000 dinars.[79]

The construction of the mosque of Sultan Inal cost 12,000 dinars, which probably refers only to the sanctuary without the minaret and dome, which were built at an earlier stage.[80]

The restoration of the Rab' Zahiri, a large apartment complex built by al-Zahir Baybars along with a qaysariyya and a house belonging to the waqf of his madrasa, was estimated at 3,000 dinars by the surveyors who inspected it, as indicated in their detailed report preserved in a court document.[81] This amount included the building materials, and the complete reconstruction of major parts of the rab', which was in a ruined condition. The rab' was a construction of stone, brick and timber, which consisted of two storeys with seventy-five apartments built above shops.

Sultan Qaytbay paid 1,000 dinars for the repair of the ablutions fountain of the Citadel's mosque, 5,000 dinars for the restoration of the mosque of 'Amr[82] and 10,000 dinars for the restoration of al-Azhar mosque in 1473; a later restoration at al-Azhar, sponsored by a merchant, cost 15,000 dinars.[83] This may have included the new gates and the addition of a minaret in the sultan's name. Qaytbay's fort in Alexandria was estimated at over 100,000 dinars, and the same amount is indicated for rebuilding the bridges of Giza, and for the restoration of the Prophet's mosque in Medina in 1481 after the devastation caused by a fire.[84] The restoration of the

bridge of Abu 'l-Manajja cost 7,000 dinars, and that of the bridge of Shubramant cost 5,000 dinars.[85] For the restoration of the Umayyad mosque of Damascus following the fire of 1479, the governor required 58,700 dinars, but the sultan allocated only 15,000 and eventually paid 22,500 dinars. As this amount could not cover the entire restoration expenses, sponsors among the notables of the city made important contributions.[86]

According to Ibn Iyas, Qaytbay paid in 1471 the sum of 20,000 dinars for the refurbishment of the Great Iwan of al-Nasir Muhammad in the Citadel, which he hardly used, however, as he held his court in the Hawsh area. Jawhari, who reported that 10,000 dinars were allocated for the works, later added that the sultan must have paid a total of c.50,000 dinars to refurbish the Iwan and also build a new loggia in the Hawsh complex of the Citadel.[87] This indicates that the effective costs exceeded the forecast, confirming Ibn Iyas' estimation, and would leave 30,000 dinars for the construction of the loggia. Qaytbay's ceremonial tent, which cost 33,000 dinars, exceeded the combined costs of building a loggia and restoring a palace.[88]

The costs of the quarter of Azbakiyya, including the civil engineering works and the excavation of the pond, amounted to more than 200,000 dinars.[89] The trousseau of Azbak's daughter cost 100,000 dinars,[90] as much as the trousseau of one of Barsbay's wives a few decades earlier.[91] Sultan al-Ghawri's transformation of the hippodrome beneath the Citadel with new residential structures, where he transferred his court, cost 80,000 dinars,[92] and his ceremonial barge, the *dhahabiyya*, cost 22,000 dinars.[93]

During the Circassian period the price of a royal Mamluk was 10,000 dirhams or 500 dinars,[94] which is similar to what al-Nasir Muhammad paid for a first-class Mamluk.[95] Al-Nasir Muhammad was ready in exceptional cases to pay much more: he purchased Sarghitmish for 85,000 dirhams or 4,250 dinars, and Malkutimur al-Hijazi for 50,000 dirhams or 2,500 dinars.[96] Al-Zahir Baybars was by comparison a bargain; although he cost only 800 dirhams (c.40 dinars), his first buyer returned him to the merchant after discovering a defect in one of his eyes.[97]

A first-class horse in the Circassian period cost over 200 dinars,[98] but al-Nasir Muhammad paid far more, between 60,000 and 70,000 dirhams (3,000 to 3,500 dinars) for an Arab horse, whereas his father Qalawun never paid more than 5,000 dirhams for a horse.[99] The monthly wage or *jamakiyya* of a royal Mamluk, not including payment in kind, amounted to 20,000 dinars during Barquq's reign, 30,000 in 1425, 38,000 in 1464, 40,000 in 1465 and 46,000 during Qaytbay's reign.[100] According to these figures the construction costs of an average mosque did not much exceed the monthly wage of a royal emir.

The figures presented here for mosques refer only to the cost of their construction; the endowment of a religious foundation with the creation of a waqf, however, required far more resources. A comparison of the religious and secular expenses of the Mamluk aristocracy indicates that, due to the various methods of acquisition of building materials and the exploitation of the labour force, the actual construction costs can be considered modest in relation to what the Mamluks spent on luxury items purchased on the market, often imported at prices they could not dictate.

–8–

The Growth of the Metropolis

Urban visions and building zeal

When the Mamluks came to power, the Egyptian capital was a city in transition. The Nile had just undergone a natural process that shifted its bed further to the west of the city, opening up new land along the shores of Fustat and Qahira. Under the Fatimids and Ayyubids, Fustat and its satellites had expanded and fused into a thriving metropolis, while Qahira was still a residential precinct. Salah al-Din's wall, designed to encompass Fustat and Qahira, was never completed. His Citadel on the Muqattam hill between the two cities was a powerful military construction, which did not yet have the glamour of the palatial tradition bestowed on it by the Mamluks. Its residential structures were hardly ready in time for al-Malik al-Kamil (r.1218–38), the first monarch to dwell there permanently, and then the last Ayyubid sultan, al-Salih Najm al-Din, turned his back on the Citadel, and in the years 1239–44 built a new one on the island of Rawda opposite Fustat, to include his own quarters and the residences and offices of his emirs.

While Fustat continued to be the commercial, industrial and residential centre of the Ayyubid capital, al-Salih's citadel at Rawda attracted the emirs to dwell in its vicinity. The two agglomerations of the Egyptian capital had their respective congregational mosques, the mosque of al-Hakim serving Qahira and the mosque of 'Amr serving Fustat. Salah al-Din transformed the Fatimid palaces of Qahira into residences for the new Ayyubid aristocracy or into madrasas, and he founded a khanqah and a hospital in the palatial quarter.

The major monumental constructions established by the Ayyubids in the double capital were the two citadels and the

walls, along with the colossal causeway built on forty arches by the vizier Qaraqush in Giza to allow traffic in that area during the flood season.[1] Among the number of madrasas founded by the Ayyubids in Qahira and Fustat,[2] those of al-Kamil and al-Salih Najm al-Din were the most prominent in Qahira. The mausoleum of Imam Shafi'i in the southern cemetery, built by al-Malik al-Kamil with the largest dome in Cairo, and the madrasa which Salah al-Din built alongside, were too remote from the centre to have an impact on its urban development.

With Qahira as the new focus, the Mamluks transformed Cairo into the foremost Muslim city and one of the largest capitals in the world. By the end of their sultanate, the metropolis stretched from the mausoleum of Imam Shafi'i in the south to the mosque of Yashbak, today in Abbasiyya in the north, and from the port of Bulaq along the Nile to the desert in the east. This gigantic area was not a homogeneous agglomeration, however. While Qahira in the north was the focus of Mamluk monumental patronage, Fustat gradually lost its significance. Even as a port it was superseded by Bulaq to the west of Qahira. An urban void remained between the two cities.

The southern cemeteries, which had developed in connection with Fustat, retained their religious significance due to the presence of saints' tombs and shrines dedicated to holy persons from the early Islamic period. With Qahira's expansion, new cemeteries with princely monuments emerged in the desert on its northeastern and southeastern sides.

Instead of the fusion envisaged by Salah al-Din, Qahira thrived and expanded on all sides without fully merging with Fustat. Fustat did not receive the same quality of Mamluk architectural patronage that was bestowed on Qahira. Only the

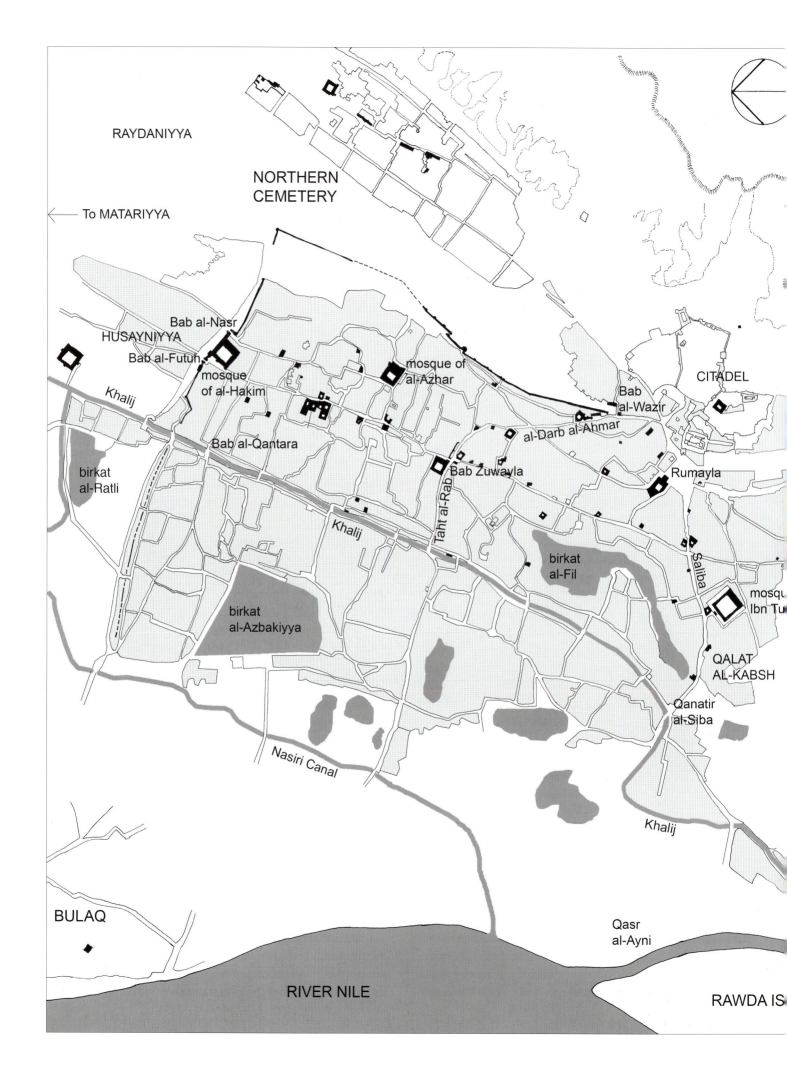

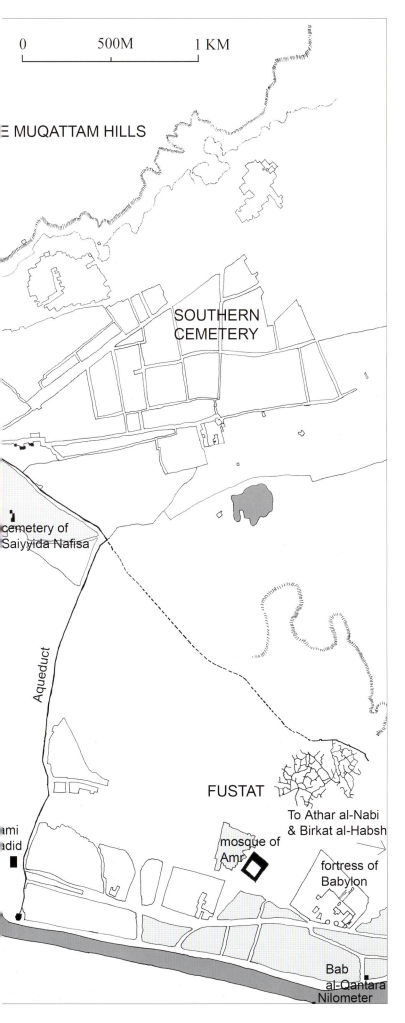

THE MUQATTAM HILLS

SOUTHERN
CEMETERY

cemetery of
Saiyyida Nafisa

Aqueduct

FUSTAT

To Athar al-Nabi
& Birkat al-Habsh

mosque of
Amr

fortress of
Babylon

ami
adid

Bab
al-Qantara
Nilometer

Fig. 10. Map of Mamluk Cairo, key to toponyms.

quarter around the mosque of Ibn Tulun, the former al-Qata'i', at the northern periphery of greater Fustat, with the Saliba artery connecting it with the Citadel and the Khalij, was integrated in Qahira. Of the nine madrasas built in Fustat during the Mamluk period, only Aybak's was a royal foundation.[3] The others were sponsored by emirs, bureaucrats and merchants. The mosque of 'Amr, however, which enjoyed the status of the first Muslim sanctuary on Egyptian soil, was continuously maintained and renovated. Mamluk Fustat was an industrial zone, with pottery kilns, oil and sugar presses and a shipyard. Other luxury crafts also seem to have existed there, such as textiles and a carpet industry mentioned in the fourteenth century.[4] The shift of the commercial centre from Fustat to Qahira did not occur abruptly with the arrival of the Mamluks; rather, it took more than half a century to complete.

Under the Mamluks, Qahira lost its fortified character and expanded far beyond its Fatimid and Ayyubid walls, which disappeared behind buildings.[5] The capital was remote enough from the Mediterranean not to be within reach of the Crusaders, who menaced the Mamluk coasts. Christian raids on the Mamluk port cities after the fall of the Crusader kingdoms in Syria and Palestine were a constant source of trouble to the Mamluks, but Alexandria rather than Cairo suffered the physical consequences. On the eastern front, southern Anatolia and the Jazira provided a buffer zone that could delay an attack on Cairo coming from Asia. In fact, the raids of the Mongols and of Timur, which inflicted much harm on Syria and on the Mamluk Empire in general, did not reach Egypt. The battle with the Ottomans that decided the final fate of the Mamluks was fought in northern Syria at Marj Dabiq. Because Cairo was defended far beyond its own surrounding territory, the Mamluks did not need to fortify it. They continuously consolidated the Citadel, however, against internal rather than external threats.

Unlike Fustat, built along the Nile shore, Qahira was built further east along the canal or Khalij, which connected the Nile with the northeastern outskirts. Because the canal also provided Cairo with drinking water from the Nile, its maintenance was always handled by the rulers, as a matter of vital importance. The landscape of the Khalij and the several ponds between the Nile and the city, which were flooded by the Nile during the summer and filled with vegetation during the rest of the year, contributed to the character and lifestyle of the capital. This green area attracted residential quarters and provided open spaces for leisure and pastimes. Until the late thirteenth century the major pond was Birkat al-Habash south of Fustat. With the growth of Qahira, however, it was superseded by the northern ponds, the major one being Birkat al-Ratli until the pond of Azbakiyya was dug in the late fifteenth century.

The first religious foundation of the Mamluk period, the funerary madrasa of Shajar al-Durr (1250), was built in the cemetery of Sayyida Nafisa in the southeastern outskirts of the Citadel, which already included important Fatimid shrines.[6] It stood next to a palace surrounded by gardens. No ruler had been buried in this cemetery before. Six years later, in 1256/7, her husband and successor al-Mu'izz Aybak founded his madrasa alongside commercial structures in southern Fustat. It seems to have been an important building, located within the southern wall built by Salah al-Din near the gate Bab al-Qantara, overlooking the Nilometer of Rawda to the west.[7] Aybak's preference to build in Fustat rather than in Qahira indicates that the old capital maintained its prestige at that time. Aybak, however, used al-Salih's citadel at Rawda as a quarry for his buildings, and his emirs followed his example.[8] This was the first and last foundation of a Mamluk sultan to be built that far south in the capital.

Sultan al-Muzaffar Qutuz (r.1259–60) built a madrasa at Hadarat al-Baqar, west of the Citadel, in the quarter where the mosque of Sultan Hasan was later erected.[9] Sultan Qalawun and his son al-Ashraf Khalil followed Shajar al-Durr's example and erected funerary madrasas in 1283–4 and 1288 in the cemetery of Sayyida Nafisa. Qalawun's foundation was dedicated to his wife.

Having spent much of his reign in campaigns against the Crusaders in Syria, which he integrated into the Mamluk Empire, al-Zahir Baybars (r.1260–77) was not motivated by an urban vision when planning his buildings in Cairo. However, his decision to reintroduce the multiple *khutba*s in the capital had a significant impact on its future development. Salah al-Din, following the Shafi'i principle that only one Friday mosque should serve an urban agglomeration, had confined the *khutba* of Qahira and Fustat to the mosques of al-Hakim and 'Amr Ibn al-'As respectively, and cancelled the Friday sermon of the mosques of al-Azhar, al-Aqmar, Ibn Tulun and al-Salih Tala'i'.[10] In the Ayyubid period, the *khutba* was held also in two other agglomerations besides Fustat and Qahira: in the southern cemetery near the mausoleum of Imam Shafi'i, in a mosque founded by Salah al-Din and turned into a Friday mosque by al-Malik al-Kamil in 1210–11, and in the citadel of Rawda, in a mosque founded by al-Malik al-Salih.[11]

During Baybars' reign, Fustat still enjoyed Mamluk patronage, and the sultan was interested in the development of the island of Rawda. Out of faithfulness to his master al-Salih Najm al-Din, or because Fustat was still promising, Baybars restored the citadel of Rawda, which had suffered despoliation under Aybak and his emirs, and he reinstated the *khutba* in an old mosque there so that the island had two Friday mosques.[12] At the same time the southern quarters of Qahira, the Hilaliyya and the quarter of Ibn Tulun, expanded with new dwellings and commercial structures.[13]

Al-Zahir Baybars' madrasa, built in 1262–3 beside that of his master al-Salih Najm al-Din in the heart of the Fatimid city,[14] was endowed with a large rab' or apartment complex built above shops outside Bab Zuwayla. A few years later, in 1266/7, he founded his monumental Friday mosque in the northern outskirts of Zuqaq al-Kuhl.[15] Although the mosque was near the populous Husayniyya quarter, which expanded with the influx of Tatar refugees in the late thirteenth century, the area was never truly urbanized and the mosque remained in the middle of a green area until the eve of modern times.[16]

Baybars' second and forgotten Friday mosque, founded in 1273, was likewise built outside the urban core, in the southern outskirts at Mansha'at al-Maharani, to the north of Fustat.[17] This mosque, of which no trace is left, was founded on the initiative of the vizier Baha' al-Din Ibn Hanna to replace another one at Bustan al-Fadil that had been swept away by a heavy Nile flood a decade earlier, in 1261–2. Already in Maqrizi's time the neighbourhood of Baybars' mosque was abandoned and the building itself dilapidated. Ibn Duqmaq described it as having six doors, which indicates monumental dimensions; his first mosque at Zuqaq al-Kuhl/Husayniyya has only three.

The patronage of Baybars' high dignitaries endowed Fustat with some important buildings. The Banu Hanna, a dynasty of powerful and wealthy viziers and bureaucrats, originating from Fustat, were great patrons of their city.[18] Ibn Muhammad Baha' al-Din Ibn Hanna built a madrasa at Zuqaq al-Qanadil,[19] and a ribat in 1269–70 near Birkat al-Habash.[20] His son Fakhr al-Din Muhammad built a mosque at Dayr al-Tin south of Fustat in 1273[21] and his other son Muhyi al-Din built a ribat in the city.[22] His grandson Taj al-Din Muhammad (d.1307/8), who became the vizier of Qalawun in 1294, built a shrine for the relics of the Prophet, the Ribat al-Athar, south of Fustat between Birkat al-Habash and the Nile, which he endowed with a garden, Bustan al-Ma'shuq, where he owned residential structures.[23]

The emir Mu'izz al-Din Aybak al-Afram (d.1296) was another patron of Fustat.[24] He started his career under the Ayyubid sultan al-Salih and continued as deputy sultan under his Mamluk successors, accumulating a legendary fortune that was estimated to have included one eighth of Egypt's land. He built in 1265 a mosque in an eastern suburb of Fustat, al-Rasad, and he sponsored a ribat in the city.[25] His most spectacular achievement was the urban development at the pond of Shu'aybiyya, situated on the northern side of Birkat al-Habash. He transformed part of the pond, which had an area of 54 *faddan*s, into a walled garden with a dam (*jisr*), and developed the rest of its land to be sublet for the construction of residences overlooking the Nile. In 1294, during the reign of Qalawun, al-Afram built a Friday mosque there.[26] At that time the shifting of the Nile to the west freed a strip of land along the Fustat shore, which made room for a new road, encouraging people to build in the area.[27]

Baybars' efforts to upgrade Rawda were in vain, as al-Mansur Qalawun, following Aybak's example, dismantled the recently restored citadel to provide his own religious complex within Qahira with building materials. This gave Qahira the definite edge over Fustat. The triangle of Qalawun's complex facing the two madrasas of al-Salih and Baybars, and surrounded by the commercial structures of their endowments, established Qahira's triumph as the cultural, religious and commercial centre of the Mamluk sultanate (Fig. 11).

Baybars and Qalawun's foundations were followed by other royal buildings in the centre of the Fatimid city: al-Nasir Muhammad's madrasa (1295–1304) started by his predecessor al-'Adil Katbugha, Baybars al-Jashnakir's khanqah (1307–10) and the multifunctional complexes of al-Zahir Barquq (1384–6), al-Mu'ayyad Shaykh (1415–20), al-Ashraf Barsbay (1423–4) and Qansuh al-Ghawri (1504–5). One should also add Janbalat's funerary mosque (1500) along the exterior wall of Bab al-Nasr, which was destroyed by Napoleon's troops in 1801.[28]

Al-Nasir Muhammad was spurred by an urban vision that inspired him to redesign and conceive the capital in the global terms of a cityscape rather than just an accumulation of individual monuments.[29] He was the first to combine monumental religious patronage with far-reaching urban planning and design. His urban transformation programme began in the 1320s, once he had fully consolidated his authority, more than a decade after the end of his second reign in 1309.[30] The extensive use of corvée and prisoners of war, and a high budget, supported the magnitude of his building programme. Although his schemes might have disregarded financial considerations and imposed a heavy toll on his successors, as commented by Ayalon, Cairo continued for centuries to make use of the monuments, hippodromes, streets and infrastructure he established.

Civil engineering projects formed a substantial element of his building programme. Crossed by a number of new bridges, the Khalij was no longer Qahira's western boundary but, rather, the link to its western bank, which could now easily merge with the main city. More than sixty *hikr*s or leaseholds, consisting of orchards and new territory on the west bank of the Khalij left behind by the Nile bed, were granted by al-Nasir Muhammad to his emirs for urban development. Al-Nasir pushed forward the urbanization of the western bank of the Khalij by digging in 1325 a new canal connecting the Nile with the old one, which it joined north of Baybars' mosque. This canal led Nile water to the village of Siryaqus about thirty kilometres north of Cairo, and it nurtured the Khalij at the same time. Between the two canals, al-Nasir dug the Nasiriyya pond, which attracted the construction of new aristocratic mansions. The sultan chose Siryaqus, a village near his hunting ground, to build a major khanqah with his mausoleum and a pleasance complex with a hippodrome. The creation of this complex was not directly connected with Cairo's urban growth; however, by placing it on the caravan road, al-Nasir addressed the visitor entering the capital with an overture of pious, ceremonial and commemorative architecture that was exclusively associated with his name.

The sultan orchestrated his metropolitan schemes with his emirs, whom he urged to build, encouraging them with legal privileges on the land and with material support. This enabled him to transform the Birkat al-Fil or Pond of the Elephant into an aristocratic residential area, which included the mosques of the emirs Ulmas (1329–30), Qawsun (1329–30) and Bashtak (1336).[31] The old Qata'i' north of Fustat had already been upgraded by Sultan Lajin in 1296 after a long period of neglect, when he renovated the mosque of Ibn Tulun and enlarged its waqf and founded a hippodrome in its vicinity. Nearby, along Saliba street, the emir Sanjar built his funerary complex in 1303–4, and a palace behind it on the hill of Qal'at al-Kabsh.

In the Citadel, al-Nasir replaced the old mosque and the palaces with new ones. For the construction of the Hawsh, which comprised private apartments overlooking a pasture ground for cattle and sheep, land had to be carved out of the Muqattam rock. The sultan's project, however, to supplement the aqueducts by conducting water from the Nile up to the Citadel through a canal dug in the Muqattam hill and hydraulic installations had to be abandoned due to insurmountable difficulties.

Al-Nasir's urban vision is best manifested in his scheme to upgrade the quarter beneath the Citadel, Hadarat al-Baqar, where Sultan Hasan later built his mosque. He conceived a complex of palaces as a spectacular architectural ensemble for him to look at from his palace in the Citadel. It consisted of two palaces for his favourite emirs and in-laws, Yalbugha al-Yahawi and Altinbugha al-Maridani, alongside four great so-called 'stables' for the emirs Qawsun, Tashtumur and Aydighmish, and another called Istabl al-Jawq.[32] Further west, the palace of Baktimur, called Istabl Baktimur, was built on the site of the hippodrome of Sultan Lajin. Such 'stables' must have been important palaces, like the one called Istabl Qawsun, whose stunning portal and ruins still attest to its grandeur (Fig. 32).[33] The term 'istabl' has to be interpreted here as a palace with a great stable complex in connection with the horse market and the hippodrome of Rumayla, located in the same neighbourhood beneath the Citadel.

The building initiatives of al-Nasir's reign included the cemeteries as well. Maqrizi commented about the urbanization of the cemetery south of the Citadel: 'The emirs followed by the military and other people built tombs, monasteries, markets, mills and baths, so that the southern and eastern cemeteries were urbanized. Roads multiplied and streets were pierced through. Many wished to dwell there because of the magnificent castles that were erected, which were called tombs, and because of the charities bestowed upon the inhabitants of the cemeteries.'[34]

The northern cemetery spread on the site of al-Zahir Baybars' hippodrome, the Maydan al-Qabaq, along Qahira's desert flank. This used to be the major venue for military exercise and tournaments, and it also included a falconry and a dais called mastaba built by Baybars in 1267. Al-Nasir transferred the falconry to Fustat at Birkat al-Habash, letting the cemetery expand on the hippodrome's ground.[35] This was not the end of this mastaba-hippodrome, however, which was relaunched in the late fourteenth century by Sultan Barquq, and referred to throughout the fifteenth century as the Mat'am al-Tayr or Birds' Feeding Ground;[36] it became the major venue for regal rituals and sports until the end of the Mamluk period. Al-Nasir also abolished another hippodrome built by al-Zahir Baybars along the Nile, which he turned into a garden, and he built instead two new ones more remote from the centre: the Maydan al-Mahara at Qanatir al-Siba', between the two canals, and the other one along the Nile shore at Bustan al-Khashshab, between Fustat and Qahira. The latter was used as a residence for foreign ambassadors, and it was maintained and restored by later sultans, including Qaytbay, who added a palace to it. Al-Nasir's hippodrome along the Nile, abandoned by Barquq, was restored by Sultan al-Mu'ayyad Shaykh, who occasionally gave audiences and dwelt in its premises.[37] Most of al-Nasir Muhammad's hippodromes fell into disrepair during the fifteenth century and their ceremonial tradition was forgotten.

Whereas the early decades of the fourteenth century saw the proliferation of funerary khanqahs and madrasas, the emirs of al-Nasir's third reign turned instead to the foundation of Friday mosques; about thirty new ones in the city and its suburbs contributed to the expansion of the metropolitan area. The multiplication of the *khutba*, already authorized by al-Zahir Baybars, was fully established during al-Nasir's reign. The Friday mosques in the suburbs formed the nuclei of new quarters, or consolidated areas still in the process of urbanization. The dissemination of Friday mosques was a service to the community at the same time as it expanded and decentralized the city. People were no longer compelled to go out of their quarters to perform the Friday prayer or in search of learning opportunities. Moreover, the markets that spread beside the mosques and emirs' palaces stimulated economic activity in various neighbourhoods. During the reign of al-Nasir, the *khutba* was also installed in the madrasa of al-Mu'izz Aybak in Fustat.[38]

The patrons' concern for urban expansion behind the dissemination of Friday mosques is evident in the case of the mosque of the emir Husayn on the western Khalij bank. To attract worshippers, the emir built a bridge across the canal in its vicinity and even took the controversial decision to pierce a gate in the city's west wall to facilitate access to his mosque.[39]

During al-Nasir's reign, eight mosques were built at Husayniyya, six in the northwestern outskirts including Bulaq, six in the southwestern zone, ten within Qahira, sixteen between Bab Zuwayla and the mosque of Ibn Tulun, four in the southern cemetery and three in the Fustat/Rawda area.[40]

Whereas the immediate northern and southern expansions proved to be durable and consistent with the city's organic needs, the western expansion, except for Bulaq and the street leading to it, did not survive the crises of the late fourteenth century. Al-Nasir's major mosque, called al-Jami' al-Jadid or the New Mosque, was built in 1312 north of Fustat along the Nile shore not far from his hippodrome. It may have been intended to boost the urbanization of the area to connect the northern suburbs of Fustat with the southern suburbs of Qahira. Already Shajar al-Durr's madrasa and palace at Sayyida Nafisa, and al-Zahir Baybars' second mosque at Mansha'at al-Maharani, had set the trend for patronage in this zone. Like Baybars' mosque, al-Nasir's New Mosque was abandoned by the time Maqrizi was compiling his *Khitat*.[41]

As Gaston Wiet put it, the powerful-looking mosque of Sultan Hasan was the architectural response to the monumentality of the Citadel and to the greatness of Rumayla square, which it faced. This monument was the culmination of the building activity that continued after al-Nasir's death in 1340, notwithstanding the great calamity of the Black Death in 1348. Cairo is estimated to have lost during the Black Death between one third and two fifths of its population.[42] However, the building zeal of the Mamluk aristocracy went on uninhibitedly because, ironically, such catastrophes released heirless funds and new *iqta'* land to the state treasury, which the sultans could allocate for building mosques. Cairo witnessed in the three decades after al-Nasir's death the founding of an important number of religious monuments, which included the mosques of Aslam al-Baha'i, 1344–5; Aydumur al-Bahlawan, 1346; Aqsunqur, 1346–7; Qutulbugha al-Dhahabi, 1347; Arghun Shah al-Isma'ili, 1347; Tughay, 1348; Manjaq al-Yusufi, 1349; al-Kharrubi, 1349; Shaykhu, 1349 (mosque) and 1349 (khanqah); Sarghitmish, 1356; Nizam al-Din, 1356; Sultan Hasan, 1356–63; Badr al-Din al-'Ajami, 1357; al-Jamali Yusuf, 1357; Tatar al-Hijaziyya, 1360; Bashir Agha al-Jamdar, 1360; Mithqal al-Anuki, 1361–9; Taybugha, 1366; Sultan Sha'ban, 1368–9; Asanbugha, 1370; anonymous, 1370; Uljay al-Yusufi, 1373; Ibn al-Ghannam, 1373; and al-Baqari, 1374.[43] This list does not include monuments that disappeared soon afterwards, such as the madrasa built by Sultan Sha'ban in 1375 near the Citadel and destroyed by his successor Sultan Barquq in 1411.

Maqrizi described fourteenth-century Cairo with nostalgia, while he was contemplating a city that was still suffering from the economic disaster inflicted by Timur's invasion of Syria in 1400, and from a series of natural catastrophes. For the historian it seemed like the end of a world. At that time, in the early fifteenth century, many of Cairo's quarters and its markets were devastated, and monuments were falling to ruin, such as Aqsunqur's mosque, which was deprived of its estate in Aleppo. However, in this case as in others, new sponsors emerged to re-endow and revive the religious monuments that stood in viable quarters and were needed by the inhabitants, whereas monuments in non-viable areas, such as south Fustat or in quarters created during al-Nasir's overstretched and arbitrary urban expansion, could not be maintained. At the same time as Maqrizi mourned the glorious past, Sultan al-Mu'ayyad Shaykh was erecting great religious and secular monuments, including a palace in the northern outskirts.

Thus, the building zeal of the Mamluk ruling establishment did not diminish even in times of severe economic crises. Cairo expanded again with the development of Bulaq and the growth and urbanization of the northern cemetery.

During the fifteenth century the northern cemetery, in which so far only emirs had founded funerary structures, began to attract the sultans' attention as well. Faraj Ibn Barquq, Barsbay, Inal, Khushqadam, Qaytbay, Qansuh Abu Sa'id (1499) and al-'Adil Tumanbay (1501) built there. Except for the funerary monument of al-Zahir Khushqadam,[44] which disappeared entirely, and al-'Adil Tumanbay's funerary complex, of which only the dome is extant, they all survive, at least partly, to the present day. The layout and architecture of the northern cemetery increasingly acquired urban features, with an emphasis on facades and street perspectives. This explains why Qansuh Abu Sa'id's mausoleum, which, as can still be seen today, obstructed the road and caused anger among many people.[45]

The monuments of the Circassian sultans attest to the continuing vigour and innovation in the building craft. Urban concerns also continued to guide building activities to the end of the Mamluk period. In the early fifteenth century the upgrading of a number of madrasas and zawiyas to Friday mosques[46] promoted further decentralization. Moreover, no fewer than eighty mosques were built in the capital between 1412 and 1516. Ibn Taghribirdi mentioned intensive urbanization projects in the desert area northeast of Cairo and in Bulaq during this period.[47]

Navigation on the Nile was always important for Egypt's economy. Fustat served as the port for ships carrying agricultural goods from Upper Egypt and merchandise from the Red Sea trade via Qus to the capital, and further towards Alexandria and Damietta on the Mediterranean. During the fifteenth century, with the growing importance of Mediterranean trade,[48] Bulaq's importance as a port increased, and it became a commercial and industrial centre with an increasing number of mosques and palaces.

The building zeal in the vicinity of the Citadel continued. The new expansion, however, left behind some gaps in the urban fabric, such as the area between Bulaq and the Khalij. In the second half of the fifteenth century landscape transformation became fashionable among the great emirs, who took initiatives to fill the voids and rehabilitate dilapidated zones within the metropolitan area.

Unlike Sultan al-Nasir Muhammad, who built a residential complex in the village of Siryaqus outside Cairo,[49] the later sultans did not found palaces or hunting pavilions in the remote countryside or the provinces, but kept their pleasance venues and the grazing grounds of their horses in Cairo's closer

Fig. 11. Plan of Bayn al-Qasrayn.

vicinity, along the shores of the Khalij, the ponds and the Nile, or even in the desert. Sultan al-Mu'ayyad Shaykh built a residential complex at Kaum al-Rish, in the northern suburb along the canal, to substitute Siryaqus. His new palace, called al-Khamas Wujuh or Pentagon, was built on the ruins of a Fatimid palace of the same name.[50] Al-Mu'ayyad, who gave his audiences there, encouraged his courtiers to build residences nearby, to be close to his court.[51] Perhaps inspired by his frequent navigation on the Nile, he founded a great khanqah on the western Nile shore of Giza, facing the island of Rawda. It was originally a belvedere (manzara), which he acquired and rebuilt in 1420.[52] During al-Mu'ayyad's reign, in 1417, the emir 'Abd al-Ghani al-Fakhri demolished all buildings along the Nile shore from the quarter of Maqs in the north to Qantarat al-Muski in the south – an area which, according to Maqrizi, was equivalent to a Syrian town – in order to set up a garden in

the vicinity of his residence.[53] According to Ibn Taghribirdi the sultans promoted the western outskirts along the Nile shore to provide themselves with venues for entertainment and music performance.[54]

In the mid-fifteenth century the reigns of Jaqmaq and Inal introduced a period of consolidation rather than expansion. Jaqmaq chose not to be a building patron, and to look, rather, after the architectural legacy of his predecessors. Inal demonstrated concern for urban maintenance; in 1455 he ordered the demolition of a large number of buildings that obstructed the roads along the Nile shore. Ibn Taghibirdi praised this measure, which took several days to complete, with the argument that the Nile shore belonged to all, not just a few individuals. The historian repeated his praise of Inal in 1457, when the sultan built a rab' and two hammams in the city centre, whereby he enlarged the street that had become increasingly encroached upon over time, by placing the buildings behind the previous street line.[55]

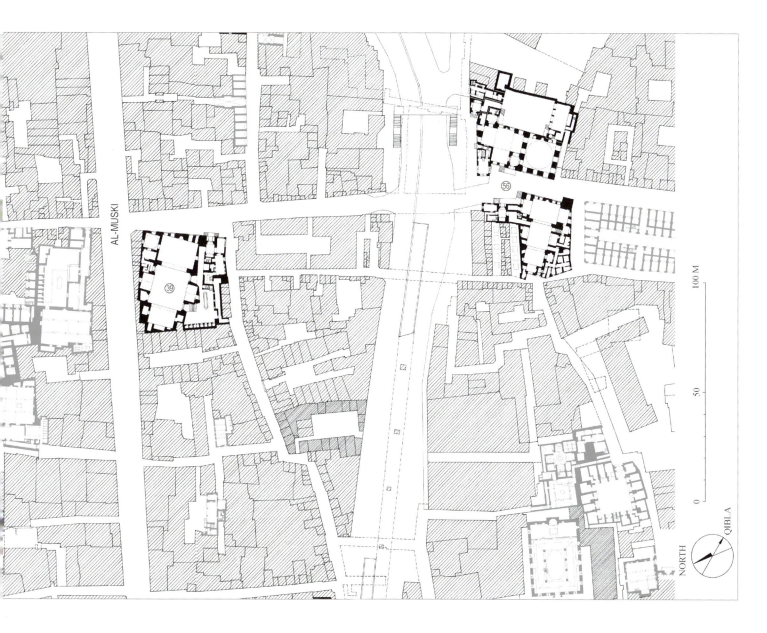

In the second half of the fifteenth century the emir Janibak, the great secretary or *dawadar* of Sultan Khushqadam, launched an ambitious project, comparable to al-Afram's at Fustat two centuries earlier. It consisted of a walled garden covering an area of 120 *faddan*s (c.125 acres), connected through a gate on its northern side at Qanatir al-Siba' with the emir's palace, while on its southern side another gate led to a Sufi complex for dervishes from the east (*a'jam*), which included two unequal domes and a minaret. The creation of the garden entailed a bold civil engineering project. The wasteland on which the garden was set up contained a pond and a mound, and was frequented by marginal people. Janibak levelled the mound to fill in the pond and prepared the ground for the garden, which had a quay along the Nile shore. Ibn Taghribirdi, an eyewitness, described it as unparalleled in garden history and a wonder that took only a short time to achieve.[56] The project, begun in January 1459, was completed before his death in August 1463. Janibak's Sufi foundation seems to have replaced an earlier one

on this site, the khanqah founded in 1310 by Arslan, a *dawadar* of al-Nasir Muhammad. Like al-Afram's transformation of the outskirts of Fustat, such a project could only have been carried out by a powerful and wealthy patron, such as Janibak.

When Qaytbay came to power in 1462 the metropolis had already reached considerable dimensions and contained a wealth of religious and secular monuments, which needed to be preserved. Perhaps inspired by Jaqmaq, who preferred to renovate rather than establish new foundations, Qaytbay took this task to heart. His monumental patronage was guided by a strong desire to maintain and restore religious and secular monuments in the capital and other cities of Egypt, Syria and the Hijaz. In addition to his funerary mosque in the southern part of the northern cemetery, and his mosques at Qal'at al-Kabsh and Rawda, Qaytbay restored many buildings in the capital, including the mosque of 'Amr at Fustat, the mausoleum of Imam Shafi'i, the shrine of Sayyida Nafisa, al-Azhar mosque, the madrasa of Sanjar al-Jawli, the madrasa Suyufiyya and the

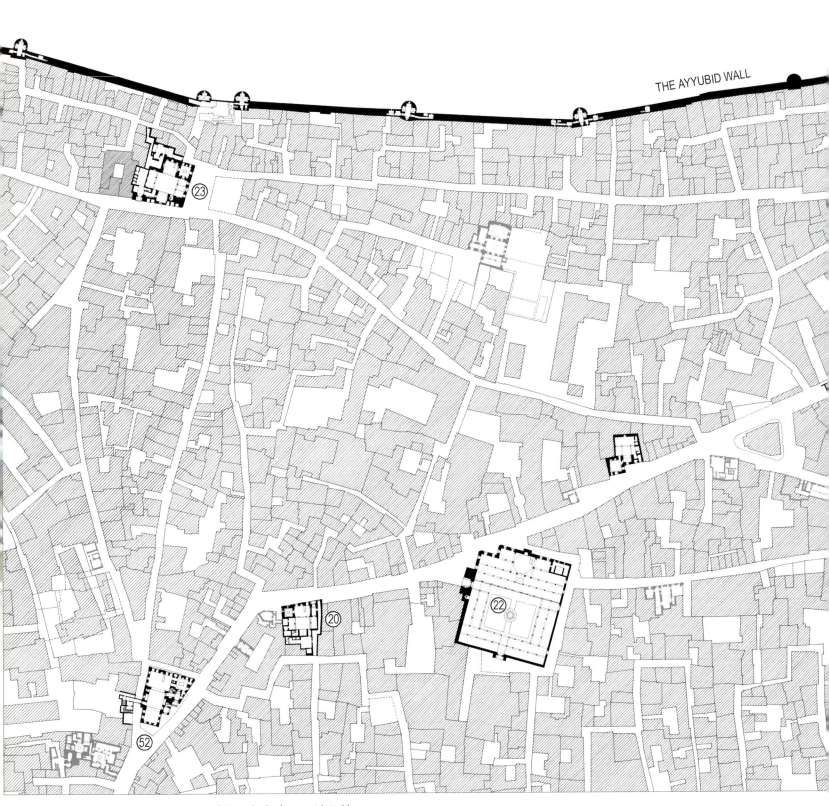

QIBLA

NORTH

0   50   100 M

THE AYYUBID WALL

㉓

㉒

⑳

㊵

Fig. 12. Plan of the quarter of al-Darb al-Ahmar with Tabbana street.

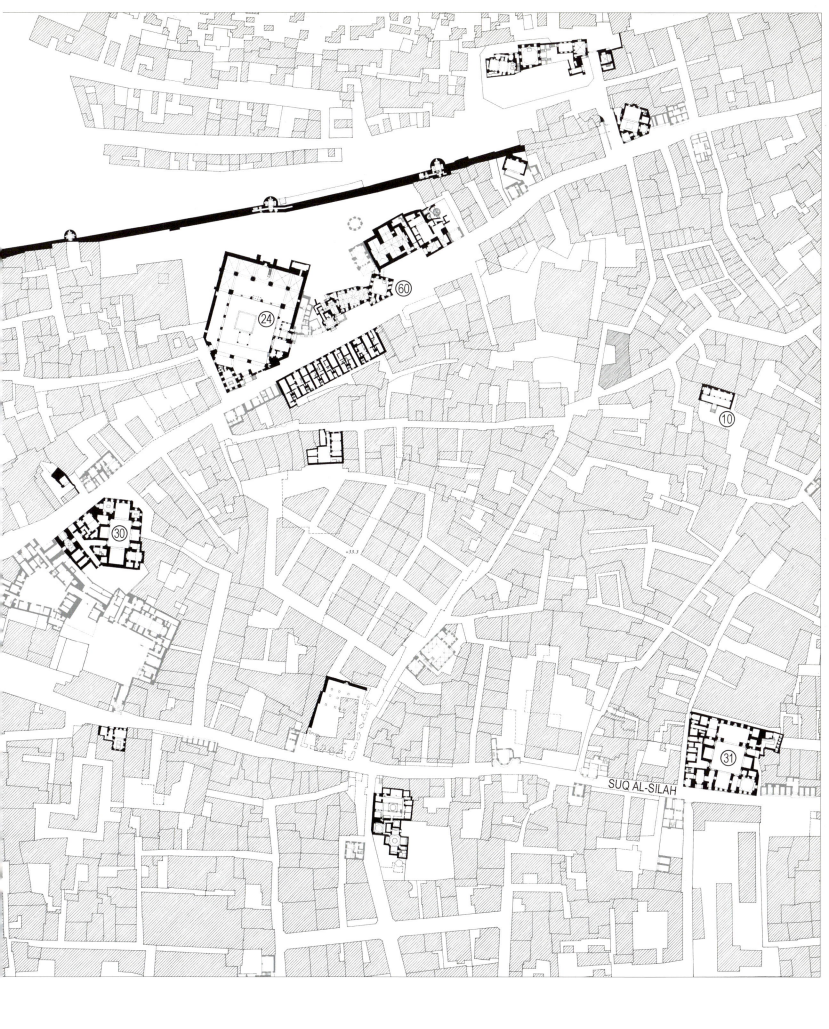

24

60

10

30

31

+33.3

SUQ AL-SILAH

khanqahs of Shaykhu and Faraj, and he rebuilt the mosque of the emir Sultan Shah and the one called Jami' al-Rahma.[57] His restorations included also bridges and dams. He not only restored the mosques but also rehabilitated their waqf estates by refurbishing and reconstructing their commercial structures and dwellings, thus revitalizing the commercial infrastructure of the city.[58] The list of monuments that carry his name is very long.[59]

In the Citadel, Qaytbay renovated the monuments of al-Nasir Muhammad: the Great Iwan, the mosque (whose dome he rebuilt) and the aqueduct. He transformed the Hawsh area, which used to be the harem of the Bahri Mamluk sultans, adding new structures to it, and making it a lavish venue for his audiences. While the sultan concentrated his efforts on the rejuvenation of the monumental heritage rather than opening up new urban vistas, his most powerful emirs, Azbak min Tutukh and Yashbak min Mahdi, pursued ambitious landscape and urban schemes in the western and northern suburbs.

Yashbak min Mahdi, Qaytbay's great secretary, might have been inspired by the example of his predecessor, Janibak, when he set out to transform the northern suburb between Matariyya/Raydaniyya and Husayniyya, and urbanize areas that were void or dilapidated. He first built in Matariyya a small domed mosque with a pond and gardens, which Sakhawi qualifies as beyond description.[60] Later, he upgraded the area between Husayniyya and Raydaniyya with residential and commercial structures, a pond with orchards and a domed mosque.

On a comparable scale and similar was Azbak's new quarter, Azbakiyya. The great *atabak* or commander-in-chief of the army launched a project to rejuvenate the western bank of the Khalij by digging a large pond to cover a poorly urbanized and dilapidated area. Along the pond's southern shore, Azbak built a new quarter on both sides of a street, with a mosque, apartment buildings and commercial structures, including shops, a qaysariyya and a double hammam next to a palace with a pond view. The project began in 1476 and was completed in 1484.[61]

Qaytbay must have blessed these urban projects; his interest in urban matters is reflected in Yashbak's embellishment campaign for the capital. Yashbak's initiatives, which included clearing the streets and painting facades, were, however, unpopular because they led to the demolition of a large number of illegally built shops, booths and dwellings, causing the ruin of many people.[62] Because urban maintenance was not institutionalized, such an initiative, which caught people by surprise, was perceived as a tyrannical measure. However, Yashbak found a fervent advocate in Maqdisi (also known as Qudsi), who composed a tract in favour of the action in which he argued that, according to the four *madhhab*s of Islamic law, the initiative was not only legal and legitimate but should have occurred a hundred years earlier. Looking back at Cairo's glorious past, he praised the city's original layout, designed

with open spaces.[63] Yashbak's campaign was justified because public streets should be accessible to all, not misused by a few individuals. The poets also celebrated the event – 'the veils were lifted from Cairo and burdens carried away, the earth vibrated with joy and sparkled with lights' – and Ibn Iyas compared Cairo to a dazzling bride.

Unlike Qaytbay, who built his funerary complex in the cemetery, Sultan al-Ashraf Janbalat (r.1500) erected his funerary mosque next to Bab al-Nasr outside the wall, and Sultan al-Ghawri managed with dubious waqf manipulations to acquire land in the very heart of the city along the main avenue.

Although his reign did not exceed a hundred days, Sultan al-'Adil Tumanbay in 1501 contributed to the expansion of Raydaniyya near the Mat'am al-Tayr, not far from Yashbak's quarter, with what seems to have been a formidable religious-funerary complex with residential and commercial structures.[64] Only the mausoleum dome stands today.

While the suburbs evolved according to economic circumstances and princely patronage, the north–south axis from Qahira to the Citadel, along with its southern extension, al-Darb al-Ahmar and Saliba with their ramifications, maintained its great significance throughout the Mamluk period (Figs 10, 12). Along this axis the major royal monuments as well as the important markets were concentrated. More than in any other medieval Islamic city, the markets of Cairo were integrated with the religious and residential buildings rather than segregated in exclusively commercial structures. Shops and booths were built beneath mosques and palaces, or combined with apartments of the rab' type. The rab', an apartment complex for middle-class tenants, was a decisive factor in this integration, as it could also be combined with commercial buildings of the caravanserai type.[65] The major markets stretched along the main thoroughfares of Qahira, around the royal mosques and madrasas. According to Maqrizi's description of the main thoroughfare before it suffered the catastrophes of the late fourteenth and early fifteenth centuries, it included the trades of goldsmiths, coppersmiths, glass and candles, and various outlets for textiles, all kinds of military outfits, fashion articles, amber, fur and toys, along with the slave market. Here were the major commercial buildings of the khan, qaysariyya and wakala type, which functioned as markets of local and imported goods, including agricultural products, and also as factories and banks; these buildings included dwellings as well.[66] A major commercial centre was around the Khan al-Khalili, where the emir Jarkas al-Khalili founded a khan during the reign of Sultan Barquq in the late fourteenth century with which he endowed the distribution of bread in the Holy Cities. Qaytbay added a new khan in this quarter, which al-Ghawri acquired and rebuilt.[67] The two beautiful gates built by these sultans recall the prestige of this quarter, which was the major centre of foreign trade in the late fifteenth century, hosting the markets of slaves and precious stones (Figs 33, 35).[68] Commercial structures and shops were also dispersed around all the mosques and in the vicinity of princely residences.

There was no strict social segregation in Cairo's quarters. The palaces of the Mamluk emirs were scattered in various quarters of the capital, within the premises of the Fatimid city, in the vicinity of the Citadel and in the suburbs. They were not secluded by enclosures; rather, their facades were integrated in the urban fabric, adjoining mosques, shops and ordinary dwellings. Although the chronicles refer to locations favoured by the emirs and other notables, such as the shores of the ponds or the Khalij, these were not exclusively aristocratic quarters. The residential complexes of palaces and gardens created by al-Afram, Janibak, Yashbak and Azbak included religious alongside commercial structures and middle-class dwellings, which were rented. Due to the structure of society, based on the emirs' households of Mamluks with their administrative staff and slaves, princely residences included various juxtaposed categories of dwellings. A Mamluk's palace did not always remain in the possession of his family, especially if he fell in disgrace. Upon an emir's death, along with the rest of his estate, the palace often reverted to the sultan, who would then grant it to the successor in office as part of his remuneration.

The Mamluk capital included some open spaces called rahbas, used to host markets rather than fulfil ceremonial functions. Only Rumayla square at the foot of the Citadel was used for ceremonies and parades. Here was the hippodrome built in the Ayyubid period and rebuilt by al-Nasir Muhammad. At the end of the Mamluk period, al-Ghawri established an outpost of his court in this hippodrome by adding to it residential structures and pavilions with gardens, adding a last touch of brilliance to Cairo before it fell to the Ottomans.[69] The other hippodromes also functioned as ceremonial outposts of the Citadel, hosting polo and military tournaments accompanied by parades and processions, princely weddings, congregational prayers and occasionally also the sultan's audience. They were walled and combined with gardens and pavilions, and, like golf courses today, they attracted elegant residences in their neighbourhoods.[70]

In the summer the flooded ponds and the Khalij were the major centres for private and popular amusements. While the sultans and emirs celebrated their feasts in waterside residences, and with private boats, the populace pitched tents and hired boats. Cairo's taverns were also concentrated along the waterfront.[71] The lifestyle connected with the ponds and the Khalij, as portrayed in Mamluk narrative, historical and poetical literature, mingled princely glamour with popular amusement in profane and frivolous pastimes.

On the eastern, desert, side of the city, the cemeteries with their madrasas, khanqahs and residential structures did not belong to the dead alone, and they were never called 'cities of the dead', as they have been baptized in modern tourist jargon. Instead, the Mamluks blurred the line between city and cemetery with the integration of their funerary monuments in the urban fabric, and the foundation of madrasas and khanqahs in the cemeteries. Maqrizi described the ambivalence of such cemeteries in the following poem:

Two worlds meet in the graveyard,
that of Life and that of Beyond,
– what a beautiful place to stay!
While the hermits wander around the tombs and pray
the revellers let continuous music play;
how many nights did we listen to the tone
of music softening the hardest stone,
while the moon fills the world with beams that shining flow
and his joyous face smiles on kindred faces below.[72]

– 9 –

The Metropolitan Architectural Style

The singularity of Cairo

The sources of Mamluk architecture can be sought mainly in the regional traditions of Egypt and Syria. The nomadic origins or cultural affinities of the Bahri Mamluks with Central Asia or the Black Sea had no bearing on the concepts that shaped their architecture. Nor was the Mamluks' obsessive hospitality towards foreign scholars accompanied by a corresponding attitude towards architects and artists; the evolution of Mamluk architecture was essentially indigenous. The patrons adopted the architectural culture they encountered in their territory. It may be a truism to add that this was a characteristic of Islamic architecture in general, which often remained faithful to regional building traditions even when adopting universal Islamic concepts such as the hypostyle mosque or the madrasa plan.

Foreign influences were introduced to Mamluk architecture in the details rather than the concepts. The facade of Qalawun's complex with its Norman Sicilian inspiration, the tile mosaics of some fourteenth-century monuments and the Seljuk Anatolian design of the portals of Sultan Hasan's and Umm al-Sultan Sha'ban's madrasas were decorative rather than architectural concepts. Like collector's items, they displayed the patrons' international vision and aspirations for originality. When Maqrizi praised the mosques of Sultan Hasan and al-Mu'ayyad Shaykh by comparing them with the monuments of the ancient Persian kings, he was inspired by the literature dealing with ancient and legendary marvels of architecture, and by the literary genre of 'mirror of princes', rather than referring to actual models. Even within Egypt and Syria the architecture of the great cities remained rooted in their own regional traditions.

The unification of Egypt and Syria under Mamluk rule did not lead to a decisive merging of architectural styles, although it did promote some exchange of patterns.

With its long history as a centre of political power, the Fustat/Qahira agglomeration had already accumulated a wealth of great monuments before the Mamluks emerged on the scene. Some characteristic features of Mamluk Cairene architecture, such as the ingenious adjustment of facades to the street alignment, and facade panelling, were already developed in the Fatimid period. They appeared for the first time in the small Aqmar mosque, which was built in 1125 by the vizier al-Ma'mun al-Bata'ihi. When the Mamluks introduced the concept of the princely mausoleum, they adopted the style and technique of Fatimid and Ayyubid dome architecture. The continuity of Fatimid building traditions can also be witnessed in the arcades of Baybars' mosque and its portal facades. The Mamluks' sense of urban aesthetics has its roots in Bayn al-Qasrayn street: this was where the Aqmar mosque was built, and where the earliest major monuments of the Mamluks were built on the site previously occupied by the Fatimid palace complex, and where also the Ayyubid sultans had erected major monuments. Here the *genius loci* prevailed. The unconventional concept of subduing a mosque's layout to the aesthetics of the street was thus rooted in the Fatimid palatial city of Qahira and its ceremonial rituals.[1] Also, some of the decorative repertoire of Mamluk architecture, in particular stucco carving, followed Fatimid/Ayyubid Cairene tradition.

Judging by stylistic criteria, the metropolitan building workshops that worked for the sultan also served the emirs and their high-ranking civilian elite. Not all the sultans' monuments

Fig. 13. The madrasa of Ibn al-Sabuni in Damascus.

belonged to a higher category of architectural excellence. Many did not substantially differ in style from those erected by the emirs, the royal mosques being rather *primus inter pares*. There is enough evidence to believe that the vanished mosque of Qawsun, of which a magnificent portal survives, belonged to the same order as the two mosques of Sultan al-Nasir Muhammad on the Nile shore and at the Citadel. Like the latter, it also had two minarets decorated with glazed tiles, and a dome that was even slightly larger than the sultan's.[2] The bureaucrat Qadi Yahya Zayn al-Din bestowed on Cairo a far more significant monumental heritage than did his master Sultan Jaqmaq. Judging by his domed mosques, Yashbak min Mahdi was perhaps a bolder patron of architecture than his master Qaytbay. Qurqumas' funerary complex in the desert and Qanibay's funerary mosque beneath the Citadel are of no lesser merit than Sultan al-Ghawri's own funerary complex. However, the sultans always maintained the privilege of location, and their monuments were more densely inscribed than the others. No emir built along the main avenue of Qahira, which remained a royal preserve. The prestige of building there is confirmed by Barquq and Barsbay, who marked their presence with funerary buildings, although they ultimately preferred to be buried in the cemetery.

In the provinces, the direct involvement of the sultan was confined to fortifications and civil engineering works, while urban development and the founding of mosques and colleges were delegated to their deputies, the governors, and to local dignitaries. The sultans, however, restored and maintained the major mosques and shrines across their territory. The provincial governors practised an intensive pious and monumental patronage, although their religious foundations did not have the same prodigious boarding facilities for foreigners as those of the capital. Moreover, while no significant monuments by Egyptian merchants are known in the Qahira area, local notables erected religious buildings in the suburban Fustat area and other cities of Egypt, and remarkable buildings in prestigious locations in Syrian cities, such as the mosque of al-'Attar (1350), built by a spice dealer in Tripoli, or the madrasas of the merchants Afridun al-'Ajami (1348) and Ahmad Ibn al-Sabuni (1459) in Damascus[3] (Fig. 13).

Syrian architecture remained faithful to its regional schools and at the same time comparatively conservative, retaining Ayyubid traditions in the architecture of domes, minarets and portals to the end of the Mamluk period. The stylistic discrepancy between Syrian and Cairene architecture is best exemplified in the two mausoleums built by Khayrbak for himself in Aleppo and Cairo at the end of the Mamluk period (Figs 15, 16), both of which follow their respective local tradition. Mamluk waqf

Fig. 14. The mosque of al-Utrush in Aleppo.

Fig. 15. [opposite] The mausoleum of Khayrbak in Cairo.

Fig. 16. The mausoleum of Khayrbak in Aleppo.

of the metropolitan vertical panelling, the facades in Damascus are generally striped horizontally with ablaq masonry, with the exception of occasional signs of Cairene inspiration visible in the panellings of the madrasa of Afridun al-'Ajami, or the mosque of al-Utrush (1399–1414) in Aleppo (Fig. 14).[6]

The *pièce de résistance* of Syrian monuments is always the portal. In Damascus it was often centrally placed in the facade and emphasized by a pronounced pishtaq, a raised portal facade, a carved fluted semi-dome on muqarnas and polychrome marble panels. Sometimes also glazed tile elements added colour to the portal, as in the striped work of Arak al-Silahdar's portal (1350), or in the medallion of the facade of the Taynabiyya mosque (1399).[7] Today not much decoration survives in Syrian mosques except on the mihrabs.

Some Syrian influences on Cairene architecture took place in the early Bahri period, such as the adoption of the muqarnas vault in portals and perhaps also the cruciform madrasa plan. Baybars' striped palace in Damascus, al-Qasr al-Ablaq, inspired al-Nasir Muhammad to build his own in Cairo, and the Duhaysha palace of his son al-Salih Isma'il was erected with ablaq or striped masonry stones and the help of craftsmen from Syria. Pendentives were adopted in domes in Aleppo earlier than in Cairo.[8] The panels with geometric interlace designs in Sultan Hasan's and Sultan Barquq's vestibules are of Syrian style.

The necessity of maintaining and restoring the Umayyad mosque of Damascus and the need to restore its mosaics required the production of glass mosaics in Syria, which also served other buildings, such as the mausoleum of Baybars and the funerary mosque of Tankiz. Al-'Umari reported that the fire of 1340 at the Umayyad mosque destroyed cases of glass tesserae that were produced at that time for the maintenance of the mosque.[9] It cannot be excluded therefore that the glass mosaic decoration of some Bahri Mamluk mihrabs in Cairo was made of glass imported from Syria.

The painted blue and white tiles that decorate the mosque of Ghars al-Din al-Khalili (1423) in Damascus seem also to be related to the restoration of the Umayyad mosque by al-Mu'ayyad in 1419, following its destruction during Timur's invasion, as some remains of tiles *in situ* reveal.[10] Similar tiles were used in Cairo in the late fifteenth and early sixteenth centuries as external decoration.[11]

However, the importation of individual decorative or even architectural elements did not have an impact on Cairene architecture as a whole, in its quality of 'a play of light and volume' as defined by Le Corbusier. This importation could have taken place through portable objects, including drawings, or by oral communication, or even through the participation of individual craftsmen. Yet a whole style of architecture in its three-dimensional properties cannot be duplicated by individual craftsmen alone, but by the collective participation of workshops.

documents regarding Syria have not come to light to enable scholars to carry out the same kind of research about the status and functions of religious foundations as they have done for Cairo. From available information it appears that, unlike in the capital, the khanqah did not significantly figure in Mamluk patronage in Syria, and the madrasas lacked extensive boarding accommodation. As in the capital, however, Mamluk religious buildings in Syria were essentially the funerary monuments of their founders. Indeed, compared with the capital, the smaller dimensions of the madrasa premises in Damascus, Aleppo, Tripoli and Jerusalem in relation to the mausoleums emphasized even further the funerary significance of these monuments. Some monuments consist of a pair of equivalent domed chambers located on either side of the entrance, one for the mausoleum, the other for the mosque.[4] As in Cairo, Syrian mausoleum domes are Mecca-oriented and overlook the street, preferably occupying a corner.

It is also interesting to note that, although Syria had easier access to wood, timber occupied a far more significant place in Cairo's roofing systems than in Syrian architecture.

With the exception of some minarets that stand out for their dimensions, such as those of al-Qal'i in Damascus (1420s), the Great Mosque of Tripoli (1293)[5] and the minaret of Mankalibugha in Aleppo (1367), monumentality was not a feature of Syrian mosques. Unlike Cairo, the minaret was not an obligatory element in the architecture of the Syrian funerary madrasa, nor was fenestration associated with architectural aesthetics. Instead

Whereas Sultan al-Nasir Muhammad contributed with craftsmen and materials for the construction of the mosques and palaces of his favourite emirs in Cairo, he does not seem to have done so in Syria. The architecture of Tankiz's monuments in Syria was not indebted to the capital.

Within Egypt itself the metropolitan architectural and artistic skills did not extend to the provincial cities of Qus and Alexandria, despite their economic importance in the Bahri period.[12] In the provinces, masonry was used only for fortifications; religious monuments were made of brick. For example, the mosque of al-Mu'ini in Damietta (c.1450), although built with a four-iwan plan, was a brick interpretation of metropolitan masonry architecture; its marble pavement, however, could compete with the best of Cairo.[13] The development of characteristic provincial features that never appeared in Cairo, such as the concave transitional zone of domes in Upper and Lower Egypt, the pronounced tapering of minarets and the use of brick compositions as decorative elements, point to regional and probably itinerant workshops that had few contacts with the capital. The minarets of Alexandria, Fuwa and Rosetta, made of brick, had little in common with those of Cairo. The mihrab of the mosque of 'Amr in Qus is a provincial interpretation of Cairene models.[14]

Our scarce information on the architecture of Alexandria suggests that regional traditions also prevailed there. No Mamluk sultan is directly associated with any major new mosque or urban project in Alexandria. The port city declined while maintaining on the whole the urban layout inherited from the pre-Islamic past. However, its fortifications, which were described by travellers and documented by the scholars of the *Description de l'Egypte* as spectacular monumental works, reveal the sultans' direct patronage. For obvious strategic reasons, the rulers of all periods took continuous and direct care of the construction and maintenance of the fortifications. Whenever a sultan or an important emir visited the city he inspected the walls and ordered their restoration, along with the famous Ptolemean lighthouse, which continued operating until its collapse in the mid-fourteenth century. Although the maintenance of the Alexandria canal, which brought Nile water to the city, belonged to the sultan's competence, it did not take place on a regular basis.

The only royal waqf document known so far to refer to imperial Mamluk patronage in Alexandria is that of al-Nasir Muhammad, which mentions his dedication of the revenue of a number of commercial structures there, including a glass factory, to his khanqah in Siryaqus. The sultan thus used Alexandria's commercial resources, which were dedicated to the privy, without endowing the city with any major monument.

Qaytbay seems to have been the only sultan who took the initiative to reproduce the metropolitan architectural style in the provinces. The chroniclers explicitly report that he sent teams of craftsmen from Egypt to Jerusalem and Medina. Qaytay's madrasa in Medina vanished; the one in Jerusalem has only partly survived. Its vestiges and the waqf description indicate that it was also in the metropolitan style.[15] It remained a stylistic singularity in Jerusalem, and also the only significant Mamluk religious monument to be erected by a sultan there.[16] A waqf document of Sultan Hasan refers to the foundation of a madrasa-mosque to teach the four rites of Islamic law to one hundred students in Jerusalem, but nothing is known about the actual building.[17] One could speculate that it was appropriated by the emir Taz, whose madrasa in Jerusalem was founded c.1361, the year of Sultan Hasan's assassination. Its architecture is of the local style.[18]

This dissemination of the metropolitan style by Qaytbay is related to his multiple travels in his empire, which he undertook more than any of his predecessors, and to his pilgrimage. On his travels he inspected buildings and gave orders for restorations. In Jerusalem, he disliked the initial madrasa founded by his predecessor Khushqadam, probably in the local style, and ordered its reconstruction by craftsmen from Egypt. Qaytbay's shrine dedicated to the Sufi saint Shaykh Ibrahim al-Dasuqi in the Egyptian provinces also seems to have been built by Cairene craftsmen, as suggested by a nineteenth-century engraving.[19] However, even Qaytbay's dissemination of the metropolitan style outside Cairo was not consistent. The style of his minaret at the Prophet's mosque in Medina did not conform to that of contemporary Cairene minarets. It was built with a rectangular first storey and topped with a ribbed cupola in the style of the early fourteenth century, which had been out of fashion for one and a half centuries. The latest extant minaret to display this style was that of Qawsun's funerary khanqah, datable to 1336, but, interestingly, this type of minaret continued to be built in the Lower Egyptian city of al-Mahalla al-Kubra until the seventeenth century.[20] This suggests that some of the craftsmen sent by Qaytbay to Medina were recruited in the Egyptian provinces rather than in the capital. When Qaytbay sponsored the restoration of the Umayyad mosque of Damascus following the fire of 1479, he did not send craftsmen from Egypt. His minaret at the southwest corner of the mosque is in the Damascene style.

The metropolitan style was closely associated with the authority of the sultan, who controlled the royal construction works and its building trade. Considering the vast array of skills and manpower that Mamluk construction, conservation and civil engineering in Cairo required, a substantial corps of craftsmen and engineers needed to be permanently occupied in the service of the State, and the sultan would not have been able to spare builders for other cities.

Thus, building workshops did not travel from place to place like their European homologues, following the requirements of the market, nor were they organized in autonomous guilds. Rather, they were recruited and controlled by the state, which also had the power to impose forced labour, and frequently made use of it. This does not necessarily mean that craftsmen lived in a condition of servitude but that the ample employment opportunities in the capital must have dominated the labour market.

The modes of transmitting architectural knowledge also contributed to the disparity between the capital and the provinces. The art of building was not a theoretical science that could be learned from books or drawings. No elevations comparable to those of Gothic cathedrals are known in the Muslim world that would have disseminated architectural knowledge and styles across regions. The profile of a Cairene Mamluk dome or minaret could be duplicated elsewhere only through the collective work of entire teams of masons, which would have implied the dispatch of workshops from the capital.

The sheer magnitude of the Mamluk building activity in the capital generated a quality of architecture that could not be duplicated elsewhere. It speeded up the rhythm of metropolitan architectural evolution, widening the gap between the capital and other cities.

The Mamluk architectural style of Cairo remained basically exclusive to the capital also because of its intimate relationship with the Mamluk aristocracy. As Ayalon wrote, 'few military aristocracies in Islamic history were as bound to the capital and as closely identified with it, in almost total disregard of the other towns, as were the Mamluks in relation to Cairo'.[21] The presence of the sultan's court with the royal Mamluks and the military elite, who were directly involved in Cairo's urban development and aesthetics, contributed to the creation of a city 'made to their measure'.

– 10 –

The Evolution of Mamluk Architecture in Cairo

The formation of an architectural identity

Mamluk religious monuments show a high degree of individuality, which reflects their major purpose as memorials erected by individuals for themselves. As suggested by the monuments, and confirmed by the chroniclers, the creation of a new building involved the patron's choices and taste, so that a historical periodization of Mamluk architecture according to the reigns of the major sultans almost imposes itself. Rather than being the implementation of a theoretical concept or an abstract vision generated in an architectural workshop, the religious monuments were essentially a flexible composition of modules combined ad hoc, according to the requirements of each site. Ideas were pragmatically subordinated to the particular circumstances of a building's location and its patronage. Because each monument was designed to take account of a variable street perspective and other urban requirements, its layout was singular.

The individuality of the religious monuments is reflected also in the general lack – with a few exceptions – of monumentality in princely Mamluk architecture. Considering the wealth and power of the Mamluks, the reason for the moderate proportions of their monuments, compared to Timurid or classical Ottoman counterparts, was due to the deliberate choices of the patrons, who preferred to sponsor multiple individual foundations that could be completed within their period of tenure, rather than colossal projects whose completion they might not witness. The incomplete mosques of Sultan Hasan, and that of Sha'ban, which was also unfinished and dismantled following his death, both built on a grandiose scale, were not encouraging examples to be followed. Al-Zahir Baybars, al-Nasir Muhammad, Faraj, al-Mu'ayyad, Barsbay, Qaytbay and al-Ghawri all preferred to build more than one mosque in the capital rather than concentrating their resources on one colossal monument. Moreover, the sheer number of mosques, required to fulfil the funerary-commemorative needs of the aristocracy, was not compatible with architecture of monumental dimensions. The consequence in the long run was that princely foundations were reduced to neighbourhood mosques and funerary oratories with residential features, which was propitious for urban development and renewal.

While the composition of Mamluk monuments varied, the funerary dome and minaret were constant leitmotifs. They arose in Cairo as respective symbols of commemoration and worship; the harmonious combination of mausoleum and minaret marked the silhouette of individual mosques, and, collectively, created a distinctive skyline for the city. This composition, unprecedented either in Fatimid or Ayyubid architecture, where funerary monuments played a less significant role, became a characteristic visual attribute of the Mamluks, almost as much as the blazon.

When Evliya Celebi described the stone double domes of the mosque of Sultan Janbalat, he noted that 'the old architects while adorning Cairo displayed skill by designing every dome and minaret with an individual pattern'.[1] As the most prominent features in a mosque's profile, the dome and minaret displayed most effectively the creativity of the Mamluk builders and decorators. Indeed, the density of monuments in the city made necessary this articulation of individual features. The builders scrupulously harmonized the mutual proportions of the minaret and dome; even in buildings where the minaret and the dome were not juxtaposed, their proportions were designed to create a harmonious composition from the street perspective. This is the case in the funerary complex of Tankizbugha (1362–3),[2] built on a hill in the northern cemetery, where the minaret stands at the portal, separated from the dome by a courtyard, and in the funerary khanqah of Qawsun (1336).[3] This coupling of the minaret with the dome was emphasized in the view of Mamluk Cairo published in the early sixteenth century by Pagano in Venice, which depicts the city full of mosques, each one represented with a dome beside a minaret.[4]

Inspired by the heritage of the Egyptian capital, where the Fatimids had already pioneered the design of street-adjusted mosque facades, the Mamluks developed a sensitive handling of architecture to enhance street vistas; at the same time they created new aesthetic concepts and architectural solutions that reflected their assumed role in history. Baybars ushered in the new era with Syrian inspirations in his madrasa, and with the novel and spectacular combination in his mosque of a large dome and three gates surmounted by minarets. The essential features that were to characterize the metropolitan style throughout Mamluk history were already established by 1285 in the complex of Sultan Qalawun. Within three decades the Mamluks had created a new, distinctive architecture in the capital.

Although it was al-Nasir Muhammad who expanded the metropolitan area with a colossal infrastructure, Mamluk architecture was already well articulated before his patronage during his third reign transformed the city. Too many of the major buildings founded by this sultan have now vanished to allow a fair assessment of the architecture of his reign, but the fact that the earliest major monument he built was the Great Iwan (1313) in the Citadel points to the secular outlook of his programme. Pictures from the eighteenth and nineteenth centuries of this vanished palace, along with the extant monumental portal of Qawsun's palace, convey a grandiose image of the quality of palatial architecture at the time, which seems to have surpassed the architecture of contemporary mosques (Figs 117–121). Literary descriptions of the Mamluk lifestyle and references to building costs suggest that a worldly emphasis prevailed in the building programme of al-Nasir Muhammad and his elite. Because of the nature of the waqf system, and the continuous reuse and alteration of Mamluk palaces in the Ottoman period,[5] however, the architectural legacy of the Mamluks consists essentially of religious buildings. At any rate, the building boom of al-Nasir Muhammad's third reign stimulated the art of architecture, and led to its apogee in the second half of the fourteenth century, culminating in the mosque of Sultan Hasan.

With al-Nasir's death the great urban expansion came to an end, while the Black Death in 1348 released funds that the ruling establishment could channel into new pious foundations. Manjaq's palace and his mosque, built in 1349, have disappeared, but his remaining minaret and the ruins of a gate and a sabil give evidence of high architectural quality.[6] Shaykhu and Sarghitmish, eminent figures of Sultan Hasan's troubled and interrupted reign, erected monuments of great originality in the 1350s, and the sultan himself built the most extraordinary of all mosques of the time. Notwithstanding the ravages of the Black Death, the designs of buildings from the 1350s to the 1370s are more ingenious than those from the 1320s to the 1340s. The construction of Sultan Hasan's mosque-madrasa, built entirely of stone, and his palace in the Citadel promoted a new generation of masons whose skills marked the architecture of subsequent years. The muqarnas of the sultan's palace at the Citadel was praised by Maqrizi for being carved out of one block.[7] The contemporary Sultaniyya mausoleum, also built entirely of stone, the remains of the funerary complex of Tankizbugha (1362–3), and the madrasas of Uljay and Umm al-Sultan Sha'ban, with their stone minarets and domes, all attest to the triumph of masonry in the third quarter of the fourteenth century. Sha'ban's own funerary madrasa, begun in 1375 near the Citadel, never completed and demolished shortly after his death, had two domes and an iwan, which according to Maqrizi surpassed that of Sultan Hasan's mosque. This was also the period when the dome masons, having fully mastered their craft, moved on to create more sophisticated decorative designs. Although Sultan Hasan's rule was short, its architectural impact continued in the next four decades, as Barquq's mosque reveals.

In sum, the architecture of the Bahri Mamluks was of a heterogeneous nature, assimilating novel and foreign ideas. A variety of forms and patterns co-existed in ground plans and in the designs of domes, minarets and portals.

Sultan Barquq's funerary madrasa (1386) did not make a significant addition to the Mamluk architectural repertoire; its interior is inspired by Sultan Hasan's mosque, while the exterior is adjusted to the perspective of Cairo's main street. By comparison, the funerary khanqah (1411) of his son Faraj, built on a riwaq plan with integrated living units, twin minarets and large twin masonry domes is one of the most remarkable monuments of the Mamluk period, despite the grave political crisis of that period. Neither did Faraj confine his building activity to the cemetery; his small mosque, the Duhaysha (1408), built opposite Bab Zuwayla, introduced a new type of philanthropic foundation, whose purpose was to serve the urban neighbourhood with a primary school, a fountain house and small oratory.

Sultan al-Mu'ayyad's funerary complex (1420) is an urban interpretation of Faraj's khanqah, with smaller mausoleums and three minarets, and a layout that returns to the more classical riwaq plan without living units. His twin minarets on the towers of Bab Zuwayla were a great achievement of design and civil engineering. His hospital, with its awesome facade, is also proof of a dynamic architectural school at that time, coupled with high-quality craftsmanship in decoration. The contemporary mosques of Qadi 'Abd al-Basit and 'Abd al-

Ghani al-Fakhri maintained the architectural dimensions of the late fourteenth century.

Barsbay's funerary khanqah (1432) introduced an urban look to the architecture of the northern cemetery. It is the first complex to show a decentralized concept where the dwellings were separated from the religious structures and articulated as a rab' juxtaposed to the mosque. This complex displays in its dome carvings novel and bold designs with geometric star compositions. Another noteworthy monument of Barsbay's reign is his domed zawiya dedicated to the Rifa'i order, which shows a novel interpretation of the domed space that is distinct from that of the funerary dome. During this period, the mosque in the form of a residential qa'a became common.

No outstanding royal monument survives from the period between Barsbay's and Qaytbay's reigns. Jaqmaq's mosque (1451) does not meet the standards associated with royal patronage. However, the mosques of his majordomo Zayn al-Din Yahya (1444, 1450, 1452) maintained princely architectural patronage and displayed some innovative decorative features. Inal's complex in the cemetery (1451–6), built in three stages, lacks a comprehensive concept.

An important missing link in this history of Mamluk architecture is the funerary complex of Sultan Khushqadam (1461–7), which was erected in the northern cemetery and has now vanished without trace.[8] Not even its exact site or the date of its disappearance are known, nor did Evliya Celebi refer to it. The great Sufi complex of Janibak al-Dawadar, built during Khushqadam's reign on the Nile shore, with two domes and a minaret, which disappeared last century, was an interesting contribution of the 1460s (Figs 271, 272). However, we are left with an architectural gap for the reign of this flamboyant sultan.

The mosques of the Qaytbay period show a refinement of proportions, and innovation in decorative techniques and patterns. Perhaps more than ever before in Mamluk architectural patronage, the mosque became auxiliary to the urban environment. The architecture of that period was not standardized, however. The spectacular urban foundations of Azbak min Tutukh and Yashbak min Mahdi combine urban and landscape design, thereby revealing a new creative impetus in architecture. The lofty mosque of Yashbak at Raydaniyya, although it belongs to an inherited tradition of domed sanctuaries, creates an unprecedented sense of space by skilfully manipulating the proportions between the cubic chamber and its dome. Moreover, its plain, massive exterior, linked to a monumental elevated passage, must have been an unusual spectacle at that time.

Finally, the reign of al-Ghawri in the first decades of the sixteenth century introduced architectural concepts that departed from the precious, richly carved small buildings of the preceding period. The Qaytbay style of carving went out of fashion and monumentality was favoured, as the sultan's mausoleum, his

minaret at al-Azhar mosque (1509), and the funerary complex of Qurqumas reveal. A new form of rectangular minaret was created, and masonry vaults replaced wooden ceilings in the mosques of Qanibay (1506) and al-Ghawri at Sabil al-Mu'mini (1503). When compared with the architecture of Qaytbay's reign, the funerary complex of al-Ghawri, straddling the heart of the city with its monumental dome and minaret adorned with blue tiles, appears ironically to usher in a new trend in Mamluk architecture.

Despite the economic and political decline, the last decades of Mamluk rule did not suffer a decline in the quality of architecture, either in Egypt or in Syria. Mamluk architecture was brought to an end by the Ottoman conquest in 1517 without going through a phase of decadence.

The layout

A citizen of Mamluk Cairo, including members of the religious establishment, might not have assessed the beauty of a mosque in terms of its plan but, rather, in terms of its general appearance, its decoration and its craftsmanship. However, an architectural historian who looks at ground plans always finds surprises in Mamluk religious architecture. The variety and flexibility of plans indicates that they were not a matter of religion but, rather, of convenience and aesthetics.

The classical hypostyle or riwaq plan, consisting of arcades surrounding a courtyard, had not been in use between the reign of al-Zahir Baybars and the third reign of al-Nasir Muhammad, the religious monuments of that period being predominantly funerary khanqahs and madrasas with cruciform or truncated cruciform plans. The multiplication of Friday mosques during the third reign of al-Nasir Muhammad, following the traditional concept, which associates Friday mosques with arcades, led to the revival of this plan. The riwaq plan was adopted in the mosques of Emir Husayn (1319),[9] Bashtak (1336),[10] Ulmas, Sitt Miska/Hadaq,[11] Qawsun, al-Maridani, Aqsunqur and Arghun Shah al-Isma'ili (1347),[12] but its use diminished in the late fourteenth century.

One may not be speculating too far to argue that the revival of the riwaq plan was due to the urban expansion, which required the foundation of new Friday mosques, rather than to a purely stylistic 'renaissance of the riwaq mosque', devoid of functional relevance, as implied by Michael Meinecke. The traditional association of the classical riwaq plan with the Friday mosque was not a canonical issue, however; it was, rather, an inherited pattern that was given up when a more convenient alternative was found. Although few of the riwaq mosques included the founder's mausoleum, the combination of a funerary chamber with this plan disturbed the symmetry when the building had to be accommodated in the street perspective. Urban constraints compelled the architect to truncate the plan in the mosques of Ulmas, Aqsunqur and Shaykhu. This may explain why al-Nasir Muhammad and Qawsun, who could afford more than one foundation, built in addition to their Friday mosques a khanqah with a mausoleum outside the urban centre, al-Nasir in Siryaqus and Qawsun in the cemetery.

The cruciform plan was more flexible. Mamluk architecture used two types of cruciform plan, the four-iwan and the two-iwan/two-recess version. The difference between them is in the size of the lateral iwans, which in the second case were reduced to small recesses. The first cruciform madrasa was that of al-Zahir Baybars; in Qalawun's madrasa the lateral iwans were too small to justify a cruciform description. This truncated cruciform plan persisted in the fully roofed qa'a common in Mamluk residences and late mosques. In all plans the pointed arch prevailed.

The layout of the funerary Friday mosque of the emir Aslam al-Baha'i, built shortly after al-Nasir's death, presented a pioneering device. Although not a grand monument, it is the earliest Friday mosque built on a cruciform plan and including residential units. A decade later, when Sultan Hasan built the first royal Friday mosque in Cairo to be combined with a madrasa, he confirmed the separation of the Friday mosque from the riwaq plan, thus opening up new possibilities in the architecture of funerary mosques in the city.

This development did not exclude, as often in Mamluk architecture, occasional returns to traditional forms. The funerary complex of Sudun min Zada (1401) in the quarter of Suwayqat al-'Izzi, which has now disappeared, brought back the riwaq or hypostyle plan to the city. It was a small building, with the main arcade three aisles deep, and the three others consisting of only one aisle. The sources describe it as a Friday mosque and a madrasa for the Shafi'i and Hanafi schools,[13] and the waqf document defines it only as a Friday mosque. There were no living units for students, only a couple of apartments for staff members.

The monumental mosque of al-Mu'ayyad Shaykh is also built on a riwaq plan. Its layout is symmetrical, but the exterior walls had to be adjusted to the street alignment. Riwaq mosques built in the suburbs were more likely to maintain the symmetry of the plan, as demonstrated by the mosques of Sitt Hadaq in Nasiriyya, Zayn al-Din Yahya in Habbaniyya and Bulaq, Jaqmaq's mosque built by Lajin al-Sayfi (1543) and Azbak's vanished mosque in Azbakiyya.

The hypostyle mosques of the Mamluks contain important collections of pre-Islamic columns and capitals, although spoils in themselves could not provide a sufficient number of columns and capitals to satisfy their building zeal. Rather than produce their own columns or piers, however, the Mamluk builders, wherever possible, preferred to make use of columns taken from ancient buildings, notwithstanding variations in size. To cope with this problem they erected the columns on plinths of different heights. The lack of consistency in the configuration of columns was obviously not perceived as disturbing.

The flexibility of the cruciform plan might have been a reason why it was more often used in funerary monuments than the hypostyle or riwaq plan. It was more suited to an irregular plot than the classical riwaq plan because it could absorb the plot's irregularity in the spaces between the iwans, and it allowed for adjustment to the format of the iwans and the living units between them. The courtyards of the mosques (masjid) of Almalik al-Juqandar (1319) and Ahmad al-Mihmandar (1325) and the funerary Friday mosque of Aslam al-Silahdar[14] might have been originally roofed, as they are today, although this cannot be ascertained.[15]

The mosque of Tatar al-Hijaziyya (1348–60),[16] due to its position and orientation in a narrow plot in the Jamaliyya quarter, has a quite odd layout, with two iwans, each equipped with a mihrab. In the eastern iwan, which is the larger, the mihrab is in the lateral rather than the middle wall, whereas the smaller lateral iwan has an axial mihrab. The mosque of Qutulbugha al-Dhahabi (1347) and the funerary mosques of Aytimish al-Bajasi (1383), and Qanibay al-Muhammadi (1413)[17] are built with only one iwan facing a covered space.

The mosque of Jamal al-Din al-Ustadar (1407–8)[18] has a four-iwan or cruciform layout, in which the main iwan and the courtyard are wider than they are deep. The mosques of Sidi Madyan (1467)[19] and Abu Bakr Ibn Muzhir (1479) display a modified cruciform plan with both the qibla iwan and the opposite one facing the central space with a triple instead of the usual single arch. The mosque of Janim al-Bahlawan (1479)[20] is also wider than it is deep, with four naves parallel to the qibla wall. The two western naves are truncated on their northern side to make room for the domed mausoleum added later (1510), which occupies the corner of the building and overlooks the street. The floor of the second nave from the west is sunken like a courtyard.

The Mamluks gradually abandoned the vaulted iwans inherited from their Ayyubid predecessors, which prevailed in the early Bahri period and were gradually replaced with a flat wooden-ceiling iwan opening on the courtyard with an arch.

Whereas living units overlooked the courtyard in earlier madrasas, Sultan Hasan's madrasa-mosque was the first to transfer the students' cells to the corners and behind the iwans, thus dedicating the entire inner space to the iwans, with no room left for cell windows to overlook the courtyard; this arrangement was repeated in the funerary complexes of Barquq and Barsbay in the city. In a number of smaller madrasas, however, windows of living units are pierced in the iwans or the courtyard. Some cruciform madrasas lack the lateral iwans, such as the madrasas of Inal al-Yusufi (1392–3) and Mahmud al-Ustadar, also known as Mahmud al-Kurdi (1395).[21] In both buildings the lateral walls of the courtyard are pierced instead with the windows of adjacent students' cells that occupy three storeys.

During the fifteenth century royal Friday mosques were reduced to a small scale, and the four-iwan plan acquired the

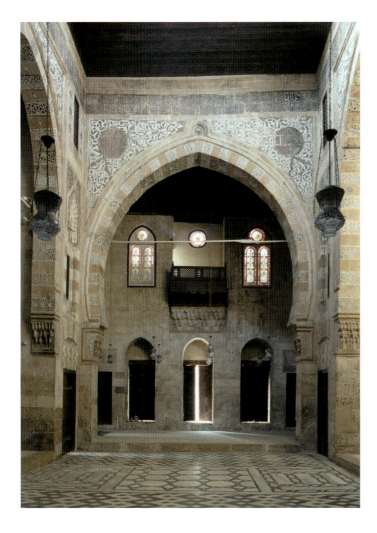

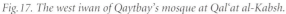

Fig. 17. The west iwan of Qaytbay's mosque at Qal'at al-Kabsh.

Fig. 18. Lateral recess in Qaytbay's mosque in the cemetery.

features of the residential oblong qa'a. Here, the open courtyard was replaced by a reduced central space, slightly lower than the surrounding iwans and lateral recesses, and often roofed with a wooden lantern or ceiling. In waqf documents the central space of a qa'a is not called 'sahn' or 'courtyard' but 'durqa'a', which is a composite Persian–Arabic term meaning 'door-hall', and the lateral recesses are called 'sidilla' instead of 'iwan'. The durqa'a was pierced with symmetrical doors and windows.[22] The decoration of the qa'a extended from the iwans and recesses to include the central walls between them, achieving a unity of space; in the mosques of Inal, Qurqumas and al-Ghawri, the marble dado of the iwans and recesses is extended to the durqa'a.

The qa'a plan appeared first in mosques built by emirs before it was also adopted in royal architecture. The funerary mosque of Jawhar al-Lala (1430)[23] is the earliest known mosque to have the full architectural and decorative features of the qa'a, followed a decade later by the funerary madrasas of Jawhar al-Qanqaba'i attached to al-Azhar mosque, and Taghribirdi, both erected in 1440 (Fig. 19). All three have richly decorated interiors with polychrome marble.

The adoption of the domestic qa'a plan points also to the high architectural status of the Mamluk urban residence in Cairo, and to the lifestyle of its notables. The few remaining residences of the Mamluk period were built, decorated and furnished of the same materials and in the same styles as the mosques, and probably by the same craftsmen.

Besides the urban funerary mosque, madrasa or khanqah, another type of funerary structure existed in the cemeteries, consisting of an enclosed complex with an iwan flanked by a domed mausoleum. In the mausoleum called Turbat al-Sitt in the northern cemetery, datable to the early fourteenth century and attributed to Princess Urdutakin, a wife of al-Nasir Muhammad, the iwan is flanked on the other side by a non-funerary domed room.[24] Another wife of al-Nasir Muhammad, Tughay, built further to the north a funerary khanqah with two unequal funerary domes flanking the iwan.[25] Qawsun's funerary khanqah and the later Sultaniyya in the cemetery south of the Citadel had two equal mausoleum domes flanking a prayer hall.[26] The layout was adopted in funerary architecture also within the city, where it appears in the funerary madrasa of Sultan Sha'ban's mother and in al-Mu'ayyad's mosque. The

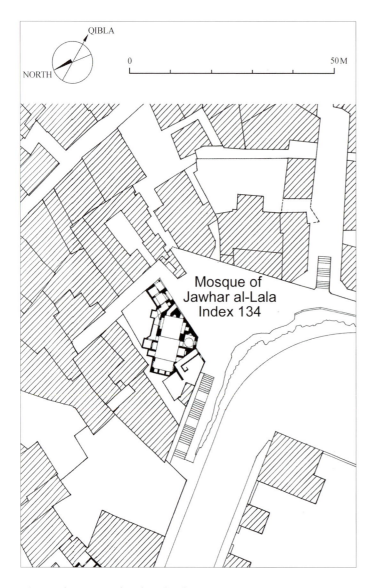

Fig. 19. The mosque of Jawhar al-Lala.

maintained residential features even after they had acquired architectural forms of their own in the thirteenth and fourteen centuries. In the late fifteenth century the mosque, madrasa and khanqah fused together into a multifunctional religious foundation, as described in waqf documents, with reduced or no boarding regulations. While clear-cut distinction between madrasa, khanqah and jami' subsided, the multifunctional foundation adopted new residential forms; the apartment complex replaced cells integrated in the main building. As a result of the merging of institutions, the term 'madrasa' lost its initial meaning, and eventually it was used to describe an architectural form.

Waqf documents and inscriptions of the late Mamluk period apply the term 'madrasa' to mosques built on the qa'a plan, even when they do not include a teaching curriculum. Although it is called 'madrasa' by its inscription, the funerary mosque of Qaytbay was defined by its waqf as only a Friday mosque with a Sufi service, like all other mosques of that period. At the same time, however, the riwaq mosque of Azbak in Azbakiyya, which fulfilled exactly the same functions, is described as jami' in its foundation deed. Similarly, the waqf deed of Sudun min Zada (1401) describes his riwaq mosque as having the 'shape of a jami'' (*'alā hay'at jāmi'*). According to their waqf stipulations the difference between individual religious foundations lay in their architectural form rather than their function.

Since the Fatimid period, Cairene architects had used the device of adjusting the Mecca-oriented mosque to a diverging street alignment by increasing the thickness of the facade wall, which absorbed the discrepancy between the two axes, and thus preserved the inner symmetry of the building. In Mamluk architecture this device was used in connection with the cruciform and the qa'a plans rather than with the riwaq plan, with the exception of the mosque of al-Mu'ayyad Shaykh.

Since the Mamluk mausoleum including its burial crypt also had to be Mecca-oriented, and the founder required it to be visible from the street, the optimal positioning of the mausoleum in the context of the city was adjacent to the prayer hall and integrated in the facade. A window between the mausoleum and the prayer hall communicated prayers performed in the sanctuary to the tomb, thus bestowing blessings on it, while the windows overlooking the street kept the memory of the deceased ever-present in the city.

Funerary structures within the city therefore increased the constraints facing the designer, and required more flexibility in architectural design.[28] The optimal location of a funerary mosque with a courtyard was the western side of a north–south oriented street, as in Bayn al-Qasrayn, Cairo's main avenue. The facade there corresponds to the mihrab wall, and allows the sanctuary along with the adjacent mausoleum to overlook the street. If built on the eastern side of the street, the sanctuary would be on the inner side of the courtyard, and the main facade

funerary complex of Tankizbugha, with a mausoleum in the middle of what seems to have been a prayer hall, is unusual.

In mosques of small size built during the fifteenth century, the dikka or bench used for the *iqama*, which is a second *adhan* or call to prayer performed on Fridays, was no longer placed in the main iwan but elevated as a balcony on the central wall of the opposite iwan, and was reached by an inner passage. This device had appeared in Bahri Mamluk architecture in the mosque of al-Nasir Muhammad at the Citadel, followed by the mosque of Aslam al-Baha'i. Later, the mosques of Qaytbay in the quarter of Qal'at al-Kabsh,[27] Abu Bakr Ibn Muzhir, Azbak al-Yusufi, Janim al-Bahlawan, al-Ghawri and Qurqumas were equipped with a elevated bench set between an upper and a lower window, creating an exquisite loggia composition.

In the Ayyubid period the first madrasas and khanqahs were housed in residences, which could easily meet their boarding requirements. Due to the necessity of accommodating their communities of students and Sufis, madrasas and khanqahs would correspond to the west iwan or arcade. In the madrasa of Sarghitmish, built on Saliba street, the main iwan, being on the inner side of the courtyard, does not overlook the street. As Christel Kessler has demonstrated, the founders in such cases preferred to separate the mausoleum from the prayer hall and place it on the street side instead.

In mosques without a courtyard there was no such problem, as in the funerary complex of Barsbay, built on the east side of the cemetery road. The mausoleum on the northern side of the building is adjacent to the mosque, which is built with a broad format and with the same depth as the mausoleum, so that both contiguous structures overlook the road. By eliminating the courtyard, the architect adjoined the mihrab wall of the funerary chamber to that of the mosque.

The choices made by the Mamluk patrons in cases of conflicting demands clearly indicate that they gave priority to prestige over piety. This secular thinking in religious architecture is particularly evident in the rare cases where the mihrab has been omitted in the mausoleum. As a rule, mausoleums had a mihrab, and waqf deeds define the mausoleum as an oratory (masjid). However, in the smaller of the two mausoleums in the madrasa of Sha'ban's mother, and also in Barsbay's first mausoleum in the city, the mihrab had to be omitted altogether to make a place for the only possible window to overlook the street.[29] In Shaykhu's mosque it was replaced by a window communicating with the sanctuary.

There was an implicit consensus to avoid placing the mausoleum behind the sanctuary, so that worshippers would not pray towards it. However, there are two exceptions to this rule. One of them is the mosque of Emir Husayn, of which little remains,[30] where a small mausoleum is placed behind the mihrab wall, and connects with the mosque through a window and a door. The prominent exception is Sultan Hasan's mosque, but it does not seem to have provoked any reprimand from religious scholars, nor does the founder's piety seem ever to have been questioned.

The difficulty facing the builders of funerary monuments is evident in the cases where the Mecca orientation had to be modified or manipulated, as in the mosques of Ulmas, Sultan Sha'ban's mother, and Khayrbak, where the orientation axis of the mausoleum diverges from that of the mosque. Two different Mecca orientations were tolerated here, a geographical one and a traditional one associated with the early mosques built by companions of the Prophet.

In most funerary complexes the depth of the mausoleum was either inferior or equal to that of the adjacent prayer hall. Exceptions to this rule can be found in some royal buildings; the size of Qalawun's mausoleum exceeds that of the madrasa's prayer hall, and the depth of Qaytbay's and al-Ghawri's mausoleums exceeds that of their respective sanctuaries, which are, however, wider.

Fig. 20. The minaret of Zawiyat al-Hunud.

The acquisition of the right urban plot was, of course, a matter of power and prestige, which a sultan was more likely to possess than an emir. This explains why the main artery of Bayn al-Qasrayn became the principal site of royal architecture.

Minarets[31]

The architectural evolution of the dome and the minaret did not take place at the same pace, however. Masonry supplanted brick earlier in minaret than in dome architecture. The mason's signature on the minarets of al-Mu'ayyad suggests that Ibn al-Qazzaz was probably a specialized minaret builder, who was responsible only for these structures. In Tripoli in Lebanon, the signature of *al-mu'allim* Ibrahim al-Mahdi on the portal of the mosque of al-'Attar indicates that he built the portal and the marble minbar, while another signature on a side door of the same building gives the name of a different builder, who must have worked on the rest of the mosque.[32] In this very specialized environment the minaret mason may have been the *avant-garde*. Specialization, however, does not exclude coordination.

Brick and stone were used intermittently in the minaret architecture of the early Bahri Mamluk period. Al-Zahir Baybars' minarets above the entrances of his mosque must have been light brick constructions, and were perhaps similar to the anonymous exquisite minaret of Zawiyat al-Hunud datable to the 1250s[33] (Fig. 20) which follows the style of al-Salih Najm al-Din's minaret. An impressive minaret in the same style that once stood in the

cemetery of Sayyida Nafisa most likely belonged to Shajar al-Durr's madrasa. Represented in a drawing by Pascal Coste, it complements our picture of the early Mamluk minaret (Fig. 63). The balustrades of the balconies were made of wood, and the decoration included carved stucco muqarnas, keel-arched niches, lozenges and medallions. The Cairene minarets were the only ones in Islamic architecture to combine varying sections – rectangular, octagonal and circular – in one shaft. The origin of this feature goes back to the Fatimid period, as the minarets of the mosque of al-Hakim show. The early medieval reconstructions of the upper structures of the Ptolemaic lighthouse of Alexandria, including those made during the Fatimid period, are described in a number of accounts as consisting of a circular, domed upper section set above an octagonal middle one carried by the original rectangular shaft.[34] This does not necessarily suggest that the ancient lighthouse inspired minaret architecture but, rather, that the medieval Egyptian techniques of building towers, which might go back to ancient traditions, were applied to tower architecture in general.

The strange minarets of Fatima Khatun's (Umm al-Salih) funerary madrasa and the mosque of al-Baqli (1297)[35] belong to a different style, which might have been used in the thirteenth century and later abandoned.

The royal minarets of Qalawun, and those of al-Nasir Muhammad's mosque at the Citadel, were the only ones before the 1340s to be built of stone. The minarets of al-Nasir's madrasa, al-Muzaffar Baybars' khanqah and Sunqur al-Sa'di's khanqah are brick structures. At the minaret of Sanjar a masonry shaft carries an upper brick construction.

The stone minarets of al-Nasir Muhammad in the Citadel show unprecedented features of tile mosaic decoration and have a slender profile; the balustrades of their balconies are the second earliest, after Sanjar's minaret, to be made of pierced stone instead of timber. The cylindrical profile of the western minaret remained singular in Cairene architecture because of its pronounced tapering. The combination displayed in the northern minaret of a rectangular first storey with a circular second storey was later echoed in the minarets of the sultans Faraj and Barsbay.

In the second quarter of the fourteenth century, the use of masonry in minaret construction led to architecture and decoration of unprecedented quality, which eventually inspired the dome builders. Although the minaret of the funerary khanqah of Qawsun (1335–6) continues a tradition inherited from the Ayyubid period, it is made entirely of stone and hence has a more slender and elegant profile. The next step was to replace this rectangular-octagonal-cylindrical shaft, surmounted by a ribbed helmet, with a slender octagonal or octagonal-circular

Fig. 21. [opposite] The minaret and mausoleum at the funerary khanqah of Qawsun.

Fig. 22. [left] The 'southern' minaret.

Fig. 23. [right] The minaret of Qaytbay's mosque at Qal'at al-Kabsh.

tower surmounted by an octagonal pavilion crowned with a bulb on muqarnas. Most minarets of the late fourteenth century were entirely octagonal, but in the fifteenth century they combined an octagonal first with a circular second storey. By eliminating the rectangular shaft the minaret became a particularly graceful sculpture that gave Cairo's skyline its characteristic Mamluk cachet. This style was the creation of *mu'allim* al-Suyufi, the only Mamluk architect (*ra'is al-muhandisin*) to be mentioned by Maqrizi, who credited him with the building of Aqbugha's minaret at al-Azhar mosque, built in the 1340s. The top of Aqbugha's minaret collapsed a long time ago, but that of the minaret of Maridani, also attributed to al-Suyufi, is the earliest extant to display the bulb top.[36] The minaret of Bashtak (1336) also belongs to the first generation of this style, as does perhaps the so-called 'southern minaret' in the eastern cemetery. This style was maintained to the end of the fifteenth century.

Among the finest of the Bahri Mamluk minarets is the one known as the 'southern minaret', a masterly carved monumental sculpture, undated and anonymous. It has been recently attributed to a mosque, which Qawsun is reported to have built near his khanqah. It would be unusual to build two minarets of different styles so close to one another, but this cannot be entirely excluded.[37] In any case, the style of its carving suggests a date in the 1330s. The first and third storeys are octagonal and the middle one circular. Today the restored bulb rests directly above the octagonal third storey without a pavilion; the minaret might originally have been surmounted

Fig.24. The funerary khanqah of the princess Tughay.

by a fourth storey consisting of the pavilion topped by the bulb, as was probably the case with Aqsunqur's original minaret. The middle section of a minaret shaft was the principal area to catch the eye with a display of novel designs, while the first and the third storeys remained rather constant.

Besides the western minaret of al-Nasir Muhammad, those of Bashtak, Aqsunqur and Mahmud al-Ustadar (Mahmud al-Kurdi) (1395) are entirely cylindrical and therefore unusual. The minarets of Asanbugha (1370) and Qanibay al-Muhammadi (1413)[38] have a triangular base and a hexagonal first storey, an anomaly that may be due to space constraints.

The minaret was preferably placed on one side of the portal or the other, supported by a solid buttress. It rarely stood directly above the entrance, as is the case with the minaret of al-Nasir Muhammad's madrasa, which is a light structure carried by the entrance passage. It was usually reached by a staircase leading from the mosque to the roof, which was not connected with the staircase inside the minaret. The four late Mamluk minarets of Azbak al-Yusufi, al-Ghawri, Qaytbay at al-Azhar and Khayrbak have double parallel staircases, recalling the Ottoman northwest minaret of the Uç Serefeli mosque in Edirne (1438–47), which has three superimposed staircases.[39] The reign of al-Ghawri introduced for the first time the totally rectangular minaret, with double and quadruple bulbs at the summit.

Domes

Until the mid-fourteenth century, Bahri Mamluk domes displayed two types of profile: one that curves immediately above the drum (Baybars al-Jashnakir, Sunqur al-Sa'di), and one that curves above a cylindrical section at nearly one third of the dome's height. The latter prevailed in the long run, being favoured for ribbed brick and carved masonry domes. Among the anomalies of this period is the dome of Mughultay al-Jamali (1329–30), which has a peculiar elongated shape and a rounded summit.

Masonry domes emerged in Cairo's landscape in the mid-fourteenth century. The dome masons seem to have learned from minaret architecture. Christel Kessler demonstrated that early stone domes were imitations of the ribbed stone cupola, which crowned fourteenth-century minarets.[40] The builders first tried their skills on small domes, such as that of Ahmad al-Qasid (c.1335), and gradually worked on a larger scale, improving the quality of the masonry and widening the repertoire of their carved patterns, in the process of which they exploited the potential of stone. The earliest masonry domes were coated with plaster to conceal the vertical joints between the stone blocks, which disturbed the appearance of the ribbed surface. In the next stage, however, the masons learned to make use of the decoration by concealing the joints in the ribs' recesses. With the anonymous dome attributed to Tankizbugha (c.1359),[41] carved with alternating concave and convex ribs, and that of Uljay al-Yusufi (1373), carved with twisted ribs, Mamluk masons opened a new era in the decoration of domes. The first is the only masonry dome with a profile curving from the base. It is also unusually constructed above the high transitional zone, which ends with a flaring muqarnas cornice that is pronouncedly wider than the drum, creating a space like a gallery around the dome. The dome of Tankizbugha's funerary complex (1362–3) has the conventional profile.

The patterns carved on stone domes evolved from ribs to zigzag and other geometric and floral all-over designs, and culminated in geometric star compositions. The experimental and problematic phase of applying geometric stars to a domical surface is visible on the mausoleum dome of Barsbay in the cemetery, where the stars, which rise at the base of the dome, become distorted as they ascend towards the apex. The smaller domes in the same enclosure show an improvement of the designer's skills. On Qaytbay's domes for his sons' and his own mausoleum, the designer reversed the pattern, so that it radiates from a central star around the apex of the dome downwards to the base, without conflict with geometric rules and aesthetics (Figs 27, 263).

The development of masonry domes, however, did not lead to a halt in the construction of brick or plastered wooden domes. Interestingly, the transitional zones of the late brick domes of Qijmas al-Ishaqi (Fig. 29), Abu'l-'Ila and Sultan al-Ghawri's mausoleums were made of stone, and treated both inside and outside in the same manner as masonry domes. Their architecture thus differed from that of their Bahri predecessors made entirely of brick.

For the inner transitional zone, Mamluk architecture made use of squinches as well as pendentives.[42] The squinches were inherited from the Fatimids and Ayyubids, who had developed the multiple-tier formula. The multi-tiered squinch has a muqarnas configuration, each tier of niches corresponding to a bracket in the wall, while on the exterior the tiers appear as steps. Structurally, however, this type of squinch is not a genuine one, but just a facing disguising a structural pendentive consisting of a series of beams set across the corners. Nevertheless, we will call it according to its appearance.

Whereas the dome of al-Salih Najm al-Din has no external drum, Qalawun's architects introduced the high octagonal

Fig.25. The funerary complex of Tankizbugha, mausoleum.

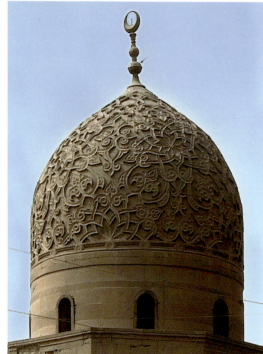

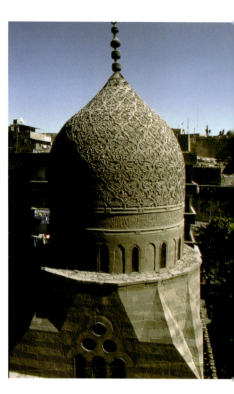

Fig. 26. The funerary dome of Aytimish al-Bajasi.   *Fig. 27. The mausoleum dome of Qaytbay's sons.*   *Fig. 28. The funerary dome of Qanibay Qara.*

drum, which can also be seen on the subsequent domes of the mausoleums of al-Nasir Muhammad and Ulmas, and above Aqsunqur's mihrab. Because of its pronounced height and width in relation to the dome, the drum of these domes appears as a transitional zone between the rectangular chamber and the spherical part. In the second half of the fourteenth century, however, the drum was detached from the transitional zone and integrated in the dome proper.

The earliest extant muqarnas pendentive in Cairo appears in wood in the dome added by Sultan Lajin in 1295–6 above the mihrab of the mosque of Ibn Tulun. The wooden dome of al-Nasir's mosque at the Citadel displays the same device on a larger scale, followed by the domes of al-Maridani's mosque and Sultan Hasan's mausoleum.[43]

Brick pendentives, which were rather rare, were used in the mausoleums of Fatima Khatun, the so-called 'Turbat al-Sitt', built in the early fourteenth century,[44] and Sarghitmish. The pendentives of Fatima Khatun's mausoleum are pseudo-pendentives used as filling for structural squinches, which is the opposite of the traditional device mentioned above, where the muqarnas pendentives are disguised as squinches. The earliest known genuine pendentives to be made of brick are those of the shallow domes that surround the courtyard of the mausoleum of Qalawun. They are spherical, unlike those of the dome of Turbat al-Sitt. Late brick domes were supported by stone pendentives.

Pendentives were predominantly adopted in masonry. They first appear as decorative devices in the portal vaults of al-Muzaffar Baybars (al-Jashnakir) and Sunqur al-Saʿdi. The earliest true stone pendentives – i.e. associated with a dome – are in the vestibule of Sultan Hasan's mosque, and they are spherical. Pendentives carved with muqarnas decoration were the typical transitional device of the masonry domes of the fifteenth century.

The early masonry domes were built with squinches copied from the architecture of brick and plastered wooden domes;[45] they were subsequently replaced by pendentives carved with muqarnas, which are structurally often a combination of pendentive and squinch. This evolution did not prevent the occasional use of plain squinches in brick, as in the mosque of Aqsunqur, and in stone, as in the two mausoleum domes of Tankizbugha (c.1359, 1362–3) and the funerary madrasa of Sultan Shaʿban's mother.

There are a number of Mamluk wooden domes in Cairo. Some were built over the mihrab area as in the mosques of al-Zahir Baybars, al-Nasir Muhammad and al-Maridani, and smaller ones crown the mihrab area of the mosques of Zayn al-Din Yahya in Bulaq and Habbaniyya. Others are funerary domes, such as those of the sultans Hasan and Barquq, both rebuilt in recent times, and the dome of the funerary madrasa of al-ʿAyni (1411–12). They also rest on wooden pendentives.[46] It is noteworthy that the external transitional zone of wooden domes differs entirely from that of stone or brick domes, lacking the stepped profile. This was already the case in the mausoleum dome of Imam Shafiʿi, where the transitional zone is hidden behind a screen wall. The transitional zones of the dome of al-Nasir Muhammad in the Citadel and at Maridani's mosque are encased in a rectangular base. At Sultan Hasan's mausoleum the transitional zone is included in the octagonal drum in the Qalawun tradition, whereas in Barquq's dome only a cylindrical drum is visible on the outside.

The need to build higher funerary domes in limited space prompted the Mamluk builders to raise the transitional zone above the rectangular chamber. Moreover, the aesthetic concern to harmonize the proportions of the dome and minaret as a composition must have led the builders to accentuate the transitional zone, which eventually became a characteristic feature of the Cairene mausoleum profile. In most Mamluk domes, the combined transitional zone and the dome proper are taller than the facade below. This height was particularly pronounced in the case of the monumental mausoleum of Sultan al-Ghawri, as shown in a reconstruction drawing by the Comité (see Fig. 303).

In the search for a decorative scheme for the transitional zone of domes, the builders looked again at the architecture of stone minarets. The transitional zone of domes, in the forms

Fig. 29. The brick dome of Qijmas al-Ishaqi.

of steps at the corners, was replaced in the fifteenth century by undulating or prismatic triangles to smooth the transition from the cubic to the spherical space. These forms were borrowed from minaret architecture, which had, by the first half of the fourteenth century, already developed devices to decorate the bases of minarets and their transitional zones, which fulfilled a similar function between the rectangular base and the octagonal or circular shaft. In the late fifteenth century the display of carved patterns increased on the transitional zones of domes and minarets. The prismatic triangles of domes could be either multiple-tiered or, as in the case of Ghawri's and other later domes, a pair occupying the corner (Figs 28, 306).

In the second half of the fourteenth century a group of exotic domes appeared in Cairo. These are the two domes of the funerary madrasa of Sarghitmish, the twin masonry domes of the Sultaniyya mausoleum and the mausoleum dome of Yunus al-Dawadar (before 1382). They all have a high drum, with a muqarnas frieze; with the exception of Yunus' dome, they were built with a double shell.[47] A nineteenth-century photograph shows the vanished mausoleum of Sudun min Zada, built in 1402, with a bulbous dome, which can be recognized as made of wood and covered with lead tiles.[48] Its profile and inscription band recall the fountain dome of the mosque of Sultan Hasan. However, the waqf document of Sudun describes the monument with a masonry mausoleum dome. Unless we assume that the patron changed his mind after the waqf document was compiled, the bulbous dome in the photograph should be seen as a later reconstruction.[49]

Although the domes of Sarghitmish and the Sultaniyya mausoleum recall Timurid architecture, the fact that they pre-date their Timurid homologues by several decades excludes a Central Asian inspiration. Michael Meinecke suggested a common prototype for the Timurid and Mamluk domes in western Iran or Iraq of the Jalayirid period.[50] The examples he provided show a high drum and a double shell, but not a bulbous profile; this might have a Cairene origin. Two wooden domes with a bulbous profile in the khanqah of Shaykhu might have inspired the design of Sarghitmish's dome over the prayer hall (Fig. 158). Nineteenth-century photographs and drawings of this dome before its reconstruction show that it was made of plastered wood and very similar to Shaykhu's. The same profile appears in the wooden fountain dome of Sultan Hasan's mosque. Sarghitmish might have imported the device of the high drum and the double shell in his other brick funerary dome, but this dome is not bulbous. It seems, therefore, that two traditions merged in the architecture of these exotic domes: the Cairene wooden bulbous dome and the foreign double-shell dome with a high drum. It is interesting to note that the bulbous dome with high drum continued to be built until the nineteenth century in the provincial architecture of Lower Egypt.

In the fifteenth century, another type of dome architecture was developed as roofing for zawiyas and mosques. The funerary khanqah of Barsbay in the cemetery includes a domed zawiya whose architecture is quite distinct from that of funerary domes. Its transitional zone, consisting of squinches, is set within – and not, as usual, above – the rectangular space, and the relationship between the elevation and the diameter of the chamber produces a space that is more appropriate for a large gathering than the traditional mausoleum. Two domes of this type were built in the 1460s by the emir Janibak, the great secretary of Sultan Khushqadam, also in connection with a zawiya, and two others by Yashbak min Mahdi, Qaytbay's great secretary. None of them had a funerary function. The last of this series is the dome of the zawiya of Shaykh Damirdash, built probably during the reign of Qaytbay in the northern outskirts, not far from Yashbak's large dome. Although contemporary Ottoman architecture had already developed the single-dome mosque, the Mamluk domed mosques share only the concept, not the architectural details, with their Turkish counterparts.

The dome as a roofing device was also used in secular architecture in palaces, and in hammams, as indicated in waqf documents.

Facades and fenestration

Very few Mamluk mosques were built to be free-standing. The continuous uninterrupted line of the facades of the buildings of Qalawun, al-Nasir Muhammad, Barquq and al-Kamil that characterizes Bayn al-Qasrayn street, and the contiguous facades of Qurqumas' and Inal's funerary complexes in the northern cemetery, are a phenomenon unique to Cairo.

Qaytbay's funerary mosque was integrated in a quarter where it was connected on three sides to other structures. Also, the mosque of Qanibay Qara, which today is free-standing on a hill beneath the Citadel, was no exception; it was once connected to a residential structure located on its western side.

Most Mamluk monuments had two street facades, a feature that led to the development of the corner as an important aesthetic factor. From the late Bahri period a corner was occupied by the composite structure of the sabil-maktab, which appears for the first time at the madrasa of Uljay al-Yusufi, and eventually became a standard feature of a religious complex. The structure consisted of a manned water-house or sabil, with two large corner windows, surmounted by the classroom of a primary school for boys, the maktab, overlooking the street through an arched wooden loggia. Both the sabil and the maktab already belonged to the auxiliaries of a mosque, but only at this

stage were they combined in an architectural composition that characterized the facade.

As was also the case in Syria, the corner was a favoured place for a mausoleum, because it promoted a more intensive communication with the street. At the outset of Mamluk rule the mausoleum of al-Salih Najm al-Din added to his madrasa by Shajar al-Durr was built to occupy a corner in the facade, which allowed more space for windows. Al-Muzaffar Baybars' and Sarghitmish's mausoleums also project boldly in the street. Qalawun's madrasa projects beyond the mausoleum and the portal with three facades. These movements in the facade precluded symmetry, which, unlike in Damascus, does not seem to have been of any interest to the Cairene architects. At the same time, however, the symmetry of the interior was pursued even though it entailed costly adjustment devices.

Folding facades with projections and recessions to adjust the building to the street became an aesthetic factor that broke the monotony of big walls in narrow streets. In the architecture of the late fifteenth century the corner treatment is particularly refined, as can be seen at the mosques of Azbak al-Yusufi and Qijmas al-Ishaqi, and at Qaytbay's funerary mosque. When ample space was available, as was the case with the khanqah of Faraj, or the mosque of Qanibay Qara beneath the Citadel, the facade was unfolded to take advantage of the site, without being fully symmetrical, however (Fig. 317).

Mamluk builders inherited from their Fatimid and Ayyubid predecessors the tradition of panelling facades with recesses pierced with windows, even when windows were not necessary. Although the Fatimid mosque of al-Salih Tala'i' received enough light from its courtyard, large rectangular windows had been pierced on three facades to allow visual communication with the street. The Ayyubids adopted this system in the madrasa of al-Salih Najm al-Din, and the madrasa of al-Zahir Baybars followed suit. However, the facades of Baybars' mosque at Husayniyya are neither panelled nor do they have rectangular windows in their lower part, the walls being pierced only with arched upper windows. The mosque of al-Nasir Muhammad at the Citadel, although built on a similar plan, had large rectangular windows on three sides. As the mosque already received enough light from its large courtyard, the windows might have had a ceremonial significance, for communication with the square, where it once faced the royal palaces. As in Baybars' mosque but unlike urban mosques, its facades are without recessed panels.

In the mosques of Sitt Hadaq (1339–40) and Maridani, both built with the riwaq plan, the recessed panels with windows appear on only two of the four facades, those built along major streets. Unlike Maridani's mosque, however, the recesses of Sitt Hadaq's mosque have no lower rectangular windows, only upper tripartite windows.

The tripartite window with an oculus above a double arched opening appears for the first time in the monuments

Fig. 30. The portal of the mosque of Emir Husayn, no longer extant.

of Qalawun and his wife, becoming henceforth a constant feature of Mamluk facades. The tripartite window corresponds, however, to a single-arched window on the interior wall. The mosque of Sultan Hasan shows an exception to this rule: the wall between the mausoleum and the prayer hall is pierced with a pair of tripartite windows on both sides that mirror the arrangement of the mausoleum's exterior walls. A single-arched window was an alternative to the tripartite window on the upper facade wall.

This inner arched window, called a 'qamariyya' in waqf documents, has a stucco grille filled with coloured glass. The qamariyyas were a relieving device as well as a decorative one that adorned the facade and added colour to the interior, rather than serving as a source of light. In the khanqah of Faraj Ibn Barquq, which is very bright anyway, qamariyyas are nonetheless pierced in the qibla wall. They are not axially placed in relation to the arcades, indicating that their purpose was, rather, connected to the recessed panels of the rear facade of the sanctuary. At the madrasa of Sultan Sha'ban's mother the symmetry of the exterior fenestration made it necessary to include blind windows in the facade. Due to the primacy of the street perspective, the facades were designed according to their own aesthetics, separately from the inner configuration, so that the exterior rarely reveals the interior, being rather a dressing.

As a rule, all the windows in a panelled facade were included in the recessed panels of the wall, with the exception of the traditional oculus above the mihrab niche, which for obvious structural reasons is set in the thicker part of the wall. The mosque of Aqsunqur has the earliest mihrab oculus in Cairo; in the mosque of Maridani, built slightly earlier, an arched window is pierced above the mihrab. The mihrab oculus became a traditional feature of Cairene mosques; at the funerary khanqah of Princess Tughay, however, it was replaced by a magnificent carved stucco medallion, and at the mosque of Khayrbak it was replaced by an arched window. The oculus appeared earlier in Damascus, in the funerary madrasa of al-Zahir Baybars, where it is enhanced on the facade by a framing interlace rosette. In the mosque of Sultan Hasan the oculus is not restricted to the mihrab wall but repeated in the three other walls of the mausoleum, and in the four iwans. In the fifteenth century, the mihrab oculus is often coupled with another symmetrical one on the opposite wall, as in the khanqahs and mausoleums of Faraj and Barsbay, and in the mausoleum of Qaytbay.

In a mosque where the iwans do not open on the street but receive their light from the courtyard, windows could be omitted altogether. This is the case at the khanqah of Baybars al-Jashnakir, which is equipped with airshafts for ventilation, and in the madrasa of Sultan Sha'ban's mother. At the mosque of Sultan Hasan the three minor iwans have very few openings in their walls, and the windows of the main iwan overlook the mausoleum.

The facades of the mosque of Sultan Hasan display a revolutionary treatment of panelling and fenestration, notably the novel treatment of the recessed panels on the north and

Fig.31. The portal of the mosque of Bashtak.

Portals and entrances

In the classical riwaq mosque three entrances were placed axially, the main one being opposite the mihrab, and the lateral ones in a symmetrical position. This arrangement was followed in the mosques of Baybars, al-Nasir Muhammad and al-Maridani, but no longer in the later period. In cruciform mosques, the axial location of the four iwans excluded the placement of axial entrances, which would otherwise have cut through the iwans. The bent entrance, which was a feature of residential architecture, prevailed. The bent entrance also resulted from the usual discrepancy between the inner axis and the street axis of the mosque, as was already the case at the Fatimid mosque of al-Aqmar. In madrasas and khanqahs, which included living quarters, the bent entrance had the advantage of protecting the privacy of the resident community.

As elsewhere, in Mamluk architecture the portal was a prominent element in the design of a facade; however, due to the panelling and fenestration of the facade and the addition of the sabil-maktab, the Cairene portal was less of a focal point than in Syria. The portal was a mason's task, always being built of stone and lavishly panelled with marble. As with other architectural features, the Bahri craftsmen created a variety of portal designs.

Al-Zahir Baybars' madrasa introduced the Syrian portal with a semi-dome on muqarnas, whereas his Friday mosque went back to Fatimid devices. Qalawun's marble ablaq portal is not architecturally emphasized, neither is Sanjar's, unlike the portal of al-Muzaffar Baybars' khanqah, which is the grandest of the early Bahri period. The main portal of al-Maridani's mosque is in the shape of a vaulted iwan and in Aqsunqur's mosque the vault is reduced to a shallow arched recess. The portal vault of the mosque of the emir Husayn (1319) displays a spectacular sunrise pattern deeply carved within a pointed arch.[51] Among the variations introduced in the Bahri period, the semi-dome over muqarnas prevailed in the second half of the fourteenth century. The most impressive masonry muqarnas of the Muslim world are found in some fourteenth-century portals in Cairo. Ulmas' remarkable portal with a deep, flat ceiling of muqarnas was emulated in the mosque of Bashtak and the oratory at his palace. The portal of Qawsun's palace, signed by Muhammad Ibn Ahmad Zaghlish al-Shami (i.e. of Damascus), combines a muqarnas shallow vault with a semi-dome (Figs 31, 127). The design of the un-finished portal of Sultan Hasan, with its gigantic muqarnas cascade, remained singular, and that of Umm al-Sutan Sha'ban's madrasa was the last grand muqarnas portal of the Bahri period.

south facades, each pierced with eight pairs of superimposed rectangular windows, each pair corresponding to a student's cell. The tall, narrow and densely pierced recesses produce an unprecedented visual effect, by which the aesthetic role of fenestration acquired a new dimension. Although this arrangement was not repeated in subsequent Mamluk architecture, it opened new perspectives for the art of fenestration, which can be seen at the madrasa of Uljay al-Yusufi, built a decade later. The profusion and the symmetrical arrangement of windows in this monument were epoch-making. In the cruciform mosques of al-Fakhri (1418) and Janibak al-Ashrafi (1427), multiple qamariyyas are pierced in the iwans, although the latter are sufficiently lit by the courtyard.

In the architecture of the fifteenth century, the art of fenestration was fully exploited: the walls became diaphanous, as in the main hall of al-Mu'ayyad's hospital, and the peak of translucency was achieved in the funerary mosque of Qurqumas. Here, although the courtyard was open to the sky, as the crenellation indicates, the densely pierced walls were reduced to a framework for light.

In Mamluk buildings large rectangular windows with iron grilles were located near the floor, thereby establishing visual contact between the mosque and the street. In this position they fulfilled the pious function of spreading its message beyond its premises.

Fig.32. [opposite] The portal vault of the palace of Qawsun.

Fig. 34. Qaytbay's portal at his madrasa at Qal'at al-Kabsh.

In the fifteenth century the use of muqarnas vaults diminished in portal architecture in favour of groined trilobe
vaults resembling squinches. There is a parallel between
portal vaults and dome architecture; the portal conch, being a
semi-dome, was constructed to seem supported by muqarnas
pendentives or squinches. The portal seems, therefore, to have
become a miniature experimental field for the development
of dome architecture. The earliest masonry pendentives are in
the portal of Baybar's khanqah, and the elaborate muqarnas
pendentives of Sarghitmish's portal anticipate those of later
masonry domes. Likewise, the trilobe portal vault inspired the
configuration of the trilobe squinches in the domes of Yashbak
at Matariyya and Husayniyya. The trilobed and groined
portal vault was decorated with ablaq patterns like those of
contemporary mihrabs.

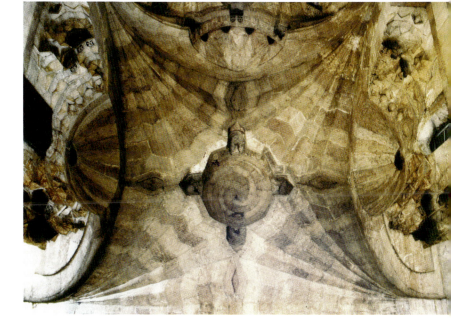

Fig. 33. [opposite] Qaytbay's portal at the Khan al-Khalili bazaar.

Fig. 35. Al-Ghawri's portal vault at the Khan al-Khalili bazaar.

The most impressive groined vault of the late Mamluk period can be seen at al-Ghawri's portal at the bazaar of Khan al-Khalili (1511) (Fig. 35);[52] it is the elaboration of an earlier device introduced in the vestibule of Uljay al-Yusufi's madrasa and was further developed in that of al-Mu'ayyad's mosque.

The khanqah of al-Muzaffar Baybars shows the earliest use of the maksala, which is a stone bench on either side of the entrance recess, and a regular feature in portals henceforth. The exception to this rule is the mosque of al-Nasir Muhammad at the Citadel. Here the absence of a bench must be related to the ceremonial character of the building. Subsequent mosques include both features. From the time of the mosque of Sultan Hasan the mosque's entrance bay developed into a vestibule, a rectangular space with a frontal wall that included a bench or mastaba. The frontal wall of vestibules of the Circassian period is pierced with a window connected to the mosque's interior.

Materials and techniques of decoration[53]

Stone-carving was the medium of facade decoration and inscriptions. Carved stucco, widely employed for interior decoration in the Bahri period, was also used externally on brick domes and minarets. Its use receded when stone substituted brick. Some decorative features, such as the keel-arched niche with radiating hood, remained a constant decorative element from the Fatimid period to the end of the Mamluk period; whereas the early ones were decorated with stucco, they were later carved in stone.

The shafts of the minarets of the mid-fourteenth century were often decorated with two-coloured stones inlaid in geometric patterns. This type of decoration, which tended to be obscured by Cairo's dust, was eventually replaced by more effective carvings. The stone and marble carvings on the facades of Sultan al-Mu'ayyad Shaykh's mosque and hospital have singular designs executed in unusual high-relief that were not subsequently repeated. Instead, the masons of his successor Barsbay were more concerned with the new challenge of carving domes with geometric star compositions. Similarly, the characteristic stone-carving style of Qaytbay's reign, with its dual composition of smooth straight lines interwoven with grooved curves, did not continue in the architecture of his successor, al-Ghawri. This style, which is found in earlier Anatolian masonry decoration, may have been introduced by craftsmen from there. It should be recalled that Mamluk territory in the fifteenth century stretched as far as the city of Divrik, as indicated by a decree inscribed on a panel in the name of the sultan's deputy, Qansuh al-Ashrafi, who was probably the later Sultan al-Ghawri. In the late fifteenth century, panels of carved stone or inlaid marble, or a combination of both, were inserted and framed by mouldings in the manner of the

Fig. 36. Carved panel in the wakala of Qaytbay near al-Azhar mosque.

facades of several monuments, suggesting the mass production of standard elements that could be integrated according to need (Fig. 36).

Qaytbay's reign introduced a revival of stucco in internal decoration, as the splendid inner decoration of the dome of Yashbak, called the Fadawiyya, demonstrates. It is, however, very different in technique and patterns from the stucco of the Bahri tradition, based on the Ayyubid style. The mosque of Qaytbay at Rawda, and his sabil on Saliba street were also adorned with shallow stucco carvings.

The arts of the Qaytbay period display new patterns in the floral repertoire of architectural decoration, and in the decorative arts and book illumination. For the first time in Mamluk art, we find naturalistic flower motifs integrated between arabesques, in masonry, stucco, marble carving and inlay.

Although the Mamluks never aspired to cover their buildings with glazed tiles, they occasionally used this medium for external touches in architectural decoration (Fig. 39). The first episode began during the reign of al-Nasir Muhammad, when tile mosaics in the Ilkhanid style were applied on minarets, domes and facades (Figs 37, 115), and also in Maridani's mosque on the exterior and the interior. The mihrab of the madrasa of al-'Ayni (1411–12), no longer extant but documented in a drawing by Jules Bourgoin, was entirely decorated with tile mosaics of Anatolian craftsmanship.[54] Mamluk tiles from the fifteenth century in museum collections decorated with underglaze painting in blue, white and black, with chinoiserie patterns, suggest a new fashion in Mamluk architectural decoration inspired by Chinese pottery. They were used in tympanums, as one in the name of Sultan Qaytbay (1495–6), and another in the name of Sultan Janbalat (1500–1), indicate.[55] The beautiful ceramic blazons of Qaytbay show the high quality achieved during this period (Fig. 33).[56] Al-Ghawri's lapis blue tiles applied to his dome and minaret, and the ceramic elements on

Fig.37. Tile mosaic inscription at the dome of the princess Tughay.

Fig.38. Lintel of marble inlay in the mosque of Qijmas al-Ishaqi.

Fig.39. Fifteenth-century painted tiles on the facade of the Kamiliyya madrasa.

the shaft of his minaret at al-Azhar and on the stone dome of Arzumuk (1503–5),[57] suggest the presence of a specialized workshop in Cairo, which continued to work in the early Ottoman period, as many examples indicate.

Glass paste was more commonly used to add a touch of blue on external and internal decoration, and another kind of black-and red-coloured paste or stucco was applied in the late fifteenth century as inlay in decorative and epigraphic marble friezes.

Marble decorated portals and the lintels of doors and windows. The Mamluk joggled lintels of ablaq or polychrome marble are a major element in facade decoration, and they became particularly elaborate in the fifteenth century. The most remarkable examples are at the mosques of al-Mu'ayyad, Faraj (Duhaysha) and Qijmas al-Ishaqi, and at Qaytbay's sabil-maktab in Saliba street (Figs 38, 296). In interior decoration, polychrome marble characterizes the dados, mihrabs and pavements. The extent of marble dados varied; in the mosque of al-Nasir Muhammad at the Citadel, it ran around all four arcades, whereas in the mosque of Maridani and al-Mu'ayyad it was restricted to the prayer hall. In the cruciform mosques of

Fig. 41. The marble and glass mosaic triple mihrab of the madrasa of Aqbugha.

Mithqal, Umm al-Sultan Sha'ban, Sultan Hasan, Sarghitmish and al-Mu'ayyad Shaykh only the qibla hall is decorated.[58] In the qa'a mosque the entire space was equally panelled. However, Qaytbay's mosque, unlike the adjoining mausoleum, has no dado.

The decoration of early Mamluk mihrabs followed the Fatimid and Ayyubid tradition of carved stucco filling the conch and the spandrels.[59] A series of Bahri mihrab conchs were decorated with glass mosaics: the ones of the mausoleums of Shajar al-Durr (1250) and al-Salih Najm al-Din (1250), the madrasa of Qalawun (1285), the main mihrab of the mosque of Ibn Tulun redecorated by Sultan Lajin (1296), the madrasas of Taybars (1309–10) and Aqbugha (1339) attached to al-Azhar (Figs 40, 41) and the mosque of Sitt Miska (1339). The

Fig. 40. [opposite] The marble and glass mosaic mihrab of the madrasa of Taybars.

painted glass tiles that decorate the mihrab of the ribat of Ibn Sulayman al-Rifa'i remained singular. Nevertheless, marble mosaic, which was a characteristic of Mamluk decoration, prevailed throughout the entire Bahri period and its use was never abandoned. Fine specimens were still produced in the late Mamluk period, in the mosques of Qijmas al-Ishaqi and Abu Bakr Ibn Muzhir, and at al-Ghawri's funerary complex. Four early Mamluk mihrabs have a painted wooden conch with arabesques in relief, made of a glued amalgam of leather, linen and gypsum, a technique used by the ancient Egyptians. Three of these conchs were part of restoration work carried out on earlier buildings.[60]

Some Bahri Mamluk marble mihrabs were treated like portal conchs and niches, with marble ablaq motifs radiating either from the base in a sunrise motif or from the apex downwards.[61] The earliest known stone mihrab with an ablaq radiating motif is that of Shaykhu's khanqah; in the mid-fifteenth century, stone mihrabs became widespread, either carved, made of ablaq-

Fig. 42. Marble pavement at the Mamluk mosque of al-Mu'ini in Damietta (c.1450).

patterned masonry or combining carving with ablaq, as in the mihrabs of Inal's, Qaytbay's and Qurqumas' mausoleums. The mihrab niche was integrated in the design of the qibla wall together with the window recesses.

In some Mamluk funerary complexes, the mausoleum and, notably, its mihrab were more lavishly decorated than that of the adjoining mosque. This was the case in the funerary complexes of Qalawun, al-Muzaffar Baybars, Faraj Ibn Barquq and Barsbay in the cemetery. At the madrasa of Uljay neither of the two mihrabs is decorated. The mihrab of Qadi 'Abd al-Basit's mosque is plain, whereas the facades of the mosque display polychrome marble decoration. In the funerary mosques of al-Mu'ayyad Shaykh, Jawhar al-Lala and Mahmud al-Ustadar (al-Kurdi), the mihrab of the mausoleum has no decoration, in contrast to the mihrab of the sanctuary. The treatment of the mihrab appears, therefore, to have been a matter of individual choice. In the late fifteenth century the discrepancy between the two mihrabs disappears, but they are always decorated with different patterns.

It is interesting to note that, although the blazon had a political significance in material culture as a symbol of the Mamluk status, its positioning in architecture was not canonized, and appears rather haphazard. In Baybars' madrasa, the panther is set in the tympanums of the facade windows, as were later blazons as well. However, Qalawun's facade does not display any, although he was reported to have had a blazon, which, according to Michael Meinecke, was the fleur-de-lis.[62] The blazon could be carved in various locations on the facade:

in a portal niche, within an exterior or interior inscription band, painted on a ceiling, or integrated in other decorative elements, such as the stucco grilles of windows, marble slabs and woodwork; in the late Mamluk period, the royal blazon was often placed in the spandrels of the portal arch. In Qaytbay's funerary mosque it appears in the window lunettes, and in his mosque at Qal'at al-Kabsh it is set in the spandrels of the iwan arches. On the mausoleum of the emir Tarabay, we find the tripartite epigraphic blazon, which is the form reserved for the sultan, but instead of including the sultan's name it contains the *shahada*, the formula stating that there is no God but Allah and Muhammad is His Prophet.

Some internal decorative features remained constant throughout the entire Mamluk period, such as the polychrome marble dado of the sanctuary and the qamariyyas, but there were also short-lived fashions, such as the decoration of mihrabs with glass mosaics. Other features evolved steadily over a long period of time, such as the marble inlay of pavements.

The floors of mosques and mausoleums were paved either with stone or with polychrome inlaid marble, which could be quite lavish (Fig. 42). It is not always possible to tell the extent to which Comité restorations are involved in their present configuration, nor should one exclude modifications introduced in the Ottoman period. It is also not certain when the Mamluks began to pave open courtyards. The pavement of Qalawun's madrasa is described in the waqf deed as made of polychrome marble. The earliest extant open courtyard to display a polychrome marble pavement is that of Shaykhu's mosque. In the mosque of Sultan Hasan only the courtyard is paved with polychrome marble, which displays the most outstanding mosaic composition of the Bahri period; although the Comité restored it, the complex design must be original. In the following period, open courtyards were regularly paved with marble mosaics. In the mosque of al-Mu'ayyad, the sanctuary and the courtyard were originally paved with polychrome marble.

There is a clear evolution in the design of marble pavements. Bahri designs consisted of a variety of rectangular panels with broad geometric and braided compositions exclusively associated with pavements, but in the fifteenth century more delicate and intricate mosaic compositions appeared, which also included arabesques and other motifs borrowed from wall decoration. In Barsbay's mosque in the cemetery, the style of the floor mosaics recalls the cosmatesque decoration of Qalawun's mausoleum walls; the marble may have been taken from an earlier building. Some mosques have a polychrome pavement but no dado, as in the cases of Qadi 'Abd al-Basit, Barsbay in the cemetery, and Qaytbay. In others sanctuaries, however, like al-Mu'ayyad's and al-Ghawri's mosques, the walls as well as the floors were decorated. Almost all royal mausoleums have polychrome marble dado and pavement. In al-Ghawri's complex, the sabil

Fig. 43. Ceiling of Qaytbay's sabil-maktab at Saliba.

pavement displays unprecedented intricate star compositions. The adornment of some dados with marble roundels, which seem to have been sliced from ancient columns, was a borrowing from pavement design. We find such roundels in the sanctuaries of al-Mu'ayyad and al-Ghawri.

The increasing emphasis on floor decoration corresponds to the decreasing dimensions of courtyards, revealing at the same time inspiration from residential architecture, where the central marble fountain of the reception hall was an eye-catching device.

There is a general resemblance between the design of courtyard pavements and late Mamluk carpets, based on a geometric division of a rectangular space, consisting of a central motif surrounded by rectangular or polygonal compartments. In the mausoleum of al-Muzaffar Baybars and the mosque of Barquq, and, according to Maqrizi, in the madrasa of Taybars, the inlaid patterns were shaped as mihrab niches parallel to the qibla wall. The latter used to be covered on Fridays with carpets that were woven with mihrab patterns.[63] It thus appears that the decorated floors did not make carpets superfluous.

The Mamluk craftsmen were not imaginative in the design of capitals, for which they did not develop their own style.

Rather, they retained the inherited bell-shaped capital, which was also used for the bases of columns. They also relied more often on capitals of pre-Islamic origins, and occasionally on spoils from Crusader buildings in Palestine and Syria, which they used to flank exterior and interior decorative niches and mihrabs. The possibility that Mamluk craftsmen copied pre-Islamic and Gothic capitals to fill gaps cannot be excluded. Another use of spoils was to build the threshold of mosques with ancient Egyptian stone blocks, many of which are no longer *in situ*, having been removed to the Egyptian Museum.[64] The significance of this custom seems to be apotropaic.

One of the glories of Mamluk art that still requires investigation is the fact that the painting and gilding of wooden ceilings often recalls book illumination (Fig. 43). The remains of painting on the ceiling of Barsbay's complex in the city, for example, show rosettes that are similar to illumination patterns in a Koran manuscript of Sultan Sha'ban.[65] The ceilings of sabils were always lavishly painted, as they were seen by all those who reached through the window grille for a cup of water. Wood was used for inscription bands around courtyards of Bahri madrasas. Wooden tie beams stretched across arches were also used for the suspension

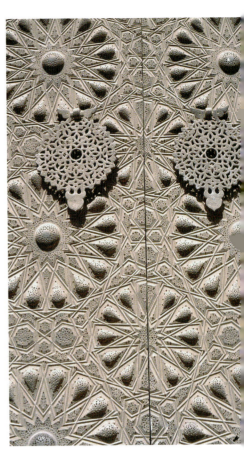

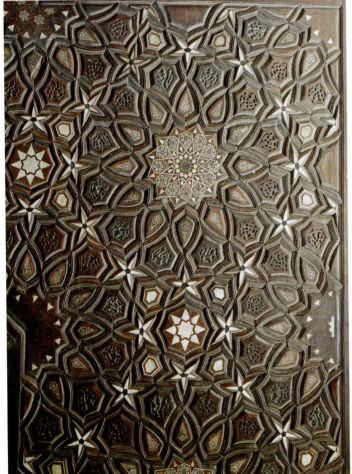

Fig. 44. [above left] The minbar of the mosque of Qijmas al-Ishaqi.

Fig. 45. [above right] The bronze door of Sultan Hasan, at the mosque of al-Mu'ayyad, detail.

of lamps and usually painted. Carved and painted wood appears in the muqarnas transitional zones of domes and ceilings.

Waqf documents indicate that turned wood, a Cairene speciality, was used for lanterns, loggias, the doors of niches that held water jars, and screen walls, such as those of Qalawun's mausoleum and Maridani's sanctuary.

Among the artefacts associated with religious buildings, the wooden minbar occupied a prominent place (Figs 44, 46).[66] Many splendid examples are still *in situ*, along with windows, doors and kursis or benches for Koran readers; they, too, need to be surveyed and studied.[67] Several craftsmen's signatures on minbars have been recorded by Hasan 'Abd al-Wahhab.[68] One of them was in the mosque of Abu 'l-Ma'ati in Damietta; the woodworker Ahmad Ibn Yusuf dated his work to 771/1369. It is also remarkable that the woodworker Ahmad Ibn 'Isa al-Dimyati (d. 1492) was honoured with a biographical entry in Sakhawi's encyclopedia, and credited for having made the minbars of the mosques of Abu Bakr Ibn Muzhir, al-Ghamri

Fig. 46. Detail of the minbar of al-Ghamri in the mosque of Barsbay in the cemetery.

(c.1480),[69] and the sanctuary of Mecca; the first is *in situ*, the second, a magnificent specimen, is now in the khanqah of Barsbay in the cemetery. Ahmad was born in Damietta, which is still famous today for its woodwork, and worked in Cairo.[70] His son, Muhammad, learned the carpenter's craft from his father, but he practised the career of a scholar.[71] Another contemporary woodworker was 'Ali Ibn Tanin, who signed his name on the magnificent minbar of the mosque of Abu 'l-'Ila, founded c.1485.[72] Normally the kursi as well as the dikka and the windows and doors of a mosque would be made in the same style as the minbar, and their patterns always consisted of geometric star compositions. Whereas the Bahri minbars were largely monochrome, those of the following period combined wood with ivory, and sometimes also included elements of silver and gold. In the Circassian period they were usually inscribed with the founder's name, and sometimes also included the foundation date of the mosque. Unlike the Ottomans, the Mamluks did not favour built-in stone or marble minbars, although two minbars made of marble and one of stone survive, and Maqrizi mentioned a marble minbar in the mosque of al-Khatiri, which has not survived.[73] The stone minbar added by Qaytbay to the khanqah of Faraj emulates the geometric decoration of woodwork on the sides, but its rail is carved in the style of architectural decoration.

A mosque's main door was made of wood clad with sheet bronze (Fig. 45). More, too, needs to be known about their metalworking techniques and patterns. Since Fatimid times, geometric star compositions were the characteristic feature of door decoration, but the bookbinding pattern was also already current in the early Bahri period. It consists of a bronze central medallion and quarter medallions in the corners, pierced with arabesques to reveal the wooden ground behind them. A door of this style, which is in the Islamic Museum in Cairo, made during the reign of Qalawun, bears the name of the emir Shams al-Din Sunqur al-Tawil.[74] This pattern was also used in the door of Uljay al-Yusufi's madrasa and frequently in fifteenth-century monuments. However, Barquq, 'Abd al-Ghani al-Fakhri and Ghawri returned to the full bronze surface in their main entrance doors. The most lavish examples are the doors of Sultan Hasan's mosques; besides the main door, which is at the mosque of al-Mu'ayyad Shaykh, the one between the mausoleum and the prayer hall is remarkable, inlaid with silver and gold floral motifs with Chinese lotus flowers. As a unique occurrence, also, the marble minbar of this mosque has a bronze door.

Epigraphy

Neither programmatic intentions nor an evolution in the selection of Koranic inscriptions are discernible in Mamluk epigraphy. The content and disposition of Mamluk monumental inscriptions combined routine with individual choices. The use of the Verse of the Throne on the drum of funerary domes was universal, as was the Koranic verse 11, 44, which refers to the qibla, traditionally inscribed on mihrabs.[75] However, the inscriptions of the mihrab of Zayn al-Din Yusuf and the mosque of Zayn al-Din Yahya in Bulaq are not Koranic, and the mihrab of Sarghitmish includes the Verse of the Throne.

Although the rule seems to have been the absence of rules in the choice of Koranic texts,[76] historical inscriptions were more premeditated, and, occasionally, as in the case of the fountain of the emir Ya'qub Shah al-Mihmandar commemorating Qaytbay's victory over the Ottomans, intended to celebrate a specific event.

In a few cases, prayers and invocations were inscribed, as on the dome of Aydumur al-Bahlawan (1346) and the mosque of Ulmas al-Hajib. Qaytbay's inscription on his wakala, with which he endowed the holy city of Medina, is a pious poem, which might have been his own composition.[77] Poetry was rare in Mamluk religious buildings except in the mausoleum of Sunqur al-Sa'di, which was inscribed with excerpts from Hariri's *Maqamat*, and in the mausoleum of Qurqumas, inscribed with excerpts of Busiri's *Burda*, a hymn on the Prophet. The prayer formula *a'udhu bi-'l-llah min al-shaytan al-rajim*, 'I implore God to protect me against Satan the cursed', which always precedes the *basmala* in recitations, was occasionally applied on inscriptions. It occurs in the sanctuaries of Sultan Hasan, Inal,[78] in the sabil of Qaytbay in Saliba street, in his mosque in Rawda, and in the mausoleum of Qansuh Abu Sa'id (1499).[79]

Royal buildings were generally more extensively inscribed than others. Elsewhere, the density of inscriptions varied greatly. Some monuments are almost bare of inscriptions, such as the mosque of Abu Bakr Ibn Muzhir, whereas the mosque of Azbak al-Yusufi, built only slightly later, is full of inscriptions. In some cases a band usually dedicated to an inscription has not been filled in, as those on the facade of Sanjar's double mausoleum and along the courtyard of Sultan Hasan's mosque.

Facades were, as a rule, carved with an inscription band and a gilded tiraz, and foundation inscriptions usually run across the portal. The absence of a tiraz band along the facades of al-Nasir's mosque at the Citadel, and of an inscription band across the portal, is remarkable; the foundation text is written instead on a slab above the doors, as is the case at the mosque of al-Zahir Baybars.

Inscriptions on minarets were placed beneath the balconies, but not all minarets were inscribed. Some inscriptions are only Koranic, others are historical.

Mamluk monumental calligraphy is distinct from book calligraphy. The style of monumental inscriptions is *thuluth*, sometimes integrating elements of *muhaqqaq*;[80] the latter was the prevailing style in Mamluk Koran manuscripts. Kufic script, which plays an exceptional role in Sultan Hasan's mosque, was revived in

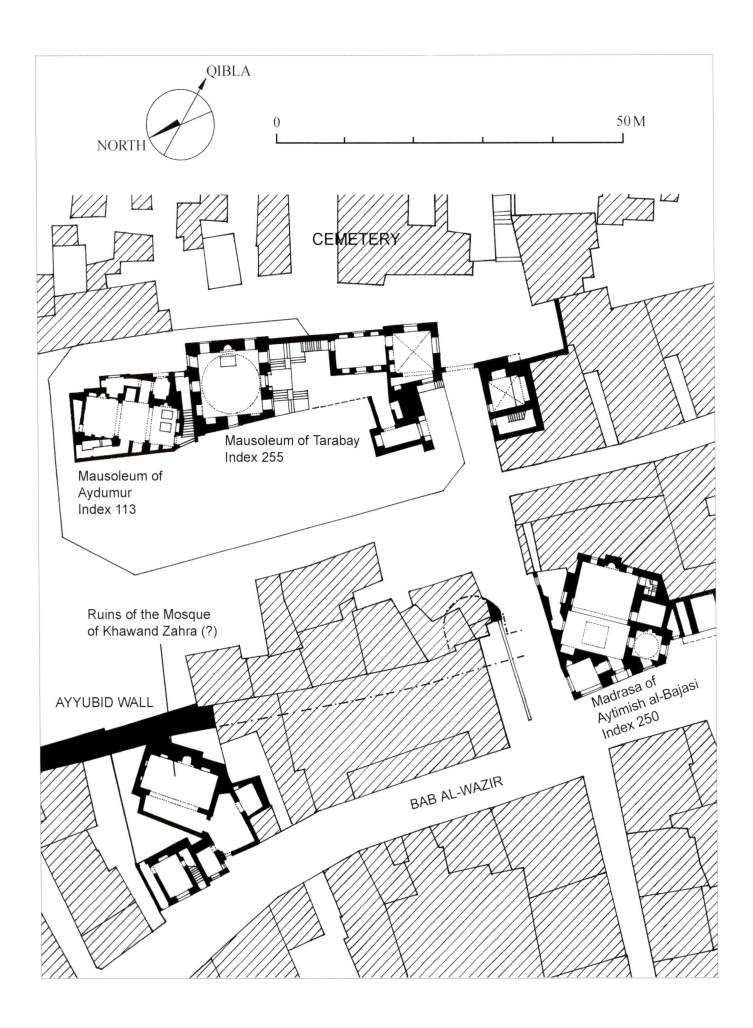

QIBLA

NORTH

0   50 M

CEMETERY

Mausoleum of Tarabay
Index 255

Mausoleum of
Aydumur
Index 113

Ruins of the Mosque
of Khawand Zahra (?)

AYYUBID WALL

Madrasa of
Aytimish al-Bajasi
Index 250

BAB AL-WAZIR

marble inlay in the interiors of fifteenth-century mosques, starting perhaps with Yashbak's northern domed mosque. An inlaid marble frieze, above the dado of the mosque of Jawhar al-Lala, with pseudo-Kufic patterns, anticipates the revival of the Kufic script, which is also a phenomenon of late Mamluk metalwork. Square Kufic, which appears for the first time in the marble panels of Qalawun's mausoleum, was often used subsequently, and also in woodwork, as can be seen on the minbar that is at present in the mosque of Barsbay in the cemetery.

The reign of al-Ghawri witnessed a renaissance of calligraphy. The style of the carved tiraz in his religious complex is remarkably beautiful, as are the interior Kufic and *thuluth* inscriptions inlaid in marble. The calligraphic images of birds, vases and lamps, and mirror compositions, in his mausoleum were innovations that continued in Ottoman calligraphy.

Epigraphy is not always helpful when trying to define the function of a monument. As will often be pointed out in the following catalogue, there is a general discrepancy between the monumental epigraphy and the waqf document in the definition of a foundation. Many late Mamluk mosques are defined by their inscriptions as a madrasa, although their waqf deeds clearly indicate that they were only mosques.[81] The term 'turba' is commonly used in inscriptions of mausoleums, and on the facades of religious complexes that include a mausoleum, such as the madrasa of the emir Aytimish al-Bajasi (1383) in Tabbana street,[82] and the khanqah of Sultan Faraj in the northern cemetery. In the latter, however, another inscription mentions the term 'khanqah'.[83] Furthermore, the neutral term 'makan' was commonly used on civil architecture, but it also appears on religious monuments, as in the funerary complexes of Sanjar, the khanqah of Shaykhu, the mosque of Faraj called Duhaysha and the funerary complex of Tarabay (1503–4).[84] The epigraphy masons were not always perfect; as the catalogue will show, mistakes of spelling, and even dating, occurred in the inscriptions.

Oddities

Many irregularities in Mamluk monuments can be attributed to the urban constraints that confronted the architect, who was obsessed with the street perspective and restricted by the Mecca orientation. However, there are also oddities that cannot be explained by these factors. For example, the mosque of Sitt Hadaq, also called Miska, which is built on the hypostyle plan with piers facing the courtyard, has a mihrab that is positioned awkwardly off the axis of the building. Even less understandable, albeit less pronounced, is the off-axis position of the mihrab of Faraj's

Fig. 47. [opposite] The mausoleum of Tarabay at Bab al-Wazir.

Fig. 48. The mausoleum dome of Tarabay.

khanqah, a monument that can be considered a masterpiece of masonry and design. Although it is hardly noticeable, this mistake could have been eliminated even subsequently without much difficulty.

The most conspicuous oddity in Mamluk architecture appears in the mausoleum dome of the emir Sayf al-Din Tarabay al-Sharifi (1504), built next to a small gate opening on the cemetery in the Bab al-Wazir quarter (Figs 48, 49).[85] The extraordinary feature here is the way the southwest corner of the rectangular base of its transitional zone has been set askew in relation to the corner of the walls below, so that we see two corners at variance with one another instead of being aligned. The deviation of the dome base from the alignment of the western facade is towards the south and Mecca. Such a deviation is not unusual in Mamluk architecture; we see it in the mausoleums of al-Nasir Muhammad and Barsbay in the city. There, however, it is kept behind the facade wall and does not protrude beyond it. Here, by contrast, it has been emphasized by twisting the corner of the building in a visible manner that attracts attention and provokes surprise. It seems to signal the correct orientation of the mausoleum, which, along with the

Fig. 49. The mausoleum dome of Tarabay, dome base.

gate and the wall connected to it, is oriented too far to the east; it amounts to at least 17° from the orientation of the mosques of Aqsunqur, Manjaq and Aytimish al-Bajasi in the vicinity (Fig. 47).[86] In this case the patron could have been particularly scrupulous to advertise the correction. This is only a symbolic correction, however; the dome base could not be twisted as far as the Mecca orientation requires, otherwise it would have almost intersected the square of the mausoleum chamber.

A decorative oddity appears in the loggia of Emir Mamay's palace built in 1496. The capitals of its columns are lotus-shaped in Ancient Egyptian style. This is the only extant artistic reference to Ancient Egypt in Cairene Islamic architecture; the cornice with reed or papyrus motif on the minarets of Qalawun, noticed by Creswell and repeated on the minarets of Shaykhu and Manjaq, is rather ambiguous and could be accidental rather than an intentional imitation.[87]

Appendix to Chapter 10

Building Materials
and Construction Methods

by Philipp Speiser

Building materials

Little has been published on the building technology used by the Mamluks. In 1887 Julius Franz Pasha, chief architect of the *Comité de la Conservation des Monuments d'Art Arabe* in Cairo, published his observations on the two topics in his book *Die Baukunst des Islams*.[88] In 1892 *L'Art arabe* appeared, written by Jules Bourgoin, first director of the College of Fine Arts in Cairo and also a member of the Comité, containing some detailed observations. More recently Jacques Revault made important contributions to this subject in the volume of *Palais et Maisons du Caire* dedicated to the Mamluk period.[89] Michael Burgoyne's observations on construction methods and materials used in the Mamluk monuments of Jerusalem are the most recent and accurate so far.[90]

As mentioned earlier in this book, ancient monuments yielded an enormous amount of building material: pharaonic columns and capitals of granite, and Roman ones made of porphyry gained from the Egyptian Mons Claudianus.[91] It is unlikely that the Mamluks themselves quarried granite or porphyry. But its use was very much in fashion. In some instances marble columns were painted red, as in the madrasa of al-Nasir Muhammad in Cairo. According to Franz Pasha, the quarries of pharaonic and Roman times were not used in the Islamic period. Whereas hard stone, such as granite, was preferably taken from ancient ruins,[92] the Mamluks quarried limestone from the Muqattam hill in the area of al-Jabal al-Ahmar.[93] It was carried in carts drawn by oxen to the construction sites, which gave the stone blocks the name *hajar 'ajjali* because of the wheeled vehicles (*'ajal*) that transported them.[94]

Fig. 50. Structure of a late Mamluk wall.

Marble was quarried in Edfu and Aswan in Upper Egypt as well as in Alexandria and in the vicinity of Cairo, but it was rarely of good quality. Superior marble came from various Roman monuments in the Nile valley and the Delta.[95]

Until the thirteenth century, forests in Upper Egypt provided Cairo with wood, which was later replaced with imports from Syria, Anatolia and Europe. Sometimes expeditions were sent to Cilicia in pursuit of wood.[96] Besides local palm trunks used for structural purposes within the walls of modest buildings, sycamore and conifer woods were imported. The best quality existed in the cedar forests situated in today's Lebanon. Local trees, mainly palm trees, sycamores and various types of acacia, yielded a poor quality of timber that was, therefore, hardly used in building.

For the structural parts of their buildings, the Mamluk builders used stone masonry, red brick bonded with lime mortar, timber and sometimes marble, granite and porphyry elements. The structural parts of roofs and ceilings were made of timber, which was also used for stairs, small domes, ceilings, loggias, screens and railings. Timber was also used in the casings of ceilings, lintels, door frames, door leaves and frieze panels.

The analysis of historic mortars reveals a mixture of slaked lime and sand to which sometimes a small proportion of gypsum was added. In some cases lime mortar was mixed with small quantities of sieved charcoal or crushed red brick; those additives slowed the drying process down and therefore the mortar became much harder and water-resistant. Wall plaster had more or less the same composition as the ordinary lime mortar but was often reinforced with flax fibres.[97] For the rubble core of cavity walls, clay – mainly Nile mud – was used in large quantities.

Construction methods

Masonry

Three types of stone masonry are most common in Cairo: A) facings of dressed stone; B) plastered rough stones; or C) a mixture of both. All three follow the principle of a cavity wall formed by an inner and outer shell made of stone, and an inner core made of rubble and clay.

Dressed stone masonry shows a large format (approx. 65 to 70 cm x 35 to 40 cm x 35 to 40 cm). Rough masonry used smaller-sized (50 to 70 cm x 20 to 25 cm x 30 cm) stones (Figs 50, 51).

In Egypt especially, brick was very much in use, probably more than in Palestine and Syria. Brick was used mainly because of its reduced weight for upper storeys, internal cross-walls, tunnel vaults, domes (until the fourteenth century) and, because of its water resistance, public baths. Apart from those technical qualities it had the advantage of being cheap to produce in a country where clay was easily available. The brick structure was built according to the classical order with header and stretcher, and was occasionally reinforced with horizontal timber beams.[98]

Foundations

Foundations were usually conceived as masonry with a rubble core using rough stones (in Egypt called *dabsh*) of the following dimensions: 50 to 70 cm x 20 to 25 cm x 30 cm for the two facing

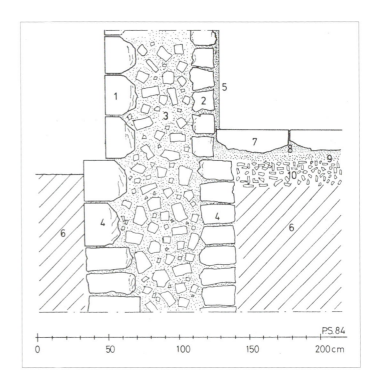

Fig.51. Load-bearing cavity wall (P. Speiser). [1] dressed stone facing; [2] rough stone; [3] rubble core; [4] foundation; [5] plaster coating; [6] soil; [7] flagstone; [8] mortar; [9] sand.

walls. The foundations were slightly wider than the masonry on top of it. The depth of the footing trench depended on the building ground and the height and weight of the structure itself.

Pavements

Three types of pavements can be identified. Limestone flags (thickness 15 to 25 cm) were, because of their weight, used on the ground floor only.[99] For upper floors much thinner lime-stone slabs (thickness c.5 cm) were laid out.[100] Both types were arranged in a longitudinal or diagonal fashion on a thick layer of sand and lime mortar. The joints were grouted with diluted gypsum afterwards, and the surface flattened. According to the importance of the building, floors were covered by mosaics made of marble and other hard stones.

Stairs

Stairs usually have one, two or four flights; spindle stairs are found in minarets only. The materials used were timber, stone or, in some cases, red brick. In Cairo the Mamluks favoured a special type of self-supporting stair, which was assembled in the following manner. After tracing the course of the stairs on the walls, the horizontal support structure was put in place (course by course), consisting of small limestone slabs bound together with gypsum. The substructure under each landing was slightly curved and was left to dry for several days. Then the individual steps, consisting of a vertical and horizontal tread, were built. First the vertical element was positioned, and then

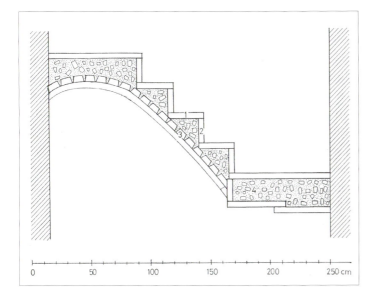

Fig. 52. Section of a self-supporting staircase made of limestone slabs (P. Speiser). [1] step; [2] reed; [3] supporting arch; [4] rubble core.

the cavity between the horizontal tread and the substructure was filled with a mixture of rubble and lime mortar. Finally, the horizontal tread, embedded in lime mortar, was put in place. This process continued until the last step. Once the mortar was dry the stair was statically self-supporting. Clearly, such a sophisticated construction needed specialized craftsmen; a small number of craftsmen still practised this skill in Cairo in the late twentieth century (Fig. 52).[101]

Roof and ceiling

Ceilings and roofs were usually flat or domed, rarely vaulted. The load was carried by beams mainly made out of cedar (their dimensions varying according to the span), on top of which palm-fibre mats were spread, preventing sand and dust descending from the upper layers and acting as a separating layer. Over the mats was placed a course of rubble mixed with clay or lime mortar (thickness 10 to 15 cm). The top layer, in the case of an internal space, would consist of the floor pavement.

For roofing, a very thick layer of mortar containing especially water-resistant clay (*tina aswally*) was spread out, and subsequently tamped.[102] In one instance the upper layer over the beams consisted of cylindrical ceramic vessels placed upside down. The reason for this must have been to reduce weight, or for insulation against the outside temperature.[103]

When ceilings were decorated, exposed beams were covered on three sides with decorated panels, and the interspace between beams was divided by small transverse beams, forming caissons.[104] Technically more elaborate are the suspended ceilings. Decorated planks or grilles with hexagonal openings closed by cups of papier mâché were fixed underneath the beams.[105]

Vaults

Vaults were often used to cover rooms located in basements or on the lower floors. The most common type is the simple or straight vaulting, made of stone or red brick.[106] It was used frequently to cover corridors and other narrow rooms. Larger spaces and iwans were covered in a similar way, and in some cases also by cross-vaults.[107] Vaults made of brick were usually covered with plaster. In the case of stone, plastering depended on the treatment of the vault's surface. In order to ensure the distribution of vertical loading, a thick layer of rubble mixed with clay or lime mortar was spread on top of it.

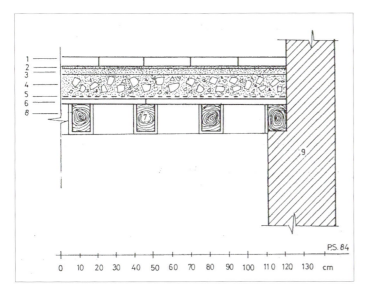

Fig. 53. Ceiling with exposed beams (P. Speiser). [1] limestone slabs; [2] mortar; [3] sand; [4] rubble; [5] mats made of palm fibre; [6] underfloor; [7] beam; [8] varced lining; [9] masonry.

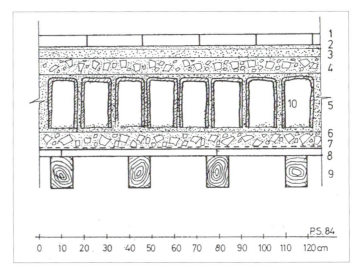

Fig. 54. Ceiling with vessels made of burnt clay (P. Speiser). [1] limestone slabs; [2] mortar; [3] sand; [4] rubble; [5] mortar; [6] rubble; [7] mats made of palm fibre; [8] underfloor; [9] beam. [10] cylindrical vessels made of burnt clay.

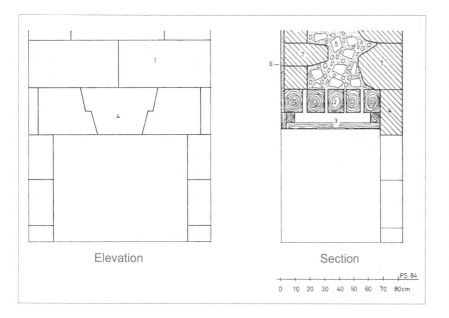

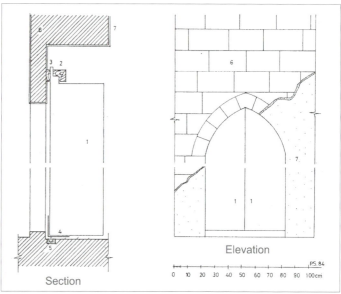

Fig. 55. Lintels in a two-tier wall (P. Speiser). [1] dressed stone lacing; [2] lintel beams; [3] cover of lintel; [4] joggled keystone; [5] rubble core; [6] plaster; [7] rough stone.

Arches and lintels

In terms of structure, the most important part of any opening in the masonry is the treatment of its upper part. The two basic solutions to this are either an arch formed by brick or wedge-shaped stones, or a lintel. Concerning the latter, several solutions were in use, depending on the masonry and the taste of the builders. Lintels in Cairo were usually mixed constructions, in that only the visible part was made of joggled stone, or in some

cases made of a thin stone revetment blending in with the dressed masonry of the facade. The remaining thickness of the wall was taken up by a series of timber beams. In the case of a plastered wall all the lintels were made of wood. Lintels in Jerusalem were, instead, made of solid joggled stonework. In many cases relieving arches made of stone or brick were placed above.[108]

Doors

If the opening featured a lintel and the walls were plastered, a timber frame was fastened onto the masonry, which is the most common way of installing a door. If the opening featured an arch, a timber frame was very difficult to fix; consequently, the door leaf was fastened behind a short recess (of the surrounding masonry) serving as a frame. Sometimes the door leaves were reinforced by strips of forked iron nailed on the leaves underneath.[109]

Fig. 57. Door without frame (P. Speiser). [1] double-leafed door; [2] cross-beam; [3] cylindrical socket; [4] metal spindle; [5] socket; [6] brick masonry; [7] plaster.

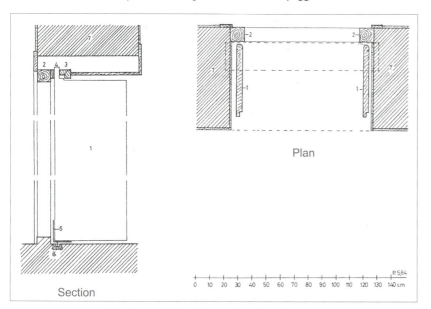

Fig. 56. Door with timber frame (P. Speiser). [1] double-leafed door; [2] frame; [3] cross-beam; [4] cylindrical socket; [5] metal spindle; [6] socket; [7] masonry.

Windows

Windows in hot climates are intended to introduce light and fresh air, and in most cases during the Mamluk period they were filled with grilles made of forked iron. The famous wooden *mashrabiyya* was, according to Franz Pasha, introduced in the Circassian period, and was much in fashion under the Ottomans, when timber might have become cheaper. In winter, windows were closed with timber boards or cloth. In some madrasas, examples of internal wooden shutters have survived, but it is unclear to what extent they were also used in domestic architecture.[110] Standard window openings consisted sometimes of timber frames into which the iron bars of the grille were inserted, or the bars were inserted directly into the stone masonry.[111] Occidental-type windows with movable wings and stained glass were unknown at that time.

Windows with stucco grilles filled with coloured glass consisted of a timber frame in which two layers of stucco were fixed, which were subsequently carved and their openings closed by pieces of white and coloured glass. They were protected from the outside with grilles made of copper wire fixed onto the facade.

Conclusion

Mamluk building materials are limited to stone, red brick and timber. There are no specific Mamluk building methods. They evolved from Fatimid and Ayyubid architectures, as well as from Crusader architecture and building technology.

Fig. 58. The minaret of Qawsun and the Sultaniyya double mausoleum on the right, with the mausoleum dome of Qawsun on the left.

NORTHERN
CEMETERY

To 48, 49 & 50

BULAQ

RIVER NILE

RAWDA ISL

hippodrome

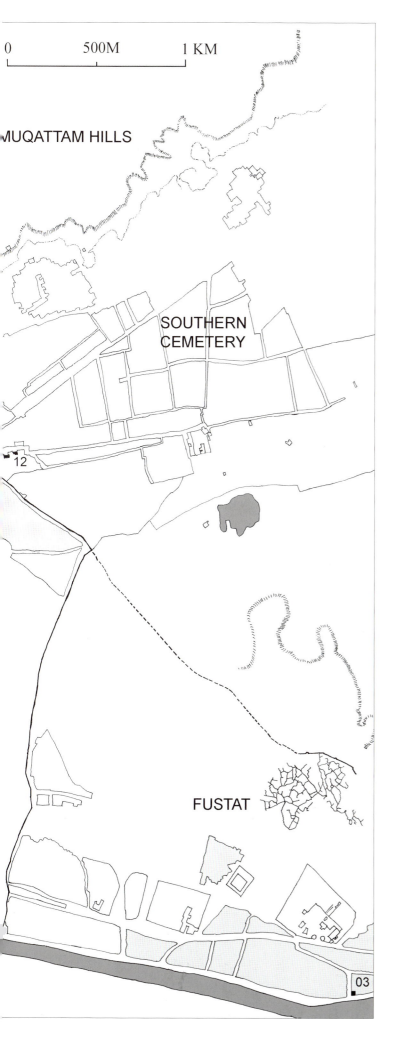

1   The mausoleum of al-Salih Najm al-Din Ayyub
2   The mausoleum of Shajar al-Durr
3   The madrasa of al-Mu'izz Aybak
4   The madrasa of Sultan al-Zahir Baybars
5   The Great Mosque of Sultan al-Zahir Baybars at Husayniyya
6   The mausoleum of the Abbasid caliphs
7   The mausoleum of Fatima Khatun (Umm al-Salih)
8   The funerary complex of Sultan al-Mansur Qalawun
9   The funerary madrasa of Sultan al-Ashraf Khalil
10 The mausoleum and ribat of Ahmad Ibn Sulayman al-Rifa'i
11 The so-called mausoleum of Mustafa Pasha or ribat of Emir Janibak
12 The zawiya of Shaykh Zayn al-Din Yusuf
13 The funerary madrasa of Sultan al-Nasir Muhammad Ibn Qalawun
14 The funerary complex of Emir Sanjar al-Jawli
15 The funerary khanqah of Sultan al-Muzaffar Baybars (al-Jashnakir)
16 The funerary khanqah of Emir Sunqur al-Sa'di
17 The New Mosque (al-Jami' al-Jadid) of Sultan al-Nasir Muhammad
18 The mosque of Emir Qawsun
19 The mosque of al-Nasir Muhammad at the Citadel
20 The mosques of Emirs Almalik al-Juqandar (A) and Ahmad al-Mihmandar (B)
21 The funerary mosque of Emir Ulmas al-Hajib
22 The Friday mosque of Emir Altinbugha al-Maridani
23 The funerary mosque of Emir Aslam al-Baha'i al-Silahdar
24 The mosque of Emir Aqsunqur al-Nasiri
25 The mosque and khanqah of Emir Shaykhu al-'Umari
26 The madrasa of Emir al-Sayfi Sarghitmish
27 The madrasa and Friday mosque of Sultan Hasan
28 The Sultaniyya mausoleum
29 The madrasa of Emir Sabiq al-Din Mithqal al-Anuki
30 The madrasa of Umm al-Sultan Sha'ban, Khawand Baraka
31 The madrasa of Emir Uljay al-Yusufi
32 The funerary complex of Sultan Barquq
33 The funerary khanqah of Sultan Faraj Ibn Barquq
34 The mosque and sabil-maktab called Duhaysha
35 The funerary complex of Sultan al-Mu'ayyad
36 The hospital of Sultan al-Mu'ayyad
37 The madrasa of 'Abd al-Ghani al-Fakhri
38 The mosque of Qadi 'Abd al-Basit
39 The funerary complex of Sultan Barsbay in the city
40 The funerary khanqah of Barsbay in the northern cemetery
41 The madrasa of Sultan Jaqmaq at Darb Sa'ada
42 The funerary complex of Emir Taghribirdi
43 The mosque of Qadi Zayn al-Din Yahya along the Khalij (Azhar street)
44 The mosque of Qadi Yahya at Bulaq
45 The mosque of Qadi Yahya at Habbaniyya
46 The funerary complex of Sultan Inal
47 The funerary complex of Sultan Qaytbay
48 The dome of Yashbak at Matariyya (today Qubba)
49 The domed mosque of Yashbak at Husayniyya/Raydaniyya, Qubbat al-Fadawiyya
50 The zawiya of Shaykh Damirdash
51 The mosque of Qadi Abu Bakr Ibn Muzhir
52 The funerary mosque of Emir Qijmas al-Ishaqi
53 The sabil-maktab of Sultan Qaytbay in Saliba street
54 The mosque of Emir Azbak al-Yusufi
55 The cistern of Ya'qub Shah al-Mihmandar
56 The funerary complex of Sultan al-Ghawri near the hippodrome
57 The two mosques (A, B) of Sultan al-Ghawri near the hippodrome
58 The funerary mosque of Emir Qanibay Qara
59 The funerary complex of Emir Qurqumas
60 The funerary madrasa of Emir Khayrbak

Fig. 59. Map of Cairo, key to monuments.

Fig. 60. Panoramic view of the northern cemetery and the Citadel in the background, from the minaret of Qaytbay with his dome in the foreground.

–11–

The Successors of the Ayyubids

1. The mausoleum of al-Salih Najm al-Din Ayyub (1250)[1]

The first two monuments of the Mamluk period were simultaneously a homage to the last Ayyubid sultan, al-Salih Najm al-Din, and a celebration of the new era. They are perhaps the most politically significant monuments of Mamluk architectural history. Their founder was a woman, Shajar al-Durr, the widow of the last Ayyubid sultan and herself the first Mamluk ruler, whose career personifies the transition.

Shajar al-Durr built a mausoleum in honour of her husband and her own funerary madrasa in the same year, 1250. The circumstances suggest that they must have been built almost simultaneously. During that year, Shajar al-Durr occupied Egypt's throne for a period of three months (May–July), to bridge the gap of transition and uncertainty following al-Salih's death. The end of her reign was not, however, the end of her power, as she continued to exert political authority under the rule of her successor, al-Mu'izz Aybak, whom she married after her abdication. Seven years later she killed him, and was herself killed by members of his clan.

Shajar al-Durr's first husband, the Ayyubid sultan al-Salih, died during the French invasion of the Egyptian city of Mansura, which ended with the triumph of his Mamluk soldiers. As the dead sultan could not be granted the honour of a timely royal burial, his corpse was brought secretly from Mansura to his palace at Rawda, to prevent the enemy from taking advantage of his death. There it remained almost a year, from Sha'ban 647/November 1249 to Rajab 648/October 1250.

Fig. 61. The mausoleum of al-Salih Najm al-Din Ayyub.

Shajar al-Durr must have built al-Salih's mausoleum between his death and the burial ceremony, which was attended by Aybak and the Ayyubid shadow-sultan, the child al-Ashraf Musa. Besides honouring the sultan, who had been the godfather of the Mamluks, al-Salih's mausoleum was a memorial to a Mamluk victory. A marble inscription slab above the entrance commemorates al-Salih as having died bravely in the jihad against the 'defeated Franks' (*al-faranj al-makhdhulin*) in the town of Mansura, although they were not yet defeated at the time of his death. This is a rather standard formula referring to enemies.

The allegiance to al-Salih is confirmed by the status his madrasa acquired in the early Mamluk period. Al-Mu'izz Aybak established in its premises the *mazalim* court, an institution that channelled petitions from the population to the ruler and had occupied a significant place in the Ayyubid State. Sultan al-Zahir Baybars eventually transferred this court to the Citadel, but the madrasa continued to be a major tribunal where the chief judges sat, as did Ibn Khaldun when he was appointed chief qadi of the Maliki rite.

Aybak also installed the ceremony of investiture of new emirs at the mausoleum of al-Salih. After the construction of Qalawun's complex, however, this ceremony was transferred there. According to al-Zahiri, who wrote in the fifteenth century, the sultans' investiture initially took place in al-Salih's mausoleum before it was transferred to the Qasr in the Citadel.[2]

The subsequent construction of al-Zahir Baybars' and Qalawun's madrasas, adjoining and facing al-Salih's mausoleum respectively, was another sign of the allegiance of the early Mamluks to their Ayyubid master; seeking his vicinity, like that of a patron saint, was a kind of aspiration towards receiving his blessing. Al-Zahir Baybars' son and successor, Baraka, enlarged the endowment of al-Salih's madrasa with the addition of the prestigious goldsmiths' market to its estate.[3]

The inscription slab of the mausoleum, which glorifies al-Salih's heroism and victory, gives the full date of his death, 15 Sha'ban 647/23 November 1249, but does not mention the date of the building or the founder's name. The date is repeated in another inscription on a wooden frieze inside the mausoleum.

With the omission of the foundation's date, the gap between the sultan's death and his burial was ignored, while the omission of the founder's name bestowed on the monument a more collective identity.

In order to make room for the mausoleum on the northern side of the madrasa, the residence of the teacher of Maliki law had to be demolished. The square domed chamber (c.21 m high, 10.9 m per each side) is adjacent to the madrasa al-Salih had built earlier in 641/1243–4 in the heart of Qahira. It projects onto the street, with two facades pierced with large rectangular windows. The facades are panelled with keel-arched recesses, which include windows in their lower part, in conformity with the facade of the madrasa. The mausoleum is set askew behind the facade following the orientation towards Mecca, while the thickness of the facade wall increases to absorb the angle between the inner walls and the street-aligned facade. This device, developed in the Fatimid period, became a permanent feature of Mamluk Cairene architecture.

The profile of the funerary dome curves right above the base like the dome of Imam Shafi'i's mausoleum, and its transitional zone is stepped on the exterior corresponding to three inner tiers.

The mausoleum had the largest mihrab at that time, and is the earliest to show marble panelling. As with the mihrab of Shajar al-Durr's mausoleum, its conch was once decorated with glass mosaics, of which nothing now remains.

Whereas the architecture of the mausoleum conforms to Ayyubid tradition, the concept of attaching the founder's mausoleum to a religious building was a novelty in Cairo. With this monument and her own mausoleum, Shajar al-Durr established a tradition that was henceforth a major characteristic feature of Mamluk monumental patronage. Although Shajar al-Durr must have been inspired by Ayyubid Syria, which in turn was inspired by Seljuk Iran, where the practice of attaching a mausoleum to a religious foundation had emerged, the specific circumstances of al-Salih's death at that particular time played a decisive role in the commemoration of the last Ayyubid sultan with a funerary monument.

Shajar al-Durr appointed the vizier Baha' al-Din Ibn Hanna as supervisor of her endowments, to be succeeded by his descendants.

2. The mausoleum of Shajar al-Durr (1250)[4]

Shajar al-Durr's initiative to erect a mausoleum for al-Salih paved the way for her self-sponsored mausoleum, which was from the outset attached to a madrasa, located in the cemetery of Sayyida Nafisa. From her funerary complex only the mausoleum dome survives; it once adjoined a hammam and a palace connected to a garden.

A renovated and undated inscription with the name and titles of Shajar al-Durr indicates that the mausoleum was founded during her short reign and prior to her marriage to Aybak. It was the first royal foundation ever to be erected in this cemetery, situated to the southeast of the Citadel and north of Fustat. The cemetery was associated with saints and relatives of the Prophet, including Sayyida Ruqayya and Sayyida Nafisa, after whom the place is named. The sanctity of the cemetery might have motivated Shajar al-Durr's choice of the site, but also its vicinity to the royal residence in the Citadel would have played a role. Shajar al-Durr and Aybak abandoned al-Salih's recently founded citadel at Rawda, and returned the royal residence to the Citadel on the Muqattam hill. At that time Fustat and Qahira were still on an equal footing; the balance had not yet swung in favour of the latter. The cemetery of Sayyida Nafisa had the advantage of being located between the

Fig.62. The mausoleum of Shajar al-Durr.

two cities. The choice proved to be fortunate; although Shajar al-Durr died in disgrace, and her body was dumped from the walls of the Citadel, popular faith associated her with the sanctity of her neighbours in the cemetery, and in the long run her mausoleum acquired the status of a shrine.

A drawing made by Pascal Coste in 1823 shows a remarkable free-standing minaret in this cemetery, of a design very similar to that of al-Salih Najm al-Din's minaret in the city. It is depicted as a brick construction with a ribbed helmet atop an octagonal middle section carried by a rectangular shaft. Its decoration consists of keel-arched niches, lozenges and medallions similar to that of the dome. It stands beside the ruins of a monument that included an iwan, which the troops of the French expedition (1798–1801) had badly damaged. The only royal structure to have

Fig.63. The minaret of Shajar al-Durr (Pascal Coste).

been built in this area that would correspond to the style of the minaret was Shajar al-Durr's madrasa.

Shajar al-Durr's mausoleum is a brick construction with stucco decoration. Measuring 7 m in diameter and 14 m in height, the domed chamber is smaller than al-Salih's, and the angular and keel-shaped profile of its dome is also different. The dome rests on a two-tiered stepped transitional zone, resembling the anonymous dome commonly associated with the Abbasid caliphs, which is located near the mosque of Sayyida Nafisa in the same neighbourhood. The chamber has three doors and the mihrab is salient.

Except for the northwestern side with the axial entrance, the exterior walls are decorated with shallow keel-arched panels with medallions and lozenges in their spandrels, similar to those on the minaret of al-Salih and the one depicted by Coste. On the northwestern side, small upper niches replace the panels, leaving bare the lower part of the walls. The presence of doors instead of windows on the lateral sides suggests that it opened onto an inner space.

The interior transitional zone of the dome displays two rows of stucco keel-arched niches forming a large muqarnas alternating with tripartite windows with a corresponding profile. The niches show the remains of painting that once outlined the muqarnas composition.

Keel-arched stucco panels, finely carved in the Ayyubid manner, decorate the upper parts of the three doors and the spandrels of the mihrab niche.

The most remarkable feature is the mihrab conch, with its glass mosaic decoration showing a tree with fruits made of mother-of-pearl. The name 'Shajar al-Durr' means 'trees of pearls'. The mihrab conch is the earliest extant case of glass mosaic decoration in Cairo. The sources refer to the mosque of 'Amr as having been decorated with mosaics, probably added in the Umayyad period. It is also interesting to note that the Fatimid caliph al-Hafiz (r.1131–49) added glass decoration to the mihrab of the mausoleum of Sayyida Nafisa,[5] which is likely to have inspired the decoration of that of Shajar al-Durr.

Due to its location and its initial attachment to a madrasa, Shajar al-Durr's mausoleum has a lower architectural profile and less of an urban character than the mausoleum of al-Salih.

3. The madrasa of al-Mu'izz Aybak (1256–7)[6]

Shajar al-Durr's second husband and successor on the Mamluk throne, Mu'izz al-Din Aybak al-Turkumani, built a madrasa at the southern edge of Fustat, which disappeared a long time ago. The

Fig.64. The mausoleum of Shajar al-Durr.

Fig.65. The mausoleum of Shajar al-Durr, glass mosaic mihrab.

choice of the location is somewhat surprising considering that the ceremonial centre had already shifted to Qahira. Moreover, Aybak himself had contributed to the decline of Fustat's prestige by dismantling al-Salih's fortress at Rawda.

Although Maqrizi did not include Aybak's madrasa in his list of religious foundations, according to Ibn Duqmaq's account it was part of an important urban complex.[7] Built in 654/1256–7, shortly before Aybak's assassination, the complex was located in a commercial area near the southern gate, Bab al-Qantara. It faced on one side a square (rahba) and overlooked the Nile on the other side, with the Nilometer at the southern tip of Rawda. The madrasa was described as having an extraordinarily long vestibule, compared to which it itself appeared small.

The *mawqufat* or endowment estate consisted of a double hammam called Hammam al-Sultan, an apartment house (rab') and a commercial building called Dar al-Wakala, but earlier

known as the Dar al-Mulk. This Dar al-Mulk, which was the former palace of the Fatimid vizier al-Afdal Shahinshah, was located on the other side of the square, which was called Rahbat al-Kharrub, previously known as Rahbat al-Hinna and even earlier as Rahbat Dar al-Mulk. The evolution of the square's name from Rahbat Dar al-Mulk or 'Place of the Royal Palace' to the 'Place of the Hinna' and 'Place of the Saint John's bread' (*calgarroba*) reflects the transformation of the residence from a palace into a commercial building for agricultural products, which probably came from Upper Egypt and were unloaded at the harbour of Fustat.

The hammam was close to the Dar al-Mulk, connected to it by a vaulted passage, which led to the Nile shore. The madrasa's estates also included a share of three quarters of the land situated across the street on the rear side of the madrasa. Unlike Shajar al-Durr's madrasa, Aybak's was not a funerary structure; he was buried in an unknown grave in the cemetery.[8]

–12–

The Reign of al-Zahir Baybars

4. The madrasa of Sultan al-Zahir Baybars (1263)[1]

Al-Zahir Rukn al-Din al-Salihi Baybars, the first great Mamluk sultan, and one of the most heroic figures of Islam, was also a pious patron, who sponsored several religious foundations and erected many military, civil and palatial buildings in Egypt, Syria and the Hijaz.

The tradition of building madrasas, established by the Ayyubid rulers, was immediately adopted by their Mamluk successors. Following the example of Shajar al-Durr, Aybak and al-Muzaffar Qutuz (1259–60),[2] Baybars' first religious foundation was also a madrasa. We do not know whether Qutuz's madrasa included a domed mausoleum, but Baybars dedicated his madrasa exclusively to God: it was not to be used for his burial.[3] He also ordered that no forced labour should be employed in its construction. The madrasa taught the Shafi'i and Hanafi *madhhab*s, the former taking place in the main iwan, the latter in the opposite one; Koran and Hadith were taught in the lateral iwans.

Construction began in Rabi' II 660/March 1262 and was completed in Safar 662/December 1263. The sultan endowed it with a large apartment complex named al-Rab' al-Zahiri after its founder. The rab' was built on the street of Taht al-Rab', which runs parallel to the southern wall of Qahira, near Bab Zuwayla.

The madrasa was adjacent to al-Salih Najm al-Din's madrasa and mausoleum on the site of the Fatimid great palace. Although only a fragment of a wall survives, Maqrizi's and Evliya's descriptions, as well as pictures from the eighteenth

Fig. 66. The madrasa of al-Zahir Baybars, remains of foundation inscription.

and nineteenth centuries, convey some idea of its architecture. Its plan consisted of four iwans around a courtyard. Unless Shajar al-Durr's, Aybak's and Qutuz's madrasas were already built on this plan, which is not unlikely, Baybars' would be the earliest cruciform madrasa in Cairo.

The remains of the facade wall projects c. 10 m into the street. Evliya Celebi described the madrasa as having a three-storeyed

minaret, which was presumably beside the portal. Louis-François Cassas' drawing in the late eighteenth century shows the top of a minaret in Ottoman style, which indicates that at that time it was either entirely rebuilt or its upper structure had been replaced. This drawing, executed from the south perspective, shows only the top of the minaret, which suggests that it was located on the northern side of the portal, otherwise the shaft would have been visible in the picture. Other illustrations confirm that it was not on the southern corner. The minaret collapsed in 1874, and the madrasa was pulled down shortly afterwards except for a wall fragment. Its magnificent bronze door today adorns the entrance of the French embassy in Cairo. Its date, 661/1262–3, is written in ciphers, and is the earliest known date in Mamluk epigraphy to be written in this form.[4]

The facade was divided into recessed panels crowned with muqarnas and including the windows. The portal, a recess with a semi-vault on muqarnas, was a novelty imported from Syria, where earlier examples exist.

5. The Great Mosque of Sultan al-Zahir Baybars at Husayniyya (1267–9)[5]

The monumental mosque built by al-Zahir Baybars in the northern suburb was the first Friday mosque to be founded in Qahira for a century. The previous one was built in 1167 by the Fatimid vizier al-Salih Tala'i'.

The date inscribed on the panel of the main gate is Rabi' II 665/January 1267, seven years after al-Zahir Baybars' access to power. The damaged inscription of the southern gate also indicated, according to Max van Berchem, the same foundation date. The inscription in the dome area mentions the following year 666/1267–8. Maqrizi wrote that the construction began in Dhu'l-Hijja 666/August–September 1268, and was completed in Shawwal 667/June 1269. The mosque took one and a half years to build.

The site

The choice of the site of al-Zahir Baybars' mosque in the northern suburb of Husayniyya is not obvious. Remote from the urban centre, the site seems to have been chosen for pious reasons rather than urban considerations. In fact, this area, situated between Zuqaq al-Kuhl, a green zone along the Khalij, and the popular Husayniyya quarter, was not defined by a toponym of its own. The site was occupied at that time by a hippodrome built by Qaraqush, the vizier of Salah al-Din. Although Maqrizi associated the mosque with Husayniyya,

Fig. 67. [opposite] The madrasa of al-Zahir Baybars in context, reconstruction.

according to his own description of this quarter the mosque was not exactly there. Husayniyya in his text refers, rather, to the quarter further east, and north of Bab al-Futuh, which is not close to the Khalij shore but bordered to the east by the cemetery of Bab al-Nasr and the desert.[6] Twenty years later, the waqf document of Qalawun described the neighbourhood of Baybars' mosque as Zuqaq al-Kuhl and mentioned that it consisted of gardens.[7] This vagueness about the locality of the mosque indicates the marginality of the area.

During the reign of Katbugha, in 1295, Mongol refugees were settled in Husayniyya, in an area described by Maqrizi as previously empty (*fada'*).[8] Henceforth, and until the crises provoked by Timur's invasion, the quarter between Bab al-Futuh and Raydaniyya in the northeast became one of the most populous with markets and a number of mosques, but this did not include the neighbourhood of Baybars' mosque.

Baybars is reported to have gone in Rabi' II 665/January 1267, accompanied by a team of engineers, in search of a place suitable for his Friday mosque. His courtiers suggested the site of a pasture ground for camels, but the sultan preferred the site of his polo ground, emphasizing that this was the location of his pastimes and leisure (*wa huwa nuzhati*).[9] These words suggest the sultan's pious intention in the choice of the site, by which he intended to sacrifice his playing ground. The chronicler Baybars al-Mansuri emphasized the pious transformation of the site with the words: 'he ordered the construction of a mosque in the hippodrome of Qaraqush outside Cairo; it was converted from a polo ground to performing the adhan, and from a tournament arena to a recitation (venue) of the Koran' (*min lu'b al-suljan ila i'lan al-adhan wa min halbat al-aqran ila talawat al-qur'an*).[10]

There is also another pious interpretation, not mentioned by Maqrizi but later by Ibn Taghribirdi and Sakhawi, which is the presence in this neighbourhood of the zawiya of Shaykh Khidr, the controversial patron saint of al-Zahir Baybars, who, before he fell in disgrace, accompanied the sultan on his travels and military campaigns, and whom the sultan visited whenever he went to his mosque.[11] This zawiya was sponsored by Baybars, who endowed it with the land around it. Ibn Shaddad mentioned the vicinity of the mosque to the zawiya, and Sakhawi wrote that Baybars followed the advice of his mentor Shaykh Khidr to build a mosque there.[12] Ibn Taghribirdi also attributed the choice of the site to Shaykh Khidr.[13] The waqf document of Sultan Qalawun confirms that the zawiya was very near the mosque, separated from it by a garden.

Another significant pious association of the mosque is the fact that its dome was built with spoils from the sultan's victorious campaign against the Crusaders in Jaffa.[14] Baybars, accompanied by his sons, personally conducted the demolition work of Jaffa's citadel in 1268, and he ordered its wood to be used for the dome and its marble for the mihrab of his future

Fig.68. The mosque of al-Zahir Baybars.

mosque in Cairo. The building material, taken as a trophy from the Crusaders, conferred a pious and political significance upon the monument at a time when the Crusaders had not yet been fully evicted. The final battle would be won by al-Ashraf Khalil two decades later.

The imposing structure with its unprecedented large dome suggests that the mosque might have been conceived as a ceremonial venue, which seems to be confirmed by the historian Baybars al-Mansuri, who reported that the sultan received ambassadors in his mosque.[15]

It should also be recalled that, when Baybars installed the Abbasid caliph in Cairo, the ceremony took place in tents pitched in a garden in the northern suburb, from where the procession crossed the city, passing through Bab al-Nasr.[16] This event might have contributed to bestowing a memorial and ceremonial character on this site.

Baybars' project apparently did not include an urban scheme for the development of the neighbourhood; no commercial structures are mentioned as endowment estate that would have contributed to its urbanization. Rather, he endowed the mosque with the surrounding land, to be leased on a long-term basis.

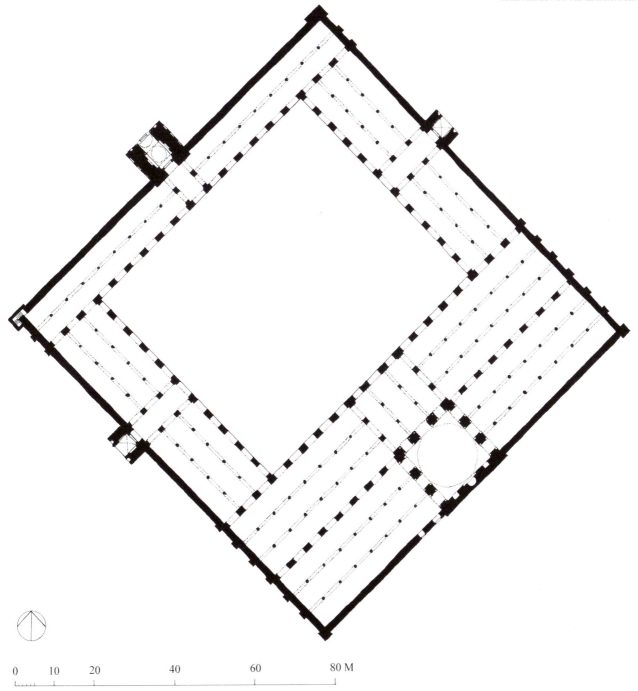

0   10   20   40   60   80 M

The layout

Fig.69. The mosque of al-Zahir Baybars.

The location of the mosque to the northwest of the city walls had the disadvantage of making the mosque turn its back on the city and on visitors coming from there. This disadvantage was compensated for by the large dome, visible at a distance centring the qibla wall, thus outweighing the absence of a portal and minaret facing the onlooker from the city.

Today the mosque is only a reminiscence of what it once was. It lacks the dome, the minarets, the original roof and most of the decoration. It is slightly over 10,000 sqm internally, and the walls are c.12m high including the crenellation. They are made of dressed stone on the exterior and plastered brick inside. Three of the four corners show

unequal rectangular buttresses; the western corner includes the staircase. Buttresses to consolidate the arcades of the prayer hall are also visible on the exterior lateral walls of the mosque.

The arched windows pierced along the upper walls of the mosque have inner and outer grilles of fine carved stucco, none of which has been preserved intact.

The plain exterior walls of the mosque belong to a different order from the facade of Baybars' madrasa, lacking the recessed panels with two rows of windows. Whereas Baybars' madrasa had an inscription band or tiraz running along its facade, as the pictures show, the mosque lacks this feature, its foundation inscriptions appearing instead in slabs above the mihrab and inside the entrance bays.

The mosque has a main axial gate and two lateral ones. All three gates project from the facade, following the model of the gate of the Fatimid mosque of al-Hakim.

The main gate is the largest of the three (11.8 m wide), projecting 8.8 m beyond the facade. Its vaulted entrance is emphasized by a cushion voussoir, a feature that characterizes Bab al-Futuh, the Fatimid city gate. The entrance arch is flanked on each side by a deep niche with a shell-shaped hood set within a rectangular recess crowned with muqarnas. Another pair of shallow keel-arched niches adorns the upper part of the wall. The side walls of the gate are carved with three shallow keel-arched recesses surmounted by lozenges and medallions of Fatimid and Ayyubid style. Niches with radiating hoods and strapwork in their spandrels are carved in the entrance passage, which is roofed with a shallow masonry dome on spherical pendentives as in the Fatimid gate Bab al-Nasr, whereas the passages of the lateral gates are roofed with a cross-vault.

Above the doorway of the main gate is a slab with the foundation inscription in *thuluth* script. The gate once supported a rectangular minaret, of which a remaining stub was depicted in the *Description de l'Egypte*, decorated with a keel arch.[17] Considering that it was carried by the portal vault, the minaret is likely to have been a light brick structure comparable to that of al-Salih Najm al-Din. Evliya mentioned three minarets, one above each gate. This description is confirmed by Ibn Shaddad, who referred to '*thalāth mabādin* [sic] '*alā thalāth abwāb*', or three *mabādin* above three gates. The word *mabādin* does not have any meaning, and is obviously a misreading of the manuscript, based very likely on a confusion of dots. If we change the dots and read '*mi'ādhin*' instead, which would be the plural of *mi'dhana*, a form that regularly occurs in Mamluk waqf documents for 'minaret', the sentence would mean 'three minarets above three gates'. As Ibn Shaddad was a contemporary of Baybars, and very well informed about his buildings, we have every reason to believe his account although today only the main gate reveals the support of a minaret. The mosque of Baybars would have had one minaret more than al-Hakim's, a number that remained unique in Mamluk architecture.

The lateral gates are smaller than the axial one, and their dimensions differ slightly, the northern being 8.1 m wide, with a projection of 4 m. Its entrance passage has an arched voussoir carved with a double zigzag. The southern gate is slightly larger, and its voussoir is carved with scallops. Their side walls lack the carved recesses of the main gate, displaying instead ablaq masonry, the second earliest occurrence in Cairo after the ablaq of the bridge of Abu 'l-Manajja, also built by Baybars.[18]

According to Maqrizi, the sultan wished the portal of his mosque (he mentions only one) to resemble that of his madrasa.

However, none of the three portals shares any architectural or decorative feature with the madrasa's portal. Perhaps Maqrizi was not thinking of a formal resemblance but a more abstract one, the originality of the design or the high quality of the craftsmanship. The portals of Baybars' mosque recall rather the projecting portal of the mosque of al-Hakim, and their vaults are citations from the Fatimid gates of Badr al-Jamali.

The maqsura

According to Qalqashandi, the maqsura in a mosque belongs to the insignia of royalty. This was the area in front of the mihrab enclosed by a grille and reserved for the monarch. The word 'maqsura' refers to the grille and the area it encloses.

Since the early history of mosque architecture, the mihrab area was emphasized by a cupola or a transept, or a combination of both, which is the case in this mosque. However, the monumentality of Baybars' dome, covering the space of nine bays, was an innovation in Cairo, and the most spectacular feature about the mosque. With a diameter of nearly 15.4 m it was equal to the dome of Imam Shafi'i, the largest in Cairo hitherto, which equalled the size of the mihrab dome of the Great Mosque of Isfahan built by Malikshah (r.1072–92). The construction of Baybars' dome, however, was not a matter of architectural prowess, because it was made of wood, like that of Imam Shafi'i. Ibn Shaddad and Evliya described it as covered with lead, also like the dome of Imam Shafi'i. According to Ibn Shaddad, it was a double-shell dome, with enough space between the shells to allow a person to pass.

Inside the sanctuary, the maqsura was screened from the prayer hall by walls pierced on both sides with three arched openings, and it was connected to the courtyard through the transept. This consisted of three naves running perpendicular to the mosque's arcades, which are parallel to the qibla wall. The two side arcades of the transept, which were connected with the prayer hall, were built with piers, the two inner ones with columns.

The maqsura with its transept presented an impressive architectural ensemble, measuring c. 20 x 36 m from the qibla wall to the court facade; it was almost like an autonomous sanctuary within the mosque. Baybars, who built a domed hall in the Citadel in 1266 and a dome in the Nilometer, and restored the Dome of the Rock in Jerusalem in 1263 and the dome of the Umayyad mosque in Damascus in 1269–70, was obviously sensitive to the solemn significance of the dome.[19] Baybars' maqsura was echoed in the Great Iwan built by Sultan al-Nasir Muhammad in the Citadel, as depicted by Louis-François Cassas and in the *Description de l'Egypte*. It had a basilical plan, with the central aisle covered by a large dome preceded by a tripartite transept.[20]

When Evliya Celebi visited Baybars' mosque in the seventeenth century he was impressed by the size and the lavishness of the painted dome. The whole qibla area was decorated with precious polychrome marble, and glass mosaics representing trees and

Fig. 70. The mosque of al-Zahir Baybars, maqsura area.

plants. At that time the neighbourhood was thinly inhabited and a public passage led through the mosque.[21]

The use of glass mosaics is not surprising considering that the mihrabs of the mausoleums of Shajar al-Durr and al-Salih Najm al-Din were similarly decorated. Baybars' mausoleum in Syria, built by his son Baraka in 1277 and completed by Qalawun in 1282, is also decorated with glass mosaics representing trees and plants.

K.A.C. Creswell has drawn a parallel between the layout of the sanctuary, with a large dome over the mihrab, and that of the Artukid mosque of Mayyafariqin, completed in 1157–8, which likewise had a dome covering nine bays. The idea of a large dome over the mihrab originated in the Great Mosque of Damascus, where the Seljuk vizier Nizam al-Mulk reconstructed an Umayyad structure, and he elaborated the concept further in the Great Mosque of Isfahan.

The four arcades face the courtyard with pointed arches supported by piers, whereas columns support the inner arches. The three minor riwaqs are composed of three aisles running parallel to the wall with a perpendicular aisle or transept on piers

Fig. 71. The mosque of al-Zahir Baybars, detail of window grille.

cutting through them to connect the gates with the courtyard. The treatment of the mosque's arcades with piers and pointed arches recalls the mosque of al-Hakim.

The arched windows in the upper wall with fine stucco grilles must have been a major decorative element in the mosque. They are set above a stucco frieze of arabesques, framed by another beautiful epigraphic band in Kufic that once ran along the whole interior.

The design of al-Zahir Baybars' mosque was not defined by the urban aesthetic criteria that characterized subsequent architecture of the Mamluks. Rather, it imposed itself on its urban environment with strict symmetry and horizontal monumentality, counterbalanced by the imposing dome and the three minarets. Whereas stone characterized the exterior decoration of the mosque, mainly in the gates, carved stucco was reserved for the interior and the double stucco grilles of the windows.

With the exception of the dome, the architecture of the mosque is in the Cairene tradition of monumental mosques. The reference to the mosque of al-Hakim is not surprising considering that Baybars' mosque was the first Friday mosque built in Cairo since the Fatimid period, and the first monumental mosque after al-Hakim's. The mosque of al-Hakim itself borrowed features from Ibn Tulun's mosque, the earliest monumental mosque in Egypt.

The stone carving on the gates, with niches, lozenges and medallions, is in the decorative tradition of al-Hakim's mosque, al-Aqmar mosque, the Ayyubid madrasa of al-Salih and the mausoleum of Shajar al-Durr. The exquisite stucco carving, which characterizes the friezes and window frames and grilles, is also rooted in the Ayyubid art of Egypt.

While the location of the mosque might have been a gesture of allegiance to Shaykh Khidr, its architecture, with the dome recalling the patron's victory over the Crusaders and also the mausoleum of Imam Shafi'i, emphasizes two poles of the sultan's reign: jihad and orthodoxy. With these associations it stands out as the most pious of all Mamluk mosques. Baybars had a pronounced sense of commemoration and continuity. He built a monument of victory, Mashhad al-Nasr, in Syria to celebrate his triumph over the Mongols at 'Ayn Jalut.[22] His restoration of al-Salih's citadel on the island of Rawda was a gesture of allegiance to his master, which he accompanied with the reinstatement of Ayyubid ceremonials and regalia.[23]

6. The mausoleum of the Abbasid caliphs[24]

Baybars was also most likely to have been the founder of the so-called mausoleum of the Abbasid caliphs, next to the mosque of Sayyida Nafisa. This anonymous domed structure bears great resemblance with the mausoleum of Shajar al-Durr. It shares with it the keel-arched profile of the dome, and the keel-arched niches and lozenges on the facades. The interior, as Creswell rightly noticed, is decorated with the most splendid stucco ornaments in Egypt. The window grilles are shaped as arabesques. The chamber includes several cenotaphs and epitaphs, the earliest of which is dated 640/1242–3 and belongs to Abu Nadla, an envoy of the Abbasid caliph of Baghdad. Two cenotaphs bear the names of sons of al-Zahir Baybars who died in 1266 and 1269, two epitaphs mention the second and the fourth shadow Abbasid caliphs, and the others belonged to children of other Cairene Abbasid caliphs. Whereas Creswell attributed the mausoleum to the Abbasid ambassador, L. Ali Ibrahim and Meinecke assigned it to Baybars. Suyuti, citing al-'Umari, wrote that the second caliph, who died in 701/1303, was buried in the cemetery of Sayyida Nafisa in a mausoleum built for him; however, the style of the architecture and decoration of the mausoleum suggest an earlier date. It is likely that Baybars built the mausoleum for his sons, who died during his lifetime, and included in it the pre-existing tomb of Abu Nadla. Al-Nasir Muhammad would eventually order that the new caliph al-Hakim bi-Amr Allah, who was the first to die in Egypt and whose caliphate lasted almost forty years, be buried in this mausoleum.

Baybars also founded a collective mausoleum called Hawsh al-Zahir Baybars.[25] Yusufi located it in the area where later the emir Baktimur built his monumental khanqah that disappeared a long time ago, which was in the southern cemetery, to the east of Birkat al-Habash. According to Ibn Shaddad, Baybars dedicated this mausoleum to his Mamluks. The fact that Baybars built a mausoleum for his Mamluks strongly suggests that he must have also dedicated a monument to his dead sons, the so-called mausoleum of the Abbasid caliphs.

Fig.72. The mihrab conch of the mausoleum of the Abbasid caliphs.

– 13 –

From al-Mansur Qalawun to al-Nasir Muhammad

7. The mausoleum of Fatima Khatun (Umm al-Salih) (1283–4)[1]

Like al-Zahir Baybars, al-Mansur Sayf al-Din Qalawun al-Alfi was a Kipchak Turk from the Black Sea. He was recruited at the relatively advanced age of twenty for the court of the Ayyubid sultan al-Malik al-'Adil. The high price of 1,000 dinars paid by his master for him earned him the nickname 'al-Alfi', 'the Thousander'. His career continued on the ascendant during the reigns of al-Salih, Aybak and al-Zahir Baybars. Like Baybars, he defended Syria against the Mongols and pursued the war against the Crusaders. He also followed his predecessor's example, in consolidating diplomatic and commercial relations with the Mongols of the Golden Horde, Byzantium and other Christian kingdoms, and adopted a pragmatic trade policy to encourage foreign merchants to deal with the Mamluk Empire.

Ibn Duqmaq and Maqrizi attributed the funerary madrasa known by the name of 'Fatima Khatun', or 'Umm al-Salih', to Qalawun's wife, the mother of his son al-Salih. All sources agree that Qalawun founded this building in 682/1283 and dedicated it to his wife, who died in Shawal 683/December 1284–January 1285, and that al-Salih, his son and heir to the throne, was buried there next to his mother when he died prematurely in Sha'ban 687/September 1288. The building was completed in Rabi' I 683/May–June 1284. The monument itself has no dating inscription. The emir Sanjar al-Shuja'i supervised the construction.

Today a domeless mausoleum alongside a portico and the rectangular stub of a minaret are all that survive from the funerary madrasa. Old photographs show that the profile of the dome was very similar to that of al-Ashraf Khalil's mausoleum, and that the madrasa had a facade with arched recesses and a system of fenestration of the same style as the sultan's complex, built later in the city. The octagonal drum of the dome, which is pronouncedly high, must have given the profile of the dome an unprecedented character, which was copied in the mausoleum domes of Qalawun, al-Ashraf Khalil and al-Nasir Muhammad in the city. The treatment of the inner transitional zone is different in each individual case, however. Although the high octagonal drum was used earlier in Syrian funerary domes, the profile of the Qalawunid domes is quite distinct from that of the Syrian predecessors and should be seen as an innovation in its own right.

At the mausoleum of Umm al-Salih, each facet of the drum includes a recess with a double-arched window surmounted by an oculus. This tripartite bay system was used in the early Gothic architecture of the Crusaders in Syria, at the reception hall of the Krak des Chevaliers or Hisn al-Akrad, but it appeared earlier in the Norman architecture of Sicily, from where Qalawun's architecture seems to have been inspired.

The minaret, of which only the rectangular first storey survives, appears in nineteenth-century photographs as surmounted by an unusual upper structure in the shape of a slender elongated octagonal pavilion on a rectangular base; the pavilion was surmounted by a cupola. The minaret of al-Baqli (c.1297) is very similar, although its cap was replaced with a bulb at a later date.[2]

The portal and the minaret are placed at an angle with the funerary chamber, in order to follow the street alignment. This

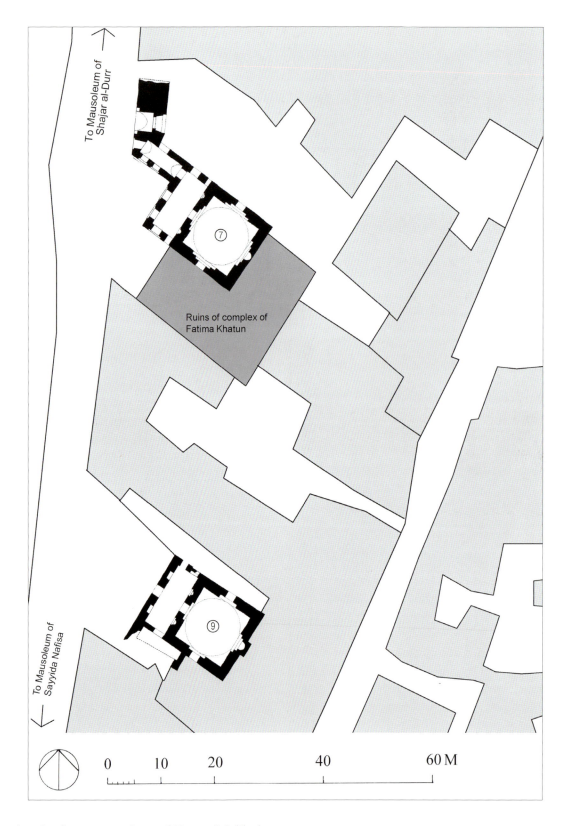

To Mausoleum of
Shajar al-Durr

Ruins of complex of
Fatima Khatun

To Mausoleum of
Sayyida Nafisa

0   10   20   40   60 M

Fig. 73. The mausoleum of Fatima Khatun (Umm al-Salih) and al-Ashraf Khalil in context.

adjustment makes the funerary madrasa of Umm al-Salih the earliest monument in the cemetery to exhibit urban features.

A corridor leads from the entrance to a vestibule, which precedes the mausoleum. The door to the mausoleum is flanked on each side with a mihrab.

The mausoleum chamber, 10.4m wide, is larger than Shajar al-Durr's, but of the same dimensions as the mausoleum of al-Salih Najm al-Din. The interior transitional zone shows a combination of squinches, including three-tiered muqarnas pendentives that reach deep down into the corners.

Fig.74. [top] The funerary madrasa of Fatima Khatun (Umm al-Salih) (nineteenth-century photograph).

Fig.75. [far left] The funerary madrasa of Fatima Khatun (Umm al-Salih), minaret (nineteenth-century photograph).

Fig.76. [left] The funerary madrasa of Fatima Khatun (Umm al-Salih), rectangular shaft of the minaret.

Fig.77. [above] The funerary madrasa of Fatima Khatun (Umm al-Salih), squinch-pendentive of dome.

8. The funerary complex of Sultan al-Mansur Qalawun (1284–5)[3]

Fig. 78. The facade of Qalawun's complex with the mosque of Barquq on the right.

The architecture of Qalawun's funerary complex was one of the most remarkable artistic works of medieval Egypt. The mausoleum was the first to be built by a sultan for himself in the heart of Qahira, and the hospital was an unparalleled philanthropic achievement at that time.

Unlike most subsequent sultans, Qalawun did not build his funerary complex immediately after his accession to the throne, but almost five years later, and after having erected the funerary madrasa for his wife. Nuwayri wrote that after Qalawun saw the mausoleum he had ordered for his son

Axonometric reconstruction of Bayn al-Qasrayn

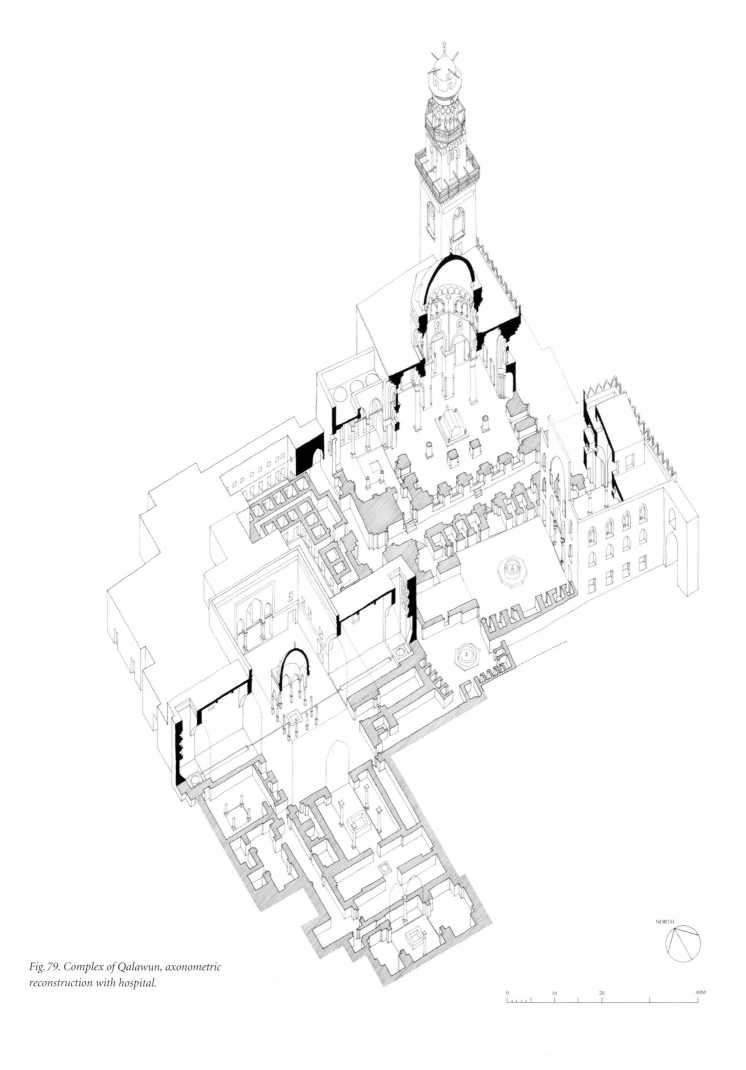

NORTH

0   10   20   40M

Fig. 79. Complex of Qalawun, axonometric reconstruction with hospital.

al-Salih (meaning that of his wife) he decided to build one for himself. This remark suggests that there may still have been at that time some reluctance about the idea of a self-sponsored royal mausoleum. Aybak and al-Zahir Baybars refrained from following Shajar al-Durr's example, and did not add a mausoleum to their respective madrasas. The historians agree that the major concern of Qalawun in this foundation was the sponsorship of a hospital.

According to all accounts and also to the epigraphic evidence, Qalawun's complex was erected within only thirteen months, which even by Mamluk standards is an astonishing speed for a monument of such dimensions. The inscription at the entrance dates the whole complex between Rabi II 683/1284 and Jumada 684/July–August 1285.

The hospital was the first part to be built, between Rabi' II 683/June–July 1284 and Ramadan 683/November–December 1284. It took less than six months to complete. The mausoleum was erected between Shawwal 683/December 1284–January 1285 and Safar 684/April–May 1285, taking only four months to complete. The madrasa was built between Safar 684/April–May 1285 and Jumada I 684/July–August 1285, also in four months. These dates also give the sequence of the construction.

Qalawun's dismantling of the citadel of al-Salih to use it as a quarry for his own monument must have saved him considerable time and expense. Moreover, the emir Sanjar al-Shuja'i, who supervised the project, used hundreds of Mongol prisoners of war,[4] and forced all builders in Fustat and Cairo to work exclusively on the project, using brutal means to extract maximum labour from the men. He even forced passersby to participate in the work, and as a consequence people avoided using the street. These controversial methods, which also included the eviction of the dwellers of the Qutbiyya palace to make way for his hospital, provoked some religious scholars to admonish people to boycott such foundations.

According to the surviving waqf documents, Qalawun endowed his complex mainly with urban estates. The hospital received the lion's share of the revenue, which Maqrizi estimated at one million dirhams (50,000 dinars) per year. The estate included three qaysariyyas, described as covered markets with shops and booths, and a large number of booths along the street, as well as a hammam, all of which were built near the complex. Two other hammams were in the neighbouring quarter of Khurunfish, and an apartment complex was elsewhere in the city centre. Furthermore, Nuwayri mentions estates in Syria, and Ibn Duqmaq a qaysariyya in Fustat,[5] which are not mentioned in the original document.

A waqf document of Qalawun's son and successor al-Ashraf Khalil, dated 17 Rajab 690/July 1291,[6] expresses his wish to share the booty of his victories against the Crusaders in Syria and Palestine with his deceased father, by endowing the latter's mausoleum with land from Acre and Tyre conquered by the

sword. Another document, dated Muharram 691/January 1292, adds large estates in Cairo to the endowment of Qalawun's madrasa.[7] These additions did not lead to an increase in salaries, which remained the same as stipulated in Qalawun's original deed.

During the reign of al-Nasir Muhammad there was a substantial restoration of the complex, which took five months of work and was completed in Muharram 726/December 1325. The initiative for this restoration was taken by the emir Jamal al-Din Aqush, who also carried the costs. In addition, he added a hall to the hospital and ordered a large tent over one hundred cubits long to cover the street.[8] In the mid-eighteenth century the emir 'Abd al-Rahman Katkhuda, in his function as supervisor of the hospital, undertook substantial restoration works on the building.[9]

A biographer of Qalawun, Shafi' Ibn 'Ali, gave an interesting version of the circumstances that accompanied the foundation of the sultan's complex. He wrote that the sultan ordered the hospital and the mausoleum but not a madrasa; this was added on the initiative of the emir Sanjar al-Shuja'i. The sultan was angry and almost refused to enter the madrasa when he went for the first time to visit the hospital.[10] According to the historian Qirtay, Qalawun's explicit wish was to place his mausoleum right opposite that of al-Salih, and not the madrasa, as is actually the case.[11] Whether this report is true or not, it is interesting for showing the significance attached to this site. Indeed, the location of Qalawun's funerary complex facing the two adjoining madrasas of al-Salih Najm al-Din and al-Zahir Baybars epitomizes a chain of allegiance (Figs 11, 67). Qalawun, as Baybars before him, served al-Salih, and he was related by marriage to Baybars.

Qalawun's disagreement with the proceedings, according to the two sources, albeit for different reasons, implies that he did not regularly inspect the construction site, as was the custom among most Mamluk sultans, otherwise he would have not been surprised by the final design. In Jumada II 899/April 1494 the commander-in-chief Azbak added the *khutba* to the madrasa, not without a legal controversy, however, because this measure did not conform to the founder's stipulations.[12]

The layout

The layout of Qalawun's complex is the earliest Mamluk example to demonstrate an articulated urban aesthetic. The location of the minaret at the northern corner beside the mausoleum, the projection of the madrasa onto the street, and the slight angle between the portal and the rest of the facade reflect a developed sense of urban perspective.

Despite Shafi'i's claim that the foundation of a madrasa was not intended by Qalawun, the layout of the complex does not betray an alteration in the design. Sanjar is likely to have included the madrasa in his scheme from the outset.

The complex was built on the western side of the street, with the mausoleum separated from the madrasa by a passage that led straight to the hospital in the rear.

The mausoleum, whose width exceeds that of the madrasa, is on the northern side of the passage. The minaret, protruding on the northern corner of the building, is not attached to the madrasa but to the mausoleum; neither does it stand near the entrance as was common practice. This positioning of the minaret shows the earliest artful juxtaposition of dome and minaret, which will characterize Mamluk funerary architecture henceforth. It signals the complex to the passerby who enters the city from the northern gates, following the traditional procession itinerary.

The minaret originally faced that of al-Zahir Baybars' madrasa, as suggested by Cassas' drawing. For an observer coming from the north, the two towers must have faced one another in the heart of the old city. They were not equal, however; the dimensions of Qalawun's facade and the proportions of the minaret surpassed those of Baybars' madrasa.[13]

The minaret begins at roof level, supported by a powerful buttress. The facade of the buttress is also panelled with a pair of shallow recesses, which seem to have included arched blind windows. The recesses contain the only muqarnas on this building, which cannot be original, its style being of the late Ottoman period. The recesses with muqarnas could have been added by 'Abd al-Rahman Katkhuda when he restored the complex in the mid-eighteenth century.

The minaret is a three-storeyed masonry tower, the upper section of which was rebuilt in brick by al-Nasir Muhammad following the destruction of the original by the earthquake of 1303. The cap was probably added in the late Ottoman period. Measured from ground level, the total height of the minaret, according to Creswell, is 56.2m. It was the first stone minaret to be built after the two minarets of the mosque of al-Hakim, constructed almost three centuries earlier. Six *mu'addhin*s were appointed to perform the call for prayer.[14]

Qalawun's complex, measuring 20.2m in height and 35.1m for the length of the facade, was of remarkable dimensions and its decoration was extraordinary in the history of Cairene architecture. The facade is panelled with a row of pointed-arch recesses, which include three superimposed levels of windows. This configuration departs from local tradition and from the arrangement of al-Zahir Baybars' madrasa, which is panelled with recesses crowned by a rectangular muqarnas frieze.

The triple window, composed of two arched openings surmounted by an oculus, is the earliest in Cairene architecture after those of the complex of Umm al-Salih, which seems to have introduced this feature. The triple window is in the upper level, above the arched windows and the lower rectangular ones.

The section of the mausoleum facade that corresponds to the mihrab is solid in its lower part and lacks the rectangular

Fig. 80. Cathedral of Amiens, main portal, relief representation of a church.

and arched windows; its upper part above the mihrab, however, is pierced with a triple window that is taller than all the others on the facade. The same device is used to signal the madrasa's mihrab on its facade. The recesses of the madrasa are shallower and less elaborate than those of the mausoleum.

The madrasa projects on the left-hand side of the entrance, its northern facade overlooking a lane that leads to the hospital. Along its southern lateral wall was a trough for animals. It emitted a bad odour and was replaced by the emir Aqush with the present sabil in the course of the refurbishments of 1325.

Creswell rightly pointed out the Western influence on the architecture of Qalawun's windows. He found the earliest case of a triple window in the tower of the cathedral of Monreale in Sicily, built in the early twelfth century during the Norman period. The triple-light is not the only Norman Sicilian feature in Qalawun's complex. The entire facade design with its double-framed and pointed recess arches recalls the facade of the cathedral of Palermo as it was before restoration. The

Fig.81. The mausoleum of Qalawun, interior.

Fig.82. The mausoleum of Qalawun, mihrab.

marble mosaics and the layout of the mausoleum with its canopy dome also point to Norman Sicily.[15] The problem with associating Qalawun's style with Norman Sicilian architecture is the gap in time. When Qalawun's complex was built this style had been abandoned in Sicily, which had shifted towards the Gothic style. Considering that the arts of Norman Sicily were strongly influenced by Fatimid art, one may think that the stylistic sources of Qalawun's monument should be found in Cairo. However, there is nothing in the extant architecture of Cairo from the Fatimid and Ayyubid periods that could be connected with Qalawun's facade and suggest a continuity of local traditions. The problem remains to explain how influences from Norman Sicily could appear in Cairo more than a century after this architecture went out of fashion there. Yet, in this period of Crusades, artistic exchanges cannot be excluded. Windows of the same type appear in the Crusader fort, the Krak des Chevaliers. In the cathedral of Amiens (1220–70) a relief in the portal depicts a monument with a facade treated with pointed recesses and triple bays similar to those of Norman architecture and Qalawun's mosque (Fig. 80). The Norman device may have reached Cairo through Crusader builders.

The entrance

The portal, with a shallow recess panelled with marble, is not architecturally emphasized; the arch of its recess, however, stands out as the only horse-shoe arch of the entire facade otherwise characterized by pointed arches. It includes a pointed arch with black and white strapwork adorning its spandrels. A triple window above the door contains a wrought iron grille, which Creswell attributed to Crusader craftsmanship.

The long passage leading from the entrance between the madrasa and the mausoleum to the hospital is covered with a wooden ceiling, which does not seem to be original. The walls do not reveal any original support for it, and the manner in which it cuts through the tip of the arched windows pierced in the side walls suggests that it was a later addition. Without the ceiling, more light would enter the mausoleum, which is now rather dark. The upper floor behind the portal was occupied by an apartment for a guardian, which would have bridged the first part of the passage, while on the side of the madrasa students' living units overlooked the passage.

The mausoleum

According to the document included in Ibn al-Zahir's chronicle of al-Ashraf Khalil, the foundation appointed an imam of any madhhab, fifty Koran readers who should perform their recitation in shifts day and night, and six attendants to the mausoleum recruited among Qalawun's and Khalil's manumitted slaves.[16] The domed chamber or qubba was more than a burial place. It was administered by a group of privileged royal eunuchs, who continued to cultivate in great pomp the

namus al-mulk or regal ceremonies in these premises 'after the sultan's death like in his lifetime', as reported by Maqrizi, in whose time the tradition was still going on. Moreover, the qubba included courses of Islamic law according to the four madhhabs, endowed by Qalawun's grandson al-Salih Isma'il, a son of al-Nasir Muhammad. Another grandson, al-Mansur Sayf al-Din Abu Bakr, made an endowment for Koran recitations to be performed there. The mausoleum also included a library and a collection of costumes that belonged to the sultans who were buried there: Qalawun, al-Nasir Muhammad and al-Malik al-Salih 'Imad al-Din Isma'il.

Most significantly, Qalawun's mausoleum substituted al-Salih's dome as the venue of the ceremony of investiture of emirs. This tradition came to an end with the Qalawunid dynasty – i.e. with the beginning of the Circassian hegemony under Sultan Barquq.

While the dome of al-Salih marked the allegiance of the first Mamluks with their Ayyubid patron and predecessor, the dome of Qalawun marked a new era of Mamluk power and dynastic continuity, which remained exceptional in the history of the sultanate.

The area of the mausoleum (21 x 23 m) surpasses that of the madrasa (17.5 x 15.5 m). Unlike later funerary complexes, the two structures are not adjacent, but separated by a passage. The present dome was built by the Comité in 1903 as a copy of the dome of al-Ashraf Khalil. The original one had to be removed in the eighteenth century by the Ottoman emir 'Abd al-Rahman Katkhuda in the course of his restoration. Its drum, which has retained traces of a stucco inscription, is original.[17]

Access to the mausoleum was originally from the west through a porticoed courtyard (13 x 10 m; 12 m high), which is singular in Mamluk architecture. It has an eastern and western arcade, each roofed with three shallow brick domes on spherical pendentives supported by piers with tie beams across their arches. The northern portico, which is roofed by a tunnel vault, faces the courtyard with a single arch. The southern wall includes the entrance to the mausoleum. It is much higher than the three porticos surrounding the courtyard and is lavishly decorated with stucco carvings. The central space (6.5 x 6.07 m) is open to the sky, and originally had a decorative fountain or fawwara. Al-Jabarti reported that 'Abd al-Rahman Katkhuda removed 'the dome' of the courtyard as he did with the mausoleum dome. Most likely this dome was that of the fawwara rather than a dome roofing the courtyard. It is difficult to imagine a dome over the courtyard, considering that the facade wall of the mausoleum is higher than the three others. A dome supported by the walls of the courtyard would have cut through the magnificent decoration of the mausoleum entrance. Like the portal of the main facade, this inner facade is pierced with several openings. Above the door an arched grille window flanked by two smaller ones is surmounted by a triple-light composition with a double arch and an oculus.

The whole window composition is framed by bands of fine stucco carvings.

In the centre of the rectangular mausoleum chamber an octagonal baldachin of piers alternating with columns carries the dome. Due to the octagonal structure there is no transitional zone here.

The decoration of the mausoleum is the most lavish in medieval Cairene architecture. Covering all the walls, it consists of painted wood, carved marble and stucco, and panels of marble mosaics. The style of the marble mosaics of the Qalawun mausoleum belongs to the cosmatesque tradition of decoration, which goes back to Roman times and was cultivated by papal patronage in eleventh-century Italy.[18] Interestingly, however, the southern Italian and Sicilian cosmatesque work often appears in association with geometric patterns of Islamic influence. Early medieval Alexandria and Constantinople seem to have been centres of this craftsmanship.[19] We do not know what happened to this tradition in Egypt prior to Qalawun's reign, and whether it was revived or continued in Qalawun's complex. Considering the various Sicilian influences on the architecture and decoration of the Qalawun complex, Sicily might have been the source of a revival of this decoration. Baybars' mausoleum in Damascus has comparable marble mosaics in the spandrels of its mihrab that must have been part of Qalawun's contribution to this monument.

The mihrab of the mausoleum is the largest and the most lavish Mamluk mihrab. It is flanked by three pairs of marble columns, each pair of a different colour. Diverging from the pointed arch used in the entire complex, but like the portal arch, the mihrabs of the mausoleum and the madrasa stand out with a horse-shoe profile. The mihrab conch is decorated with marble mosaics and the voussoir is of ablaq marble. Three rows of small niches flanked by colonettes and filled with geometric mosaics of marble and mother-of-pearl alternate with friezes of carved marble. Stucco is used extensively in the decoration of the arches, perpetuating the style of Baybars' mosque.

The wooden screen, which separates the funerary space of the octagonal canopy from the surrounding space, was added by al-Nasir Muhammad, as the remains of its inscription indicate.[20]

The madrasa

According to Maqrizi the madrasa was dedicated to the teaching of the four *madhhab*s of Islamic law, Hadith as well as medicine. A fragmentary waqf document includes a detailed description of its architecture and restoration but no mention of its functions.

The madrasa consisted of two unequal major iwans and two recesses called 'suffa' in the waqf deed, which literally means 'recess'. The plan was therefore not cruciform like that of Baybars' madrasa but closer to the shape of al-Salih Najm al-Din's madrasa, which had two blocks consisting each of two

Fig. 83. The madrasa of Qalawun, court facade.

iwans built across a courtyard with cells on the lateral sides. The document also describes the courtyard as 'durqa'a', which is the term generally used for the central space of a residential hall, instead of the word 'sahn' which defines the open courtyard. This terminology reflects the residential Cairene origin of the layout, which could have been inspired from the Fatimid palace previously standing on this site.

The waqf deed describes the west iwan and the lateral recesses as roofed with a flat wooden ceiling. The southern one had a window overlooking the qaysariyya built nearby by the sultan as part of his endowment. During 'Abd al-Rahman Katkhuda's restoration of the complex the original southern recess or suffa was replaced by the present triple-arched shallow recess, and six doors that existed on this side of the courtyard were removed. The northern recess was vaulted during the Comité

Fig. 84. The madrasa of Qalawun, central nave.

restoration. Both recesses were built shorter than the two iwans to make room for an upper storey of cells. The southern wall included six doors leading to the dwellings and annexes.

The original entrance to the cruciform madrasa was on the left-hand side of the passage and opened into the northern corner of its courtyard through a vestibule connected to a staircase leading to the cells. The present entrance is a former window.

The courtyard was originally paved with polychrome marble. Excavations in 1971 brought to light the remains of an octagonal central fountain, also mentioned in the waqf deed. Living units occupied three storeys between the three minor iwans. Despite decay and modifications, the prayer hall still reveals outstanding features. It has a basilical plan with a central nave higher and wider than the lateral ones, with which it communicates on each side through four arches supported by three columns.

The sanctuary faces the courtyard with a tripartite two-storeyed facade consisting of a central arch flanked by two smaller ones, and surmounted by similar arched openings. These were originally surmounted by three oculi, one above two, and not only one, as is the case today. This composition is set within an arched recess. A nineteenth-century painting by Adrien Dauzat (1804–66) shows this original arrangement before a modern restoration altered it.[21] In the course of these modifications the ceiling was rebuilt on a lower level, concealing part of the stucco decoration of the central nave, and one oculus replaced the former triple composition on the sanctuary's facade. Flanking the triple arch of the facade, on each side of the central nave a rectangular entrance surmounted by two superimposed arched windows leads to each of the side naves.

Creswell, who recognized that the original roof of the central nave was higher than the present, assumed that it was originally carried by light arches resting on the brackets still visible on the walls and supporting tie beams. Dauzat's painting, however, only partly confirms this assumption. The brackets of the side walls supported only tie beams, which strengthened the walls to carry the high flat roof, but there were no wooden arches. The tie beams were placed on the upper part of the walls, below the rectangular windows, and not where they are today, right above the capitals of the columns, where they restrict the view of the interior and disturb the design of the sanctuary.

Due to its projection into the street the prayer hall of the madrasa is bright, receiving light from upper and lower windows on three sides in addition to the arches facing the courtyard.

The soffits and voussoirs of the arches are decorated in the same style of stucco carving as those of the mausoleum. The mihrab, with a horse-shoe arch, is smaller and less elaborate than that of the mausoleum and, instead of marble mosaics, its conch is decorated with glass mosaics and mother-of-pearl, representing vegetal scrolls on a gold ground. The use of a deep red colour in these mosaics is remarkable.

The hospital

Interestingly, the most public part of the complex, the hospital, is not visible from the main street, although its description leaves no doubt that it was a most lavish building and the most important hospital and medical centre of its time in the entire Muslim world. It continued to fulfil its function until the late Ottoman period, and travellers who visited Egypt in pre-modern times always mentioned it in their accounts. Evliya, who was a great traveller, attested that there was no hospital in the Arab, Persian or Turkish worlds comparable to this one. He praised the effect on the patients of the running water from the fountains. Water obviously played a significant role in Qalawun's architecture, as the fountains in the courtyards of the mausoleum and the madrasa show. The hospital was demolished in 1910, leaving only a few traces, which include stucco carvings, wall recesses, two marble basins and wooden beams of Fatimid origin.

As the waqf document stipulated, the hospital offered its charitable services to all Muslim men and women, rich or poor, from any country, origin or race, and whatever their illness might be. Besides medical treatment by specialized physicians, who were to reside in the hospital and work in shifts day and night, the hospital provided drugs, boarding facilities, food and clothing, straw fans against the heat, shrouds and burial services for the dead. The patients were to be served their food in individual ceramic and glass-lidded vessels! The hospital should lift the spirit of the patient (*idkhāl al-surūr ʿalā ʾl-marīḍ*). Moreover, the waqf deed praises the beauty of the hospital as being 'a magnificent building, unparalleled in the universe, famous in the whole world for its fine qualities' (*al-badīʿ bināʾuhu, waʾl-maʿdūm fī ʾl-āfāq mithāluhu waʾl-mashhūr fī ʾl-aqṭār ḥusn waṣfihi*), which is a very unusual occurrence in a legal document of this kind.[22]

Al-Nuwayri mentions that the patients had fully furnished beds with mattresses, pillows, blankets and quilts which, according to the waqf deed, were made of cotton.

The chief physician of the hospital was required to devote part of his time to medical study (*ishtighal biʾl-ʿilm*) in a dedicated area, sitting on a mastaba or bench. It is not clear from this passage, which does not refer to students, whether 'study' means research or teaching; Maqrizi mentions medical teaching in the madrasa. The hospital also included laboratories for the production of medical drugs.

Although the document gives a detailed description of the functions of the hospital, it does not include a detailed description of the building. It indicates, however, that it consisted of several wards and various clinics attended by general physicians, orthopædists, surgeons and ophthalmologists, also serving outpatients. The space of the hospital was divided into wards according to pathological categories, such as ophthalmology, surgery and internal and other diseases, and it included a ward for women.

According to Maqrizi, the hospital was the transformed Fatimid palace of Sayyidat al-Mulk, a granddaughter of the caliph al-Muʿizz; it later became the residence of Qutb al-Din Ahmad, the son of the Ayyubid sultan al-Malik al-ʿAdil, and was known afterwards as al-Dar al-Qutbiyya. It remained in the possession of his descendants until Qalawun acquired it. The emir Sanjar al-Shujaʿi, who was in charge of the construction of Qalawun's complex, maintained the layout of the palace as it was (*ʿalā ḥālihā*) with its four iwans and fountains. This seems plausible considering the remarkably short time it took to complete the building.

Fig. 85. The madrasa of Qalawun, mihrab conch.

A description by Evliya Celebi and a plan by Pascal Coste and another by Max Herz, in addition to a few remaining walls, allow a general reconstruction of the complex.[23]

The hospital was reached through the corridor between the madrasa and the mausoleum. It had a polychrome marble portal facing the entrance to the mausoleum's courtyard. The central courtyard of the hospital had a broad format (21 x 33 m). Evliya, confirming Maqrizi's description, mentioned in the centre of the courtyard a water basin surmounted by a domed canopy resting on twelve columns, which collected the water flowing down from the wall fountains (shadirwan) of the two opposite iwans. Two marble inlaid basins connected to the shadirwans have survived.[24] The style of their decoration, which is the same as in the mausoleum, suggests that Qalawun redecorated the palace. The fact that the endowment deed mentions the beauty of the decoration in unusually expressive terms seems to emphasize the sultan's additions to the old palace.

In Coste's drawing, the courtyard is centred by a small oratory in the shape of a rectangular canopy, which must have been added by 'Abd al-Rahman Katkhuda when he restored the complex in the eighteenth century. Coste's drawing shows a carved band running along the facades of the courtyard and round the arches of two vaulted iwans. An arcade with a wooden ceiling must have been added in the eighteenth century by 'Abd al-Rahman Katkhuda around three sides of the courtyard. Coste also depicted two oblong iwans, 13 m deep, facing each other along the east–west axis. Each had a shadirwan or fountain in its rear wall connected with a channel that conducted the water to the central basin. In Coste's plan, however, the stream ended in a basin at the entrance of the iwan and not in the courtyard, where the central fountain was replaced by the oratory. The northern and southern iwans, which have different configurations, were connected with other rooms and cruciform structures with a courtyard, each with a central basin.

The cruciform wing with a central basin behind the southern iwan was dedicated to female patients. On the southern side of the women's wing the waqf document mentions a hammam. The northern iwan led to the physician's residence, the western to the courtyard of the male patients, and the northeastern corner led to two courtyards each with a central basin surrounded by cells, for the male and female mental patients. Rooms of various size and purpose occupied the corners of the courtyard between the iwans. Another hammam belonging to the hospital and a waterwheel complex were near the northern tract; the kitchen was in the southwestern corner.

Fig. 86. The mausoleum dome of al-Ashraf Khalil.

9. The funerary madrasa of Sultan al-Ashraf Khalil (1288)[25]

Sultan al-Ashraf Khalil (r.1290–93) was not initially designated to succeed his father Qalawun; this happened only because the heir to the throne, his brother al-Salih, died prematurely. Khalil himself was eventually assassinated. However, he had the privilege to lead the final battle, already prepared for by his father, which resulted in the eviction of the Crusaders from the Holy Land.

Al-Ashraf Khalil built his funerary madrasa in 687/1288, prior to his access to the throne, probably immediately after he was designated by his father as his successor, upon al-Salih's death. This date is indicated in a foundation inscription naming him with royal titles. Three years later, with the booty of his victory against the Crusaders in Acre, he enlarged the endowments of his father's mausoleum and madrasa and his own, as stipulated in a waqf document dated Rajab 690/July 1291.

Al-Ashraf Khalil's waqf thus explicitly commemorated this victory, and linked it to his father's funerary complex and to his own funerary madrasa by stating that he was endowing them with the revenue of land in Acre and Tyre, seized from the Crusaders by his sword.

Fig. 87. The mausoleum dome of al-Ashraf Khalil, squinch.

The funerary madrasa was built outside the city centre, in the cemetery of Sayyida Nafisa, near to the tomb of Fatima Khatun or Umm al-Salih, where his brother had been buried, and not far from the funerary madrasa of Shajar al-Durr (Figs 59, 73).

The madrasa, which taught the four rites of Islamic law, has disappeared without leaving any trace; only the mausoleum stands today. The waqf stipulated the appointment of twenty Koran readers in the mausoleum.

Maqrizi wrote that the emir Jamal al-Din al-Ustadar, Barquq's majordomo, dismantled it to build a minaret at al-Azhar mosque.[26] The absence of any vestige of the madrasa or a visible sign of the mausoleum being connected with the madrasa led Creswell to believe that they were separate structures.[27] The initial waqf deed, which would have included a description of the complex, has not been found. However, the complementary deeds copied in Ibn 'Abd al-Zahir's chronicle describe the mausoleum as 'adjacent' (*mulāsiqa*) to the madrasa, which is the same term used in the document to refer to the mausoleum of Qalawun.[28] This suggests that Khalil may have adopted for his funerary madrasa a layout similar to that of his father, with a passage between the mausoleum and the madrasa. The mausoleum of al-Ashraf is the same size as that of Fatima Khatun and is very similar to it. The rectangular base is built of stone. The dome, sloping from the base, has buttresses.

The inner transitional zone differs from its predecessor in that it returns to the pre-Mamluk device of muqarnas squinches. An interesting feature is the stucco frieze above the transitional zone with interlocking circles filled with stucco grilles; every third one is an oculus. The mihrab is inscribed with Koran III, 187–91.

10. The mausoleum and ribat of Ahmad Ibn Sulayman al-Rifa'i (c. 1291)[29]

Literary sources indicate that the Mamluk dignitaries were the most significant, albeit not the only, sponsors of pious foundations of the Bahri period. Bureaucrats and Sufis, and occasionally professionals and merchants, also figure among the patrons, but only a few non-princely monuments survive from that time. For this reason, the mausoleum and ribat of Ahmad Ibn Sulayman al-Rifa'i, and the zawiya of Zayn al-Din Yusuf, deserve attention.

The architecture of the ribat of Ahmad Ibn Sulayman al-Rifa'i does not belong to the princely order; however its decoration is of artistic and art-historical interest.

The meanings of the terms 'zawiya' and 'ribat' have varied between countries and across periods, and even within the same period the words have multiple uses. In Mamluk Cairo the ribat and the zawiya seem to have fulfilled similar functions. They were often founded by or for a Sufi, whose mausoleum they may include after his death. Unlike the khanqah, the ribat and the zawiya were often associated with a specific Sufi order or with an individual shaykh, and they did not always include boarding facilities. Moreover, their shaykhs were not necessarily appointed by the sultan. Because the shaykh's mausoleum bestowed a holy character on a zawiya or a ribat, these foundations acquired the status of a shrine and pilgrimage site, being continuously restored and embellished by their community.

The ribat of Ahmad Ibn Sulayman al-Rifa'i is located in the vicinity of Suq al-Silah or the weapon market, not far from the mosque of Sultan Hasan. The present structure, which has not preserved any historical inscription to identify the founder, includes the mausoleum of the shaykh, who, according to an inscription on the wooden cenotaph, died in 690/1291. So far no biographical entry on this shakyh is known. The mausoleum is attached to what Maqrizi calls a 'riwaq', which in contemporary sources and in waqf documents meant either an arcaded hall in a mosque or an apartment.[30] In this particular case the term refers to the arcaded prayer hall next to the mausoleum, which must have also been a gathering venue.

No facade has survived. A nineteenth-century photograph with a panoramic view of Cairo shows in this location a minaret, which must have belonged to the building. The minaret had a rectangular first storey and a damaged upper structure built in the early Mamluk style. A recently published album of photographs from the nineteenth century shows another panoramic view of this area, which includes the minaret before it was damaged.[31]

The riwaq (15 x 6.2 m), made of masonry and reconstructed by the Comité, consisted of two naves parallel to the qibla wall. It has preserved its original stucco mihrab, which is conspicuously in the Fatimid tradition and therefore an archaic feature. Its profile is keel-arched and its conch carved with hoods radiating from the base towards the extremities to form a muqarnas voussoir. It is framed by a stucco frieze with cartouches inscribed with a Koranic text.

The present configuration suggests that the mausoleum was added to the ribat after the shaykh's death. It stands on its eastern corner, connected with it through openings on two sides.

Were it not for its outstanding decoration, the small dimensions of the brick mausoleum (3.2 m diameter) would place it rather outside the mainstream of Mamluk funerary

Fig.89. The ribat of Ahmad Ibn Sulayman al-Rifaʿi, mausoleum interior.

Fig.90. The ribat of Ahmad Ibn Sulayman al-Rifaʿi, mihrab detail.

architecture. It is a brick domed structure, which has lost its exterior plaster and decoration. The exterior transitional zone of the dome is relatively high to compensate for its small diameter. It has a three-step composition with triple windows below the octagonal drum. The transitional zone corresponds to an inner three-tiered muqarnas composition, which conceals both the transitional zone and the drum, an anomaly noted by Creswell.

The flamboyant interior decoration contrasts with the modest scale of the dome. The dome itself, along with the transitional zone of the drum and the mihrab wall, are entirely covered with fine stucco carvings that still show remains of paint. An epigraphic band runs along the base of the dome. The mihrab was flanked

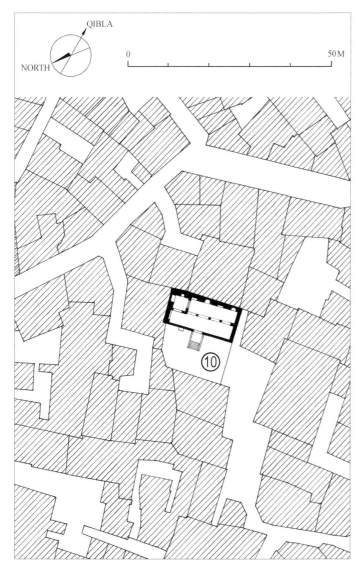

Fig.88. The ribat of Ahmad Ibn Sulayman al-Rifaʿi.

with a pair of round-arched niches filled with geometrical rosettes, of which only one survives in a very ruined condition. The arch of this niche is adorned with elements of painted glass, which is the great surprise of the mausoleum's decoration. However, these coloured elements, once embedded in the carved stucco, are now almost entirely gone. They are of elongated hexagonal or round shapes, and made of what Stefano Carboni identified as *verre églomisé*, which consists of a layer of painted glass covered by a second glass layer like a sandwich. The painted patterns consisted of arabesque scrolls in green and brown with black contours.

The combination of this pattern with a hexagonal shape appears earlier in painted stucco in the decoration of a hammam in Fustat, probably of the Tulunid period, fragments of which are now in the Islamic Museum in Cairo. There was a tradition of using glass in Cairene architectural decoration. Coloured glass was commonly used in qamariyyas, to fill stucco window grilles and occasionally for mosaics. Coloured glass was also used in the stucco decoration of the Fatimid dome added by Caliph al-Hafiz to al-Azhar mosque.[32] Many Mamluk monuments show elements of turquoise glass paste inlaid in stone or marble. Glass elements were also integrated in the decoration of the Abbasid palaces in Samarra, and in Iran in the twelfth century. However, the use of the technique of *verre églomisé* in this mausoleum is singular. Carboni found a contemporary parallel to Ibn Sulayman's decoration only in Italy, in an Islamic-inspired geometric design. Considering that the funerary complex of Qalawun, built only a few years earlier than the present mausoleum, bears parallels with Norman Sicilian architecture and with Amalfian decorative devices, the Italian connection of the *verre églomisé* in this mausoleum is less difficult to envisage than it may seem. The lavish decoration of this building suggests the sponsorship of a high-ranking sponsor.

11. The so-called mausoleum of Mustafa Pasha or ribat of Emir Janibak (thirteenth century–c.1465)[33]

This enigmatic monument, with no foundation inscription, but popularly known as the mausoleum of Mustafa Pasha, is located on the northern side of the zawiya of Zayn al-Din Yusuf, in the northern part of the southern cemetery. Creswell identified the monument as the ribat of Shaykh Yusuf al-'Ajami al-'Adawi on the basis of a deficient interpretation of a passage in Sakhawi's *Tuhfa*, and dated it to 1269. Although Creswell's dating, which is supported by his stylistic analysis, is plausible, Sakhawi's text suggests another patron.

Sakhawi's text clearly identifies the building on the northern side of the zawiya of Zayn al-Din Yusuf as a ribat with a mausoleum, built initially by an emir called Azdumur

al-Salihi.[34] The title 'al-Salihi' suggests that he lived in the second half of the thirteenth century. Sakhawi also mentioned a tomb there dated 672/1273. In the mid-fifteenth century when this ribat was in ruins, the emir Janibak appropriated it as a turba for himself, where he appointed fifty Sufis, Koran readers and a large staff. He renovated, painted and decorated it (*zakhrafahu wa bayyadahu*). He also repaired its hydraulic installations, and made substantial additions that included a graveyard with a loggia or maq'ad, a kitchen, a stable, an ablution fountain, a sabil and a maktab, so that the area began to thrive with the foundation. Ibn Taghribirdi reported that Janibak was buried in 1463 in the turba he had built outside the cemetery gate, Bab al-Qarafa, which corresponds to the location of this ribat.

We have mentioned this prominent emir, Sayf al-Din Janibak Ibn 'Abd Allah al-Zahiri, earlier in the book as the founder of a fabulous garden on the Nile shore with a Sufi complex and a residence. During Jaqmaq's reign, in 1445–6, he was appointed

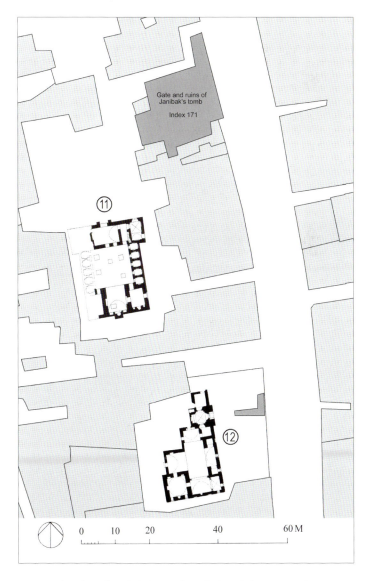

Fig 91. The ribat of Janibak (Mustafa Pasha), and the zawiya of Zayn al-Din Yusuf to the south.

Fig. 92. The ribat of Janibak (Mustafa Pasha), iwan.

governor of Jedda, where he made a great fortune in the Indian trade, which allowed him to acquire vast land properties from the *bayt al-mal*. He was the great majordomo of Inal, and later he became the great secretary or *dawadar* of Khushqadam. Janibak is reported to have founded a funerary complex in the cemetery south of the Citadel. He died in 1463.

The building consists of an iwan and a number of cells overlooking an open courtyard. It is reached through an arched door framed by a voussoir of intersecting arches of stone inlay, and set within a rectangle framed by an unusual carved band. This northern door leads to a cross-vaulted vestibule that opens into a courtyard with a southern brick-vaulted iwan adjoined by a small chamber. The mihrab of the iwan and a triple mihrab in the adjoining room have a keel-arched profile, and their niches are set askew eastwards in relation to the qibla wall, which is on a south–north axis. The mihrab niches and the lower part of the walls are undecorated. The courtyard has a row of cells on the northern side, which according to Creswell's reconstruction faced other cells on the opposite side.

The angular profile of the triple window above the main mihrab and the keel-arched profile of the mihrabs attribute the construction of the iwan to the early Mamluk period. The frontal walls of the iwan and the adjoining room are richly decorated in their upper part with stucco carvings. Koranic inscription bands in *thuluth* script frame the iwan's frontal wall and the triple mihrab of the side room; another band running around the arch of the main mihrab is in Kufic. The inscriptions in the side room are only in *thuluth*.

An isolated portal, on the eastern side of the ribat and along the cemetery road, is inscribed with the name of Janibak with his titles as great secretary and deputy sultan, and his blazon. It has a trilobe vault in the style of the period and is in a very ruined condition. Van Berchem read the inscription on the main portal, which refers to the foundation as including a qubba or dome. The dome, which has not survived, would have overlooked the street between the gate and the ribat in a space that is empty today, and would have been connected to the hawsh and other structures mentioned by Sakhawi. Van Berchem saw the ruins of these structures shortly before they totally vanished, and he read in a second inscription on a side portal the date Rajab 869/March 1465, which is two years later than the year of Janibak's death. Creswell mentioned another reading by the Comité, according to which the date was 864/1460, which is more likely.

Creswell, who mentioned Janibak's foundation in his *Chronology*, did not connect it to the ribat when he discussed it in his main book. Sakhawi's account, however, strongly suggests

Fig. 93. The ribat of Janibak (Mustafa Pasha), decoration of iwan.

that the two structures became linked when Janibak appropriated the ribat. When Janibak integrated the ribat in his funerary complex, he probably modified the axis of the mihrab niches.

Creswell's dating of the building was based on the style of the door facade, which he compared with Ayyubid and Seljuk Anatolian examples. Sakhawi's text also confirms the date suggested by the architecture of the iwan, which indicates the second half of the thirteenth century. He did not mention, however, the obvious western Islamic style of the stucco decoration in the iwan, which Farid Shafi'i noticed and compared with the decoration of the mosque of Taza (1294) in Morocco.

The Moroccan or Andalusian origin of the stucco design in the iwan is obvious; the problem is the dating, and whether Janibak redecorated the interior with the present stucco, or kept the original decoration and restored it. The style of the *thuluth* inscriptions and the arabesques are early Mamluk. However, Sakhawi's text is explicit about the redecoration of the previous building. One would assume that one of the most glorious emirs of the fifteenth century, as Janibak was, would not have appropriated a building one and half centuries old without redecorating it.

The lobed arches of the stucco decoration, combined with inscribed cartouches and knots, recall the arts of the Marinids in Morocco, who ruled from 1217 to 1420, and whose artistic traditions continued long after their reign. An Andalusian origin is also possible. Another datable example of carved stucco of Moroccan or Andalusian origin is an arched panel in the mosque of al-Mu'ayyad, built in 1420; its composition of lobed arches combined with cartouches, knots and bands of beads (dotted circles), although more elaborate and of higher quality, resembles the pattern of this iwan; its inscriptions are all Kufic.[35] Shafi'i, who mentioned this panel in the same article, did not comment on its style. As shown by Creswell and Shafi'i, western Islamic decorative elements appear occasionally in Ayyubid and Bahri Mamluk architecture; the presence of this kind of craftsmanship in fifteenth-century Cairo is a curiosity. Maghrebi craftsmen on their way to the east, or migrants from Andalusia, might have found an opportunity to exercise their skills in Cairo. However, considering the integration of Mamluk stylistic elements in this decoration, the possibility that it was executed by a local workshop using western Islamic patterns should be seriously considered.

Whereas the style of the inscription bands and the arabesques of the iwan date the decoration to the early Mamluk period, the decoration of the adjoining room might be attributed to a later restoration. The lobed arches and arabesques here, which appear as a less fine interpretation of the iwan's carving, and the absence around the central mihrab of the frieze of beads that frames the two others, point to an inconsistency that might be due to the involvement of different craftsmen. Although faithful restoration was not common at that time, Janibak, while refurbishing the ribat, might have tried to maintain the original style.

–14–

The Early Period of al-Nasir Muhammad's Reign

12. The zawiya of Shaykh Zayn al-Din Yusuf (1298–1325)[1]

The zawiya of Shaykh Zayn al-Din Yusuf is the only extant religious foundation of the Bahri Mamluk period to be defined by its inscriptions as a zawiya. Although the inscriptions do not name a founder, they indicate that the mausoleum and the zawiya were dedicated to the Sufi shaykh Zayn al-Din Yusuf, who introduced to Cairo the 'Adawiyya Sufi order.

The zawiya was also known by the founder of the order, 'Adiy Ibn Musafir, Zayn al-Din's ancestor. He was a famous mystic, who died in 1162 in the Kurdish area of Hakkar, near Mosul. In his genealogy, documented in the foundation inscription, Shaykh Zayn al-Din Yusuf is identified as a descendant of the Umayyad caliphs, which implies that he was of Qurayshi descent, like the Prophet.

Zayn al-Din left Mosul and migrated to Syria, where he was given an *iqta'* and the title of emir, which he rejected, however. He preferred to withdraw instead to a place called Jabal Far, where he led a most lavish lifestyle, surrounded by slave girls and using silk brocades and gold and silver vessels. When Sultan al-Ashraf Khalil sent two of his high-ranking emirs to take Zayn al-Din's oath of allegiance, the latter treated them in a most haughty manner.

Although the sources do not mention the circumstances of Zayn al-Din's arrival in Cairo, an event that took place during the reign of al-Ashraf Khalil may be related to the presence of his Sufi order in the Egyptian capital. In 1293 a shaykh named 'Abd al-Hamid, sent by the Kurdish prince 'Ala' al-Din al-Hakkari, arrived in Cairo to ask the sultan for the insignia of

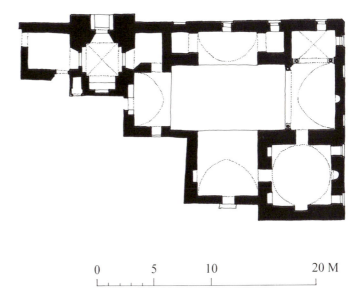

Fig. 94. The zawiya of Zayn al-Din Yusuf.

the *futuwwa*, which literally means 'chivalry' and refers to a kind of mystic guild or fraternity, for himself and his people. He then vowed his allegiance to the sultan with a pledge to fulfil the jihad.[2] The encounter between Khalil and the Hakkari envoy might have opened the door for Zayn al-Din, who came shortly afterwards with his wealthy Kurdish community to settle in Egypt. According to Ibn Habib, the Sufis of this zawiya were Kurds.

However, the situation changed after al-Nasir Muhammad succeeded Khalil. This sultan felt threatened by the growing political power of the Kurds in his kingdom, suspecting them

Fig. 95. The zawiya of Zayn al-Din Yusuf.

of subversive schemes. In 1333 he jailed one of their leaders in Syria, and he dismantled the zawiya in Cairo, dispersing its community. According to Sakhawi, the dismantling of the zawiya took place forty years after Zayn al-Din's death (697/1298), which would be in 1338.

The zawiya later became associated with the famous Qadiriyya order, whose founder, Shaykh 'Abd al-Qadir al-Jaylani, had been a close friend of 'Adiy Ibn Musafir, Zayn al-Din's ancestor. When some of his descendants introduced the Qadiriyya order to Egypt in the late fourteenth or early fifteenth century, they occupied the zawiya of Zayn al-Din, which was by then abandoned. Considering the political significance of Zayn al-Din, it is not surprising that the zawiya had the attributes of princely architecture. Although it is the only monument to be

called a zawiya by its inscription, it must have been a foundation similar to the more modest ribat of Ahmad Ibn Sulayman, and to the ribat known as the mausoleum of Mustafa Pasha.[3]

The building took shape in more than one phase, as attested by the three different dates indicated in the inscriptions, as well as by the layout itself. A slab with a foundation text defines the mausoleum as a qubba or dome, and gives the genealogy of the shaykh and the date of his death and of the foundation of the mausoleum as 697/1298.

Another inscription in the mausoleum calls it a 'maqam', which means 'mausoleum', and gives the date Rabi' 725/February–March 1325, without indicating to what this date refers. A third date, 736/1335–6, is mentioned in an inscription on the isolated portal outside the building; it states that this is the zawiya of Zayn al-Din.

Fig. 96. The zawiya of Zayn al-Din Yusuf, dome interior.

In her study of this zawiya, L. Ali Ibrahim has argued that the mausoleum was originally built in 1298 as a commemorative funerary structure for the shaykh, and that the building was modified at a later date, in 725/1325, to include a courtyard surrounded by four iwans. Irregularities in the plan should be attributed to the later additions. She argued that the absence of a founder's name suggests that the original structure was not a full-fledged pious foundation, but only a turba. The turbas were funerary buildings, mostly located in a cemetery, consisting usually of a mausoleum adjacent to a prayer hall, and dependencies within an enclosure. Their endowment would include a Sufi service – i.e. the provision for Sufis to practise their *hudur* or session in the premises to invoke a blessing to the dead.

L. Ali Ibrahim further interprets the date 736/1335–6, inscribed on the isolated portal outside the main building where the inscription that describes the monument as a zawiya is to be found, as the date when the turba was converted into a zawiya, meaning that the zawiya was a posthumous foundation. However, the chronicle of Ibn Habib, which was published after the publication of L. Ali Ibrahim's article, associates Zayn al-Din with a zawiya in Cairo from the outset, thus excluding the idea of a posthumous addition.[4]

The fact that the term zawiya appears only in the later inscription is indeed significant. The gate in which it is included was built during the period of al-Nasir's persecution of the Sufi order and its Kurdish community. Members of the order might have tried to rehabilitate or reform their organization to regain legitimacy and appease the sultan. The absence of a founder's name and the use of the word 'zawiya' confirm the religious function of the foundation while declaring its low profile. This did not prevent, however, the dismantling of the zawiya shortly afterwards.

The building stands on the western side of the cemetery road. It has a rather low stone facade, with only one tier of windows, and a raised muqarnas portal on the north side. The unusually small rectangular windows are set within relatively tall arched recesses crowned with distinctive stone carvings. The facade has no tiraz band; the foundation inscriptions are written on slabs. Inscribed bands with references to Zayn al-Din and his genealogy, and Koran passages, are inside the building.

The eastern facade is pierced with four windows; the two at the extremity are set within trilobe-arched recesses framed by a thick moulding. The two in the middle are crowned with muqarnas and are framed by a rectangular moulding. The southern facade's windows are crowned with keel-arched niches. Remarkable lintels carved with arabesques and inscriptions add to the decoration of the windows.

The dome, attached to the prayer hall on its western side, does not overlook the main road, but only a side lane to the south. However, due to the low facade, it is fully visible from the road. There is no minaret and no trace of one.

The dome is ribbed, and the exterior transitional zone is decorated with bands of carved stucco that frame all its facets and include the twenty keel-arched bays of the drum and the stucco Koranic inscription that runs along its base. Its interior is equally ribbed; its decoration is exceptional, with flat ribs displaying alternating patterns of finely carved stucco. The ribs end down at the base of the dome in a row of small niches flanked by a pair of colonettes. The lower part of the domed chamber has a polychrome marble dado and inlaid panels with square Kufic inscriptions. All four iwans are vaulted and connected by a stucco epigraphic band that runs along the whole interior.

The mihrab of the sanctuary is the only one before that of Zayn al-Din Yahya in Bulaq to have a historical instead of a Koranic text.

The four iwans are all of different sizes. That of the sanctuary is shallow compared with common practice, whereas the adjacent mausoleum is deeper and protrudes slightly on the rear side. The sanctuary is extended on the road side by a cross-vaulted space with a window. The west iwan, which also communicates with the mausoleum, is the largest, and the one facing the sanctuary is reduced. The T-shaped east iwan is the shallowest.

The cruciform plan also differs from its contemporaries by not having cells between the iwans. There was formerly an upper floor, added at a later stage, which was removed during restoration works.

13. The funerary madrasa of Sultan al-Nasir Muhammad Ibn Qalawun (1295–1303)[5]

This madrasa was initially founded by Sultan al-'Adil Katbugha, who ruled from Muharram 694/December 1294 to Muharram 696/December 1296 during the interim preceding al-Nasir Muhammad's second reign, and it was completed by the latter, who celebrated its inauguration in 703/1303, during his second reign.

Al-Nuwayri indicated that Katbugha built the mausoleum and the prayer iwan, and al-Nasir completed the building and added the minaret. According to Maqrizi, Katbugha carried out the construction up to the top of the inscription band.

The inscription carved on the facade is in the name of al-Nasir Muhammad, beginning on the right-hand side of the portal with the words 'has ordered the building of this madrasa'. However, it ends on the other side with the date 695/1296, which is the date of Katbugha's foundation, during al-Nasir's absence. It thus seems that al-Nasir replaced Katbugha's name in the first section of the inscription with his own, without altering the second section with the initial foundation date. When back in power, al-Nasir acquired and enlarged the waqf estate in Dhu 'l-Hijja 698/September 1299 to complete the construction in his own name; this is confirmed in another inscription in the portal recess, which dates the foundation of the qubba and the madrasa to the year when the sultan regained his throne, just before he left for Syria to meet the invading army of Ghazan Khan.

Like Qalawun's and Khalil's madrasas, this one taught the four madhhabs of Islamic law. According to the waqf stipulations, the main iwan was dedicated to the Malikis, the Hanbalis were in the one opposite, the Hanafis in the northern iwan and the Shafi'is in the southern. For some unknown reason, the Hanafis and Hanbalis exchanged their positions. The priority locations given to the Maliki and Hanbali madhhabs does not correspond to their importance in Egypt, neither does it conform to the common practice in Mamluk madrasas, where the Shafi'is usually occupied the main iwan. Some special political considerations may have prompted al-Nasir's choice. Although the waqf associated the four madhhabs with the four iwans, the cruciform plan was also used in madrasas teaching one or two madhhabs, as in the case of al-Zahir Baybars' foundation.

The madrasa had eight mu'adhdhins, four teachers, an imam for the madrasa and another for the mausoleum, a librarian, an undefined number of readers and students in the madrasa, and twenty-five Koran readers and one Hadith teacher in the mausoleum. Commercial structures, dwellings and hammams in different quarters in Cairo, and a share in a commercial building, a khan in Damascus, belonged to the endowment.

The dome disappeared a long time ago, and the extant high drum is in the same style used in earlier Qalawunid architecture. The minaret is a brick structure ingeniously supported by the walls of the passage that leads between the madrasa and the mausoleum to the courtyard. Together with the dome, it forms a slight angle with the facade wall, following the Mecca orientation. Although the minaret of al-Salih Najm al-Din was similarly built above a passage, this device remained a rarity in Mamluk Cairo, where the minaret usually stands on a solid buttress on one side of the portal.

In contrast to Qalawun's monumental but discreetly decorated minaret next door, the rectangular first storey of this minaret is flamboyant, with finely carved stucco. At the top a *thuluth* historical inscription, with the name of al-Nasir Muhammad, begins on the northern side of the minaret. The inscription and the decoration on this side do not cover the entire wall of the minaret, leaving a bare vertical space along the edge over the entire length of the shaft. As already mentioned, the minaret was erected later than the dome, and very close to it. As a result, the dome must have concealed the western edge of the minaret's northern wall, and the first part of the inscription would have been invisible if it had been applied where the wall begins.

The stucco decoration of the minaret consists of medallions, lozenges, keel-arched niches, and panels filled with geometric and floral lace-like patterns. Towards the top, a row of niches with lobed arches between colonettes are filled with minute geometric patterns recalling the Mamluk decoration of the mihrab of al-Azhar mosque. A band of ornate Kufic script runs across this arcade. The rectangular shaft is crowned with elaborate muqarnas sculptures.

Only this rectangular section is original; the second storey is of a later style. It has an octagonal shape with a keel-arched panel on each side, all framed by a continuous moulding. Green glass or ceramic elements fill the loops of the moulding that runs around the keel-arched panels. It is likely that this section was built by Sultan Inal, when he enlarged the street in 1457 and founded two hammams and a qaysariyya further north near the Ayyubid madrasa of al-Malik al-Kamil.[6] Its style is akin to that of the octagonal section of his own minaret in the cemetery, which is, however, unlike this brick and stucco structure, built in stone. The upper structure must be from the Ottoman period.

The most remarkable feature about the facade is the Gothic portal, a trophy brought by Katbugha from a church in Acre during al-Ashraf Khalil's triumphant campaign against the Crusaders in 1291. It is, therefore, not without symbolic significance, considering that this battle was the second major achievement after the victory of the Mamluks against the Mongols; these victories earned the Mamluks their uncontestable legitimacy.

Fig. 97. The funerary madrasa of al-Nasir Muhammad.

The narrow facade contrasts sharply with the monumentality of Qalawun's, next door. Its contiguity to Qalawun's building to form one continuous wall might have been inspired by al-Zahir Baybars' madrasa across the street beside al-Salih's mausoleum (Figs 11, 67).

The mihrab protrusion on the facade and the window above it are very close to Qalawun's minaret, so that almost half of the inner qibla wall is set against its wall, concealed from the street.

As in Qalawun's complex, the minaret and the dome stand close to each other, but here it was due rather to the lack of an alternative option than conscious design, the two elements sharing the entire space available.

The minaret is also very close to Qalawun's, and both face Baybars' minaret across the street, so that the three of them must have created an interesting towering composition, laden with political symbolism that transcended the original function of the minaret. A few metres further south is al-Salih's minaret.

Fig. 98. The funerary madrasa of al-Nasir Muhammad, portal.

Fig. 99. The funerary madrasa of al-Nasir Muhammad, minaret.

The marble portal consists of a pointed arch with a triple recess flanked by three slender columns on each side. At the apex of the arch the word 'Allah' has been inserted in a loop. It is interesting that Maqrizi praised the craftsmanship and decoration of this portal as among the most wonderful works ever done by a human being (*min a'jab mā 'amalathu aydī banī ādam*). Considering the truly magnificent portals that existed at that time in Cairo, such as those of the mosques of Sultan Hasan, Bashtak and al-Mu'ayyad, or the portal of Qawsun's palace, one wonders if this admiration was due to its symbolic significance or its exotic character.

The madrasa has a cruciform plan with four vaulted iwans facing the courtyard (Fig. 11) and three floors of living units occupying the corners between them. The vaulted iwans are all of different size, even the lateral ones. In most cruciform buildings, while the sanctuary iwan is larger than the one opposite, the lateral ones are of the same size. A wooden frieze suggests that there might have been originally an inscription

band around the courtyard, as can still be seen at the zawiya of Zayn al-Din Yusuf.

The mausoleum has a large mihrab flanked by a beautiful pair of marble columns with Gothic capitals, which might also have come from the church that provided the portal.

The only remaining decoration in the madrasa is the carved stucco mihrab. It is visibly smaller than that of the mausoleum and included within a larger arched panel, also carved in stucco. An arched window above the mihrab has a stucco grille of a later date, which disturbs the decoration of the mihrab wall. It seems as if this window was originally blocked from within to make room for the stucco decoration and was reopened at a later date (Figs 97, 99). The conch of this mihrab has no parallel in Cairo. Its high-relief carving displays pierced bosses resembling *repoussé* metalwork on a ground of complex arabesques recalling Iranian stucco of Tabriz style. The artistic connection with Tabriz may be related to al-Nasir Muhammad's marriage to a Mongol princess following his entente with the

Fig. 100. The funerary madrasa of al-Nasir Muhammad, interior view.

Ilkhanid court. During his reign, Persian craftsmen worked in Cairo and influenced the decorative arts. However, at the time when the madrasa was completed, diplomatic relations between Mamluks and Mongols had not yet developed. Unless the conch was decorated at least a decade later, the craftsman who carved this mihrab would not have come by diplomatic arrangement, but rather as a refugee.

The circumstances had led al-Nasir Muhammad to take over this building, but, once his power was consolidated during his third reign, he preferred to be buried elsewhere, in the funerary khanqah he built in the village of Siryaqus. Ironically, neither the madrasa's nor the khanqah's mausoleum ever housed the sultan's remains. In fear of unrest following his death, due to the rivalry between his emirs, he was buried secretly at night without ceremony in his father's mausoleum.[7]

The sultan launched the village of Siryaqus in 723/1323 as a leisure ground with a hippodrome and gardens, with palaces for himself and his entourage. He later added the khanqah, which was inaugurated in 725/1325 with a solemn celebration. It was the most privileged Sufi foundation at that time; its generous endowment allowed its community to enjoy higher living standards than any other contemporary khanqah. In the following year, 1326, the canal known as the Nasiri Khalij was dug to irrigate the area and facilitate the transport of goods to Siryaqus. Eventually the place grew and prospered as a town and pleasance area.

Unfortunately, the description of the buildings is missing in the waqf deed. We only know that the mosque had a riwaq plan.[8] Maqrizi's statement that it was a Friday mosque is contradicted by the stipulations of the waqf deed, which describes it as a masjid only, without Friday prayer and without mention of a *khatib* among the staff. Beside it were three dwelling compounds, two for twenty Sufis each, and a hostel to house sixty needy guests or *fuqara'*. The complex was supposed to include the graves of the principals of the khanqah; the other Sufis were to be buried in a cemetery outside the premises.

Fig.101. The funerary madrasa of al-Nasir Muhammad, mihrab.

Al-Nasir was a great sponsor of Sufism. Besides the Sufis accredited to his first mosque, and his funerary khanqah in Siryaqus, he sponsored the zawiya called Qubbat al-Nasr for mystics from Persia (*a'jam*) in the northern end of the northern cemetery. All three buildings vanished long ago.

14. The funerary complex of Emir Sanjar al-Jawli (1303–4)[9]

The founder of this funerary complex, identified in the chronicles as the emir Sanjar al-Jawli, began his career in Syria during the reign of al-Zahir Baybars. He was appointed emir during al-Nasir Muhammad's second interim reign, when Salar and Baybars al-Jashnakir shared power. Despite the eight years he spent in prison, he remained one of al-Nasir's favourites until that sultan's death. He was governor

of Gaza, where he founded important pious foundations, including a big hospital. His patronage extended to Hebron and other cities in Syria and Palestine. The inscription of his mausoleum described him as the majordomo of al-Nasir Muhammad.

Sanjar's buildings in Cairo seemed to have been limited to a palace next to this funerary complex with the double mausoleum for Salar and himself. Besides being a prominent emir who had the merit of conquering al-Karak from the Crusaders, Sanjar was a scholar in his own right of the Shafi'i *madhhab* and the author of fatwas and theological treatises. He taught and issued an *ijaza* or certificate to the historian al-Safadi. His interest in Shafi'i scholarship is remarkable considering that the Mamluks adhered to Hanafism. When he died in Cairo in 745/1345 he was almost a centenarian.

Fig.102. [opposite] The funerary complex of Sanjar al-Jawli, rear view.

Fig. 103. The funerary complex of Sanjar al-Jawli.

Salar, to whom Sanjar dedicated the larger and more decorated of the two mausoleums, died much earlier, in 1310. His glamorous career began during Qalawun's reign and ascended during al-Nasir's second reign, when he was appointed deputy sultan. With Baybars al-Jashnakir he held the office of regent to the young sultan. When Baybars usurped the throne in 1309, and took the title 'al-Muzaffar', Salar continued to hold the office of deputy sultan, but then turned against his new master and helped al-Nasir to recuperate the throne. Having celebrated al-Nasir's return, Salar asked him for permission to retire to his estate at al-Shawbak, in present-day Jordan. At that time Salar was in his fifties. The sultan agreed to his retirement, but after a while summoned him back and threw him into jail, leaving him to starve to the point of eating his shoe. Salar died at the very moment he heard the message of his amnesty; Sanjar was allowed to take care of his friend's funeral.

The sultan confiscated Salar's legendary fortune. He was renowned as a dandy, who gave great attention to his clothes

and even designed costumes, such as the *salariyya*, which became fashionable and was named after him.

The friendship between Sanjar and Salar must have begun prior to the foundation of the double mausoleum in 1303–4. During the regency period, Salar acted as Sanjar's mentor, taking his side openly and fervently on more than one occasion when he was accused of embezzlement by Baybars al-Jashnakir. This strained the relationship between the two regents so that Sanjar, to avoid further embarrassment to Salar, began to sell his belongings to refund the deficit claimed by Baybars al-Jashnakir. He might have relied for this on Salar's fabulous wealth.

In the absence of a waqf document, it is difficult to identify the function of the various spaces in this enigmatic monument. The singular circumstances that led Sanjar to the foundation of a double mausoleum – his gratitude to his mentor, and the commemoration of a faithful friendship – had an undeniable impact on the monument's architecture.

It is not clear whether the funerary complex included a madrasa or a khanqah. Maqrizi listed it under both entries, and he wrote that the institution included both a college curriculum and a Sufi service. Maqrizi, however, wrote at a time when the fusion between madrasa and khanqah had taken place, which was not yet the case when the foundation was established.

The inscription on the entrance, which does not name a founder, calls it only a 'makan' or 'place', which usually refers to a secular building or a mausoleum. The inscriptions of the mausoleums describe them as 'turba' and associate them with the two emirs, Salar and Sanjar. Al-Safadi, who was Sanjar's contemporary, also uses the term 'makan' to describe this foundation.

The initial function of the building might have been merely a funerary one. This is suggested by the fact that only the mausoleums are Mecca-oriented, whereas the rest of the complex with the halls and living units surrounding a central space is not. The main iwan did not initially have a mihrab; the present one, which is not axially placed, is a modern addition. There is, however, an original stucco mihrab in the exterior courtyard.

The singular layout of the complex, the location of the mausoleums and their position within the complex, and the use of the words 'makan' in the foundation inscription and 'turba' in contemporary texts, suggest that this was in the first instance a commemorative funerary monument, probably with a Sufi service. Having limited boarding facilities, it might not have been originally conceived as a substantial madrasa or khanqah. Sanjar, whose palace was located on the rear side of the monument, being himself a scholar, might have used it as a working and gathering place for a small community. In a further development, or through the subsequent enlargement of the endowment, a fully pledged khanqah or madrasa might have been added to the double mausoleum.

Fig. 104. The funerary complex of Sanjar al-Jawli, mausoleum dome of Salar, transitional zone.

The layout

The complex stands on Saliba street, a major artery of the medieval city, not far from the mosque of Ibn Tulun. Perched on the rocks of the hill called Jabal Yashkur, it faces the passerby coming down from the Citadel with a facade that can be considered one of the boldest of Mamluk architecture, dominated by a graceful minaret beside two unequal domes.

The facade is panelled with window recesses, as is common in Mamluk mosques, and bears an uninscribed band.

The two adjoining mausoleums, being built on an east–west axis, are almost parallel to the street. The domes are ribbed on the exterior and decorated with an inscribed band of carved stucco in the drum. Their profile, unlike that of al-Muzaffar Baybars' (al-Jashnakir) mausoleum, curves after about one third of the dome's height.

The entrance, at an angle to the rest of the facade, is not architecturally emphasized; it is simply set in a recess crowned with muqarnas, like the window recesses.

The rectangular shaft of the minaret, made of stone, is more slender and elongated than its predecessors. Its decoration recalls Qalawun's minaret, each side having an arched panel resting on muqarnas and flanked with colonnettes. One of its windows is framed with a horse-shoe arch, and another one has a triple composition. Also, the style of the muqarnas atop the rectangular shaft recalls Qalawun's minaret. The upper structure is slender and made of brick. The octagonal elongated section is crowned with a cornice of muqarnas beneath the circular pavilion with a ribbed cupola.

A special feature of the minaret is the portal at the entrance of its stairway above the roof of the mosque. It has a trilobed arch and two small maksalas or benches on both sides. Only the minaret of Bashtak, built in 1340, has a portal to its staircase. The minaret is inscribed with the Koran verse XXIV, 36.

As the building is on the slope of a hill, a staircase leads from the main entrance to the upper floor, where the complex is located, whereas the back entrance opens on a flight of steps that leads down to the communal rooms.

Fig. 105. The funerary complex of Sanjar al-Jawli, stone screen.

The funerary compound

The funerary compound consists of a cross-vaulted corridor, a kind of portico before the funerary chambers overlooking an open courtyard. The view on the courtyard is screened by a set of large pierced stone panels, which are a most remarkable feature in this monument. Each of the four screen panels is carved with an individual intricate floral design, one of them showing grapes. Pierced panels of smaller size are set between the arches in the walls of the corridor as a decorative device, and others are used as window grilles in the living units.

The stone screens and panels of this building are unprecedented and they became the prototype of the stone parapets that henceforth characterized minaret balconies, replacing the former wooden ones, as already shown in this minaret. We may assume that the minaret here was the first to have such parapets. The next stone parapets are on the minarets of al-Nasir Muhammad at the Citadel.

The two domed chambers are reached from the corridor through their individual doors, and they communicate with each other through inner doors. The first door leads to the larger of the two mausoleums, where Salar was buried, which is also more decorated. Its prayer hall has fine geometric marble mosaics in the conch and the spandrels, and the lower part is also panelled with marble. A wooden inscription band runs along the walls. The transitional zone of this dome consists of an octagonal belt of niches and muqarnas pierced with windows corresponding to the profile of the muqarnas elements. The interior of both domes is, unlike the exterior, not ribbed, thus differing from their Fatimid predecessors and from the mausoleum of Zayn al-Din Yusuf, where the flutes of the domes are structural. The inscription includes the Koran verse III, 181–91; Sanjar's inscription has the Koran verse II, 284–6.

Two doors opposite the prayer niche lead from Salar's to Sanjar's funerary chamber. Here, the prayer niche is without marble, and its conch is carved instead with flutes radiating from the apex towards the base, ending in a row of small niches. It recalls some Bahri portals, and is unusual for mihrab decoration in Cairo. The transitional zone of the dome is similar to the previous one.

The small and squat masonry dome at the end of the corridor is a later addition; it was most likely built to roof the tomb of the emir Bashtak, who died in 1341 in prison, and was buried in this building in 1347–8.[10]

The courtyard behind the screen includes tombs, but we do not know whether it was initially planned to be a graveyard. It is framed on two sides by modern buildings. The eastern wall, which belongs to the living compound, is carved with a fine stucco inscription band and includes a small stucco mihrab in the southeast corner. The orientation of this mihrab diverges from that of the mausoleums.

The common room

On the left-hand side of the staircase is the undefined structure of a madrasa or khanqah, which consists of a hall (9.3 x 8.7 m), without original mihrab, attached to a kind of covered courtyard surrounded by cells built on two levels. The lower ones have a window with a pierced stone grille above their doors, whereas the upper ones have pierced panels above their small windows. A stucco inscription band runs along the wall above the windows with the Koranic verses XXV, 62–70, and XXX, 182.

This covered courtyard is connected to another slightly raised area with a vaulted small iwan on its northern side. As both spaces are roofed, the interior is dark. Creswell assumed convincingly that they were originally open to the sky and that there was another iwan opposite the one on the north wall.

15. The funerary khanqah of Sultan al-Muzaffar Baybars (al-Jashnakir) (1307–10)[11]

Al-Muzaffar Baybars held the office of jashnakir or sultan's taster before he was sultan for a short period. During the interim following al-Nasir Muhammad's second reign, Baybars usurped the throne, only to pay with his life on the sultan's return. In revenge, the sultan closed the funerary khanqah that al-Muzaffar Baybars had built in the Jamaliyya quarter, confiscated its estate and obliterated his royal titles from the foundation inscription. The khanqah was reopened in 726/1326 after al-Nasir had established his own great khanqah at Siryaqus.

According to Maqrizi, the khanqah had been founded in 706/1306 while Baybars was emir, and it was completed in 709/1310 during his sultanate, as attested by the foundation inscriptions. This is also corroborated by the waqf documents.

Function

Three waqf deeds define the functions of the complex, indicating that it combined a khanqah with a ribat. These were not, however, two distinct architectural units but, rather, two communities sharing the complex. The khanqah was dedicated to a maximum of four hundred Sufis, offering boarding facilities to one hundred of them, preferably foreigners. The others were non-resident.

The ribat, whose community was allocated the courtyard with the sanctuary and one of the lateral iwans, consisted of one hundred persons; thirty of them could enjoy boarding facilities. Unlike the khanqah community, the ribat members were not described as Sufis but as poor (al-fuqara' wa 'l-maskana) with the 'qualities of zawiya people'.[12] Priority of admission was given to the founder's manumitted slaves, followed by demobilized soldiers. The documents thus define the ribat as an institution

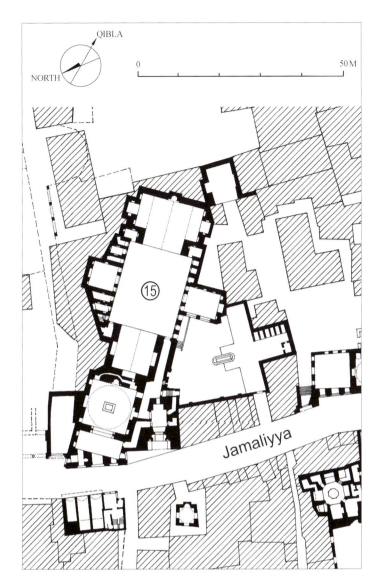

Fig. 107. The funerary khanqah of al-Muzaffar Baybars (al-Jashnakir).

dedicated to the same kind of community as the zawiya. This ribat was a kind of asylum without a strict curriculum. Considering that the ribat was allocated two iwans and the courtyard, and that thirty of its members were lodged in the complex, it is likely that they occupied the cells overlooking the courtyard. Their right to use the main iwan suggests a priority status.

In addition to the cells surrounding the courtyard, a living compound on the northeastern side of the complex would have once been used for the khanqah's dwellers.

This khanqah is the oldest extant in Cairo. It was preceded by the one built by Salah al-Din, which disappeared long ago, and by the khanqah of Aydakin al-Bunduqdar, built during Qalawun's reign in 1283–4, of which only the founder's mausoleum survives.

Fig. 106. [opposite] The funerary khanqah of al-Muzaffar Baybars (al-Jashnakir).

The layout

The complex is located in the Jamaliyya quarter, parallel to Bayn al-Qasrayn, on the site of the Fatimid vizier's residence that once faced a western gate of the caliph's great palace.

The waqf documents indicate that the khanqah was built prior to the mausoleum and the minaret by referring to their forthcoming construction. It can be assumed that their location was already determined. There were not many options anyway. As Mamluk priorities dictated, the mausoleum had to be on the street side, and preferably in harmonious juxtaposition with the minaret, which obviously was also attached to the facade. The layout must therefore have been planned by the time the deed was compiled. It was common practice in the Mamluk period to begin the construction of a religious monument with the prayer hall and use it before the rest of the building was completed.

At a distance to the south, the building emerges as a harmonious conjunction of dome and minaret, while from nearby the portal is impressive.

The funerary khanqah occupies an area measuring 70 x 30 m. The mausoleum is built on an axis parallel to that of the khanqah, which is at an angle with the street alignment, the gap being absorbed by the thickness of the walls.

The plan has some irregularities that are not easy to interpret. The facade, 12 m high, projects from the street, with a salient of 9.5 m and 10.2 m on both sides respectively. According to Creswell's calculation, Baybars took 300 sqm from the main street. Within this salient the mausoleum projects further so that the facade forms a two-stepped salient.

The projection of the mausoleum cannot be explained by lack of space, since the vestibule, which precedes the mausoleum on the street side, is unnecessary. The projection with the vestibule was, rather, a means to stretch the funerary chamber onto the street, without detaching it from the khanqah to which it is contiguous. The mausoleum of al-Salih Najm al-Din, which also projects beyond the madrasa's facade, may have served as an example. The salient here also projected the minaret, to make it, like Qalawun's, visible from a distance. The projection seems therefore to have been intended to add prominence to the facade.

The facade

A carved tiraz band with the foundation inscription runs from the southern side of the projecting facade through the portal recess and continues further north. It starts with the Koranic verse XXIV, 36–8.

The portal is an impressive structure with a deep and elaborate entrance hall that anticipates the vestibules of later mosques. It faces the street with a round arch with a cushion voussoir (Fig. 108). A shallow recess in the frontal wall, which includes the door, is crowned with a half dome on two muqarnas pendentives

Fig. 108. The funerary khanqah of al-Muzaffar Baybars (al-Jashnakir), portal.

with an oculus between them. This recess is flanked by a pair of niches on the sides; two others adorn its flanks. The conchs of the four niches display a sunrise motif in black and white marble. Engaged marble colonettes with Gothic capitals, probably spoils from Crusader monuments or perhaps imitations, occupy the corners of the recess between the outer and the inner niches. An epigraphic band in black and white inlaid marble runs along the inner portal recess on both sides of the entrance.

The portal recess has a pair of maksalas or stone benches flanking the entrance. 'Maksala' means literally 'a place to relax or be lazy'. This is the earliest documented case of a device that will henceforth characterize Mamluk portals. The bronze door is original. The block of granite in the threshold, carved with hieroglyphs, belongs to an ancient Egyptian monument. This is also a characteristic feature of Mamluk buildings.[13]

The projection of the mausoleum facade added light to the interior through the pairs of rectangular windows pierced in each of its lateral sides, in addition to the three other pairs of windows in the main facade wall. There are no arched windows here. The lower windows are larger than the upper, but the central

one stands out as the largest of the whole set. This window has a story associated with it. According to Maqrizi, its iron grille once belonged to the palace of the Abbasid caliph in Baghdad. It was brought to Egypt in the Fatimid period along with the turban of Caliph al-Qa'im following the rebellion that overthrew him in 1075. It was eventually incorporated in the Fatimid vizier's palace, which stood on the site of the khanqah and which Salah al-Din used as his residence. Apart from its size, nothing in the present appearance of this grille distinguishes it from others.

The mausoleum dome, like that of al-Salih Najm al-Din, curves near the base. The minaret stands on the right-hand side of the portal, slightly recessed behind the portal, perhaps to be better viewed from the courtyard. It is a brick construction, 18m above roof level, with a rectangular first storey decorated with stucco keel-arched niches and crowned with bunches of muqarnas, which are very similar to those on the minaret of al-Nasir's madrasa. The second storey is cylindrical, which is unusual. The circular pavilion with a ribbed helmet at the top shows the remnants of green tiles. The use of glazed tiles in architectural decoration here precedes the fashion, introduced two decades later, of tile mosaics in Ilkhanid style.

As it is a light brick construction, the minaret has no articulated buttress visible on the plan; it is carried by the portal walls. A nineteenth-century photograph shows a very similar minaret in the quarter of Tabbana, now disappeared, which was most likely built during the reign of al-Nasir Muhammad.[14]

The interior

The mausoleum (11.3 m side) is reached through an entrance on the left-hand side of the corridor, which leads further to the khanqah. It is preceded by the above-mentioned projecting vestibule (11.4 x 4.7 m), which opens into the domed chamber with a large pointed arch. A screen of turned wood partly fills the arch and includes the door to the funerary chamber. It bears an inscription with the date 709/1310.

As the domed chamber does not overlook the street directly it is relatively dark. Light is introduced only through the five pairs of superimposed rectangular windows pierced in the wall of the vestibule. Their light is rather subdued due to their deep recesses, corresponding to the thickness of the facade walls.

Fig. 109. [right] The funerary khanqah of al-Muzaffar Baybars (al-Jashnakir), mihrab of mausoleum.

Fig. 110. [below] The funerary khanqah of al-Muzaffar Baybars (al-Jashnakir), interior view.

The ground plan reveals a thin passage behind the mausoleum mihrab connecting two cupboard recesses of the qibla wall with the rear wall of the western iwan of the khanqah.

Contrasting with the sparsely decorated khanqah and its bare mihrab, the mausoleum's walls, floor and mihrab are lavishly decorated with black and white inlaid marble. The option for black and white instead of polychrome marble decoration is as subtle as it is striking. The conch of the mihrab is inlaid with a radiating motif, which, unlike the facade niches, starts from the apex rather than from the bottom of the conch. The pavement of inlaid marble shows a row of seven mihrabs parallel to the qibla wall. Maqrizi reports that the marble of Baybars' khanqah and residence originally belonged to the Fatimid caliph's palace and was found in an underground cache in the neighbourhood.

An epigraphic band in wood runs along the walls and frames the mihrab. Its Koranic inscription is LXVII, 13–4 , and that of the mihrab is II, 39.

The transitional zone of the dome is the earliest to be composed of four instead of the usual three tiers of niches.

One reaches the courtyard (19.7 x 16.4m) through the long, bent corridor. The plan of the khanqah is cruciform. The height of the courtyard's surrounding walls, 15.4 m, surpasses that of the facade, which is to be explained by the three storeys of cells. The main iwan (9.8 x 12.1m) is vaulted and has a T-shaped ground plan with a smaller arched recess equipped with an airshaft on each side; all four iwans have no windows and no decoration; the stone mihrab is plain except for a moulding. This intended and pronounced simplicity suits the dedication of the iwan as a gathering hall for the humble community of the ribat.

The iwan opposite the sanctuary is also vaulted and equipped with an airshaft recess in the central wall. Two smaller unequal iwans with a tunnel vault and a mihrab are on both sides of the courtyard. Between the iwans are small cells of varying size occupying the ground and two upper floors. The only decoration of the courtyard is in the carved hoods of the window recesses, designed with rhythmical variations displaying keel arches, pointed arches and muqarnas crests.

16. The funerary khanqah of Emir Sunqur al-Sa'di (1315–21)[15]

Little is recorded about the founder, and what is known does not throw any light on the character of this original monument. Emir Sunqur al-Sa'di, who made his career during al-Nasir Muhammad's third reign, was his in-law (sahr), but the exact relationship is not clear. He was secretary of the army, na'ib al-jaysh, before he was sent to Tripoli in 1323 for reasons related to a conflict with the mighty emir Qawsun. He died there in 1328. He was renowned for his passion for building, hunting

and falconry, and for agriculture. This monument shows that he was also a person with literary taste.

Sunqur's foundation is one of the earliest of al-Nasir's third reign. It is located in the quarter of Hadarat al-Baqar behind the mosque of Sultan Hasan, and consisted of a mausoleum, perhaps a khanqah and a ribat or asylum for women. In the Ottoman period it became a tekke for the dervishes of the Mawlawi order.

An undated inscription on one of the four wooden cenotaphs in the mausoleum indicates the founder's name. The text of this inscription is unusual for its composition and the unusual length of the series of titles preceding Sunqur's name. Another panel on the same cenotaph in the name of the Sufi shaykh Sadaqa indicates the date Rabi' I 715/June 1315 while stating that this is his darih. This term, which means 'shrine' or 'mausoleum', would refer to the building, suggesting that the mausoleum was dedicated to him. Maqrizi also dates the monument to that year, but he does not mention Sadaqa. He describes the foundation as a madrasa with a ribat for women. The inscription of the mausoleum gives the date 721/1321.

Ibn Hajar mentions Sadaqa Ibn al-Sharabishi as a wealthy notable from Cairo who made an endowment for this foundation, which he calls a khanqah. However, in his entry on Sunqur, Ibn Hajar described it as a madrasa. Sadaqa's patronym Sharabishi, 'the sharbush maker',[16] points to a mercantile background. His titles in the inscription of the cenotaph define him as a mystic, which suggests that the foundation was a khanqah rather than a madrasa. The date of his death (745/1345) in Ibn Hajar's reference, however, is thirty years later than the one on the cenotaph. Ibn Hajar refers to Sadaqa as a rich sponsor rather than a shaykh, but he may have also have been a wealthy Sufi, who co-sponsored the foundation, and therefore acquired the privilege of being buried there. Sunqur probably established this foundation for himself, and later included Sadaqa's tomb in it. It was not common Mamluk practice, however, to dedicate a mausoleum of this quality to a shaykh, or to include shaykhs in princely mausoleums. The circumstances of this funerary foundation thus remain somehow enigmatic.

The facade with a minaret and a dome are all that remain today from the Mamluk period. The madrasa or khanqah, which has recently been excavated, had a courtyard with a central fountain surrounded by cells.

The portal recess is crowned with a half-dome resting on muqarnas. The half-dome is filled with a double sunrise motif in ablaq masonry radiating from two points at the base. This pattern was repeated in the conch of the mihrab of Sultan Hasan's madrasa. Joggled lintels, like those at al-Muzaffar Baybars' khanqah, adorn the entrance. Also, as in the previous building, the portal recess

Fig. 111. The funerary complex of Sunqur al-Sa'di.

Fig. 112. The funerary complex of Sunqur al-Sa'di, dome

includes a pair of maksalas. A small, handsome window is pierced above the door, as in all Mamluk portals. This one displays a pair of Gothic-style colonettes. Above the portal arch a horizontal stucco panel is carved with a geometric interlacing pattern that goes back to the Fatimid and Ayyubid periods, when it was used on the south minaret of al-Hakim's mosque, above some stucco mihrabs, and on the exterior decoration of Imam Shafi'i's mausoleum.

As in al-Muzaffar Baybars' khanqah, the minaret is juxtaposed with the dome in a harmonious composition. Both brick structures are adorned with stucco carvings of high quality.

The minaret, 32 m high, has a singular silhouette with a particularly slender shaft. The reduced octagonal section is surmounted by a section of profuse stucco muqarnas beneath the ribbed helmet. The muqarnas here is characterized by unusual small niches. Traditional keel-arched niches decorate the rectangular and the octagonal sections of the shaft.

The dome curves near the base, and its lower part is carved with bands of stucco decoration that include the entire transitional zone

and the drum with its windows. As in all Mamluk mausoleums, the inscription contains the Verse of the Throne. The windows alternate with blind niches, and share with them the fine stucco grilles. A set of twenty-four grilles, corresponding to eight windows and sixteen niches, displays six alternating patterns, which are repeated four times. The patterns are very fine and analogous to the stucco of the minaret of al-Nasir Muhammad's madrasa.

The transitional zone consists of three steps underlined by the stucco ribbons and adorned with medallions. The grilles of the windows in the transitional zone are larger than those of the drum.

The domed mausoleum chamber has a plan that is not quite square, 7.8 x 8.4 m, so that the dome has a slightly elliptic base. With only one lower window, the chamber is dark. Its most remarkable feature is in the epigraphy. A fine stucco inscription band runs along the upper part of the rectangular walls, concluding with the date 721/1321. The date is written in numbers rather than in letters. Along with the date on the bronze door of al-Zahir Baybars' madrasa, it is an exception in Mamluk epigraphy.

The date on the dome is six years later than the one on Sadaqa's cenotaph. It may refer to the completion of the building, or to its decoration, which for some unknown reason was delayed.

Another, lower, inscription band runs from one end of the qibla wall to the other, passing round the mihrab arch. As the mihrab is particularly tall, the inscription band at its apex touches the upper epigraphic band. The inscribed text is set in cartouches alternating with decorative medallions.

The only Koranic text in the mausoleum is the beginning of the Verse of the Throne inscribed in a medallion at the apex of the dome. The text inscribed in both bands is not Koranic, not even religious. It has been read and published by 'Abd al-Rahman Fahmi Muhammad, who identified its content as excerpts from the *Maqamat al-Hariri*. The *Maqamat* or sketches of al-Hariri (1054–1122) is a collection of narratives describing the adventures of a vagabond, Abu Zayd al-Saruji, who travels from one place to another making his living by unscrupulous means, but ultimately, through genius, wit and eloquence, he earns forgiveness and ultimately repents for his mischief. The hero's cynicism notwithstanding, the *Maqamat* has always been valued as a great work of literature in the Arab world for its wit and for the prowess of its language. However, it was a bold decision to inscribe a passage from it in a mausoleum instead of Koranic verses. This extraordinary choice, which points to a patron of special calibre and a literary connoisseur, perhaps even to an eccentric, is, however, in accordance with the culture of the time. Several Mamluk illustrated manuscripts of the *Maqamat* were produced in the first third of the fourteenth century, and it is worth speculating whether Sunqur might have been among such patrons.

The upper band contains a passage from the eleventh *maqama*, which is one of most accomplished of al-Hariri's book. The scene takes place in a cemetery at Sava in Iran, where the hero arrives and encounters a funeral. He joins the mourners and gives a most eloquent sermon, from which the inscription includes a passage.

The inscription begins with a *basmala* and ends with a pious formula, both of which have been added to the original text. The inscribed passage is not a faithful copy of the original passage because it excludes the phrase 'You let your friend be vermins' food then listen to the tunes of pipe and lute'.[17]

[In the Name of God, the Compassionate, the Merciful]
Let for this aim work all human workers,[18]
remember well, all you forgetters,
brace yourselves, you non-achievers,
open your eyes, you keen observers,
what is the matter with you?
You do not wail for buried relatives,
nor fear the thump when graves are filled in cemeteries,

you ignore our time's calamities,
do not prepare your own obituaries.
You do not weep for tears in others' eyes,
you do not care when someone dies,
are not concerned by a fellow's burial,
ignore the wailing in a funeral.
You carry the bier to the tomb
with your mind set towards home.
You see that your friend is laid to rest
yet only think of what for yourself is best.
So often for lack of food you cried,
but forgot your beloved ones who died.
(You let your friend be vermins' food
then listen to tunes of pipe and lute.)
[Oh God, take us to you as your believers!]

The text of the lower band, which runs around the mihrab hood is from the forty-first *maqama*, called the Tanisiyya for its location in the city of Tanis in the Egyptian Delta.

O sons of Adam, how poor they are and weak,
support in this world on shaky grounds they seek.
They ask the unworthy for protection,
they cling to this world so stupidly,
are attached to it so eagerly,
like mad dogs they fight ferociously,
but for their end not prepare sagaciously.
(I swear by Him
who made both seas[19] *divide,*
who to both moons[20] *set light,*
who set both stones[21] *upright):*
If reason were to rule man's thinking
he would not join in bouts of drinking.
If he remembered the life he led,
tears of blood would he then shed.
Thinking of the judgement to face at last
should remind him of what has passed,
if he became aware of the final sanctions
he would make good his ugly actions.
How strange, how strange, that they aspire
to be engulfed by hellish fire,
because it's gold they so admire
and richness they so much desire.
Omens (that are quite astonishing,
are greying hair that's so admonishing,
and the setting sun, a sign for perishing,
yet you see no reason to relent
nor for your) shameful (deeds to repent).
[Grant us your mercy by your Mercy, Oh God,
God's prayers upon our Prophet Muhammad and his kin
In the year 721.]

–15–

Al-Nasir Muhammad's Third Reign and After

17. The New Mosque (al-Jami' al-Jadid) of Sultan al-Nasir Muhammad (1312)[1]

The first mosque (1311) built by al-Nasir Muhammad after his return to the throne for the third and definitive time was in the northern outskirts of Fustat along the Nile shore, north of his hippodrome, the Maydan al-Nasiri. The mosque disappeared centuries ago but it was exceptionally well documented by Ibn Duqmaq, who described it as being a large riwaq or hypostyle mosque, with a domed maqsura in front of the mihrab, opening through three entrances on the sanctuary. The maqsura dome was supported by ten columns, described by Maqrizi and Ibn Duqmaq as thicker than the rest, which suggests that they were piers supporting the dome and secluding the maqsura from the sanctuary; each of the three sides was connected with the sanctuary, as in al-Zahir Baybars' mosque, which explains the three reported entrances; these entrances might have had the shape of a triple opening, as in the case of Baybars' mosque. The qibla wall had three mihrabs, the main one being within the maqsura and the two others on either side of it. The mosque had three axial entrances in addition to an entrance near the main mihrab, which connected the mosque with the *qa'at al-khataba* or the preacher's hall. Ibn Duqmaq mentioned a minaret at the western entrance. He also mentioned a second maqsura, for the use of a Sufi community attached to the mosque, in the northern arcade, which must have been an enclosure without a dome. It is not clear whether it included cells or was merely a gathering hall. This is the only enclosure for Sufis to be mentioned in the context of a riwaq mosque.

Maqrizi wrote that the mosque overlooked the Nile to the west and a garden to the east, and that it was one of Cairo's finest recreation venues (*muntazahat*). He dates the foundation to Muharram 711/May 1311, and its completion to Safar 712/June 1312. Its preacher was a Shafi'i judge.

The mosque measured 120 x 100 cubits (*dhira' al-'amal*), which would be equivalent to c. 60 x 50 m. It had sixteen iron-grilled windows. Three were in the qibla wall, one on the west side of the mihrab and two on the east side, six were pierced in the southern wall and seven were in the northern wall, three of which belonged to the enclosure of the Sufis. This left the western facade, which faced the Nile, without windows. The eastern and northern windows overlooked gardens.

When Evliya Celebi saw the mosque, which was near the great waterwheel of al-Ghawri's aqueduct, its prayer hall had been demolished.[2] The columns were of various provenances, as was the case in all hypostyle mosques of the period. Evliya mentioned two minarets; the second might have been added at a later date. He read the date as 721, which must be a misreading, since other contemporary sources date its construction between 711 and 712/1312–3.

18. The mosque of Emir Qawsun (1330)[3]

Although it was founded later than al-Nasir Muhammad's first construction of his mosque of the Citadel, the mosque of Qawsun will be discussed at this stage, because of its relationship to the reconstructed mosque of al-Nasir.

Sayf al-Din Qawsun, who originated in Central Asia, was the cup-bearer of al-Nasir Muhammad, and enjoyed the double privilege of being his son-in-law and brother-in-law. He was one of the wealthiest and mightiest emirs of his time, and he

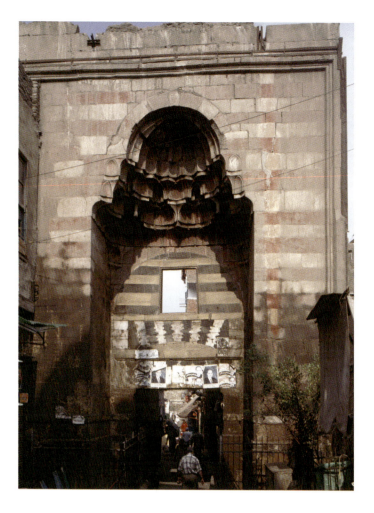

Fig. 113. The mosque of Qawsun, external entrance.

built the monumental palace in the quarter west of the Citadel, of which the most magnificent muqarnas portal of the Mamluk period survives. His career came to a brutal end during the reign of Kujuk, and he died in 1342 in jail after his property was confiscated. Besides this mosque, he built a funerary khanqah in the cemetery south of the Citadel, of which a mausoleum dome and a magnificent minaret have survived.[4]

The monumental mosque was built on the riwaq plan without a mausoleum, perhaps anticipating the patron's later foundation of a funerary khanqah, in 1336–7. As a result, its layout was strictly symmetrical. The mosque was demolished when Muhammad 'Ali street was pierced last century, and replaced by a new construction. Only the remains of a wall with stucco windows and a portal on Surujiyya street are preserved (Fig. 113).

According to Maqrizi, the construction work began in 730, and the inaugural Friday prayer took place in Ramadan 730/June–July 1330. This indicates a short building period of a maximum of nine months, which is not surprising considering that Qawsun had the possibility of using forced labour.

From the remains of the mosque and the eyewitness descriptions by A.C.T.E. Prisse d'Avennes and August Mehren

(1867–8), Creswell reconstructed its plan, which is analogous to that of al-Nasir Muhammad's mosque at the Citadel, with four parallel arcades in the qibla wall and two in each of the lateral riwaqs. He estimated the size of the mosque to be 68.9 x 62 m, with the qibla hall 26.5 x 23.3 m, and the west riwaq 11.8 m deep. According to this reconstruction, which was published by Meinecke, the dome of c. 15 m diameter would have been larger than those of Baybars and al-Nasir Muhammad at the Citadel. Mehren wrote that the dome was supported by ten marble columns, as in al-Nasir Muhammad's mosque after its reconstruction, and Prisse d'Avennes, who mentioned columns with Corinthian capitals, which have been moved to the Islamic Museum, added that the maqsura area was surrounded by a wooden grille of beautiful work. Also like al-Nasir's mosque, this one had two minarets. The remaining wall includes pointed arch windows, which corresponded to the centre of each nave, above a frieze of stucco carving; this window arrangement recalls al-Zahir Baybars' mosque.

According to Maqrizi, a craftsman from Tabriz built the two minarets of Qawsun's mosque in 730/1330 on the model of the mosque of 'Ali Shah in Tabriz (c. 1310–20).[5] The Tabrizi craftsman came to Cairo with Aytimish, the Mamluk envoy, who signed the peace treaty with the Ilkhanid ruler Abu Sa'id in 723/1323. Evliya Celebi mentioned only one minaret at the southern entrance, decorated with tiles. As one would expect a minaret to be near the entrance on the western wall, the two minarets appear to have not been symmetrically placed. Jabarti reported the collapse of a minaret in 1215/1800–1 on the side of the street called Darb al-Aghawat, which would correspond to the western wall – i.e. the axial entrance. Today a magnificent portal with an inscription with the date 730/1330 opens on Surujiyya street on the southern side of the mosque. It bears a sundial made by Ahmad al-Hariri in 785/1383–4.[6] Creswell identified in the masonry of this portal what could be the rectangular base of a minaret. The portal did not lead directly into the mosque but was connected to a passage 4 m long and 3 m wide connecting the street with a lane leading to the mosque.

Creswell mentioned in his notes another gate, a structure 6.3 m wide with a pointed arch leading to a tunnel vault (3.9 x 2.2 m). Its arch is framed by a moulding that curls into a loop at its apex, the earliest known use of this decorative device. Creswell rightly compared this gate with those of al-Zahir Baybars' mosque.

19. The mosque of al-Nasir Muhammad at the Citadel (1318–35)[7]

This royal mosque, where the sultans regularly performed their Friday prayer, was not the first to be built in the Citadel. Rather, its construction belonged to the comprehensive reconstruction and refurbishing scheme undertaken by al-Nasir Muhammad in the royal precinct, in the course of which he demolished the previous mosque, whose foundation went back to the Ayyubid period. The new mosque, which was not exactly on the same site, was larger than the previous one.

The palatial context of the mosque

The first building al-Nasir erected after returning to the throne, and in the same year, 710/1310, was the Great Iwan. Two years later he completed the New Mosque and rebuilt the hippodrome beneath the Citadel, and in 1313–14 he built the Striped Palace in the Citadel, overlooking the hippodrome that had been completed months earlier. Overlooking a large esplanade between the two main gates of the Citadel, the mosque faced the palace complex of the Striped Palace, al-Qasr al-Ablaq, and the Great Iwan, al-Iwan al-Kabir. The architecture of the mosque echoed that of the palatial complex.

In 718/1318 the sultan replaced the old mosque of the Citadel with a new one. Two inscription panels at the western entrance and southern portals state that the mosque was built in 718/1318, which is also the date indicated by Maqrizi, who added, however, that it was rebuilt on a larger scale in 735/1335. When Maqrizi wrote that the mosque was demolished and reconstructed twice, he was implying that al-Nasir's first mosque of 1318 was the first 'reconstruction' of the old Citadel mosque, and his reconstruction of 1335 was the second 'reconstruction'.

Al-Nuwayri, who died in 1333, before the reconstruction, reported that in Safar 718/April–May 1318 al-Nasir Muhammad demolished dwellings of emirs, storerooms (*farashkhana, hawa'ijkhana, tashtakhana*), the kitchen and the Mint in order to rebuild the mosque (meaning the old mosque) on their site.[8] The qibla riwaq was completed the same year, in Rajab/August–September, so that prayer could take place there immediately, and the marble decoration was completed in the following month of Sha'ban. He endowed the mosque and selected eighteen *mu'adhdhin*s and three chief *mu'adhdhin*s to work in three shifts. This means that six *mu'adhdhin*s performed in one shift – i.e. three on one minaret.

Al-Yusufi copied the text of al-Nuwayri, but located it mistakenly in his account of the year 1335 instead of 1318.[9] According to Dawadari, the construction of the mosque took four months and twenty-five days during the year 1318.[10]

Years later, in Sha'ban 733/1333, al-Nasir set out to rebuild the Great Iwan; the demolition lasted until Rabi' II 734/1334.

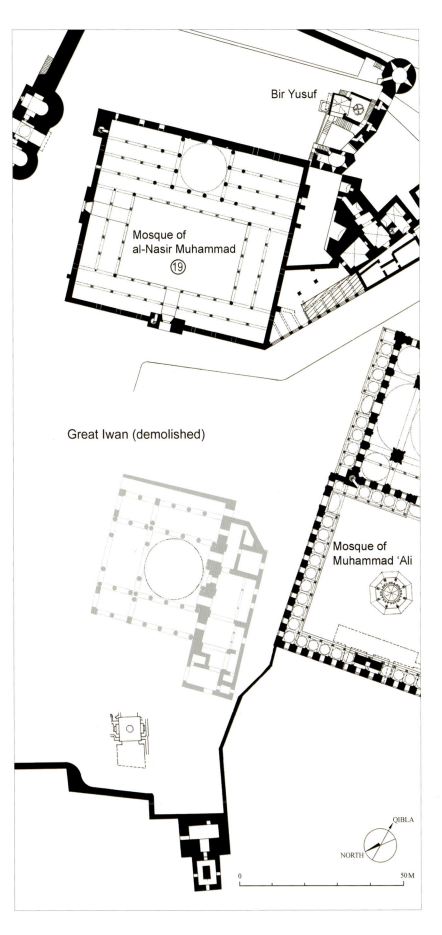

Fig. 114. The mosque of al-Nasir Muhammad at the Citadel in context.

173

The Iwan was enlarged and its dome was built higher than the previous one.[11] He then undertook remodelling works at the mosque in 1335. Referring to these works, al-Dawadari wrote that the interior of the sanctuary was demolished and rebuilt with higher arcades and a higher dome. In the course of these works, the sultan brought huge columns from Ashmunayn in Upper Egypt. This was a colossal undertaking, for which the governors of the Upper Egyptian provinces had to recruit a large number of people to secure their transport on the Nile. In Cairo and Fustat 'thousands' of people were also recruited to bring the columns to the Citadel.

The columns carried from Upper Egypt were not only for the mosque but for the Great Iwan as well, according to Maqrizi's text. The reconstruction of the mosque must have been adapted to that of the Iwan. As both structures depended on ancient columns and the production of ceramic tiles for their respective domes, co-ordinated construction would have been sensible, in as much as both structures, as shown below, complemented one another in their impact on the Citadel's skyline.

The dome of the maqsura was, like the dome of the Great Iwan nearby, covered with green tiles. Al-Nasir must have carefully positioned these two green domes so that the mosque's dome was visible to the onlooker from the caravan road and the cemetery, while the dome of the Great Iwan addressed Rumayla square and the hippodrome. The secular dome faced the city and the religious one the cemetery. Similarly, the two main gates of the Citadel, according to 'Umari, were respectively on the side of the city facing the horse market near the hippodrome, and the cemetery. The mosque was thus part of the sultan's monumental and ceremonial vision of the Citadel.

Al-Nasir planned his hypostyle mosque in the Citadel with the same layout and with similar dimensions as his earlier New Mosque, al-Jami' al-Jadid, which also had a domed maqsura, with the difference that he replaced the piers used in the earlier maqsura with pharaonic columns in the later one. The mosque of Qawsun adopted this layout, also with columns instead of piers.

The facades diverge from the contemporary urban style. They lack the tiraz inscription band as well as the recesses that would include the windows. The large rectangular windows pierced along the lower part of the facade are now walled. Another row of arched windows is pierced in the upper part of the walls.

The mosque (c. 57.6 x 60 m) has four arcades parallel to the qibla wall in the main riwaq, and two arcades in the three other riwaqs. It has four entrances, one next to the prayer niche and three axial ones with portals that all look different. The projecting main portal lacks the stone benches (maksala)

Fig. 116. The mosque of al-Nasir Muhammad at the Citadel, courtyard.

that were common in all urban mosques since the time of the khanqah of al-Muzaffar Baybars. It is relatively plain, consisting only of a recess crowned by a ribbed conch on muqarnas. The projecting northern portal has a trilobed recess, and the southern, also projecting, has a pointed arch filled with a sunrise motif in ablaq masonry. All three portals are relatively low-profile structures, which may be explained by the fact that the mosque was integrated as an element within a wider architectural composition.

The masonry reveals two stages of construction on the facade walls, confirming that in 1335 the mosque was heightened but not broadened. Moreover, the base of the two minarets is lower than the roof level, which is against the rule of Mamluk minaret architecture, suggesting that the actual structures belonged to the original construction.

The designer put the emphasis above rather than below the roof level by covering the dome with green glazed tiles and decorating the two minarets with tile mosaics, leaving the facade relatively plain.

The reason why al-Nasir Muhammad raised the walls of the mosque in 1335 almost simultaneously with the enlargement of the Iwan's dome, requiring columns to be transported from afar, was obviously to emphasize the dome of the mosque. By raising the roof level, and with the transitional zone of the dome protruding high above the roof, he accentuated the prominence of the dome and increased its visibility from the caravan road and the cemetery, which was part of the royal procession itinerary. In the course of these works, the arcades of the main riwaq were rearranged. Christel Kessler noticed that the previous mosque had three instead of the present four arcades, which means that the prayer hall was entirely hollowed

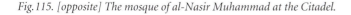

Fig. 115. [opposite] The mosque of al-Nasir Muhammad at the Citadel.

Fig. 117. The mosque and the Great Iwan of al-Nasir Muhammad (Pascal Coste).

Fig. 118. The Citadel with the Great Iwan of al-Nasir Muhammad (Louis-François Cassas).

Fig. 119. The Great Iwan of al-Nasir Muhammad (Pascal Coste).

out and its interior rebuilt. The masonry of the external walls with the minaret at the northeastern corner indicates that the walls of the sanctuary also remained unchanged, except for their height. Considering that the sanctuary was originally built on three arcades, the first dome is likely to have been only two aisles deep (9–10 m base). The reconstruction with pharaonic columns allowed its enlargement to a depth of three aisles (c. 14 m base) with a corresponding height.

Ibn Iyas reported that the original dome of the mosque collapsed in 892/1468. Sultan Qaytbay ordered its reconstruction as well as the replacement of the pulpit, which had been demolished by the debris, with a new one made of polychrome marble. The dome was probably made of wood as the transitional zone indicates, like the dome of the Great Iwan, which collapsed in 928/1522, and which was covered with lead and tiles.[12] This

happened shortly after the Ottoman conquest, and this dome was not reconstructed. The mention of lead is interesting; as noted earlier, the dome of al-Zahir Baybars' mosque was, according to Evliya Celebi, also covered with lead, as was the wooden dome of Imam Shafi'i's mausoleum. However, the lead of al-Nasir's dome was hidden under the tiles.

The position of the two minarets is not symmetrical; one flanks the west entrance and the other stands at the northeastern corner of the mosque. The latter, which is also visible from the desert outside the Citadel, addressed the barracks of the Mamluks and other official buildings, while the first, visible from Rumayla square, addressed the royal palaces.

The minarets, both masonry constructions with different shapes, look exotic in the Mamluk Cairene context. The minaret at the main entrance is composed of three cylindrical tapering storeys; two balconies with parapets of pierced stone mark the top of the first and second storeys. The shaft is carved with a deep zigzag pattern, horizontal in the first storey and vertical in the second. The upper section, which is ribbed and tapering, is crowned by a garlic-shaped structure on a cylindrical base. The bulb and the base with its inscription are entirely covered with mosaics of glazed tiles. The northern minaret is taller, and has no carving on the shaft. Its first storey is rectangular, while the second one is receding and cylindrical. The upper storey, which consists of a hexagonal pavilion also surmounted by a garlic-shaped structure, is decorated with the same type of glazed tile mosaics as the other one. The ceramic tiles on both minarets are of blue, black, white and turquoise colour. The two minarets show the earliest extant use of balcony balustrades made of pierced stone after Sanjar al-Jawli's minaret. In previous minarets they were made of timber. The idea originated in the funerary complex of Sanjar al-Jawli, where pierced stone panels were used for the first time.

A small balcony in the northern wall of the mosque connects to a staircase that leads to the roof. This balcony might have been used as a kind of tribune for an audience outside; however, it is not visible from within the mosque.

Meinecke attributed the mosaics of al-Nasir's minarets to the craftsman from Tabriz who built Qawsun's minarets. However, the two minarets were already built in 1318, as indicated by the awkward location of their base below the roof level. According to Meinecke, the tiles were added during the reconstruction of 1335. Considering that the style of the two minarets is very unusual, in particular the cylindrical shape of the western minaret, which may also be of Iranian inspiration, it seems more likely that the minarets and their tiles were designed simultaneously. We have seen that the stucco mihrab of al-Nasir's madrasa, built even earlier, was also of Iranian style. Iranians might have worked in Cairo before the entente of 1323 between al-Nasir Muhammad and the Ilkhanid court and the arrival of the craftsman who built Qawsun's minarets. In this case Qawsun would have been inspired by the sultan's mosque rather than the reverse.

However, one should not exclude the possibility of an influence from Anatolia, where tile mosaics were also extensively used, as suggested by Ülkü Bates.[13] This would explain the association of the tile mosaics with masonry, which was regularly practised in Anatolian architecture of the Seljuk and Ilkhanid periods, whereas Iranian architecture is predominantly in brick. Moreover, the deeply carved shaft of the western minaret has antecedents in Anatolian Seljuq masonry.

The use of multiple minarets was not very common in Mamluk Cairo, with the exception of al-Azhar mosque. Al-Nasir's mosque is the second extant case after the mosque of al-Zahir Baybars. The mosque of the emir Qawsun is also reported to have had two minarets, which, as already mentioned, seem

Fig. 120. The Great Iwan of al-Nasir Muhammad (Robert Hay).

Fig. 121. The Great Iwan of al-Nasir Muhammad and the city (Description de l'Egypte).

to have been like al-Nasir's and unlike the Iranian model – that is, not symmetrically placed.

The external crenellations of the mosque consist of plain arched elements of the type used in fortifications, whereas the ones around the courtyard are stepped. This relates the mosque to the Citadel walls and the Great Iwan, which was depicted by Cassas with similar external crenellations, while relating the interior to traditional religious architecture.

Arched windows are pierced in the spandrels of the arches and along the upper qibla wall. The arches are pointed and connected by tie beams.

The large windows, now walled, which are pierced in the lower part of the walls appear rectangular on the facade, but inside they are framed by pointed arches integrated within the high polychrome dado. Although Ibn Iyas reported that the Ottomans removed marbles from the Citadel, Evliya, in his description of this mosque, dedicated a long passage in praise of its fine marble mosaics, the traces of which can still be seen; the dado was higher than 5 m.

The decoration of the courtyard consists exclusively of the ablaq voussoirs of the arches and the arched windows above them, and the crenellation. In each of the four upper corners between the crenels is a sculpted structure recalling the tops of early minarets; these would have been used to tie the ropes that pulled the awnings to shade the courtyard.

The columns of the mosque are a mixture of spoils from pre-Islamic monuments. Because they are of various heights, the sizes of their bases have been adapted accordingly. However, the two columns with basket capitals that flank the entrance are equal and of Coptic style. The remains of the original coffered ceiling suggest that it was magnificent and similar to that of Qalawun's mausoleum.

The dome (14.3 m diameter), supported on three sides by three arches on granite columns, rests on wooden pendentives, which, along with the fine foundation inscription around the base, were painted and gilded.

The present decoration of the mihrab is Comité work, but old photographs show remains of similar marble inlay.

The small loggia above the axial entrance is the earliest elevated bench for the use of the *mu'adhdhin*, instead of the more common version of a bench on columns. This structure was dedicated to the *iqama*, which is a call to prayer performed on Friday within the mosque. It was also a kind of pulpit for chanting and recitations. In later, smaller, mosques of the fifteenth century the elevated dikka was commonly used.

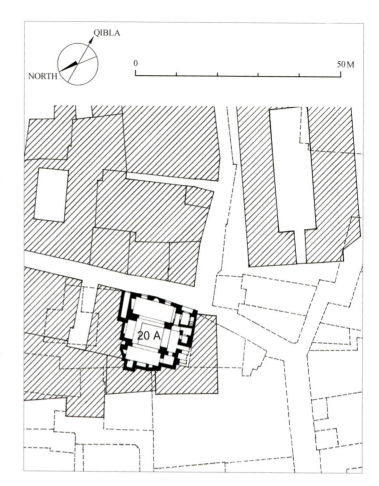

Fig. 122. The mosque of Almalik al-Juqandar.

20 (A, B). The mosques of Emirs Almalik al-Juqandar (1319)[14] and Ahmad al-Mihmandar (1325)[15]

Maqrizi described many monuments according to the functions they fulfilled at the time he was writing, as madrasas, or khanqahs, or a combination of both. Their

Fig. 123. The mosque of Almalik al-Juqandar.

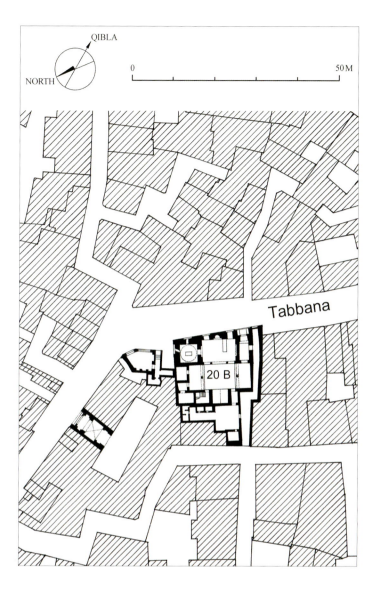

Fig. 124. The mosque of Ahmad al-Mihmandar.

The funerary mosque of the chief of protocol Shihab al-Din Ahmad al-Mihmandar (d.1348) (B) belongs to the same category (Figs 122, 123). It is called by its inscription 'turba and masjid', while Maqrizi described it as a madrasa and khanqah. There are no living units in the present building.

The minaret and the dome, unlike common practice, are not juxtaposed; the mausoleum occupies the northern corner of the building and the minaret stands at the southern edge. The present minaret is not original.

The most remarkable feature about the mosque is the facade with its deeply and beautifully carved tiraz band, which

Fig. 125. The mosque of Ahmad al-Mihmandar, portal.

inscriptions, however, often described their status in different terms. Among these cases is the mosque of the polo master Almalik al-Juqandar (A), built in 719/1319 (Figs 122, 123). Of the three religious foundations erected by this emir, it is the only one extant. It is described as a masjid by its inscription and as a madrasa by Maqrizi. The portal recess is crowned with a fine fluted semi-dome on maqurnas, and includes an oculus above the door. The plan is cruciform, and the four iwans have flat ceilings and pointed arches facing a courtyard (6.7 x 5.9m), which is roofed with a modern wooden lantern. It is not clear whether it was originally roofed. The minor iwans are lower than the main one, leaving space above for small rectangular windows overlooking the courtyard. They could have belonged to living units. The mosque had a fine stucco inscription running around the interior, which has recently been restored, awfully. The mihrab is of polychrome marble.

runs along its entire width, passing through the portal recess, where it curves above an oculus. The portal has a carved semi-dome on muqarnas pendentives, and the door is surmounted by an oculus framed by an interlocking marble rosette of remarkable quality.

The undecorated mosque has a four-iwan plan with the mausoleum adjoining the qibla iwan. The main and the lateral iwans, which are covered with wooden ceilings, open onto the courtyard with a triple and double arch respectively; only the west iwan is vaulted. The courtyard might have been originally covered.

Fig.126. The mosque of Ahmad al-Mihmandar.

21. The funerary mosque of Emir Ulmas al-Hajib (1330)[16]

Ulmas al-Hajib, the chamberlain of al-Nasir Muhammad, founded his mosque in the quarter of Hadarat al-Baqar to the west of the Citadel. An inscription above the door dates its foundation to 729/1328–9, and the completion to 730/1329–30.

Ulmas fell in disgrace and was executed three years after the completion of his mosque. Safadi reported that he imported marbles for his mosque and his adjoining palace from Syria and Anatolia and from other places overseas (*jaza'ir al-bahr*).

As was the case with the mosques of al-Maridani and Aqsunqur, the funerary mosque of Ulmas exemplifies the adjustment of the classical hypostyle or riwaq mosque to the urban environment. In other words, it shows the modifications

Fig.127. The mosque of Ulmas al-Hajib, portal.

or the loss of symmetry that this plan underwent when it had to be fitted in a given urban plot. However, this is the only one of the three to include the founder's domed mausoleum, and the second known Friday mosque in Cairo, after the mosque of Emir Husayn built in 719/1319, to include the founder's mausoleum. Although little has survived from the mosque of Emir Husayn,[17] its hypostyle plan and the location of the mausoleum behind the prayer hall are recognizable.

The funerary dome of Ulmas occupies a corner on the left and the minaret stands on the right side of the portal. The profile of the dome is more rounded than any other of the Mamluk period. Its transitional zone is pronounced in the Qalawunid tradition. It includes recesses on four sides pierced with triple windows framed with carved stucco bands. The minaret was reconstructed in 1713 (Fig.129).

Fig.128. The mosque of Ulmas al-Hajib, arcade.

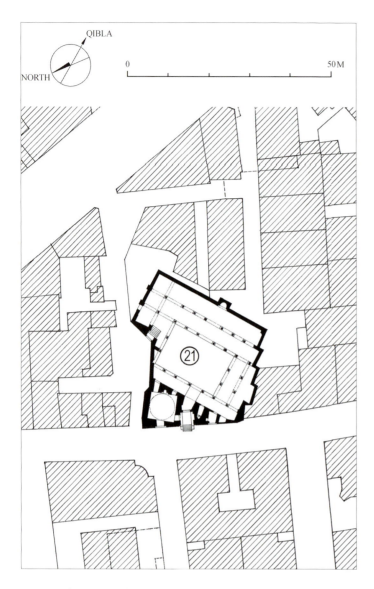

Fig. 129. The mosque of Ulmas al-Hajib.

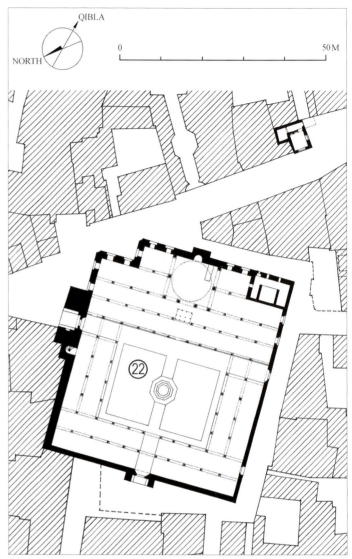

Fig. 130. The mosque of Altinbugha al-Maridani.

The portal consists of a deep recess roofed with a flat stone muqarnas, which was a novelty in Cairo that was repeated twice later, at the mosque of Bashtak (736/1336) and at the small oratory attached to Bashtak's palace in the street of Bayn al-Qasrayn (c. 738/1337–8) (Fig. 127).

The two recessed panels of the facade are pierced in their upper part with double-arched windows adorned with unusual wooden grilles shaped in arabesques that are unusual in Mamluk open woodwork, which is predominantly geometric.

The tiraz band along the facade passing along the portal recess is inscribed with an invocation rather than a Koranic verse. The drum of the mausoleum of Aydumur al-Bahlawan, built before 1346, also has such an inscription. In this text, published by C. Karim, the founder praises God and begs Him for forgiveness for his passions, lust and greed. Ulmas, who was very wealthy and had a controversial love affair with a boy from the popular quarter of Husayniyya, might have been troubled and repentant about his lifestyle. But the inscription could

also have been meant to placate the sultan, whose suspicion he feared so much that he pretended to be austere and stingy. The sultan, who was annoyed about Ulmas' love affair, executed him, however, for another reason; he suspected him of plotting to overthrow his rule.

The layout of the mosque is quite irregular. The lateral arcades are asymmetrical, and the northern one is truncated. Moreover, the mihrab is off the axis of the prayer hall, placed instead on the axis of the courtyard and the entrance.

A further irregularity due to the constraints of the site is the Mecca orientation of the mausoleum, which diverges from that of the prayer hall by almost 22°. This is one of four such cases in Mamluk funerary architecture.

The interior of the mosque, now in an advanced state of dilapidation, was originally decorated with fine stucco carvings framing the arches and filling their spandrels. The keel-arched openings in the spandrels were also framed with a band of carved stucco. As noticed by Hasan 'Abd al-Wahhab,

Fig. 131. The mosque of Altinbugha al-Maridani, west portal.

Fig. 132. The mosque of Altinbugha al-Maridani, prayer hall facade.

this decorative treatment of the arches is rather archaic, having been used in the mosque of Ibn Tulun and in Fatimid monuments, and in the Mamluk period only in the complex of Qalawun and here.

The respective mihrabs of the mosque and the mausoleum are individually decorated with polychrome marble in the style of the period. The mihrab of the mosque is surmounted by a rectangular window flanked by a pair of oculi.

22. The Friday mosque of Emir Altinbugha al-Maridani (1339–40)[18]

Altinbugha al-Maridani began his career as the cup-bearer of al-Nasir Muhammad. He became 'emir of a thousand' and chief of the police in Cairo, and married the sultan's daughter.

After a short crisis during the reign of al-Nasir's successor al-Mansur Abu Bakr, his career went on successfully under al-Ashraf Kujuk and al-Salih Isma'il. He died as governor of Aleppo in 744/1343.

Al-Maridani built his mosque when he was seriously ill, which also prompted him to make generous donations. The historian al-Yusufi praised the mosque as one of the most lavishly decorated and best built in Cairo, emphasizing its dome and minaret.

An inscription band at the west entrance dates the foundation of the mosque to 739/1338–9, and two inscriptions over the main and the northern entrance indicate the completion date as Ramadan 740/1340. A third dating inscription in the sanctuary repeats the completion date.

The sultan contributed to the mosque of his son-in-law with wood and marble, and his master builder *al-mu'allim* al-Suyufi built it. The columns, taken from the Fatimid mosque of Rashida, were spoils from ancient monuments. Koranic texts

Fig. 133. The mosque of Altinbugh al-Maridani, wooden screen.

Fig. 134. The mosque of Altinbugha al-Maridani, prayer hall.

Fig. 135. The mosque of Altinbugha al-Maridani, stucco tree in qibla wall.

are profusely inscribed on the western portal, along the facades and in the prayer hall.

Like the sultan's mosque in the Citadel, al-Maridani's mosque is built with a riwaq plan, a dome above the mihrab and three axial entrances. Due to urban constraints, however, the plan is not perfectly rectangular; the northeastern corner, between Tabbana street and a lane, is chamfered. It is, however, less irregular than the plan of Ulmas' mosque due to the absence of a mausoleum.

The minaret stands next to the main portal, which is not opposite the prayer hall but in the northern wall. The facade wall between the main portal and the corner beneath the minaret indicates that substantial consolidation work must have been executed here at a later date. The inscription band, the crenellation, and the corner colonette are missing in this section.

The stone minaret is the earliest known to have been built with an entirely octagonal shaft surmounted by an octagonal pavilion crowned with a bulb on muqarnas. The *mu'allim* al-Suyufi, who built this mosque, also designed the minaret of the madrasa of Aqbugha attached to al-Azhar mosque. The restored bulb at the top of al-Maridani's minaret is repeated on the wooden pulpit inside, which is original.[19]

The main portal has the shape of an iwan with a pointed arch. The door is included in a recess crowned with a rectangular muqarnas cresting, panelled with marble and decorated with ablaq inlaid patterns. The joggled door lintels were the most lavishly inlaid so far in Mamluk architecture. The small window with colonettes above the door is a common feature on Mamluk portals. This one corresponds to an inner window with a grille decorated with blue and white tile mosaics.

The west portal has a different design. It projects with a beautiful half-conch resting on muqarnas pendentives and decorated with a sunrise motif in ablaq stone inlay. Between the pendentives above the inscription cartouches an epigraphic medallion includes another pierced medallion decorated with tile mosaics (Fig. 131). The southern entrance is plain.

Unlike the mosque of al-Nasir Muhammad in the Citadel, the facade on the main street, which corresponds to the mihrab wall, is panelled with window recesses. Following the fenestration device of Qalawun's complex, the lower windows are rectangular and the upper ones have a double-arched composition, which corresponds to a single-arch qamariyya within. Only the northern and eastern facades and a section of the southern facade are panelled with window recesses – i.e. the most visible parts. The remaining walls, which correspond to the three minor riwaqs, are plain and blind. The tiraz band, however, which starts on the northern facade, continues along the eastern wall and further to the end of the southern wall.

The mihrab protrudes in the central recess of the facade beneath a double-arched window. This projection is a small buttress to strengthen the lower part of the wall, which is hollowed, and hence weakened, by the cavity of the mihrab set in the thinner recess wall. In later buildings a more elegant solution was found by placing the mihrab in the protruding or thicker part of the wall instead of a recess, making the buttress unnecessary. Later mosques also show an oculus instead of the arched window above the mihrab.

The facade of the courtyard differs from that of al-Nasir Muhammad's mosque at the Citadel. The pointed arches of the surrounding arcades are framed with a continuous moulding, which curls in a loop at the apex of each arch. Stucco-carved keel-arched niches and medallions alternate in the spandrels of the arcade. In the second row the spandrels of the arches are pierced with relieving oculi. The corners of the courtyard are adorned with the same kind of ribbed domical sculptures seen at the mosque of al-Nasir Muhammad.

The dome over the mihrab is similar to, but smaller than that of al-Nasir Muhammad with similar wooden painted and gilded pendentives. It is carried by eight instead of ten columns, and the arrangement of the windows in the transitional zone consists here of one oculus above two bays, instead of one over three as in the former mosque.

A remarkable feature about al-Maridani's mosque is the screen of turned wood that separates the sanctuary from the courtyard, which justifies the windows in the walls as a necessary source of light (Figs 132, 133).

The prayer hall, which is currently in bad shape, was once lavishly decorated. Remains of gilded stucco decoration with epigraphic bands forming rectangles centred by naturalistic trees adorn the qibla wall. Besides the trees bearing fruits represented in glass mosaic mihrabs of Qalawun's and Taybar's madrasas, these are the only extant naturalistic trees in Mamluk architectural decoration (Fig.135).[20] The mihrab and the dado are of polychrome marble, with friezes of small niches flanked with colonettes of blue glass paste. Panels of marble mosaics with 'Allah' inscribed in square Kufic, recalling Qalawun's mausoleum, decorate the walls of the sanctuary. On the northern wall there is an interesting foundation inscription panel of inlaid white marble. The function of the room that occupies the southeast corner of the prayer hall is not clear.

The varying size of the pre-Islamic columns of this mosque has been compensated for by the size of their pedestals. However, the columns that carry the dome are all of granite of equal size, and have ancient Egyptian capitals; they might have been brought from Upper Egypt together with those for al-Nasir Muhammad's mosque and palace in the Citadel.

The side arcades have no other decoration than the stucco medallions in their upper walls.

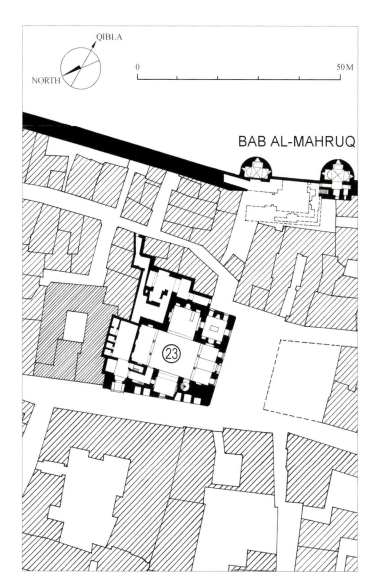

Fig.136. The mosque of Aslam al-Baha'i.

23. The funerary mosque of Emir Aslam al-Baha'i al-Silahdar (1345)[21]

Aslam al-Baha'i began his career with Sultan Qalawun and continued to advance until he became the *silahdar* or arm-bearer of al-Nasir Muhammad. After spending the years 1326–33 in jail, he was appointed governor of Gaza, and kept this office until his death in 1346 during the reign of al-Muzaffar Hajji. The mosque was built four years after al-Nasir's death, and one year prior to his own.

Located in al-Darb al-Ahmar quarter, the mosque belongs in the same architectural category as the mosques of Almalik and Ahmad al-Mihmandar, except that it was founded with the status of a Friday mosque. This is apparently an anomaly if we consider that the Friday mosques of al-Nasir's reign were generally built with a riwaq plan. Another anomaly of this Friday mosque is the presence of rooms overlooking its courtyard.

Fig. 137. The funerary mosque of Aslam al-Baha'i, marble panel in the portal.

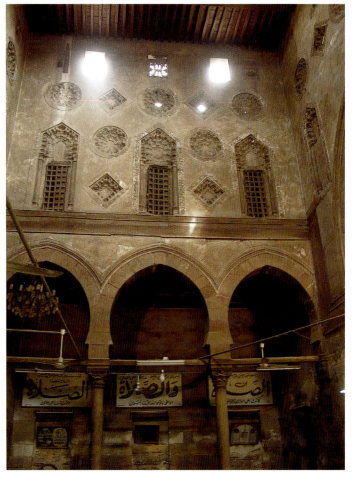

Fig. 139. The funerary mosque of Aslam al-Baha'i.

Fig. 138. The funerary mosque of Aslam al-Baha'i, marble panel in the portal.

The building has two facades, the main southern one, and a western one, both overlooking a small square, next to which Aslam's residence once stood. A sabil, a trough and a rab' also stood nearby. As in the mosque of Ahmad al-Mihmandar, the minaret is not contiguous to the mausoleum. The present one is a late reconstruction that stands at the southwest end of the main facade. The mausoleum occupies the southeastern corner.

Both facades have a portal with a dating inscription. The southern portal states that the mosque was begun in Jumada I 745/September–October 1344, and completed in Rabi' I 746/July 1345. The northwest inscription states that it was completed in Rajab 746/October–November 1345. We thus have two completion dates with a gap of about four months between them. This gap could refer to the completion of the decoration or the annexes of the mosque. According to Chahinda Karim, the masonry suggests that the mausoleum was built first and the mosque was added as a second thought. Considering that this small building took a whole year to erect, it is likely that the construction of the mausoleum was included in this period.

The main and southern portal is a shallow trilobed recess, whose major adornment is the large square marble panel above the door, centred by an oculus. The oculus is in the centre of a twenty-pointed star of carved marble surrounded by a flamboyant sixteen-petalled interlace medallion with fleurs-de-lis pointing to the centre, set within the panel. The western portal shows a conch in a trilobed recess framed by a moulding that interlocks to form a loop at the apex of the conch.

The dome, a brick ribbed construction, has along its external drum the remains of a magnificent inscription with the Verse of the Throne made of fine glazed tile mosaics of blue, green, black and white colours, and set in cartouches alternating with medallions. It shares this feature with the funerary dome of al-Nasir Muhammad's wife Tughay, built before 1349 in the cemetery.[22]

Aslam's mosque has a cruciform plan with a courtyard covered with a wooden lantern. Each of the iwans is roofed with a flat wooden ceiling; the eastern and the western face the central space with a frontal arch, and the lateral ones with three arches. As in the mosque of Almalik, the minor iwans do not occupy the entire height of the wall; the lateral ones are surmounted by windows, and the west iwan by a balcony facing the sanctuary. The windows and the balcony belong to rooms on the upper floor. The west iwan includes an elevated wooden bench; it is the second elevated dikka after that of al-Nasir's mosque at the Citadel, which is above the main entrance. They must have been for the use of the *mu'adhdhin*s. This one is also reached from within through the minaret staircase.

The walls of the courtyard have remarkable stucco decoration, consisting of niches, medallions and lozenges set between the arches and windows. A wooden inscription band runs along the walls.

The mausoleum, which communicates through a window with the sanctuary, is reached through a proper portal next to the iwan arch. It is decorated with exquisite stucco carvings; the conch and spandrels of the mihrab display fine arabesques and they are framed with epigraphic bands. A stucco medallion above the mihrab is also framed with arabesques and screened with an epigraphic stucco grille.

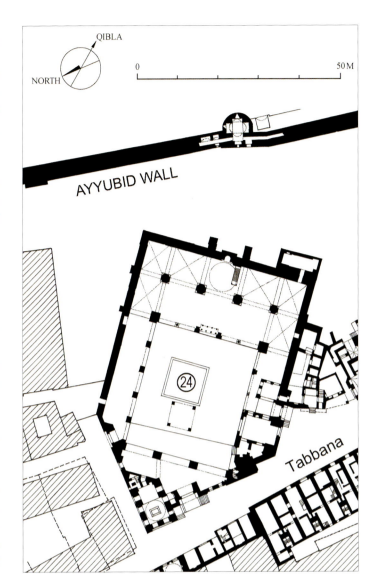

Fig. 140. The mosque of Aqsunqur.

24. The mosque of Emir Aqsunqur al-Nasiri (1346–7)[23]

The emir Aqsunqur held the office of master of the hunt and governor of Gaza and Tripoli during the reign of al-Nasir Muhammad, whose son-in-law he was. After al-Nasir's death he also married his widow. He reached the peak of his career under al-Muzaffar Hajji before he was assassinated in 748/1347. Although it was founded more than five years after al-Nasir's death, this mosque belongs entirely to the architectural tradition of that sultan's reign.

Aqsunqur's mosque stands in Tabbana street, the extension of the main avenue of Qahira leading to the Citadel. Its foundation on this site, formerly a cemetery, upgraded the area, which belonged to the sultans' procession itinerary.

The posthumous inscription of the northern portal indicates that the mosque was founded in Ramadan 747/December 1346,

and that Friday prayer was held there in Rabi' I 748/June 1347, only six months later, and that the founder died in Rabi' II 748/July 1347. According to Maqrizi, Aqsunqur built a mausoleum next to the mosque '*bi-jiwarihi*', a primary school or maktab, and a 'shop' to serve water to the thirsty, meaning a sabil. The maktab and the sabil have disappeared.

The main facade is not parallel to the courtyard, but protrudes onto the street, forming a triangle whose base is along the facade of the western arcade. The minaret stands at the southern side of the angular facade and heralds the mosque at a distance to the onlooker coming from the Citadel. The monumental minaret, entirely cylindrical, seems to have had originally four instead of the usual three storeys. This has been recorded in several nineteenth-century drawings. Although restored on a smaller scale with a reconstructed top, it is still an impressive tower.

The facades are panelled with recesses crowned with muqarnas, which include the windows. The main portal, which

Fig. 141. The mosque of Aqsunqur, minaret.

is near the summit of the triangle, has the shape of a shallow iwan. Next to it a domed mausoleum occupies the angle of the facade. There are two non-axial entrances in the lateral walls; the northern one is behind the mausoleum.

The architecture of this mosque differs in many respects from the slightly earlier mosque of al-Maridani. The walls are less high and the arcades are built on piers instead of columns with transverse arches supporting cross-vaults. This device is common in the architecture of Aleppo, where Aqsunqur had been governor, and in Tripoli.

The mihrab is surmounted by a one-bay dome with a transitional zone consisting of a plain squinch. On the exterior its transitional zone is octagonal. An oculus is pierced right above the mihrab, partly included in the transitional zone of the dome. It is the earliest extant mihrab oculus, which henceforth will become a traditional feature of Mamluk Cairene architecture. The mihrab protrudes on the rear facade, as at al-Maridani's mosque. The mihrab has a conch of carved and painted marble and the rest of its niche is in polychrome marble.

The remarkable carved and inlaid marble minbar is the earliest in Cairo to be a built-in structure, followed by the minbar of Sultan Hasan. Sultan Qaytbay built a stone minbar in the khanqah of Sultan Faraj (Figs 142, 144).

Although major transformations were made to the mosque by the Ottoman emir Ibrahim Agha in the seventeenth century, when it was badly damaged after having been restored in the fifteenth century, the original layout is still recognizable. Ibrahim Agha replaced the damaged vaults of the mosque's arcade with a wooden ceiling and redecorated the qibla wall with Turkish tiles. He also inserted his own mausoleum, a rectangular chamber, in the southern arcade in 1062/1652. This mausoleum is lavishly decorated with polychrome marble mosaics of Bahri Mamluk style, which raises the question as to whether this marble came from Aqsunqur's mausoleum, which was near the mosque.

The domed mausoleum (Fig. 143) we see today contains an inscription dedicated to Sultan al-Ashraf 'Ala' al-Din Kujuk, a son of al-Nasir Muhammad and the stepson of Aqsunqur; he was sultan for a short period in 1341–2, died in 1345, prior to the foundation of the mosque, and was buried elsewhere. His remains were moved at a later date, in Ramadan 748/December 1347, to this mausoleum. In the same month, Sultan al-Muzaffar Hajji was buried in what Maqrizi described as 'Aqsunqur's mausoleum'.[24] One might speculate that the mausoleum dedicated to Sultan Kujuk was the one built by Aqsunqur for himself and that his widow might have buried her son Kujuk there and added the inscription. On this occasion, the bodies of other sons of al-Nasir Muhammad buried earlier in this area, perhaps in a simple sepulchre, were transferred into this mausoleum. However,

Fig 142. The mosque of Aqsunqur, the prayer hall.

there is a twist to this interpretation, which is the presence in the southern arcade of the mosque of a rectangular structure with a cenotaph with an inscription from the Ottoman period, which states that Aqsunqur is buried there. The inscription, which gives the dates of the foundation and completion of the mosque, is, according to Van Berchem, the copy of an original text. But why should Aqsunqur have been buried in the side arcade when his mosque was designed in conjunction with a mausoleum? Unless this inscription is based on a misunderstanding from the Ottoman period, we may assume that Aqsunqur built his own mausoleum near the mosque, and that his remains were transferred into the mosque when this mausoleum was demolished; this might have happened at the same time as the mosque itself was damaged. The location of Aqsunqur's mausoleum next to the southern entrance and the minaret is likely, as also assumed by Meinecke. This would have allowed a small Mecca-oriented mausoleum with visual access to the street to be juxtaposed to the minaret without truncating a side arcade, as was done in Ulmas' mosque. It is interesting to note that Aqsunqur gave the privileged location to Kujuk's mausoleum by attaching it to his mosque, whereas his

Fig. 143. The mosque of Aqsunqur, stucco decoration in the mausoleum of Sultan Kujuk.

own stood outside. This would have been out of reverence for Kujuk and as an acknowledgement of his superior royal status.

According to Creswell, the masonry indicates that Kujuk's mausoleum was built at the same time as the mosque, both completed after Aqsunqur's death. Meinecke explained the irregularity of the western riwaq by the fact that the mausoleum pre-dates the mosque. However, this view cannot be supported because, unlike common practice, the mausoleum is not Mecca-oriented. Had it pre-dated the mosque, it should have been Mecca-oriented, as was the rule. At that time this quarter was not fully urbanized, and there were no serious obstacles to prevent such an important element in a funerary structure. In a mausoleum attached to a Friday mosque the absence of a mihrab is less problematic, however. The addition of the mausoleum to the western arcade of the mosque, and the constraints of the street, left no alternative but to construct it without a mihrab. This shortcoming was compensated for by the advantageous positioning of the mausoleum, which protrudes into the street, with four vertical rows of windows on three sides. A small iwan attached to the domed chamber overlooks the mosque's interior with a window and an upper oculus. The mausoleum was probably attached to the mosque during the final stage of its construction.

The transitional zone of the funerary dome consists of a small single-niche pendentive. The walls of the domed chamber and the adjoining iwan have preserved a carved stucco inscription and stucco medallions.

Fig. 144. The mosque of Aqsunqur, minbar detail.

– 16 –

The Reign of
al-Nasir Hasan and After

25. The mosque and khanqah of Emir Shaykhu al-ʿUmari (1349–57)[1]

Shaykhu al-ʿUmari al-Nasiri began his brilliant career as a recruit of al-Nasir Muhammad. His career flourished during the reign of Sultan Hasan, especially after the interim period, when Shaykhu was the major political authority in the state until his assassination in 1357. Maqrizi credited him for having acquired his fabulous fortune – his daily income amounted to 200,000 dirhams or 10,000 dinars – by honourable means.

The religious complex of Shaykhu was the first major foundation to be established after the Black Death in 1348, which is estimated to have killed about one third of Egypt's population. It was built in two phases; the funerary mosque was completed in 750/1349 and the khanqah in 756/1355. ʿAbd al-Wahhab believed that the construction of the mosque had already begun in 747/1346, because of a window grille found there, which is inlaid with silver and gold, and inscribed with the title 'al-Malik al-Muzaffar', referring to Sayf al-Din Hajji, who ruled from September 1346 to December 1347. This would mean that the mosque took three years to complete, which is rather unlikely. Shaykhu may instead have acquired the window from an earlier building.

The double building straddles Saliba street, with the mosque and the mausoleum on the northern side and the khanqah opposite. This was not the first complex to display this arrangement: in 736/1336 Bashtak had built a khanqah

Fig. 145. The mosque and khanqah of Shaykhu, south view.

Fig. 146. The mosque of Shaykhu, interior.

facing a Friday mosque, with which it was connected by a bridge across the street. Aqsunqur might also have built his mausoleum and a sabil across a side street near his mosque. With the addition of the khanqah, Shaykhu's complex acquired its distinctive character as a pious foundation, which, by embracing a thoroughfare, was fully integrated into the urban environment.

The southern end of the facades of the two buildings, which are inscribed with a Koranic band, is emphasized by similar portals surmounted by equal octagonal minarets facing each other. Approached from the southern end of Saliba street, the identical minarets above similar portals are the first to appear, heralding the pious foundation.

Despite the seven-year gap between the two buildings, their design is homogeneous. Instead of muqarnas, the balconies of the minarets are decorated with horizontal linear carvings on the first storey, and vertical ones on the second storey. The vertical design, which recalls an ancient Egyptian papyrus motif, repeats the device used at the top of the minaret of Qalawun added by his son al-Nasir Muhammad. It was also used in the minaret of Manjaq, built slightly earlier, in 1346–7. The portal vaults with a semi-dome on muqarnas are identical. Their conch is carved with arabesques, once painted.

The mosque

The portal inscription of the mosque dates its completion to Ramadan 750/November–December 1349 and defines it as a jami'. The foundation is said to have been built for Shaykh Akmal al-Din al-Rumi, who was also the principal of twenty Sufis attached to it.[2]

It has an irregular hypostyle or riwaq plan, with two arcaded halls, both of which are two aisles deep, and two lateral double-arched recesses. Besides the main portal in the southern facade, a door in the western wall and another one in the northern wall leading to the latrines are not axial.

Instead of increasing the thickness of the walls to absorb the irregularity of the plan and maintain the inner symmetry, as was usually done, the architect let the prayer hall have an irregular shape with non-parallel lateral walls. The northern wall juts out with a triangular tip and the southern wall follows the street alignment, making an angle with the inner axis. Likewise, the southern corner of the prayer hall extends along the street alignment instead of being absorbed in the masonry. There was a good reason for this unconventional solution, which was to allow the mausoleum to communicate with the sanctuary through a window. The mausoleum is a small chamber (4.8 m wide) squeezed between the vestibule, the courtyard and this extended tip of the sanctuary. The lack of space, and the need to connect the mausoleum with

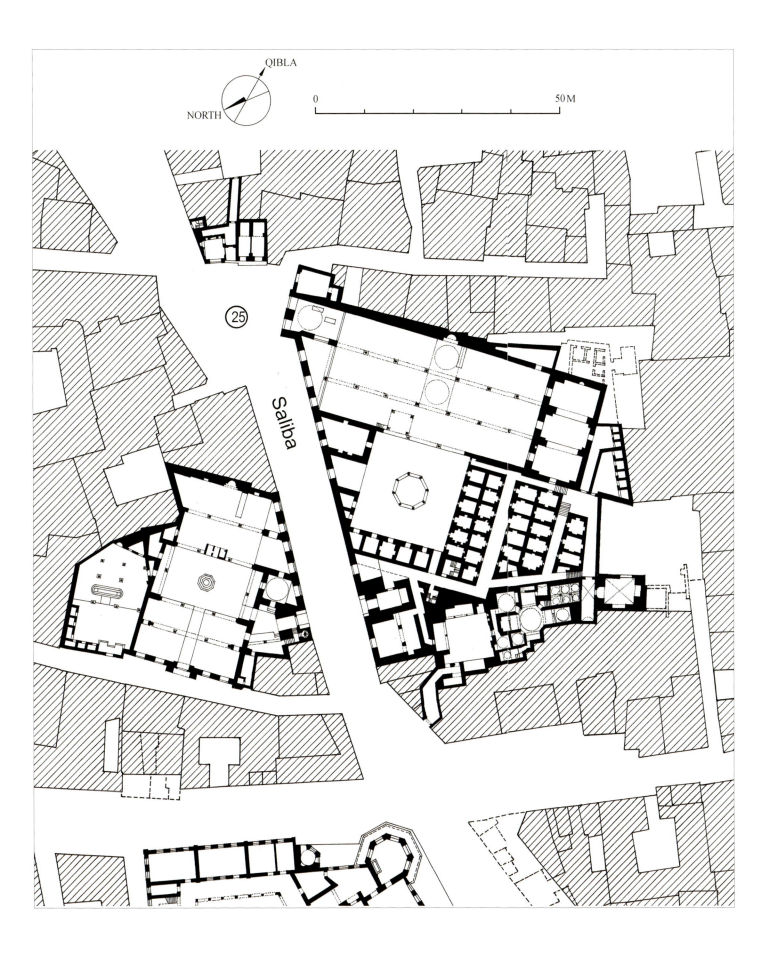

QIBLA

NORTH

0   50 M

②⑤

Saliba

Fig. 147. The mosque and khanqah of Shaykhu.

Fig. 148. The khanqah of Shaykhu, northeastern corner.

Fig. 149. The khanqah of Shaykhu, courtyard.

the mosque, imposed a second compromise, which was the elimination of the mausoleum's mihrab in favour of the window overlooking the prayer hall. The mausoleum is today bare of decoration. Two stucco window grilles in the transitional zone seem to be original.

The courtyard is the earliest extant in a riwaq mosque to be paved with polychrome marble. The mosque originally had fine stucco window grilles, which underwent restoration, as did most parts of the mosque. The mihrab has remains of the typical polychrome marble of the period. Its lower part displays eighteenth-century Tunisian tiles. A dome, which surmounted it, burnt down during the Ottoman campaign in 1517. It was most likely a light timber structure carried by the ceiling, like that of the khanqah.

In the prayer hall a dikka on columns and a minbar made of stone display the same style of carving. The dikka is dated Safar 961/January 1554, and is inscribed with the name of its mason, Hajj Sha'ban Ibn Muhammad Ibn Sa'id al-Nuqali, who probably produced the similarly carved stone minbar.

The khanqah

The khanqah was completed within seven months in 756/1355. Shaykhu had acquired more than a *faddan* of land (4200 sqm) to build the khanqah, along with two hammams, shops and dwellings. The generous endowment also included a curriculum for teaching the four *madhhab*s of Islamic law and other religious disciplines. It is thus the earliest known khanqah-madrasa of the Mamluk period. The Sufis were required to be celibate, which was not always the case in Mamluk monastic practice. The Anatolian Sufi shakyh Akmal al-Din, mentioned earlier, was the first principal of the khanqah and the supervisor of its endowment; he was also the teacher of the Hanafi *madhhab*.

The foundation inscription in the portal has a remarkable text mentioning the founder's name with the humble Sufi attribute '*al-'abd al-faqir*' or 'the poor slave', instead of the usual Mamluk titulature. The text refers to the building with the vague term 'makan' instead of 'khanqah' or 'madrasa'. The inscription on the khanqah's minaret differs from that of the mosque; it includes the Koranic passage XXII, 27, which refers to the pilgrimage. The khanqah might therefore have hosted foreign pilgrims passing through Cairo on their way to Mecca. This quarter being traditionally inhabited by Maghrebis, the khanqah might have hosted pilgrims from North Africa.

On coming down from the Citadel, before passing between the two long facades, a passerby faces the domed corner of the khanqah. This small facade is pierced with two upper and two lower windows, in accordance with the design of the two main facades of the complex. However, the upper tripartite windows here are adorned with more elaborate marble columns, and the four rectangular windows of this corner are larger than all the others. The small dome, which emphasizes this northern facade, is a plastered wooden structure with a rounded and bulbous profile. Although it appears as a domed mausoleum, this corner is only a domed space within the mosque's arcade (Fig. 148).

The lintel of the khanqah's entrance, beneath the panel of the foundation inscription, is an ancient Egyptian granite block, with a linear vertical carving along the upper edge, similar to the decoration beneath the upper balconies of the minarets.

The khanqah is built around a courtyard, with an arcaded prayer hall and living units occupying three floors on the southern and western sides. The northern side includes an iwan facing the courtyard with an arch and living units. A large dwelling compound, three storeys high, and ruined dependencies, are on the rear side of the khanqah.

As in the mosque, here also the architect did not pursue a regular plan by increasing the thickness of the walls. Instead, the prayer hall is extended along the street to include an additional irregular space, which is covered with the wooden dome on the eastern corner.

Beneath this dome is the tomb of Akmal al-Din, who died in 786/1384 during the reign of Sultan Barquq, who revered him so highly that he accompanied his funerary cortege on foot. The burial of a shaykh within a khanqah was not common in a princely foundation. This might have been by order of Barquq, or, considering his special status, by Shaykhu himself. However, no waqf document has survived to confirm this. Considering that the shaykh was the supervisor of the endowment, even Shaykhu himself might have stipulated to be buried there.

The last arch at the northern end of the arcade, which borders the domed area, is supported by a rectangular pier instead of a column. This allowed the spanning of a larger arch and the support of a dome at this corner. The windows of this domed corner of the prayer hall are particularly large, and signal the special significance of this space. Shaykhu is reported also to have been buried in the khanqah, which would mean that he changed his mind after building the mausoleum attached to the earlier mosque. This change of mind would be consistent with his self-image as a Sufi, as expressed in the foundation inscription of the khanqah.

The light dome is carried like a lantern by the wooden ceiling. Creswell attributed the construction of the dome to the restoration of Bilal Agha in 1095/1683–4. Indeed, the coarse inner woodwork is different from that of the rest of the ceiling. It is very likely, however, that Bilal restored an existing dome, as the treatment of this corner and its facade strongly suggest.

A similar bulbous wooden dome is above the mihrab. It is preceded by a lantern decorated in the same style as the rest of the ceiling. This dome could also could have been restored or rebuilt. The sole decoration on the stone mihrab is the ablaq sunrise motif in the conch, which anticipates the mihrabs of the Circassian period.

Fig. 150. The khanqah of Shaykhu, painted ceiling.

Fig. 151. The khanqah of Shaykhu, painted ceiling.

The wooden ceiling of the khanqah's sanctuary is beautifully painted in blue, white and black. A reception hall (qa'a) adjoins the sanctuary on the southern side.

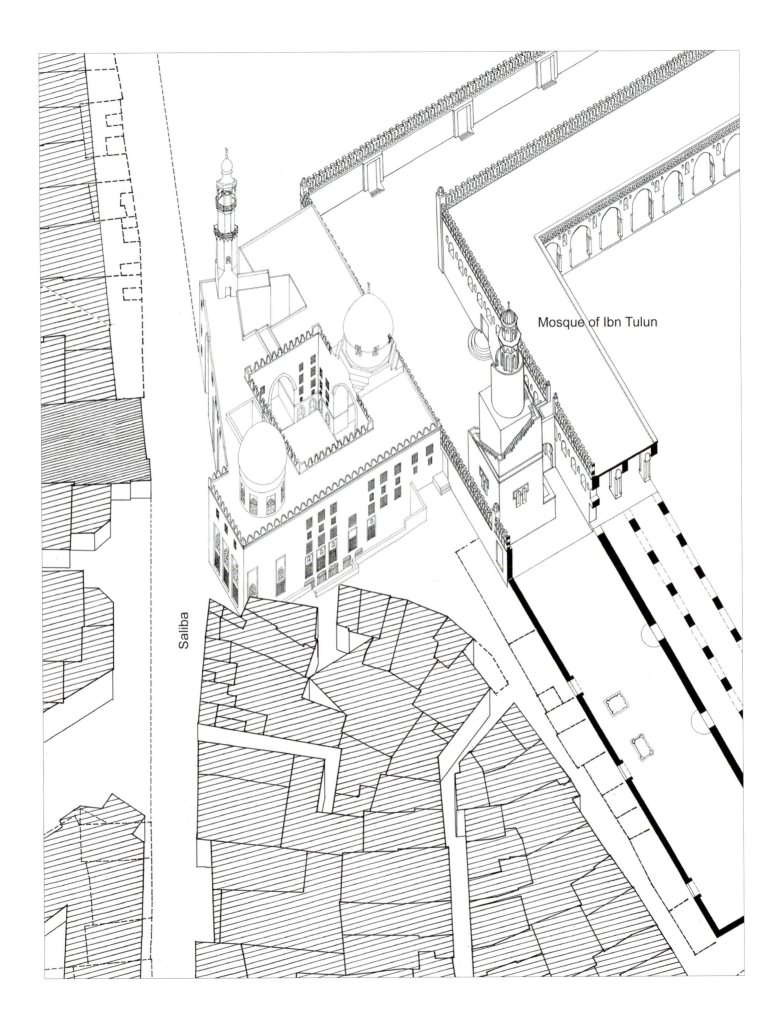

Saliba

Mosque of Ibn Tulun

THE REIGN OF AL-NASIR HASAN AND AFTER

Fig. 153. The madrasa of Sarghitmish, mausoleum dome.

Fig. 154. The madrasa of Sarghitmish, portal.

26. The madrasa of Emir al-Sayfi Sarghitmish (1356)[3]

The career of al-Sayfi Sarghitmish began in the service of al-Nasir Muhammad and reached its peak during the reign of Sultan Hasan, when he dominated the political scene for a while alongside Shaykhu. Following Shaykhu's death he enjoyed a short period of supreme authority before he fell in disgrace and was sent to jail, where he died in 759/1358.

The inscription band at the entrance dates the madrasa to 757/1356 and describes the founder as 'ra's al-nawba al-malakī' or 'chief of the royal Mamluks'. It also describes the founder as the 'mentor of scholars, the succour of the weak, and the founder of madrasas and mosques' (*murabbī 'l-ulamā', muqawwī 'l-ḍu'afā'*

Fig. 152. [opposite] The madrasa of Sarghitmish, axonometric drawing.

bānī 'l-madāris wa'l-masājid). These attributes epitomize Mamluk virtues and ideals, and the first one refers to Sarghitmish's acknowledged scholarship.

Maqrizi dates the commencement of construction works to Ramadan 756/September–October 1355 and the completion to Jumada I 757/May 1356, which indicates a construction period of approximately eight months.

The institution was dedicated to students from Iran (*a'jam*). They might have been Turkic people, as the madrasa was dedicated to the Hanafi *madhhab*, which was predominant among Turks and Turcomans, whereas Iranians at that time were mostly Shafi'i.

The layout

The monument is a remarkable specimen of Mamluk architectural innovation in the era following al-Nasir Muhammad's reign. Sarghitmish's minaret is placed on the eastern corner of

197

Fig. 155. The madrasa of Sarghitmish, mihrab dome (nineteenth-century photograph).

Fig. 156. The madrasa of Sarghitmish, minaret.

Fig. 157. The madrasa of Sarghitmish.

the facade, from where it dominates the northern courtyard or ziyada of the adjacent Ibn Tulun's mosque, as if it belonged there. Conversely, flanking the madrasa on the southeastern corner, the minaret of Ibn Tulun appears as if it were attached to the madrasa of Sarghitmish. Seen from the northern side, the silhouette of the madrasa appears as an ensemble with two prominent domes and two minarets. The octagonal minaret (24.6 m from roof level) is one of the most elegant of the period, its decoration consisting of ablaq geometric patterns. It stands on the left-hand side of a portal with a semi-vault on muqarnas. The portal is emphasized by a slight pishtaq, and the rest of the facade is 15.5 m high. The pishtaq, or elevated section of the facade emphasizing the portal, is a device common in Mamluk Syrian architecture, and was already used in the portals of the khanqah of Mughultay al-Jamali 730/1329–30, of which little remains. Its recess is crowned with a half-dome on muqarnas pendentives, which are the antecedents

of the pendentives that characterize the masonry domes of the fifteenth century. The niches of the muqarnas are carved with a sunrise motif radiating from their bases.

Along the upper walls of the facade a row of small rectangular windows belonging to living units are pierced above the recesses. This unusual feature dwarfs the recesses and disturbs the aesthetics of the facade. The windows continue along the facade of the mausoleum, where they do not correspond to living units, for the sake of consistency. The rear facade of the madrasa also displays rows of rectangular windows belonging to students' cells.

The plan of the madrasa building has an unusual combination of a cruciform or four-iwan plan with a dome over the mihrab. Due to the location of the building, the domed mausoleum is not contiguous to the prayer hall, where it would not have been visible from the main street, but adjoins the west iwan across the courtyard, where it projects boldly into the street.

Fig. 158. The madrasa of Sarghitmish, mihrab dome (Ebers).

As in the case of al-Muzaffar Baybars' mausoleum, the domed chamber does not overlook the street directly; it is preceded by a rectangular space that overlooks the street through three tiers of windows. As in the previous case, this space must have been added to emphasize the mausoleum by increasing its projection into the street. The space is roofed with vaults.

The funerary dome is a brick construction with no external transitional zone, but with a high drum adorned with muqarnas above an inscription band. The inscription, most of which had disappeared, was replaced during the recent restoration by a badly executed one. The dome consists of a double shell; the apex of the inner shell seems to be slightly above the external muqarnas frieze.

The inner transitional zone displays muqarnas pendentives instead of squinches, which are more common on brick domes; the muqarnas here lacks the elegance characteristic of Mamluk transitional zones. Between the pendentives, composite windows have a corresponding pyramidal profile. Interestingly, these four windows are not visible on the exterior, but hidden behind four of the large arched windows of the external drum. These eight arched windows are half the usual number, but their size is larger than is usual. They correspond to smaller arched windows inside the dome, and the lower part of four of them corresponds to the four windows of the transitional zone.

The double brick shell of the funerary dome and the exterior muqarnas frieze in the upper part of the drum were not common features in Cairo. The high drum and the unconventional rounded profile of the dome recall Timurid architecture, which, however, they pre-date. As discussed previously, west Iran or Iraq seem to be the source of these features. Whether they were introduced by members of the madrasa's Iranian community is difficult to tell.

The dome of the sanctuary is a Comité reconstruction based on nineteenth-century drawings and photographs, which show a plastered wooden construction.[4]

The domed space of the sanctuary is flanked by two lateral iwans with a flat wooden ceiling opening into the sanctuary through an arch. The transitional zone of the dome consists of wooden pendentives similar to those of Sultan Hasan's mausoleum.

Instead of the usual polychrome marble dado, the mihrab wall was originally decorated with remarkable panels of white marble carved with medallions in the style of bookbindings, and included Sarghitmish's name and his blazon, which was the handkerchief, the symbol of the master of the wardrobe. Some of the marble panels carved with arabesques, a mosque lamp, birds and a pair of hands holding stems, have been removed to the Islamic Museum; two are *in situ* flanking the mihrab (Fig. 159). The marble mihrab is inscribed with the Verse of the Throne. The awful present dado is not a faithful copy of the original decoration. The three other iwans, which open with an arch into the courtyard, have a flat wooden ceiling.

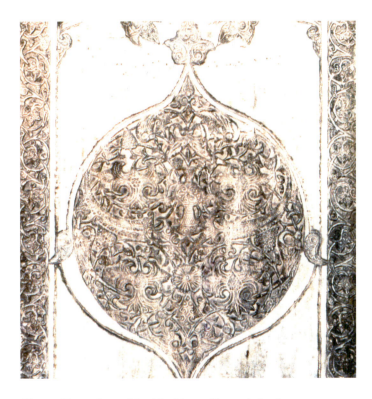

Fig. 159. The madrasa of Sarghitmish, marble panel, detail.

The courtyard is centred by an octagonal fountain in the shape of a pavilion with marble columns, which carry a recently reconstructed wooden dome. The marble floor has been restored.

The cells occupy three storeys in the corners between the four iwans. Some of them overlook the courtyard, others the street, and some have no windows at all and might have been used for storage. They are of various sizes. The interior of the mausoleum is plain, including the mihrab, whereas the cenotaph is made of beautiful carved marble.

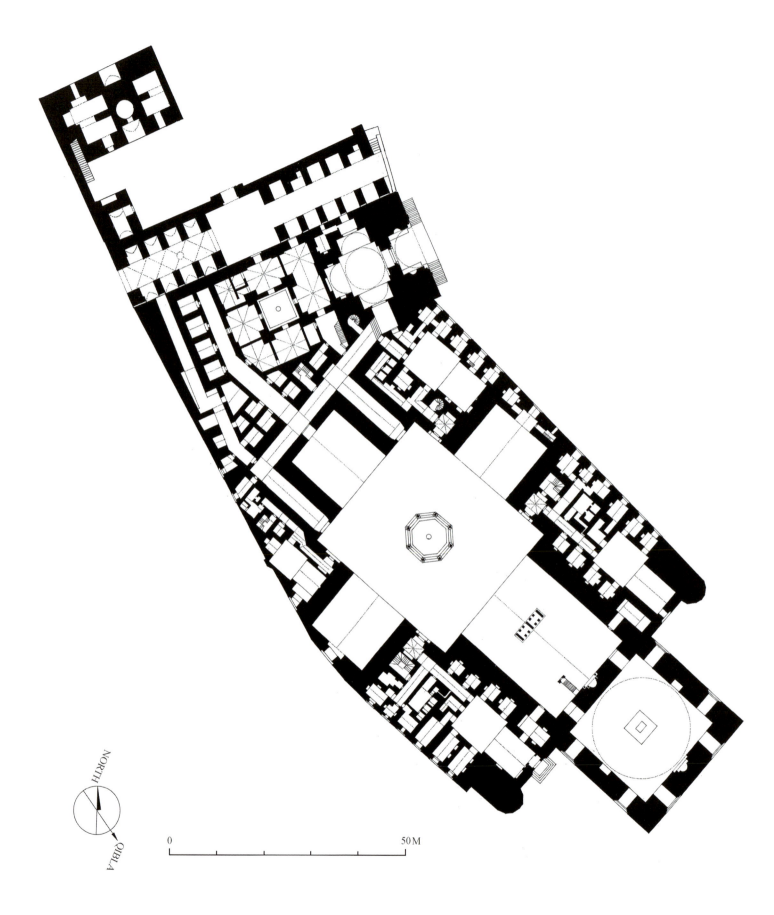

NORTH

QIBLA

0　　　　　　　　　　　　　　　　　　50 M

Fig.160. The funerary complex of Sultan Hasan.

27. The madrasa and Friday mosque of Sultan Hasan (1356–63)[5]

Founder and foundation

Sultan Hasan, the founder of the greatest mosque in the world at that time, has a rather unimpressive profile in the contemporary chronicles. Although he was the most politically minded among the sons and successors of al-Nasir Muhammad, who were either extravagant or helpless children, his reign was overshadowed by the mighty emirs Sarghitmish, Manjaq, Taz and Shaykhu.

Hasan, who himself chose this name instead of the Turkish Qamari, which was initially given to him, was raised by a stepmother and princess after his mother died when he was a small child.[6] He ascended the throne in 748/1347 at the age of only thirteen. As soon as he reached maturity, in 1350, he arrested the emir Manjaq, who, together with his brother Baybugha, fully controlled state affairs, and he took the reins of power into his own hands, appointing his favourites to key positions to the detriment of the established dignitaries. Discontented emirs arrested the sultan in 1351, and installed his brother al-Salih Salih in his place. After more than three years in prison, which he spent studying, Hasan returned to the throne in 1354, fully determined to consolidate his power and demonstrate his authority. He reshuffled the entire ruling establishment, eliminating many of his father's emirs, and promoted men of aristocratic birth, like himself, in the belief that he would find loyalty and support on their side. Hasan arrested the emir Taz, but after the interference of Shaykhu, his commander-in-chief, he sent him to Aleppo as governor instead of jailing him. Following Shaykhu's assassination in 758/1357, of which he seems to have been innocent, Sarghitmish unsuccessfully attempted to take Shaykhu's place. He was confronted by the sultan's Mamluks and was eventually arrested and left to die in jail in the same year, 1358. His property was confiscated and the Iranian Sufis of his madrasa arrested for conspiring with him. Manjaq, who had been in hiding, escaped to Syria, but was later arrested and pardoned, and sent to retire in Damascus. Immediately after Shaykhu's death, Sultan Hasan set out to build his mosque. He did not have much time, however. He was assassinated in 762/1361 shortly after inaugurating the sanctuary, while construction work was still going on in the rest of the building. His murderer was, ironically, one of his own favoured Mamluks, the commander-in-chief of the army Yalbugha al-'Umari, who rebelled against the sultan because he squandered *iqta'* land on women and indulged in other forms of favouritism. The sultan's body was hidden and not found, and the gigantic mausoleum never fulfilled its primary purpose. The mosque was never completed, although work continued after the sultan's death under the supervision of the emir Bashir al-Jamdar.

In their obituaries the chroniclers acknowledged Sultan Hasan's learning, which he acquired while in prison, his restoration of the Mecca shrine and the uniqueness of his mosque in the Muslim world. They also noted with criticism his pronounced predilection for the sons of Mamluks (*awlad al-nas*) over genuine Mamluks, and his great penchant for women and music. The contemporary Syrian historian Ibn Kathir blamed the sultan for his greed, for squandering public funds on formidable monuments that were not needed and for cutting people's wages to fill his private purse while his subjects were suffering; he added that the sultan's assassination was God's revenge. Ibn Hajar was also critical of the sultan, accusing him of being a tyrant, who squandered the public treasury, the *bayt al-mal*.

Although all Mamluk sources agree that Sultan Hasan's mosque was an extraordinary monument in the Muslim world at that time, the contemporary chronicles are not very informative about the history and the circumstances of its design and construction, or the builders and craftsmen involved. Maqrizi who wrote more than six decades later (c.1425), is still our most substantial source of information; some of the details he provided indicate that he must have had access to some kind of administrative documents regarding the construction works. His comparison of the qibla iwan with the vault of the Sasanian palace of Ctesiphon, also mentioned by other authors, including the assertion that Sultan Hasan's iwan was five cubits wider, demonstrates the great admiration this monument inspired.

No other Mamluk monument displays as many innovations as Sultan Hasan's mosque in functional, architectural and decorative terms. It is an irony of Mamluk art history that Sultan Hasan's biography cannot be harmonized with his legacy, either in terms of pious patronage or architectural achievement.

We do know that during his first reign, while still a child, Sultan Hasan, the son of a sultan, had to endure the humiliating situation of being deprived of financial resources except for the humble pocket money of 100 dirhams that a servant collected each day for him. Maqrizi commented: 'It has never been heard of that a king on his throne, who can appoint and dismiss, and who has the revenue of Egypt and Syria brought to him, has no power to spend anything of it'.[7] At the same time the income of the emir Shaykhu from his *iqta'* estates in Egypt and Syria was estimated to 200,000 dirhams a day, which was 2,000 times that of the sultan![8] Manjaq's estates in Egypt and Syria were estimated at more than 600 million dinars![9]

The deprivation Hasan endured at the beginning of his reign might explain the lavishness of his foundation, and the luxury of his lifestyle when he recovered his throne after three and a half years in jail. At that point he was determined to demonstrate that he was in full control of his resources. He built an elaborate palace, lavishly furnished at superlative costs, in the Citadel; ordered the foundation of a madrasa in Jerusalem; sponsored the mausoleum of his wife;[10] ordered

0   50 M

Fig. 162. The funerary complex of Sultan Hasan, section, east view from the courtyard.

restoration works in Mecca; probably built a mausoleum for his mother, the so-called Sultaniyya mausoleum; and erected the greatest mosque in the world.

Amounting to more than one million dinars of building expenses, his mosque was the costliest to be built in medieval Cairo. Considering that Sultan Hasan's first reign coincided with the Black Death, which killed much of Egypt's population and devastated its economy, the scale of his undertaking may appear miraculous, but it should also be recalled that the state inherited considerable fortunes as a consequence of the plague. Moreover, an austerity policy practised by Manjaq, who made severe cuts on public spending that were considered tyrannical, and Shaykhu's fabulous wealth, which also ended up in the sultan's treasury, not to mention the funds that he extorted

Fig. 161. [opposite] The funerary complex of Sultan Hasan, east view.

from his subjects, contributed to the resources that enabled Sultan Hasan to erect such a monument.

The magnitude of Sultan Hasan's foundation appears to be the expression of a personal experience rather than a reflection of the *zeitgeist*. His scheme to recover his power proved successful, and the choice of the Koranic inscription in the sanctuary affirms his victory. Eventually, his mosque rather than his rule immortalized his name.

The supervisor of the construction of Sultan Hasan's mosque

Hasan 'Abd al-Wahhab read the name of Muhammad Ibn Biylik al-Muhsini, without princely titles, following the sultan's name, in the stucco Kufic inscription in the Hanafi wing of the madrasa. Muhammad is described as the *shadd al-'imara* or supervisor of the construction work. 'Abd al-Wahhab was not able to identify Muhammad Ibn Biylik, whom he thought was an architect, nor did Ramadan in a recent interpretation of the inscription. Nasir al-Din Muhammad Ibn Biylik al-Muhsini was in fact a major emir at that time; Ibn Hajar recorded him in a biography with the *nisba* al-Jazari, adding that he was born in Egypt. Maqrizi mentioned him alternately as Muhammad Ibn Biylik and Muhammad Ibn al-Muhsini. He had a long career, during which he held positions under al-Nasir Muhammad, and was appointed governor of Cairo in 1330 after having been governor of the province of Minufiyya. He oversaw the reconstruction of al-Zahir Baybars' hippodrome, which he completed in two months. He served in Tripoli before he was appointed vizier in 754/1353, and in 755/1354 he was summoned to help reconstruct a broken dam that had flooded the province of Fayyum. During his second reign, Sultan Hasan appointed him one of his ten 'emirs of thousand', or royal emirs, who were selected from the emirs of Mamluk descent, favoured by the sultan. He fought bravely on the sultan's side in his final battle against Yalbugha al-'Umari, and survived the battle. However, he was arrested shortly afterwards in the same year, 1361, and sent to jail in Alexandria.[11] The date of his death is unknown. Muhammad, who was not young when he took charge of Sultan Hasan's mosque, was experienced in civil engineering and construction works, as well as in financial and administrative matters. The fact that Sultan Hasan appointed one of his highest-ranking emirs to supervise the construction of the mosque, and permitted his signature next to his own name on the building, confirms the extraordinary status of the undertaking. It is also interesting to note that the inscription states that Muhammad wrote it '*katabahu*', which suggests that he designed the madrasa's inscription, and probably also that of the sanctuary, both being in the same style.

The labour

The magnitude of the construction and the multitude of arts and crafts involved in the achievement appear difficult to reconcile with Maqrizi's account of the devastation caused by the Black Death in the labour market only eight years earlier. According to him, all urban and rural crafts and trades almost came to a halt due to the decimation of the population.[12] However, the fact that the mosque, although it was never completed, took three years without a day of break to erect was due less to a labour crisis than to the proportions of the undertaking. The sultan himself seems to have been disheartened by the costs that the construction required to the extent that he thought of abandoning the project, had it not been for his concern that 'people would say the king of Egypt has failed to complete his monument'. However, the initiative to undertake such a colossal royal project is likely to have attracted craftsmen from all over the Mamluk empire, including the remote Anatolian provinces, which contributed to the diversity of its design. Zahiri wrote that the sultan summoned craftsmen from all over the world. Indeed, more than any other Mamluk monument, the mosque of Sultan Hasan displays novel architectural features, some of which are rooted in Mamluk aesthetics, and others, mainly decorative elements, are borrowed from foreign traditions.

The waqf

The sultan dedicated the revenue of a considerable amount of agricultural land in Egypt and Syria, as well as half of the city of Antakia (Antioch) and its surrounding land, to his pious foundation, without including any stipulation that would point to personal profit for his own family or clan. Not just in terms of monumentality, the pious foundation itself was by far the largest ever to be sponsored in the Mamluk period. With 506 students, 200 schoolboys and 340 staff members, the size of the foundation exceeded by more than four times the khanqah of al-Muzaffar Baybars, with 200 Sufis, and the khanqah-madrasa of Barquq, with a total of 205 students and Sufis.[13] Whereas the mosque of al-Nasir Muhammad at the Citadel, which was the royal mosque where the sultans performed the Friday prayer, had only eighteen *mu'adhdhin*s, this one was supposed to have, after the enlargement of its endowment, as many as forty-eight *mu'adhdhin*s. Thirty-two were first appointed to work in two shifts of sixteen; later sixteen more were added. It was also the only Mamluk mosque to have two *khatib*s or preachers. How far and how long the founder's stipulations formulated in the waqf deed were implemented is difficult to tell. As mentioned earlier, Mamluks were already occupying the students' dwellings two decades later, and the estate of the waqf was soon diverted.

Besides the four rites of Islamic law and other religious disciplines, the madrasa also included medicine and astronomy in its curriculum. The foundation employed a physician, an ophthalmologist and an orthopædist-surgeon to provide medical care to its community, including the students and staff members who were not resident in the complex.

There was a particular emphasis on orthodoxy in this foundation, which was the first Mamluk madrasa in Cairo also to have also the status of a Friday mosque or *jami'*. After that, all sultanic foundations combined the *jami'* status with madrasa or/and khanqah functions. It was not the first Mamluk foundation to combine a madrasa with a *jami'*, however. The madrasa of al-Burtasi in Tripoli, built in 1324, was also a Friday mosque.[14]

Sultan Hasan's waqf deed does not mention any kind of Sufi involvement in the foundation, which is unlike the usual practice of that time. Ibn Iyas, who wrote one and a half centuries later, mentioned, however, that Sultan Hasan appointed Baha' al-Din al-Subki as the head of the Sufis to perform the *hudur* in his mosque.[15] The funerary madrasa that Sultan Hasan sponsored for his wife also did not include a Sufi service.[16] Thus, Sultan Hasan might have been more inclined to orthodoxy than to Sufism.

The endowment deed stipulates that the mausoleum, which is defined as a 'masjid', should be the venue for the teaching of Hadith and *tafsir* – i.e. Koranic exegesis. The main iwan was dedicated to Friday prayer and to Shafi'i teaching, the western iwan to the Hanafis, the northern to the Malikis and the southern to the Hanbalis.

Although the waqf deed describes the building in very brief terms,[17] it indicates the exact size of the burial crypt in the domed chamber dedicated to the founder and his children. It was to consist of two parts and to measure 15 x 10 *dhira'* or cubits.[18]

Chronology

Maqrizi dated the beginning of the construction work to 757/1356. Inscriptions on the mausoleum facade and in the main iwan glorify the sultan in terms indicating that he was alive when the facade and the main iwan were built. In fact, Ibn Iyas, quoting Safadi, wrote that the sultan attended the inaugural Friday prayer in Rabi' I 758/March 1357.

The waqf document compiled in Rajab 760/June 1359, and slightly modified in Jumada I 761/April 1360, refers to the qubba and the mosque with the four iwans as already standing; the minarets, living quarters, ablution fountains and primary school are mentioned as yet to be completed.[19] This indicates that the construction proceeded from the inside to the outside. The document mentions the four minaret buttresses, not the minarets themselves. It describes the layout of the four wings of the madrasa without indicating the number of living units, and it refers to the waterwheel and a rectangular pool.

In Rabi' II 762/February 1361 the minaret above the portal collapsed; according to Ibn Iyas, this minaret was the third to be built. Thirty-three days later the sultan was killed.

Inscriptions on the wooden dome of the fountain in the courtyard, above the four entrances of the madrasa and along the walls of the mausoleum chamber, give the posthumous date – the sultan being mentioned as dead (*shahid*): 764/1362–3; the cenotaph in the mausoleum is dated 786/1384.

The site

The mausoleum overlooked, to the east, Rumayla square, with the horse market near the hippodrome and along the southern side of the mausoleum. The northern facade overlooked a pre-existing aqueduct that raised water to the royal stables in the Citadel.

The madrasa covers an area of almost 8,000 sqm. In order to build his mosque on this site, Sultan Hasan had to pull down the fabulous palace of Yalbugha al-Yahawi, built three decades earlier by his father at the cost of more than twenty-one million dinars. He most probably used the foundations and building materials of Yalbugha's palace for his own construction. The visual potential of the site, which al-Nasir had selected for a complex of princely palaces to please his eyes while looking from the windows of his palace in the Citadel, must have inspired Hasan's scheme for his mosque.

The silhouette of the mosque today, having lost its original dome and one of its monumental minarets, is quite different from what it once was. Due to its location and the sturdiness of its construction, Sultan Hasan's mosque had a

strategic importance that contributed to its physical losses and, at the same time, to its legend. On several occasions, as Ibn Iyas reported,[20] it was used by Mamluk rebels as a fort, where they could entrench themselves to besiege or attack the sultan at the Citadel. On more than one occasion, therefore, sultans ordered the demolition or the blocking of the mosque's staircases, and eventually they also had to repair the damage caused to the building. In 1500 Sultan Janbalat ordered the entire mosque to be pulled down to thwart a rebel offensive from its premises. Ibn Iyas reported that the demolition works at the qibla wall of the mausoleum lasted three days, without much success, so that the sultan had to follow the advice of an emir and give up this hopeless scheme. People deplored the damage caused to the building, and poets composed admonition verses. Similar episodes also occurred in the Ottoman period, as reported by Evliya and Jabarti. These incidents enhanced the image of the mosque of Sultan Hasan as an extraordinary monument.

The dome and the minarets

The position of the mausoleum in relation to the sanctuary is unique in Mamluk architecture.[21] Placed behind the prayer hall, occupying the same width, one would think that it must have breached some unwritten law against the building of a profane mausoleum in the direction of prayer. However, this does not seem to have been the case. Mamluk historians agree about the greatness of this monument without mentioning any concerns regarding the positioning of the mausoleum.

The mausoleum of the emir Husayn, built in 1319, is also placed behind the qibla wall of its adjacent mosque, but because the mausoleum is on a much smaller scale it is not directly behind the mihrab.[22]

The waqf deed mentions a structure next to the main building for the primary school, which must have been sizeable enough to provide teaching for two hundred boys. On the western side of the madrasa the annexes, which have partly survived, included a waterwheel connected to a rectangular pool, as well as the latrines and ablution fountains. A drawing by Cassas (1785) shows on the west side of the portal a wall with a large double arch set within a recess;[23] this loggia looks as if it belonged to the primary school. Although we do not have Mamluk maktabs prior to the mosque of Uljay, all later ones have a similar appearance of a loggia, occupying a corner.

Although the mausoleum is free-standing on three sides, the architect did not use the space available to increase the number of windows and add light to the funerary chamber, which remains, perhaps deliberately, rather dark. Each of the three facades displays two pairs of windows and a central oculus. All three oculi are framed by inlaid rosettes of interlace petals in ablaq masonry. The same kind of interlace frames the conchs of the upper window recesses. It is interesting to note that, for

Fig.163. The funerary complex of Sultan Hasan, north view.

the sake of symmetry, even the fourth mausoleum wall, which separates the mausoleum from the prayer hall, displays the same window arrangement.

The pyramidal recesses of the lower windows were once filled with geometric ceramic decoration. Their profile and the hexagonal pattern of the decoration point to Anatolia.

Despite the thickness of the mausoleum walls, which would have allowed a brick structure, the dome was made of wood. With a 21m inner diameter it was the largest wooden dome ever to be built in Cairo. The reconstructed actual dome built in 1082/1671 does not resemble the original, however, which was described in 1616 by Pietro Della Valle as unique, having the shape of an egg swelling above the narrow base and contracting towards the top. According to Ibn Taghribirdi it was covered with lead.[24] Evliya described it as high, whitewashed, and artistically fashioned.[25] The wooden fountain dome inside the mosque is bulbous but not pointed. Wooden domes flaring above the drum were a fashion in Cairo at that time, as the mihrab dome of Sarghitmish's madrasa indicates, and also the domes of Shaykhu's khanqah, if they were restored according to their original appearance. However, none of these has an egg shape, which is yet another novelty of Sultan Hasan's mosque that was repeated in the Sultaniyya mausoleum.

The positioning of the mausoleum between two minarets was a further novelty, adding a new dimension to the Cairene art of juxtaposing the dome and the minaret. With two more minarets planned to flank the portal, as in Seljuk Anatolian buildings, Sultan Hasan's mosque would have had four minarets, an unprecedented number in Cairo.

The northern minaret collapsed in 1659 and was replaced by the present structure in 1671–2.[26] Ibn Kathir wrote that the original had 'a strange appearance, namely a double minaret on a single shaft' ('alā ṣifa gharība wa dhālika 'annahā manāratān 'alā aṣl wāḥid); in other words it was double-headed, a feature that reappeared at the end of the Mamluk period.[27]

Restoration is visible at the buttress and the contiguous eastern wall, where the windows look different from those of the other side. The original southern minaret is at c.84m from street level the highest of the Mamluk period. Its original counterpart may have been smaller, judging from the smaller size of its buttress.

Once the minarets of the mausoleum were erected, construction began at the first and western of the twin minarets of the portal. When it collapsed in 1361, killing many children in the

Fig. 164. The funerary complex of Sultan Hasan, south view.

primary school beneath, it was considered a bad omen for the sultan – which very soon proved to be true.

The large buttresses of the four minarets are visible on the plan. The design of the twin portal minarets would have been yet another novelty introduced by Sultan Hasan.

The buttresses of the mausoleum minarets are not of equal size. Kessler explained this discrepancy by the reuse of the expensive foundations of Yalbugha's palace, which imposed constraints on the architect, who had to confine the walls to the existing foundation platform while exactly orientating the axis of the oblong complex towards Mecca. Because the architect was particularly scrupulous to observe the exact Mecca orientation – a further testimony to Sultan Hasan's orthodoxy – he had to shift the mausoleum slightly closer to the northern than to the southern minaret, thus breaking the symmetry. Windows belonging to the living tract are pierced on each side of the mausoleum between its projecting walls and the minaret buttresses.

The northern and southern facades

The cornice of carved muqarnas, which boldly projects about 1.5 m at the summit of the entire facade, is a tour de force of masonry, and a singular occurrence in Cairene architecture. It is not symmetrical, however. On the southern side the cornice does not continue along the entire facade, and its muqarnas is in a different style. Also, the window recesses of the southern facade lack the muqarnas crest of the northern recesses.

Both the southern and northern facades are characterized by their extraordinary fenestration. Six recesses pierced with eight vertical rows of windows correspond to four storeys of cells each with two superimposed windows. This configuration, which gives the facades a contemporary look, was a further outstanding feature, which added a new dimension to the art of fenestration in Mamluk architecture. However, it was not to be repeated elsewhere. Both facades have an oculus set in a recess above two superimposed windows, corresponding to the middle of the northern and southern iwans. The northern and main facade is 150 m long.

The southern facade displays a series of corbels in its lower part, which suggests that they carried a roof. It might have covered a market along the walls of the mosque. This is confirmed by Evliya, who mentions beneath the mosque about fifty shops built of stone. The west side of the complex includes the annexes with a waterwheel, latrines and ablution fountains, and a row of arcaded units, which could be shops connected with the weapon market.

The portal

The gigantic portal of Sultan Hasan, c. 38 m high, is visible from Rumayla square and the Citadel due to its projection and its askew position in relation to the rest of the facade. It turns towards the Citadel at an angle of 17° from the facade to reveal its grandeur and novelty.

Neither the muqarnas vault nor the carved decoration of the portal was completed. The portal design consists of a magnificent rectangular arabesque-carved frame doubled by another external frame of interlocking bands framing carved rectangles. The arabesque frame has been completely carved on the sides except for the upper line above the portal vault, where a layer of stone facing has not been put in place. Its pattern is akin to the illuminations designed by Abu Bakr, known as Sandal, in a Koran manuscript of 1313.[28] This is not the only evidence of an influence of Sandal's work on the decoration of Sultan Hasan's mosque, as will be shown below.

The interlocking framing bands were outlined in the lower part of the walls and only a fragment has been carved. Similarly, the opulent chinoiserie floral motifs are outlined with thin carved lines still to be elaborated. They are the only instance of chinoiserie in Mamluk architecture. Chinoiserie

Fig.165. The funerary complex of Sultan Hasan, portal.

Fig.167. The portal of the Gök madrasa in Siwas.

Fig.166. The funerary complex of Sultan Hasan, facade detail with Gothic panels.

had already been introduced into the Mamluk decorative arts some decades earlier, in glass and metalwork. It also appeared in contemporary book illumination.

Deeply carved marble medallions outside and inside the portals recall a Seljuk Anatolian decorative tradition. On each side of the portal recess, slender marble slabs, one with a floral meander of Gothic style and the other with enigmatic

Fig.168. The funerary complex of Sultan Hasan, facade detail with chinoiserie.

Fig.169. The funerary complex of Sultan Hasan, portal niche.

Fig.170. The funerary complex of Sultan Hasan, vestibule vault.

architectural representations that do not quite fit with the rest of the wall, must have been spoils from a Gothic monument, most likely from Antakia, which belonged to the mosque's estate, and which still included at that time Christian monuments and its entire ancient walls, as the waqfiyya indicates (Fig.166).

The side walls of the portal recess are decorated with a pair of marble niches with a muqarnas conch of Anatolian style (Fig.169). The geometric patterns that fill the niches beneath the conch are also inspired by Sandal's illumination of al-Muzaffar Baybars' (al-Jashnakir's) Koran.[29] Above the niches are inlaid marble slabs with Koranic phrases in Kufic script from the Sura of Victory, *surat al-fath*, which are also inscribed in carved panels of square Kufic above the niches. This sura is also inscribed in the prayer iwan.

With its twin minarets, the design of this portal with the profile of the muqarnas vault reveals an Anatolian Seljuk inspiration, in particular the portal of the Gök madrasa in Siwas, built in 1271 (Fig.167).[30] The big gap between the dates

of the two monuments naturally excludes an attribution to the same craftsmen. Moreover, the dimensions of Sultan Hasan's portal are so much greater than its Anatolian predecessor that it is difficult to believe the latter could have been a source of inspiration. The similarity, which is in the general design rather than in the details, may have been transmitted by a drawing. This seems to be confirmed by the fact that the portal of another Anatolian madrasa, the Khatuniyya in Qaraman, built more than a century later, in 1382, is also in the style of the Gök madrasa.[31]

The awesome entrance vestibule is a masonry space surrounded by three muqarnas vaulted recesses, which the waqf document describes as 'iwans' (Fig.170). This arrangement of a central dome flanked by half-domes is of Byzantine origin, but its masonry execution here suggests, rather, an influence from Armenia, where such masonry vaults were common, without muqarnas.

The central recess within the vestibule's frontal wall is entirely panelled with marble, and contains a bench, called a

Fig.171. [opposite top] The funerary complex of Sultan Hasan, marble panel in the vestibule.

Fig.172. [opposite bottom] The funerary complex of Sultan Hasan, carved panel in the vestibule.

mastaba in the waqf deed, which is the first of its kind in Cairo. The recess contains a magnificent red and white inlaid marble panel in the Syrian style filled with a geometric composition, and flanked on each side with a carved medallion design set in a geometric interlace composition. The lateral walls of the bench recess are also carved with panels filled with geometric designs, with hexagonal stars again recalling Sandal's illuminations (Fig.169).[32]

The quality of the architecture and decoration of this vestibule is so unusual and impressive that it suggests a ceremonial function, which is, however, not confirmed by the sources.

The interior

A bent passage leads to the courtyard, passing beneath the wing of the madrasa dedicated to the teaching of the Maliki school. The four monumental iwans fully dominate the courtyard of the mosque, with no living units to share the inner space. Unlike previous madrasas, where living units overlook the courtyard, the residential space here is totally separate from that of the public Friday mosque. This separation may be related to the double function of the complex, as a madrasa dedicated to the academic community and a Friday mosque accessible to the general public. Only the entrances of the four wings of the madrasa, placed at the corners between the three minor iwans, are enhanced by their polychrome marble inlaid lintels. The onlooker in the courtyard of the mosque does not perceive the impressive four-storeyed structures, which dominate the facades, concealed behind the inner walls. The dwellings were conceived as an outer shell.

Above the four iwans, beneath their apex and the crenellation, an empty space marked by a horizontal moulding that runs along the entire courtyard, might have been intended to contain an inscription.

The monumentality of the main iwan has been acknowledged by Mamluk historians to have no parallel, and to exceed the proportions of the vault of the Sasanian palace at Ctesiphon. The iwan is panelled with a marble dado, which is much lower on the lateral walls than on the central one, thus emphasizing the qibla. The mihrab, which is flanked by a pair of columns with capitals of Gothic style, has a conch carved and inlaid with a triple sunrise motif. The minbar is made of marble, like that of Aqsunqur, but without inlay work. Its glory is, rather, in its bronze door with geometric star compositions. The bench for the *mu'adhdhin*s is carried on marble columns, also displaying an unusual polychrome zigzag design.

Fig.173. The funerary complex of Sultan Hasan, fountain.

The stucco inscription band, which runs along the entire upper wall of the sanctuary, is unparalleled in Mamluk mosque interiors (Figs 175, 176). It is a revival of Kufic script in monumental epigraphy in a style borrowed from the chapter headings of Bahri Mamluk Koran manuscripts, which was inspired from Baghdad.[33] The ground of scrolls against which the text is set, however, includes Chinese lotus flowers that do not feature in the aforementioned illuminations, but this pattern was used for the first time in illumination in a Koran manuscript dated 1356 – i.e. to Sultan Hasan's reign – but which was donated in 1369, probably illegally, by Sultan Sha'ban to his mother's madrasa.[34]

A signature on the edge of the inscription band attributes the work to 'Abd Allah Muhammad al-Yamani 'Abd (?).[35] The *nisba* 'al-yamani' suggests either a Yemeni craftsman or a craftsman who worked in Yemen. Although stucco was a major decorative medium in Rasulid architecture in contemporary Yemen, no comparable inscription band is known to me. In the Hanbali madrasa there are some loose epigraphic stucco slabs written in Kufic, which contain fragments of the text inscribed in the iwan; they could be templates for the monumental epigraphy of the mosque. Comparable but less elaborate Kufic inscription bands are in the iwans of the madrasas; the one in the Hanafi wing names the sultan and the supervisor of the construction works.

The text of the Koranic inscription of the sanctuary, a fragment from the Sura of Victory, LXVIII, 1–6, which begins with 'We have given you a glorious victory so that God may

Fig.174. The funerary complex of Sultan Hasan, main iwan.

forgive you your past and future sins…', and which is also fragmentarily applied in inlaid marble on the portal, must have been selected by the patron to celebrate the recovery of his throne following the years of humiliation. The Koranic text is preceded by the formula '*a'ūdhu bi-'l-llāh min al-shayṭān al-rajīm*', which was not common in the epigraphy of this period.

The mausoleum chamber (12 m diameter) (Fig. 177) is entirely panelled with a polychrome dado, and its inscription band below the transitional zone of the dome is made of wood with high-relief white characters, instead of the usual gilded inscriptions. The huge wooden pendentives were painted and gilded.

According to Maqrizi, the marble was added by the eunuch Bashir al-Jamdar after the sultan's death. The use of marble in the mosque's interior is rather restrained, and particularly when compared with the lavish marblework of the portal. This might not have been the initial intention of the founder, but the result of his premature death.

The minor iwans are unadorned in contrast with the lavish polychrome marble pavement of the courtyard, which displays a central rectangle surrounded by a cruciform composition with eight rectangles, filled with three different patterns. Although the floor has been restored, its ingenuous design is probably another creation of Sultan Hasan's workshops (Fig. 173).

The central rectangle is occupied by the fountain, an octagonal structure with a bulbous wooden dome carrying a dating inscription. The profile of the dome recalls the domes in the khanqah of Shaykhu. It is the earliest extant fountain of this kind.

In the northern and southern iwans the oculus in the upper wall has a fine stucco arabesque grille, and the lower of two rectangular windows is set in an arched recess. In the western iwan the middle window is missing, and the recess window overlooks a rear passage.

The four madrasa wings have no direct communication between them, but only through the courtyard. Only the Maliki madrasa can be accessed directly from the entrance. A corridor, which connects the entrance vestibule with the Maliki madrasa and further to the courtyard, turns around the west iwan, branching off to the ablution area, and bends back to the courtyard without giving access to the Hanbali wing.

Each of the four wings of the madrasa is centred by its own courtyard with living units on three sides and a vaulted iwan on the qibla side. The size and number of the cells of the four wings of the madrasa vary, with 56, 52, 44 and 22 living units respectively for the Hanafi, Shafi'i, Maliki and Hanbali sections. The total number of 174 living units is much smaller than the number of 506 students to whom the madrasa was dedicated, indicating that the majority of the students were non-resident. The iwans of the madrasas are adorned with stucco Kufic inscriptions comparable to that of the sanctuary.

Fig. 175. *The funerary complex of Sultan Hasan, main iwan.*

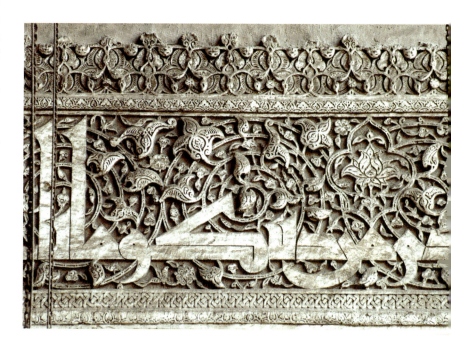

Fig. 176. *The funerary complex of Sultan Hasan, inscription of the main iwan.*

Fig. 177. The funerary complex of Sultan Hasan, interior of the Hanafi madrasa.

Fig. 178. The funerary complex of Sultan Hasan, mausoleum.

Fig. 179. The funerary complex of Sultan Hasan, pavement.

28. The Sultaniyya mausoleum (1350s)[36]

This exotic double mausoleum, located in the cemetery on the southeastern side of the Citadel, is anonymous and undated. Its popular name, 'Sultaniyya', means 'royal' or 'sultanic', and its architecture also suggests this.

Its founder has been identified by fortuitous documentary evidence. The waqf deed of the Ottoman governor Masih Pasha of 1578, which describes his religious complex built to the west of the Sultaniyya, refers to one of its boundaries as adjacent to the mausoleum of Sultan Hasan's mother. Creswell refuted this information as not precise enough to identify the monument. However, Evliya Celebi's account confirms Masih Pasha's waqf deed; he mentions the building of Sultan Hasan's mother as next to those of Masih Pasha and Qawsun, which can only refer to the Sultaniyya, because those three prominent monuments are close to each other in this part of the cemetery.

Sultan Hasan's mother died while he was small, and he was adopted and raised, according to Maqrizi, by his stepmother Ardu, the Tatar mother of Sultan Kujuk. Maqrizi contradicted himself elsewhere and named Tughay as his adoptive mother, which Ibn Taghribirdi repeated.[37] Tughay, al-Nasir Muhammad's

Fig.180. The Sultaniyya mausoleum, rear view.

favourite wife, died in 1348 and was buried in a well-known funerary khanqah in the northern cemetery.

Considering that his mother died early and that she was not a princess, this imposing masonry monument, with a vaulted iwan in the style of Sultan Hasan's own madrasa, seems to have been a memorial of special significance to the founder, especially when compared with the turbas of the princesses Tughay and his wife Tulubiyya,[38] both of which are brick constructions.

The monument is composed of two similar but not identical domes placed on either side of the stone vaulted iwan. On the western and opposite side a stone minaret must have once been attached to a wall enclosing the funerary complex. No portal or facade has survived.

This layout has been used in earlier funerary architecture in the cemetery, in the mausoleum of Qawsun nearby (1336), which was built likewise with two domes, and the so-called Turbat al-Sitt, which is datable to the early fourteenth century.[39] As in Qawsun's complex, the minaret of the Sultaniyya occupied the northern corner of the enclosure, and its design is very similar to Sultan Hasan's. With Qawsun's minaret next to it the two monuments form a remarkable composition.

The exterior rear walls of the Sultaniyya double mausoleum show the same kind of pierced recesses with muqarnas cresting common in urban architecture, but without an oculus over the mihrab. Lower rectangular and upper arched windows are pierced in the walls on all sides.

was much larger it might have been the wooden model that was copied in stone in the Sultaniyya mausoleum, making use of the potential of masonry and adding carved ribs to the surface.

The drum of the northern dome displays a shallow carving of square Kufic inscriptions, which was often used in Mamluk marble and woodwork, but its external use was more widespread in Iran and Anatolia (Fig. 180). The other drum, which is plain, may not have been completed. The masonry of the inner shell of the northern dome is shaped with concentric stone courses,

Fig. 181. The Sultaniyya mausoleum, west view.

Fig. 182. The Sultaniyya mausoleum, detail of minaret.

The domes' unusual bulbous and pointed profiles, and the high drums, are striking on Cairo's skyline. A muqarnas cornice runs along their base and they have a double-shell like Sarghitmish's brick mausoleum dome. Whereas Sarghitmish's dome differs by its rounded profile and smooth surface, however, Sultan Hasan's dome was described as bulbous and pointed and may have looked like the Sultaniyya's. Although it

unlike the southern dome, where the stone courses radiate from the apex. This recalls the treatment of the conchs in the pendentives of the mausoleum of Sultan Sha'ban's mother, which are not all identical but display two different patterns, a radiating and a concentric one.

The pendentives of the two domes are also not alike, but one thing they have in common is that they differ from any other pendentives in Cairo; they look awkward and somehow alien. Those of the northern dome have their muqarnas niches following a vertical line across the muqarnas tiers instead of being arranged alternately. They are surmounted by a frieze of miniature niches running around the dome and carved with a radiating pattern. Miniature niches with a radiating pattern, which also appear in the muqarnas pendentives of the portal of Sarghitmish's madrasa, in the muqarnas capital of the engaged columns at Sultan Hasan's portal and in the muqarnas of Umm al-Sultan Sha'ban's portal, are a very common feature in Seljuk Anatolian muqarnas carving.

The mihrabs of the iwan and the two funerary chambers are in stone. That of the iwan has a conch carved with muqarnas, like the side niches of Sultan Hasan's portal and that of the mausoleum of Tankizbugha (1362–3), which is rare in Cairo but common in Anatolia. The vanished ceramic mihrab of the madrasa of al-'Ayni, which was of Anatolian origin, also had a muqarnas conch.[40] The mihrab spandrels are also carved.

Although the design of the Sultaniyya and the related domes recalls the Timurid domes of Central Asia, their earlier dating precludes a direct Timurid influence. A common prototype from western Iran or Iraq, as suggested by Meinecke, explains the high drum and the double shell of Cairene and Central Asian domes. However, the bulbous dome was not unknown to the Cairene builders, as the dome of the fountain of Sultan Hasan

Fig. 183. The Sultaniyya mausoleum, northern dome.

indicates. The domes of Shaykhu's khanqah, if their design is original, would be yet earlier specimens.

The stone vaulted iwan, the style of the minaret, the muqarnas conch of the mihrab and the pointed and bulbous dome profile, which connect the Sultaniyya to the madrasa of Sultan Hasan, confirm Evliya's report and Masih Pasha's waqf deed in attributing the Sultaniyya to the reign of that sultan – i.e. between the 1350s and

the 1360s. Furthermore, the imposing appearance of this monument, together with its novel features, point to a royal patron with a taste for bold innovation. That patron most likely was Sultan Hasan.

29. The madrasa of Emir Sabiq al-Din Mithqal al-Anuki (1361–9)[41]

Mithqal was a eunuch whose career began in the service of Anuk, al-Nasir Muhammad's son. He was of Abyssinian origin, as a *nisba* included in his titles indicates. He reached the peak of his career

Fig. 184. The madrasa of Mithqal al-Anuki, south iwan.

under Sultan Sha'ban, who appointed him commander of the royal Mamluks, *muqaddam al-mamalik al-sultaniyya*. He died in 1375 and was buried according to his will in the mausoleum of his friend Shaykh Ibn al-Labban in the cemetery.

Mithqal's madrasa is located in the street called Darb Qirmiz in the Jamaliyya quarter, which is on the eastern side of Bayn al-Qasrayn, in the heart of the old Qahira.

Fig. 185. The madrasa of Mithqal al-Anuki.

two floors to accommodate a total of seven upper living units. This is the only known case in Cairene architecture where an iwan has been cut to accommodate a residential structure. We have seen that the height of the minor iwans of the mosques of Almalik and Aslam al-Silahdar was reduced to make space for a room above it. Here, however, the living units have been integrated within the lateral iwans. This was done in an aesthetic manner by using screens of turned wood to conceal the dwellings. The arched windows of the living units around the courtyard are also faced with wooden screens and surmounted by oculi with fine stucco grilles.

The mihrab, which is surmounted by the traditional oculus, is of polychrome marble and flanked by a pair of columns with Gothic capitals. There is no marble dado; instead, polychrome marble is used in the pavement, whose design displays a geometric motif with a central square including another filled with a circle, and surrounded by rectangles on the four sides, and squares in the four corners. This is a simplified version of the layout of Sultan Hasan's pavement.

30. The madrasa of Umm al-Sultan Sha'ban, Khawand Baraka (1368–9)[42]

The madrasa associated with Sultan Sha'ban, a grandson of al-Nasir Muhammad, and his mother Lady (Khawand) Baraka (d.774/1373), stands south of Bab Zuwayla in Tabbana street. Baraka is described as one of the greatest women of her time, for her piety, generosity and beauty. Her pilgrimage convoy was described as one of the most glamorous.

The inscriptions, which give the date 770/1368–9, state that Sultan Sha'ban founded the madrasa and dedicated it to his mother. The sultan, born in 1353–4, was at that time a child, which suggests that his mother was the de facto founder. The madrasa taught the Shafi'i and the Hanafi *madhhab*s. Neither its inscriptions, nor the foundation deed or the chronicles, describe it as a Friday mosque. It is indeed unlikely that, at a time when Friday mosques were not yet the standard princely foundations that they later became, a princess would have been granted this privilege when the sultan himself had not yet founded his own Friday mosque.[43] However, a minbar was added at a later unknown date by a Mamluk emir with the name of 'Ali, but otherwise unidentifiable.

In 777/1375, Sha'ban founded his own monumental madrasa and Friday mosque, which Maqrizi described as having two domes and an iwan surpassing that of Sultan Hasan. Built at the foot of the Citadel, on the site later occupied by al-Mu'ayyad's hospital, it was lavishly decorated.[44] With the two domes it followed the model of Qawsun's funerary khanqah and the Sultaniyya double mausoleum. Sha'ban was assassinated before

The building is undated, but Maqrizi described it as a foundation for teaching the Shafi'i *madhhab*, with a primary school and a trough. The founder's titles, according to the inscriptions, suggest that he built the madrasa between 1361 and 1375.

The madrasa was built, like most emirs' mosques, next to the founder's residence. No minaret has survived. The recessed panels and fenestration of its facade as well as the portal with muqarnas, conform to the traditional arrangement of the period.

To make up for the limited space available, 21 x 21 m, the builder has adjusted the cruciform plan of the madrasa at the expense of symmetry, to provide a maximum of teaching room. The main iwan is extended to the north by an additional space that cannot be seen from the courtyard. Similar extensions enlarge the opposite west iwan on two sides. The lateral iwans were given a small format to make room at the rear. The two large iwans, which occupy the entire height of the building, left little space for upper living units. For this reason the lateral iwans have been divided into

Fig. 186. The funerary madrasa of Sultan Sha'ban's mother.

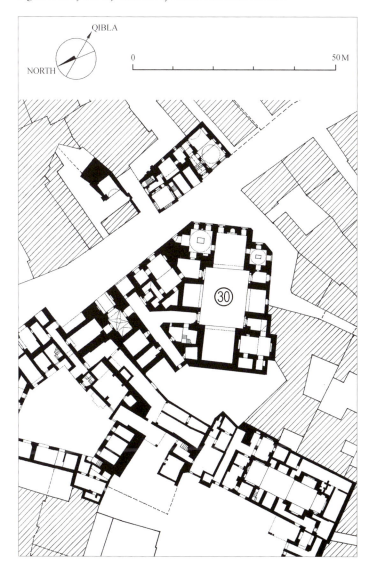

Fig. 187. The funerary madrasa of Sultan Sha'ban's mother.

its completion, and buried in his mother's funerary foundation. His own building was eventually dismantled by Sultan Faraj in 1411 to reuse its material.[45]

Lady Baraka is buried under the larger dome of her madrasa. The smaller one, which might have been dedicated to other members of the family or clan, eventually received Sha'ban's remains.

The layout

The exterior appearance of this monument with its grand portal and elaborate facade on the Tabbana street does not correspond to the interior configuration. Rather, the facade disguises the interior, so that the main portal leads to the dependencies, whereas a small portal on the side street leads directly to the main part of the madrasa. As a result, the windows of the main facade correspond to rooms and apartments that fill the space between Tabbana street and the madrasa proper.

This rather awkward layout is a most revealing case of bold architectural manipulation to accommodate a religious-funerary monument in an unaccommodating plot. The architect proved to be a master of compromise, but compromise *per se* excludes perfection.

The madrasa has three facades on a corner of Tabbana street with a lane. The minaret, which is unconventionally separated from the portal of the main facade, is juxtaposed instead with the larger funerary dome at the corner between the main and middle part of the facade. This dome–minaret juxtaposition would not have been possible had the minaret been erected near the portal. The smaller funerary dome occupies the corner between the middle and the side facade.

The design of the relatively high facades (c.18 m high) with three tiers of windows is imposing. The lower windows are rectangular, the others are arched. The elaborate fenestration is an adornment of the facade rather than a need for openings; an upper window, which corresponds to the prayer iwan, is blind.

The two unequal masonry domes are separated by the prayer hall; the large dome is adjoined by the minaret. Both are finely carved with flutes ending in festoon-like curves at the base. The stone minaret is octagonal, and its middle section is decorated with a carved zigzag. Its upper structure has recently been replaced in the same style as the original one, which can be seen in a nineteenth-century photograph.

The pyramidal muqarnas vault of the portal, which is unique in Cairo, is of Anatolian style. The pyramidal vault was probably designed by the same craftsmen who introduced Seljuk elements at the mosque of Sultan Hasan. The marble decoration and the design of the muqarnas, however, are of Mamluk craftsmanship (Figs 188, 189).

The deep portal recess is entirely roofed with a remarkable muqarnas rosette connected to the pyramidal opening. This device is comparable to the muqarnas vault of Qawsun's

Fig. 188. The funerary madrasa of Sultan Sha'ban's mother, portal.

Fig. 189. The funerary madrasa of Sultan Sha'ban's mother, portal detail.

palace, and to the muqarnas ceiling of Bashtak's portal, which open respectively on the facade with a conch.

A novel feature is the carved inscription band, which begins on the right-hand side and ends on the left-hand side of the portal recess, where it runs around three arched recesses. The lateral ones have radiating hoods made of polychrome marble inlay, and the central one includes a triple window similarly decorated. The triple window is not common in portals. Shallow carvings fill the spandrels of the portal vault.

On the left-hand side of the portal a sabil faces the street with a rectangular window with iron grille, framed by a wooden lattice screen with a geometric composition. On the right-hand side of the portal a trough for animals bears the epigraphic blazon of Sultan Sha'ban. It is surmounted by a wooden loggia that might have belonged to a primary school. The portal leads to a vestibule connected to a long and bifurcating passage, which leads to the madrasa on one side and to the annexes on the other.

The first thing to be seen by the visitor entering the building through the main entrance is a three-storeyed complex of rooms and apartments, probably intended for the madrasa staff.

On the left-hand side the passage leads to a second shallow portal with a rectangular muqarnas cresting and two small maksalas or portal benches. This entrance leads through a bent

passage to a vaulted iwan, which might have been a teaching room, and further to the main part of the madrasa.

The madrasa is built on the cruciform plan, with the two domed mausoleums connected to the main iwan. Due to the lack of space the smaller and southern dome has no mihrab, the space available having been used instead for a window on the street. The mihrab of the northern and larger domed chamber is flanked by two windows in the middle facade and a third window at the end of a long, bending recess opening in the main facade.

The transitional zone of the two domes consists of plain squinches. Such squinches, common in Syria, were rare in Cairo. They were used only in the dome of Aqsunqur's mosque, in the two mausoleums attributed to Tankizbugha (1359, 1362–3) and in this madrasa. Here, the transitional zone in both domes has two squinches with radiating masonry, and the two others have concentric masonry. Such alternation in the treatment of the masonry appears also in the decoration of the twin domes of the Sultaniyya mausoleum.

The recent restoration has brought to light remains of a green colour in the masonry of the domes.[46] The exterior inscriptions in the drums were gilded on a green ground.

Christel Kessler has demonstrated that the Mecca orientation of the madrasa deviates by 10° east of the normal Mamluk qibla of 127°, in order to accommodate optimally the two mausoleums adjacent to the prayer hall with their windows on the street. The 117° qibla orientation used in this building was common in mosques of the earlier Islamic period, but then abandoned later because of its geographical inaccuracy. However, it continued to be legally acceptable because it was associated with sanctuaries founded by the companions of the Prophet.[47]

The iwans have no windows but their interiors are sufficiently lit through the courtyard. A wooden inscription band once ran around the entire courtyard and the four iwans. Only the main iwan was panelled with polychrome marble, which also adorns the mihrab. At the base of the conch with a radiating motif, a small triangle includes a pious formula inscribed in black paste on a white marble ground. The wooden ceiling of the southern iwan has preserved its beautiful painted decoration.

No living quarter for students has survived, only a few rooms and apartments between the main entrance and the madrasa. A ruined structure on the southwestern corner of the madrasa might have once included living units.

31. The madrasa of Emir Uljay al-Yusufi (1373)[48]

Uljay al-Yusufi al-Nasiri began his career under Sultan Hasan and became commander-in-chief of the army under Sultan al-Ashraf Sha'ban. He married Khawand Baraka, Sha'ban's mother and Sultan Hasan's sister. Upon her death in 774/1373, however, a confrontation with the sultan over her estate ended his career as well as his life. Trying to escape the sultan's soldiers, he threw himself in the Nile and drowned, to the sultan's regret. Divers recovered his body so that he could be buried in his mausoleum, in Muharram 775/June 1373.

This madrasa was also a Friday mosque, following the example of Sultan Hasan's complex, and was dedicated to the teaching of the Shafi'i and Hanafi *madhhab*s. Its waqf deed is not recorded.

The inscriptions of the portal indicate the date Rajab 774/January 1373, contradicting Maqrizi's attribution of the monument to 768/1366–7. At that time Uljay was not yet commander-in-chief.

The monument stands on the Suq al-Silah or weapon market street, occupying two corners. Coming from Rumayla square, the striking and characteristic feature of the monument is the masonry dome at the southern corner carved with curved oblique flutes and harmoniously matching the minaret. The architect's skilful handling of the proportions of both structures creates the illusion that the minaret stands next to the dome, although it is actually next to the portal, separated from the mausoleum by the western iwan.

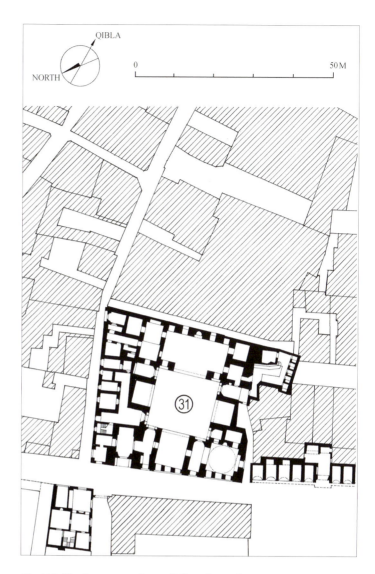

Fig. 190. The funerary madrasa of Uljay al-Yusufi.

The carved oblique flutes, which appear here for the first time on a dome, were current as decorative patterns for columns and colonettes. They adorn colonettes on the facade of the mosque of al-Maridani, and the tall engaged columns of Sultan Hasan's mausoleum facade. The flutes of these columns, however, end in straight lines at the base and the summit. On the stone dome of Aytimish al-Bajasi, built in 1383,[49] the flutes rise straight above the base before they bend in a diagonal direction.

Uljay's stone minaret is one of the most graceful of the Bahri period (Fig. 191). Its bulb rests on a carved rosette with projecting petals, and the shaft is decorated with ablaq inlaid masonry.

The facade displays a dense fenestration in three tiers of windows inserted in a large rectangular recess flanked by two keel-arched ones. A network of ablaq stripes and arches, which are unique in Cairo, covers the entire facade.

The composite sabil-maktab at the corner appears here for the first time, and will henceforth characterize Mamluk architecture. The present structure is heavily restored, however.

At the madrasa of Uljay's wife, Sultan Sha'ban's mother, built slightly earlier, the sabil does not occupy a corner, neither is it connected to the primary school or maktab.

The muqarnas of the portal vault is structured like that of Sultan Hasan's complex. Uljay's blazon, the cup, is set in a cartouche above the door and appears in the interior in stucco window grilles. The spectacular groin vaults of the vestibule are unprecedented in the fourteenth century, and will inspire the builders of the next century (Fig. 193). The deeply carved groins rise from the four corners to culminate in a central cruciform vault. A trilobed groined recess forms an elegant transition between the vaulted ceiling and the central vestibule wall. The next impressive example of this can be seen at the mosque of Sultan al-Mu'ayyad Shaykh, fifty years later.

Like the facade, the interior of Uljay's madrasa is characterized by an unprecedented density of windows pierced in symmetrical arrangement (Figs 194, 195). The windows seen from the street belong to the second iwan and to the mausoleum, both opposite the sanctuary, revealing the whole interior to the passerby. To the viewer within, the diaphanous walls convey a special character to the inner space.

The fenestration of the prayer hall is equally dense. Instead of the usual big arch spanning its entire width, the main iwan faces the courtyard, with an arch flanked on both sides by a screen wall pierced with four tiers of rectangular windows set in a recess crowned with a muqarnas frieze. The sole purpose of this wall

was obviously to create a symmetrical arrangement to match the wall on the opposite side, where the windows are functional, belonging to the living units and to the funerary chamber.

Likewise, the qibla wall, with two upper tiers of arched windows or qamariyyas above lower rectangular windows, is more densely pierced than in any previous mosque. This window arrangement continues along the lateral walls of the prayer iwan, where light is introduced from rear spaces open to the sky. The mihrab of the prayer hall, which is made of stone with ablaq masonry in the conch above an inscription band, is the second after that of Shaykhu's khanqah to show this sober style, which becomes a characteristic of fifteenth-century mosques. There is no marble dado in the entire mosque, including the mausoleum; the designer relied instead on the effect of the windows. These have round instead of the more common pointed arches. It is not clear whether they originally had iron grilles, as is the case today, or stucco grilles with coloured glass, like those of the opposite iwan. In the latter case they would have introduced colour into the prayer hall, which would explain the absence of a polychrome dado.

The domed funerary chamber is reached from the courtyard through an oblong fore-space, with which it is connected by an arch. This space overlooks the street and the courtyard, with respectively three tiers and the adjacent iwan with two tiers of windows. Interestingly, although the qibla wall of the

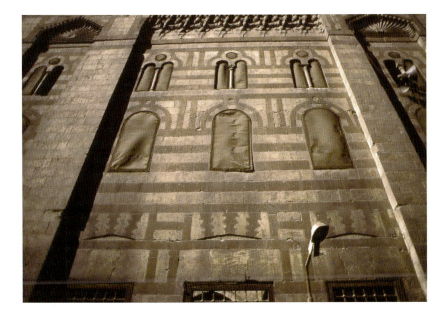

Fig. 192. The funerary madrasa of Uljay al-Yusufi, facade.

Fig. 193. The funerary madrasa of Uljay al-Yusufi, vestibule vault.

Fig. 191. [opposite] The funerary madrasa of Uljay al-Yusufi.

Fig.194. The funerary madrasa of Uljay al-Yusufi, west iwan.

Fig.195. The funerary madrasa of Uljay al-Yusufi, main iwan.

mausoleum is set against the madrasa, it is also pierced with two tiers of windows. In order to realize his concept of brightness, the architect provided open spaces behind these windows.

The southern and northern walls of the courtyard bear in their upper part stone corbels, which seem to have carried beams for the suspension of lamps, or perhaps for spanning awnings.

The mosque of Uljay al-Yusufi articulates a novel approach to fenestration as a decorative element, giving priority to light over polychromy. The symmetry and the density of the windows in this mosque's interior had a great impact on subsequent architecture. In later mosques of the qa'a plan, symmetrical non-functional windows became a standard feature of the interior design.

32. The funerary complex of Sultan Barquq (1384–6)[50]

Al-Zahir Barquq was a Circassian purchased in the Crimea and sold to the emir Yalbugha al-'Umari, who killed Sultan Hasan. He was trained in the barracks of the Circassians in the Citadel, and held the office of commander-in-chief of the army during the period of rebellion and conspiracies under the rule of the last two sultans of the Qalawun dynasty, who were both children. He eventually deposed Sultan Hajji and ascended the throne in 1382. A rebellion in Syria, however, supported by the Turcomans at the frontier, challenged his rule, and brought back Hajji to the throne in May 1389. Barquq managed to recuperate his throne in February 1390, and to keep it until his death nine years later. He also succeeded in averting an invasion of Syria by Timur. Barquq favoured the recruitment of Circassian instead of the Turkish Mamluks.

Barquq's funerary complex in the coppersmiths' market on the Bayn al-Qasrayn street was, according to the inscription in the tiraz band along the facade, and another one in the mausoleum, completed in Rabi' I 788/April 1386. This is also confirmed in the chronicles. The demolition of pre-existing structures began in Rajab 786/August 1384, and the foundations were laid in Dhu 'l-Qa'da/December of the same year. The construction works thus took one and a half years. Sultan Jaqmaq added an undated minbar inscribed with his name.

The supervisor of the construction works was the emir Jarkas al-Khalili, the master of the stables, whose name is recorded in a foundation inscription, and the master builder was the *mu'allim* Ahmad al-Tuluni, mentioned in the chronicles.[51] Jarkas himself stood on the construction site to oversee the transport of the stone blocks carried on carts from the Muqattam hill. Maqrizi attests that the workers were paid, and not forced by corvée.

After completion of the building, Barquq transferred the remains of his father from the cemetery to the attached domed mausoleum. In a testament made shortly before his death,

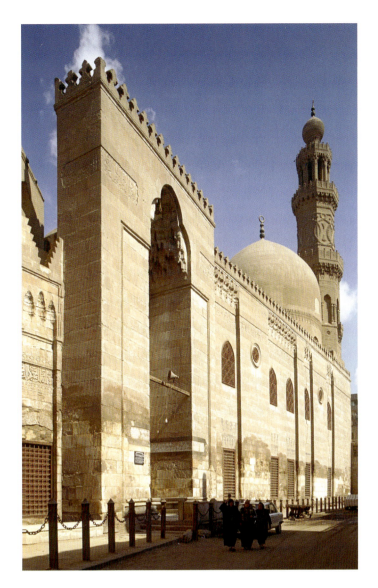

Fig. 196. The funerary complex of Barquq.

however, he ordered the construction of a funerary structure (turba) for himself in the northern cemetery. This was eventually built by his son Faraj, who also enlarged the endowment of his father's complex in the city, after it could no longer serve food to its community during the economic crisis at the turn of the century.

The waqf deed describes this complex as including a Friday mosque, a madrasa to teach the four *madhhab*s of Islamic law to 125 students, and a khanqah for 60 Sufis. The Iranian 'Ala' al-Din al-Sayrami was the first rector of the Sufis.[52]

The layout

Although Barquq inaugurated a new era in Mamluk political history, his funerary complex fully conforms to the traditions of late Bahri architecture. The building stands in the heart of the city in Bayn al-Qasrayn on the site of the Fatimid western palace, which at that time was occupied by a khan or commercial building, which Barquq demolished.

QIBLA

NORTH

0   50 M

Bayn al-Qasrayn

32

Fig. 198. The funerary complex of Barquq with the original dome (nineteenth-century photograph).

Fig. 199. The funerary complex of Barquq, minaret.

The complex has only one facade (43 m wide, 18.2 m high), adjoining the madrasa of al-Nasir Muhammad on the southern and the Ayyubid madrasa of al-Malik al-Kamil on the northern side, with no room for a sabil-maktab. The architect, however, made the best use of the space available to display a successful composition of minaret and dome.

The present dome is not original but a good brick reconstruction made in 1893 of the original wooden structure (Fig. 198). It has no exterior transitional zone; the muqarnas frieze between the drum, which is original, and the dome proper is the latest of a series, which began with the mausoleum of Sarghitmish and continued with the domes of the Sultaniyya and Yunus al-Dawadar. The waqf deed indicates that the dome was covered with lead, which was a common practice with

wooden domes. This is confirmed by a nineteenth-century photograph taken before the dome was replaced. The inner transitional zone is made of wooden pendentives.

The octagonal stone minaret (currently c. 52.8 m high above street level), like its predecessor at the mosque of Umm al-Sultan Sha'ban, is carved in the middle section, and also inlaid with marble, which is a unique case. The pattern of the carving consists of intersecting circles, which curve at their summit to form loops connected to a horizontal linear moulding (Fig. 199).

The upper arched windows and the two oculi of the respective mihrabs of the mosque and mausoleum are filled with wooden instead of stucco grilles, as in the mosques of Ulmas (1330) and Aydumur al-Bahlawan (1346).[53] The engaged columns that decorate the facades have interesting capitals with carved arabesques; in one of them, the arabesques appear in the form of rams' heads.

Fig. 197. [opposite] The funerary complex of Barquq.

Fig. 200. The funerary complex of Barquq, capital of engaged column on the facade.

Fig. 201. The funerary complex of Barquq, window.

Fig. 202. The funerary complex of Barquq, portal inscription.

Fig. 203. The funerary complex of Barquq, portal decoration.

The portal has a trilobed muqarnas vault and bears a lower marble inscription band that displays unusually ornate calligraphy (Fig. 202). The frontal wall of the vestibule is decorated with a marble inlaid panel of Syrian style similar to that of Sultan Hasan's vestibule, albeit less complex. It must have belonged to the polychrome marble, which, according to Maqrizi, the sultan brought from Syria for his mosque (Fig. 203).

This frontal wall is recessed and crowned by a fine trilobed muqarnas vault on a pair of muqarnas pendentives. A cupola roofs the vestibule, another analogy with Sultan Hasan's mosque; this one is made of brick. The bronze door is a simpler version of Sultan Hasan's. The traditional small, rectangular window in the portal's frontal wall is, however, replaced here by an oculus with an unusual grille of cast iron in the shape of a rosette.

The interior also recalls at first glance the mosque of Sultan Hasan, with the entrances to the living quarters of the madrasa placed at the corners of the courtyard. However, the main iwan here is different (Fig. 205). Instead of a vault, it is roofed with a flat wooden ceiling. The iwan has a tripartite composition, with a large central nave connected to each of the lateral naves through three arches supported by a pair of ancient Egyptian granite columns. This layout was used earlier in the madrasa of Qalawun, and slightly later in the mosque of 'Abd al-Ghani al-Fakhri (1418). The latter, however, has only a double arch on each side.

The central nave of the prayer hall (17.6 x 17.6 m) is the largest single-roofed space with a wooden ceiling in Mamluk architecture. The acquisition of the kind of timber necessary to build such a ceiling could not have been easy; the remarkable carpet-like decoration, lapis-painted and gilded, emphasized its singularity.[54] Its general design, consisting of a central medallion surrounded in geometrical arrangement by smaller ones, recalls that of the Mamluk carpets of the late fifteenth and early sixteenth centuries; some of the medallions include mushroom-like patterns, which can be found only on carpets. Four corner medallions include the Koranic phrase (XVII, 84) 'Each man behaves after his own fashion', which is traditionally inscribed in the apex of domes. The decoration was redone by the Comité.

The other iwans are vaulted and built of stone, as in Sultan Hasan's mosque. The western shows intricate joggled masonry resembling the pattern of lintels. The four entrances to the madrasa premises are set in recesses crowned with round arches with chevron-carved voussoirs. Their door openings are enhanced with arched lintels elaborately inlaid with black and white marble. Unlike Sultan Hasan's mosque, the courtyard has a Koranic inscription band running along its four walls above the iwan arches, which includes the date 788/1386. The octagonal domed fountain was reconstructed by the Comité.

The polychrome marble and wood decoration of the prayer hall follows the conventions of the Bahri period. The inlaid marble floor of the sanctuary, however, displays an unusual row of mihrabs, which have their parallels only in the mausoleum of al-Muzaffar Baybars. These are filled with marble mosaics.

The dado of the mausoleum is high and displays tiers of marble roundels, probably from slices of ancient columns. This is the earliest use of such roundels, which are common on pavements. The wooden transitional zone of the dome recalls that of Sultan Hasan. At the top of the walls and below the wooden epigraphic band, a frieze of painted wood attracts attention; it is composed of a sequence of niches filled alternately with a suspended mosque lamp or a flower.

The plain wooden minbar bears the name of Sultan Jaqmaq. One may wonder how Barquq's minbar could have disappeared

Fig. 204. The funerary complex of Barquq, vestibule vault.

only sixty years after the mosque was built. It would be incompatible, however, with Jaqmaq's puritanical character to have transferred the original minbar to his own mosque, as suggested by J. Michael Rogers.

Behind the madrasa on the western side, a large complex of dwellings for the students and Sufis and their teachers, including a stable, is today in a ruined condition.

Fig. 205. The funerary complex of Barquq, courtyard.

– 17 –

The Reign of al-Nasir Faraj Ibn Barquq

33. The funerary khanqah of Sultan Faraj Ibn Barquq (1400–11)[1]

Sultan al-Nasir Faraj, the son of Barquq, led the army to Syria after Timur's sack of Aleppo in 1400, without succeeding, however, in saving Damascus, which was sacked and burnt by Timur's troops. Faraj's reign was interrupted for two months in 1405, during which his brother 'Abd al-'Aziz replaced him. He returned to the throne, but his rule was marked by anarchy in Syria and discontent in Egypt. He was deposed by rebellious emirs, who were supported by the caliph al-Musta'in bi'l-llah. In an exceptional initiative, the emirs enthroned the caliph as a sultan for a transitional period. Faraj, who tried to resist his deposition, was eventually assassinated. Maqrizi condemned Faraj for mismanagement, for oppressive taxation and for his debauchery. Ibn Taghribirdi agreed with his colleague's assessment, but, due to his own family connections with the Mamluk establishment, his critique, expressed in a rather fatalistic tone, was less harsh.

Sultan Faraj complied with his father's wish that he be buried in the desert in the vicinity of saints and scholars rather than in his funerary complex in the urban centre. He therefore founded this funerary khanqah in the northern cemetery, for which Barquq had allocated the amount of 80,000 dinars to pay for the construction and the purchase of the endowment estate.

Barquq was buried there in 801/1399 before the building was erected. An inscription in the northern mausoleum at the base of the dome states that the turba was built by order of Sultan Barquq by his son Faraj in 803/1400–1. Another inscription beneath it states that it was completed in Jumada II

808/November 1405 by Sultan 'Abd al-'Aziz, a brother of Faraj, who ruled briefly in an interim that year. Upon his return to the throne, Faraj finished the work. The southern mausoleum was completed in 813/1410–11. The same date is given in an epigraphic slab on the sanctuary's facade. An inscription in the northwestern portal names the emir Lajin al-Turuntay as overseer of the construction. Barquq had previously appointed Yunus al-Dawadar for this task.[2]

The construction work thus began with the northern mausoleum after Barquq's death, and the prayer hall was probably built simultaneously or shortly afterwards. The southern mausoleum carries the latest date; the rest of the complex is not dated. The complex took eleven years to complete, which is a very long time by Mamluk standards. But the sultan was dethroned twice during this period of unrest. Faraj had plans to include markets in this area, but he died before completing his scheme. No waqf document survives to indicate whether a madrasa curriculum was included in this foundation, which, according to its inscriptions, combined a Friday mosque with a turba and a khanqah.

Notwithstanding the fact that this period witnessed the most severe economic and political problems that the Mamluks had to face, the architecture of this monument is one of the most original and outstanding of the Mamluk sultanate. This is also attested by Ibn Taghribirdi, who considered it as second only to Sultan Hasan's mosque, in construction and skill (*khushunat al-'amal wa 'l-imkan*).[3] Only the relatively long period it took to complete the building reveals the critical situation at that time.

Having abundant space at his disposal, the architect could afford to design a free-standing building characterized by

Fig. 206. *The funerary khanqah of Faraj Ibn Barquq, east view.*

symmetry, which is a rare feature in Mamluk ground plans. Because the area was not yet urbanized the building could be seen from all sides, and the mausoleums could be placed on the inner side of the building, where they were visible to the traveller coming along the caravan road. Each of the four facades displays an interesting composition. The rear facade on the cemetery side is characterized by a pair of monumental masonry domes with a small brick dome between them, which marks the sanctuary's mihrab. The northern and southern facades display a dome and a minaret on each extremity. The western facade addresses the city with two minarets. All the facades are panelled in the usual Mamluk style.

The western facade is pierced with an oculus between the recessed panels although there is no mihrab there. We have already seen that the oculus became a standard device to indicate the mihrab on the facade to an external onlooker. Being on the axis of the mihrab in the opposite riwaq, the oculus here signals the positioning of the mihrab located on the other side.

The building measures c. 72 x 73 m, with the western facade being 72 m wide and c. 17 m high. It has two portals, each flanked

by a sabil-maktab. The northern facade, which faces the caravan road, is connected to an arcade that might have belonged to a musalla or open space for funerary prayers. The north portal occupies a corner, and the second portal protrudes from the west facade facing the city. Both portals are enhanced by a pronounced pishtaq. The portals are not placed symmetrically, although they are connected to symmetrical entrance corridors. Whereas the north portal and the corresponding entrance passage are integrated between the north and west riwaqs, the other portal projects from the facade beyond the southwest corner of the building. It is connected to a passage leading to a sabil-maktab, which might originally have had two windows before restoration, and to a reception hall, which projects to

Fig. 207. *[opposite top] The funerary khanqah of Faraj Ibn Barquq.*

Fig. 208. *[opposite bottom] The funerary khanqah of Faraj Ibn Barquq, south view.*

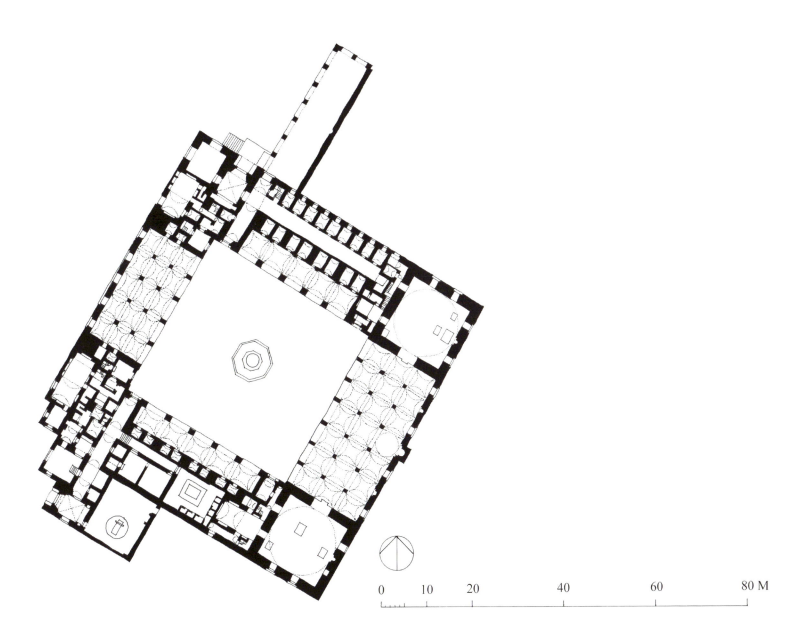

0   10   20   40   60   80 M

Fig. 209. The funerary khanqah of Faraj Ibn Barquq, prayer hall.

form a second corner with windows opening towards the city. This hall, placed between the portal and the mosque, is the reason for the asymmetry that has pushed the portal outside the rectangle of the complex. This reduced qa'a must have been

used for social gatherings, like the one in Shaykhu's complex and many other funerary monuments. The remains of a trough can be seen below the sabil.

The minarets have a rectangular first storey, which was unusual at that time, with a cylindrical carved middle section and the usual upper pavilion with a bulb crown. The carving of the middle section copies that of the minaret of Asanbugha, built in 1370 and displays an interlacing pattern.[4]

With an inner diameter of 14.3 m the domes are the largest masonry domes of the Mamluk period. Their inner height to the apex is c. 30.4 m. They rest above a high transitional zone with an undulating profile, which is a borrowing from minaret architecture. The earliest minaret with an undulating transitional zone at the base is that of the emir Bashtak, built in 1336.[5] The carved zigzag pattern of the domes had already been applied at the mausoleum of Jamal al-Din Mahmud al-Ustadar (Mahmud al-Kurdi), built in 1395.[6] It was henceforth repeated several times.

Before reaching the central courtyard, the entrance corridor opens onto a compound with a passage between the southern living units, which once occupied three floors, and what was probably a kitchen behind them. On this side there is also a courtyard with the ruins of what could have been a waterwheel or a mill.

The plan of the funerary khanqah shows a modified riwaq mosque, which remained singular in Mamluk architecture.

Fig. 210. The funerary khanqah of Faraj Ibn Barquq, side mihrab.

Fig. 211. The funerary khanqah of Faraj Ibn Barquq, dome interior.

Fig. 212. [opposite] The funerary khanqah of Faraj Ibn Barquq, minbar of Qaytbay.

The lateral arcades, which are lower than the riwaqs of the sanctuary and the opposite one, were surmounted by living units. These arcades have the double function of side riwaqs as well as porticos for the cells on the ground floor. The prayer hall and the opposite riwaq are each three aisles deep. Behind and parallel to the northern riwaq, the Sufi cells occupied three floors.

Whereas the prayer hall of Barquq's complex in the city is characterized by its broad timber ceiling, which displays carpentry skills, almost no timber is visible in this building. Instead, the arcades consist of parallel and perpendicular arches that support shallow brick domes. The domes of the sanctuary are larger than those of the other arcades. Those of the west riwaq are elliptic.

The bareness of the four riwaqs contrasts with the polychrome marble decoration of the mausoleums (Figs 213, 214). The arched windows with coloured glass introduce touches of colour in the prayer hall, where the plain stone mihrab is emphasized only by the brick dome and the oculus. There are two other side mihrabs, which are equally plain. The main mihrab, along with its oculus, is not placed exactly on the axis of the central bay, but deviates about 20 cm to the north. The side mihrabs are even more pronouncedly off the axis of their bay, as are the two arched windows above each of them. The arched windows in the entire qibla wall are not placed axially in relation to the bays, but follow instead the arrangement of the recessed panels in the rear facade. The side mihrabs follow the arrangement of the windows, which explains their asymmetrical position. The deviation of the main mihrab, however, seems to be due to a lack of precision in the workmanship rather than to any constraint, which is surprising in a monument of such quality, but the mihrab is not the only irregularity, as shown below.

Sultan Qaytbay might have been disturbed by the austerity of this sanctuary, which prompted him to add the richly carved stone minbar and the wooden bench that carries his name.

The mausoleums are entered directly from the prayer hall through a screen wall of geometric wooden lattice. The northern mausoleum includes the remains of Faraj and Barquq, and the southern is dedicated to the female members of the family. The two chambers are not identical. In the southern female mausoleum, the space between the two windows in the qibla

wall was not sufficient for the mihrab, which had to be squeezed to a format narrower than that of the northern mausoleum, or ordinary mihrabs. The distance between the eastern windows in the northern mausoleum is larger. As in the case of the sanctuary mihrab, the diverging distance between the windows of the two mausoleums seems to be due to miscalculation by the craftsmen rather than constraint.

The qibla walls of the mausoleum are panelled with a conventional polychrome marble dado, which in the male mausoleum is higher than in the other. The three other walls are plain. The cenotaphs of the two sultans are larger and more elaborate than those of their female counterparts. Both domes have their interior painted in red and black colours with the pattern of a rosette and with inscription bands. The painting is rather crude (Fig. 211).

34. The mosque and sabil-maktab called Duhaysha (1408)[7]

The small building of Sultan Faraj facing Bab Zuwayla to the south was pulled down in 1922, and rebuilt further north to enlarge the street. Nevertheless, it is interesting enough to be discussed here.

This structure had a name, Duhaysha, which means 'the Little Stunning'; the name was also given earlier to a palace in the Citadel. The fact that it was made to impress is, surprisingly enough, reiterated in its waqf deed, which is full of superlatives, written in a very unusual style for this kind of document, to emphasize the aesthetic values of this building. Phrases such as 'precious marbles', 'wonderful craftsmanship', 'gorgeous appearance', 'of perfect beauty', 'pleasing to the eyes', 'with qualities that cheer the spirit and inspire joy', 'priceless', 'stunning' and 'accomplished' occur in almost every sentence describing the building. The reason for this effervescent formulation may lie in the fact that the building and decoration material of the Duhaysha were removed from the monumental madrasa of al-Ashraf Sha'ban beneath the Citadel, which was

Fig. 213. [opposite top] The funerary khanqah of Faraj Ibn Barquq, mihrab of male mausoleum.

Fig. 214. [opposite bottom] The funerary khanqah of Faraj Ibn Barquq, mihrab of female mausoleum.

Fig. 215. The mosque and sabil (Duhaysha) of Faraj Ibn Barquq, detail of facade.

left unfinished at its founder's death. Faraj dismantled the madrasa, delegating to this task his controversial majordomo, the emir Jamal al-Din Yusuf al-Ustadar, who also helped himself to the spoils to build his own madrasa.[8] The emphasis on the preciousness of the materials might have been intended to justify the despoliation of al-Ashraf's madrasa by re-endowing its material for a new pious foundation.

Jamal al-Din Yusuf al-Ustadar oversaw the construction works, as indicated by Maqrizi and an inscription. His blazon with a pen box appears on the sabil's lunette. The inscription dates the building to 811/1408; its waqf deed is dated slightly later, to 812/1409.

The Duhaysha was not a Friday mosque but, rather, as a sabil-maktab attached to a small oratory (masjid) – or perhaps even the reverse, the sabil-maktab being foremost. There was no minaret. The inscription of the portal describes the foundation as a 'makan', which is a term more currently applied to secular buildings or mausoleums. Another one refers to the sabil. A further inscription, now in the Islamic Museum, included the Koranic verse LXVI, 21, often inscribed on sabils, referring to water. Originally the structure adjoined an apartment complex or rab', which it must have served. This small composite structure is a precursor of the free-standing sabil-maktabs with prayer hall, which were built during the reign of Sultan Qaytbay and continued to be built under the Ottomans, often in conjunction with residential or commercial structures.

The building was originally reached by a ramp as well as a flight of steps. The present polychrome marble panels of the facade, which might have belonged to the madrasa of al-Ashraf Sha'ban, are remarkable and confirm the waqf deed's praise. The tiraz band and the muqarnas were gilded.

The entrance led to the sabil, 'the sight of which quenches the thirst', and to the prayer hall. The sabil had gilded bronze window grilles and a painted ceiling, and was entirely panelled with polychrome marble. The mosque was a small room. Its pavement, the dado (almost five cubits high, i.e. c.2.5m), and the mihrab were all in 'expensive and rare' polychrome marble. Semi-precious stones were inserted in the mihrab's decoration. The wooden ceiling was painted and gilded. Photographs in the Creswell archive show some details before the mosque was pulled down. The ceiling of the maktab above the sabil had in its middle a painted wooden lantern in the shape of a cupola.

–18–

The Reign of al-Mu'ayyad Shaykh

35. The funerary complex of Sultan al-Mu'ayyad (1415–20)[1]

Al-Mu'ayyad Shaykh was purchased by Barquq at the age of ten or twelve, and Faraj appointed him governor of Tripoli. After ten years in Syria he joined the opponents of Faraj to depose him in 1412 and invest in his place the caliph al-Musta'in, whose sultanate lasted only six months. In the same year Shaykh, who had been the chief of the army, seized power, after crushing a rebellion by his former ally Nawruz, who was holding Syria. Shaykh, who took the title al-Mu'ayyad, led several campaigns to northern Syria and fought the Turcoman neighbours in southern Anatolia, the Dhu 'l-Qadr and Ramadan, during which he advanced to Konya. However, plague, the devaluation of the currency and rebellious bedouins in Upper Egypt disturbed his reign. He died in 1421 after a period of illness. The problems he had to face throughout his entire reign did not prevent him from being one of the great patrons of architecture, being at the same time extremely humble in his personal appearance and spending very little on himself.

Al-Mu'ayyad embellished Cairo with several religious and secular monuments. A mosque at Rawda, a khanqah in Giza and the palace called al-Khamas Wujuh along the Khalij in the northern outskirts are gone. He reconstructed al-Nasir Muhammad's hippodrome on the Nile shore, which had been abandoned for two decades, and built a palace on the Nile shore at Ambuba (today Imbaba), facing Bulaq.

Maqrizi reported that the sultan built this mosque on the site of a prison where he had been incarcerated, having vowed that he would build a mosque on its site, should he survive.

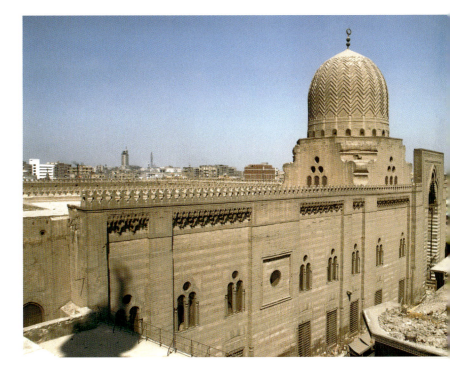

Fig. 216. The funerary complex of al-Mu'ayyad Shaykh.

Al-Mu'ayyad's funerary complex included a Friday mosque and a madrasa for the four *madhhabs*, which, unlike Barquq's foundation, was not a madrasa with a khanqah but a more integrated institution, a madrasa for Sufi students of the four rites. They were supposed to include fifty Hanafis, forty Shafi'is, fifteen Malikis and ten Hanbalis, and their respective teachers and imams. The madrasa also included two classes of twenty

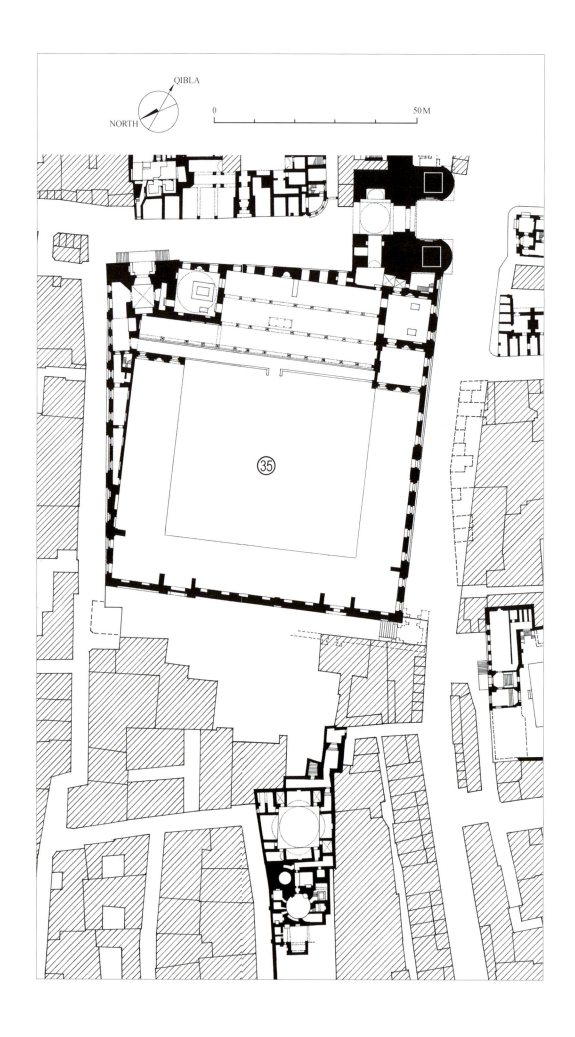

QIBLA

NORTH

0   50 M

35

students for *tafsir* (exegesis) and Hadith, and two others of ten students for Koran recitation and legal studies according to the teachings of the Hanafi jurist al-Tahawi (tenth century).

Thirty builders and one hundred workers were employed for the construction. Maqrizi, who noted that the workers were treated fairly, revealed, however, that the sultan had no scruples in taking marble and columns from other mosques and palaces, including a bronze door and chandelier from the mosque of Sultan Hasan. Books for the library were brought from the Citadel's royal collection, and Muhammad al-Barizi, the sultan's private secretary, contributed with five hundred more; he was rewarded with the appointment of his son as the preacher and librarian of the foundation. The latrines complex was built on land purchased by his majordomo, 'Abd al-Ghani al-Fakhri, who sent his Mamluks to build them, and they completed the work within twenty-five days. However, the main building was never completed. The projected dome of the second mausoleum was not erected, and, according to Maqrizi, neither were the Sufi dwellings, for which 20,000 dinars were allocated. It is not clear whether or not they were built at a later date, but they were planned as a separate multi-storeyed building with a courtyard. The present condition of the monument, which has suffered greatly and retains only a portion of its original structure, does not provide an answer to this question. Only the eastern facade and the prayer hall are original. According to the waqf deed, the complex included a hall reserved for the library. The ruins of a hammam belonging to the estate stands on the western side of the mosque.

Maqrizi, who was an eyewitness, reported that the clearing of the site began in Rabi' I 818/May 1415, three years after the sultan's accession to the throne. The digging of the foundations began in Jumada II, and the construction began in Safar 819/April 1416. The first *khutba* was held in the sanctuary in August of the same year while the rest of the building was still under construction. The inaugural celebration took place in Shawwal 822/November 1419. The inscription on the portal gives the later date of 823/1420.

The minarets

The location of the twin stone minarets above the tower of Bab Zuwayla is the most striking feature of the mosque. Their elegant profile honours their location. Their decoration is conventional, however. The minarets have an epigraphic cartouche above their doors on the roof level, both of which name the builder. The inscriptions are not identical. The one on the eastern minaret states that this 'ma'dhana' was built by Muhammad Ibn al-Qazzaz and completed in Rajab 822/August 1419. The text of the western minaret states that Sultan al-Mu'ayyad ordered the

Fig. 217. The mosque and hammam of al-Mu'ayyad Shaykh.

construction of the two 'manars', and that they were executed by Muhammad Ibn al-Qazzaz and completed in Sha'ban 823/August 1420. The use of two different terms for 'minaret', 'manar' and 'ma'dhana', is interesting but cannot be explained.

Maqrizi mentioned that one of the minarets had begun to show deficiencies and had to be pulled down in June 1418, without specifying which one. It seems that the deficient minaret was the first and eastern one, which was rebuilt in August 1419. Since the eastern minaret was completed in August 1419, and the other one the following year, we may assume that it took one year to construct a minaret, which is a long period by Mamluk standards. In this particular case, due to the structural challenge of placing them above the pre-existing Fatimid gate towers, the construction of the minarets required more skill and time than usual. Muhammad Ibn al-Qazzaz's accomplishment was admirable, which explains his pride in signing his work; however, the chronicles do not mention him. We do not know if Muhammad had been responsible for the first deficient minaret or another builder who was eventually replaced. Neither do we know whether Ibn al-Qazzaz was involved in any other construction work in the complex.

A third three-storeyed minaret stood at the west portal on a side street. Maqrizi wrote that it was smaller than the others, but was visible from the courtyard. This minaret, which collapsed in Rajab 830/1427, during Barsbay's reign, was immediately rebuilt. It disappeared in the nineteenth century.[2]

The facade

The mosque was a free-standing building with four facades and three axial entrances. To construct the southern facade the Fatimid wall had to be demolished. As its style indicates, the present facade is a nineteenth-century reconstruction.

According to the waqf document there was a richly decorated sabil-maktab at the corner of the main facade. The present shops beneath the mosque are part of the original design. Large rectangular windows are pierced in the lower part of the walls.

The elevated position of the minarets required the architect to raise the facades of the mosque to a corresponding height. Its height of c. 17.30 m exceeds the average of that time. Despite their height, the facades have only two rows of windows, unlike the madrasas of Umm al-Sultan Sha'ban and Uljay al-Yusufi, which have three.

Located next to the portal, the mausoleum dome, with a diameter of c. 10 m, is a reduced copy of Faraj's twin domes. In this monumental setting it appears disproportionately small.

The monumental main portal is the last grand portal to be built in the Mamluk period. It is enhanced by a pishtaq (23.2 m high) that is more accentuated than previous ones. Its top is at the same level as the top of the dome's transitional zone. A moulding frames the portal's trilobe vault, which vaguely echoes that of Sultan Hasan's mosque with its conch resting above a

cascade of muqarnas. The doorway is framed with a beautiful marble band carved in high relief with a geometric pattern and inlaid with polychrome stones and coloured stucco. Panels of inlaid black and white marble Kufic adorn the lateral walls of the portal recess. The door frame is of pink granite of ancient provenance. The vault of the entrance vestibule is an elaborate masonry groin vault, recalling that of Uljay al-Yusufi, flanked by half-domes on muqarnas (Figs 219, 220).

The plan

The plan of the mosque, like that of Faraj's khanqah, is hypostyle, with a pair of domed mausoleums flanking the prayer hall. However, unlike its predecessor it has no cells integrated in the riwaqs around the courtyard; the waqf deed indicates that they were in a separate compound.

The symmetry of the plan here is less accomplished than in Faraj's mosque, with the northern mausoleum encroaching into the space that in a symmetrical arrangement should have belonged to the prayer hall. Moreover, the mausoleums are less deep than the prayer hall, leaving an aisle free between them and the lateral riwaqs. The aisle in front of the northern mausoleum connects the vestibule with the sanctuary; otherwise the worshipper would have had to pass through the mausoleum before getting inside the mosque. Such a problem could not have occurred in Faraj's mosque, where the mausoleums on the opposite side of the mosque are remote from the entrances.

As the main street does not correspond to the direction of the qibla wall, the facade has been adjusted by increasing its thickness to fill the resulting angle. The northern facade also had to be adjusted to keep the lateral walls of the mosque parallel. On this side, however, instead of a massive wall of increasing thickness, a triangular space was left between the external wall following the street and the internal one parallel to the sanctuary wall; the space was used for rooms.

The arcaded hypostyle prayer hall with columns is the only one of the four riwaqs to have survived; the three others have been reconstructed in the course of the latest restoration. A row of arched windows is pierced above the arches, which are connected with tie beams. The three minor riwaqs were built with two aisles each. Pascal Coste's drawing shows the courtyard and the surrounding arcades with alternating keel-arched niches and medallions in the spandrels. This decoration can still be seen on the facade of the sanctuary, with a moulding running along the arches and curling to form a loop at their apex, as in the mosque of al-Maridani.

The two funerary chambers, which occupy the corners between the prayer hall and the lateral riwaqs, display on the wall facing the riwaqs a shallow mihrab, a feature that

Fig. 219. The funerary complex of al-Mu'ayyad Shaykh, portal.

Fig. 218. [opposite] The funerary complex of al-Mu'ayyad Shaykh, minarets.

Fig. 220. The funerary complex of al-Mu'ayyad Shaykh, lintel of main door.

marble columns roofed with a gilded wooden dome above an awning.

The sanctuary is the most richly decorated of its time (Fig. 221). According to Sakhawi the mosque was the most lavishly decorated monument ever to be built after the Umayyad mosque of Damascus,[3] and Ibn Taghribirdi praised its decoration as the most remarkable of the Mamluk period. The waqf deed indicates that the wall decoration was limited only to the prayer hall, where the polychrome marble dado is high enough to include the window and the mihrab recesses. Above the mihrab, however, a large rosette of polychrome marble replaces the usual oculus; this kind of rosette is, rather, a traditional feature of floor pavements. The marble columns of the prayer hall are pre-Islamic and of diverse size and shape, predominantly with Corinthian capitals except the four columns in front of the mihrab, which have Mamluk plain bell-shaped capitals, thus stylistically emphasizing this area. In front of the entrance to the female mausoleum two painted wooden transversal arches are set between the parallel arcades, perhaps to signal a restricted area for women. According to the waqf deed, confirmed by Coste's drawing, the floors of the sanctuary and the courtyard were paved with polychrome marble. The three other riwaqs were paved with stone.

The voussoirs of the window recesses and the spandrels of the mihrab display elaborate marble inlay of the type that would often be used in the architecture of Qaytbay's reign. The mihrab itself is in the Bahri tradition. A frieze of small niches flanked by pairs of colonettes made of blue glass paste runs along the entire qibla wall at the base of the arches of the mihrab and the window recesses. The wooden doors and panels as well as the minbar are original and of exquisite craftsmanship.

An interesting feature in the prayer hall is the presence of a pair of blind windows with stucco grilles in the upper part of the wall adjacent to the mausoleum. The carving of their grilles is in Andalusian or Moroccan style; one is geometric, the other floral, both of high quality.[4]

In contrast to the prayer hall, the walls and the mihrab of the mausoleum are bare of decoration. This is the reverse of the arrangement in the khanqah of Faraj. The cenotaph of al-Mu'ayyad was not made for him; it is carved in beautiful Kufic, which dates it to the ninth or tenth century.

Fig. 221. The funerary complex of al-Mu'ayyad Shaykh, prayer hall.

Fig. 222. The mosque of al-Mu'ayyad Shaykh, reconstructed courtyard.

does not appear in Faraj's khanqah. The mihrabs must have been intended for worshippers praying in the lateral riwaqs. The courtyard was originally centred by a fountain with

36. The hospital of Sultan al-Mu'ayyad (1420)[5]

What remains of this hospital is a glorious ruin that still reveals an ambitious monumental scheme. Only the wide facade and the remains of the main hall survive. The building was erected on the site of the dismantled madrasa of al-Ashraf Sha'ban.

Fig. 223. The hospital of al-Mu'ayyad Shaykh.

Al-Mu'ayyad might have reused its foundations and parts of its walls, which had gigantic proportions and probably contributed to the grand appearance of this hospital. In fact, the orientation of the main hall is aligned to the qibla. Al-Jawhari wrote that part of Sha'ban's madrasa on the side of the entrance (*min nahiyat al-bāb*) survived, and that the *mu'allim* Ibn 'Umar al-Tuluni was the master builder.

The construction work began in Jumada II 821/July 1418 and it was completed in Rajab 823/July–August 1420. Maqrizi noted that orders were given to finance the hospital from the sultan's endowment for this mosque. However, al-Mu'ayyad died the following year, and the hospital was given up without having provided any service during the plague of 822–3/1419–20, which took 10,000 lives in Cairo alone.[6] The building was inhabited by a group of Iranians and then used as a guesthouse for the Mamluk court until the following year, when in Rabi' II 825/March 1422, during Barsbay's reign, it was turned into a Friday mosque.

The fate of the hospital may not be surprising, considering that al-Mu'ayyad's waqf stipulates that, after the expenses of the mosque and the khanqah were settled, the balance of the revenue should revert to the sultan's descendants. The waqf deed, which gives a brief description of the hospital, does not include any specifications regarding the use of its space or any stipulations concerning the medical services to be provided, nor does it mention anything regarding the medical staff or the hospital's expenses. This is quite a contrast with Qalawun's detailed endowment deed. It seems, therefore, that the foundation of the hospital was not a thoroughly planned project. Since the maintenance of the hospital was not explicitly included in the stipulations, the descendants, who were entitled to the balance of the pious endowment, might not have been keen to diminish their own share of the revenue by including the hospital's costs. Barsbay must have made a new endowment for the mosque.

Located on the Muqattam slope beneath the Citadel, the hospital is reached by a modern staircase. Elevation, magnitude

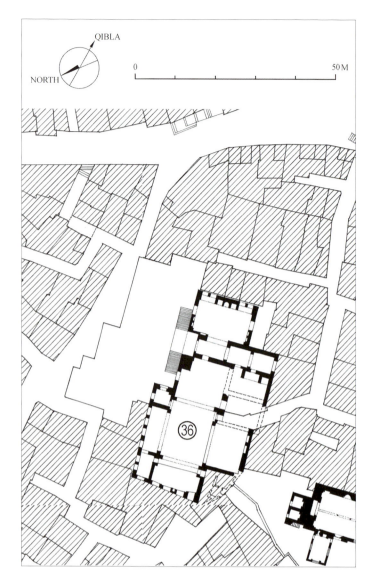

Fig. 224. The hospital of al-Mu'ayyad Shaykh.

Kufic script made of glazed lapis blue tiles. Above these are carved stone panels filled with coloured stones and perhaps also paste. More colour was displayed in the lateral walls of the portal recess, where, on either side, a roundel above a square panel inlaid with coloured stone recalls those of the vestibules of Sultan Hasan's and Barquq's mosques.

The fenestration of the main hall or qa'a is remarkable, consisting of a lower tier of four rectangular windows, with little masonry between them. Above them are four arched windows surmounted by a pyramidal composition of six oculi: one over two over three. This dense fenestration, which is repeated in the opposite wall, transforms the wall into a monumental transparent screen. The system of arched windows and oculi set in pyramidal arrangement is a standard feature of the transitional zone of domes; it was also used in the hall of the palace of Qawsun.

Fig. 225. The hospital of al-Mu'ayyad Shaykh, detail of ceramic panel on the facade.

and symmetry give the facade an awesome and regal appearance. According to its brief description in the waqf document, the entrance vestibule led to an open courtyard surrounded by various rooms that included the principal four-iwan hall with a central basin. Water flowed down from two shadirwans set in the central walls of the two axial iwans. Among the other halls, one was for female patients; there was also an oratory, a kitchen and several upper rooms, including a loggia.

The facade is raised above the street level, and it was originally reached by a spiral staircase. The portal, which is enhanced by a pishtaq, has a recess with a trilobe vault of stone muqarnas, similar to that of the sultan's mosque, built against a brick vault.

The facade is framed by a carved band of unparalleled high-relief showing a sequence of horizontal 'S'-shapes alternating with circles, all filled with coloured stones. On each side of the entrance recess are symmetrical rectangular panels of square

37. The madrasa of 'Abd al-Ghani al-Fakhri (1418)[7]

'Abd al-Ghani al-Fakhri was a high-ranking bureaucrat of Christian-Armenian origin. Under al-Mu'ayyad he ascended to the office of *ustadar* or majordomo, and finally he held the vizierate. He had a bad reputation, being regarded as an evil and dishonest tyrant, who brutally extorted money from poor villagers.

'Abd al-Ghani was buried in his madrasa in Shawwal 821/ November 1418 two months after the inaugural *khutba*, which had taken place earlier in Sha'ban/September, but before the rest of the building was completed. An inscription in the entrance indicates the date 1851–2, for a restoration, and the mosque also underwent substantial restoration by the Comité. The fine bronze door with geometric stars could be of an earlier date.

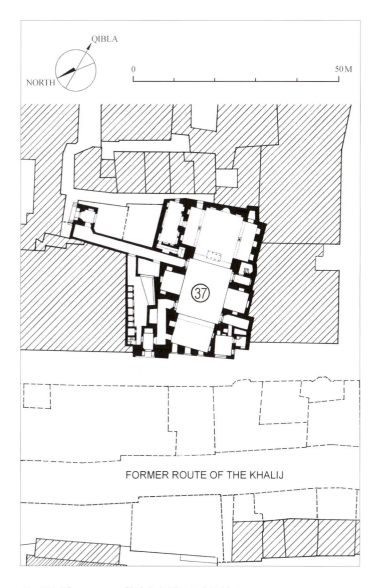

Fig. 226. The mosque of 'Abd al-Ghani al-Fakhri.

The foundation was a Friday mosque with a madrasa curriculum for teaching three *madhhab*s of Islamic law, the Shafi'i, Hanafi and Maliki, as well as Sufism.

Built along the Khalij waterfront, the mosque occupied a corner with the street called Darb Sa'ada. It has a conventional facade with a sabil-maktab at the corner, and a minaret that was replaced in the Ottoman period by the present structure. The courtyard is surrounded by four iwans roofed with a flat wooden ceiling. The proportions of the courtyard to the surrounding walls are very pleasant.

The prayer hall follows on a smaller scale the pattern of Barquq's madrasa, with two side naves separated from the central one by a double arch with a central column. The entrances to the living units of the madrasa are at the corners. The founder's mausoleum is not domed, but in the shape of a qa'a located on the northeast side of the prayer hall.

The density of arched windows and qamariyyas, which occupy three tiers in the western wall, is aesthetic rather than functional. The middle windows have a triple composition of a double arch with an oculus; the upper ones are simply arched.

38. The mosque of Qadi 'Abd al-Basit (1420)[8]

Qadi 'Abd al-Basit was a judge of Syrian origin whose career was closely associated with al-Mu'ayyad Shaykh since the time when he was governor of Damascus. Upon his access to the throne, al-Mu'ayyad appointed 'Abd al-Basit to high administrative positions, among which was the supervision of the sultan's treasury and the management of the *kiswa*, the cover for the Ka'ba, and those for other shrines prepared and dispatched on a yearly basis. His career continued under Sultan Barsbay, who appointed him supervisor of the military administration (*nazir al-juyush*). 'Abd al-Basit managed to maintain an excellent reputation of integrity and fairness until the end of his life, in 1450. He was wealthy, owned many Mamluks and dwelt in the former palace of the Bahri Mamluk emir Tankiz in the Khurunfish quarter, next to which he built this madrasa for Sufis. Maqrizi, who praised the beauty of the monument, credited the patron for having founded it with honest means.

The madrasa is one of several foundations he established in Egypt, Syria and the Hijaz. It has no mausoleum; 'Abd al-Basit was buried in the cemetery. Its inscriptions define it as a madrasa, but at that time buildings described as madrasas were Friday mosques as well. It does not include any visible living

Fig. 227. The mosque of 'Abd al-Ghani al-Fakhri, west iwan.

compound for students, although Maqrizi reported that the foundation included dwellings for Sufis.

According to an inscription band on the main and eastern facade above the portal, construction began in Jumada I 823/May–June 1420, and it was also completed in the same month. This, of course, is impossible, and must be a mason's mistake. Another inscription around the courtyard with the Koranic text II, 56, is without date. The foundation should be dated to 822, as indicated by Maqrizi, who also gave the date of the first *khutba* as Safar 823/February–March 1420.

The madrasa has two facades with two portals, an eastern and a northern one with a sabil-maktab at their corners. The minaret on the northwest corner is very similar to those of al-Mu'ayyad Shaykh above Bab Zuwayla. Its Koranic inscription is unusual (XXII, 28); it refers to pilgrimage, thus alluding to the founder's office.

The lintels of the windows and the entrances have a remarkable decoration of polychrome marble mosaics.

The mosque has a cruciform four-iwan plan; the iwans are roofed with timber and face the courtyard through a pointed arch. The main iwan has a 'T'-shape with two lateral recesses. The mihrab is plain, and the walls are bare of decoration, contrasting with the floor, which is paved with fine polychrome inlaid marble with a geometric design. Above each of the two windows flanking the mihrab there is a single-arch qamariyya, which corresponds to the composite triple windows on the facade. Each of the two qamariyyas, like the mihrab, is surmounted by an oculus, so that this qibla wall has three oculi.

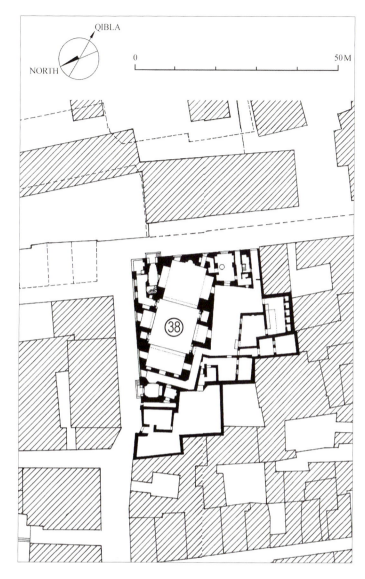

Fig. 229. The mosque of 'Abd al-Basit.

Fig. 228. [opposite] The mosque of 'Abd al-Basit.

–19–

The Reign of al-Ashraf Barsbay

39. The funerary complex of Sultan Barsbay in the city (1423–4)[1]

Barsbay began his career as a Mamluk of Barquq, and he served under his son Faraj. He was promoted during the reign of al-Mu'ayyad, serving as governor of Tripoli and great secretary (*dawadar*) before he ascended to the throne in Rabi' II 825/April 1422. His reign was marked by the threat of increasing European power in the Mediterranean, but he managed to avenge the sack of Alexandria of 1365 by seizing Cyprus, which remained under the control of the Mamluks to the end of their rule. Like his predecessor, he led a campaign in southern Anatolia to contain the Turcomans. In an attempt to improve the economic situation of the empire, battered by his military campaigns in Cyprus and Diyarbakr, Barsbay took an active and controversial role in trade policy; he transferred the entrepôt of the Indian trade from Aden to Jedda, to the great advantage of the Mamluks, and, internally, he introduced a monopoly in the sugar trade, extending state control over commerce.

Barsbay was a pious ruler, and a great sponsor of religious foundations. In addition to his two funerary complexes, he built a mosque in the village of Siryaqus next to the khanqah of al-Nasir Muhammad and another unidentifiable mosque south of Bab al-Nasr, and he transformed the hospital of al-Mu'ayyad into a mosque. He made important restorations at al-Azhar and the mosque of Sultan Hasan. He is not associated with the construction of palaces.

Fig. 230. The funerary complex of Barsbay in the city.

In order to acquire the plot of land, which was occupied by important commercial waqf properties, Barsbay resorted to *istibdal*, by which he gave the previous waqf a new equivalent estate to compensate for his acquisition of the one he needed for his mosque. He is credited for having offered fair deals.

The estate of the endowment was considerable, consisting of major commercial structures of the wakala and khan type, alongside dwellings in the close vicinity of the mosque, and elsewhere in the city, and also agricultural land. The largess of the endowment is to be explained by the personal interests of the sultan, who dedicated the balance of the revenue, once the running costs of the building and the pious foundations were covered, to the private use of his children and descendants.

With this foundation the sultan acquired a prestigious place in the heart of the city as his master Barquq has done earlier. However, the monument has no outstanding architectural features. Ultimately, Barsbay preferred to be buried in the cemetery in a monument of more architectural ingenuity and less philanthropic significance.

The foundation incorporated a Friday mosque and a khanqah for sixty-five Sufi students who belonged to the four

Fig. 231. The funerary complex of Barsbay in the city, prayer hall.

Fig. 232. The funerary complex of Barsbay in the city.

schools of Islamic law, and their superiors. The foundation provided stipends for twenty Hanafi, twenty Shafi'i, and ten students for each of the other schools of law. The stipends of the Hanafis were higher than the rest.

The inscription band on the facade of his multifunctional complex, which begins with the Koranic text XLVIII, 1–3, names Qadi 'Abd al-Basit as the supervisor of the construction, and indicates the foundation date as Sha'ban 826/July–August 1423 and the date of completion as Jumada I 827/April 1424. The complex took nine months to build once the clearing of previous buildings was completed, which had begun in Rajab 826/June 1423. The inaugural Friday prayer was on 7 April 1424, immediately after the completion of the prayer hall.

The building has three facades with a sabil-maktab at the southeastern corner. The ribbed portal's conch is set above a muqarnas transitional zone. When Janus, the king of Cyprus, was captured and paraded in Cairo, his hat was suspended in the portal, where it allegedly could still be seen in the seventeenth century. The minarets and the dome are carved with the same patterns used in the funerary khanqah of Faraj. The alignment of the minaret does not follow the facade, but the inner orientation of the prayer hall.

The general layout is similar to that of Barquq's complex along the same street, with the difference that all four iwans here are roofed with a flat timber ceiling. Also, the vestibule, unlike Barquq's vault, is made of painted timber. Only the west iwan and the sabil have kept their original painting, which is of high quality. The living units of the students and Sufis, which are located between the iwans and on the rear side of the building, are not visible from the courtyard.

The inscriptions in the prayer hall and the west iwan opposite are a resumé of the endowment deed. Such inscriptions are very common in Syria, but this one is exceptional in Cairo. They were a security measure to safeguard the endowments in case of alteration or disappearance of the manuscript copies.

The small mausoleum has only one window in the centre of its qibla wall, instead of a mihrab. This exceptional absence of a mihrab, as in the case of the smaller mausoleum in the madrasa of Umm al-Sultan Sha'ban, is due to lack of space and the priority given to a window overlooking the street. In the mausoleum of Shaykhu, the mihrab had to give way to a window communicating with the sanctuary.

The mausoleum contains the tombs of a son and a wife of Barsbay. As in al-Mu'ayyad's mosque, windows with fine stucco grilles are pierced between the mausoleum chamber and the prayer hall. These are not original, however; they were remodelled after the windows of the sultan's mosque in the cemetery.[2]

The only truly remarkable feature in this mosque is the marble pavement in the sanctuary with its intricate polychrome mosaics; right in front of the mihrab a square filled with a medallion inlaid with curved patterns not common hitherto in pavements recalls wall decoration.

Fig. 233. The funerary khanqah of Barsbay in the cemetery, the mosque.

40. The funerary khanqah of Sultan Barsbay in the northern cemetery (1432)[3]

The function of this funerary complex, built in the northern cemetery south of Faraj Ibn Barquq's khanqah, represents a quite different concept from that of Barsbay's urban foundation. Whereas the latter has a rather conventional design, this funerary complex built eight years later in the desert is a remarkable monument even though the pious foundation it sheltered, with a staff of only twenty-nine, was rather small. A comparison between the two endowments reveals substantial differences in their respective scope. This one can be described as a turba or funerary complex with Sufi services that conform to its location in the cemetery. The emphasis of its composition, which included a Friday mosque, is on the mausoleum; the two Sufi foundations, the khanqah and the zawiya with its hospice, bestowed an aura of Sufism on the founder rather than serving as an academic institution for a large group of beneficiaries.

The inscription indicates the completion date as Dhu 'l-Hijja 835/August 1432. Beside the mosque and the mausoleum, the complex included two sabils and hydraulic structures.

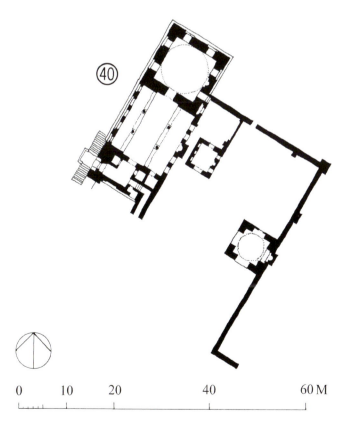

Fig. 234. The funerary khanqah of Barsbay in the cemetery.

the Rifaʿi order, but its exact curriculum is not defined in the document. Maqrizi reported that in 1438, during Jaqmaq's reign, an Iranian shaykh called Hasan al-ʿAjami was beaten and paraded in the streets. This man had succeeded upon his arrival in Cairo in gaining access to Barsbay and enjoyed his confidence, so that he eventually became influential and wealthy. The sultan built for him a 'large dome' in the *sahra'*, meaning the desert and the northern cemetery, which he generously endowed. After Barsbay's death, however, some dignitaries, disturbed by the shaykh's financial abuses, denounced him to Jaqmaq, who jailed him and exiled him to the Upper Egyptian town of Qus.[4] One may speculate whether this dome was the one built for the shaykh, although he is not mentioned as belonging to the Rifaʿi order.

Fig. 236. The funerary khanqah of Barsbay in the cemetery, dome of family member.

Fig. 237. The funerary khanqah of Barsbay in the cemetery, mosque interior.

On the eastern side of the mosque a graveyard includes the tombs of Barsbay's brother and other emirs of his entourage and scholars, combined with a musalla or open prayer place for funerals. Three small domed mausoleums were built in this graveyard for the sultan's parents, his brother Yashbak and his namesake the emir Yashbak the treasurer; one of them has lost its dome (Figs 235, 236).

The mosque, called 'madrasa' in the waqf deed, provided teaching only of the Hanafi *madhhab* and for only four Sufi students. The khanqah was dedicated to seventeen Sufis and their superior. The zawiya across the street consisted of a domed structure, called 'qubba' and 'zawiya' in the waqf deed, with a hospice, to house Sufi travellers. The qubba was dedicated to

The terminology of the epigraphy of the monument does not exactly correspond to that of the waqf deed. Whereas the mosque is called a madrasa in the deed, the monumental inscription at its entrance refers to a khanqah. An inscribed waqf text in the sanctuary uses only the term 'turba'.

The main structures have survived except for the hospice of the zawiya. The khanqah with the dwellings and the sabil located on the southern side of the mosque are in a ruined condition.

The complex displays interesting and innovative features. It was built on both sides of the cemetery road, which was already becoming a street with urban character. The eastern side is occupied by the mausoleum, and the attached mosque is adjoined further south by the khanqah and flanked to the east by the graveyard.

As in the case of Faraj's khanqah, the panelled facade has an oculus corresponding to that of the mihrab on the opposite wall. The portal, if it was restored according to the original pattern,

Fig. 235. [opposite] The funerary khanqah of Barsbay in the cemetery, domes of Barsbay and Yashbak.

would be the earliest to have a trilobed groin vault. The original minaret has been replaced by the present ugly structure.

The sultan's mausoleum occupies the northern corner of the complex and is free-standing apart from on the southern side, which is connected to the mosque. Its upper arched windows are larger than those of the mosque. The exterior width of the mosque is equal to that of the mausoleum. Inside, however, the

Fig. 238. The mausoleum of Barsbay in the cemetery, mihrab.

Fig. 239. The mausoleum of Barsbay in the cemetery, detail of the marble mosaic decoration.

thicker walls of the mausoleum, which bear the stone dome, reduce its inner width.

The layout of the mosque, with its broad format and no courtyard, is unprecedented in Mamluk royal architecture. It consists of three aisles parallel to the qibla wall, with two arcades of three arches resting on four columns (Fig. 237). In the waqf deed the mosque is described as having two iwans separated by a durqa'a. The durqa'a or covered courtyard is the sunken central aisle, which connects the entrance to the mausoleum. The mosque therefore appears almost as a great vestibule that leads from the entrance to the mausoleum, to which there is no other access. This layout, which appends the mosque to the mausoleum, allowed the latter to overlook the cemetery on three sides with the maximal number of windows while still adjoining the prayer hall. Had there been a courtyard the mausoleum would have been separated either from the prayer hall or from the street. Had the mosque been built on the opposite side of the street, the building could have had a courtyard while retaining the same advantages. We do not know the reason why the mausoleum was placed on this side of the road, but it might have been for consistency with Faraj's khanqah, which is similarly located.

Due to its broad format and windows on both sides overlooking the road and the cemetery, the mosque is very bright. In contrast to the bare walls and the plain stone mihrab, the floor is decorated with fine marble mosaics that recall some of the best decoration of the Bahri period. It cannot be excluded that they were taken from an earlier building. The beautiful minbar originally belonged to the mosque of al-Ghamri (1451) (Fig. 46).[5]

The sultan's mausoleum has the earliest masonry dome to be carved with a geometric star pattern. As observed by Kessler, the quality of the two smaller mausoleums included in the adjoining graveyard indicates that the sultan's dome was built first, in an experimental phase, and that techniques had improved by the time the smaller domes were carved. On the sultan's dome the geometric composition has not been successfully adapted to the diminishing surface area of the dome towards the apex, and the continuity of the design appears disrupted. In the two other mausoleums, the geometric star composition is more evenly spread on the domical surface.

The transitional zone, as in Faraj's domes, has an undulating profile. The interior of the mausoleum is conventionally treated with muqarnas pendentives in the transitional zone and an elaborate marble dado and pavement.

The external transitional zone, as in Faraj's domes, has an undulating profile. Its interior is conventionally treated with muqarnas pendentives. Unlike the bare walls of the mosque, the mausoleum chamber is panelled with an elaborate polychrome dado and a freeze of fine marble mosaic of the same quality displayed in the sanctuary's pavement. Also the mausoleum's floor is paved with exquisite polychrome marble.

The extended facade of the Sufi dwellings built as a rab' conveys an urban appearance to the building. From the structures on the opposite side of the cemetery road, which were for the use of the Sufis of the Rifa'i order, only the domed zawiya has survived. It is the earliest known of this type of domed structure. The building is free-standing, the walls of the rectangular chamber are relatively low and the dome rests on a stepped exterior transitional zone, which corresponds to inner trilobed pendentives, the earliest of their kind in Cairo. The scallops in their upper niches were probably added in the course of a late embellishment, probably in the nineteenth century, along with the plaster coating. There are traces left of a painted inscription band in the lower part of the dome, and another one in the rectangular walls.

Further south, on the same side, a brick dome stands alone, surrounded by modern buildings. This anonymous and undated monument is popularly known by the name of 'Khadija Umm al-Ashraf', and could be in fact the mausoleum of al-Ashraf Barsbay's mother. The carved stucco design on its surface has only one parallel in Cairo, the mausoleum dome of the emir Taghribirdi, built in 1440, which this one must have pre-dated.

Fig. 240. The funerary khanqah of Barsbay in the cemetery, dome of zawiya.

Fig. 241. The funerary khanqah of Barsbay in the cemetery, zawiya interior.

–20–

The Reign of al-Zahir Jaqmaq

41. The madrasa of Sultan Jaqmaq at Darb Sa'ada (1451)[1]

Sultan al-Zahir Sayf al-Din Abu Sa'id Jaqmaq, who added 'Muhammad' to his name, was purchased by Barquq and served his successors al-Mu'ayyad, Tatar and Barsbay. His character stands out among his peers, characterized by extreme piety and humility, an utmost austerity in his lifestyle and hostility to regal paraphernalia and all manifestations of power. At the same time, he was liberal and philanthropic, and spent considerable funds in favours and donations, mainly to scholars and men of religion. Trying to follow Barsbay's example, who subdued Cyprus, Jaqmaq started three military campaigns against the Knights Hospitaller of Rhodes to stop their raids on the Mamluk coasts, which were all unsuccessful.

A remarkable feature of Jaqmaq's reign was that he refrained from immortalizing himself with a funerary monument; he was buried in the mosque of Qanibay al-Sharkasi, the master of the stables and one of his favourite emirs. This mosque, of which only the minaret survives, was built near the gate of the hippodrome beneath the Citadel.[2] Jaqmaq restored a number of mosques and took particular care of the maintenance of bridges and dams in Egypt and Syria, and he made an endowment for a public kitchen to serve porridge (*dashisha*) and distribute clothes to the poor in Mecca and Medina.[3] Although Ibn Taghribirdi did not attribute any religious monument to Jaqmaq, and Sakhawi explicitly said that he did not build any madrasa, three

Fig. 242. The madrasa of Jaqmaq, minaret.

Fig. 243. The madrasa of Jaqmaq.

buildings bear inscriptions in his name, which suggest that he might have only restored or reconstructed existing structures. Sakhawi, however, added that Jaqmaq was keen to have his name inscribed on the mosques he restored. The plain minbar of Barquq's mosque, for example, bears his name.[4]

One of the three buildings bearing his name is a Friday mosque, of which only little remains, whose foundation in 854/1450 Sakhawi attributed to Lajin al-Sayfi. Another Friday mosque at Dayr al-Nahhas near Fustat has disappeared. Only this madrasa, in the street called Darb Sa'ada, which Creswell rightly described as mean and shabby, survives. This is the reason why it has been included here, as a variant in Mamluk monumental patronage.

The date of the madrasa, built in 1451, thirteen years after Jaqmaq's access to the throne and two years prior to his death at the age of nearly eighty, is significant. It reveals that, unlike almost all other sultans, who erected their monuments immediately after their access to power, Jaqmaq was not keen on monumental patronage. The circumstances of this foundation are not clear; it is very likely that it was built, as assumed by 'Abd al-Wahhab, to replace the Ayyubid Fakhriyya madrasa, founded in 1225 in the area. The minaret of the latter had collapsed in 1445, demolishing the facade and neighbouring buildings, and the sultan ordered its reconstruction, which the secretary of the privy and the army (*nāẓir al-khāṣṣ wa 'l-jaysh*) al-Jamali Yusuf executed in 855/1451, the date indicated in the inscription. It is also possible that this was a new madrasa said by Sakhawi to have been founded by Yusuf near the Ayyubid one, both of them being in the latter's neighbourhood.[5] The sultan's name was always given as Muhammad Jaqmaq, which he had preferred to be called since his accession to the throne. In fact, nothing in the present structure appears to be Ayyubid; the reconstruction, albeit a very modest one, must have been radical. An inscription on the portal and another on a wooden door indicate the date of its completion as Muharram 855/ February 1451. Most likely the sultan reused the waqf of the Ayyubid madrasa. The foundation inscription refers to a madrasa, and it is not clear whether it also included a *khutba*.

The building is squeezed in the street of Darb Sa'ada, its facade forming an angle. The portal and the sabil-maktab are on one side, and the minaret on the other. Unlike royal minarets of the time, only the lower section of this one is made of stone, the upper structure being of brick. The possibility that this is the original upper structure cannot be excluded. This style of minaret was generally built of stone, including the upper bulb and its pavilion. The Mamluk builders were not used to constructing such a slender structure in brick, which may not have been stable enough. For this reason, they may have preferred to build the upper structure of wood. An old photograph of the minaret of Khayrbak, which is also a brick construction, shows that its upper structure was likewise made of plastered wood. The stucco decoration in the minaret's middle section is singular, displaying interlocking moulding bands connected with loops of the type that decorate contemporary stone portals.

The madrasa has a four-iwan plan and its interior is without decoration or inscriptions. Small rectangular windows are pierced in the lateral walls of the main iwan, pointing to contiguous living units, as later in the mosque of Sultan Inal in the cemetery. In the madrasas of Jamal al-Din Mahmud al-Ustadar (Mahmud al-Kurdi) and Inal al-Yusufi, built in the late fourteenth century, we find cell windows overlooking the central space or durqa'a, but not the prayer hall.

42. The funerary complex of Emir Taghribirdi (1440)⁰

This small monument founded by the emir Taghribirdi, Sultan Jaqmaq's great secretary, occupies a corner of Saliba street with a lane. Two foundation inscriptions date its construction to Jumada I and Jumada II 844/October and November 1440, and describe it as a madrasa.

The facades display the usual arrangement, with two levels of windows and an oculus in the mihrab protrusion, the sabil-maktab occupying the southwestern corner. The minaret on the left-hand side of the elevated portal has a rectangular first storey following the fashion of the early fifteenth century. Its middle shaft is carved with a geometric star composition.

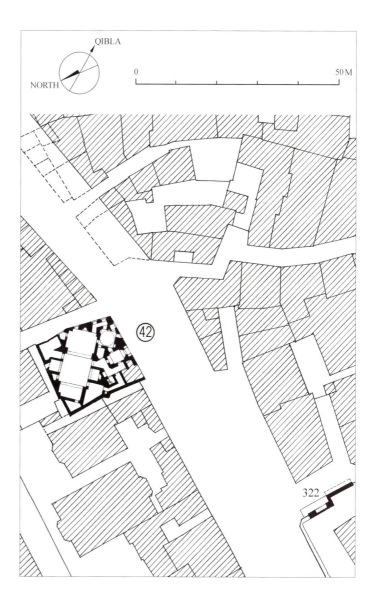

Fig. 245. *The funerary mosque of Taghribirdi.*

Fig. 244. *The funerary mosque of Taghribirdi.*

The dome on the right-hand side of the portal has a surface decorated with an interlacing pattern borrowed from the repertoire of minaret stone carvings, the prototypes being the minarets of Asanbugha, Faraj and Barsbay and the vanished minaret of Qanim al-Tajir. The same pattern can be seen on the dome of Umm al-Ashraf, opposite Barsbay's funerary khanqah. However, unlike the minarets that provided the carving pattern, these two domes are brick constructions decorated with stucco. Brick domes normally had no carved surface, but were either plain or ribbed, the ribs being part of the brick construction, not applied stucco.

The plan of Taghribirdi's funerary mosque is ingenious. To accommodate the Mecca orientation of the mosque and the mausoleum within the given plot, the architect set the mosque diagonally to the facade, at an angle of almost 45°, and filled the space left between the mosque and the exterior walls with rooms and recesses rather than solid masonry. The small mosque of Jawhar al-Lala (1430) has a similar plan (see Fig. 19).[7]

Fig. 246. The mosque of Qadi Yahya on the Khalij, Azhar street.

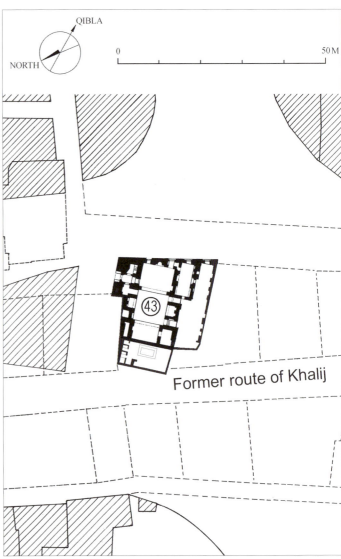

Fig. 248. The mosque of Qadi Yahya on the Khalij before restoration.

Fig. 247. The mosque of Qadi Yahya on the Khalij, Azhar street, main iwan.

43. The mosque of Qadi Zayn al-Din Yahya along the Khalij (Azhar street) (1444)[8]

Zayn al-Din Yayha was a high-ranking bureaucrat of Christian origin, whose career reached its peak when he became Sultan Jaqmaq's majordomo. This allowed him to accumulate an enormous fortune, which he was accused of having acquired by extortion and dishonest means. He founded several religious buildings, and among his charitable works were the supply of water for the pilgrimage caravan, and a mortuary (*maghsal*). His monumental legacy and its artistic significance overshadowed the shabby contributions of his patron Jaqmaq. Following the death of his patron and mentor, his career came quickly to a miserable end. Qaytbay confiscated his estate and sent him to jail, where he was tortured and died in 874/1469.

An interesting aspect of Yahya's monumental patronage is the foundation of several mosques instead of erecting one outstanding monument. These buildings, however, reveal artistic acumen and refinement in the decoration and in the quality of the furniture. Yahya's religious patronage might have been motivated by the heavy accusations made against him, and his need to appease his opponents, gain recognition and please his pious master. As his wealth and power grew, he might have found it necessary to keep proving his piety.

The exact number of his religious foundations is not known. Several foundation deeds were compiled in his name, of which only one is known. Three mosques have survived, but the waqf document refers to a khanqah near his funerary mosque and to other small oratories, including a ribat, which are no longer extant.[9] The present waqf deed includes a long list of commercial and residential buildings in Cairo and the provinces, which indicate that Zayn al-Din Yahya was a man of fabulous wealth.

Zayn al-Din Yahya's earliest known mosque, completed in Sha'ban 848/1444, is a funerary jami'. The free-standing structure we see today was initially part of a large complex in the quarter called Bayn al-Surayn, which was mainly inhabited by Christians. The complex included an extensive residential complex for the use of the founder and his Mamluks, with dwellings varying in size including a villa with a garden, described in the waqf deed as lavishly decorated. They were located on the southern side of the mosque, and equipped with multiple loggias, balconies and windows overlooking either the Khalij or a garden. The waqf deed also refers to a khanqah previously built by the founder in the same quarter. A waterwheel supplied the residences and the mosque with water from the Khalij. Attached to the residence was also a sabil or public water-house, for which there was no room here. In addition, the mosque provided direct access to the Khalij. The complex also included the tomb of a shaykh called Faraj that must have pre-dated it.

Although it has been heavily restored this mosque is interesting because of its urban context at the time when it was built. The description of this ensemble conveys the impression of it being the residential complex of a refined gentleman to which philanthropic neighbourhood services were attached, rather than it being just a mosque in a residential quarter.

The mosque underwent substantial restorations by the Comité at the end of the nineteenth century, and again in the 1940s. The main walls, the first gallery of the minaret, and the painted wooden ceiling of the porch are original. The southern facade was rebuilt.

The mosque was reached via a flight of steps, and the lower floor was occupied by a shop in the south facade; latrines, ablution fountains and storerooms were on the west side. Its three facades are panelled with window recesses. The main portal is in the northern facade with the minaret on the northeastern corner; the second portal is in the southern facade with the funerary chamber

on the southeast corner surmounted by the triple-arched loggia of the primary school. The use of a trilobe groin-vault in the southern portal is one of the earliest of its kind; the earlier portal is in Barsbay's khanqah in the cemetery and looks heavily restored.

The founder added his mausoleum next to the prayer iwan. It is not domed, but in the shape of an irregular rectangle overlooking the street with four windows, three on the southern and one on the eastern or qibla facade. Because of the eastern window there was no room left for a mihrab. The absence of a mausoleum dome may be a concession to the orthodoxy of Yayha's patron, Sultan Jaqmaq. The funerary chamber occupies the corner beneath the maktab, leaving no room for a sabil, which was put instead in another building together with the waterwheel and the residence. Between the prayer hall and the mausoleum there is a room for the *khatib* or preacher.

The mosque was built on the qa'a plan. The stone mihrab was in the style of the mihrab of Shaykhu's khanqah that became very common in the late Mamluk period. Its restrained decoration consists of an ablaq sunrise motif in the conch, below which is a Koranic text carved inscription band (II, 144) that refers to the qibla. According to the waqf document the original decoration of the mosque was very lavish; it included painted and gilded wooden ceilings, polychrome marble, qamariyyas with coloured glass, and doors of inlaid wood. The inlay of the magnificent wooden minbar included silver. The marble pavement of the central space displays a geometric design with roundels.

The waqf deed refers to an inscription band, no longer extant, along the west iwan with excerpts of the waqf stipulations. Originally this iwan had three lower rectangular windows, now walled up, connected to a wooden loggia. The loggia overlooked the Khalij with five wooden arches on marble columns, three on the west and two on the north facade; it was also equipped with two bookshelves. An apartment contiguous to the mosque overlooked its west iwan through a small window, and the Khalij through other windows.

The maktab on the upper floor also had a triple wooden arch, as was common practice.

44. The mosque of Qadi Yahya at Bulaq (1448–50)[10]

Five years later, in 852/1448, Yahya founded a second Friday mosque with a Sufi service in the suburb of Bulaq, the port of Cairo at that time. Its architecture is totally different from the previous mosque, being a return to the classical type.

The building was completed, according to an inscription on the southern portal, in Sha'ban 852/September 1448. The inaugural prayer took place in the following Ramadan. Sakhawi, however, dated the completion to Dhu' l-Hijja 853/January–February 1450.

Fig. 249. The mosque of Qadi Yahya at Bulaq, courtyard.

Built outside the urban centre, it is a fully symmetrical hypostyle or riwaq mosque. The facades, as usual panelled with window recesses, are pierced with three axial portals with foundation inscriptions and ablaq marble decoration. The lower windows are rectangular and surmounted by triple windows, with an oculus above a double arch. The vault of the main portal in the western facade is trilobed and groined, and is framed by a double band of moulding that interlocks at the apex, whereas the side portals are set in recesses with a rectangular muqarnas cornice above roof level.

The facades of the courtyard are decorated with a double-band moulding running along the arches to curl in a loop at their apex. The spandrels of the arches are pierced with oculi in the shape of rosettes. The arcades run parallel to the walls, with tie beams across the arches.

The mihrab conch is also framed by a moulding, which consists of two bands interlocking to form a chain of loops, a device that was used earlier on the portal of the mosque of Emir Taghribirdi.

Here, the bands interlock in a loop at the apex of the mihrab arch, and they continue further up to include a rectangular panel pierced with a large oculus above, creating a pleasing relief composition. The conch has a twin sunrise ablaq pattern, and two inscription bands; the oculus has a stucco grille with coloured glass.

Interestingly, the stone mihrab is inscribed with a historical text naming the founder and giving credit to his patron, the sultan. The bay in front of the mihrab is covered with a wooden dome, which has been reconstructed. This domed bay appears as a canopy structure with a pair of arches running perpendicular to the arches of the parallel arcade.

The mosque, which was severely damaged, did not preserve any original decoration. The surviving octagonal section of the minaret is built in stone and bears the remarkable feature of a faceted carved transition to the first gallery instead of the usual muqarnas. This device was later emulated in the minaret of Qaytbay at Qal'at al-Kabsh and at the minaret of Yashbak at Imam al-Layth.[11]

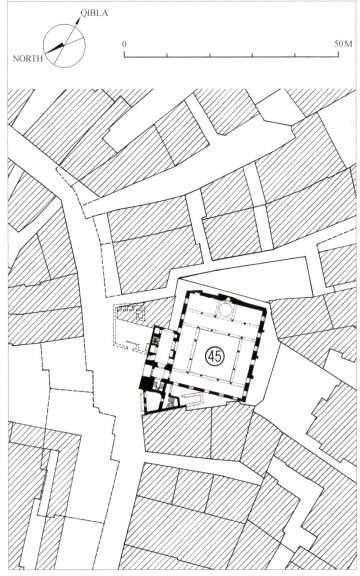

Fig. 250. The mosque of Qadi Yahya at Habbaniyya.

45. The mosque of Qadi Yahya at Habbaniyya (1452)[12]

The third mosque of Yahya was built in the quarter of Habbaniyya, and it was completed in 856/1452. This mosque also has a riwaq plan with a wooden dome over the mihrab, but it is smaller than the mosque at Bulaq, with only one arcade instead of two in each of the three minor riwaqs. Unlike the Bulaq mosque, which has three straight axial entrances, this has only one portal, which is off the mihrab's axis and connected to a bent entrance. There was a sabil-maktab on its right side.

The portal recess is elegant. Its vault has a trilobe profile with a semi-dome carved with muqarnas and resting on elaborate groins. The recess is framed by the same kind of chain moulding as in the portal of Taghribirdi and the mihrab of Yahya's mosque at Bulaq. The earliest occurrence in Cairene

Fig. 252. The mosque of Qadi Yahya at Habbaniyya, mihrab.

architecture of a double band with loops is at the Fatimid gates of Bab Zuwayla. This motif was borrowed from manuscript illuminations, where it appears much earlier.

The stone mihrab is carved with bands radiating from the base of the conch towards the arch, which they frame with a polylobed voussoir. This device was copied a few years later in the mihrab of Sultan Inal's mosque. Yahya's mihrab is inscribed with a Koranic passage, and a foundation inscription with the founder's name and an acknowledgement to his sultan, as in the mosque at Bulaq. The wooden dome above the mihrab, a rare feature in fifteenth-century architecture, has three-tiered muqarnas squinches.

Fig. 251. The mosque of Qadi Yahya at Habbaniyya, courtyard.

265

– 21 –

The Reign of al-Ashraf Inal

46. The funerary complex of Sultan Inal (1453–61)[1]

Sultan al-Ashraf Inal al-'Ala'i was purchased by Barquq, manumitted by Faraj, and appointed by Barsbay governor of Edessa and Safad. Jaqmaq appointed him governor of Gaza, great secretary and finally commander-in-chief of the army. He led Jaqmaq's second and third expeditions to Rhodes, but, facing insurmountable difficulties, he preferred to return rather than sacrifice his soldiers in vain.

The funerary complex of Sultan Inal in the northern cemetery is an odd building. The main facade of the mosque, which overlooks the main road, is separate from the mausoleum dome and the minaret that stand respectively to its northern and southern sides, connected to it by an enclosure wall. The bases of both the minaret and dome and the enclosure wall are of the same height, and substantially lower than the roof of the mosque, which clearly indicates that the complex was built in more than one stage; in fact, it was built in three phases. The mausoleum and minaret were built first; a khanqah or complex of living units for Sufis was inserted in the second stage, and the mosque was the last structure to be added. Today the whole complex is in a semi-ruined condition.

The inscription on the dome dates its foundation to the beginning of Muharram 855/February 1451, and indicates the founder's title as *atabak*, or commander-in-chief of the Mamluk army. Ibn Iyas, who did not mention the mausoleum, reported that in Dhu 'l-Qa'da 859/October–November 1455 the secretary of the privy, al-Jamali Yusuf, built for Sultan Inal a magnificent madrasa with a zawiya in front of it and an enclosure for the burial of the sultan's clan. It cost more than 12,000 dinars. According to Ibn Taghribirdi, Inal demolished the turba he had built before he became sultan in order to build a madrasa at its place; this is contradicted by the epigraphic evidence.[2] The completion of the religious complex was celebrated with the inaugural Friday sermon in Rajab 860/June 1456, during the third year of Inal's reign. He himself could not attend, however.

The monumental epigraphy confirms the literary sources, and reveals the building sequence. An inscription at the northern entrance of the enclosure refers to a khanqah and dates it to Muharram 858/January 1453, whereas the inscriptions on both portals of the mosque use only the term 'madrasa', which was then equivalent to a mosque, and give the date Rabi' I 860/February 1456. Another long foundation inscription around the courtyard mentions the secretary of the army and the privy as the supervisor of the construction, without naming him, and states that the mosque was begun in Dhu 'l-Qa'da 859/October 1455 and completed in Rabi' I 860/February 1456. This monumental structure took four months to build and probably four months to decorate, since it was inaugurated in June. Van Berchem noted in the courtyard a sundial dated Rabi' I 871/October 1466 and signed by Badr al-Din al-Tibi(?) al-Mardini.

The sequence of dates indicates that the turba was erected while Inal was an emir, and the khanqah, with its complex of living units on the west side of the complex, was added as soon as he ascended the throne, followed by the mosque.

The large complex was surrounded by an enclosure. The design of the facade, with its trilobe groin-vaulted portal, recessed windows and mihrab oculus in the protruding section

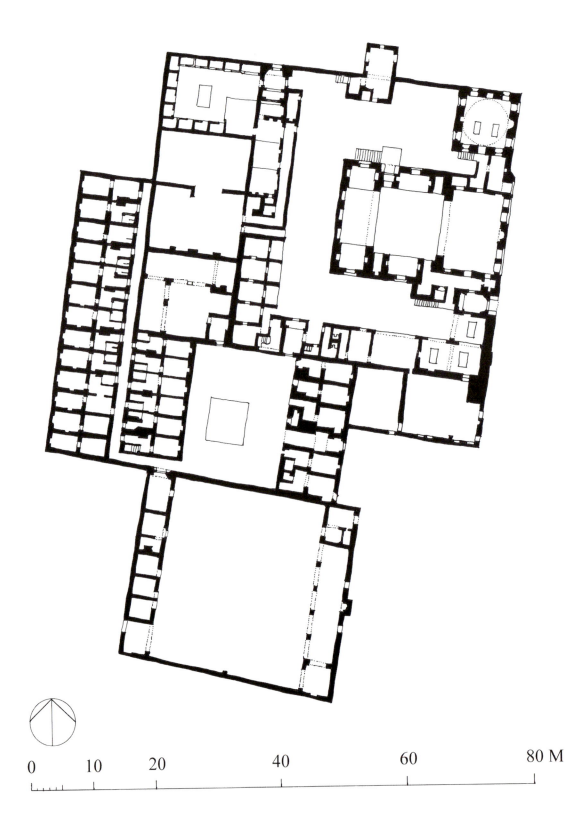

0   10   20   40   60   80 M

Fig. 253. The funerary complex of Inal.

Fig. 254. The funerary complex of Inal, main facade.

Fig. 255. The funerary complex of Inal, east portal.

Fig. 256. The funerary complex of Inal, minaret.

of the wall, is conventional. The mausoleum, which is relatively small, occupies the northeastern corner of the enclosure: the zigzag carving of its dome begins above a series of loops at the base, filled with bulbs of blue glass paste. The minaret displays a profusion of carvings, anticipating the taste of the Qaytbay period; its middle section displays a three-dimensional zigzag pattern. It is interesting to note that the initial funerary enclosure, although only a turba, included a minaret.

The khanqah with its dependencies stands on the eastern side of the enclosure and is in an advanced state of ruin. It is a fine masonry construction, which includes a complex of dwellings of the rabʿ type, latrines and other dependencies.

The complex can also be reached from the north, where the remains of a sabil are beside the entrance of the enclosure. The mausoleum is on the left-hand side of the onlooker, who faces the northern facade of the mosque.

The mosque is a monumental qaʿa open to the sky. The mihrab is made of carved stone without inscription. It is a copy of that of the mosque of Qadi Yahya at Habbaniyya, and, as is to be expected, its carving differs from that of the mausoleum's

Fig. 257. The funerary complex of Inal, mihrab conch.

mihrab. This one, also of stone, is carved with arabesques in the conch and geometric stars in the lower part. A Koranic inscription runs across the recess below the conch.

The west iwan is extended on the sides with two lateral recesses, making it wider than the east iwan. Both iwans have three tiers of openings in their lateral walls, suggesting the existence of passages or cells behind the walls. However, the plan published by Van Berchem does not indicate any space there for living units. Nothing survives of the wooden ceiling and the marble dado whose traces are visible in the whole interior, including the courtyard. A carved inscription band runs across the qibla iwan, and another along the courtyard above the four arches.

No waqf deed survives to document the exact functions of the complex, and its ruined state does not allow a clear analysis. Due to the three stages of construction, the building lacks the harmony of a comprehensive design; however, the result is interesting, because it confirms a development begun by Barsbay, which then continued to the end of the Mamluk period. As in Barsbay's complex, the living units of the khanqah were no longer in the form of cells integrated in the main building, but consisted of a separate rab' with duplex apartments, which must have been occupied by the Sufis with their families. And as in the complex of Barsbay, this one also is reported to have included a zawiya on the opposite side (*tijaha*) of the main building. We do not know whether a residential hall existed, as was usually the case.

The whole ensemble had the character of a quarter rather than a funerary mosque with dependencies, anticipating the buildings of Qaytbay, al-'Adil Tumanbay and Qurqumas.

Fig. 258. [opposite] The funerary complex of Inal, west iwan.

Fig. 259. The funerary complex of Inal, ruins of khanqah.

Fig 260. The funerary complex of Inal, latrines.

– 22 –

The Reign of al-Ashraf Qaytbay

47. The funerary complex of Sultan Qaytbay (1472–4)[1]

Sultan al-Ashraf Qaytbay (872–901/1468–96) was purchased by Barsbay and served Jaqmaq, Inal, Khushqadam and Timurbugha, who appointed him commander-in-chief. He was already of advanced age when he ascended the throne, which he did only reluctantly. Qaytbay's reign was overshadowed by the rebellion of the Dhu'l-Qadr, the vassals of the Mamluks in Little Armenia, and the growing power of the Ottomans and their interference in Asia Minor, which was a continuous headache to the Circassian sultans. Military expeditions against the Ottomans and the Dhu 'l-Qadr cost the state more than seven million dinars. Despite the military threats, economic problems, a devastating plague and a cattle epidemic, as well as unrest in the army and a rebellion of the bedouins, Qaytbay's reign of almost twenty-nine years, only surpassed in length by that of al-Nasir Muhammad, was a golden age for architecture and the decorative arts. His endeavours to improve commercial relations with Europe and boost export trade led to the revival of many crafts, and his pious patronage favoured the refinement of architecture and, most of all, its decoration. This complex was the first in a long series of pious and architectural achievements of Qaytbay's reign.

Although Qaytbay's mosque is described by its inscription as a madrasa, both the waqf deed and Ibn Iyas describe its function as that of a mere Friday mosque with a Sufi service, like most mosques of the later Mamluk period. The staff included five Koran readers, but there is no reference to any teaching of law or religious sciences, nor does it dictate a particular madhhab for the preacher (*khatib*) or the imam. The only teaching stipulated in the foundation deed is

Fig. 261. The funerary complex of Qaytbay.

To Rab' of Qaytbay

Drinking trough

Loggia

Mausoleum of
Qaytbay's sons

47
Funerary complex
of Qaytbay

Gate

0   10   20   40   60   80 M

Fig. 262. The funerary complex of Qaytbay.

Fig. 263. The funerary complex of Qaytbay, mausoleum.

Fig. 264. The funerary complex of Qaytbay, portal.

that of the primary school or maktab. Forty Sufis and their shaykh were affiliated to the mosque to gather daily for a service, dedicating prayers to the founder and his descendants. The waqf, however, does not stipulate that they had to dwell in the premises, as was the case in the early khanqah. Ibn Iyas mentioned only thirty Sufis and the name of Shaykh Abu 'Abd Allah al-Qaljani al-Maghribi as their rector. The shaykh belonged to the Maliki *madhhab*, which is surprising.[2] One may speculate and explain this by the fact that the mosque was built in the vicinity of the shrine of the mystic shaykh and saint 'Abd Allah al-Minufi (d.749/1348), who was a Maliki.[3] The waqf stipulations do not mention any *madhhab* to be given preference in the rituals.

The date inscribed on the portal of the mosque is 877/1472–3. Inscriptions in the prayer iwan and the west iwan give Rajab of that same year, or December 1472; the central space is dated Ramadan, which corresponds to February 1473, and the mausoleum was completed almost two years later, in Rajab 879/November 1474. The gate leading to the quarter bears the

same date. The minbar is dated Rabi' I 878/August 1473, more than a year prior to the inaugural prayer, which was celebrated, according to Ibn Iyas, in Rajab 879; at the same time Qaytbay appointed the religious staff.

Ibn Iyas dated the beginning of the construction works in Shawwal 874/April 1470; three years of construction is unusual in the Mamluk period, but this project included a substantial quarter with structures on both sides of the street, most of which have vanished. Today the mosque, a maq'ad or loggia, and another funerary mosque dedicated to the sultan's deceased sons, the remains of a gate and a sabil, a drinking trough for animals, a hall and an apartment building are extant. According to the very detailed descriptions of the waqf deed, however, this quarter also included a stable, a waterwheel and a number of dwellings. The waqf deed also refers to the mausoleum of a relative of Qaytbay nearby.

Evilya Celebi described Qaytbay's quarter as a summer resort with gardens in the shape of a triangle, which took three hours to walk around.

The funerary mosque faces the onlooker coming from the north and blocks the road, which at this point bends to the east. From the south – i.e. from the Citadel – an arched gate with royal blazons in the spandrels led to Qaytbay's quarter. Unlike its appearance today, the mosque was originally connected on the western and southern sides with other structures. On its northern side, an apartment complex faced another one across the street, dedicated to the Sufis and their shaykh; beside it were the ablution fountains and latrines. A ruined, half-buried but impressive apartment complex with a trilobed grand portal, located further north, on the west side of the road, is not mentioned in the waqf deed. It is not known whether, as was usually the case, it included shops in the lower part.

The positioning of the mosque indicates that Qaytbay diverted the original road further east. The reason could have been his desire to achieve an optimal visual perspective by placing the mosque across the road, as was done three years later by Sultan Qansuh Abu Sa'id on the opposite northern side of the cemetery. Unlike Qansuh, Qaytbay does not seem to have been criticized for obstructing the way.

The mosque combines moderate dimensions with excellent proportions and exquisite stone carving. The elaborate portal

Fig. 265. The funerary complex of Qaytbay, west iwan.

has a groin-vaulted trilobe recess with ablaq stones and carved muqarnas. The sabil-maktab occupies the northeastern corner, with a double arch on the northern side and a triple one on the eastern. The minaret stands on the western side of the entrance. The mausoleum protrudes into the street on the southeastern corner of the mosque, adding a third facade to the mausoleum, thereby increasing its visibility from the north and adding light to the interior through the pair of superimposed windows in its northern projection.

The minaret is a jewel of late Mamluk architecture and carved masonry; a twisted band surrounds the neck of the bulb like a necklace.

The dome's design turns upside down the concept initiated in Barsbay's star domes. Here the design is conceived around a central star that radiates from the apex down to the base, instead of a row of stars departing from the base towards the apex. The basic geometric design is rendered in plain relief lines, whereas the arabesque filling consists of grooved stems and leaves, so that their design is accentuated by shadow lines. The brightness of the geometric lines thus contrasts with the darker grooved arabesques, conveying a multi-layered appearance to the carved decoration.

The entire transitional zone of the dome, which is at least as high as the cylindrical section of the dome before it curves, is framed with a carved moulding that underlines its composition. The undulating steps at the corners are beautifully carved.

The vestibule, which includes the door to the sabil room, communicates through a large window above a marble bench with the interior of the mosque. The passage leading to the mosque includes the usual recess for water jars, the mazmala, and is roofed with an elaborate groin vault.

Although there is nothing new about the arrangement of the interior, the fenestration creates a pleasing effect. To the onlooker facing the mihrab, the wall looks like a luminous screen. The four rectangular windows in the lower wall appear like a strip of light interrupted only by the mihrab and the thin masonry between the windows. The mihrab and the windows are of the same height and are set in a sequence of five arched recesses with ablaq voussoirs. The central recess includes the conch of the mihrab; the others include painted stucco in their lunettes. The mihrab is of stone with a conch adorned only with ablaq inlaid and carved patterns. The upper part of the wall is filled with two pairs of qamariyyas separated by the mihrab oculus, which introduce coloured light through their grilles of stucco and glass.

The central space is roofed with a wooden lantern, which is not the original one. Unlike in Qaytbay's mosque at Qal'at al-Kabsh, the west iwan here lacks the elevated dikka, and is pierced with three large lower windows surmounted by an oculus between two arched qamariyyas. As in Inal's mosque, the west iwan is flanked by two lateral recesses. In the adjacent mausoleum, however, the walls are of panelled polychrome marble, while the stone mihrab is of carved and ablaq masonry (Fig. 267). The cells of the muqarnas pendentives, which support the dome, are finely carved.

Outside the mosque, in the lower part of a wall the mosque near the entrance of the mausoleum, is a curious marble panel (arrow on the plan), carved with a double arch filled with arabesques and vegetal motifs (Fig. 268). At first glance, the panel appears as if it belonged to a Christian building because the arabesques, which are different in each of the two arches, are designed to suggest the profile of an Armenian cross; however, the floral patterns, which are consistent with the style of the period, and the name 'Muhammad al-N-sh-t-y'(?), which is carved on one of the pair of posts that flank the panel, point, rather, to a workshop of Qaytbay. The masonry indicates that this wall is a later addition and that the panel was originally a balustrade in an open platform overlooking a hall adjoining the mosque to the west. This hall, which is filled with cenotaphs of a later date, faces with a triple pointed arch a small courtyard and a ruined unidentifiable multistoreyed building on the opposite side.

Further west, another building, known today as the Kulshani mausoleum, is described in the waqf deed as a madrasa and mausoleum for the dead sons of Qaytbay; it is also called the 'old turba', which suggests that it pre-dates the sultan's mosque. It is interesting that the waqf deed describes this structure also as 'a madrasa, which is a turba', confirming that the term 'madrasa' at that time referred to a covered prayer hall rather than a teaching institution (Fig. 269).

The madrasa, reached through a shallow trilobed portal, is an undecorated and uninscribed oblong prayer hall with a plain mihrab in the front wall. Its northern and eastern wall are pierced with two tiers of windows; the upper arched ones are now blocked. The mausoleum, protruding beyond the northwestern corner of the hall, is roofed with a small masonry dome carved with arabesques. Here, the design follows the concept of Barsbay's domes, with rosettes radiating from the base, with the difference, however, that the stars are rendered in a floral interpretation, as rosettes. Although the design is less complex than that of Qaytbay's dome, it displays its characteristic grooved arabesques of this period. The muqarnas pendentives of the dome are also adorned with fine carvings.

Whereas the so-called madrasa is parallel to Qaytbay's mosque, the maq'ad or loggia, located on its west side, deploys its broad facade in a perpendicular position, so that the two structures form a corner in what used to be a courtyard (Fig. 262). Both structures, which have similar oblong shapes, and numerous windows in their broad side overlooking a courtyard, appear to complement one another.

The maq'ad is a loggia borrowed from residential architecture of the fifteenth century. In houses and palaces it had the

Fig. 266. The funerary complex of Qaytbay, mausoleum.

Fig. 267. The funerary complex of Qaytbay, mausoleum mihrab.

shape of a loggia overlooking the courtyard and facing north. This one, like that of al-Ghawri's mausoleum, was of the type described in the waqf deeds as 'qibti', which refers to a closed hall pierced with multiple windows instead of being open with arches.[4] It is built above a row of rooms, probably for

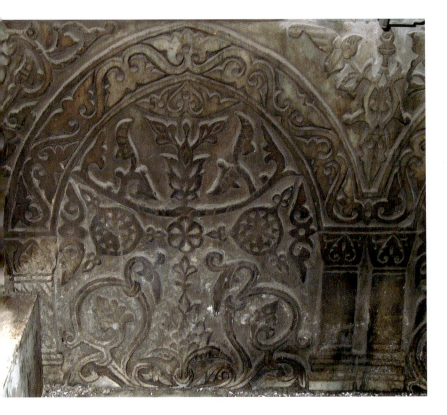

Fig. 268. *The funerary complex of Qaytbay, detail of marble panel near mausoleum.*

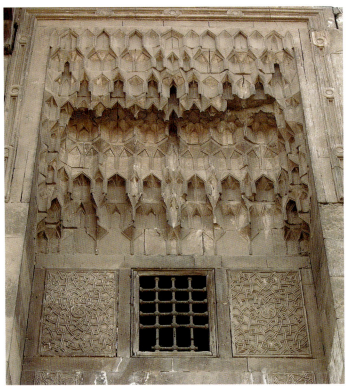

Fig. 270. *The funerary complex of Qaytbay, loggia portal.*

Fig. 269. *The funerary complex of Qaytbay, funerary madrasa for Qaytbay's sons and loggia to the right.*

storage, and has a fine portal recess with rectangular muqarnas. With two tiers of windows densely arranged along the entire northern wall, the interior is bright, and probably cool in the summer. The only decoration extant is the painting of the wooden ceiling.

48. The dome of Emir Yashbak at Matariyya (today Qubba) (1477)[5]

The small domed mosque facing the Qubba palace is today hardly recognizable as the jewel of late Mamluk architecture it once was. A late nineteenth-century minaret and concrete decoration added to its surface in the 1960s have badly transformed its appearance. A photograph published by Hasan 'Abd al-Wahhab shows the dome prior to the post-revolution cosmetics.

The dome was built by Yashbak min Mahdi, Qaytbay's great *dawadar*, who was at that time equivalent to a grand vizier and the second man in rank after the sultan. It was part of a pleasance complex, begun in Safar 882/May–June 1477, which included a madrasa amid gardens and residential structures; during Qaytbay's and al-Ghawri's reigns it became a royal resort. Sultan Qaytbay preferred this complex to Azbakiyya with its large pond and waterfront quarter. The European travellers Joos Van Ghistele and Felix Fabri, who visited this quarter in

Fig. 271. The dome of Janibak at al-Qasr al-'Ayni (nineteenth-century photograph).

Fig. 272. The dome of Janibak at al-Qasr al-'Ayni, squinch (nineteenth-century photograph).

Fig. 273. The dome of Yashbak at Matariyya/Qubba before alteration.

Fig. 274. The dome of Yashbak at Matariyya/Qubba (Le Brun 1700).

1483, praised it in enthusiastic terms for its lavish decoration and beautiful site, benefiting annually from the Nile flood, which transformed the scenery around it. Van Ghistele described the residence as one of the most beautiful in the world. Fabri

mentioned a terrace overlooking a panorama. He called the place the summer residence of the sultan. Pierre Belon du Mans (1547) mentioned a terrace and a pergola. Evliya Celebi rightly compared the dome, which he attributed to Sultan al-Ghawri, to

Fig. 275. The dome of Yashbak at Matariyya/Qubba, interior.

Fig. 276. The dome of Yashbak at Matariyya/Qubba, mihrab detail.

Yashbak's large dome further south in Husaniyya/Raydaniyya. Another traveller, Charles Le Brun (1700), made a drawing of the complex that shows the dome adjoining what seems to be a residence and a polygonal structure, which should be a waterwheel. The residence is depicted as having a small dome.

Ibn Iyas mentioned a palace and a pool one hundred cubits long built by Sultan al-Ghawri near Yashbak's dome.[6] A waqf deed of al-Ghawri mentions briefly two ponds and a *qubba sultaniyya* or sultan's dome, indicating that he had appropriated it, and in fact many travellers eventually attributed the complex to al-Ghawri.

The small domed mosque (c.11m wide and 5.8m high to the apex of the dome) is interesting for its architecture and some aspects of its decoration. Unlike funerary domes it was plain on the outside and without an exterior transitional zone. Also, the ratio of the width to the height differs from that of Mamluk funerary domes. Its architecture copies the dome of the Rifa'i zawiya built by Barsbay and the domes of Janibak at Qasr al-'Ayni (Figs 271, 272). The transitional zone, which is here set within the cubic space, consists of squinches combined with spherical pendentives. They are trilobed and similar to the vaults of earlier portals of the fifteenth century. Their twin lower arches crown the twin windows that occupy the corners (Fig. 275).

Above the polychrome marble dado a beautiful inscription frieze of black and white marble inlay includes Koran texts XXXIII, 56, and III, 26–7, written in foliated Kufic. This is the earliest example of a Kufic revival, which appears in the reign of Qaytbay in architecture and also in metalware, suggesting that it may have been due to Yashbak's initiative. The dome and the drum were repainted in the early twentieth century.

49. The domed mosque of Emir Yashbak at Husayniyya/Raydaniyya, Qubbat al-Fadawiyya (1480–2)

Two years after the foundation of the dome at Matariyya, Yashbak planned a second comparable complex with a larger dome and closer to the city.

Yashbak's urban project, which recalls Janibak's domed zawiyas and his huge garden along the Nile, mentioned earlier, combined a mosque with residential and pleasance structures to upgrade the northern suburb. Azbak's quarter or Azbakiyya, which survived longer, and is documented in a waqf deed, also belonged to this category. Both Yashbak's and Azbak's quarters included the creation of water bodies for which hydraulic works were necessary. Neither Janibak nor Yashbak or Azbak included a mausoleum in his complex; Janibak and Yashbak founded funerary structures in the cemetery.

Yashbak's quarter was founded in the suburb that Ibn Iyas called alternately Husayniyya and Raydaniyya. In fact, it was to the north of Husayniyya and south of Raydaniyya, today Abbasiyya. In the Ottoman period the quarter was called Yashbakiyya. The mosque was originally called Qubbat Yashbak, and in the nineteenth century it was called Qubbat al-'Azab. Its modern name is Qubbat al-Fadawiyya.

According to Sakhawi and Ibn Iyas, who indicated the month of Dhu 'l-Hijja, just after Qaytbay departed on pilgrimage in 884/1480, Yashbak pulled down some buildings including a cemetery to the north of Husayniyya, and conducted water to create a pond surrounded with gardens 'for the view'. He then built a sabat or elevated causeway roofed with a trellis that led to a domed mosque and several markets. On the desert side, further east, he built a funerary complex with a madrasa and a Sufi foundation. Both Ibn Iyas and Sakhawi emphasized Yashbak's intention to embellish the city with a pleasure ground.

Yashbak's complex at Raydaniyya was built in connection with the Mat'am al-Tayr or Birds' Feeding Ground, mentioned earlier as a kind of hippodrome and place for falconry, and a major venue for ceremonies and parades since the reign of

Fig. 278. The dome of Yashbak at Raydaniyya/Husayniyya.

Fig. 277. The dome of Yashbak at Raydaniyya/Husayniyya.

Barquq. The Mat'am was always associated with the mastaba, which literally means 'bench', suggesting that it was a structure equipped with a dais and perhaps also benches for spectators comparable to those of a stadium. This feature may have distinguished the mastaba from the common hippodrome. In fact, a waqf deed of Sultan al-Ghawri mentions a maydan or hippodrome in this area.

Several reports and travellers' accounts of the late fifteenth century and later referred to a very long walled structure in this area with stone benches or steps for spectators, which they associated with equestrian spectacles. These descriptions, in spite of their incoherence, suggest that Yashbak's elevated passage was connected to or overlooked the mastaba. Pagano's view of Cairo shows a long structure, resembling his representation of the aqueduct north of Fustat, leading to a dome. Its scale confirms the monumentality of this structure.[8]

Also, commercial structures and a caravanserai are mentioned by Leo Africanus, Evliya Celebi and Monconys. In the seventeenth century, al-Nablusi mentioned a palace and residences overlooking a great panorama and a pond supplied by a waterwheel. Evliya, like Nablusi, called the place 'Yashbakiyya'. He and Edward Pococke attributed the dome to an unnamed emir who wished to celebrate Qaytbay's pilgrimage. They both emphasized the lavishness of its decoration, and referred to residences and dwellings for the Sufis.

The domed mosque is all that survives today from Yashbak's quarter. Ibn Iyas referred to it as a Friday mosque. Although not mentioned, it most likely had a minaret, probably free-standing.

An inscription band at the entrance states that Sultan Qaytbay ordered the construction of the dome, but Ibn Iyas and Sakhawi leave no doubt that Yashbak was the founder. He died, however, in late Ramadan 885/November–December 1480, before the building was completed; in Shawwal 886/November–December 1481 Qaytbay ordered its completion. The reason for the sultan's appropriation of the building could be that Yashbak died before setting up the waqf. Since his estate had to revert to the sultan upon his death, Qaytbay might eventually have endowed the mosque in his own name from his own or public funds.

The portal is 5.25 m above street level and is reached today by a staircase, the prayer hall being built above a vaulted ground floor of unknown function. On both sides of the portal, traces can be seen in the wall of where the elevated passage abutted against it. Because the passage led directly to the dome, the portal is reduced to a shallow rectangular recess with a muqarnas crest, leading without a vestibule or a bent entrance directly to the sanctuary.

The plain dome rises above the cubic space without an external transitional zone, unlike the Rifa'i dome and Yashbak's dome further north. The exterior walls lack the usual window recesses, the only recess being that of the portal.

A Koranic inscription, xxx, 50, at the portal reads 'Behold then the tokens of God's Mercy: how He resurrects the earth

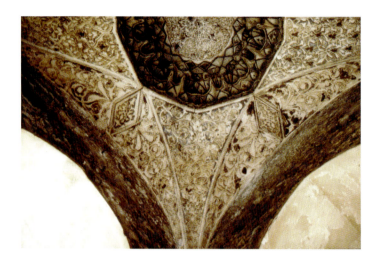

Fig. 279. The dome of Yashbak at Raydaniyya/Husayniyya, squinch detail.

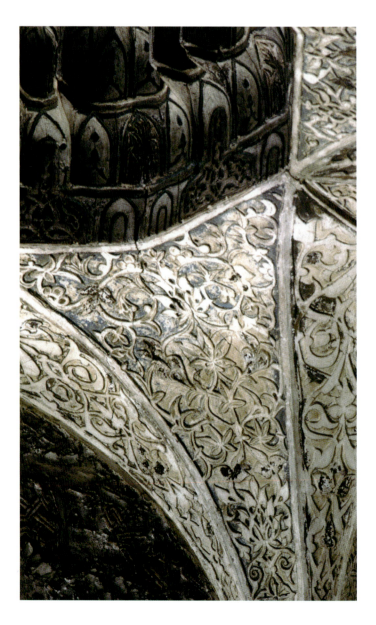

Fig. 280. The dome of Yashbak at Raydaniyya/Husayniyya, squinch detail.

after death', which appears to be a reference to the upgrading of the area undertaken by Yashbak, who replaced ruins and tombs with gardens and handsome buildings.

The domed chamber, which measures 14.3 m inside, and 19.9 m on the outside, is the largest chamber in the Mamluk period to be roofed by a brick dome. By comparison with contemporary mosques, fenestration here is reduced, which leaves the interior relatively dark. This is, however, compensated by the loftiness of the dome and its magnificent stucco painting before the recent disastrous 'restoration'.

The inner transitional zone repeats the device already used in Yashbak's northern dome, consisting of trilobed squinches set within the cubic space, not above it, and alternating with spherical pendentives. Their lower twin arches are set above two corner windows, which throw light on their painted stucco decoration. However, the proportions of the dome in relation to the cubic space it covers were unprecedented. Also, the contrast between the plain exterior and the colourful, lavish interior deviates from the aesthetic norms of that period.

Except for the marble dado, which has recently been replaced, the entire space above the dado is decorated with carved, painted and gilded stucco. A multitude of geometric and floral patterns are displayed in the transitional zone and inside the dome, some of which have no known parallel in Mamluk architectural decoration, and seem to have been inspired from book illumination. Others belong to a new floral repertoire, with naturalistic flowers that were not common hitherto in Mamluk decoration, but were used in the stone carving, metalwork and book illumination of the Qaytbay period (Figs 279, 280).

The decoration of this mosque represents a revival of stucco wall decoration, in a style quite distinct from that of the Bahri period. The mosque of Qaytbay at Rawda was also decorated with stucco. The pattern of the painting inside the dome may have inspired the exterior carved decoration of the dome of Qanibay Qara near the Citadel.

There are two inscription bands, one in the drum, and another directly above the squinches. The lower has the Koranic text III, 18, 26, referring to God's majesty and His power over life and death. The upper commemorates the pilgrimage of Qaytbay, giving its date, 884/1480. This is the only monument to celebrate this event. Qaytbay's pilgrimage was praised by contemporary historians as a significant event because he was the first sultan to perform it after al-Ashraf Sha'ban, more than a century earlier.[9] He was the fourth sultan to perform the pilgrimage, and the only one of the Circassian period. It remains open to debate whether this inscription was formulated by Yashbak or Qaytbay. Yashbak died nine months after the sultan's return from pilgrimage. It is also possible that Qaytbay added this inscription when he completed the building after Yashbak's death.

This was not the last in the series of Mamluk domed zawiyas and mosques. The earliest Mamluk domed zawiya to be mentioned was the now vanished Qubbat al-Nasr, which Maqrizi attributed to Sultan al-Nasir Muhammad, who dedicated it to Sufis from Iran.[10] The last domed zawiya of this architectural type is that of Shaykh Damirdash.

One characteristic the domes have in common is that they were all built outside the urban centre, in the cemetery or within a green residential area, and, therefore, do not bear the typical urban features of Mamluk architecture of an emphasized facade adjusted to the street vista.

50. The zawiya of Shaykh Damirdash (1470s–90s)[11]

Shaykh 'Abd Allah Shams al-Din Damirdash al-Muhammadi was the founder of one of the major Sufi orders of Egypt, a branch of the Khalwatiyya, which originated in Azerbayjan in the fifteenth century. He was captured in Tabriz at the age of fifteen and brought to Sultan Qaytbay. This may have been in 1468, after the Aq Qoyunlu ruler Uzun Hasan conquered Azerbayjan.[12] Uzun Hasan then sent the keys of Tabriz and other cities to Qaytbay along with other gifts, which also included two Circassian Mamluks, to confirm his allegiance to the Mamluk sultan. The two Circassians could well have been Damirdash and his companion Shahin, both of whom had the patronym al-Muhammadi. They went back to Tabriz, where they met Shaykh 'Umar al-Rawshani, a partisan of

Fig. 281. The dome of Damirdash.

Fig. 282. The dome of Damirdash, interior.

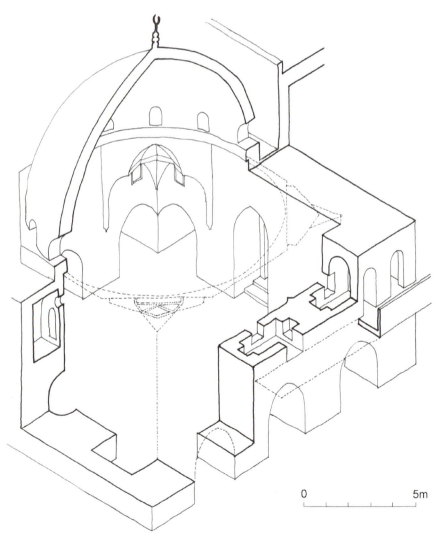

0   5m

Fig. 283. The dome of Damirdash, axonometric view.

Uzun Hasan, who initiated them into Khalwati Sufism, and eventually they returned to Cairo. Damirdash asked the sultan for permission to build a zawiya and cultivate an orchard in the northern outskirts of Cairo, not far from Yashbak's dome in present-day Abbasiyya. Damirdash divided the revenue of his orchard into three equal shares, to maintain the zawiya, finance other philanthropic causes and secure an income for his progeny. He died in Dhu'l-Hijja 930/October 1524, and was buried in a corner of his domed zawiya. This zawiya was unlike the usual ones in the city or its suburbs; it had a rural character, sustaining itself from the agricultural yield of the orchard.

The zawiya is not dated, but according to the sources it should be attributed to the reign of Qaytbay. Today it is hidden within the modern Damirdashiyya mosque, which surrounds it on all sides. Its architecture perpetuates the design of the two domes of Yashbak. The transitional zone consists likewise of trilobed squinches, which, unlike Barsbay's zawiya and Yashbak's domes, however, are not combined with spherical pendentives. The dome is a brick construction, and the sides of the chamber measure c. 9.5 m, slightly shorter than Yashbak's first domed mosque, the side of which measures 11 m. No original decoration has survived.

The domed mosque bears an interesting and singular feature, which is the presence of small vaulted cells set in the thickness of the north, east and south walls, and accessible from an exterior gallery. Originally the west wall might also have included cells, which were removed to make room for the present three high entrances, which do not look original. Today there are eight cells in the walls besides others in the modern part of the building. These cells (c. 2 m long) were devoted to the *khalwa* or retreat exercise, a notable practice of the Khalwatiyya order, as its name indicates.

The great significance of the building is its patronage by a Sufi shaykh, who, while emulating princely architecture, adapted it to the specific requirements of the Damirdashiyya order, in an unprecedented design.

51. The mosque of Qadi Abu Bakr Ibn Muzhir (1479–80)[13]

Qadi Zayn al-Din Abu Bakr Ibn Muzhir al-Ansari (d. 892/1487) was a bureaucrat, who already occupied high positions in the state administration during Khushqadam's reign. In Ibn Iyas' chronicle he is referred to as Qaytbay's private secretary (*katib al-sirr*). Along with the sultan's master builder Badr al-Din Ibn al-Kuwayz, he oversaw the refurbishment of the Great Iwan of al-Nasir Muhammad at the Citadel, where Qaytbay planned to hold audiences, but never did. The titles inscribed in Abu Bakr's mosque describe him as the secretary of the chancellery.

Fig. 284. The mosque of Abu Bakr Ibn Muzhir.

Fig. 285. The mosque of Abu Bakr Ibn Muzhir.

The mosque does not have any carved inscription; only the wooden ceiling of the sabil-maktab is dated 884/1479, and the wooden minbar of the mosque is dated 885/1480.

The building occupies the corner of two small streets in the quarter of Khurunfish, which is west of the main avenue of Qahira. The beautifully carved minaret, with a star adorning its middle section, stands near the trilobed portal in the eastern facade. The sabil-maktab is at the western corner of the southern facade next to the second portal. The facades are not elaborate, probably due to the location of the building in a side street.

The architecture of this small monument is typical of the period, and yet, as is often the case, it displays original and individual features. The plan is a variation on the qa'a pattern. Rather than the oblong qa'a, its format is almost square, with the two major iwans facing the central space with a triple arch supported by a pair of columns. This plan is similar to that of the mosque of Barsbay in the cemetery, and the mosque of Shaykh Madyan (1465). It was also repeated in the mosque of Janim al-

Fig. 286. The mosque of Abu Bakr Ibn Muzhir, mihrab.

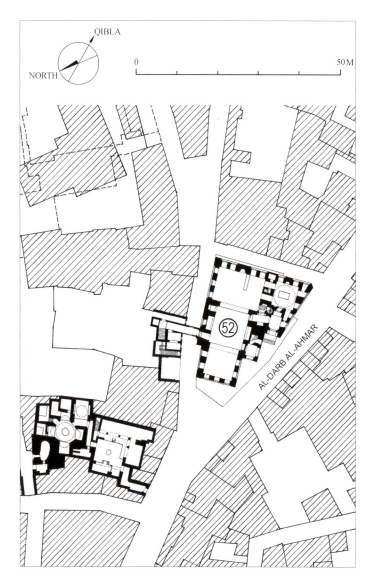

Fig. 287. The mosque of Qijmas al-Ishaqi.

Fig. 288. The mosque of Qijmas al-Ishaqi, main facade.

Bahlawan (1478) in Surujiyya street, and in the mosque of the Sufi shaykh al-Dashtuti (1506).

The arched recesses in Abu Bakr's mosque are framed by a moulding that runs along the whole interior. As on contemporary portals, it is composed of a double band interlocking into loops, like a chain.

The spandrels of the mihrab arch and of the windows were decorated by 'Abd al-Qadir al-Naqqash, who used a new marble-inlaid design and signed his name in a mirror composition, as he did also in Qijmas' mosque, built the same year. The mihrab has a flamboyant conch with a sunrise motif of inlaid marble in red, black and white, which radiates to include the spandrels (Fig. 286). The lower part of the niche is decorated with intricate geometric patterns in polychrome marble mosaics and turquoise glass paste, which is a real surprise in a monument of this period and points yet again to a revival of a traditional craft.

The western or second iwan includes a recess in its frontal wall, where the *mu'adhdhin*'s bench is elevated as a wooden loggia with a balustrade of turned wood, reached from an inner staircase. It is set below the ceiling between two qamariyyas. A similar dikka appears in Qaytbay's mosque at Qal'at al-Kabsh.

52. The funerary mosque of Emir Qijmas al-Ishaqi (1479–82)[14]

Qijmas al-Ishaqi was governor of Alexandria in 1470, where he built two mosques, one of them with an attached mausoleum, and another one in the Roman Serapeum, as well as a ribat and a caravanserai. He was appointed in 1475 master of the stables in the capital, and in 1480 he was sent to Damascus as governor, where he died and was buried in 1487 in a madrasa he had built there. Al-Sakhawi attributes to Qijmas another turba in Cairo.

Fig. 289. [opposite] The mosque of Qijmas al-Ishaqi, west view.

Fig. 290. The mosque of Qijmas al-Ishaqi, southeast view.

Fig. 291. The mosque of Qijmas al-Ishaqi, mihrab detail.

His funerary mosque in Cairo is located in the quarter called al-Darb al-Ahmar, to the southeast of Bab Zuwayla. It is one of the most interesting monuments of the late Mamluk period, both in terms of architecture and decoration. It is popularly known by the name of 'Shaykh Abu Hurayba', who was buried in the mausoleum in 1852.

Several inscriptions give a series of dates between 884/1479 and 887/1482 and some indicate the founder's title as *amir akhur*, which suggests that the foundation was begun while he was master of the stables and before he was appointed to Damascus in 1480. They refer to the building as a Friday mosque (*jami'*). The inscription at the portal dates the completion to Muharram 886/March 1481; that of the vestibule is dated earlier, Sha'ban 884/October–November 1479. An inscription in the qibla iwan in the stucco windows bears the date Rabi' I 885/May–June 1480, and an epigraphic band along the upper walls of the courtyard mentions Ramadan 885/November 1480. The kursi or bench of the *mu'adhdhin*, now in the Islamic Museum Cairo, is dated 887/1482–3 and describes the founder as governor of Damascus. The sequence indicates that the portal, and perhaps the facade as well, was the last part of the building to be completed.

The mosque is a free-standing building at the bifurcation of Darb Ahmar street with two lanes. An elevated covered passage connects it to a structure with a trough for animals on the other side of the northern lane. This ingenuous layout made optimal use of the plot, which is in the shape of a right-angled triangle. It was built, as is common in Cairo, above a row of shops. To the onlooker coming from the gate of Bab Zuwayla,

Fig. 292. The mosque of Qijmas al-Ishaqi, window lintel.

the facade unfolds with two projections on the western side, where the minaret and the dome stand near the portal. A small sabil occupies the first projection behind the main facade, and the portal is in the second projection. No maktab surmounts this sabil, but the structure across the lane above the trough that overlooks the street with a wooden double arch could be one. No waqf document is available to clarify the functions of the building.

The brick dome rests on a masonry transitional zone articulated with triple prisms at the corners. The middle section of the stone minaret is bare of decoration, unlike its contemporaries. The simplicity of the upper structures contrasts with the lavishness displayed in the dense and innovative decoration of the facade, mainly in the stone carvings and polychrome marble inlay of the lintels of the windows and the portal recess. In the main facade, a rectangular recess crowned with muqarnas includes two tiers of three windows, the upper ones being arched.

The intricate inlaid marble patterns of the lintels have no equivalent precedents in Cairo. The engaged colonettes at the corners of the facade are carved with registers of various alternating designs, which is a novelty of the Qaytbay period. The style and quality of the carving recalls that of Qaytbay's dome.

A remarkable feature of the facade is the chain moulding, consisting of two bands intercepted with loops that run around carved panels. This type of carved panel became a standard feature of late Mamluk facades.

The entrance vestibule connects through a sliding door with the small mausoleum chamber. This door and another one in a window at the mosque of Abu Bakr Ibn Muzhir are the only known sliding doors from the Mamluk period.

The interior is a qaʿa with elaborate decoration. Woodwork, stone carving, polychrome marble inlay and stucco windows display the highest quality of craftsmanship. Unlike Qaytbay's mosque the walls here are panelled with a marble dado. Carved stone panels, like those on the facade, are set in the inner walls.

The *pièce de résistance* of the decoration is the mihrab, framed by a flamboyant inlaid voussoir and spandrels that recall

Fig. 293. The mosque of Qijmas al-Ishaqi, lintel of carved stone on facade.

the decoration of the mihrab of Sultan al-Mu'ayyad. The conch is decorated with geometric marble mosaics. Beneath the conch, the mihrab niche is panelled with white marble slabs inlaid with a black and red paste, with the design of a central rosette composed of scroll formations radiating towards the edges. In the heart of the rosette, the artist 'Abd al-Qadir, who also worked at the mosque of Abu Bakr Ibn Muzhir, signed his name in a mirror composition, designed in a pattern reminiscent of the later *tughra*s of the Ottoman sultans (Figs 291, 292). He also signed the similar marble inlay of the window spandrels. The pattern of the rosette is novel in mihrab decoration, but it recalls contemporary Mamluk metal vessels made for export to Europe in the so-called 'Veneto-Saracenic' style. The positioning of a craftsman's signature in the middle of the mihrab, where not even sultans dared to put their names, was bold, if not blasphemous. This ostentatious way of signing also has its parallels in the above-mentioned metalware. The technique used here, of inlaying marble with a kind of coloured stucco, was previously adopted in the inscriptions of the northern domed mosque of Yashbak at Matariyya. However, its application here to create very thin curves of arabesques is unprecedented.

53. The sabil-maktab of Sultan Qaytbay in Saliba street (1480)[15]

One of the characteristic features of Qaytbay's charitable patronage was the foundation of a number of fountains and troughs in Cairo and elsewhere. Some of them were attached to religious buildings, but many others were either free-standing or attached to secular buildings such as wakalas or rab's: for example, the sabil-maktab of Qaytbay next to his wakala behind al-Azhar mosque. This kind of sabil, usually surmounted by a maktab, became very common in the Ottoman period. It should also be recalled that the idea of attaching a sabil-maktab to a residential-commercial complex was not an innovation of Qaytbay's reign; the Duhaysha of Sultan Faraj outside Bab Zuwayla seems to have been the first of this type. However, no such structures are yet known to have been built between Faraj's and Qaytbay's reigns.

Unfortunately, no description of the Saliba structure is included in the known waqfs of Qaytbay, but it cannot be excluded that it was built near a commercial building or an apartment complex, which would explain why only two facades are decorated. However, we have waqf descriptions of two other, no longer extant, autonomous sabil-maktabs. One of them refers to a building consisting of a sabil with a mihrab and a sizeable cistern, surmounted by a maktab and including two apartments. The mihrab signals that the structure was also an oratory. The other description refers to a sabil in the street of

Fig. 294. The sabil-maktab of Qaytbay at Saliba street.

Fig. 295. The sabil-maktab of Qaytbay at Saliba street.

Taht al-Rab' along the southern Fatimid wall opposite a mosque built by Qaytbay, which is perhaps the mosque of Fatima Shaqra founded in Jumada II 873/December 1468–January 1469 in this location.[16] The sabil had three facades each with a large grille window; it was richly panelled with marble and had a painted

Fig. 296. The sabil-maktab of Qaytbay at Saliba street, detail of west facade.

and gilded wooden ceiling. The maktab occupied, as usual, the upper floor; a shop and an apartment were included in the structure. The sabil-maktab behind al-Azhar mosque included two apartments.[17] Usually one of the apartments was reserved for the teacher at the maktab, and the other would have been rented for the profit of the endowment.

Situated on Saliba street in a prominent spot, where the street rises more steeply towards the Citadel, this monumental sabil-maktab is visible at a distance. It has two elaborate facades on a corner of Saliba street with a lane. The height of the facade, at 17 m, exceeds by two metres that of Qaytbay's funerary mosque and equals that of a three-storeyed modern building. It was built to dominate the street, like the double mausoleum of Sanjar at the opposite end.

The facades bear two inscription bands, one at the portal stating that Qaytbay issued the foundation order in Dhu 'l-Hijja 884/February–March 1480 (*amara bi-inshā'*), and the other one starting above the portal and running along the entire double facade, indicating the slightly earlier date of Ramadan, corresponding to November–December 1479, as the date of completion (*faragh*). It is obviously a mistake that the order for the foundation is dated later than its completion.

In Dhu 'l-Hijja 884 Qaytbay was on pilgrimage, and he returned in Muharram 885/March–April 1480. Shortly afterwards, he went to inspect his madrasa at Qal'at al-Kabsh, built in 1475, and on his way back to the Citadel he visited this sabil-maktab. Ibn Iyas wrote on one occasion that the overseer of its construction was the emir Tanibak Qara, who held several prominent positions. However, the historian added later in the emir's obituary that he was the founder of this sabil, which cost him a huge sum, and he dedicated it to the sultan.

The west facade includes the portal to the right and the sabil window to the left. The trilobe portal, which is of the same style used in contemporary mosques, is flanked on each side by three tiers of grilled windows.

On the northern facade four tiers of rectangular windows of various sizes belong to rooms and apartments on the second floor. On the upper northwest corner a tall wooden balcony projects before the double arch of the maktab and continues along the entire northern facade.

As a typical decorative feature of this period, a chain moulding runs along the portal and the corner windows framing the inscription band and the decorative carved and inlaid panels. A royal blazon is carved on either side of the corner. The polychrome inlaid marble decoration of the facade is, alongside that of the mosque of Qijmas al-Ishaqi, one of the most magnificent of Qaytbay's reign.

The bars of the western grille window are engraved with the repeated signature of the craftsman, Zayn al-'Abidin al-Zardakash, alternating with the name and titles of Sultan Qaytbay.[18] The word zardakash suggests that Zayn al-'Abidin worked in the royal armoury or zardakhana. Whereas Qalqashandi defined the zardakash as a craftsman specialized in the production of armours,[19] the chronicles refer regularly to the great zardakash as an emir of the second class in charge of the royal armoury; minor officials are also associated with this function.[20] Ibn Iyas mentioned among the notables and craftsmen deported by Sultan Selim to Istanbul in 1517 a zardakash called Zayn al-'Abidin Ibn Mahmud al-A'war.[21] This was forty-seven years later; if it was the same man who signed his name on the bars, he must have been of an advanced age when he was deported. He was probably a master craftsman, not an emir.

The monumentality of the structure is even more striking within. The fountain room at the corner, behind the large grille windows, is lofty and beautifully decorated with a marble inlaid shadirwan, which is a fountain attached to the southern wall facing a muqarnas wooden niche on the opposite side, as in residential halls. The wooden ceiling is painted and gilded. Next to this hall another room includes a staircase down to a huge cistern. A modern high staircase leads to two upper floors; the one at the top is occupied by a bright hall with high windows opening on the balcony and overlooking Saliba street. This must have been the classroom of the maktab. Because the upper floors were ruined and were rebuilt by the Comité, their exact original arrangement is not quite clear. At least two apartments would have been included in the building. Today the rooms on the inner sides of the second and third floor are occupied by offices.

54. The mosque of Emir Azbak al-Yusufi (1494–5)[22]

Azbak al-Yusufi was purchased by Jaqmaq and he became an 'emir of thousand' in 876/1471–2; he served as the great treasurer and supervisor of the privy, and head of royal Mamluks at Qaytbay's court from 894/1488–9 to 901/1495–6, and after the latter's death he served his son al-Nasir Muhammad. He died in 904/1499 at the age of almost eighty.

Azbak's small mosque off Saliba street, in the shape of a qa'a, does not introduce any novel artistic features to the architecture of the Qaytbay period. However, what makes it worth mentioning is, unlike Abu Bakr Ibn Muzhir's mosque, the profusion of its exterior and interior inscriptions with Koranic texts and with dates referring to the stages of construction.

The tiraz band indicates that the order for its construction (amara bi-inshā') was issued in Jumada II 900/March 1495; the portal's inscription gives a later date for construction (ansha'a), Sha'ban 900/May 1495. The courtyard's inscription indicates the completion date as Safar 900/November 1494; the wooden panels above the doors of the courtyard are dated Rajab 900/April 1495. The foundation is described therein alternately as makan, madrasa and jami'. Ibn Iyas reported the inaugural khutba in Ramadan 900/May–June 1495.

The epigraphy is confusing; the completion date of the interior precedes the 'order for construction' referred to in the tiraz. However, it can be assumed that the sanctuary, which had to be given the Mecca orientation, was laid out, as usual, at the outset, before the completion of the external walls. The available information suggests that the mosque was completed within less than a year, which the lack of a mausoleum dome must have facilitated.

Because of its location on the bifurcation of two streets leading eastwards to Saliba, the mosque's facade follows the corner to display most of its decoration on the eastern side to an onlooker coming from that direction. On the northern facade the minaret stands near the portal and the sabil-maktab occupies the northeast corner. On the eastern facade the mihrab oculus is framed by a rectangular chain moulding, which includes above the oculus an epigraphic band glorifying Sultan Qaytbay. The sultan's blazon appears above the eastern window of the sabil, set in the centre of a panel inlaid in a sunburst motif, thus representing the sultan as the sun; this panel is framed by a chain moulding, like the oculus. The sultan's blazon appears again on the northern facade between the portal and the other sabil window, framed by a similar moulding. Azbak's own multiple-icon blazon is carved within the portal recess above the entrance.

The interior is almost conventional, with a stone mihrab displaying an ablaq inlaid motif in the shape of the word 'Allah'. Like the mosque of Qaytbay at Qal'at al-Kabsh, built

Fig. 297. The mosque of Azbak al-Yusufi.

Fig. 298. The mosque of Azbak al-Yusufi, detail of west facade.

Fig. 300. The mosque of Azbak al-Yusufi.

in 1475, the walls of the courtyard, including the spandrels and voussoirs of the arches, are densely carved with arabesques; a chain moulding frames the architectural elements and their carved surfaces. The carving differs from that of contemporary facades, being shallower. The lunettes of the windows are adorned with carved and painted stucco and Kufic inscriptions. Their present condition does not allow an exact identification of the pattern, which appears unusual. The marble pavement is intricate.

Azbak was buried in the northern recess or small iwan of his mosque, which overlooks the street through a grille window opening on the entrance vestibule. Mubarak read an inscription on a wooden screen across the small iwan indicating the date of the death of Azbak's daughter, Rabi' I 879/July 1474, and another inscription on a marble panel indicating the date of his son's death, Rabi' I 888/April 1483. Azbak having lost both

Fig. 299. The mosque of Azbak al-Yusufi, marble pavement.

children more than ten years before the mosque was founded, these inscriptions may be only commemorative rather than indicating that they were buried there.

55. The cistern of Emir Ya'qub Shah al-Mihmandar (1495–6)[23]

The domed structure built by Ya'qub Shah al-Mihmandar at the foot of the Muqattam hill facing the Citadel from the east is a very unusual building, erected by an unusual patron. The monument is not a mausoleum, although the shape of its dome might suggest this, but, rather, the superstructure of a cistern, and in fact it is a memorial.

Its founder, Ya'qub Shah Ibn Usta 'Ali al-Arzinjani, was born in 1407–8 in Arzinjan in northeastern Anatolia, from where he moved as a child to Tabriz with his aunt, where she was married to a high dignitary at the court of Qara Yusuf of the Qara Qoyunlu dynasty. When Iskandar succeeded Qara Yusuf on the throne, Ya'qub Shah moved with his aunt to settle in

Fig. 301. The cistern of Ya'qub Shah al-Mihmandar.

Cairo. He joined the Mamluk elite, being highly esteemed for his multilingual skills; he translated diplomatic correspondence from Turkish, Persian, Tatar and Indian languages, which prompted Qaytbay to appoint him as *mihmandar* or chief of protocol. Being integrated in the Mamluk establishment, he assumed several administrative tasks in the state apparatus, which earned him wealth and influence. He also built a mosque, which no longer exists.

Ya'qub Shah dedicated this structure to the commemoration of his master's military achievements. A long and extraordinary inscription praises the sultan in unconventional terminology of a rather epic style. The text provides a vivid account of the battle that took place in southern Anatolia in 1486 between the Mamluk army led by the commander-in-chief Azbak and the Ottomans, and the eventual deportation of Herzekzade Ahmad, the head of the Ottoman troops, to Cairo. He was eventually released, to turn again in 891/1490 against the Mamluks, who once more defeated him, this time in Kayseri. The inscription, which describes the campaign as 'jihad', thus treating the Ottomans as infidels, gave a strong political message at a critical time when the greatest concern of the Mamluks was the Ottoman expansion, which a decade later terminated their history. Judging from the unusual style of the inscription and Ya'qub Shah's career, he is very likely to have himself composed its text.

It is interesting to note that the monument, dated by its inscription to 901/1495–6 with no reference to the month, was built several years after the victory it intended to commemorate. At the end of that year Qaytbay died.

A shallow trilobed portal leads into a cross-vaulted vestibule next to the domed room. The brick dome rests on a four-tier transitional zone. A niche in the facade must have included a fountain. The inscription refers to two domes and two cisterns. The masonry of the present structure indeed suggests that parts of the original building have disappeared. The design of a domed fountain resembling a mausoleum had already been initiated in Qaytbay's sabil in Jerusalem, which has a carved masonry dome.[24]

−23−

The Reign of
al-Ashraf Qansuh al-Ghawri

56. The funerary complex of Sultan al-Ghawri (1502–4)[1]

Al-Ashraf Qansuh al-Ghawri was purchased in Circassian lands by Qaytbay. He was called 'al-Ghawri' after the barracks al-Ghawr, where he was garrisoned. He participated in the military campaign against the Ottomans in 1484, and was subsequently appointed governor of Tarsus, then chamberlain of Aleppo. During the reign of Qaytbay's son, al-Nasir Muhammad, he was governor of Malatya in southern Anatolia.

The reign of Sultan al-Ghawri marks the finale of Mamluk pious and artistic patronage. Despite the miserable economic and political situation of the Mamluk State, the sultan pursued to the very end of his reign a passion for regal pomp, spending considerable funds and confiscating properties to build representative buildings.

To acquire this prime location in the very heart of Qahira for his funerary complex, al-Ghawri confiscated and demolished several buildings in the quarter, which included a madrasa founded by the eunuch Mukhtass, and markets, dwellings and commercial structures, provoking harsh criticism.

The sultan's mausoleum was designed to be more than just a royal funerary chamber; it was to shelter relics of the Prophet and a Koran volume said to have belonged to the Caliph 'Uthman, which would bestow on it the status of a pilgrimage site. These holy relics had been kept hitherto in the building called Ribat al-Athar, which allegedly had fallen into disrepair.

Fig. 302. The funerary complex of al-Ghawri.

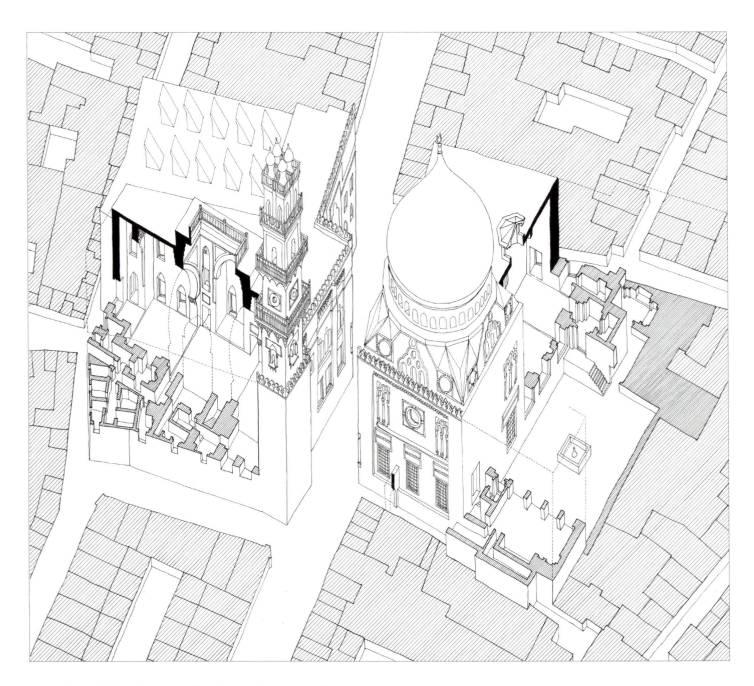

Fig. 303. The funerary complex of al-Ghawri, axonometric reconstruction.

It was founded by the vizier Taj al-Din Ibn Hanna (d.1303), who had purchased the relics from a family in Yanbuʿ in the Hijaz, and installed them in a ribat he built for them on the Nile shore south of Fustat. Ever since, the ribat had been a lively and well-endowed place of pilgrimage.[2] Sultan al-Ashraf Shaʿban endowed it with a madrasa for Shafiʿi teaching, and Sultan Barquq built a quay on the Nile to facilitate access to its premises. The transfer of the relics from the ribat to al-Ghawri's mausoleum was celebrated with a grand procession.

The layout

The funerary complex has a remarkable layout as a double architectural composition, with two blocks straddling the main street in the heart of medieval Cairo. The western block consists of a mosque with its minaret; the eastern one

is a funerary complex, which includes the mausoleum, a hall called khanqah, a maqʿad, a graveyard and a sabil-maktab. The facades of the two buildings display two projections, that of the minaret buttress on the southwestern corner and that of the sabil-maktab on the opposite one. An inscription inside the western building dates the completion of the madrasa to Rabiʿ I 909/August–September 1503. This is also the date indicated by Ibn Iyas for the inaugural *khutba*, which took place three months after the completion of the building was celebrated in Dhu ʾl-Hijja 908/May–June 1503. The sabil-maktab was completed in Dhu ʾl-Hijja 909/May–June 1504, and the relics of the Prophet were brought to the mausoleum in Jumada I 910/October–November 1504.

The dome had to be pulled down in Shawwal 917/January 1512 and must have been rebuilt immediately. A year later, in Safar 919/April–May 1513, it was pulled down again and rebuilt by Rabi' I/May–June of the same year. The sultan himself sat on the roof of the madrasa under a canopy to supervise the works.

Both buildings are built above shops connected to markets stretching along the side streets. A wooden roof linked the two blocks and provided shade for the street, as is shown in an engraving by David Roberts and mentioned in the waqf deed. This roof must have concealed the view of the minaret and the dome to a passerby coming from the north. Timber was an expensive imported commodity; al-Ghawri had to acquire wood from the Ottomans to build military ships to protect Mamluk interests in the Red Sea.[3]

Al-Ghawri's complex was designed to reveal its minaret-and-dome composition to an onlooker coming from the south. Girault de Prangey recognized this when he depicted the complex in his album published in 1846. Although the minaret and the dome are separated by the street, they were nonetheless conceived as a single, harmonious composition, united by their blue ceramic decoration. The dome, which collapsed in the nineteenth century, was made of brick and covered with blue tiles, as was the upper storey of the minaret. One may wonder whether the idea of decorating the dome with tiles was perhaps motivated by the fact that Qaytbay's dome represented the perfection of dome masonry, very difficult to surpass, thus prompting his successor to look for something novel. This was achieved with the monumentality of the architecture and the blue tiles. The scheme proved too bold to last, however.

The waqf deed describes the tiles that covered the dome and the top of the minaret as 'of lapis blue colour' (*qashānī azraq lāzūrdī*), which must have been similar to the blue ceramic decoration of the sultan's minaret at al-Azhar. Girault de Prangey's drawing shows the remains of tiles near the base of the dome, and a drawing by Coste shows the tiled upper storey of the minaret. The first stipulation of the waqf refers to the maintenance of the tiles, which should be replaced as soon and as often as needed. Although al-Nasir Muhammad had the domes of his mosque and palace in the Citadel adorned with ceramic tiles, Cairene craftsmen were not familiar with the construction of tiled domes, which may perhaps explain their structural problem and the fact that none of them survived.

For the tiles of his funerary complex and his minaret at al-Azhar, al-Ghawri must have established a ceramic workshop, which also produced the blue ceramic pear-shaped elements that adorn the carved stone dome of Arzumuk's mausoleum in the cemetery, built in 909–10/1503–5.[4] This workshop survived the Ottoman conquest; it produced the tiles that cover the

Fig. 304. The funerary complex of al-Ghawri, mosque portal

domes of Sulayman Pasha's maktab attached to his mosque at the Citadel (1528), along with the cap of its minaret, and the tiles of the mausoleum of Shaykh Sa'ud, sponsored by that pasha.

The mosque

The facades of the two buildings are not identical, but they have similar portals, each with a trilobe vault on muqarnas, a fine epigraphic band of high-quality calligraphy, and high-relief carving running along their upper walls. The facade of the mosque lacks the usual recessed panels that would have included the three tiers of windows, which, therefore, appear awkward. The marble panelling of the portal recesses is in black and white. Dots of white marble inlaid in the masonry of the facade punctuate its design. The engaged columns at the corner of the mosque and the mausoleum have capitals of Coptic and Byzantine styles, which indicate that Mamluk craftsmen were imitating pre-Islamic designs.

The massive minaret at the corner of the mosque is visible from near Bab Zuwayla, and has a novel design. It is

Fig. 305. The funerary complex of al-Ghawri, mausoleum facade.

a four-storey rectangular tower of conspicuous height, which originally had a four-headed upper structure. Ibn Iyas wrote that this was the first four-headed minaret ever to be built in Cairo. Pascal Coste's drawing shows that blue tiles covered the entire upper section including the four-headed top, and that they were pierced in the middle to be nailed to the wall. Nails were also driven between the tiles to provide additional support. An inscribed cartouche was included in the ceramic revetment. This is the earliest known minaret in Cairo to have an entirely rectangular shaft, and it was followed by the minarets of Qanibay. The present two balconies have wooden balustrades. Besides the muqarnas below the balconies, only ablaq inlaid masonry decorates the shaft, which is a return to Bahri Mamluk traditions. White marble dots are inserted in the stone to emphasize the ablaq design.

In Jumada II 911/November 1505 the minaret began to reveal structural deficiencies at the top, and had to be rebuilt. Ibn Iyas noted that the upper structure was rebuilt in brick, which

suggests that the original might have been in stone. This top, however, collapsed in the nineteenth century and was replaced with the present five-headed structure.

The mosque, called a madrasa, is described only as a Friday mosque in the waqf deed. It has a qa'a plan open to the sky, which was originally covered with a net (*shabaka sharit*) to deter birds and their droppings. The royal epigraphic blazon is carved in the spandrels of the iwans' arches. The two large iwans differ from the usual pattern; the main one has itself a composition similar to that of a qa'a, with two small raised iwans on each lateral side, which broaden its format in relation to the central space, on which it opens through a rectangular wooden frame. The western iwan is 'T'-shaped, being extended by a central recess, which includes an elevated *mu'adhdhin*'s bench, reached by an inner staircase. This dikka, entirely made

Fig. 306. [opposite] The funerary complex of al-Ghawri, mausoleum.

Fig. 307. The funerary complex of al-Ghawri, mausoleum facade.

of wood, is set between a large lower rectangular window and an upper triple window. It adds to the residential character of the interior. The durqaʻa is paved with polychrome marble displaying roundels in the centre. This block included eighteen living units for the staff, part of which overlook the main street with rectangular windows.

As in al-Muʾayyad's mosque, the marble dado of the prayer iwan is extended higher than the mihrab, which is decorated with marble mosaics. Above the dado, which adorns the whole interior, is a fine marble inscription band in black Kufic letters inlaid on a white background; it recalls that of Yashbak's northern dome, which is, however, inlaid with a black paste. In the mausoleum a similar device was used, but with the inscription in *thuluth* instead of Kufic.

The funerary compound

Unlike the mosque, the main facade of the funerary compound is panelled with recesses crowned with a rectangular muqarnas crest, which include lower rectangular and upper triple windows. The main portal leads to an unusual vestibule with two opposite entrances, the one on the right-hand side leading to the mausoleum, and the other leading to the khanqah. Each of these entrances is enhanced by a trilobed portal. This block has the sabil-maktab on its northwestern corner and its northern facade includes a side entrance. The sabil-maktab projects onto

Fig. 308. The funerary complex of al-Ghawri, mosque, courtyard and qibla iwan.

the street with three facades. As already mentioned, this type of sabil configuration appeared during Qaytbay's reign. The northern facade wall is aligned to the street, making an angle with the inner khanqah wall, which leaves an empty triangular space between the two. The northern entrance, which leads to a graveyard for members of the sultan's clan, is plain on the outside but emphasized by a portal on the courtyard side, which is unusual. The graveyard is surrounded on three sides by a maqʻad, the mausoleum and the oratory called 'khanqah' in the waqf deed. The maqʻad facing north is similar to that of Qaytbay, a hall densely pierced with windows that overlook the graveyard. Its upper wall, however, is distinguished by an unusual elaborate muqarnas cornice. The mausoleum chamber and the adjoining khanqah occupy the western and northern sides, and are accessible from the graveyard as well as through the main entrance.

The sultan's mausoleum diverged from contemporary practice by being detached from the Friday mosque, and adjoined instead by a prayer hall defined in the waqf deed as a khanqah. This was not a khanqah in the traditional sense of a boarding institution for Sufis, but consisted only of a prayer

hall for Sufi gatherings, without living units attached to it.[5] There is no reason at this stage to believe that the splitting of the khanqah from the mosque was a response to some significant change in Sufi rituals. The stipulations of al-Ghawri's waqf indicate, rather, that the foundation was structured like all its contemporaries, the only difference being that the *hudur* or Sufi session was held in a separate oratory. The positioning of the khanqah next to the mausoleum served the design of a double building intended to dominate the heart of the city. Moreover, it had the advantage of allowing the sultan to build a monumental funerary chamber in the city centre, with a width equal to that of the mosque, which would not have been feasible had it been adjacent to the mosque. Only the mausoleum of Sultan Hasan is as wide as the adjoining mosque.[6]

Together with that of the mausoleum of Qanibay, the external transitional zone of al-Ghawri's dome, which takes the form of a pair of triangles at each corner, is an innovation. It replaces the device of multi-tiered triangles.

The inner transitional zone consists of very tall pendentives that rise from the rectangular walls below the top of the windows, which are tripartite on the facade and single-arched within. Usually pendentives begin above the rectangular space; this may have been an additional precaution to ensure the stability of the dome after it had shown structural deficiencies. Because its lower part is concealed in the cubic space, the transitional zone appears shorter on the exterior than the interior. Although the dome is made of brick its pendentives are of the type used in masonry domes, thus departing from the traditional construction of earlier brick domes.

The internal diameter of al-Ghawri's dome is 12.5 m, and, judging from the height of its transitional zone, the top of which is 24 m from the floor, its internal height would have been c. 36 m, almost that of the minaret. The mausoleum dome was surpassed in dimensions only by Sultan Hasan's wooden and Faraj's masonry domes.

The lofty funerary chamber is pierced on all sides with windows; three on each of the southern and western walls overlook the street and two more are in the eastern wall on either side of the mihrab, one overlooking the maq'ad, the other overlooking the graveyard. The northern wall includes the door and two windows communicating with the khanqah. The walls are densely decorated with shallow carvings on their upper part with a polychrome marble dado and mihrab.

The dado of the mausoleum is surmounted by an inlaid marble inscription frieze, in a fine and novel *thuluth* script. The patron's interest in calligraphy is reflected in the extraordinary black marble panels in the vestibule and flanking the inner mausoleum door entrance (Figs 312, 313). Their patterns, inlaid with a golden paste, are unprecedented in Mamluk art, displaying calligraphic compositions in mirror configuration or in the shape of vases, trees and stylized birds.

Fig. 309. The funerary complex of al-Ghawri, mosque, west iwan, bench recess.

Fig. 310. The funerary complex of al-Ghawri, mosque dado.

Fig. 311. The funerary complex of al-Ghawri, dome interior.

Fig. 313. The funerary complex of al-Ghawri, inlaid marble panel in the mausoleum (Prisse d'Avennes).

Accurate drawings of these panels, some of which are today in a deteriorated condition, are included in Prisse d'Avennes' album. Calligraphic figures had already appeared in Ottoman art by 1458.[7] Mirror calligraphy had appeared in a window grille of the Fatimid mosque of al-Hakim (990–1003), but it does not seem to have evolved in Egypt until the reign of Qaytbay, as the signatures of 'Abd al-Qadir al-Naqqash demonstrate.[8]

The khanqah is a 'T'-shaped hall with a mihrab, decorated like the mausoleum and the mosque with a polychrome marble dado and pavement. Each of the three mihrabs of the complex has a distinct pattern of marble mosaics. The polychrome marble pavement of the sabil, displaying a dense composition of twenty-pointed geometric stars, is one of the most elaborate in Cairo.

Fig. 312. The funerary complex of al-Ghawri, inlaid marble panel in the mausoleum (Prisse d'Avennes).

Fig. 314. The mosque of al-Ghawri near the hippodrome (57A).

57 (A, B). The two mosques of Sultan al-Ghawri near the hippodrome (1503, 1509–10)⁹

Sultan al-Ghawri introduced substantial changes to Mamluk court ceremonial, notably by transferring the venue of his court from the Hawsh compound within the Citadel to the hippodrome at Rumayla beneath it. The reconstruction works at the hippodrome began in Rabi' I 909/September 1503, and they were completed in Jumada I of the same year, which is a period of about two months. Many poems were composed to celebrate the inauguration of the complex, which Ibn Iyas described as a 'paradise on earth'. There, the sultan held most of his audiences, and received numerous foreign embassies that came to Cairo during his reign.[10]

While restructuring the hippodrome built by al-Nasir Muhammad, al-Ghawri built two small mosques beside it.

After the disappearance of all traces of the hippodrome, the connection between these two mosques and the hippodrome was forgotten. However, a close look at the topography of the Citadel's neighbourhood reveals that the sultan's ceremonial and architectural programme for the area also included a pious element.

The complex covered an oblong area, still recognizable today, between Rumayla square opposite the mosque of Sultan Hasan on the northern side, and the mosque near the cemetery on the southern end, discussed here (see maps). Ibn Iyas described the maydan as walled with two main gates, a monumental one and another one adjoined by a qasr, which is an elevated residential structure;[11] both gates were closed with chains. A reception complex included a loggia and an audience hall, a qasr and a manzara, which is a belvedere or a structure commanding a view. These buildings are likely to have been on the eastern side of the hippodrome and connected with the staircase and the gate through which the sultan descended from the Citadel. They were set amid a garden planted with imported fruits and they overlooked a pool nurtured by two aqueducts, one, no longer extant, near the mosque of Sultan Hasan on the northern side of the maydan, and the other, extant, on its southern side near the cemetery, where it ends today. Al-Ghawri restored this old aqueduct in Jumada II 914/ October 1508.

The pool, more than forty cubits long, was built after the hydraulic installations were completed. It served as a decorative element in the palatial complex, and at the same time served

Fig.315. The mosque of al-Ghawri near the hippodrome (57A).

as a tank for the irrigation of the garden. Next to the garden was the hippodrome itself where the lancers' games took place, which al-Ghawri reinstated after they had been neglected in the previous years.

With the exception of the remains of the two mosques, which were part of the renewal scheme for the area, nothing survives of the maydan itself, except Ibn Iyas' description, which conveys a general picture of it. When Evliya Celebi described the hippodrome in the seventeenth century as a magnificent walled garden with four gates with iron doors, and including a castle, it was being used by the Ottoman governors for military exercises and pastimes.[12] The map of late eighteenth-century Cairo in the *Description de l'Egypte* shows the boundaries of the hippodrome and the four gates: a northern one, to the southeast of the mosque of Sultan Hasan, presumably the main entrance; an eastern one, connected to the Citadel; a southern one in the area called 'Arab Yasar, formerly Hawsh al-'Arab; and a western one facing the quarter on the western side of Saliba street (Fig. 59).

The first mosque is an interesting oratory (57A), not a Friday mosque, located on the northern side of the street that was once parallel to the hippodrome's southern wall. The mosque is the only structure that survived from a complex known in the Mamluk period as Sabil al-Mu'mini (Figs 314, 315). The present structure has no inscription, but two cartouches with the name of Sultan al-Ghawri. Ibn Iyas mentioned its foundation in 909/1503, the year when the hippodrome was refurbished, and he described it instead as a sabil belonging to a complex, which included a mortuary (*maghsal*), a waterwheel and a trough for animals.[13] In fact, a musalla, which is an oratory for funerary prayer, and a sabil were built on this site by the emir Baktimur al-Mu'mini (d. 1369–70) during the reign of Sultan Sha'ban, which explains the name of the complex as Sabil al-Mu'mini.[14] Sultan Qaytbay restored it during the plague of Shawwal 903/June 1498.[15] The mortuary of Sabil al-Mu'mini is often mentioned in the chronicles as the venue where the sultans performed funerary prayers for members of their family or other high dignitaries.

In his brief mention of the mosque of al-Ghawri at Sabil al-Mu'mini, Ibn Iyas referred specifically to its stone vaults, which are indeed its most remarkable feature. The layout consists of six vaulted bays in two rows parallel to the qibla wall, four of which are roofed with shallow stone domes on spherical pendentives, while the two others, which are in the front row, have cross-vaults, a combination adopted also at the mosque of Qanibay on the northern side of the hippodrome. With the exception of the central arch, which is set between the two piers, all arches are connected to piers embedded within the walls. The mosque has no entrance but is open to the exterior with its three front arches. This arrangement is consistent with its function as an open oratory attached to the mortuary, which

itself probably had an enclosure. All the arches of the mosque are round, which is an unusual feature at that period. Today the walls are bare of any decoration.

The bay mosque had appeared in a number of regions since the early Islamic period.[16] It was built in India, Spain, North Africa, Oman, Yemen, Mosul, Iran and Anatolia, and in Egypt in Alexandria, Rosetta, Aswan and Cairo, where it was used in the mashhad of Tabataba, in the Fatimid Aqmar mosque and in the khanqah of Faraj Ibn Barquq. The plan has a pre-Islamic tradition; it characterizes the architecture of Greek and Hellenistic cisterns around the Mediterranean. The Alexandrian cisterns were built in this manner, as was also the Western Mosque or al-Jami' al-Gharbi in that city, probably built by Salah al-Din.[17]

The second mosque (57B), which al-Ghawri founded in the vicinity of the hippodrome, was a Friday mosque. As indicated by Ibn Iyas and the map of the *Description de l'Egypte*, it was close to the southern gate in the area of 'Arab Yasar or Hawsh al-'Arab. The mosque is dated by Ibn Iyas and its inscription to 915/1509–10. Only the minaret has been preserved.[18] It is a modest structure whose only remarkable feature is the position of its minaret; instead of being erected above the roof level of the mosque, it flanks one of its corners so that the muqarnas of its first balcony is at the height of the mosque's crenellation.

58. The funerary mosque of Emir Qanibay Qara (1506)[19]

Qanibay Qara was purchased by Qaytbay, who appointed him to various positions in Egypt and Syria before he became the *amir akhur* or master of the stables in 1497 during the reign of Qaytbay's son, al-Nasir Muhammad. He maintained this office during al-Ghawri's reign and until his death in 1515. He was a great soldier, who commanded several military campaigns against bedouins in Egypt and Syria. His nickname, 'al-Rammah', is a tribute to his skill as a spear thrower. Ibn Iyas criticized him for being cruel and ignorant, for exploiting the workers he employed, and also for his illicit appropriation of waqf estates, adding that no one mourned his death, which came as a relief to many. Qanibay built two Friday mosques in Cairo. The first, undated but described in the waqf deed, was near the Nasiriyya pond and a hippodrome. This mosque has recently been demolished and badly rebuilt. It had a rectangular double-headed minaret.

The mosque beneath the Citadel, overlooking Rumayla or Ramla square, was the more important of the two because it included the founder's mausoleum.

The foundation deed describes it as a madrasa and Friday mosque, but, as was usual at that time, it included a Sufi

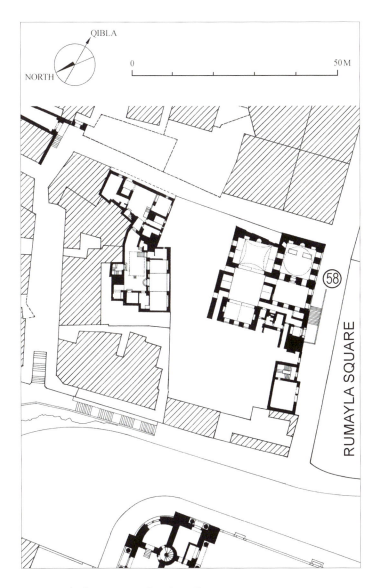

Fig. 316. The funerary complex of Qanibay Qara.

curriculum in addition to Koran recitations and religious chanting. There is no mention of courses in religious studies or of living units for students.

The foundation inscription published by Van Berchem, which refers to the mosque as a madrasa, dates it to Shawwal 911/March 1506. Another inscription published by Hasan ʿAbd al-Wahhab dates the mausoleum three years earlier, to Shaʿban 908/February 1503.

The waqf deed states that the founder made his endowment in Rajab 908/January 1503, i.e. six months after he was appointed master of the stables in Muharram of that year. However, the document was not authenticated until 920/1514–15. The document does not include a description of the mosque, but describes the residential structures next to it. It seems, therefore, that Qanibay set up the endowment of the complex

Fig. 317. The funerary complex of Qanibay Qara.

while the mausoleum was being built, and before the mosque was completed. He made several additions and modifications to the endowment, the latest of which was authenticated in 921/1515, shortly before his death. The founder reserved all that remained from the waqf revenue, once the expenses of the two mosques and other charitable deeds were covered, for himself and his descendants.

Elevated above Rumayla square, the monument reveals a spectacular facade (41.6 m long and c.18 m high), making full use of the ample space available, to command the panorama of the Rumayla square and the hippodrome. To the south of this building, facing the mosque of Sultan Hasan, was the aqueduct established in the Bahri period. Considering Qanibay's office as the master of the stables, and his quality as a great horseman who excelled in the art of the spear, the location of his funerary mosque near the great hippodrome was probably not a coincidence. His first mosque was also in the vicinity of a hippodrome.

The mosque and the adjoining mausoleum are built above a cross-vaulted ground floor originally dedicated to storage facilities. The complex is reached today by a ramp and a staircase. Initially it was not free-standing, but was adjoined on its western side by a residence, described as a qasr and accessible through the vestibule of the mosque. The residence consisted of several halls, one of them with a fountain in its middle surmounted by a wooden dome, rooms of various size, a kitchen, a bathroom, storerooms, a number of individual apartments and a garden. The main structures overlooked

Fig. 318. The funerary mosque of Qanibay Qara, qibla iwan.

The interior differs from contemporary qa'a mosques in the roofing of its iwans. The main iwan is covered with a shallow masonry dome on spherical pendentives, of the same type used in the sultan's mosque at Sabil al-Mu'mini, and supported by four arches set in the walls, which, unlike the pointed arches of the opposite iwan, are rounded. The sanctuary's dome is surrounded by a carved Koranic inscription, followed by the founder's name without a date. The opposite iwan has a cross-vault, also framed by a Koranic inscription. The courtyard, which is open to the sky, has a foundation inscription on the upper part of the walls with the date.

The mihrab of the sanctuary is not surmounted by the usual oculus, but instead by a composite window of three arched openings surmounted by a triple composition of one-over-two oculi, of the type common in the transitional zone of domes. This is the only window in the main iwan, which receives sufficient light from the courtyard. Instead of lower rectangular windows, the stone mihrab is flanked by a niche on either side, one of them for containing books, the other for the use of the *khatib*, as stated in the waqf deed. The mausoleum dome is reached from the prayer hall. Its stone mihrab is surmounted by an oculus between two arched windows.

The mosque has remarkable decoration. The entire inner walls, including the vaults, are of striped masonry. Marble is used only for the dado of the mausoleum, and is kept very low. Stone carvings of fine quality, and novel geometric and arabesque patterns, distinct from those of Qaytbay's period, adorn the lintels of the windows and the pendentives of the sanctuary dome. Both mihrabs are made of carved stone with different patterns.

Rumayla square. This qasr was dedicated to the use of the founder and his family.

The masonry dome occupies the southeastern quarter of the facade. It is carved with an overall pattern of lobed lozenges filled with arabesques. The design is less complex and the quality of the carving shallower than that of Qaytbay's dome.

The minaret, a good reconstruction by the Comité in 1916, stands on the other side of the facade on the left-hand side of the portal, between it and the sabil-maktab. It has a rectangular shaft with a double-headed upper structure. The double bulb was used earlier in the minaret of Sultan Janbalat's mosque, built in 1500 and destroyed during the French occupation.[20] It might not have been the first such case since, as mentioned earlier, Ibn Kathir described one of the minarets of Sultan Hasan as having a double top. Sultan al-Ghawri's minaret at al-Azhar mosque and the earlier minaret of Qanibay at Nasiriyya also display this device. The sabil-maktab was reconstructed in 1939, on the basis of old photographs.

59. The funerary complex of Emir Qurqumas (1506–7)[21]

Qurqumas min Qaliyy al-Din began his career with Qaytbay, who appointed him master of the stables. After a short setback during the reign of al-'Adil Tumanbay (1501), when he was imprisoned in Syria, he regained prestige and power during the reign of al-Ghawri, who appointed him commander-in-chief of the army. Qurqumas had an excellent reputation, and his death in 916/1510 was mourned by many. Al-Ghawri joined the large crowd of his funerary cortege to the mortuary of Sabil al-Mu'mini, where he dismounted, kissed the bier and wept.

The complex is in the northern cemetery; the mausoleum was the first structure to be erected, as indicated by its inscription with the completion date Dhu 'l-Qa'da 911/April 1506. The inscription at the main entrance dates the completion of the complex to Rajab 913/November 1507.

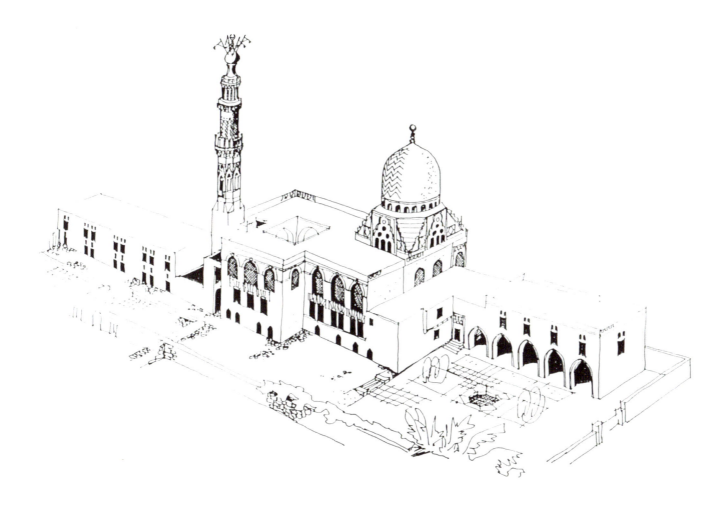

Fig. 319. The funerary complex of Qurqumas, axonometric west view.

As usual in this period, the complex consisted of a Friday mosque with a Sufi service. Although it is called a madrasa in the waqf deed it had no teaching curriculum, nor was it tied to a specific *madhhab*. Neither the waqf deed nor the epigraphy of this complex mentions the term 'khanqah'.

As the collection of his waqf deeds attests, Qurqumas had already begun in 898/1493 – i.e. while he was an emir of Qaytbay – to acquire estates, initially as a private investment. In 905/1500 he appointed, along with other staff, three Koran readers to perform recitations in a mausoleum (turba) he founded before the present funerary dome. It is described as being in the vicinity of Barquq's tomb, which does not correspond to the location of the present complex. It seems, therefore, that Qurqumas founded an earlier and more modest building, which he abandoned after he became commander-in-chief in favour of the present one. He continued to add estates to his endowment, which included agricultural land in Egypt, real estate in various parts of Cairo and a qaysariyya in Damascus.

In Rajab 916/October 1510, and again later in Ramadan of the same year, shortly before his death and during his last illness, he modified and finalized the stipulations of his endowment, which were authenticated after his death in Sha'ban 917/ October–November 1511.

Once the costs of the pious foundation were covered, all remaining revenue from the endowed estate was to revert to his descendants, and, if none were left, to the progeny of his manumitted slaves. Besides the maintenance personnel, a preacher, an imam, twenty-two Sufis and their shaykh, six Koran readers, a reader of al-Bukhari's Hadith compendium, and seven schoolboys and their teachers were to be attached to the foundation; this is a rather modest number of beneficiaries in relation to the size of the building, which is one of the most monumental of the Mamluk period. Parts of the funerary complex, such as the qasr and other structures on the opposite side of the road, were dedicated to the private use of the founder's family.

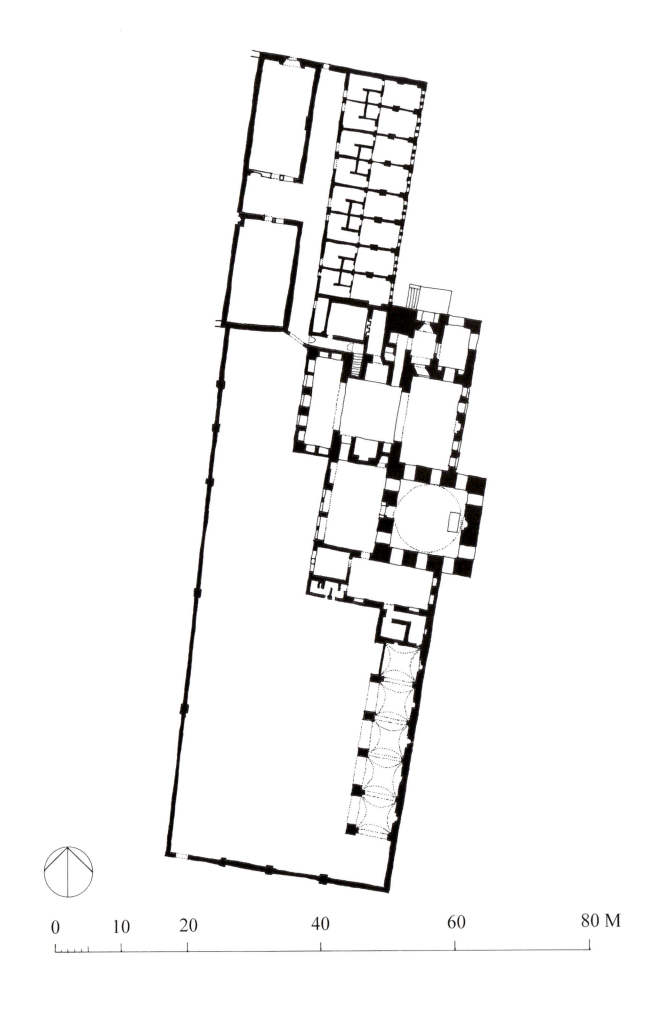

0   10   20   40   60   80 M

Fig. 321. The funerary complex of Qurqumas with the complex of Inal in the rear.

Fig. 322. The funerary complex of Qurqumas, qasr and mausoleum.

The layout

The layout appears at first glance similar to that of Sultan Qaytbay's complex, with the minaret on the right-hand side of the portal, the sabil-maktab on the left and the mausoleum dome protruding at the southern end of the eastern facade. As in Qaytbay's case, the mosque was connected on its northern side with residential structures. Here, they consist of an apartment building with eight units built on two storeys, which today are in a ruined condition. The south side of the complex extends to include a residential hall, described as a qasr in the waqf deed (Fig. 309). Qanibay's funerary complex near the Citadel also included a qasr, albeit a more elaborate one with the full attributes of an autonomous residence. A waqf description of the complex of al-'Adil Tumanbay further north also mentions extensive residential structures.[22] It should be recalled that the maq'ads of Qaytbay's and al-Ghawri's funerary complexes were also residential structures, probably fulfilling similar functions.

The main facade of Qurqumas' complex extends over a length of c. 107 m adjoining Inal's buildings. Together the two facades are almost 200 m long.

The dimensions of the minaret, which is over 25 m high from the roof, are similar to Qaytbay's. The inner side of the mausoleum is 10 m long, and the inner height to the apex of the dome is c. 30 m.

Across the street, which was originally narrower than is the case today, there was a rab' with sixteen apartments and storerooms, a lavatory complex with ten latrines, and a domed ablution fountain. On its rear or eastern side another block included a well with a waterwheel, a kitchen and a trough. Nearby, a stable was not yet completed when the endowment was finalized. This residential compound faced the qasr attached to the mausoleum, conveying to the southern section of the complex a rather secular character. Seen from the west, the building appears almost as a villa, with its arcade and the strikingly dense fenestration of the upper structures.

Seen from the east, the dense rhythmic arrangement of the windows characterizes the facade. The mihrabs of the mausoleum and the mosque are signalled on the outside by their respective oculi, which are both set symmetrically between the upper and lower windows. The upper arched windows differ from the norm by their remarkable size, which almost equals that of the lower rectangular ones, leaving little masonry between them.

Fig. 320. [opposite] The funerary complex of Qurqumas.

The mosque, in the form of a qa'a, has a central space open to the sky, and its iwans, moreover, are densely pierced with windows, with minimal masonry (Figs 325, 329). The main iwan includes large windows on three sides, as does the iwan on the opposite side, where the wall facing the mihrab is pierced with three lower rectangular windows and a large central arched window above them, flanked by two narrower ones. The central window is the largest arched window in a Mamluk mosque. The lower windows had iron grilles, while the upper ones had grilles of turned wood, of the type later known as mashrabiyya.

On the mihrab's axis, an elevated wooden *mu'adhdhin*'s bench, placed beneath the central large window, conveys an impression of a palatial interior. The dikka is reached by an inner passage and staircase, as in the mosques of Azbak al-Yusufi, Janim al-Bahlawan and al-Ghawri. A polychrome dado adorned the whole inner space of the mosque.

Unlike Qaytbay's mausoleum, which is preceded by an open space next to the mosque on its west side, and unlike any other mausoleum, that of Qurqumas opens on its west side on a lofty loggia, with four lower rectangular windows surmounted by three huge arched openings overlooking the open courtyard on the rear side. It is a singular case, where the upper windows are larger than the lower ones. This wall appears, rather, as a screen, with more light than masonry, an effect emphasized by the height of the walls and the open space beyond (Fig. 319). The loggia also fulfilled the function of a mausoleum for the founder's manumitted slaves, who were buried in a crypt underneath its floor; it was also a gathering room for the *simat*, which means 'meal' or 'banquet'.

The interior of the monumental mausoleum chamber, connected by a pair of windows with the mosque, conforms to contemporary funerary architecture. The stone mihrab is, as usual, decorated differently from the mihrab of the mosque. Unlike the mosque, the mausoleum has no marble dado. However, the waqf deed mentions an inscription band of marble and stucco and a marble pavement, which no longer exist.

The inscription band includes excerpts of the famous poem *al-Burda* by the Mamluk poet al-Busiri, which is a hymn to the Prophet;[23] it was originally gilded.

The mosque and mausoleum, built on the second floor above storerooms and ablution fountains, commanded a panoramic view of the cemetery and the city further west.

On the southern side of the mausoleum, a door leads to a small apartment with windows overlooking the road and the open courtyard, and connected to the qasr. The latter is a large rectangular hall with four composite windows on each of its side walls and one on the southern wall. The windows consist of

Fig. 324. The funerary complex of Qurqumas, qibla iwan.

Fig. 323. [opposite] The funerary complex of Qurqumas, minaret detail.

Fig. 325. The funerary complex of Qurqumas, west iwan.

Fig. 326. The funerary complex of Qurqumas, mausoleum pendentive.

a rectangular opening surmounted by a double-arched window with grilles of pierced stone without glass, as the waqf deed specifies. There were no stucco window grilles in this complex; the grilles were either made of stone, iron or wood. This novel feature confirms the designer's concern with light, which the architecture of this monument so clearly shows.

Seen from the west, the qasr stands above a hall facing a graveyard with five pointed arches supported by piers, corresponding to five vaulted bays. The hall, whose function is not defined in the waqf deed, might have been a musalla or prayer place for the dead. It has three plain mihrabs on its frontal wall and originally included bookshelves. On the northern side of the graveyard, the apartment complex overlooks a courtyard that once included storerooms and dependencies.

The architecture of Qurqumas' complex, with its diaphanous walls, interacted with the bright desert environment. The bold fenestration on an unprecedented scale, combined with the loftiness of the building, displays a masterly manipulation of light. This architecture of luminosity was the final development of Mamluk architecture.

60. The funerary madrasa of Emir Khayrbak (1502–21)[24]

Bilbay al-Jarkasi, better known as Khayrbak Bilbay, was recruited by Qaytbay and appointed governor of Aleppo during al-Ghawri's reign, a position he retained until the Ottoman conquest in 1517. As a reward for his collaboration with the Ottomans, Sultan Selim appointed him the first governor of the Egyptian province, with the title of *malik al-umara'*. This appointment of a Mamluk emir to govern Egypt on behalf of the Ottomans aimed to achieve a smooth transition to the new regime. He ruled for five years, and died in 928/1522.

Khayrbak had built a mausoleum earlier in Aleppo, which is entirely in the regional style. This one, which stands in Tabbana street next to the mosque of Aqsunqur, was built during the early reign of al-Ghawri, in 908/1502, as indicated by an inscription in the dome that gives Khayrbak's title as chief chamberlain. It pre-dates by twenty years the present mosque, which was founded during his tenure as governor, and was thus the first princely mosque to be established under Ottoman rule.[25] Its architecture is entirely Mamluk, however. The madrasa has no dating inscription, but its foundation deed was compiled in 927/1521.

Unlike all princely foundations of the late Mamluk period, this madrasa was not a Friday mosque, but merely a madrasa to teach Hadith, as indicated in the waqf deed. Khayrbak might not have been authorized by the Ottoman sultan to found a Friday mosque in his own name. After his death, however, in 937/1531, a minbar and the *mu'adhdhin*'s bench were added, indicating that the mosque had since acquired the status of a Friday mosque.[26] Although it is elevated, this dikka, unlike those of Abu Bakr Ibn Muzhir, Azbak al-Yusufi, al-Ghawri and Qurqumas, was not reached by an inner staircase, but by an external ladder, confirming that it was not initially planned.

Khayrbak's endowment was enlarged by the emir Janim al-Hamzawi, who was his deputy and close associate since the first days of the Ottoman conquest. He added the sabil on the opposite side of the entrance passage.

The layout

The felicitous juxtaposition of the mausoleum dome with the minaret projecting into the street and visible at a distance made this monument one of the most photogenic of medieval Cairo, as numerous nineteenth-century drawings and photographs attest. The carved decoration of the masonry dome displays two superimposed and intertwined patterns of repetitive curved lozenges and scrolls of arabesques. The outlines of the lozenges are in flat plain relief, contrasting with the grooved arabesque stems. This decoration is similar to but more complex than that of Qanibay's dome built slightly later.

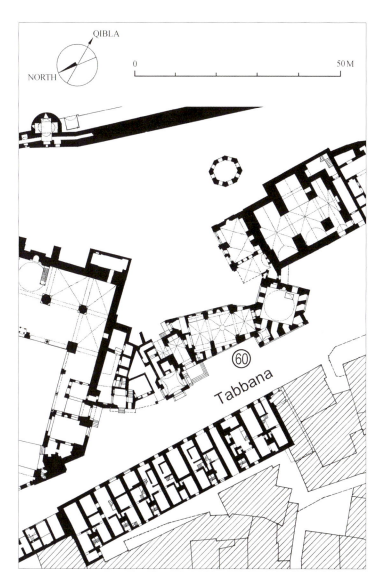

Fig. 327. The funerary mosque of Khayrbak.

Fig. 328. The mosque of Khayrbak, detail of minaret and dome.

The brick minaret stands above a small vaulted space, connected to the mausoleum, and its first storey includes a double staircase reached through two entrances. The minaret's shaft is decorated with carved stucco, and previously, according to a drawing by Girault de Prangey, it had a wooden bulb at the top, like the one on Jaqmaq's minaret. Such wooden bulbs are likely to have been original, considering that these minarets were made of brick and could not have supported the kind of upper structure found on comparable stone minarets. It seems that the builder could not copy in brick the octagonal pavilion surmounted with a bulb that is common on stone minarets. Most probably it would have had an unsatisfactory appearance, the plaster would not have weathered well, and the structure itself might have become unstable.

The date of the minaret is uncertain. If it was built in the second phase of the construction, it would be the only minaret built under Ottoman rule in the Mamluk style prior to the minaret of al-Burdayni, erected a century later.[27]

The photogenic composition of the dome and minaret was accomplished by twisting the plan in the boldest manner ever achieved in Mamluk architecture. The facade displays two major projections onto the street. The southern one includes the mausoleum, whose southern facade is broken into an obtuse angle. The sabil-maktab later added by Janim al-Hamzawi projects on the northern corner. The decoration of the facade is in the traditional style. The trilobed groin-vaulted portal leads to the sabil-maktab on the left-hand side, and to the mosque on the right, and further to a courtyard on the eastern side of the mosque, bordered by Salah al-Din's city wall. This courtyard was used as a graveyard.

The walls of the building show a pronounced adjustment to the street, which, however, failed to solve the problem of the qibla orientation of the complex, which is utterly squeezed between the street on the western side and a pre-existing palace and the city wall on the eastern side. This palace, built by the emir Alin Aq in the late thirteenth or early fourteenth century, was

Fig. 329. The funerary mosque of Khayrbak, interior.

the residence of many subsequent emirs, including Khayrbak himself. Due to these constraints, the qibla of the mosque diverges by 29° from that of the mausoleum, which is the largest known discrepancy in a Mamluk funerary monument, and, ironically, it is the mosque that has the more problematic orientation.

An irregular feature of the rear or east facade is the arched window in the protruding section of the wall, which includes the mihrab. Normally the windows are pierced in the recessed part of the screen walls, with the exception of the traditional oculus above the mihrab. The arched window here replaces the traditional mihrab oculus.

The prayer hall has an unconventional layout, consisting of three cross-vaulted bays connected by two transverse arches. The central bay, which includes the mihrab, has a canopy structure; it is set between the transverse northern and southern arches and two lateral arches supported by piers inserted in the east and west walls. The apex of its vault is pierced with an octagonal opening, which might have been adorned by a small wooden lantern. The eastern arch partly conceals two qamariyyas in the qibla wall. This feature, along with the defective orientation of the wall and the absence of a mihrab oculus, suggest that the qibla wall was erected at an earlier date and was not intended to include a mihrab. The mihrab is squeezed between a pair of rectangular windows set in arched recesses of the same size. These windows left no room for a minbar, for which there was no need, as this was not initially a Friday mosque.

A marble frieze inlaid with arabesques of black and red paste runs above the mosque's dado. In the mausoleum a similar frieze is inscribed with a Koranic text in *thuluth* script.

Along with the mosque of Qanibay beneath the Citadel, and the mosque of al-Ghawri at Sabil al-Mu'mini, this was the third late Mamluk mosque to be entirely roofed with masonry vaults.

The mausoleum on the southern end of the prayer hall has a portal with a trilobed groin vault and a pair of maksalas, which are the stone benches common on Mamluk portals. This portal configuration is an external rather than internal feature, but it may be explained by the fact that the mausoleum pre-dates the mosque and the entrance might have belonged to its original facade. However, no break is visible between the masonry of the mausoleum and that of the eastern wall of the mosque. This may be due to a refacing of the walls, but it could also indicate that this wall was built simultaneously with the mausoleum as part of a simpler structure before a madrasa was added. An inner staircase concealed behind what seems to be a cupboard door connects the mausoleum with the palace; its curve is recognizable on the southern facade.

Fig. 330. The funerary mosque of Khayrbak, detail of sabil decoration.

The sabil-maktab added later is a separate structure with its own entrance on the northern side of the mosque, from which it is separated by the entrance passage. The sabil hall has a marble fountain in a niche, and is covered with a shallow dome on spherical pendentives. The walls between the pendentives are carved with a pattern that recalls the decoration of late Mamluk 'Veneto-Saracenic' metal vessels (Figs 9, 330).

The Mamluk Sultans

Bahri Mamluks (Turks)

title (laqab)	name (ism)	son of (ibn)	start of reign CE	AH	end of reign CE	AH	note
	Shajar al-Durr		May 1250	648	July 1250	648	
al-Mu'izz 'Izz al-Din	**Aybak**		July 1250	648	April 1257	655	
al-Mansur Nur al-Din	**'Ali**	Aybak	April 1257	655	Nov. 1259	657	
al-Muzaffar Sayf al-Din	**Qutuz**		Nov. 1259	657	Oct. 1260	658	
al-Zahir Rukn al-Din	**Baybars**		Oct. 1260	658	July 1277	676	
al-Sa'id Nasir al-Din	**Baraka Khan**	Baybars	July 1277	676	Aug. 1279	678	
al-'Adil Badr al-Din	**Salamish**	Baybars	Aug. 1279	678	Nov. 1279	678	
al-Mansur Sayf al-Din	**Qalawun**		Nov. 1279	678	Nov. 1290	689	
al-Ashraf Salah al-Din	**Khalil**	Qalawun	Nov. 1290	689	Dec. 1293	693	
al-Nasir Nasir al-Din	**Muhammad**	Qalawun	Dec. 1293	693	Dec. 1294	694	1st reign
al-'Adil Zayn al-Din	**Katbugha**		Dec. 1294	694	Dec. 1296	696	
al-Mansur Husam al-Din	**Lajin**		Dec. 1296	696	Jan. 1299	698	
al-Nasir Nasir al-Din	**Muhammad**	Qalawun	Jan. 1299	698	April 1309	708	2nd reign
al-Muzaffar Rukn al-Din	**Baybars**	Jashnakir	April 1309	708	Feb. 1310	709	
al-Nasir Nasir al-Din	**Muhammad**	Qalawun	Feb. 1310	709	June 1341	741	3rd reign
al-Mansur Sayf al-Din	**Abu Bakr**	Muhammad	June 1341	741	Aug. 1341	742	
al-Ashraf 'Ala' al-Din	**Kujuk**	Muhammad	Aug. 1341	742	Jan. 1342	742	
al-Nasir Shihab al-Din	**Ahmad**	Muhammad	Jan. 1342	742	June 1342	743	
al-Salih 'Imad al-Din	**Isma'il**	Muhammad	June 1342	743	Aug. 1345	746	
al-Kamil Sayf al-Din	**Sha'ban**	Muhammad	Aug. 1345	746	Sep. 1346	747	
al-Muzaffar Zayn al-Din	**Hajji**	Muhammad	Sep. 1346	747	Dec. 1347	748	
al-Nasir Nasir al-Din	**Hasan**	Muhammad	Dec. 1347	748	Aug. 1351	752	1st reign
al-Salih Salah al-Din	**Salih**	Muhammad	Aug. 1351	752	Oct. 1354	755	
al-Nasir Nasir al-Din	**Hasan**	Muhammad	Oct. 1354	755	March 1361	762	2nd reign
al-Mansur Nasir al-Din	**Muhammad**	Hajji	March 1361	762	May 1363	764	
al-Ashraf Zayn al-Din	**Sha'ban**	Husayn	May 1363	764	March 1377	778	
al-Mansur 'Ala' al-Din	**'Ali**	Sha'ban	March 1377	778	May 1381	783	
al-Salih Salah al-Din*	**Hajji**	Sha'ban	May 1381	783	Nov. 1382	784	1st reign
al-Zahir Sayf al-Din	**Barquq**	Anas	Nov. 1382	784	May 1389	791	1st reign
al-Mansur Salah al-Din*	**Hajji**	Sha'ban	May 1389	791	Feb. 1390	792	2nd reign

* Same sultan using two different titles.
Name components in colour are normally used together to identify an individual sultan, e.g. al-Zahir Baybars.

Burji Mamluks (Circassians)

title (laqab)	name (ism)	son of (ibn)	start of reign CE	start of reign AH	end of reign CE	end of reign AH	note
al-Zahir Sayf al-Din	**Barquq**	Anas	Feb. 1390	792	June 1399	801	2nd reign
al-Nasir Zayn al-Din	**Faraj**	Barquq	June 1399	801	Sep. 1405	808	1st reign
al-Mansur 'Izz al-Din	**'Abd al-'Aziz**	Barquq	Sep. 1405	808	Nov. 1405	808	
al-Nasir Zayn al-Din	**Faraj**	Barquq	Nov. 1405	808	May 1412	815	2nd reign
al-Musta'in*	**'Abbas**	al-Mutawakkil	May 1412	815	Nov. 1412	815	
al-Mu'ayyad Sayf al-Din	**Shaykh**		Nov. 1412	815	Jan. 1421	824	
al-Muzaffar	**Ahmad**	Shaykh	Jan. 1421	824	Aug. 1421	824	
al-Zahir Sayf al-Din	**Tatar**		Aug. 1421	824	Nov. 1421	824	
al-Salih Nasir al-Din	**Muhammad**	Tatar	Nov. 1421	824	April 1422	825	
al-Ashraf Sayf al-Din	**Barsbay**		April 1422	825	June 1438	841	
al-Aziz Jamal al-Din	**Yusuf**	Barsbay	June 1438	841	Sep. 1438	842	
al-Zahir Sayf al-Din	**Jaqmaq**		Sep. 1438	842	Feb. 1453	857	
al-Mansur Fakhr al-Din	**'Uthman**	Jaqmaq	Feb. 1453	857	March 1453	857	
al-Ashraf Sayf al-Din	**Inal**		March 1453	857	Feb. 1461	865	
al-Mu'ayyad	**Ahmad**	Inal	Feb. 1461	865	June 1461	865	
al-Zahir Sayf al-Din	**Khushqadam**		June 1461	865	Oct. 1467	872	
al-Zahir	**Yilbay**		Oct. 1467	872	Dec. 1467	872	
al-Zahir	**Timurbugha**		Dec. 1467	872	Feb. 1468	872	
al-Ashraf	**Qaytbay**		Feb. 1468	872	Aug. 1496	901	
al-Nasir	**Muhammad**	Qaytbay	Aug. 1496	901	Oct. 1498	904	
al-Zahir	**Qansuh**		Nov. 1498	904	June 1500	905	Khamsmi'a
al-Ashraf	**Janbalat**		June 1500	905	Jan. 1501	906	
al-Adil Sayf al-Din	**Tumanbay**		Jan. 1501	906	April 1501	906	
al-Ashraf	**Qansuh**		April 1501	906	Aug. 1516	922	**al-Ghawri**
al-Ashraf	**Tumanbay**		Aug. 1516	922	April 1517	923	

Shadow Abbasid caliph appointed as interim sultan.

Name components in colour are normally used together to identify an individual sultan, e.g. al-Zahir Baybars.

Notes

Chapter 1

1 Some scholars, however, contest this etymology, with the arguments that the term 'baḥariyya' was already used in the Fatimid and Ayyubid periods to designate an army corps, and that the association with the Nile does not appear prior to the fifteenth century: 'Abbadi, p. 97.

2 Sakhawi, *Daw'*, III, p. 74.

3 Fabri, p. 915.

4 See below.

5 Darrag, *Barsbay*, pp. 25ff.; Behrens-Abouseif, 'Ghawri', p. 85.

6 He was Circassian, but 'Turk' here refers rather to his Mamluk origin. Sakhawi, *Daw'*, III, p. 71.

7 Haarmann, 'Altun'.

8 Holt, 'Ancestry'.

9 Maqrizi, *Khitat*, II, p. 220.

10 Rogers, 'Mamluk–Mongol Relations'.

11 Haarmann, 'Ideology', p. 183.

12 George Saliba, 'Theory and Observation in Islamic Astronomy: The work of Ibn al-Shāṭir of Damascus', *Journal for the History of Astronomy*, 18 (1987), pp. 35–43; Victor Roberts, 'The Solar and Lunar Theory of Ibn al-Shāṭir: A Pre-Copernican Model', ISIS, 48 (1957), pp. 428–32; King, 'Astronomy', p. 74.

13 Ibrahim, *Maktaba*, pp. 38f; Behrens-Abouseif, 'Cairene Notable', pp. 27, 131; Amin, *Awqaf*, pp. 255–9.

14 Flemming, 'Literary Activities', pp. 253f.

15 Sakhawi, *Daw'*, X, p. 274.

16 Maqrizi, *Khitat*, II, p. 395; Ibn Taghribirdi, *Manhal*, IX, pp. 236f., XI, pp. 213ff.

17 Maqrizi, *Khitat*, II, p. 401.

18 Azzam, p. 81.

19 Sakhawi, *I'lan*, transl. Rosenthal, pp. 224, 236.

20 Sakhawi, *I'lan*, transl. Rosenthal, pp. 289f.

21 See on this subject Salim, VIII.

22 Bauer, 'Ibrahim al-Mi'mar'.

23 Maqrizi, *Suluk*, III, pp. 962, 1058.

24 Maqrizi, *Khitat*, II, p. 125.

25 Maqrizi, *Suluk*, IV, pp. 436, 1206.

26 Maqrizi, *Suluk*, IV, p. 918.

27 Flemming, 'Literary Activities', p. 252.

28 Behrens-Abouseif, 'European Arts and Crafts'.

Chapter 2

1 The case of the caliph 'Abbas al-Musta'in is exceptional; he was involved in the rebellion against Faraj, and eventually appointed sultan for a transitional period (May–November 1412).

2 Maqrizi, *Khitat*, II, p. 243; Suyuti, *Husn*, II, pp. 45–92.

3 Ibn Iyas, III, pp. 300f.

4 Maqrizi, *Khitat*, II, p. 243.

5 Schimmel, 'Sufismus und Heiligenverehrung'; idem, 'Glimpses'.

6 This was temporarily challenged by Sultan Barquq, who gave preference to the Hanafi judge.

7 Schimmel, 'Kalif und Kadi'.

8 Mawardi, p. 6.

9 Ibn Iyas, I/1, p. 308.

10 Tarsusi, pp. 11, 13f.; see also Menasri's comments, pp. 61–3.

11 Qudsi, pp. 101–31. Turk here refers to all Mamluks, including the Circassians; Haarmann, 'Rather Injustice'.

12 Amin, *Awqaf*, pp. 248f.; Petry, *Elite*, pp. 61–72; Fernandes, 'Education', pp. 94f.

13 Walter J. Fischel, *Ibn Khaldūn in Egypt*, Berkeley/Los Angeles 1967, chapters 4, 5.

14 Fernandes, 'Baybars', p. 25.

15 Van Berchem, pp. 242ff.

16 Maqrizi, *Khitat*, ii, pp. 432, 433.

17 Long pointed headgear.

18 Maqrizi, *Suluk*, ii, p. 494. The Khanqah Rukniyya is that of al-Muzaffar Baybars (al-Jashnakir).

19 Ibn Iyas, iii, p. 90; Fernandes, 'Education', p. 98.

20 Ibn Iyas, iii, p. 100.

21 Fernandes, 'Education', p. 95.

22 Maqrizi, *Khitat*, ii, p. 370.

23 Maqrizi, *Suluk*, iii, p. 359.

24 Fernandes, *Khanqah*, pp. 11, 96ff.

25 Amin, *Watha'iq waqf Sultan Hasan*, p. 5.

26 Geoffroy, pp. 253–9.

27 Amin, *Awqaf*, p. 226.

28 Maqrizi, *Suluk*, iv, p. 202.

29 Sabra, pp. 85ff.

30 Van Berchem, p. 370.

31 Amin, *Awqaf*, pp. 72–82.

32 Ibn Shaddad, p. 344; Dar al-Whata'iq 126/20, survey protocol, d.865/1461.

33 Amin, *Awqaf*, p. 65; Suyuti, *Fatawi*, i, pp. 154ff.

34 Darrāǧ, *Acte de waqf*, pp. 12–29.

35 Maqrizi, *Suluk*, iii, pp. 345ff.; Ibn Hajar, *Inba'*, i, pp. 273f.

36 Ibn Taghirbirdi, *Hawadith*, i, p. 17.

37 Nuwayri (al-Sakandari), xxxii, p. 63.

38 Ibn Iyas, i/2, p. 205.

39 Escovitz, pp. 149–57.

40 Ibn Iyas, iv, p. 69.

41 Maqrizi, *Khitat*, ii, p. 408.

42 Maqrizi, *Khitat*, ii, p. 276.

43 Ibn Iyas, iv, p. 68.

44 Escovitz, pp. 150–62.

45 Ibn Taghribirdi, *Nujum*, xv, p. 348.

Chapter 3

1 Mawardi, pp. 16, 83, 100–3, 188f.

2 Ibn 'Abd Allah, pp. 163f.

3 Ibn Iyas, iii, p. 117.

4 Ibn Khaldun, *Muqaddima*, p. 451.

5 Ibn Khaldun, *Muqaddima*, p. 316.

6 Ibn Khaldun, *Ta'rif*, p. 351.

7 Ibn Taghribirdi, *Nujum*, xiv, p. 154.

8 Amin, *Awqaf*, pp. 343ff.

9 Maqrizi, *Suluk*, ii, p. 135; al-Qudsi cited by Haarmann, *Geschichte*, p. 250.

10 Ibn Iyas, iv, p. 91.

11 Maqrizi, *Khitat*, ii, p. 384.

12 Ibn Iyas, i/2, p. 350.

13 W.M. Brinner, 'Ibn Iyas', *EI* 2nd ed.

14 Maqrizi, *Khitat*, ii, p. 407f.

15 Maqrizi, *Suluk*, ii, p. 423.

16 Maqrizi, *Khitat*, ii, pp. 314f.

17 Maqrizi, *Suluk*, ii, pp. 640f; idem, *Khitat*, i, p. 425, II, p. 188.

18 Maqrizi, *Khitat*, ii, p. 326.

19 Grabar, 'Inscriptions'.

20 Van Berchem, pp. 547ff.

21 Ibn Iyas, i/2, p. 413.

22 Ibn Iyas, i/2, p. 353; Ibn Taghribirdi, *Nujum*, xi, p. 302.

23 Ibn Taghribirdi, *Manhal*, vii, p. 90; idem, *Nujum*, x, p. 239; 'Abd al-Wahhab, *Masajid*, pp. 243–6; Homerin, 'Domed Shrine'; Kessler, *Domes*, pp. 27, 29.

24 Kessler, *Domes*, p. 27.

25 Ibn al-Hajj, iii, pp. 263f., 267ff.

26 Ibn al-Hajj, iii, pp. 263–74; 'Abd al-Sattar 'Uthman, pp. 107–11; Leisten, 'Between Orthodoxy and Exegesis'.

27 Meri, 'Ziyara', *EI* 2nd ed.; Taylor, *Vicinity*.

28 Dar al-Watha'iq 126/20; Meinecke, *Architektur*, ii, p. 17.

29 Behrens-Abouseif, 'Qaytbay's Investments'.

30 Garcin and Taher, 'Ensemble de waqfs'; idem, 'Les Waqfs'; Behrens-Abouseif, *Azbakiyya*, pp. 22–5; Waqf of Azbak, Dar al-Whata'iq 198.

31 Maqrizi, *Suluk*, iii, p. 206.

32 Meinecke, *Architektur*, ii, p. 25.

33 Van Berchem, p. 370.

34 Maqrizi, *Khitat*, ii, pp. 275ff.; Van Berchem, pp. 44–8; Creswell, *Chronology*, pp. 49–51; 'Abd al-Wahhab, *Masajid*, pp. 53–8; Rabbat, 'al-Azhar', pp. 57f.

35 Ibn Iyas, iii, p. 99.

36 Maqrizi, *Khitat*, ii, pp. 252f.; Ibn Duqmaq, iv, pp. 16, 70f.

37 Maqrizi, *Khitat*, ii, p. 268; Creswell, *Chronology*, pp. 41f.; idem, *MAE*, ii, pp. 223–33.

38 Maqrizi, *Khitat*, ii, p. 306; Creswell, *MAE*, ii, p. 73; Meinecke, *Architektur*, ii, pp. 116, 192, 421, 457.

39 Meinecke, *Architektur*, ii, pp. 258, 308, 417, 456.

40 Maqrizi, *Khitat*, ii, p. 429; Meinecke, *Architektur*, ii, pp. 314, 329, 455.

41 Homerin, 'Domed Shrine'.

42 Sakhawi, *Daw'*, iii, p. 73.

43 Newhall, chapter 4.

44 Maqrizi, *Khitat*, ii, pp. 427f.

45 Index No. 146; Meinecke, *Architektur*, ii, p. 62; O'Kane et al., *Documentation*, No. 146.2.

46 Maqrizi, *Khitat*, II, p. 394.
47 Ibn Iyas, I/2, p. 560; Behrens-Abouseif, *Minarets*, pp. 173f.
48 Abd Ar-Raziq, 'Trois fondations', pp. 97–111; C. Williams, 'Sitt Hadaq'.
49 Speiser, chapter 5.
50 'Abd Ar-Raziq, 'Trois fondations', pp. 98–126.
51 Harithy, 'Turbat al-Sitt'.
52 Index No. 80; Van Berchem, pp. 740f.; Meinecke, *Architektur*, II, p. 239.
53 Index No. 61; Van Berchem, pp. 408, 747; Creswell, *Chronology*, p. 135; Sakhawi, *Daw'*, XII, pp. 44f.
54 Abd Ar-Raziq, *La Femme*, pp. 19–27; Van Berchem, pp. 556ff.; Asalbay built her mosque during her son's reign.
55 Index No. 58; Mubarak, II, p. 128; Creswell, *Chronology*, p. 138.
56 Amin, *Watha'iq waqf al-sultan Hasan*, p. 5.
57 Maqrizi, *Khitat*, II, p. 420f.; O'Kane et al., *Documentation*, No. 146.2.
58 Index No. 195; Ibn Iyas, III, pp. 12, 30, 100, 104, 302, 326, 427, 469, IV, p. 64; 'Abd al-Wahhab, *Masajid*, p. 247; Creswell, *Chronology*, p. 138.
59 Maqrizi, *Khitat*, II, pp. 305, 312.
60 Ibn Iyas, III, pp. 280, 363. This was the former Kaum al-Rish where there used to be a Fatimid belvedere, which Sultan al-Mu'ayyad rebuilt.
61 Ibn Iyas, III, p. 181.
62 Ibn Taghribirdi, *Hawadith*, II, p. 217.

Chapter 4

1 Ibn Hajar, *Inba'*, IV, p. 170.
2 Ibn Taghribirdi, *Nujum*, pp. 347f.
3 Ibn Hajar, *Durar*, II, p. 305.
4 Index No. 519; Ibn Iyas, III, p. 283; 'Abd al-Wahhab, *Masajid*, pp. 273–5.
5 Ibn Iyas, III, pp. 306, 431; Sakhawi, *Daw'*, X, pp. 136, 160.
6 Ibn Iyas, III, pp. 124, 306, 431; Van Berchem, pp. 47, 674f.; 'Abd al-Wahhab, *Masajid*, p. 156; O'Kane et al., *Documentation*, Nos 97.33, 97.109, 97.111.
7 See waqf discussion in Behrens-Abouseif, *Fath Allah*.
8 Maqrizi, *Khitat*, II, p. 253.
9 Safadi, XXII, No. 4, pp. 30f.
10 Maqrizi, *Khitat*, II, p. 315.
11 Maqrizi, *Khitat*, II, p. 324.
12 Maqrizi, *Khitat*, II, p. 391.
13 Maqrizi, *Khitat*, II, pp. 315, 391.
14 Ali Ibrahim and O'Kane, 'Tiled Mihrab'.
15 Maqrizi, *Khitat*, II, p. 463.
16 Index No. 140; Maqrizi, *Suluk*, III, pp. 339, 461; Van Berchem, pp. 242ff.

17 Maqrizi, *Khitat*, II, p. 327.
18 Van Berchem, p. 669.
19 Maqrizi, *Khitat*, II, p. 331; Van Berchem, pp. 581f., Behrens-Abouseif, *Minarets*, pp. 180f.
20 Garcin, 'L'Insertion', pp. 164ff.
21 Index No. 12; Ibn Iyas, III, pp. 259, 392, IV, p. 97, V, pp. 215, 267f.; Mubarak, IV, p. 110.
22 Qalqashandi, IV, p. 32.
23 Maqrizi, *Khitat*, II, p. 326; Meinecke, *Architektur*, II, p. 150.
24 Maqrizi, *Khitat*, II, p. 369.
25 Maqrizi, *Khitat*, II, p. 370.
26 Ibn Hajar, *Inba'*, I, pp. 146f; *Durar*, III, p. 26; Labib, p. 113.
27 Maqrizi, *Khitat*, II, p. 313.
28 Labib, pp. 112f.
29 Sakhawi, *Daw'*, VIII, pp. 260f.; Ibn Iyas, III, p. 293; Samhudi, II, pp. 605, 618.
30 Ibn Hajar, *Inba'*, II, pp. 196f.
31 Jawhari, *Nuzha*, II, p. 193.
32 Jawhari, *Nuzha*, II, pp. 336f.; Behrens-Abouseif, *Fath Allah*, pp. 7, 27–38.
33 Maqrizi, *Khitat*, II, p. 392; Van Berchem p. 246.
34 Maqrizi, *Khitat*, II, p. 325. I could not find the meaning of *kimakht*, but it may be equivalent to *kamkha*, a type of silk embroidered fabric. Jawhari (*Nuzha*, I, p. 295, II, p. 73.) mentioned it to be spread before the sultan's horse in processions.
35 Maqrizi, *Khitat*, II, p. 331.
36 Maqrizi, AFS ed., IV/1, p. 673.
37 Index No. 340; 'Abd al-Wahhab, *Masajid*, pp. 276–80.
38 Ibn Hajar, *Inba'*, IX, pp. 157ff.

Chapter 5

1 Ibn Iyas, V, p. 37.
2 Ibn Iyas, IV, p. 61.
3 Ibn Taghribirdi, *Hawadith*, VIII, p. 457.
4 Ibn Taghribirdi, *Hawadith*, I, pp. 117ff.
5 Ibn Taghribirdi, *Nujum*, XV, p. 457.
6 Ibn Taghribirdi, *Hawadith*, VIII, pp. 456f.
7 Qudsi, p. 116.
8 Zahiri, p. 88.
9 Maqrizi, *Khitat*, II, pp. 220f; Qalqashandi, IV, pp. 45ff.
10 Bora Keskiner drew my attention to this possible interpretation.
11 Qalqashandi, IV, pp. 6ff.
12 Maqrizi, *Suluk*, IV, pp. 61, 679, 689.
13 Maqrizi, *Suluk*, IV, p. 1221.
14 Ibn Taghribirdi, *Hawadith*, VIII, pp. 446ff.
15 Ibn Iyas, III, p. 32.
16 Ibn Taghribirdi, *Hawadith*, II, pp. 299, 307.

17 Jawhari, *Inba'*, p. 285.

18 Ibn Iyas, III, p. 339.

19 Maqrizi, *Khitat*, II, p. 92.

20 'Umari, p. 112.

21 Martel-Thoumian, *Civils*, p. 68.

22 Ibn Hajar, *Inba'*, III, pp. 325f.

23 Zahiri, pp. 86ff.

24 Qalqashandi, IV, pp. 44ff.; 'Umari, pp. 100ff.

25 Ibn Taghribirdi, *Nujum*, IX, p. 180.

26 See on this subject, Joergen S. Nielsen, 'Maẓalim', *EI*, 2nd. ed.; idem, *Secular Justice in an Islamic State: Maẓālim under the Baḥrī Mamlūks 662/1264–789/1387* (Istanbul 1985).

27 Contrary to N. Rabbat's statement in 'The Ideological significance of the Dar al-'Adl in the Medieval Islamic Orient', *International Journal of Middle East Studies*, 27 (1995), pp. 13–28, esp. p. 18, that the 'Dār al-'Adl' ceremony was downgraded, and at times totally suspended.

28 Maqrizi, *Suluk*, III, p. 566.

29 Maqrizi, *Suluk*, III, p. 943; idem, *Khitat*, II, pp. 207f.; Ibn Taghribirdi, *Nujum*, XII, p. 108; idem, *Manhal*, III, p. 336; Behrens-Abouseif, 'Citadel', pp. 61–4.

30 Ibn Taghribirdi, *Nujum*, XVI, p. 297.

31 Zahiri, p. 87; Ibn Iyas, III, pp. 60f., 77, 432.

32 Qalqashandi, IV, p. 7.

33 Dawadari, *Kanz*, p. 88.

34 Maqrizi, *Khitat*, II, p. 107.

35 Ibn Taghribirdi, *Hawadith*, III, p. 448.

36 Ibn Taghribirdi, *Nujum*, XI, p. 230.

37 Maqrizi, *Suluk*, IV, p. 622.

38 Jawhari, *Nuzha*, p. 295.

39 Zahiri, p. 86.

40 Ibn Taghribirdi, *Nujum*, XIV, p. 26.

41 Maqrizi, *Suluk*, III, p. 521; Ibn Taghribirdi, *Nujum*, XI, pp. 302f.

42 Ibn Taghribirdi, *Hawadith*, VIII, pp. 489 n.3, 529; idem, *Nujum*, XIV, p. 65.

43 Isma'il, 'mawakib'.

44 Jawhari, *Inba'*, p. 362.

45 Ibn Iyas, III, p. 121.

46 Ibn Taghribirdi, *Hawadith*, II, p. 341.

47 Ibn Taghribirdi, *Nujum*, XII, pp. 45ff.

48 Maqrizi, *Khitat*, II, p. 381.

49 Ibn Tahribirdi, *Nujum*, VIII, pp. 165–8.

50 Ibn Taghribirdi, *Nujum*, VI, pp. 612–5.

51 Maqrizi, *Suluk*, IV, pp. 724f.

52 Ibn Iyas, III, pp. 76f.

53 Ibn Iyas, III, pp. 162f.

54 Ibn Taghribirdi, *Nujum*, XV, p. 435; Maqrizi, *Suluk*, IV, p. 614.

55 Ibn Iyas, II, pp. 228, 324.

56 Maqrizi, *Suluk*, III, p. 252.

57 Ibn Taghribirdi, *Nujum*, IX, pp. 181, 189.

58 Maqrizi, *Suluk*, III, p. 491.

59 Ibn Taghribirdi, *Hawadith*, VIII, p. 541.

60 Ibn Taghribirdi, *Hawadith*, VIII, p. 502.

61 Maqrizi, *Suluk*, IV, pp. 435, 494, 499, 501, 502, 529, 537; 'Ayni, pp. 323, 356, 373.

62 Maqrizi, *Suluk*, IV, pp. 501ff., 534, 537; Ibn Taghribirdi, *Nujum*, XIV, p. 99.

63 Maqrizi, *Suluk*, IV, p. 480; Ibn Taghribirdi, *Nujum*, XIV, p. 64.

64 Maqrizi, *Suluk*, IV, pp. 501, 537.

65 Ibn Iyas, IV, pp. 276f.

66 Maqrizi, *Suluk*, III/1, p. 132; Qalqashandi, IV, p. 46.

67 Qalqashandi, III, p. 513.

68 Ibn Iyas, III, p. 330, IV, p. 298.

69 Behrens-Abouseif, 'European Arts and Crafts', p. 49.

70 Maqrizi, *Suluk*, IV, p. 487; Ibn Taghribirdi, *Nujum*, XIV, pp. 78f.

71 Ibn Taghribirdi, *Nujum*, XIV, p. 97; Maqrizi, *Suluk*, IV, pp. 531f.

72 On a similar occasion, Barsbay rode out to the southern outskirts near Birkat al-Habash, at al-Rasad, where he stood for a while and prayed for the flood: Maqrizi, *Suluk*, IV, p. 749.

73 Maqrizi, *Suluk*, IV, pp. 458, 459.

74 Ibn Taghribirdi, *Hawadith*, VIII, p. 469.

75 Ibn Iyas, III, p. 162.

76 Maqrizi, *Suluk*, II, p. 240.

77 Ibn Taghribirdi, *Hawadith*, VIII, p. 593.

78 Safadi, XVI, No. 481, pp. 447f.; Dawadari, *Kanz*, IX, p. 305; Ibn Hajar, *Durar*, II, No. 2025, p. 322; 'Abd Ar-Raziq, *La Femme*, p. 298.

79 Maqrizi, *Suluk*, II, p. 177.

80 Ibn Iyas, III, p. 104.

81 Ibn Iyas, IV, pp. 409f.

82 Ibn Iyas, IV, pp. 433, 441.

83 Ibn Taghribirdi, *Hawadith*, II, pp. 228f.

84 Other high officials recovering from illness were also celebrated with lights and music, and people anointing themselves with saffron.

85 Ibn Iyas, IV, p. 61; Melog, 'Mahmal'.

86 Ibn Iyas, IV, p. 325.

87 Ibn Iyas, IV, pp. 187, 206.

88 Ibn Iyas, V, pp. 38–45.

89 Ibn Iyas, V, p. 72.

90 Maqrizi, *Suluk*, III, p. 547, IV, p. 508.

91 Maqrizi, *Suluk*, IV, p. 302ff.

92 Maqrizi, *Suluk*, IV, pp. 302, 313ff.; Ibn Taghribirdi, *Nujum*, XIV, p. 26; al-'Ayni, *Sayf*, p. 332.

93 Ibn Iyas, IV, p. 212.

94 Nuwayri, XXIX, p.165.
95 Maqrizi, *Khitat*, II, p.183.
96 Maqrizi, *Suluk*, III, pp.626, 679.
97 Ibn Taghirbirdi, *Hawadith*, I, p.17.
98 Maqrizi, *Suluk*, IV, pp.1106, 1161, 1223, 1226.
99 Ibn Taghribirdi, *Hawadith*, II, p.219.
100 Jawhari, *Inba'*, pp.202, 244, 405.
101 Jawhari, *Inba'*, pp.334, 387.
102 Jawhari, *Inba'*, pp.383ff, 387, 396, 413.
103 Jawhari, *Inba'*, pp.9f.; Ibn Taghribirdi, *Hawadith*, III, p.673.
104 Maqrizi, *Suluk*, IV, p.1179.
105 Maqrizi, *Suluk*, II, p.285.
106 Maqrizi, *Khitat*, II, pp.219ff.
107 Tarsusi, pp.73f.
108 Ibn Taghribirdi, *Hawadith*, I, p.17; Maqrizi, *Suluk*, IV, p.530; Irwin, 'Privatization'.
109 Ibn Iyas, IV, pp.302, 312, 318, 320.
110 Ibn Iyas, V, p.92.
111 Necipoğlu, pp.254ff.; J.M. Rogers, 'Mehmed the Conqueror between East and West', in: *Bellini and the Orient*, exhibition catalogue, London 2006, pp.80–97.

Chapter 6

1 Maqrizi, *Khitat*, II, p.424.
2 James, *Qur'ans*, p.116.
3 Ibn Iyas, IV, p.69.
4 James, *Qur'ans* is the major source on the subject; idem, *Master Scribes*, pp.150–93; Atil, *Renaissance*, pp.24–47.
5 Martin Lings and Yasin Hamid Safadi, *The Qur'an*, London 1976, cat.90–2; Atil, *Renaissance*, cat.7, 8.
6 *Islamische Buchkunst aus 1000 Jahren*, Berlin 1980, cat.19; Atil, *Renaissance*, cat.9.
7 Flemming, 'Literary Activities'.
8 Ibn Taghribirdi, *Manhal*, IV, p.299.
9 Atil, 'Mamluk Painting'; idem, *Renaissance*, pp.250–3.
10 Maqrizi, *Khitat*, II, p.69.
11 For a documentation of Mamluk palaces and residences, see Garcin et al., *Palais*.
12 Labib, pp.104f., 328.
13 Leo Africanus, II, pp.206f.; Labib, pp.267f., 314f., 332.
14 Maqrizi, *Khitat*, II, pp.71f.; idem, *Suluk*, II, pp.481, 880f.
15 Ibn Iyas, III, pp.162f.
16 Maqrizi, *Khitat*, I, pp.373–7, II, pp.86–108; Raymond and Wiet, pp.85–216.
17 Labib, pp.293f., 327.
18 Mayer, *Costume*, Appendix I.
19 Jawhari, *Nuzha*, II, pp.73, 210, 211.
20 Ibn Iyas, III, p.200, V, p.24.

21 Ibn Taghribirdi, *Manhal*, VII, pp.5–13; Maqrizi, *Suluk*, II, pp.98ff.
22 Maqrizi, *Khitat*, II, p.101.
23 Maqrizi, *Khitat*, II, pp.72f.
24 Maqrizi, *Khitat*, II, p.73.
25 Jawhari, *Inba'*, p.261.
26 Abd ar-Raziq, *Femme*, pp.138ff.
27 Maqrizi, *Khitat*, II, p.68.
28 Maqrizi, *Khitat*, II, p.105.
29 Ibn Taghribirdi, *Hawadith*, I, p.67; Othman Mohd. Yatim, *Chinese Islamic Wares in the Collection of Muzium Negara*, Kuala Lumpur 1981, p.18.
30 Mayer, *Costume*, is a major source on this topic; Maqrizi, *Khitat*, II, pp.201, 216ff.
31 Maqrizi, *Suluk*, II, pp.524f.
32 Maqrizi, *Khitat*, II, pp.98f., 103.
33 Mustafa, *Index to Ibn Iyas*, IV (*Mustalahat*) p.430.
34 Ibn Iyas, IV, pp.200, 417, V, pp.41, 75.
35 Meinecke, 'Löwe, Lilie'; see also Mayer, *Saracenic*, and Meinecke, 'Heraldik'.
36 Ibn Shaddad, p.340; Rice, *Baptistère*; Behrens-Abouseif, 'Baptistère'; Meinecke, *Architektur*, I, p.30.
37 Al-Ashraf Khalil hall in the Citadel, called al-Rafraf, was likewise described as a domed pavilion on columns, with mural painting depicting emirs and dignitaries. Maqrizi, *Khitat*, II, p.213.
38 Qalqashandi, XIII, pp.162–6.
39 Allan, *Nuhad Es-Said Collection*, pp.24, 86f.
40 Balog, II, VII–X.
41 Ibn 'Abd al-Zahir, *Rawd*, p.82.
42 Oliver Watson, *Ceramics from Islamic Lands: Kuwait National Museum, The Al-Sabah Collection*, London 2004, pp.57f., 408–15.
43 Maqrizi, *Khitat*, II, pp.91, 92, 102, 104, 105, 136, 191; Raymond and Wiet, pp.233, 260.
44 Wiet, *Lampes et bouteilles*, pls LVIII–LXI.
45 It is mentioned in al-Nasir waqf deed for the Siryaqus khanqah, published by Amin, Appendix to Ibn Habib, II, p.432.
46 Melikian-Chirvani, 'Cuivres'; Lay A. Levenson (ed.), *Circa 1492, Art in the Age of Exploration*, exhibition catalogue, New Haven/London 1991, p.203, No. 95.
47 Melikian-Chirvani, 'Venise'; Allan, J.W. 'Venetian-Saracenic Metalwork: The Problem of Provenance', in: *Venezia e l'Oriente Vicino: Atti del Primo Simposio Internazionale sull Arte Veneziana e l'Arte Islamica*, Venice 1986; Behrens-Abouseif, 'Veneto-Saracenic'; Tim Stanley, *Palace and Mosque: Islamic Art from the Middle East*, London 2004, pp.90, 99; The generally accepted Mamluk attribution of this group had been recently contested by Sylvia Auld with purely speculative arguments in favour of an Aq Qoyunlu provenance that suffers from lack of

evidence of comparable material: *Renaissance Venice and Mahmud al-Kurdi*, London 2004, pp. 104–7; idem., 'Maître Mahmûd et les métaux inscrustés au XVe siècle', in: *Venise et l'Orient (828–1797)*, Paris 2006, pp. 212–25.
48 Jawhari, *Nuzha*, I, p. 135.
49 Marinetto, 'La Alfombra'.
50 Wiet, *Lampes et bouteilles*, pl. XC.
51 Qalqashandi, IV, p. 11.
52 Maqrizi, *Khitat*, II, pp. 98f.
53 Jawahri, *Inba'*, p. 261.
54 Ibn Tulun, pp. 51f.; Ibn Taghribirdi, *Manhal*, VI, p. 241; Maqrizi, *Khitat*, ed. A.F.S., IV/2, p. 664; idem, *Suluk*, III, pp. 272f.
55 Maqrizi, *Khitat*, II, pp. 101, 105; this quarter is also mentioned in the restoration protocol of the Rab' Zahiri dated 865/1461: Dar al-Watha'iq, 126/20.

Chapter 7

1 Qalqashandi, IV, p. 22; Zahiri, p. 115; on the building craft, see Behrens-Abouseif, 'Muhandis'.
2 Maqrizi, *Suluk*, II, p. 130.
3 Maqrizi, *Khitat*, II, p. 309; Ibn Hajar, *Durar*, I, p. 421.
4 Ibn Hajar, *Durar*, I, p. 418; Maqrizi, *Khitat*, II, p. 309.
5 Maqrizi, *Suluk*, II, pp. 71f., 438f., 453, 459f.
6 Maqrizi, *Suluk*, II, p. 813.
7 Qalqashandi, IV, p. 194, XI, p. 90.
8 Dar al-Watha'iq, 126/20, protocol of restoration dated Rabi' II 865/January–February 1461.
9 Maqrizi, *Suluk*, II, pp. 679f., 687, 702; idem, *Khitat*, II, pp. 73, 212; A.F.S ed., III, p. 680.
10 Maqrizi, *Khitat*, II, p. 384.
11 Ibn Taghribirdi, *Hawadith*, I, p. 16.
12 Sakhawi, *Daw'*, I, p. 243.
13 Meinecke, *Architektur*, II, p. 289.
14 Meinecke, *Architektur*, II, p. 336.
15 Ibn Iyas, II, pp. 390, 427, III, pp. 181f., 240, 283, 343, IV, p. 35, V, p. 161; Sakhawi, *Daw'*, III, p. 98.
16 Ibn Iyas, III, pp. 145, 170, 188, 293.
17 Two small cartouches on each side of the entrance bay read ''amal Muhammad Ibn Ahmad' and 'Ahmad Zaghlish al-Shami' respectively. According to 'Abd al-Wahhab, these are two names, and they refer to decorators. It is more likely, in my view, that the signature names one person, who is the builder, not the decorator, of the portal vault. 'Abd al-Wahhab, 'Tawqi'at', p. 555.
18 Van Berchem, pp. 298, 319, 350, 402, 470, 557.
19 Maqrizi, *Suluk*, II, p. 749.
20 Maqrizi, *Suluk*, II, pp. 228, 642; Nuwayri al-Sakandari, *Ilmam*, V, p. 196.
21 Maqrizi, *Suluk*, II, pp. 640f.; idem, *Khitat*, I, p. 423, II, pp. 188, 310, 517.
22 Nuwayri al-Sakandari, *Ilmam*, V, p. 196.
23 Maqrizi, *Suluk*, II, p. 302.
24 Jawhari, *Inba'*, p. 483.
25 Loiseau, 'Les Avatars du lit'.
26 Maqrizi, *Suluk*, III, p. 265; idem, *Khitat*, II, pp. 165–71.
27 Dawadari, IX, p. 266.
28 Maqrizi, *Suluk*, II, p. 334.
29 Van Berchem, pp. 465–72.
30 Ayalon, 'Payment', pp. 47f.; Labib, pp. 266f., 273f.
31 Maqrizi, *Suluk*, II, p. 130.
32 See the discussion of this subject in 'Abd al-Wahhab, 'al-Athar al-manqula'.
33 Maqrizi, *Khitat*, III, p. 276.
34 Maqrizi, *Khitat*, III, p. 371.
35 Maqrizi, *Suluk*, II, p. 334.
36 Maqrizi, *Suluk*, IV, p. 776; idem, *Khitat*, II, p. 92.
37 Van Berchem, pp. 740f.
38 'Abd al-Wahhab, 'al-Athar al-manqula', p. 267.
39 Ibn Taghribirdi, *Nujum*, XIV, pp. 43f.
40 Maqrizi, *Suluk*, II, p. 102.
41 Maqrizi, *Suluk*, II, p. 69; Van Berchem, pp. 465–72.
42 Amin, *Awqaf*, pp. 341–61.
43 Maqrizi, *Suluk*, IV, pp. 636f.
44 Ibn Iyas, IV, p. 52.
45 Maqrizi, *Suluk*, IV, pp. 346, 534, 712, 753; Ibn Taghribirdi, *Nujum*, XIV, p. 99.
46 Safadi, X, p. 340. This rate of 1/20 was valid throughout the Bahri period.
47 Abd al-Zahir, *Rawd*, p. 81.
48 Maqrizi, *Khitat*, II, p. 308.
49 Nuwayri, XXXIII, p. 201.
50 Amin, *Watha'iq waqf al-sultan Hasan*; idem, appendix to Ibn Habib, III, pp. 30, 82.
51 Maqrizi, *Suluk*, II, p. 406.
52 Maqrizi, *Suluk*, II, p. 309.
53 Maqrizi, *Khitat*, II, pp. 309, 325.
54 Maqrizi, *Suluk*, II, p. 815.
55 On the palaces, see Maqrizi, *Khitat*, II, pp. 51–79.
56 Also Ibn Taghribirdi, *Nujum*, IX, p. 188.
57 Maqrizi, *Suluk*, II, p. 130; idem, *Khitat*, II, p. 68.
58 Maqrizi, *Khitat*, II, p. 72; this extraordinary amount is repeated in the new *Khitat* edition by A. Fu'ad Sayyid: III, pp. 233–5.
59 August 2006.
60 Maqrizi, *Khitat*, II, p. 212.
61 Maqrizi, *Suluk*, II, pp. 632f, 679.
62 Maqrizi, *Khitat*, II, p. 212.
63 Maqrizi, *Suluk*, II, p. 130; idem, *Khitat*, II, p. 71.
64 Maqrizi, *Suluk*, II, p. 288, II, p. 536.

65 Maqrizi, *Suluk*, II, p. 814.
66 Ibn Taghribirdi, *Nujum*, IX, pp. 175f.
67 Maqrizi, *Suluk*, II, p. 125.
68 Maqrizi, *Khitat*, II, p. 211.
69 Maqrizi, *Khitat*, II, p. 210; idem, *Suluk*, II, p. 129.
70 Maqrizi, *Khitat*, II, p. 276.
71 Maqrizi, *Suluk*, III, p. 937; Jawhari, *Nuzha*, I, p. 496.
72 Jawhari, *Nuzha*, I, p. 476.
73 Maqrizi, *Suluk*, IV, p. 776.
74 Maqrizi, *Khitat*, II, pp. 328ff.
75 Maqrizi, *Suluk*, IV, p. 776.
76 Maqrizi, *Suluk*, IV, p. 457.
77 Maqrizi, *Suluk*, IV, p. 449.
78 Ibn Taghribirdi, *Hawadith*, II, p. 217.
79 Maqrizi, *Suluk*, IV, pp. 445, 452.
80 Ibn Iyas, II, p. 331.
81 See chapter 2 n. 61.
82 Ibn Iyas, III, pp. 63, 99.
83 Ibn Iyas, III, pp. 124, 306, 431.
84 Ibn Iyas, III, pp. 156, 169f., 188.
85 Ibn Iyas, III, pp. 240, 278f.
86 Behrens-Abouseif, 'Fire', p. 285.
87 Ibn Iyas, III, p. 61; Jawahri, *Inba'*, pp. 294, 339.
88 Ibn Iyas, III, p. 200, V, p. 24.
89 Ibn Iyas, III, p. 117.
90 Ibn Iyas, III, p. 412.
91 Jawhari, *Inba'*, p. 132.
92 Ibn Iyas, IV, p. 56.
93 Ibn Iyas, IV, p. 276.
94 Jawhari, *Inba'*, p. 8.
95 Maqrizi, *Suluk*, II, p. 214.
96 Maqrizi, *Suluk*, II, p. 536; Ibn Hajar, *Durar*, V, p. 127.
97 Maqrizi, *Suluk*, I, p. 627.
98 Jawhari, *Inba'*, p. 100.
99 Maqrizi, *Suluk*, II, p. 225.
100 Ayalon, 'Payment', pp. 51ff., 275f.

Chapter 8

1 Maqrizi, *Khitat*, II, pp. 151–2; MacKenzie, pp. 69ff.; Ibn Jubayr, p. 27.
2 Korn, II, pp. 11–43.
3 I am using here S. Denoix's figures, excluding the madrasas of Sanjar al-Jawli and Sarghitmish along the Saliba artery: Denoix, *Décrire*, pp. 95f.
4 Maqrizi, *Khitat*, II, p. 72.
5 Raymond, *Cairo*, pp. 7–80; Abu-Lughod, pp. 13–25; Denoix, *Décrire*, chapters 7–8.
6 Maqrizi, *Khitat*, I, p. 343; Behrens-Abouseif, 'Lost Minaret'.
7 Maqrizi, *Suluk*, IV, p. 302; idem, *Khitat*, II, p. 184; Ibn Duqmaq, IV, p. 92; Ibn Taghribirdi, *Nujum*, VII, p. 14. This madrasa was not included by Maqrizi in his list of religious monuments.
8 Ibn Duqmaq, IV, p. 96.
9 Ibn Iyas, I/1, p. 308.
10 Maqrizi, *Khitat*, II, pp. 276f.
11 Maqrizi, *Khitat*, II, pp. 290, 297, 297.
12 Maqrizi, *Khitat*, II, p. 297.
13 Ibn Shaddad, pp. 359ff.
14 Baybars was buried in Damascus in a mausoleum built by his son.
15 Maqrizi, *Khitat*, II, p. 430; Ibn Taghribirdi, *Nujum*, V, pp. 161f.
16 Maqrizi, *Khitat*, II, pp. 22, 136, 300.
17 Ibn Duqmaq, IV, p. 119; Maqrizi, *Khitat*, I, pp. 345f., II, p. 298.
18 Safadi, XXII, pp. 30f.
19 Maqrizi, *Khitat*, II, p. 370.
20 Maqrizi, *Khitat*, II, p. 427.
21 Ibn Duqmaq, IV, p. 78; Maqrizi, *Khitat*, II, pp. 298f.
22 Ibn Duqmaq, IV, p. 101.
23 Maqrizi, *Khitat*, II, pp. 159, 429; Safadi, I, p. 217, No. 146.
24 Safadi, IX, p. 478, No. 4438; Denoix, *Décrire*, p. 99.
25 Ibn Duqmaq, IV, pp. 55, 101; Maqrizi, *Khitat*, II, p. 298.
26 Maqrizi, *Khitat*, II, pp. 158f., 165; Ibn Duqmaq, IV, pp. 55, 78.
27 Safadi, IX, p. 478; Denoix, *Décrire*, p. 99.
28 This mosque, mentioned by Ibn Iyas (IV, pp. 8, 169) in his chronicle, was destroyed by French troops, as recorded by al-Jabarti, who described it with admiration. He used the plural *qibab* for domes and I assume they were a pair: Jabarti, III, p. 159.
29 Ayalon, 'Muslim City'; idem, 'Expansion and Decline'; Raymond, *Cairo*, chapter 4.
30 Ibn Taghribirdi, *Nujum*, IX, pp. 178–210.
31 Salmon, chapter 5.
32 Maqrizi, *Khitat*, II, pp. 71–3.
33 Garcin et al., pp. 51–9.
34 Maqrizi, *Khitat*, II, p. 444.
35 Maqrizi, *Khitat*, II, pp. 111f.
36 Behrens-Abouseif, 'Northeastern'.
37 Maqrizi, *Suluk*, IV, p. 529; Ibn Taghribirdi, *Nujum*, XIV, pp. 95, 96, 99.
38 Ibn Taghribirdi, *Nujum*, IX, p. 195.
39 Maqrizi, *Khitat*, II, p. 307.
40 Raymond, *Cairo*, p. 136.
41 Maqrizi, *Khitat*, I, pp. 343, 345, II, p. 304.
42 Dols, pp. 169ff.
43 This list is based on Creswell's brief chronology and the 'Index of Mohammedan Monuments', and does not include free-standing mausoleums.

44 This monument did not survive and its exact foundation date is not known.

45 Ibn Iyas, III, pp. 424, 437.

46 Maqrizi, *Khitat*, II, p. 331.

47 Ibn Taghribirdi, *Nujum*, XI, pp. 186f.; Raymond, *Cairo*, p. 179.

48 On Bulaq see Hanna.

49 See J. Williams, 'Siryaqus'.

50 Ibn Taghribirdi, *Nujum*, XIV, pp. 94, 105f.; idem, *Hawadith*, II, p. 217; Maqrizi, *Suluk*, IV, pp. 526, 528, 538, 541.

51 Ibn Taghribirdi, *Nujum*, XIV, p. 105.

52 Al-'Ayni, IV, pp. 108f.

53 Maqrizi, *Suluk*, IV, p. 386.

54 Ibn Taghribirdi, *Nujum*, XV, p. 348.

55 Ibn Taghribirdi, *Nujum*, XV, p. 118; idem, *Hawadith*, II, p. 307.

56 Ibn Taghribirdi, *Hawadith*, II, p. 321, III, pp. 566–9, IV, pp. 766–9, 800–3; idem, *Manhal*, IV, pp. 243–8; *Nujum*, XVI, pp. 322f.; Ibn Iyas, II, pp. 406, 449; Sakhawi, *Daw'*, III, pp. 57–9.

57 Sakhawi, *Daw'*, VI, pp. 201ff.; Ibn Iyas, III, p. 329.

58 Behrens-Abouseif, 'Patrons of Urbanism', 'Qaytbay's Investments'; Newhall, pp. 264f.

59 Meinecke, *Architektur*, II, pp. 396–442; Van Berchem, pp. 431–547; Creswell, *Chronology*, pp. 139–49; Ibn Iyas, III, pp. 329f.; Sakhawi, *Daw'*, VI, pp. 201–11.

60 Sakhawi, *Daw'*, X, pp. 272–4; Ibn Iyas, III, pp. 134, 160, 173, 189; Behrens-Abouseif, 'Northeastern', 'Mamluk Suburb'.

61 Behrens-Abouseif, *Azbakiyya*, pp. 3–25.

62 Ibn Iyas, III, pp. 127f., 138; Raymond and Wiet, pp. 54f.

63 Maqdisi, *Fawa'id*.

64 Evliya Çelebi, pp. 397, 484, 1043. A description of the complex is included in the archive of al-Bab al-'Ali, 265/230, pp. 171f.

65 Ali Ibrahim, 'Middle-class'.

66 Raymond and Wiet, *Marchés*; Labib, chapter 8.

67 Maqrizi, *Khitat*, II, p. 94; Ibn Iyas, III, pp. 100, 329, IV, pp. 230, 237, 243, 248; Raymond and Wiet, *Marchés*, pp. 143–5, 223–7.

68 Leo Africanus, II, pp. 206f.

69 Ibn Iyas, IV, pp. 56, 60, 137f, 172ff.

70 Maqrizi, *Khitat*, II, pp. 197ff.

71 Behrens-Abouseif, *Azbakiyya*, pp. 19–22.

72 Maqrizi, *Khitat*, II, pp. 244f.

Chapter 9

1 Behrens-Abouseif, 'The Façade of the Aqmar-Mosque in the Context of Fatimid Ceremonial', *Muqarnas*, IX (1992), pp. 29–38.

2 Meinecke, *Architektur*, I, fig. 29.

3 Salam-Liebich, pp. 68ff.; Meinecke, *Architektur*, I, pp. 109, 193; for the Mamluk architecture of Syria, this is the major study to consult.

4 Meinecke, *Architektur*, I, p. 111.

5 This minaret might be a Crusader tower.

6 Meinecke, *Architektur*, I, pls 128, 129.

7 Degeorge, p. 134.

8 Creswell, *MAE*, II, p. 146.

9 'Umari, *Masalik*, I, p. 193.

10 See Meinecke, 'Syrian Blue-and-white'; Carswell, 'Six Tiles'; Degeorge, figs, pp. 145–7; Gibbs, pp. 35f.

11 Prost, pp. 11–12, pls IV, VI.

12 On Egyptian provincial architecture, see 'Abd al-Wahhab, 'Tarz'; Behrens-Abouseif, 'Notes'; Garcin, 'Le Caire et la province'.

13 Evliya, p. 740; Mubarak, XI, p. 55 ; 'Abd al-Wahhab, 'Tarz', p. 19, pls 9, 10; *The Mosques of Egypt*, II, pl. 241; Meinecke, *Architektur*, II, p. 380.

14 Garcin, 'Le Caire et la province', p. 60.

15 See the architectural survey in Walls, *Geometry*.

16 Baybars and Faraj each sponsored a zawiya in Jerusalem: Richards in Burgoyne, *Jerusalem*, p. 68.

17 Amin, *Watha'iq waqf al-sultan Hasan*, p. 4.

18 Burgoyne, pp. 399ff.

19 Ebers, I, p. 85.

20 *The Mosques of Egypt*, II, pl. 215.

21 Ayalon, 'The Muslim City', p. 319; idem, 'Studies', p. 205.

Chapter 10

1 Evliya, pp. 211f., Arabic transl., p. 289.

2 Index No. 85; Hamza, 'Tankizbugha'.

3 Index Nos 290, 291.

4 See the publication of this view by Warner, *True Description*.

5 Isma'il, *al-Usul al-mamlukiyya*, pp. 58f.

6 Index Nos 138, 247; Van Berchem, pp. 207ff.

7 Maqrizi, *Khitat*, II, p. 212.

8 Meinecke, *Architektur*, II, p. 388.

9 Index No. 233; Van Berchem, pp. 169f.; Creswell, *MAE*, II, pp. 269f.

10 Index No. 205; Evliya, p. 229, Arabic transl. p. 308.; Creswell, *MAE*, II, p. 269f.; Meinecke, *Architektur*, II, p. 173.

11 Index No. 252; Van Berchem, pp. 193f.; C. Williams, 'Sitt Hadaq'; 'Abd Ar-Raziq, 'Trois fondations', pp. 97–111.

12 Index No. 253; Van Berchem, pp. 198–200; Meinecke, *Architektur*, II, p. 201.

13 Index No. 127; Sakhawi, *Daw'*, III, p. 275; Mubarak, V, p. 21; Dar al-Watha'iq 58/10, dated 804H.; Meinecke, *Architektur*, II, p. 299; Warner, *Monuments*, p. 109

14 Karim, 'Aslam'.

15 O'Kane, 'Domestic and Religious', p. 159.

16 Index No. 36; Speiser, chapter 5.

17 Index Nos 242, 250, 151.

18 Index No. 35.

19 Index No. 82.

20 Index No. 129; Herz, *Ganem el-Bahlaouan*.

21 Index Nos 118, 117.

22 Amin and Ali Ibrahim, *Architectural Terms*, p. 50.

23 Index No. 134.

24 Index No. 300; Harithy, 'Turbat al-Sitt'.

25 'Abd Ar-Raziq, 'Trois fondations', pp. 111–26.

26 Ali Ibrahim, 'Great Hanqah'.

27 Index No. 223.

28 Kessler, 'Funerary Architecture'.

29 Kessler, 'Mecca-oriented'.

30 Creswell, *MAE*, II, pp. 269f.

31 For the evolution of Mamluk minarets, and for drawings and photographs, see Behrens-Abouseif, *Minarets*.

32 Salam-Liebich, pp. 69ff.

33 Index No. 237; Creswell, *MAE*, II, pp. 140f.

34 Behrens-Abouseif, 'Lighthouse'.

35 Index No. 156.

36 The top was restored by the Comité on the basis of the original remains.

37 Abu 'l-'Amayim; my previous dating (*Minarets*, pp. 85f.), of this minaret to 1340s should be corrected to a decade earlier; its identification still poses problems.

38 Index Nos 185, 151.

39 G. Goodwin, *A History of Ottoman Architecture*, London 1987, p. 99.

40 This discussion of the evolution of the masonry domes is based on Kessler, *Domes*.

41 Index No. 298, Kessler, *Domes*, pl. 9.

42 On the transitional zone of domes, see Ali Ibrahim, 'Transitional Zones'.

43 Meinecke, *Architektur*, I, p. 89.

44 Harithy, 'Turbat al-Sitt', figs 5, 6.

45 Meinecke, *Architektur*, I, p. 91.

46 Creswell, *MAE*, II, p. 237, n. 7; Ali Ibrahim and O'Kane, 'Tiled Mihrab', pl. XIVa.

47 Creswell, *Chronology*, pp. 114f.; Kessler, *Domes*, p. 16.

48 Ihsanoğlu et al., pl. 83.

49 Dar al-Watha'q, 58/10; excerpts published by 'Abd al-Sattar 'Uthman, pp. 469–73, 485f.

50 Meinecke, *Architektur*, I, p. 127, pl. 78c.

51 Creswell, *MAE*, II, pl. 103.d.

52 Index No. 56.

53 Clerget, I, pp. 194ff.; Garcin et al., *Palais et Maisons*, pp. 221–58; Riederer in: Meinecke et al., *Restaurierung*, pp. 140f.; Meinecke, 'Baumaterialien'.

54 See Ali Ibrahim and O'Kane, 'Tiled Mihrab'.

55 Prost, p. 11, pl. IV/1.

56 Marilyn Jenkins, *Islamic Art in the Kuwait National Museum*, London 1983, p. 85.

57 Kessler, *Domes*, fig. 40.

58 The recent restoration wrongly added a dado to the entire courtyard and to the three other iwans.

59 Creswell, *MAE*, II, pls 106–14.

60 Ali Ibrahim, 'Four Mihrabs'.

61 Creswell, *MAE*, II, pl. 113.

62 Meinecke, 'Heraldik', p. 251.

63 Maqrizi, *Khitat*, II, p. 383.

64 'Abd al-Wahhab, 'al-Athar al-manqula'.

65 James, *Qur'ans*, fig. 141.

66 On the style of the Bahri minbars, see Karnouk, 'Minbar'.

67 Sixty years ago in his documentation of Cairo's monuments and in his articles, Hasan 'Abd al-Wahhab drew attention to the original wooden furniture and the modern restoration works. This work needs now to be updated.

68 'Abd al-Wahhab, 'Tawqi'at', pp. 547f.

69 Van Berchem, p. 581.

70 'Abd al-Wahhab, *Masajid*, II, p. 228, figs 165, 167, 168; Sakhawi, *Daw'*, II, p. 59.

71 Sakhawi, *Daw'*, VII, p. 35.

72 'Abd al-Wahhab, *Masajid*, II, figs 209, 210.

73 Marble minbars are in the mosques of Aqsunqur and Sultan Hasan; Qaytbay added a stone minbar to Faraj's khanqah. Maqrizi (*Khitat*, II, p. 312) mentions a marble minbar in the mosque of al-Khatiri.

74 'Abd al-Wahhab, 'al-Athar al-manqula', p. 267.

75 Van Berchem, pp. 145, 437, 540.

76 This is also confirmed by Bernard O'Kane, on the basis of the epigraphic database (*Documentation*) he and his team have undertaken on the monuments of Cairo. Personal communication by O'Kane.

77 Van Berchem, p. 495.

78 It is not published.

79 O'Kane et al., *Documentation*, Nos 164.1, 324.2, 519.1.

80 Ali Ibrahim, 'Zawiya', p. 106.

81 Van Berchem, pp. 533ff.

82 Ministry of Waqf 1143 ; Van Berchem, p. 295ff.

83 Van Berchem, pp. 295, 316.

84 Van Berchem, p. 434, n. 1.

85 Index No. 255; *Dalil*, pp. 61f.; Van Berchem, pp. 579f.

86 Warner, *Monuments*, p. 135, map 8.

87 Index No. 51; Van Berchem, pp. 541–7; Creswell, *MAE*, II, p. 195.

88 Franz Pascha, *Die Baukunst des Islams*, Darmstadt 1887, pp. 34–66. (=Die Baustile. Historische und technische Entwicklung. Des Handbuches der Architektur, zweiter Teil 3. Band zweite Hälfte).

89 Garcin et al., *Palais et maisons du Caire*, I, pp. 219–40; Philipp Speiser, 'La Restauration du Palais Bastak', *L'habitat traditionnel dans les pays musulmans autour de la Méditerranée*, III, Cairo 1990, pp. 809–26, pls CCXXXIII–CCXLIV; idem, *Erhaltung*, pp. 174–6, 184f.; figs 71, 73, Pls 35b, c and 38a, b.

90 Burgoyne, pp. 88–97.

91 Large blocks of granite were reused in the construction of the gate of the mosque of Mu'yyad Shaykh in Cairo and the fortress of Qaytbay in Alexandria.

92 On the ancient quarries cf. Rosemarie and Dietrich D. Klemm, *Steine und Steinbrüche im Alten Ägypten*, Berlin/Heidelberg/New York 1992; on some Egyptian quarries, see U.F. Hume, *The Building Stones of Cairo's Neighbourhood and Upper Egypt*, Cairo 1910.

93 The so-called 'red stone' is famous for its durability.

94 Ibn Iyas, I/2, p. 350.

95 Cf Burgoyne, p. 41.

96 G. Wiet, 'Deux Princes ottomans à la cour d'Egypte', *Bulletin de l'nstitut d'Eypte*, XX (1937–38), pp. 149f.; Heyd, II, p. 538; Ibn Taghribirdi, *Hawadith*, II, p. 255, III, p. 470; Labib, pp. 111, 330, 488.

97 On the use of traditional building materials in the nineteenth century, see Edouard Mariette, *Traité pratique et raisonné de la construction en Egypte*, I, Alexandra, pp. 71–4.

98 This construction mode was in use since pharaonic times and derived from mud-brick structures.

99 Burgoyne, p. 90.

100 In Egypt they are called *massarani*, with reference to the quarries of Massara.

101 I had several of this type of stairs reconstructed in 1980 and 1983; see Speiser, *La Restauration*, p. 821f. fig. 8 and pl. CCXLb.

102 Since the late nineteenth century, cement tiles have been used instead.

103 Speiser, 'La Restauration', p. 823, fig. 10, pl. CCLXII A.

104 Franz Pascha, *Baukunst*, p. 40, fig. 30; Speiser, *Erhaltung*, p. 184 fig. 71a, b.

105 Speiser, 'La Restauration', pl. CCXLI B.

106 Burgoyne, p. 90f.

107 On the use of vaults or flat ceilings, see O'Kane, 'Domestic and Religious', pp. 157–9.

108 Curiously enough the empty space between arch and lintel is often blocked by brick or small stone.

109 Cf. the Bab al-'Askar, which is part of the Bashtak-Palace in Cairo.

110 The only case known to the author of externally fixed shutters is at the fortress of Qaytbay in Alexandria.

111 Burgoyne, p. 93ff.

Chapter 11

1 Index Nos 38, 169; Maqrizi, *Khitat*, II, pp. 374f., 380, 420; Van Berchem, pp. 104ff.; Creswell, *MAE*, II, pp. 100–4; Kessler, 'Funerary', p. 258.

2 Zahiri, p. 86.

3 Maqrizi, *Khitat*, II, p. 102.

4 Maqrizi, *Khitat*, I, p. 343; Sakhawi, *Tuhfa*, pp. 118f.; Van Berchem, pp. 116f.; Creswell, *MAE*, II, pp. 136f.; Behrens-Abouseif, 'Lost Minaret'.

5 Sakhawi, *Tuhfa*, p. 136. The date indicated here for the renovation of the mausoleum's decoration 582/1186 is not compatible with the reign of al-Hafiz, and is likely to be a misreading of 532/1137–8.

6 Ibn Taghribirdi, *Nujum*, VII, p. 14.

7 Ibn Duqmaq, IV, pp. 12f., 30, 35, 53f., 80, 92f., 104; Maqrizi, *Suluk*, IV, p. 302; idem, *Khitat*, II, p. 184.

8 Meinecke, *Architektur*, II, p. 2.

Chapter 12

1 Index No. 37; Ibn Shaddad, p. 344; Ibn 'Abd al-Zahir, *Rawd*, pp. 90f.; Maqrizi, *Khitat* II, pp. 82, 378f.; Safadi, X, pp. 339–43; Ibn Taghribirdi, *Nujum*, V, pp. 190–97; Evliya, p. 209, Arabic transl. p. 286; Creswell, *MAE*, II, pp. 143–54, pl. 45a, b.; Meinecke, *Architektur*, I, pp. 26f., I, pp. 6–51. Besides the nineteenth-century illustrations published by Creswell, figs 72, 73, pl. 45a, b; Ravaisse, pp. 450f.; a watercolor painting by Amadeo Preziosi in 1862 depicts part of Baybars' madrasa: Caroline Juler, *Les Orientalistes d'Ecole Italienne*, Paris 1994, p. 129; Van Berchem, pp. 119f.

2 Ibn Iyas I/1, p. 308.

3 Maqrizi, *Khitat*, II, p. 300.

4 'Abd al-Wahhab, 'al-Athar al-manqula', p. 264.

5 Index No. 1; Ibn Shaddad, p. 346; Maqrizi, *Khitat*, II, pp. 299ff.; Van Berchem, pp. 121–23; Creswell, *MAE*, II, pp. 155–72; Bloom, 'The Mosque of Baybars'; Humphreys, 'Expressive Intent'; Meinecke, *Architektur*, II, p. 26.

6 Maqrizi, *Khitat*, II, p. 21.

7 Maqrizi, *Khitat*, II, p. 136; Amin, appendix to Ibn Habib I, pp. 238–41.

8 Maqrizi, *Khitat*, II, p. 23.

9 Maqrizi, *Khitat*, II, p. 197.

10 Baybars al-Mansuri, p. 59.

11 Maqrizi, *Khitat*, II, p. 430; Thorau, pp. 225ff.

12 Ibn Shaddad, p. 346; Sakhawi, *Tuhfa*, pp. 22ff.

13 Ibn Taghribirdi, *Nujum*, VII, p. 163.

14 Ibn 'Abd al-Zahir, *Rawd*, p. 293.

15 Baybars al-Mansuri, p. 117.

16 Maqrizi, *Suluk*, I, pp. 452ff.

17 Behrens-Abouseif, *Minarets*, pp. 170f.

18 Creswell, *MAE*, ɪɪ, pp. 149, 158.

19 Meinecke, *Architektur*, ɪ, p. 33.

20 Behrens-Abouseif, 'Citadel', figs 6, 7, 9.

21 Evliya, p. 199, Arabic transl. p. 276.

22 Leisten, pp. 19f.

23 Ibn 'Abd al-Zahir, *Rawd*, p. 71.

24 Index No. 276; Suyuti, *Husn*, ɪɪ, p. 62; Sakhawi, *Tuhfa*, p. 136; Creswell, *MAE*, ɪɪ, pp. 88–94; Meinecke, *Architektur*, ɪɪ, p. 24; Ali Ibrahim, 'Zayn al-Din', p. 82 n. 23.

25 Ibn Shaddad, p. 247; Yusufi, pp. 155, 156; Sakhawi, *Tuhfa*, pp. 390, 391. The term *hawsh* here means graveyard.

Chapter 13

1 Index No. 274; Ibn Duqmaq, ɪᴠ, pp. 125; Maqrizi, *Khitat*, ɪɪ, p. 394; Baybars al-Mansuri, p. 236; Creswell, *MAE*, ɪɪ, pp. 180ff., pls 60 a, b; Meinecke, *Architektur*, ɪ, p. 43, ɪɪ, pp. 60f.

2 Archive of Prisse d'Avennes, *Bibliothèque Nationale*, Paris; Behrens-Abouseif, *Minarets*, pp. 71, 72.

3 Index No. 43; Ministry of Waqf 1010; waqf description of the hospital published in: Amin, appendix of Ibn Habib, ɪ, pp. 295ff.; Issa, pp. 44–69; waqf description of the madrasa published in: Sayf al-Nasr, 'Madrasat al-sultan al-mansur'; Maqrizi, *Khitat*, ɪɪ, pp. 379ff., 406ff.; Nuwayri, xxxɪ, pp. 105–13; Mubarak, ᴠ, pp. 99f.; Coste, pl. xᴠɪɪ; *Toutes les Egypte*, pp. 125f.; Herz, *Baugruppe*; Creswell, *MAE*, ɪɪ, pp. 191–212; 'Abd al-Wahhab, *Masajid*, pp. 114–23; Meinecke, 'Mausoleum'; idem, *Architektur*, ɪɪ, p. 61; Northrup, pp. 119–24; Denoix et al., *Khan al-Khalili*, p. 35; al-Haddad, *al-Sultan al-Mansur*, pp. 109–82.

4 Northrup, p. 122.

5 Ibn Duqmaq, ɪᴠ, p. 38.

6 Ibn 'Abd al-Zahir, *Altaf*, fols 97–116; Moberg, 'Waqf-Urkunden'.

7 Ibn 'Abd al-Zahir, *Altaf*, fols 131–58.

8 Nuwayri, xxxɪɪɪ, pp. 200f.; Maqrizi, *Suluk*, ɪɪ, pp. 273f.

9 Jabarti, ɪɪ, p. 6.

10 Shafi', p. 408.

11 Cited by Northrup, p. 119.

12 Ibn Iyas, ɪɪɪ, p. 301.

13 Although Baybars's madrasa, as depicted by Cassas in the eighteenth century, had been altered by dwellings on the upper floor, its recesses, which are slightly lower than the portal vault, and include two tiers of windows, indicate the original height of the facade.

14 Ibn 'Abd al-Zahir, *Altaf*, fol. 108v.

15 Behrens-Abouseif, 'Sicily'.

16 Ibn 'Abd al-Zahir, *Altaf*, fol. 107.

17 Jabarti, ɪɪ, p. 6; Issa, pp. 69ff.

18 Pajares-Ayuela, pp. 42ff.

19 S.A. D'Aniello, 'Il Pavimiento Musivo del Duomo di Salerno' in: Agostino Cilardo (ed.), *Presenza Araba e Islamica in Campania*, Naples 1992, pp. 237–49, esp. p. 241.

20 Van Berchem, p. 133.

21 Lynne Thornton, *Les Orientalistes*, Paris 1983, p. 32.

22 This kind of praise occurs also in the waqf deed of Sultan Faraj's Duhaysha, as discussed below.

23 Evliya, pp. 262f., Arabic transl. pp. 346ff.

24 Creswell, *MAE*, ɪɪ, pl. 63.

25 Index No. 275; Ibn 'Abd al-Zahir, *Altaf*, fols 116–31; Maqrizi, *Khitat*, ɪᴠ/2, ed. AFS, p. 673; idem, *Suluk*, ɪ, p. 769; Moberg, 'Waqf-urkunden'; Van Berchem, pp. 141f.; Creswell, *MAE*, ɪɪ, pp. 213–8; Meinecke, *Architektur*, ɪɪ, p. 67.

26 Maqrizi, *Khitat*, ɪɪ, p. 276.

27 Ibn Duqmaq, ɪᴠ, pp. 124f.; Maqrizi, *Khitat*, ɪɪ, p. 239; idem, *Suluk*, ɪ, p. 790.

28 Ibn 'Abd al-Zahir, *Altaf*, fols 152v; 177.

29 Index No. 245; Maqrizi, *Khitat*, ɪɪ, p. 428; Ali Ibrahim, 'Four Cairene Mihrabs'; Creswell, *MAE*, ɪɪ, pp. 220f.; Behrens-Abouseif, *Minarets*, p. 175; Carboni, 'Painted Glass'.

30 Amin and Ali Ibrahim, *Architectural Terms*, p. 57.

31 Ihsanoğlu et al., pl. 41.

32 Creswell, *MAE*, ɪ, p. 55.

33 Index Nos 279, 869; Sakhawi, *Tuhfa*, pp. 187f.; Ibn Taghribirdi, *Manhal*, ɪᴠ, pp. 243–8; idem, *Nujum*, xᴠɪ, pp. 322–4; idem, *Hawadith*, ɪᴠ, pp. 800ff.; Van Berchem, pp. 411–21; Creswell, *MAE*, ɪɪ, pp. 178–80; idem, *Chronology*, p. 136; Shafi'i, pp. 32f.; Meinecke, *Architektur*, ɪɪ, p. 384.

34 I could not find his biography.

35 *The Mosques of Egypt*, ɪɪ, pl. 239.

Chapter 14

1 Index No. 172; Ibn Habib, ɪ, p. 207; Maqrizi, *Khitat*, ɪɪ, pp. 435 ff.; Van Berchem, pp. 148 ff.; Creswell, *MAE*, ɪɪ, pp. 229ff.; Ali Ibrahim, 'Zawiya'.

2 Franz Taeschner, *Zünfte und Bruderschaften im Islam*, Munich 1979, pp. 221–225; Ibn 'Abd al-Zahir, *Altaf*, fol. 91.

3 See the entry on this building below.

4 Laila Ali Ibrahim told me that this new information invalidated some of her arguments in her article.

5 Index No. 44; Nuwayri, xxxɪɪ, pp. 60–74; Maqrizi, *Khitat*, ɪɪ, p. 382; Van Berchem, pp. 152–5; Creswell, *MAE*, ɪɪ, pp. 234–40; Behrens-Abouseif, *Minarets*, pp. 73f.; Little, 'Mamluk Madrasahs'.

6 Ismail, 'Qaysariyya'.

7 Maqrizi, *Khitat*, ɪɪ, pp. 304f.

8   Amin, appendix to Ibn Habib, II, pp. 401ff.; J.A. Williams'
    interpretation of the document is not exact.
9   Index No. 221; Maqrizi, *Suluk*, II, pp. 24, 674; idem, *Khitat*,
    II, pp. 398, 421; Ibn Hajar, *Durar*, II, pp. 266, 276f.; Safadi,
    XV, pp. 482f., 242 ff.; XVI, pp. 55f.; Ibn Taghribirdi, *Manhal*,
    VI, pp. 5–13; Van Berchem, pp. 157–60; Creswell, *MAE*, II,
    pp. 242–8; 'Abd al-Wahhab, *Masajid*, pp. 124–30.
10 Maqrizi, *Suluk*, II, p. 748.
11 Index No. 32; Maqrizi, *Khitat*, II, p. 416; Creswell, *MAE*,
    II, pp. 249–53; Van Berchem, pp. 161–6; 'Abd-al-Wahhab,
    Masajid, pp. 131–5; Fernandes, 'Baybars'; Behrens-
    Abouseif, *Minarets*, p. 172, fig. 106.
12 This phrase confirms the equivalence of ribat and zawiya
    in Egyptian terminology of the time.
13 'Abd al-Wahhab, 'al-Athar al-manqula', p. 256.
14 Behrens-Abouseif, *Minarets*, p. 173.
15 Index No. 263; Maqrizi, *Khitat*, II, p. 397; Ibn Hajar,
    Durar, II, pp. 273, 304f.; Yusufi, p. 440; Ibn Iyas, I/1, p. 458;
    Van Berchem, pp. 733–6; Creswell, *MAE*, II, pp. 267ff.;
    'Abd al-Rahman Fahmi, 'Maqama'.
16 The *sharbush*, as described by Maqrizi in connection with
    the market where it was sold, is a ceremonial cap.
17 The phrases in rectangular brackets are additions to the
    text of the *maqama*; those in round brackets have been
    omitted.
18 Koran, XXXVII, 59.
19 The two seas: sweet and salty water.
20 The two moons: sun and moon.
21 The two stones: the stone in the Ka'ba and Abraham's
    stone altar in Jerusalem.

Chapter 15

1   Ibn Duqmaq, IV, pp. 76f.; Maqrizi, *Khitat*, II, p. 304; Evliya,
    pp. 309f., Arabic transl. pp. 396f.; Meinecke-Berg, 'Quellen
    zur Topographie'; Meinecke, *Architektur*, II, p. 110.
2   Also in Ibn Iyas, IV, p. 110.
3   Index No. 202; Creswell Archive, Ashmolean Museum,
    Oxford; Maqrizi, *Suluk*, II, p. 320; idem, *Khitat*, II,
    p. 307; Mubarak, V, pp. 387f.; Prisse d'Avennes, p. 128;
    Mehren, II, pp. 44f; Van Berchem, pp. 179f.; 'Abd al-
    Wahhab, *Masajid*, pp. 139–42; Meinecke, *Architektur*, I,
    fig. 29, II, p. 155.
4   Ali Ibrahim, 'Great Hanqah'.
5   Maqrizi, *Suluk*, II, p. 320; idem, *Khitat*, II, p. 307;
    Evliya, p. 227, Arabic transl. p. 306; Donald N. Wilber,
    The Architecture of Islamic Iran in the Ilkhanid Period,
    Princeton 1955, pp. 146ff.
6   The bronze door of this gate is, according to Creswell,
    No. 1057 in the Islamic Museum.

7   Index No. 143; Nuwayri, XXXII, p. 283; 'Umari, pp. 79ff;
    Maqrizi, *Khitat*, II, pp. 206, 209, 212, 321; idem, *Suluk*,
    II, pp. 123, 129, 184, 380; Evliya, pp. 213f., Arabic transl.,
    pp. 291f.; Meinecke, 'Fayencemosaikdekorationen', pp. 97–
    107; idem, *Architektur*, II, p. 122; Rabbat, *Citadel*, pp. 187f.;
    Christel Kessler, unpublished paper in the Creswell
    Archive, Ashmolean Museum, Oxford.
8   The same information is in Ibn Abi 'l-Fada'il, pp. 57, 58
    (Arabic text).
9   Yusufi, p. 241.
10 Dawadari, IX, pp. 293, 382.
11 Dawadari, IX, p. 238.
12 Ibn Iyas, IV, pp. 245, 441.
13 Bates, pp. 39, 45 n. 5.
14 Index Nos 115, 24; Maqrizi, *Khitat*, II, p. 392; Van Berchem,
    pp. 170f.; Creswell, *MAE*, II, pp. 270–2.
15 Maqrizi, *Khitat*, II, p. 399; Van Berchem, pp. 172–7;
    Creswell, *MAE*, II, pp. 273f.
16 Index No. 130; Safadi, IX, p. 371; Maqrizi, *Khitat*, II, p. 307;
    Mubarak, IV, p. 60; Van Berchem, p. 176; 'Abd al-Wahhab,
    Masajid, pp. 136–8; Kessler, 'Funerary Architecture', p. 265;
    Behrens-Abouseif, *Minarets*, p. 162; Karim, 'The Mosque
    of Ulmas'.
17 Creswell, *MAE*, II, p. 162.
18 Index No. 120; Maqrizi, *Khitat*, II, p. 308; Yusufi,
    pp. 265ff.; Safadi IX, pp. 364ff.; 'Abd al-Wahhab,
    Masajid, pp. 147–51; Van Berchem, pp. 190f.; Meinecke,
    Architektur, II, p. 178.
19 Karnouk, 'Minbar', p. 123.
20 O'Kane, 'The Arboreal Aesthetic'. Laila Ali Ibrahim told
    me that there were similar ones in the funerary khanqah
    of Tughay, which vanished years ago.
21 Index No 112; Maqrizi, *Khitat*, II, p. 309; Van Berchem,
    pp. 195f.; Karim, 'Aslam'.
22 Abd Ar-Raziq, 'Trois Fondations', pp. 111–26.
23 Index No. 123; Maqrizi, *Khitat*, II, p. 309; Mubarak,
    IV, pp. 44f.; Van Berchem, pp. 197f., 200–6; Creswell,
    Chronology, pp. 102ff.; 'Abd al-Wahhab, *Masajid*,
    pp. 152–5; Behrens-Abouseif, *Minarets*, pp. 91f.; Meinecke,
    'Aqsunqur'; idem, *Architektur*, II, p. 134.
24 Maqrizi, *Suluk*, II, pp. 744, 748.

Chapter 16

1   Index Nos 147, 152; Maqrizi, *Khitat*, II, pp. 321, 421;
    idem, *Suluk*, II, p. 17; Mubarak, V, pp. 34–7; Van
    Berchem, pp. 231–42; 'Abd al-Wahhab, *Masajid*,
    pp. 156–9; Kessler, 'Funerary', pp. 259, 263; Meinecke,
    Architektur, II, pp. 223f.
2   Maqrizi, *Suluk*, II, p. 864.

3   Index No. 218; Ministry of Waqf 3195; Maqrizi, *Khitat*, II, p. 403; Mubarak, V, p. 38; 'Abd al-Wahhab, *Masajid*, pp. 160–4; Van Berchem, pp. 240ff.; Kessler, 'Funerary'; Ibrahim, 'Min al-watha'iq'; Meinecke, 'Fayencemosaikdekorationen', p. 133; idem, *Architektur*, II, p. 223.

4   Ebers, I, p. 347.

5   Index No. 133; Dar al-Watha'iq, Nos 40/6, 365/85 and waqf publication: Amin, *Watha'iq waqf al-sultan Hasan*, also appendix in: Ibn Habib II and Harithy, *Waqf Document*; Ibn Kathir, XIV, p. 278; Maqrizi, *Khitat*, II, pp. 316ff.; idem, *Suluk*, II, pp. 745, 842, III, pp. 60–3; Ibn Hajar, *Durar*, II, pp. 124f.; Zahiri, p. 31; Ibn Taghribirdi, *Manhal*, V, pp. 125–32; idem, *Nujum*, X, pp. 187, 302–18; Ibn Iyas, I/1, p. 560; 'Abd al-Wahhab, *Masajid*, pp. 165–81; Herz, 'Sultan Hassan'; Van Berchem, pp. 251–73; Wiet, 'Sultan Hasan'; Rogers, 'Seljuk Influences'; Meinecke, *Architektur*, I, pp. 115ff.; Kessler, *Sultan Hasan*; Meinecke, *Architektur*, II, pp. 224f.; Ramadan, 'Kitabat'.

6   Maqrizi mentioned once Ardu, and once Tughay, as Hasan's stepmother; Ibn Taghribirdi mentioned only Ardu.

7   Maqrizi, *Suluk*, II, p. 751.

8   Maqrizi, *Khitat*, II, p. 314.

9   Ibn Taghribirdi, *Manhal*, XI, p. 277.

10 The mausoleum of Princess Tulubiyya, Sultan Hasan's wife, is in the northern cemetery. She died in 765/1364. Ibn Taghribirdi, *Manhal*, VII, p. 31; Amin, *Watha'iq waqf al-sultan Hasan*, p. 51. It is not known, however, if Tulubiyya was his only wife. The foundation included five students and a Hadith teacher, twenty primary-school boys and their teacher, Koran readers, an imam and servants.

11 Ibn Hajar, *Durar*, IV, p. 31; Maqrizi, *Suluk*, II, pp. 323, 334, 565, 671, 919, III, pp. 13, 61, 63, 65; Ibn Taghribirdi, *Nujum*, X, pp. 311ff., 317.

12 Maqrizi, *Suluk*, II, pp. 782–6.

13 Amin, *Watha'iq waqf al-sultan Hasan*, p. 30; Fernandes, *Khanqah*, pp. 71, 74f.

14 Salam-Liebich, p. 35.

15 Ibn Iyas I/2, p. 561.

16 See below, the discussion of the Sultaniyya.

17 Harithy, *Waqf*, pp. 5–10.

18 Amin, *Watha'iq waqf al-sultan Hasan*, p. 51.

19 Amin, *Watha'iq waqf al-sultan Hasan*, pp. 55–7.

20 Ibn Iyas, I/2, pp. 257, 412, 443, II, p. 201, III, pp. 367, 371, 391, 455, 458f., 464; Ibn Taghribirdi, *Nujum*, XV, pp. 271 273.

21 Maqrizi, *Suluk*, II, pp. 28f.

22 Creswell, *MAE*, II, p. 269.

23 Louis François Cassas, Cat. No. 100.

24 Ibn Taghribirdi, *Hawadith*, II, p. 218.

25 Evliya, p. 203, Arabic transl., p. 281.

26 Aḥmad Jalabī 'Abd al-Ghanī, *Awḍaḥ al-ishārāt fī man walā miṣr al-qāhira min al-wizarā' wa'l-bāshāt*, ed. F.M. al-Māwī, Cairo 1977, p. 187; Ḥusayn Ibn

Muḥammad al-Warthilānī, *Nuzhat al-anẓār fī faḍl 'ilm al-tā rīkh wa'l-akhbār*, Beirut 1974, p. 266.

27 Ibn Kathir, XIV, p. 277; 'Abd al-Wahhab, *Masajid*, p. 285.

28 James, *Qur'ans*, cat. 3, fig. 32.

29 James, *Qur'ans*, cat. 1, fig. 25.

30 Rogers, 'Seljuk Influences'.

31 Aslanapa, p. 204.

32 James, *Qur'ans*, fig. 32.

33 James, *Qur'ans*, pp. 18, 55, 190–5.

34 James, *Qur'ans*, cat. 24, pp. 180f.

35 Ramadan, p. 23.

36 Index Nos 288, 289; Ministry of Waqf 2836; Farida Maqar, 'The Sultaniyya Mausoleum' (unpublished MA thesis), AUC 1969; Evliya Celebi, p. 230, Arabic transl. p. 309; Creswell, *Chronology*, p. 129; Meinecke, 'Fayence-mosaikdekorationen'.

37 See Sultan Hasan's entry above; Ibn Taghribirdi, *Nujum*, X, p. 232.

38 Van Berchem, pp. 740f.; Ibn Taghibirdi, *Manhal*, VII, p. 31.

39 Ali Ibrahim, 'Great Hanqah'; Harithy, 'Turbat al-Sitt'.

40 Ali Ibrahim and O'Kane, 'Tiled Mihrab'.

41 Index No. 45; Meinecke et al., *Restaurierung*, pp. 29–56; Meinecke-Berg in: Meinecke et al., *Restaurierung*, pp. 57f.

42 Index No. 125; Maqrizi, *Khitat*, II, pp. 399f.; Van Berchem, pp. 278–8; 'Abd al-Wahhab, *Masajid*, pp. 182–7; Kessler, 'Mecca-oriented'.

43 Leonor Fernandes drew my attention to the colophon of the Koran of Sultan Sha'ban's mother, which indicates that it was sponsored for her 'madrasa', whereas the colophon of Sha'ban's Koran indicates that it was sponsored for his 'Friday mosque'.

44 Ali Ibrahim, 'Great Hanqah'.

45 Maqrizi, *Khitat*, A.F.S. ed., IV/2, pp. 661f.; idem, *Suluk*, III, p. 282.

46 This information was kindly given to me by Dina Bakhoum.

47 Kessler, 'Mecca-oriented', n. 4; Maqrizi, *Khitat*, II, pp. 256–64.

48 Index No. 131; Maqrizi, *Khitat*, II, p. 399; Ibn Taghribirdi, *Manhal*, III, pp. 40–4; Van Berchem, pp. 289–91; 'Abd al-Wahhab, *Masajid*, pp. 188–91.

49 Kessler, *Domes*, p. 14.

50 Index No. 187; Dar al-Watha'iq 51; Maqrizi, *Khitat*, II, p. 418, A.F.S. ed., IV/2, pp. 679ff.; idem, *Suluk*, III, pp. 519, 544, 546, 946; Jawhari, *Nuzha*, I, pp. 134ff.; Mubarak, VI, p. 4; Van Berchem, pp. 297–306; Creswell, *Chronology*, pp. 120f.; 'Abd al-Wahhab, *Masajid*, pp. 192–7; Rogers, 'Stones of Barquq'; Mostafa, *Barquq*.

51 Behrens-Abouseif, 'Muhandis'.

52 Ibn Iyas, II, p. 372.

53 Index No. 22; Creswell, *Chronology*, p. 102.

54 *The Mosques of Egypt*, II, pl. 99.

Chapter 17

1 Index No. 149; Ibn Hajar, *Inba'*, IV, p. 28; Jawhari, *Nuzha*, I, p. 496; Maqrizi, *Khitat*, I, p. 381, II, p. 464; Van Berchem, pp. 316–31; Mostafa, *Kloster und Mausoleum*.
2 Maqrizi, *Suluk*, III, p. 937.
3 Ibn Taghribirdi, *Nujum*, XIV, p. 43.
4 Behrens-Abouseif, *Minarets*, p. 105, pl. 43.
5 Ali Ibrahim, 'Transitional Zones', pp. 15, 20.
6 Kessler, *Domes*, pp. 18–22.
7 Index No. 203; the monument and its waqf have been studied by Mostafa et al., *Farag*.
8 Maqrizi, *Khitat*, II, pp. 401ff., A.F.S. ed., IV/2, pp. 664ff.

Chapter 18

1 Index No. 190; Ministry of Waqf 938; waqf published in 'Abd al-'Alim, pp. 113–69; Maqrizi, *Khitat*, II, pp. 238, 408; Jawhari, *Nuzha*, II, pp. 365f.; Prisse d'Avennes, pp. 136ff.; Coste, pls. XXVII–XXXI; Van Berchem, pp. 335–43; Mubarak, v, pp. 124–32.
2 Maqrizi, *Suluk*, IV, pp. 658, 744.
3 Sakhawi, *Daw'*, III, p. 310.
4 Shafi'i, 'West Islamic', p. 43, fig. 17.
5 Index No. 257; Maqrizi, *Suluk*, II, p. 610; idem, *Khitat*, II, p. 408; Jawhari, *Nuzha*, II, p. 428.
6 Maqrizi, *Suluk*, IV, pp. 486, 492.
7 Index No. 184; Maqrizi, *Khitat*, II, p. 328; Sakhawi, *Daw'*, IV, pp. 248ff.; Van Berchem, pp. 334f.; 'Abd al-Wahhab, *Masajid*, pp. 215–7.
8 Index No. 60; Maqrizi, *Khitat*, II, p. 331; idem, *Suluk*, IV, p. 662; Mubarak, v, pp. 44–6; Van Berchem, pp. 344–9, 770f.; 'Abd al-Wahhab, *Masajid*, pp. 202–6.

Chapter 19

1 Index No. 175; Ministry of Waqf 880, Dar al-Watha'iq 92; Maqrizi, *Khitat*, II, pp. 330f.; Van Berchem, pp. 349–60; 'Abd al-Wahhab, *Masajid*, pp. 221–4; Darrag, *Barsbay*, chapter XI; idem, *Acte de waqf*, pp. 56f.; Fernandes, *Khanqah*, p. 83.
2 *The Mosques of Egypt*, II, p. 81.
3 Index No. 121; Ministry of Waqf 880; Darrag, *Acte de waqf*, pp. 29–34; Mubarak, IV, pp. 57–59. Fernandes, 'Sufi Foundations'; Van Berchem, pp. 365–74; 'Abd al-Wahhab, *Masajid*, pp. 225–8; Kessler, *Domes*, pp. 23f.
4 Maqrizi, *Suluk*, IV, p. 1100.
5 *The Mosques of Egypt*, II, p. 83.

Chapter 20

1 Index No. 180; Ibn Taghribirdi, *Manhal*, IV, pp. 275–312; idem, *Nujum*, xv, p. 435; idem, *Hawadith*, I, p. 16; Sakhawi, *Daw'*, III, pp. 71–4, VI, p. 232; idem, *Tibr*, pp. 114f., 346; Mubarak, v, p. 98; Creswell, *Chronology*, pp. 132f.; Van Berchem, pp. 392–3; 'Abd al-Wahhab, *Masajid*, p. 242 n. 1.
2 Van Berchem, pp. 381f.; Behrens-Abouseif, *Minarets*, fig. 57.
3 I thank Corinne Morisot for drawing my attention to Jaqmaq's waqf document, dated Muharram 857/1453, in the collection of the Institut Français d'Archéologie Orientale, Cairo.
4 'Abd al-Wahhab, *Masajid*, p. 196.
5 Maqrizi, *Khitat*, II, p. 367; Ibn Taghribirdi, *Manhal*, XII, p. 226; Sakhawi, *Daw'*, x, pp. 322f.
6 Index No. 209; Van Berchem, pp. 379f.; Kessler, 'Funerary', p. 264; Behrens-Abouseif, *Minarets*, figs 21, 22, pls 43, 49, 53.
7 Garcin and Taher, 'Ensemble de waqfs'.
8 Index No. 182; Sakhawi, *Daw'*, x, pp. 233f.; al-Jawahari, *Inba'*, pp. 172f.; Dar al-Watha'iq 110/17 b. The document is in a fragmentary condition with many passages missing; Van Berchem, pp. 383–91; Creswell, *Chronology*, pp. 130f.; *The Mosques of Egypt*, II, p. 86; 'Abd al-Wahhab, *Masajid*, pp. 234–7.
9 Warner, *Monuments*, p. 113.
10 Index No. 344; Sakhawi, *Tibr*, pp. 217, 270; 'Abd al-Wahhab noticed that in the inscription the word 'khamsin' for 'fifty' is missing, indicating instead 802, which is obviously an error: *Masajid*, pp. 238–40.
11 Behrens-Abouseif, *Minarets*, pp. 126, 134.
12 Index No. 204; 'Abd al-Wahhab, *Masajid*, pp. 241f.

Chapter 21

1 Index No. 158; Ibn Taghribirdi, *Nujum*, XVI, p. 38; idem, *Manhal*, III, pp. 209–12; Ibn Iyas, II, pp. 331, 333; Van Berchem, p. 394.
2 Ibn Taghirbirdi, *Nujum*, XVI, pp. 94, 97.

Chapter 22

1 Index Nos 99; 100, 101, 104; Ministry of Waqf 888, Dar al-Whatha'iq 187; Sakhawi, *Daw'*, VI, pp. 201–12; Ibn Iyas, III, pp. 45, 100, 329–32; Evliya, pp. 295f.,352, Arabic transl. pp. 335, 383; Mayer, *The Buildings of Qaytbay*; Mubarak, v, pp. 69–75; Van Berchem, pp. 431–9; Grabar, 'The Inscriptions'; Kessler, *Domes*, pp. 30f.; Newhall, pp. 128–44.
2 Ibn Iyas, III, p. 102.

3 Ibn Taghribirdi, *Manhal*, VII, p. 90; idem, *Nujum*, X, p. 239; Sha'rani, II, p. 2.

4 Amin and Ali Ibrahim, pp. 113f.

5 Ministry of Waqf 502; Ibn Iyas, III, pp. 134, 171; Sakhawi, *Daw'*, X, pp. 272–7; Fabri, pp. 365, 377f.; Van Ghistele, p. 77; *Le Voyage en Egypte de Pierre Belon Du Mans 1547*, Cairo, p. 112; C. Harant, *Voyage en Egypte*, Cairo 1971, p. 83; Evliya, pp. 254, 481, Arabic transl. pp. 336, 601; Van Berchem pp. 534.f.; 'Abd al-Wahhab, *Masajid*, pp. 258–60, 269ff.; Behrens-Abouseif, 'Four Domes'; idem, 'Northeastern Extension'; idem, 'The Qubba'.

6 Le Brun, fig. 78.

7 Index No. 5; Ibn Iyas, III, pp. 160, 173, 189; 'Abd al-Ghanī al-Nablūsī, *al-Ḥaqīqa wa 'l-majāz*, Cairo 1986, pp. 251f.; Evliya, p. 481, Arabic transl. pp. 335f., 600; Seigneur de Villamont, *Voyage en Egypte des Années 1589, 1590, 1591*, Cairo 1971, pp. 206f.; O. Dapper, *Description de l'Afrique*, Amsterdam 1686, p. 58; Leo Africanus, p. 212; De Monconys, *Le Journal des Voyages*, Lyon 1665, I, 78, Lyon 1665, pp. 205f.; R. Pococke, *A Description of the East and Some Other Countries*, London 1743, I, p. 31; 'Abd al-Wahhab, *Masajid*, pp. 269–75; Behrens-Abouseif, 'Suburb' p. 20; idem, 'Northeastern', pp. 179f.

8 See Pagano's view in Warner, *Description*.

9 Sakhawi, *Daw'*, VI, p. 206; Ibn Iyas, III, pp. 150f., 177.

10 Maqrizi, *Khitat*, II, p. 433.

11 Sha'rani, *Tabaqat*, II, pp. 147f.; al-Ghazzī, *al-kawakib al-sā'ira bi a'yān al-mi'a 'l-'āshira*, 3 vols (ed.) J.S. Jabbur, Beirut 1979, I, p. 192; Mubarak, IV, p. 112; Behrens-Abouseif, 'Unlisted Monument'.

12 Ibn Taghribirdi, *Hawadith*, III, pp. 675, 699.

13 Index No. 49; Ibn Iyas, III, p. 61; Mubarak, V, pp. 113f.; Van Berchem, pp. 505–8; Creswell, *Chronology*, p. 144.

14 Index No. 114; Sakhawi, *Daw'*, VI, p. 213; Mubarak, IV, pp. 48f.; Van Berchem, pp. 509–13; 'Abd al-Wahhab, *Masajid*, pp. 261ff.; Behrens-Abouseif, 'Veneto-Saracenic', p. 151; O'Kane et al., *Documentation*, No. 114.

15 Index No. 324; Ibn Iyas, III, pp. 164, 430; Van Berchem, p. 492.

16 This sabil probably stood on the site of the one built by Hasan Agha in the nineteenth century; Waqf of Qaytbay 888, pp. 39ff., 194, 197ff., 234; Ibn Iyas, III, pp. 43, 300; Newhall, pp. 157–63.

17 Ministry of Waqf 888, pp. 194, 197ff., 234f.

18 I thank Baha Tanman for drawing my attention to this signature.

19 Qalqashandi, IV, p. 12.

20 Popper, XV, pp. 93f.

21 Ibn Iyas, V, pp. 186, 231.

22 Index No. 211; Ibn Iyas, III, p. 309, 414; Mubarak, IV, pp. 55f.; Van Berchem, pp. 527–38.

23 Index No. 303; Ibn Iyas, III, p. 180; Sakhawi, *Daw'*, X, p. 280; Ibn Iyas, III, pp. 226, 269, 275f.; Van Berchem, pp. 547–54; Rogers, 'Inscription'.

24 Burgoyne, pp. 607f.

Chapter 23

1 Index Nos 66, 67, 189; Ministry of Waqf 882; Ibn Iyas, IV, pp. 52f., 58f., 68f., 84, 249, 299, 306; Mubarak, V, pp. 61–6; Van Berchem, pp. 572–6; Girault de Prangey, p. 80; *Toutes les Egypte*, p. 129; Prost, pp. 13f., pl. IV/2; Creswell, *MAE*, II, p. 73; 'Azzam, I, p. 28; 'Abd al-Wahhab, *Masajid*, pp. 286–94; Behrens-Abouseif, 'Sultan al-Ghawri'.

2 Maqrizi, *Khitat*, II, p. 429.

3 Ibn Iyas, IV, pp. 202, 285, 355, 365f.

4 Kessler, *Domes*, pl. 40.

5 Behrens-Abouseif, 'Function and Form'. In the waqf deed of the khanqah of Barsbay in the cemetery the term 'khanqah' designates the apartment complex attached to the funerary mosque.

6 In the khanqah of Barsbay in the northern cemetery the mausoleum's side equals the depth of the adjoining prayer hall.

7 Roxburgh, cat. 246, pp. 288f., 439.

8 Creswell, *MAE*, I, pl. 21c.

9 Index Nos 148, 159; Creswell, *Chronology*, p. 156; Meinecke, *Architektur*, II, p. 459.

10 Ibn Iyas, IV, pp. 56, 60, 137f., 172ff., 176.

11 Amin and Ali Ibrahim, p. 90.

12 Evliya, p. 171, Arabic transl. p. 244.

13 Ibn Iyas, IV, pp. 56, 74.

14 Ibn Taghribirdi, *Nujum*, XI, p. 112.

15 Maqrizi, *Suluk*, III/2, p. 52; Ibn Iyas, I/1, p. 563, I/2, pp. 115, 352, II, pp. 118, 404, 443, III, pp. 153, 302, 379.

16 G.R.D. King, 'The Nine Bay Domed Mosque in Islam', *Madrider Mitteilungen*, 30 (1989), pp. 332–382; O'Kane, 'Origin, Development and Meaning of the Nine-Bay Plan in Islamic Architecture', in: Abbas Daneshvari (ed.), *A Survey of Persian Art from Prehistoric Times to the Present*, XVIII, Costa Mesa 2005, pp. 189–244.

17 Behrens Abouseif, 'Notes'.

18 Ibn Iyas, IV, pp. 160, 484; Van Berchem, pp. 594f.; Behrens-Abouseif, *Minarets*, p. 157.

19 Index No. 136; Ministry of Waqf 1019; Ibn Iyas, IV, pp. 450–53; Van Berchem, pp. 569–72, 586ff.; 'Abd al-Wahhab, *Masajid*, pp. 281–5; Kessler, *Domes*, p. 35.

20 Jabarti, III, p. 159.

21 Index No. 162; Ministry of Waqf 901; Ibn Iyas IV, pp. 197f.; Van Berchem, pp. 592ff.; Misiorowski, *Qurqumas.*

22 Evliya, pp. 397, 484, 1043. A description is included in the archive of al-Bab al-'Ali, 265/230, pp. 171f.

23 O'Kane et al., *Documentation*, No. 162.14.

24 Index No. 248; Dar al-Watha'iq 294; Mubarak, IV, p. 110; Van Berchem pp. 565–9; Kessler 'Funerary', pp. 265f.;

Behrens-Abouseif, *Egypt's Adjustment to Ottoman Rule*, Leiden/New York 1994, pp. 182ff., 232f.

25 It is not the first religious foundation of the Ottoman period; the Takiyyat Ibrahim al-Kulshani was founded slightly earlier in 1519, and completed in 1524.

26 Van Berchem, p. 568.

27 Behrens-Abouseif, *Minarets*, p. 161.

Bibliography

A) Historical sources

al-ʿAynī, Badr al-Dīn, *al-Sayf al-muhannad fī sīrat al-malik al-Muʾayyad Shaykh al-Maḥmudī*, F.M. Shaltut (ed.), Cairo 1966–7.

Baybars al-Mansurī al-Dāwādar, *Zubdat al-fikra fī tārīkh al-hijra*, Donald S. Richards (ed.), Beirut 1998.

Cassas, Louis-François, *Voyage pittoresque de la Syrie et Basse-Egypte*, Paris 1799.

al-Dawādārī, Ibn Aybak, *Kanz al-durar wa jāmiʿ al-ghurar*, IX, H.R. Römer (ed.), Cairo 1960.

Evliya Çelebi, *Seyahatnamesi: Misir, Sudan, Habeş (1672–1680)*, X, Istanbul 1938; Arabic transl. Muhammad ʿAlī ʿAwnī, Cairo 2003.

Fabri, Felix, *Le Voyage en Egypte*, 3 vols, Cairo 1975.

von Harff, Arnold, *The Pilgrimage of Arnold von Harff*, transl. Malcolm Letts, London 1946.

Ibn ʿAbd Allāh, al-Ḥasan Ibn al-ʿAbbās, *Āthār al-uwal fī tartīb al-duwal*, Cairo n.d.

Ibn ʿAbd al-Hādī, *Thimār al-maqāṣid fī dhikr al-masājid*, Muḥammad Asʿad Aṭlas (ed.), Beirut 1975.

Ibn ʿAbd al-Ẓāhir, *al-Rawḍ al-zāhir fī sīrat al-malik al-Ẓāhir*, ʿAbd al-Azīz al-Khuwaytir (ed.), Riyadh 1976.

— *al-Rawḍa ʾl-bahiyya al-zāhira fi khiṭaṭ al-muʿizziyya al-qāhira*, Ayman Fūʾād Sayyid (ed.), Cairo 1996.

— *al-Alṭāf al-khafiyya min al-sīra al-sharīfa al-sulṭāniyya al-ashrafiyya*, ms. Bayerische Staatsbibliothek Munich, Cod. Ar. 405.

Ibn Abī ʾl-Faḍāʾil, Mufaḍḍal, *Ägypten und Syrien zwischen 1317 und 1341 in der Chronik des Mufaḍḍal b. Abī l-Faḍāʾil*, Samira Kortantamer (ed.), Freiburg 1973.

Ibn Duqmāq, *Kitāb al-intiṣār li wāsiṭaṭ ʿiqd al-amṣār*, Bulaq 1314/1897–8.

Ibn Ḥabīb, *Tadhkirat al-nabīh fī ayyām al-manṣūr wa banīh*, 3 vols, Muḥammad Muḥ. Amīn (ed.), Cairo 1976–86.

Ibn Hajar al-ʿAsqalānī, *al-Durar al-kāmina fī aʿyān al-miʾa al-thāmina*, 5 vols, Cairo 1966.

— *Inbāʾ al-ghumr bi-abnāʾ al-ʿumr*, 9 vols, Beirut 1986.

Ibn al-Ḥājj, *al-Madkhal*, 4 vols, Cairo 1981.

Ibn Iyās, *Badāʾiʿ al-zuhūr fī waqāʾiʿ al-duhūr*, M. Muṣṭafa (ed.), Wiesbaden/Cairo 1961–75.

Ibn Jubayr, *Riḥlat Ibn Jubayr*, Beirut 1959.

Ibn Kathīr, *al-Bidāya wa ʾl-nihāya*, 14 vols, Beirut 1966.

Ibn Khaldūn, *al-Taʿrīf bi Ibn Khaldūn wa riḥlatihi gharban wa sharqan*, Beirut 1979.

— *al-Muqaddima*, Beirut n.d.

Ibn Shaddād, *Tārīkh al-Malik al-Ẓāhir*, Ahmad Ḥuṭayṭ (ed.), Beirut 1983.

Ibn Taghrībirdī, *Ḥawādith al-duhūr fī madā ʾl-ayyām wa ʾl-shuhūr*, W. Popper (ed.), Berkeley 1931.

— *al-Nujūm al-zāhira fī mulūk miṣr wa ʾl-qāhira*, 16 vols, Cairo 1963–71.

— *al-Manhal al-ṣāfī wa ʾl-mustawfā baʿd al-wāfī*, Cairo 1956–2005.

Ibn Ṭūlūn, Muḥammad, *Iʿlām al-warā biman wuliya nāʾiban min al-atrāk bi-dimashq al-shām al-kubrā*, Muḥammad Aḥmad Duhmān (ed.), Damascus 1964.

al-Jabartī, ʿAbd al-Raḥmān, *ʿAjāʾib al-āthār fī ʾl-tarājim wa ʾl-akhbār*, 4 vols, Bulaq 1236/1820–21.

al-Jawharī al-Ṣayrafī, ʿAlī Ibn Dāwūd, *Nuzhat al-nufūs wa ʾl-abdān fī tawārīkh al-zamān*, 3 vols, Ḥasan Ḥabashī (ed.), Cairo 1970.

—*Inbā' al-ḥaṣr bi-abnā' al-'aṣr*, Ḥasan al-Ḥabashī (ed.), Cairo 1970.

Le Brun, Corneille, *Voyage au Levant*, Delft 1700.

Leo Africanus (al-Ḥasan Ibn Muḥammad al-Wazzān), *Waṣf Ifrīqiyā*, transl. Muḥammad Ḥajjī and Muḥammad al-Akhḍar, Beirut/Rabat 1983.

al-Maqdisī, Abū Ḥāmid, *al-Fawā'id al-nafīsa al-bāhira fī bayān shawāri' al-qāhira fī madhāhib al-a'imma al-arbā'a al-zāhira*, Amāl al-'Imārī (ed.), Cairo 1988. See also al-Qudsī.

al-Maqrīzī, Taqiyy al-Dīn Aḥmad, *Kitāb al-mawā'iẓ wa 'l-i'tibār bi dhikr al-khiṭaṭ wa 'l-āthār*, 2 vols, Bulaq, 1306/1888–9; 2nd edn Ayman Fu'ād Sayyid (ed.), 4 vols, London 2003.

—*Kitāb al-sulūk li-ma'rifat duwal al-mulūk*, M. Ziyāda and S. 'Āshshūr (eds), Cairo 1970–73.

al-Māwardī, *al-Aḥkām al-sulṭāniyya wa 'l-wilāyāt al-dīniyya*, Cairo 1960.

Mujīr al-Dīn, *al-Uns al-jalīl bi-tārīkh al-quds wa 'l-khalīl*, 2 vols, Amman 1973.

al-Nuwayrī, Shihāb al-Dīn Aḥmad, *Nihāyat al-arab fī funūn al-'arab*, xxxi, al-Bāz al-'Arīnī (ed.), Cairo 1992; xxxii, Fahīm Muḥ. 'Ulwī Shaltūt (ed.), Cairo 1998; xxxiii, Muṣṭafā Ḥijāzī and Muḥammad Muṣṭafā Ziyāda (eds), Cairo 1997.

al-Nuwayrī (al-Sakandarī), Muḥammad Ibn Qāsim, *Kitāb al-Ilmām*, A.S. 'Aṭiyya (ed.), 4 vols, Haydarabad 1970.

al-Qalqashandī, Abū 'l-'Abbās Aḥmad, *Ṣubḥ al-a'shā fī ṣinā'at al-inshā*, Cairo 1914–28.

al-Qudsī, Abu Ḥāmid, *Duwal al-islām al-sharīfa al-bahiyya*, Ṣubḥī Labīb and Ulrich Haarmann (eds), Beirut 1997. See also al-Maqdisī.

al-Ṣafadī, *al-Wāfī bi-l-wafayāt*, Wiesbaden 1981.

al-Sakhāwī, Muḥammad Ibn 'Abd al-Raḥmān, *al-Ḍaw' al-lāmi' li-ahl al-qarn al-tāsi'*, 12 vols, Cairo 1896.

—*al-Tibr al-masbūk fī dhayl al-sulūk*, Cairo n.d.

—*I'lān bi-l-tawbīkh li-man dhamma ahl al-tawārīkh*, Eng. transl. F. Rosenthal, *A History of Muslim Historiography*, Leiden 1968.

al-Sakhāwī, Nūr al-Dīn, *Tuḥfat al-aḥbāb wa bughyat al-ṭullāb*, Cairo 1937.

al-Samhūdī, Nūr al-Dīn 'Alī, *Wafā' al-wafā bi-akhbār dār al-muṣṭafā*, Muḥ. Muḥyī 'l-Dīn 'Abd al-Majīd (ed.), 2 vols, Mecca n.d.

Shāfi', Ibn 'Alī, *Šāfi' Ibn 'Alī's Biography of the Mamluk Sultan Qalāwūn*, Paulina B. Lewicka (ed.), Warsaw 2000.

al-Sha'rānī, 'Abd al-Wahhāb, *al-Ṭabaqāt al-kubrā*, 2 vols, Cairo 1954.

al-Shujā'ī, Shams al-Dīn, *Tārīkh al-malik al-Nāṣir Muḥammad Ibn Qalāwūn al-Ṣāliḥī*, Barbara Schäfer (ed.), Wiesbaden 1978; also B. Schäfer, *Beiträge zur mamlukischen Historiographie nach dem Tode al-Malik al-Nāṣirs*, Freiburg 1971.

al-Suyūṭī, *Ḥusn al-muḥāḍara fī tārīkh miṣr wa 'l-qāhira*, 2 vols, Cairo 1968.

—*al-Ḥāwī li-l-fatāwī*, 2 vols, Beirut 1982.

al-Ṭarsūsī, Najm al-Dīn, *Kitāb tuḥfat al-turk*, Mohamed Menasri (ed.), Damascus 1997.

al-'Umarī, Ibn Faḍl Allāh, *Masālik al-abṣār fī mamālik al-amṣār*, Aḥmad Zakī (ed.), Cairo 1924.

Van Ghistele, Joos, *Le Voyage en Egypte*, Cairo 1986.

al-Yūsufī, Mūsā Ibn Muḥ. *Nuzhat al-nuzzār fī sīrat al-malik al-Nāṣir*, Aḥmad Ḥuṭayṭ (ed.), Beirut 1986.

al-Ẓāhirī, Khalil Ibn Shāhīn, *Zubdat kashf al-mamālik*, (ed.) Paul Ravaisse, Paris 1893, repr. Frankfurt 1993.

B) Modern sources and studies

al-'Abbādī, Ahmad Mukhtār, *Qiyām dawlat al-mamālīk fī miṣr wa 'l-shām*, Alexandria 1982.

'Abd al-'Alīm, Fahmī, *al-'Imāra 'l-islāmiyya fī 'aṣr al-mamālīk al-jarākisa: 'aṣr al-sulṭān al-Mu'ayyad Shaykh*, Cairo 2003.

'Abd Ar-Rāziq, Aḥmad, *La Femme au temps des Mamlouks*, Cairo 1973.

— 'Trois fondations féminines dans l'Egypte Mamelouke', *Revue des Etudes Islamiques*, xli/1 (1973), pp. 95–126.

—*al-Badhal wa 'l-barṭala fī zaman salāṭīn al-mamālīk*, Cairo 1979.

'Abd al-Wahhāb, Ḥasan, *Tārīkh al-masājid al-athariyya*, Cairo 1946.

— 'Tawqī'āt al-ṣunnā' 'alā āthār miṣr al-islāmiyya', *Bulletin de l'Institut d'Egypte*, xxxvi (1953–4), pp. 553–8.

— 'al-Āthār al-manqūla wa 'l-muntaḥala fī 'l-'imāra 'l-islāmiyya', *Bulletin de l'Institut d'Egypte/Majallat al-Majma' al-'Ilmī al-Miṣrī*, xxxviii /1 (1955–6), pp. 243–3.

— 'Ṭarz al-'imāra al-islāmiyya fī rīf miṣr', *Bulletin de l'Institut d'Egypte/Majallat al-Majma' al-'Ilmī al-Miṣrī*, xxxviii/2 (1956–7), pp. 5–18.

Abu-Lughod, Janet L., *Cairo, 1001 Years of the City Victorious*, Princeton 1971.

Abū 'l-'Amāyim, Muḥammad, 'al-Mi'dhana al-qibliyya wa mā ḥawlahā min al-āthār khārij bāb al-qarāfa bi-l-qāhira', *Annales Islamologiques*, xxxiv/2 (2000), pp. 45–89.

Ali Ibrahim, Laila, 'Four Cairene Mihrabs and their Dating', *Kunst des Orients*, vii/1 (1970–71), pp. 30–59.

— 'The Great Ḥanqah of the Emir Qawsun in Cairo', *Mitteilungen des Deutschen Archäologischen Instituts, Abteilung Kairo*, xxx/1 (1974), pp. 37–57.

— 'The Transitional Zones of Domes in Cairene Architecture', *Kunst des Orients*, x/1–2 (1975), pp. 5–23.

— 'Mamluk Monuments in Cairo', *Quaderni Dell' Istituto Italiano Di Cultura Per la R.A.E.* (1976).

— 'The Zawiya of Shaikh Zain al-Din Yusuf in Cairo', *Mitteilungen des Deutschen Archäologischen Instituts, Abteilung Kairo*, xxxiv (1978), pp. 79–110.

—'Middle-class Living Units in Mamluk Cairo', *AARP (Art and Archaeology Research Papers)*, xiv (1978), pp. 24–30.

—'Residential architecture in Mamluk Cairo', *Muqarnas*, ii (1984), pp. 47–60.

Ali Ibrahim, Laila, and Bernard O'Kane, 'The Madrasa of Badr al-Dīn al-ʿAynī and its Tiled Miḥrāb', *Annales Islamologiques*, xxiv (1988), pp. 253–68.

Allan, James W., *Islamic Metalwork: The Nuhad Es-Said Collection*, London 1982.

—'Shaʿban, Barquq and the Decline of the Mamluk Metalworking Industry', *Muqarnas*, ii (1984), pp. 85–94.

Amīn, Muḥammad Muḥammad, *al-Awqāf wa 'l-ḥayāt al-ijtimāʿiyya fī miṣr (648–923/1250–1517)*, Cairo 1980.

—'Wathāʾiq waqf al-sulṭān Qalāwūn ʿalā 'l-bīmāristān al-manṣūrī', appendix to Abū 'l-Ḥasan Ibn Ḥabīb, *Tadhkirat al-nabīh*, i, Cairo 1976, pp. 329–96.

—*Catalogue des documents d'archives du Caire de 239/853 à 922/1516*, Cairo 1981.—'Wathāʾiq waqf al-sulṭān al-Nāṣir Muḥammad Ibn Qalāwūn', appendix to Ibn Ḥabīb, *Tadhkirat al-nabīh*, ii, Cairo 1982, pp. 231–448.

—'Wathāʾiq waqf al-sulṭān Ḥasan Ibn Muḥammad Ibn Qalāwūn ʿalā maṣāliḥ al-qubba wa 'l-masjid wa 'l-madāris wa maktab al-sabīl bi-l-qāhira', appendix to Ibn Ḥabīb, *Tadhkirat al-nabīh*, iii, Cairo 1986, pp. 341–450.

—*Wathāʾiq waqf al-sulṭān Ḥasan Ibn Muḥammad Ibn Qalāwūn ʿalā maṣāliḥ al-qubba wa 'l-masjid wa 'l-madāris wa maktab al-sabīl bi-l-qāhira*, Cairo 1986.

Amīn, Muḥammad Muḥ., and Layla Ali Ibrahim, *Architectural Terms in Mamluk Documents (648–923H/1250–1517)*, Cairo 1990.

Aslanapa, Oktay, *Türk Sanati*, 2nd edn, Istanbul 1984.

Atasi, Sarab, 'Von den Umayyaden zu den Mamluken: Aspekte städtischer Entwicklung in Damaskus', in: Mamoun Fansa, Heinz Gaube, Jens Windelberd (eds), *Damaskus-Aleppo, 5000 Jahre Stadtentwicklung in Syrien*, Mainz 2000, pp. 108–23.

Atil, Esin, *Renaissance of Islam: The Arts of the Mamluks*, Washington 1981.

—'Mamluk Painting in the Late Fifteenth Century', *Muqarnas*, ii (1984), pp. 159–71.

Aṭlas, Muḥammad Asʿad, appendix (*dhayl*) to his edition of Ibn ʿAbd al-Hādī, *Thimār al-maqāṣid fī dhikr al-masājid*, Beirut 1975.

Ayalon, David, *Studies on the Mamlūks of Egypt (1250–1517)* (reprinted essays), London 1977.

—*The Mamluk Military Society* (reprinted essays), London 1979.

—'The Great "Yâsa" of Chingiz Khân', *Studia Islamica*, xxxviii (1971), pp. 97–140.

—'The Muslim City and the Mamluk Military Aristocracy', in: *Proceedings of the Israel Academy of Sciences and Humanities*, ii (1968), pp. 311–29.

—'The Expansion and Decline of Cairo under the Mamluks and its Background', in: R. Curiel and R. Gyselen (eds), *Itinéraires d'orient: hommages à Claude Cahen*, Paris 1994, pp. 14–16.

—'Studies on the Structure of the Mamluk Army', *Bulletin of the School of Oriental and African Studies*, xv/2–3 (1953), pp. 203–28, 448–76, xvi/1 (1954), pp. 57–90.

—'The System of Payment in Mamluk Military Society', *Journal of Economic and Social History of the Orient*, i/1(1958), pp. 37–65, i/3 (1958), pp. 257–96.

ʿAzzām, ʿAbd al-Wahhāb, *Majālis al-sulṭān al-Ghawrī*, 2 vols, Cairo 1941.

Baer, Eva, 'Mamluk Art and its Clientele: A Speculation', *Assaph, Studies in Art History*, 8 (2003), pp. 49–69.

Balog, Paul, *The Coinage of the Mamluk Sultans of Egypt and Syria*, New York 1964.

Bates, Ulku, 'Evolution of Tile Revetment in Ottoman Cairo', in: *First International Congress on Turkish Tiles and Ceramics*, Istanbul 1989, pp. 39–58.

Bauer, Thomas, 'Literarische Anthologien der Mamlūkenzeit', in: Stephan Conermann and Anja Pistor-Hatam (eds), *Asien und Afrika (Beiträge des Zentrums für Asiatische und Afrikanische Studien (ZAAS) der Christian-Albrechts-Universität zu Kiel), Die Mamlūken*, vii (2003), pp. 71–122.

—'Ibrahim al-Miʿmar: ein dichtender Handwerker aus Ägyptens Mamlukenzeit', *Zeitschrift der Deutschen Morgenländischen Gesellschaft*, 152 (2002), pp. 63–93.

—'Mamluk Literature: Misunderstandings and New Approaches', *Mamlūk Studies Review*, ix/2 (2005), pp. 105–30.

Behrens-Abouseif, Doris, 'A Circassian Mamluk Suburb in the Northeast of Cairo', *AARP (Art and Archaeology Research Papers)*, xiv (1978), pp. 17–23.

—'The Northeastern Extension of Cairo under the Mamluks', *Annales Islamologiques*, xvii (1981), pp. 157–89.

—'Four Domes of the Late Mamluk Period', *Annales Islamologiques*, xvii (1981), pp. 191–2.

—'An Unlisted Monument of the Fifteenth Century: The Dome of Zawiyat al-Damirdash', *Annales Islamologiques*, xviii (1982), pp. 105–21.

—'The Lost Minaret of Shajarat ad-Durr at her Complex in the Cemetery of Sayyida Nafisa', *Mitteilungen des Deutschen Archäologischen Instituts*, Abteilung Kairo, xxxix (1983), pp. 1–16.

—'The Qubba, an Aristocratic Type of *Zāwiya*', *Annales Islamologiques*, xix (1983), pp. 1–7.

—*Azbakiyya and its Environs, from Azbak to Ismāʿīl, 1476–1979*, Cairo 1985.

—'Change in Function and Form of Mamluk Religious Institutions', *Annales Islamologiques*, xxi (1985), pp. 73–93.

—*The Minarets of Cairo*, Cairo 1985 (repr. 1987).

—*Fatḥ Allāh and Abū Zakariyya: Physicians under the Mamluks*, Cairo 1987.

—'The Citadel of Cairo: Stage for Mamluk Ceremonial', *Annales Islamologiques*, xxiv (1988), pp. 25–79.

—'The Baptistère de St. Louis, a Reinterpretation', *Islamic Art*, iii (1988–9), pp. 3–13.

—'*Muhandis, Shād, Muʿallim* – Note on the Building Craft in the Mamluk Period', *Der Islam*, lxxii/2 (1995), pp. 293–309.

—'The Waqf of a Cairene Notable in early Ottoman Cairo – Muhibb al-Din Abu al-Tayyib, Son of a Physician', in: R. Deguilhem (ed.), *Le Waqf dans l'éspace islamique*, pp. 123–32.

—'Al-Nāṣir Muḥammad and al-Ašraf Qāytbāy, Patrons of Urbanism', in: U. Vermeulen and D. De Smet (eds), *Egypt and Syria in the Fatimid, Ayyubid and Mamluk Eras*, Leuven 1995, pp. 257–74.

—'Sicily, the Missing Link in the Evolution of Cairene Architecture', in: U. Vermeulen and D. De Smet (eds), *Egypt and Syria in the Fatimid, Ayyubid and Mamluk Eras*, Leuven 1995, pp. 275–301.

—'Qāytbāy's Investments in the City of Cairo: Waqf and Power', *Annales Islamologiques*, xxxii (1998), pp. 29–40.

—'Notes sur l'architecture musulmane d'Alexandrie', in: Christian Décobert and Jean-Yves Empereur (eds), *Alexandrie Médiévale 1*, Cairo 1998, pp. 101–14.

—'Qaytbay's Madrasahs in the Holy Cities and the Evolution of Haram Architecture', *Mamlūk Studies Review*, iii (1999), pp. 129–49.

—'Sultan al-Ghawri and the Arts', *Mamlūk Studies Review*, vi (2002), pp. 71–94.

—'European Arts and Crafts at the Mamluk Court', *Muqarnas*, xxi (2004), pp. 45–54.

—'The Fire of 884/1479 at the Umayyad Mosque of Damascus and an Account of its Restoration', *Mamlūk Studies Review*, viii/1 (2004), pp. 279–96.

—(ed.), *The Cairo Heritage, Essays in Honor of Laila Ali Ibrahim*, Cairo/New York 2000.

—'Veneto-Saracenic Metalware: a Mamluk Art', *Mamlūk Studies Review*, ix/2 (2005), pp. 147–72.

—'The Islamic History of the Lighthouse of Alexandria', *Muqarnas*, xxiii (2006), pp. 1–13.

Behrens-Abouseif, D., Sylvie Denoix and Jean-Claude Garcin, 'Le Caire' in: Jean-Claude Garcin (ed.), *Grandes Villes Méditerranéennes du monde musulman médiéval*, Rome 2000, pp.177–213.

Berkey, Jonathan, *The Transmission of Knowledge in Medieval Cairo*, Princeton 1992.

Bloom, Jonathan, 'The Mosque of Baybars al-Bunduqdari', *Annales Islamologiques*, xvii (1982), pp. 45–78.

Bourgoin, Jules, *Les arts arabes*, Paris 1873.

Burgoyne, M.H., *Mamluk Jerusalem*, London 1987.

Brinner, W.M., 'Ibn Iyās', *Encyclopaedia of Islam*, 2nd edn, Leiden/London 1986.

Broadbridge, Anne F., 'Mamluk Legitimacy and the Mongols: The Reigns of Baybars and Qalawun', *Mamlūk Studies Review*, v (2001), pp. 91–118.

—'Academic Rivalry and the Patronage System in Fifteenth Century Egypt: al-ʿAynī, al-Maqrīzī, and Ibn Ḥajar al-ʿAsqalānī', *Mamlūk Studies Review*, iii (1999), pp. 85–107.

Bulletin du Comité des monuments de l'art arabe, 1882–1963.

Carboni, Stefano, 'The Painted Glass Decoration of the Mausoleum of Ahmad Ibn Sulayman al-Rifaʿi in Cairo', *Muqarnas*, xx (2003), pp. 61–84.

Carswell, John, 'Some Fifteenth-century Hexagonal Tiles from the Near East', *Victoria and Albert Museum Yearbook*, iii (1972), pp. 59–75.

—'Six Tiles', in: Richard Ettinghausenin (ed.), *Islamic Art in the Metropolitan Museum of Art*, New York 1972, pp. 99–109.

Casanova, Paul, 'Histoire et description de la citadelle du Caire', *Mémoires publiés par les membres de la Mission Archéologique Française au Caire*, vi (1891–2).

Clerget, Marcel, *Le Caire*, 2 vols, Cairo 1934.

Colloque international sur l'histoire du Caire, Cairo 1972.

Comité de Conservation des Monuments de l'Art Arabe, *Rapports de la deuxième commission*, Cairo 1882–1954.

Coste, Pascal, *Architecture arabe des monuments du Caire*, Paris 1839.

Creswell, K.A.C., *MAE: Muslim Architecture of Egypt*, 2 vols, Oxford 1952–9 (repr. New York 1978).

—*A Brief Chronology of the Muhammadan Monuments of Egypt to A.D. 1517*, Cairo 1919.

Dalīl al-āthār al-islāmiyya bi-madīnat al-qāhira, Ministry of Culture, Cairo 2000.

Darrāg, Ahmed, *L'Acte de waqf de Barsbay*, Cairo 1963.

—*L'Egypte sous le règne de Barsbay 825–441/1422–1438*, Damascus 1961.

Degeorge, Gérard, *Damascus*, Paris 2004.

Deguilhem, Randy (ed.), *Le Waqf dans l'éspace islamique: outil de pouvoir socio-politique*, Damascus 1995.

Denoix, Sylvie, *Décrire le Caire d'après Ibn Duqmâq et Maqrîzî*, Cairo 1992.

—'Topographie de l'intervention du personnel politique à l'époque mamlouke', in: S. Denoix et al. (eds), *Le Khan al-Khalili*, pp. 33–49.

Denoix, S., Charles Depaule and Michel Tuchscherer, *Le Khan al-Khalili: un centre commercial et artisanal au Caire du XIIIe au XXe siècle*, 2 vols, Cairo 1999.

Description de l'Egypte (Etat Moderne), Paris 1812.

Dols, Michael, *The Black Death*, Princeton 1977.

Ebeid, Sophie, *Early Sabils and their Standardization*, MA thesis, American University in Cairo, 1976.

Ebers, Georg, *Aegypten in Bild und Wort*, 2 vols, Leipzig 1880.

Escovitz, Joseph H., *The Office of Qâḍî al-Quḍât in Cairo under the Baḥrî Mamlûks*, Berlin 1984.

Fahmī Muḥammad, 'Abd al-Raḥmān, 'Bayna adab al-maqāma wa fann al-'imāra fī 'l-madrasa al-sa'diyya (qubbat Ḥasan Ṣadaqa)', *Bulletin de l'Institut d'Egypte*, III (1970–71), pp. 59–83.

Fernandes, Leonor, 'Three Ṣūfī Foundations in a 15th century Waqfiyya', *Annales Islamologiques*, XXVII (1981), pp. 141–56.

— 'The Foundation of Baybars al-Jashankir: Its Waqf, History and Architecture', *Muqarnas*, IV (1987), pp. 21–42.

— 'Mamluk Politics and Education: The Evidence from Two Fourteenth Century Waqfiyya [sic]', *Annales Islamologiques*, XXIII (1987), pp. 87–98.

— *The Evolution of a Sufi Institution in Mamluk Egypt: The Khanqah*, Berlin 1988.

— 'The Game of Exchange and its Impact on the Urbanization of Mamluk Cairo', in: D. Behrens-Abouseif (ed.), *The Cairo Heritage*, pp. 203–22.

Flemming, Barbara, 'Šerif, Sultan Ġawrī und die Perser', *Der Islam*, XLV (1969), pp. 81–93.

— 'Literary Activities in Mamluk Halls and Barracks', in: Myriam Rosen-Ayalon (ed.), *Studies in Memory of Gaston Wiet*, Jerusalem 1977, pp. 249–59.

Garcin, Jean-Claude, 'Le Caire et la province: constructions au Caire et à Qûs sous les Mamluks Bahrides', *Annales Islamologiques*, VIII (1969), pp. 47–61.

— 'L'Insertion sociale de Sha'rani dans le milieu Cairote', in: *Colloque international sur l'histoire du Caire*, pp. 159–68.

— 'La Méditerranéisation de l'empire mamelouk sous les sultans Bahrides', *Revista degli Studi Orientali*, XLVIII (1974), pp. 109–16.

— *Espaces, pouvoirs et idéologies de l'Egypte médiévale* (reprinted essays), London 1987.

— 'Le Système militaire mamluk et le blockage de la société', *Annales Islamologiques*, XXIV (1988), pp. 93–110.

— 'Le Caire et l'évolution des pays musulmans à l'époque médiévale', *Annales Islamologiques*, XXV (1991), pp. 289–304.

— 'The Regime of the Circassian Mamluks', in: Carl Petry (ed.), *The Cambridge History of Egypt*, I: *Islamic Egypt, 640–1517*, Cambridge 1998.

— 'Note sur la population du Caire en 1517', in: Jean-Claude Garcin (ed.), *Grandes Villes Méditérranéennes du monde musulman médiéval*, pp. 205–13.

— (ed.), *Grandes Villes Méditérranéennes du monde musulman médiéval*, Rome/Paris 2000.

— 'Outsiders in the City', in: D. Behrens-Abouseif (ed.), *The Cairo Heritage*, pp. 7–16.

Garcin, J.-C., B. Maury and J. Revault, *Palais et maisons du Caire*, I: *Epoque mamelouke*, Paris 1982.

Garcin, J.-C. and M.A. Taher, 'Un ensemble de waqfs du IX/XVe siècle en Egypte: Les actes de Jawhar al-Lālā', in: R. Curiel and R. Gyselen (eds), *Itinéraires d'Orient: Hommages à Claude Cahen (Res Orientales 6)*, Bures-Sur-Yvette 1994, pp. 309–24.

— 'Les Waqfs d'une madrasa au Caire au XVe siècle: les propriétés urbaines de Ǧawhar al-Lālā', in: R. Deguilhem (ed.), *Les Waqfs dans l'éspace islamique*, pp. 151–86.

Gaube, Heinz, *Arabische Inschriften aus Syrien*, Wiesbaden/Beirut, 1978.

Geoffroy, Eric, *Le Soufisme en Egypte et en Syrie sous les derniers Mamlouks et les premiers Ottomans*, Damascus 1995.

Gibbs, Edward, 'Mamluk Ceramics 648–923 A.H./A.D. 1250–1517', *Transactions of the Oriental Ceramics Society*, vol. 63 (1998–1999), pp. 19–44.

Girault De Prangey, *Monuments arabes d'Egypte, de Syrie et d'Asie mineure*, Paris 1846.

Grabar, Oleg, 'The Inscriptions of the Madrasah-Mausoleum of Qaytbay', in: *Near-Eastern Numismatics: Iconography, Epigraphy and History, Studies in Honor of George C. Miles*, Beirut 1974, pp. 465–8.

Green, A.H. (ed.), *In Quest of an Islamic Humanism: Arabic and Islamic Studies in Memory of Mohamed al-Nowaihi*, Cairo 1984.

Haarmann, Ulrich, 'Alṭun Ḥan und Čingiz Ḫān bei den ägyptischen Mamluken', *Der Islam*, LI (1974), pp. 1–36.

— 'Arabic in Speech, Turkish in Lineage: Mamluks and their Sons in the Intellectual Life of Fourteenth-century Egypt and Syria', *Journal of Semitic Studies*, XXXIII (1988), pp. 81–114.

— 'Ideology and History, Identity and Alterity: The Arab Image of the Turk from the 'Abbasid to Modern Egypt', *International Journal of Middle East Studies*, XX (1988), pp. 175–96.

— 'Rather Injustice of the Turks than the Righteousness of the Arabs—Changing 'Ulamā' Attitudes towards Mamluk Rule in the Late Fifteenth Century', *Studia Islamica*, LXVIII (1988), pp. 61–77.

— *Geschichte der arabischen Welt*, Munich 1991.

Al-Ḥaddād, Muhammad Hamza Isma'il, *al-Sulṭān al-Manṣūr Qalāwūn: tārīkh, aḥwāl miṣr fī 'ahdihi, munshā'ātuhu al-mi'māriyya*, Cairo 1993.

Al-Ḥājjī, Hayat Nasir, *al-Sulṭān al-Nāṣir Muḥammad wa niẓām al-waqf fī 'ahdihi*, Kuwait 1983.

Hallenberg, Helena, 'The Sultan Who Loved Sufis: How Qāytbāy Endowed a Shrine Complex in Dasūq', *Mamlūk Studies Review*, IV (2000), pp. 147–66.

Hamza, Hani, *The Northern Cemetery of Cairo*, Cairo 2001.

— 'The Turbah of Tankizbughā', *Mamlūk Studies Review*, X/2 (2006), pp. 161–83.

Hanna, Nelly, *An Urban History of Būlāq in the Mamluk and Ottoman Periods*, Cairo 1983.

al-Harithy, Howyda, 'The Complex of Sultan Hasan in Cairo: Reading between the Lines', *Muqarnas*, XIII (1996), pp. 68–79.

—'The Patronage of al-Nāṣir Muḥammad ibn Qalāwūn', *Mamlūk Studies Review*, IV (2000), pp. 219–44.

—'Turbat al-Sitt: An Identification', in: D. Behrens-Abouseif (ed.), *The Cairo Heritage: Papers in Honor of Layla Ali Ibrahim*, pp. 103–22.

—'The Concept of Space in Mamluk Architecture', *Muqarnas*, XVIII (2001), pp. 73–93.

—(ed.) *The Waqf Document of Sultan al-Nasir Hasan B. Muhammad B. Qalawun*, Beirut 2001.

Hay, Robert, *Illustrations of Cairo*, London 1840.

Herz, Max, *Die Baugruppe des Sultans Qalawun*, Hamburg 1910.

—'La mosquée d'Ezbek al-Youssoufi', *Revue Egyptienne*, I (1899), pp. 16–21.

—*La mosquée du Sultan Hassan au Caire*, Cairo 1899.

—*La mosquée de l'émir Ganem el-Bahlaouan au Caire* (Comité de Conservation des Monuments de l'Art Arabe), Cairo 1908.

—*Index général des bulletins du Comité des années 1881–1910*, Cairo 1914.

Heyd, Wilhelm, *Histoire du commerce du levant au moyen âge*, 2 vols, Leipzig 1885–6.

Holt, Peter M., 'Mamlūks', *Encyclopaedia of Islam*, 2nd edn, Leiden 1991.

—'An-Nāṣir Muḥammad B. Qalāwūn (684.74/1285–1341): His Ancestry, Kindred and Affinity', in: U. Vermeuleun and D. De Smet (eds) *Egypt and Syria in the Fatimid, Ayyubid and Mamluk Eras*, pp. 314–23.

—'The Position and Power of the Mamlūk Sultan', *Bulletin of the School of Oriental and African Studies*, XXXVIII/2 (1984), pp. 237–49.

—'The Structure of Government in the Mamluk Sultanate', in: P.M. Holt (ed.), *The Eastern Mediterranean Lands in the Period of the Crusades*, Warminster 1977, pp. 44–61.

Homerin, Emil, 'The Domed Shrine of Ibn al-Fāriḍ', *Annales Islamologiques*, XXV (1990), pp. 133–8.

Humphreys, Stephen, 'The Expressive Intent of the Mamluk Architecture of Cairo: A Preliminary Essay', *Studia Islamica*, XXXV (1972), pp. 69–119.

Ibrāhīm, 'Abd al-Laṭīf, 'Silsilat al-dirāsāt al-wathā'iqiyya: al-wathā'iq fī khidmat al-āthār', in: *Kitāb al-mu'tamar al-thānī li-āthār al-bilād al-'arabiyya*, Cairo 1959, pp. 205–87.

—*al-Maktaba al-mamlūkiyya*, Cairo 1962.

—'Min al-wathā'iq al-'arabiyya fī 'l-'uṣūr al-wusṭā: naṣṣān jadīdān min wathīqat al-amīr Ṣarghitmish', *Majallat Kulliyat al-Ādāb*, XXVII/1–22 (1969), pp. 121–58; XXVIII (1971), pp. 143–210.

Ihsanoğlu, Ekmeleddin et al., *Egypt as Viewed in the 19th Century*, Istanbul 2001.

Irwin, Robert, *The Middle East in the Middle Ages: The Early Mamluk Sultanate 1250–1382*, London 1986.

—'The Privatization of "Justice" under the Circassian Mamluks', *Mamlūk Studies Review*, VI (2002), pp. 63–70.

Ismail, Husam, 'The Qaysariyya of Sultan al-Ashraf Inal According to Waqf Documents', in: D. Behrens-Abouseif (ed.), *The Cairo Heritage*, pp. 183–90.

Ismā'īl, Muḥammad Ḥusām al-Dīn, *al-Uṣūl al-mamlūkiyya li-l-'amā'ir al-'uthmāniyya*, Alexandria 2002.

—'Ba'ḍ al-mulāḥaẓāt 'alā 'l-'ilāqa bayna murūr al-mawākib wa waḍ' al-mabānī 'l-athariyya fī shawāri' madīnat al-qāhira', *Annales Islamologiques*, 25 (1990), pp. 1–10.

Issa, Ahmed, *Histoire des bimaristans à l'époque islamique*, Cairo 1928.

James, David, *The Koran: Catalogue of an Exhibition in the Chester Beatty Library*, Dublin 1978.

—*Qur'āns of the Mamlūks*, London 1988.

—*The Master Scribes*, II, Oxford 1992.

Karim, Chahinda, 'The Mosque of Ulmas al-Hajib', in: D. Behrens-Abouseif (ed.), *The Cairo Heritage*, pp. 123–48.

—'The Mosque of Aslam al-Bahā'ī al-Silāḥdār (746/1345)', *Annales Islamologiques*, XXIV (1988), pp. 233–53.

Karnouk, Gloria, 'Form and Ornament of the Cairene Baḥrī Minbar', *Annales Islamologiques*, XVII (1981), pp. 113–41.

Kessler, Christel, 'Funerary Architecture within the City', *Colloque international sur l'histoire du Caire (1969)*, Cairo 1972, pp. 257–67.

—*The Carved Masonry Domes of Mediaeval Cairo*, Cairo/London 1976.

—'Mecca-oriented Urban Architecture in Mamluk Cairo: the Madrasa-Mausoleum of Sultan Sha'ban II', in: A.H. Green (ed.), *In Quest of an Islamic Humanism*, pp. 97–108.

—'The "Imperious Reasons" that flawed the Minaret-flanked Setting of Sultan Ḥasan's Mausoleum in Cairo' in: *Damaszener Mitteilungen*, XI (1999), pp. 307–16.

King, David A., 'The Astronomy of the Mamluks: A Brief Overview', *Muqarnas*, II (1984), pp. 73–84.

Korn, Lorenz, *Ayyubidische Architektur in Ägypten und Syrien*, 2 vols, Heidelberg 2004.

Labib, Subhi, *Handelsgeschichte Ägyptens im Spätmittelalter (1171–1517)*, Wiesbaden 1965.

Lane-Poole, Stanley, *The Story of Cairo*, London 1906.

Lapidus, Ira M., *Muslim Cities in the Later Middle Ages*, Cambridge/London/New York 1987.

Leisten, Thomas, 'Between Orthodoxy and Exegesis: Some Aspects of Attitudes in the Shari'a towards Funerary Architecture', *Muqarnas*, VII (1990), pp. 12–22.

—'Mashhad al-Nasr: Monuments of War and Victory in Medieval Islamic Art', *Muqarnas*, XIII (1996), pp.7–26.

Little, Donald P., 'Religion under the Mamluks', *Muslim World*, LXXIII (1983), pp. 165–81.

—*An Introduction to Mamluk Historiography*, Wiesbaden 1970.

—'The Nature of Khanqahs, Ribats and Zawiyas under the Mamluks', in: Wael B. Hallaq and P. Donald Little (eds), *Islamic Studies Presented to Charles J. Adams*, Leiden 1991, pp. 91–105.

—'Notes on Mamluk Madrasahs', *Mamlūk Studies Review*, VI (2002), pp. 9–20.

Loiseau, Julien, 'Les Avatars du lit: divagations du Nil et morphologies des rives à hauteur du Caire: VIIe–XVe Siècles', *Médiévales*, XXXVI (1999), pp. 7–15.

Louis-François Cassas 1756–1827 Dessinateur-Voyageur im Banne der Sphinx, exhibition catalogue, Mainz 1994.

MacKenzie, Neil D., *Ayyubid Cairo: A Topographical Study*, Cairo 1992.

Mahdi, Muhsin, *Alf Layla wa layla min uṣūlihi 'l-'arabiyya 'l-ūlā*, Leiden 1984; *The Arabian Nights*, transl. Husayn Haddawy, New York/London 1990.

Marinetto Sanchez, Purificación, 'La Alfombra del Generalife y su posible uso en la Granada Nazarí', *Cuadernos de la Alhambra*, XL (2004), pp. 155–75.

Martel-Thoumian, Bernadette, *Les Civils et l'administration dans l'état militaire mamlūk (IXe/XVe siècle)*, Damascus 1998.

—'The Sale of Office and Its Economic Consequences during the Rule of the Last Circassians (872–922/1468–1516)', *Mamlūk Studies Review*, IX/2 (2005), pp. 49–84.

Mayer, L.A., *Saracenic Heraldry: A Survey*, Oxford 1933.

— *Mamluk Costume*, Geneva 1952.

— *The Buildings of Qaytbay as Described in his Endowment Deeds*, London 1938.

Mehren, A.F., *Câhirah og Kerâfat, historiske Studier under et Ophold i Aegypten 1867–68*, 2 vols, Copenhagen 1869–70.

Meinecke, Michael, 'Das Mausoleum des Qalā'ūn in Kairo: Untersuchungen zur Genese der mamlukischen Architekturdekoration', *Mitteilungen des Deutschen Archäologischen Instituts, Abteilung Kairo*, XXVII/1 (1971), pp. 47–80.

—'Zur mamlukischen Heraldik', *Mitteilungen des Deutschen Archäologischen Instituts, Abteilung Kairo*, XXVIII/2 (1972), pp. 213–87.

—'Die Moschee des Aqsunqur an-Nasiri in Kairo', *Mitteilungen des Deutschen Archäologischen Instituts, Abteilung Kairo*, XXXIX/1 (1973), pp. 9–48.

—'Die mamlukischen Fayencemosaikdekorationen: Eine Werkstätte aus Tabriz in Kairo', *Kunst des Orients*, XI (1976–7), pp. 85–144.

—'Mamluk Architecture: Regional Architectural Traditions: Evolution and Interrelations', *Damaszener Mitteilungen*, II (1985), pp. 163–75.

—'Baumaterialien in der islamischen Architektur Ägyptens', in: *Ägypten – Dauer und Wandel*, Mainz 1985, pp. 153–9.

—'Syrian blue-and-white Tiles of the 9th/15th Century', *Damaszener Mitteilungen*, III (1988), pp. 203–15.

—*Mamlukische Architektur in Ägypten und Syrien*, 2 vols, Mainz 1993.

—'Löwe, Lilie, Adler: Die Europäischen Wurzeln der islamischen Heraldik', in: *Das Staunen der Welt* (Bilderheft der Staatlichen Museen zu Berlin-Preussischer Kulturbesitz 77/78), Berlin 1995, pp. 29–34.

Meinecke, Michael et al., *Die Restaurierung der Madrasa des Amirs Sābiq ad-Din Miṭqāl al-Ānūkī und die Sanierung des Darb Qirmiz in Kairo*, Mainz 1980.

Meinecke-Berg, Victoria, 'Quellen zur Topographie und Baugeschichte in Kairo unter Sultan an-Nasir Muhammad b. Qala'ūn', *Zeitschrift der Deutschen Morgenländischen Gesellschaft (Supplement III)* (1977), pp. 539–50.

—'Historische Topographie des Viertels', in: M. Meinecke et al., *Die Restaurierung der Madrasa des Amirs Sābiq ad-Dīn Miṭqāl al-Anūkī*, pp. 18–28.

—'Spolien in der mittelalterlichen Architektur von Kairo', in: *Ägypten – Dauer und Wandel*, Mainz 1985, pp. 153–9.

—'Cairo, the Changing Face of a Capital City', in: M. Hattstein and P. Delius (eds), *Islam, Art and Architecture*, Königswinter 2004.

Melikian-Chirvani, A.S.,'Cuivres inédits de l'époque de Qa'itbay', *Kunst des Orients*, VI/2 (1969), pp. 99–133.

—'Venise, l'orient et l'occident', *Bulletin d'Etudes Orientales*, XXVII (1974), pp. 109–26.

Meloy, John L. 'Celebrating the Maḥmal: The Rajab Festival in Fifteenth Century Cairo', in: Judith Pfeiffer and Sholeh A. Quinn (eds), *History and Historiography in Post-Mongol Central Asia and the Middle East: Studies in Honor of John Woods*, Wiesbaden 2006, pp. 404–27.

Menasri, Mohamed, *Kitāb tuḥfat al-turk. Oeuvre de combat hanafite à Damas au XVIe siècle*, Damascus 1997.

Meri, J.W., 'Ziyāra', *Encyclopaedia of Islam*, 2nd edn, Leiden 2002.

Misiorowski, Andrzej, *Mausoleum of Qurqumas in Cairo: An Example of the Architecture and Building Art of the Mamlouk Period*, Warsaw 1979.

Moberg, Axel, 'Zwei ägyptische Waqf-Urkunden aus dem Jahre 691/1292', *Le Monde Oriental*, XII (1918), pp. 1–64.

—*Ur 'Abd Allah B. 'Abd Ez-Ẓâhir's Biografi över Sultanen El-Malik El-Aśraf Ḥalîl*, Upsala 1902.

The Mosques of Egypt, Ministry of Waqfs, 2 vols, Cairo 1949.

Mostafa, Saleh Lamei, *Kloster und Mausoleum des Farağ ibn Barqūq in Kairo (Abhandlungen des Deutschen*

Archäologischen Instituts, Abteilung Kairo, Islamische Reihe), II, Glückstadt 1968.

—*Madrasa Ḫanqāh und Mausoleum des Barqūq in Kairo (Abhandlungen des Deutschen Archäologischen Instituts, Abteilung Kairo, Islamische Reihe)*, IV, Glückstadt 1982.

—'The Cairene Sabil: Form and Meaning', *Muqarnas*, VI (1990), pp. 33–42.

Mostafa, Saleh Lamei et al., *Moschee des Farağ ibn Barqūq in Kairo (Abhandlungen des Deutschen Archäologischen Instituts, Abteilung Kairo, Islamische Reihe)*, III, Glückstadt 1972.

Mubārak, ʿAlī, *al-Khiṭaṭ al-jadīda al-tawfīqiyya*, Bulaq 1306/1888–9.

Muṣṭafā, Muḥammad, *Index to Ibn Iyās, Badāʾiʿ al-zuhūr*, 4 vols, Wiesbaden 1984–93, p. 343.

Necipoğlu, Gülru, *Architecture, Ceremonial and Power*, New York 1991.

Newhall, Amy W., 'The Patronage of the Mamluk Sultan Qaʾit Bay 872–901/1468–1496', PhD dissertation, Harvard University 1987.

Northrup, Linda S., *From Slave to Sultan: The Career of al-Mansur Qalawun and the Consolidation of Mamluk Rule in Egypt and Syria*, Stuttgart 1998.

Nuwaysar, Husni, *Madrasa jarkasiyya ʿalā namaṭ al-masājid al-jāmiʿa, madrasat al-amīr Sudūn min Zāda bi-sūq al-silāḥ*, Kairo 1985.

O'Kane, Bernard, 'Monumentality in Mamluk and Mongol Art and Architecture', *Art History*, XIX (1996), pp. 499–522.

—'Domestic and Religious Architecture in Cairo: Mutual influences', in: D. Behrens-Abouseif (ed.), *The Cairo Heritage*, pp. 149–83.

—'The Arboreal Aesthetic: Landscape, Painting and Architecture from Mongol Iran to Mamluk Egypt', in: Bernard O'Kane (ed.), *The Iconography of Islamic Art, Studies in Honour of Robert Hillenbrand*, Edinburgh 2005, pp. 211–23.

—O'Kane, Bernard et al., *Documentation of the Inscriptions in the Historic Zone in Cairo* (The Egyptian Antiquities Project of the American Research Center in Egypt, Inc. (ARCE) under USAID Grant N. 263-0000-G-00-3089-00).

Pajares-Ayuela, Paloma, *Cosmatesque Ornament*, London 2002.

Pauty, Edmond, *Les Hammams du Caire*, Cairo 1933.

Petry, Carl F., 'A Paradox of Patronage During the Late Mamluk Period', *Muslim World*, LXXIII (1983), pp. 182–207.

—*The Civilian Elite of Cairo in the Later Middle Ages*, Princeton 1981.

—*Protectors or Praetorians? The Last Mamlūk Sultans and Egypt's Waning as a Great Power*, New York 1994.

—*Twilight of Majesty: The Reigns of the Mamlūk Sultans al-Ashraf Qāytbāy and Qānṣūh al-Ghawrī in Egypt*, Seattle/London 1993.

Philipp, Thomas and Ulrich Haarmann (eds), *The Mamluks in Egyptian Politics and Society*, Cambridge 1998.

Popper, William, *Egypt and Syria under the Circassian Sultans*, University of California, Publications in Semitic Philology, XV–XVI, Berkeley/Los Angeles 1955–57.

Prost, Claude M., 'Les Revêtements céramiques dans les monuments musulmans de l'Egypte', *Mémoires publiés par les Membres de l'Institut Français d'Archéologie Orientale du Caire*, Cairo 1916.

Rabbat, Nasser, 'Mamluk Throne Halls: Qubba or Iwan', *Ars Orientalis*, XXIII (1993), pp. 201–18.

—*The Citadel of Cairo*, Leiden/New York 1996.

—'Al-Azhar Mosque: An Architectural History', *Muqarnas*, XIII (1996), pp. 45–68.

—'Perception of Architecture in Mamluk Sources', *Mamlūk Studies Review*, VI (2000), pp. 155–76.

Ramaḍān, Ḥusayn Muṣṭafā Ḥusayn, 'Mulāḥaẓāt ʿalā 'l-kitābāt al-kūfiyya bi-madrasat al-sulṭān Ḥasan', *Annales Islamologiques*, XXXIX (2005), pp. 19–30.

Ravaisse, Paul, 'Essai sur l'histoire et sur la topographie du Caire d'après Maqrīzī', *Mémoires de la Mission Archéologique Française au Caire*, I/3, pp. 409–89, III/4, pp. 33–114, Cairo 1886–9.

Raymond, André, *Le Caire*, Paris 1993; *Cairo*, transl. W. Wood, Cambridge MA 2000.

—'Cairo's Area and Population in the Early Fifteenth Century', *Muqarnas*, II (1984), pp. 21–32.

Raymond, André and Gaston Wiet, *Les Marchés du Caire* (traduction annotée du texte de Maqrizi), Cairo 1979.

Rice, D.S., *The Baptistère de St Louis*, Paris 1953.

Rogers, J. Michael, 'Seljuk Influences on the Monuments of Cairo', *Kunst des Orients*, VII/1 (1972), pp. 40–68.

—'Evidence for Mamluk–Mongol Relations', in: *Colloque international sur l'histoire du Caire (1969)*, 1972, pp. 385–403.

—'The Stones of Barqūq: Building Materials and Architectural Design in Late Fourteenth-century Cairo', *Apollo*, CIII/170 (1976), pp. 307–13.

—'Ḳāhira', *Encyclopaedia of Islam*, 2nd edn, Leiden 1978.

—'The Inscription of the Cistern of Yaʿqub Shah al-Mihmandar in Cairo', in: *Fifth International Congress of Turkish Art*, Budapest 1978, p. 737f.

Rosenthal, Franz, *A History of Muslim Historiography*, 2nd edn, Leiden 1968.

Roxburgh, David (ed.), *Turks: A Journey of a Thousand Years 600–1699* (exhibition catalogue), London 2005.

Sabra, Adam, *Poverty and Charity in Medieval Islam*, Cambridge 2000.

Sadek, Mohamed-Moain, *Die mamlukische Architektur der Stadt Gaza*, Berlin 1990.

Salam-Liebich, Hayat, *The Architecture of the Mamluk City of Tripoli*, Cambridge MA 1975.

Sālim, 'Abd al-'Azīz, *Tārīkh madīnat al-iskandariyya fī 'l-'aṣr al-islāmī*, Alexandria 1982.

Sālim, Maḥmūd Rizq, *'Aṣr al-salāṭīn al-mamālīk*, 8 vols, Cairo 1962–5.

Salmon, Georges, *Etudes sur la topographie du Caire: Kal'at al-Kabch et Birkat al-Fil (Mémoires de l'IFAO, VII)*, Cairo 1902.

Sayed, Hazem I., 'The Development of the Cairene Qāʾa: Some Considerations', *Annales Islamologiques*, XXIII (1987), pp. 31–54.

Sayf al-Naṣr, Muḥammad Abū 'l-Futūḥ, 'Madrasat al-sulṭān al-manṣūr Qalāwūn bi-l-naḥḥāsīn bi-l-qāhira', *Majallat Kuliyyat al-Ādāb, Jāmiʿat Ṣanʿāʾ* (1984), pp. 77–129.

Schimmel, Annemarie, 'Kalif und Kadi im spätmittelalterlichen Ägypten', *Die Welt des Islam*, XXIV (1942), pp. 2–128.

Shafiʿi, Farid, 'West Islamic Influences on Architecture in Egypt', *Bulletin of the Faculty of Arts (Cairo University)*, XV/2 (December 1954), pp. 1–47.

— 'Sufismus und Heiligenverehrung im spätmittelalterlichen Ägypten', in: Erwin Gräf (ed.), *Festschrift Werner Caskel*, Leiden 1968, pp. 274–88.

— 'Some Glimpses of the Religious Life in Egypt during the Later Mamlūk Period', *Islamic Studies*, IV/4 (1965), pp. 353–91.

Speiser, Philipp, *Die Geschichte der Erhaltung Arabischer Baudenkmäler in Ägypten*, Heidelberg 2001.

Stowasser, Karl, 'Manners and Customs at the Mamluk Court', *Muqarnas*, II (1984), pp. 13–20.

Taylor, Christopher S., *In the Vicinity of the Righteous: Ziyara and the Veneration of Muslim Saints in Late Medieval Egypt*, Leiden/Boston/Cologne 1999.

Thorau, Peter, *The Lion of Egypt: Sultan Baybars I and the Near East in the Thirteenth Century*, transl. Peter Holt, London/New York 1982.

Toutes Les Egypte (exhibition catalogue), Marseille 1998.

'Uthmān, A.M., *Wathīqat waqf Jamāl al-Dīn al-Ustādār*, Cairo 1983.

'Uthmān, Muḥammad 'Abd al-Sattār, *Naẓariyyat al-waẓīfiyya bi-l-'amāʾir al-dīniyya 'l-mamlūkiyya bi-l-qāhira*, Alexandria 2000.

Van Berchem, Max, *Matériaux pour un Corpus Inscriptionum Arabicarum* (Mémoires publiés par les Membres de la Mission Archéologique Française au Caire), XIX/1–4, Cairo 1894–1903.

Vermeulen, U. and D. De Smet (eds), *Egypt and Syria in the Fatimid, Ayyubid and Mamluk Eras*, Leuven 1995.

Walls, Archie G., *Geometry and Architecture in Islamic Jerusalem. A Study of the Ashrafiyya*, London 1990.

Ward, Rachel, 'The Baptistère de St Louis – A Mamluk Basin made for Export to Europe', in: Charles Burnett and Anna Contadini (eds), *Islam and the Italian Renaissance*, London 1999, pp. 113–32.

— 'Brass, Gold and Silver from Mamluk Egypt: Metal Vessels made for Al-Nāsir Muhammad', *Journal of the Royal Asiatic Society*, XIV/1 (2004), pp. 59–73.

Warner, Nicholas, *The Monuments of Historic Cairo*, Cairo/New York 2005.

— *The True Description of Cairo: A Sixteenth Century Venetian View*, 3 vols, Oxford 2006.

Wiet, Gaston, *Catalogue général du Musée Arabe du Caire: lampes et bouteilles en verre émaillé*, Cairo 1929, repr. 1982.

— 'Sultan Hasan', *La Revue du Caire* (June 1938), pp. 86–92.

— *Cairo, City of Art and Commerce*, Oklahoma 1964.

— 'La Mosquée de Kafur au Caire', in: *Studies in Islamic Art and Architecture in Honour of Professor K.A.C. Creswell*, Cairo 1965, pp. 260–9.

Williams, Caroline, 'The Mosque of Sitt Hadaq', *Muqarnas*, XI (1994), pp. 55–64.

Williams, John A., 'Urbanization and Monument Construction in Mamluk Cairo', *Muqarnas,* II (1984), pp. 33–45.

— 'The Khanqah of Siryaqus: A Mamluk Royal Religious Foundation', in: A.H. Green (ed.) *In Quest of an Islamic Humanism*, pp. 109–19.

Zakarya, Mona, *Deux palais du Caire médiéval: waqfs et architecture*, Paris 1983.

Index

mawqufat: the estate belonging to a waqf (commercial buildings, agricultural land, etc.).

maydan: hippodrome.

mazalim: court of petitions or appeal, where the sultan or an emir dispenses secular justice.

mazmala: niche to hold water jars.

minbar: pulpit.

mu'adhdhin: the person who performs the call to prayer.

mu'allim: master, a craftsman's title.

muqarnas: decorative device consisting of a geometrical composition of small niches; used to be called stalactites.

musalla: open oratory, usually for funerary prayers.

Nilometer: a structure on the island of Rawda to measure the Nile flood.

pishtaq: an elevated section of a facade.

qa'a: a reception or ceremonial hall; the qa'a plan in Mamluk architecture. Consists of the iwans facing a central space with two lateral smaller iwans or recesses.

qasr: elevated palace or elevated residential structure.

qaysariyya: commercial building like khan and wakala.

qibla: the orientation to Mecca; the qibla wall is the frontal wall in a mosque that includes the mihrab.

rab': type of Cairene apartment building that could also be attached to commercial structures, built above shops.

rahba: open space, often used to include markets.

ribat: a foundation to house Sufis or the needy, often a dwelling complex in a religious building.

riwaq: arcaded hall in a mosque; the word also refers to a middle-sized apartment.

sabat: elevated passage.

sabil: a manned water house equipped with a cistern to distribute water on a charitable basis.

sabil-maktab: a Mamluk water house surmounted by a primary school for boys.

sama': Sufi chanting and musical performance.

shadirwan: decorative fountain in a wall.

shaykh: man of religion, Sufi.

tariqa: Sufi order.

tiraz: embroidered band on ceremonial gowns; epigraphic band on a facade.

tughra: royal seal or signature.

turba: grave, tomb, mausoleum, also a funerary complex that fulfills other religious functions.

ustadar: majordomo.

wakala: commercial building like khan and qaysariyya.

waqf: Islamic system of trust, with pious, private or combined purposes.

zawiya: Sufi foundation, often dedicated to an individual shaykh or Sufi order.

Glossary

ablaq: striped masonry.

adhan: call to prayer.

atabak: Mamluk title of the commander-in-chief of the army.

basmala: formula of 'b'ism Allah al-rahman al-rahim' ('in the name of God the All-Compassionate and All-Merciful').

bayt al-mal: public treasury.

cosmatesque work: a technique of marble mosaics with geometrical designs of Byzantine origin used on pavements in early medieval Italy. It is also known as *opus alexandrinum* referring to the city of Alexandria where this craft was practised. The marble decoration of Qalawun's mausoleum belongs to this style.

darih: mausoleum.

dawadar: secretary.

dikka: bench.

dikkat al-mu'adhdhinin: bench in the mosque, on columns or attached to the wall, for the iqama, which is a second call to prayer performed within the mosque before the Friday sermon.

diwan: a central office, like a ministry. The word also means a collection of poems by a poet.

ghashiya: an emblem of royalty in the shape of a gold-embroidered leather saddle.

hawsh: funerary enclosure in a cemetery; also a popular form of dwelling.

iqta': a form of land grant to remunerate the military establishment.

istibdal: swap, exchange. In waqf terminology it is a procedure that allows under specific conditions for the sale or exchange of a waqf property, which in principle is not transferable.

iwan: a hall open on one side, facing a courtyard.

jami': a congregational or Friday mosque where the khutba or Friday sermon is held.

khalij: canal.

khan, qaysariyya, wakala: commercial buildings, mostly built around a courtyard, with shops and workshops on the ground floor, and surmounted by a separate apartment complex on two or three stories. In the Mamluk period the three terms seem to refer to the same kind of building.

khanqah: a monastery for Sufis.

khatib: the preacher of Friday sermons in a mosque.

khutba: Friday sermon.

kursi: a wooden bench for a Koran reader; also throne.

madhhab: school or rite, also used for the four rites of Islamic Sunni law.

mahmal: the ritual palanquin that accompanied the pilgrimage caravan.

maksala: a small bench, which appears as a pair, on either side of a door.

maktab: primary school, today known as kuttab.

maqam: mausoleum, shrine.

maqsura: loggia, the domed and enclosed space in front of a mihrab.

masjid: mosque without Friday sermon.

mastaba: bench, dais, or an architectural structure with a dais, or including benches for spectators.

mat'am al-tayr: feeding ground for birds, falconry, the name of a hippodrome with a falconry.